Criminal Justice & Public Health

MRSA & Other Deadly Pathogens

DENNIS J. STEVENS

UNC Charlotte
Justice Writers of America

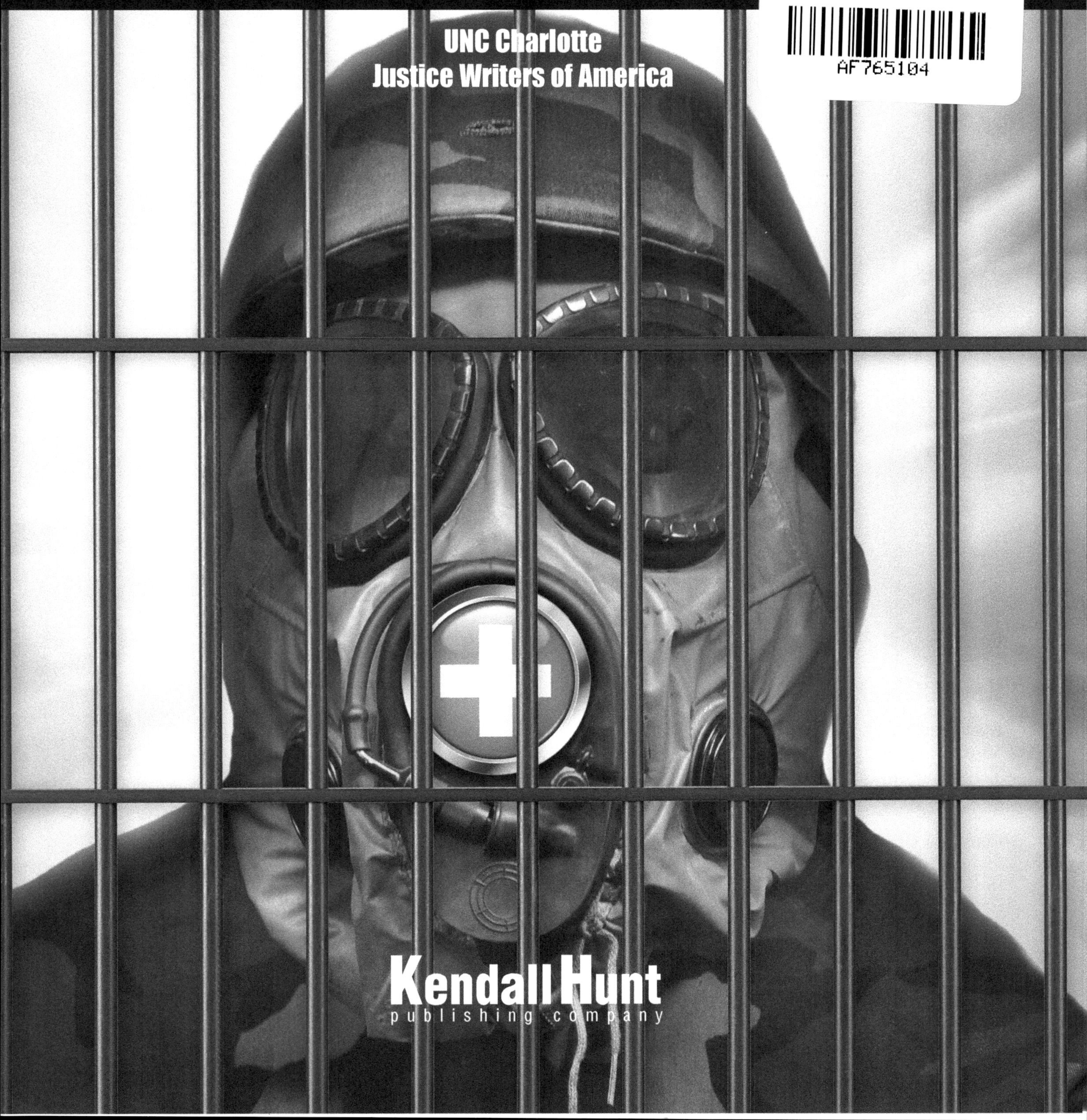

Kendall Hunt
publishing company

Kendall Hunt
publishing company
www.kendallhunt.com
Send all inquiries to:
4050 Westmark Drive
Dubuque, IA 52004-1840

ISBN 978-1-4652-6756-6

This work is dedicated to a woman whom I share a deep affinity with, Joan Gallo from Rye, New York who has patiently waited as I researched and wrote this book.

Brief Contents

Contents

Preface

One reality is that an estimated 100,000 individuals are killed annually from deadly infectious pathogens after being admitted to American hospitals, regardless of the reason he or she had been admitted to the hospital in the first place. The Centers for Disease Control (CDC) advance the idea that most of those infectious deaths were preventable. *Criminal Justice and Public Health: MRSA and Other Deadly Pathogens* is an account of the relationship between the quality of public safety services, treatment, and care provided by criminal justice personnel and their collaborative partners (firefighters, hospitals and clinics, and healthcare personnel). The experiences of Hurricane Katrina, other disasters, and the scholarly literature were used as a laboratory to predict future responses of public service and healthcare personnel during the current deadly pathogen invasion, and to predict future responses after an attack by biological weapons on the US. One finding of this work shows that both providers and individuals requiring public safety services are engaged in at-risk environments which are compounded by 'agents of compliance' that significantly complicate strategies employed by provider organizations. In part, agents of compliance include a fear of prosecution which cloud decisions to protect, treat, and admit individuals who require assistance of police, physicians and nurses, and hospitals. Regulation through criminalization of providers changes the quality of services and not in the way one would expect.

It is also theorized that the Prison Industrial Complex (PIC) of the American justice system is the catalyst of the deadly infectious pathogen invasion through the individuals under their care, custody, and employment. Both the literature and my experience tell me that prisons act as reservoirs for infectious pathogens, pumping disease into the civilian community through personnel, visitors, and released prisoners. Infectious diseases do not respect prison walls. For these reasons among others, and similar to slavery, when it couldn't be improved it was abolished which is the theme of my previous work: *The Failure of The American Prison Complex: Let's Abolish It* (Kendall Hunt, 2014).

This book is an account of public health organizations toward their fulfillment to assure conditions in which individuals can be healthy in a world invaded by antibiotic resistant mutate strains of bacteria and viruses. In the majority of cases where antimicrobials are used, the microorganisms have found a way to evade or resist antimicrobial agents and go on the offensive of attacking human beings, says the CDC. The struggle to provide and to receive quality services is, in essence, a struggle for social justice.

These agents of compliance, coupled with a lack of pharmaceutical remedies and a lack of social justice for those who seek services, fuel the infectious pathogen or superbug invasion. Accentuated throughout this work is evidence revealing that individuals of the lower social economic class most often intersect with the justice community and their collaborative partners. Generally those same individuals experience poor healthcare, tend to be less healthy than others for a variety of reasons, and once confined are more likely to be exposed and contaminated by infectious diseases placing prisoners and correctional personnel at risk.

Yet, my curiosity as a sociologist and criminologist heightened when I learned that this is also an account of people and tribes; it is a description of bureaucratic hierarchies and social class, and American greed; it's a story about the haves and the have-nots and the unintentional agenda of the Power Elite and their sophisticated approach to saving mankind from itself resulting in mass incarceration, criminalization policies, and punitive enforcement strategies that haven't changed the color of crime.

Yet, I've learned that the brave men and women in criminal justice, firefighting, and healthcare professions are not as safe as commonly believed. Who protects the protectors?

I think you will enjoy this challenging work. It is current, decisive, and contrary to many perspectives I held prior to my investigation of public health and professional performance. Largely, it will ignite your imagination, attack your peace of mind, and will lead to some anxious but worthy debates in the classroom and at home.

Dennis J. Stevens, PhD
Justice Writers of America
Charlotte, North Carolina

About the Author

Dennis J. Stevens earned a PhD from Loyola University of Chicago in 1991 with honors. He earned his masters and undergraduate degrees from Northeastern Illinois University in psychology, sociology, and education: Magna Cum Laude. Currently, he is an adjunct at the University of North Carolina–Charlotte; he has worked for the University of Southern Mississippi as Director of the Criminal Justice PhD program. Stevens was a professor at the University of Massachusetts–Boston, and chair of the criminal justice/sociology department at a North Carolina regional college. In addition to teaching traditional students, he has taught and counselled law enforcement and correctional personnel at law academies, such as the North Carolina Justice Academy and Boston Police Districts; and provided crisis intervention sessions after Hurricane Katrina for officers of the New Orleans Police Department and deputies of Jefferson Parish. Stevens has taught and led group meetings such as AA for felons at maximum-security penitentiaries, such as Attica in New York; Eastern and NC Women's Institute North Carolina; Stateville and Joliet near Chicago; CCI in Columbia, South Carolina; and MCI Framingham (women), Norfolk, and Bay State in Massachusetts.

Stevens has published twenty-one books (fourteen for academia plus four study guides) and ninety-eight scholarly and popular articles on policing, corrections, and criminally violent sexual predators. Stevens has been retained by private agencies, such as Wackenhut, to develop their "use of force" protocols; by state legislators to examine the flow of drugs into prisons, and recidivism rates among student-incarcerated prisoners by US federal agencies to study corruption among narcotic officers; and by foreign governments (e.g., the Provincial Government of Canada) to aid in prisoner research. He has been a researcher for many writers such as Frank Schmalleger and John Ortiz Smykla and editor or reviewer for many academic journals such as Journal of Police and Criminal Psychology, The Police Journal, Law and Human Behavior, Sage, Pearson, and McMillian.

As a volunteer, Stevens has guided many sexually abused children and their families through church-affiliated programs in New York, North Carolina, and South Carolina. Finally, Stevens is currently the managing director of Justice Writers of America, an organization that guides criminal justice professionals in their personal pursuits of constructing journal articles, documents, and books. Should you have questions or comments, feel free to contact the author at:

Dennis J. Stevens, Ph.D.
Justice Writers of America
Box 470073
Charlotte, North Carolina 28247
dennisj.stevens@gmail.com
crimeprofessor.com

Other Publications by the Author

Books

- The Failure of the American Prison Complex: Let's Abolish It, Kendall Hunt (2014)
- The Media and Criminal Justice: CSI Effect, Jones and Bartlett (2011)
- Wicked Women: A Journey of Super Predators, IUniverse (2011)
- Introduction to American Policing: An Applied Approach, Jones and Bartlett (2010)
- Police Officer Stress: Sources and Solutions, Prentice Hall (2008)
- Community Corrections, Prentice Hall (2006)
- Community Policing in the 21st Century, Allyn Bacon (2003)
- Case Studies of Community Policing, Allyn Bacon (2003)
- Policing and Community Partnerships, Prentice Hall (2003)
- Case Studies of Community Policing, Prentice Hall (2001)
- Measuring Performance: A Guide to Evaluative Research, (2001)
- Perspective in Corrections, Coursewise (2000)
- Inside the Mind of the Serial Rapist, Winfield (2000)

Chapters Provided by the Author for other Books

- "Women in Solitary Confinement: Health and Recidivism." Modern American Prisons, Stephen Richards (Ed). Southern Illinois University Press (2015).
- "Sexual Offenders." Prison Abolition: Unchaining Ourselves from U.S. Imperialism, Kaltefleiter, Nagel, & Nocella (Eds.) Rodopi Publishing (2012).
- "Police Stress." Encyclopedia of Psychology and Law, 2nd ed. Brian Cutler (Ed) (2007).
- "STING Tactics." Encyclopedia of Police Science, 3rd ed. Jack Greene (Ed). Jack R. Greene (Ed). Routledge (2007).
- "The History of Prisons: Continental Europe and England." The Encyclopedia of Criminology. Routledge/Taylor & Francis (2005).
- "John Wayne Gacy: The Killer Clown." In Frankie Y. Bailey and Steven Chermak (Eds.). Famous American Crimes and Trials. NY: Praeger Publishing (2005).
- "Police Officer Stress and Occupational Stressors." Policing and Strategies. Heith Copes (Ed), Prentice Hall (2005).
- "Civil Liabilities and Arrest Decisions." Policing and the Law, Jeffrey T. Walker (Ed) Prentice Hall (2002).
- "Education Programming for Offenders." In Compendium of Corrections. Compendium 2000: On Effective Correctional Programming. (pp. 57–64). Provincial Government of Canada. Correctional Service of Canada (2001).
- "Justifiable Use of Deadly Force for Law Enforcement Officers Serving U.S. Department of Energy Sites." Wackenhut Industries (1997).

E.P. Morel/Shutterstock, Inc.

CHAPTER 1

Disaster Comes in Threes

Learning Objectives

After you read this chapter, you will be better prepared to:

- Understand the role history and learning play in a healthy society and to the quality of life experiences and opportunities of an individual.
- Identify the "players" in the justice community and their collaborative partners; explain in what way each can contribute to public safety, social order, and equality.
- Comprehend the significance of political priorities toward public safety using the example of the New Orleans' Levees.
- Describe in what way dying alone can be a powerful symbol of social abandonment and failure.
- Identify and explain the relevance of the Power Elite in the discussions about Katrina strategies.
- Describe policing strategy outcomes among Katrina victims. In what way do you see those strategies as appropriate or inappropriate? What would you have done differently if you were a police officer in New Orleans during the hurricane?
- Describe some of the treatment outcomes among Katrina victims. In what way do you see treatment decisions as appropriate or inappropriate? What would you have done differently if you were a physician or a nurse in New Orleans during the hurricane?
- Explain the ideas connected to "The Emperor's New Clothes" and how it applies to welfare recipients and welfare workers.
- Describe some of the government's role among Katrina victims during the hurricane. If you were in charge, what would you have done differently and why?

Key Terms

Agents of Compliance
Collaborative Partners
Federal Emergency Management Agency (FEMA)
Lessons of History
Power Elite
National Hurricane Center
Scholarly Work
Twin Moral Impules

Words of Wisdom

History is the witness that testifies to the passing of time; it illumines reality, vitalizes memory, provides guidance in daily life and brings us tidings of antiquity.

Cicero (106 BC–43 BC)

Introduction

This book is about the at-risk occupational routines of criminal justice professionals and their healthcare partners (detailed below) who often interact with hosts or carriers of infectious diseases: hosts include suspects and perpetrators of crime, patients and colleagues, prisoners and priests, victims of crime and accidents, victims of terrorist attacks and terrorists, victims of highway accidents and family violence, and others requiring medical attention, protection, or comfort; hosts can include providers of public safety and treatment to victims of disastrous events such as the focus of this chapter—Hurricane Katrina. The story that follows is about certain victims receiving or not receiving care and services; it's about personnel and healthcare systems providing or failing to provide public safety, treatment, and care because of what I call 'agents of compliance' which includes agents of disease transmission, organizational policy and politics, and compliance regulations (detailed in the chapters ahead).

Intrusive to this story line and this entire book for that matter is an account of social justice, commerce, and politics. It is hoped that we can learn from Hurricane Katrina to provide public safety and treatment during future disasters particularly a bioweapon attack (See Chapter 10). Chapter 2 describes America's second disaster: the invasion of antimicrobial infectious diseases and pathogens including MRSA and Ebola; Chapter 2 also describes the third disaster: America's inability to combat these new disasters. What you need to know right now are the details about Hurricane Katrina and the Gulf Coast.

The Gulf Coast

Thursday night of a new university semester, I was lecturing to students enrolled in a research methods course at the University of Southern Mississippi at the Gulfport, Mississippi, campus overlooking the warm calm waters of the Gulf of Mexico. It was August 2005. My students were nervous about the amount of work required of them to complete their mandatory course for graduation; yet they were enthusiastic and determined to succeed particularly after I assured them that I anticipated their individual needs for guidance and aid, and accordingly would make time for each student, provide examples of work from former students, and assigned them graduate students as tutors.

First and Last Lecture

Little had any of us realized (although I'm sure some of my students hoped for it) that this was the first and last lecture for the semester in this classroom because over the weekend the buildings housing the university as we knew it would be turned to mud; it was common knowledge that on the horizon loomed an aggressive hurricane named Katrina. It was hurricane season on the Gulf and weather reports were clear that Katrina could, indeed, be the storm we feared. We discussed precautions such as getting cash from debit cards and bank accounts, filling bath tubs with water and vehicles with gasoline; above all, purchase an expensive manual can opener, plenty of canned food especially tuna fish, matches, candles, spoons, bar soap and a knife. Put these items in a plastic bag, and be sure to have a six pack of water and a medical kit (assorted bandages, disposable gloves, tweezers, antibiotic ointment, instant cold pack, light stick, survival wrap). It was a fun lecture because I facilitated a discussion among university students rather than being a single contributor unless I called on students. We were prepared for the storm. Students, faculty members, and staff invaded each of our e-mail networks that weekend with survival info, questions, and answers about the

Robert Kneschke/Shutterstock, Inc.

We wanted to learn more about Hurricane Katrina.

coming storm largely because two days or so before landfall, US energy companies estimated that Katrina had already reduced Gulf of Mexico oil production by more than a third.[1] Everyone knew that Katrina was on the move and advancing upon the Gulf Coast. There was mayhem at Walmart, Kroger, and CVS that weekend.

The Lessons of History

When anyone visits a physician's office for the first time, invariably answers to questions about medical history are on the list. There are questions about heredity (parents alive, heart issues), past behaviors (how much liquor is consumed), and past experiences (smokers, sleep issues); these answers are clues to someone's present condition. Physicians similar to most public (teachers, police officers, correctional officers, counselors) service providers who interact with the public are trained to be attentive to the appearance, the environment in which an individual resides, and the social relationships in which the individual participates. Scars, skin tone, eyes, speech patterns, and so on are "tells" (indicators). Health is influenced by the past—by history including biological inheritance and by the present including social environment and relationships. Whenever you return to the physician, he or she pulls out a file which contains all the notes from past visits. This file is a history of your health. Professionals understand clearly that the past and the present matter.[1]

Imagine waking up one morning unable to tell total strangers from family and friends! Collective memory is similar, though its loss does not immediately paralyze everyday private activity. But ignorance of history—that is, absent or defective collective memory—does deprive us of the best available guide for public action or social policy.[2] The American Historical Association defines historical knowledge as no more and no less than carefully and critically constructed collective memory. Therefore, this author is utilizing both documented accounts and my own accounts to describe Hurricane Katrina's impact upon the Gulf Coast in the hopes that you might take action and learn from these experiences as a police officer, a teacher, a counsellor, a policymaker, a healthcare practitioner, or as a parent. You have heard it said that those who don't know history repeat it. Yet, I think knowing history and learning from it is a greater concept. For instance, knowing your best friend's life story is one thing—learning how to complement each other as university student classmates or as intimates, is another thing. Understanding the nuances of an individual's social environment (including affluence and education or lack of it) and his or her social relationships (former friends, intimates, and family members) are relevant to your progress toward becoming a VBF (very best friend) or "your gal" or "your guy." In the descriptions that follow, decide how often the information provided could aid social policy to enhance the quality of life experiences and opportunities in the US for others and for you.

[1] The health of a society is also influenced by its past—by history, assuming a learning curve is in progress. Here's your history, and after a close look, here's the plan to further your success. Professionals tend to learn from the past as a guide in the present to aid the future.

The Eye of the Storm

When the eye of the storm hit land on Monday, August 29, 2005, at 11 a.m., Hurricane Katrina's front-right quadrant—its strongest winds and peak storm surge slammed into Biloxi and every gambling casino on the strip—it wasn't their lucky day; Katrina also hit hard Gulfport, and Pass Christian, (where I lived) Mississippi, with devastating and an unrelenting fury; its 150 mile winds and twenty foot storm surges destroyed much of those cities including the casinos, reports National Geographic.[3] Yes, weeks later we found slot machines on the beaches once we fought through the debris cluttering the roads, yards, and parks. And yes, it was devastating, and we survived despite a lack of electricity until Thanksgiving, medical necessities, food, running water, shelter, or cell phones (my children had no way of knowing if their daddy was alive or dead for weeks—my youngest, Alyssa Picou Stevens now living in Tampa, then in high school and visiting her grandparents in Houma, Louisiana; she 'smoothed-talked' her way on to a flight out of New Orleans to Boston; the flight cost over $1,000—regularly around $98.00; there is little someone from the lower class without cash and a silver tongue could do to evacuate the city; i.e., gasoline prices were as high as $50 a gallon).

New Orleans was hit three times: once by poverty, once by inefficient federal and local government, and that was before the third hit—Hurricane Katrina. Powerful politicians and their cronies including the President of the United

States and Federal Emergency Management Agency (FEMA)'s director, Michael Brown and local government failed the people of New Orleans.[2]

In New Orleans (Orleans Parish: Louisiana has parishes not counties) and Jefferson Parish (a large part of the city of New Orleans and many of its suburbs), law enforcement officers, healthcare providers, evacuee managers, and people who couldn't or wouldn't evacuate were outgunned by looting gangbangers, vicious profiteers, and a 'patch and pray' political system that permitted up to eight feet of water to flood approximately 80 percent of a city which was already below sea level.[4] The hospitals, stores, homes, churches, and jails flooded all with people in them (more details about the flooded jails later). All along the Gulf because of the surges, most homes and business were destroyed by water but few people were in those structures.

[2] White House aides at the time would tell you that President George W. Bush made his famous comment, "Brownie, you're doing a heck of a job," in order to bolster the spirits of the embattled FEMA director Michael Brown during the ordeal of Hurricane Katrina. Brown responded, "Heck of a job," and proceeded to say that 'Brownie' called Bush an "inattentive fratboy," David Jackson (2011). "Heck Of A Job, 'Brownie' Calls Bush Inattentive 'Fratboy.' *USA Today*. Retrieved April 23, 2014 at http://content.usatoday.com/communities/theoval/post/2011/06/heck-of-a-job-brownie-calls-bush-inattentive-fratboy/1#.U1gkRbQtqno

Courageous People

Many people, without government decree or assistance and despite government's redundant compliance policy demands (such as all civilians must dispose of their weapons), reached out and acted courageously in the aftermath of Hurricane Katrina; protecting children, elderly, and the homeless—which almost everyone was homeless for many weeks and months. Some slept while others kept watch for villains, hungry wildlife, and changing weather conditions. Observing and participating in human systems interacting with environment hazards can produce both laughter and sighs depending on whether you're hunted or hunting. Most of us preferred neither.

Zack Frank/Shutterstock, Inc.

New Orleans Flooded Because the Levees and Politicians Were Dysfunctional

It was a wonderful experience to be a survivor; it was amazing to witness the care and resilience of the people along the Gulf coast from Mobile, Alabama, to Houston, Texas, and everything in-between. Some commandeered boats, provided canned food (thank goodness for manual can openers) and shelter to strangers; many helped others search for lost family members and pets, asking nothing and taking nothing in return. Police officers and other public service personnel provided assistance even though they were at risk in more ways than they realized at the time (more about this thought later linked to federal prosecutions). Many public servants evacuated their family members to provide public safety to the family members of others. During crises intervention discussions at Loyola University of New Orleans a month later, I asked first responders why they provided aid to others at their own peril; a typical response was that New Orleans, or Gulfport, or Biloxi was their home; many typified, "I wanted to help people," a young Deputy from Jefferson Parish said. He had sent his new baby and wife to her parent's home in Jackson, Mississippi.

That said—along the Gulf Coast cities, colorful tents were erected two or three weeks after Katrina by the Methodists, Baptists, and the Catholics from Wisconsin to North Carolina to Texas; they provided warm blankets, smiles, and prayers; most everyone became skinny because the Katrina Diet was mandatory at least until Cheeseburgers in Paradise (the restaurant chain from Honolulu, and I still have not worn their T-shirt) arrived and provided—what else, delicious cheeseburgers; the Red Cross supplied tetanus shots (which didn't hurt a bit and it was nice to smell clean people) to long lines of exhausted people; the Salvation Army brought bottles of water and Walgreens supplied prescription medications (without charge). The first time in weeks many of us saw a toilet although it was portable it was still better than the alternatives. A wet inferno nested on our shoulders but we were sort'a prepared, helping hands, and for the most part made many of our own decisions about how we would live and how we would die if there were no other options, aside from the morally bankrupt government attempting to bayonet their way out of previous decisions and current responsibilities (see the discussion on the levees).

An Unprepared Government

The federal and local governments were unprepared or unconcerned despite previous reports that a tropical cyclone hurricane was in progress, reports the National Hurricane Center and History.com.[5,] The US Army Corp of Engineers under directive from the US government was aware of the condition of the levees as they slowly attempted to restructure them years prior to Katrina.[6,3] The Federal Emergency Management Agency (FEMA) did not professionally respond to hurricane victims until late in September; they delivered what we called "fuma' (FEMA) junk (trailers)" and anchored their junks along the shore of the Gulf in Mississippi and Louisiana; you know the results of that decision; they slip and slide on the sand and FEMA forgot to supply keys for the locks of their fuma junk doors and propane tanks for energy.

The National Guard was deployed by Friday to New Orleans and a few weeks after Katrina hit the Gulf Coast, there were paddy fresh-faced youngsters from Iowa and Arizona (at least the ones I met) whose mission was to collect weapons at the end of their shiny bayonets; many of us surmised that the Guard were collecting weapons so that the looters from Texas and gang members from LA (that's not lower Alabama) who pilfered everything and everybody including all the stray animals (all the animals were strays much like the people) would not be injured.

The US Coast Guard (not administratively part of the American military) saved more than 33,500 survivors and evacuated 9,409 medical patients after Hurricane Katrina. Over 5,600 Coast Guard personnel participated in the response efforts.[7] The number of guard members who became infected through various diseases is unknown similar to the number of police officers who committed suicide or took the lives of their immobile parent/s, children, spouses, and pets. I checked numerous sources and found very little. I did not accept the data from the tabloids, blogs, or Wikipedia largely because that data is easily manipulated by anyone (see Chapter 10 for details on the media and sensationalized information; or see Dennis J. Stevens (2011). *Media and Criminal Justice: CSI Effect*. Boston: Jones and Bartlett).

It was late in the game when veteran federal troops from Naval Air Station Pensacola, Fort Benning, and Camp Shelby among others arrived (some had weapons) to be involved with rescue activities, to enforce curfew, and to control traffic.[4]

[3] Gilbert F. White, the father of floodplain management studied the delta after a 1927 disaster and concluded that much of the suffering resulting from that disaster could have been avoided. "Floods are 'acts of God,'" he wrote in 1942, "but flood losses are largely acts of man." White argued that dams, levees, and other flood protections in New Orleans could increase flood losses because they spur new development in the floodplain, which incurs catastrophic losses when man-made flood protections fail. The phenomenon is known as the "levee effect."

City planners and developers applauded as the Army Corps of Engineers after Hurricane Betsy ravaged New Orleans in 1965. They said that the Army Corps strengthened the existing levees around the city but also threw new levees far and wide, enclosing thousands of acres of undeveloped wetlands lining the new I-10 corridor. Almost 80 percent of the estimated benefits that the corps initially used to justify the cost of the project came from the future development of those wetlands. "It was basically a development scheme," says Oliver Houck, a Tulane professor of environmental law. "They put it (levees) around New Orleans East, and the developers laughed all the way to the bank." After Katrina, two independent investigations and the Army Corps of Engineers' 25-million-dollar study painted a disturbing picture of flaws in the planning, design, and construction of the levee system prior to Katrina. *Source:* Joel K. Bourne, Jr. (2007). New Orleans: A Perilous Future. National Geographic Magazine. Retrieved December 3, 2014: http://ngm.nationalgeographic.com/print/2007/08/new-orleans/new-orleans-text

[4] President Bush attempted to change the law, but failed. The law in question is the Posse Comitatus Act, the longstanding federal statute that restricts the government's ability to use the US military as a police force.

The Posse Comitatus Act is no barrier to federal troops providing logistical support during natural disasters. Nor does it prohibit the President from using military to restore order in extraordinary circumstances—even over the objection of a state governor. What it does is set a high bar for the use of federal troops in a policing role. That reflects America's traditional distrust of using standing armies to enforce order at home, a distrust that's well-justified. There are good reasons to resist any push toward domestic militarization. As one federal court has explained: "Military personnel must be trained to operate under circumstances where the protection of constitutional freedoms cannot receive the consideration needed in order to assure their preservation. The Posse Comitatus statute is intended to meet that danger." The Posse Comitatus Act is the US federal law (18 U.S.C. § 1385, original at 20 Stat. 152) was passed on June 18, 1878, after the end of Reconstruction and was updated in 1981.

President George W. Bush and his administration seemed unaware of the devastation along the Gulf Coast, but the psychological desperation in particular was largely concentrated in New Orleans; this author easily speculates that one reason for the desperation in New Orleans was because most of those residents represented persons of color (black, brown, and yellow) and were poor and although wonderful individuals, they were largely illiterate. The thinking and the literature pretty well clarify that one perspective is that poverty, illiteracy, and people of color are pathways to prison.[8] Why help them since the industrial prison complex and the Power Elite (explained later) have much to gain from keeping folks illiterate and power.

David Burkholder/Shutterstock, Inc.

X's are where dead bodies were discovered

There were poor folks elsewhere along the coast, but in my observations, they were socialized toward being dependent upon themselves rather than socialized towards dependency on a welfare system that demands compliance and conformity. This thought is consistent with the literature; for instance, one prominent author writes that in the US, a majority of the poor and those who work with the poor are women; this thought was particularly true in New Orleans in 2005. Recipients of public assistance and the welfare public servants who served them "are trapped at the bottom of the American welfare system."[9] One implication is that their individual self-worth in the hierarchy of a bureaucratic system demands compliance which determines their personal opportunities and outcomes. I have always lectured to my students that welfare is a form of dominance over a population in particular the lower social economic class which government and its cronies (The Power Elite) must control in order to continue their lifestyles.[5] Not enough money or dignity to live respectfully like human beings, but just enough money so that they must cheat a little here and there; welfare recipients and some welfare workers might take cash jobs such as ironing clothes, watching children, and prostitution.[10] When welfare recipients cheat, government has them exactly where government want welfare recipients and welfare workers—vulnerable to arrest and imprisonment. The social worker trap similar to the welfare recipients' trap can be explained through what some researchers call "The Emperor's New Clothes" perspective.[11] This notion of self-enforcing norms (of government) tells the story of three rogues who sell a foolish monarch a "nonexistent robe that they claim cannot be seen by those who are 'unfit for office' or 'incorrigible stupid.' Fear of exposure leads the emperor and in turn each of the citizens to express admiration for the new clothes." The idea is based on the Hans Christian Andersen fable. In this model, welfare workers (as well as criminal justice professionals and their collaborate partners) must decide whether to comply with and enforce norms and laws that are supported by a few fanatics such as "the reason the US is in decline is

[5] The Power Elite: the governing elite in the US draws its selective members from three areas: (1) the highest political leaders including the president and a handful of key cabinet members and close advisers;
(2) major corporate owners and directors; and (3) high-ranking military officers.
Source: C. Wright Mills (1956). *The Power Elite.* New York: Oxford University Press.
Another source argues the elite occupies what Mills terms the top command posts of society. These positions give their holders enormous authority over not just governmental, but financial, educational, social, civic, and cultural institutions as well. A small group is able to take fundamental actions that touch everyone. Decisions made in the boardrooms of large corporations and banks affect inflation and employment. The needs of industry greatly determine the priorities and policies of educational and research organizations, and the chief economic agencies of government. The Power Elite represents a close-knit group, yet they are not part of a conspiracy that secretly manipulates events. It is said that they respect civil liberties, follow established constitutional principles, and operate openly and peacefully. They are not a dictatorship nor do they rely on terror, a secret police, or midnight arrests to get its way.
Source: H.T. Reynolds (2013). University of Delaware. Retrieved September 16, 2014: http://www.udel.edu/htr/Psc105/Texts/power.html

because of weak immigration laws or the black guy did it." They find that cascades of self-reinforcing support among each other.

Before the storm, New Orleans was among the most ghettoized cities in America. Among the nation's 100 largest metro areas, it ranked third in poverty concentration.[12] In 2000, 23 percent of the poor in metro New Orleans lived in high-poverty neighborhoods (where at least 40 percent of the population lived below the poverty line). Also, New Orleans' population was 67 percent black and brown but they raised their children in churches and smiled at their babies every second they could; their homes (not their families) were constructed of inexpensive materials patched together by government red tape and bureaucratic compliance regulation; consequently, their amenities were below standards; they were "disposable properties" that collapsed when the winds from Katrina hit; those homes washed away when the levees flooded the city.[13] The sad part of the story is that the people of Orleans Parish and much of Jefferson Parish were also considered "disposable" by the federal and local government, observers say. The social media reinforced government's sins by reporting what some fundamentalists were preaching: Katrina was actually a punishment for the wickedness of the people who live in the Gulf Coast especially New Orleans, Louisiana, or NOLA.[14] In part, the justification lays in the the Judeo Christian Bible which argues that our choices bear consequences. "Whatever a man sows, that's what he reaps" (Galatians 6:7–8). Also see Chapter 4, 9, and 10, where HIV, among other diseases are also considered consequences of sins as explained in the Judeo Christian Bible which influence law enforcement and correctional officers, physicians and nurses, performance linked to public safety, protection, and treatment.

Another assumption many of us at the time thought was that many residents particularly those who lacked social ties and did not leave their homes before Katrina, did not want to be rescued; what did it matter? They were sinners and already standing at hell's gates no matter what; they had little respect for themselves, and little incentive to think otherwise. I did not know at the time that the literature was consistent with those thoughts until years later when I read an account by Eric Klinenberg.[15] His perspective is that when someone dies alone at home, "death is a powerful symbol of social abandonment and failure." If bowling alone is a sign of a weakening of American civil society, dying alone can carry a more powerful social and symbolic meaning.[7]

[6] Hurricane Katrina damaged the city of New Orleans in what seems like biblical proportions. Some say the human suffering alone could be a part of God's plan. Reverend Franklin Graham, son of Reverend Billy Graham, suggests the city was targeted because of the city's sinful reputation. Source: NBC News. Retrieved May 13, 2014: http://www.nbcnews.com/id/9600878/ns/msnbc-morning_joe/t/hurricane-katrina-wrath-god/#.U3I9kBsU9y0

At a speech in Virginia, he said, "This is one wicked city, OK? It's known for Mardi Gras, for Satan worship. It's known for sex perversion. It's known for every type of drugs and alcohol and the orgies and all of these things that go on down there in New Orleans." Reverend Graham continued, "There's been a black spiritual cloud over New Orleans for years. They believe God is going to use that storm to bring revival."

[7] During the summer heat wave of 1995 in Chicago, "...anything that facilitated social contact, even membership in a social club or owning a pet was associated with a decreased risk of death." Over 700 Chicago residents in excess of the norm died alone in their apartments and homes during the week of July 13, 1995. Victims didn't respond to phone calls or knocks at doors or rescuers. Doors and windows were locked; there were no known relatives or friends. Victims were all members of lower social class.

Source: Jan C. Semenza, Carol H. Rubin, Kenneth H. Falter, Joel D. Selanikio, W. Dana Flanders, Holly L. Howe, and John L. Wilhelm (1996). "Heat Related Deaths During the July 1995 Heat Wave in Chicago." *New England Journal of Medicine*, 335: 84–90.

[8] Many in the Gulf finally better understood Ronald Reagan's thought: "The most terrifying words in the English language are: I'm from the government and I'm here to help."

Federal Government's Unprofessional Decisions

It's hard to tell the magnitude of the Bush administration's blunders and misjudgments, or their cost in human lives and property damage.[16] What is clear was the federal government's indifference toward New Orleans long before Katrina struck. "The Bush administration systemically stripped FEMA and the Army Corps of Engineers of authority, money and key staff; undermined their morale; and ignored warnings by state emergency managers that its actions were sabotaging FEMA's capacity to respond to disasters."[17, 8]

Once FEMA became an agency of the Department of Homeland Security, FEMA's role as an emergency planning and relief agency was diminished. FEMA no longer saw the levees in New Orleans as relevant. The Bush administration knew long before the storm hit that 100,000 New Orleans residents had no way to escape a major hurricane on their own and that the city had finished only 10 percent of its evacuation plan. Any demographic study of the city would have shown that those residents were largely seniors, impoverished, fearful of crime, and removed from proximate sources of financial and social support which is a deadly combination of a vulnerable population to traumatic outcomes during episodes of acute crisis.[18] The National Weather Service correctly predicted the force of Hurricane Katrina, but the Bush administration failed to accept the weight of the storm.[19]

The general perspective of the people of New Orleans was that government left them to die. The storm hit Monday and it wasn't until Friday that a convoy of National Guard troops and supply trucks arrived; they distributed food and water to the 20,000 residents stranded at the Superdome and convention center.[20] The Guard did not have enough water for a third of the people in the Superdome; riots broke out and injury was common. Medical attention for everyone was not available, and the few healthcare providers were frustrated because they just couldn't help anyone, they said at group meetings with this author. These providers had few supplies; many were forced to decide who should and who should not receive treatment. Water and medical supplies are part of every emergency deployment; why was NOLA a different rescue mission, some asked.

Medical Care: Who Should Receive and Who Shouldn't Receive Treatment

Concerning the clinics in New Orleans and medical care, below is an account offered by a physician after Hurricane Katrina:[21]

> On September 2, 2005, when Wildlife and Fisheries boats finally evacuated patients and staff from Charity Hospital in New Orleans, we could not fully comprehend the devastation of our health care infrastructure." Reflecting recently on the vast scope of the rebuilding effort, Fred Lopez, vice chair for education at Louisiana State University (LSU) School of Medicine, observed, "The desperate week we spent inside Charity after Katrina is the one that everybody saw on CNN, but that was the easiest week of the last six months.

Assistance to care for those injured was nonexistent after Katrina. In one of the larger hospitals, few if any healthcare providers including physicians, nurses, and helpers were available; there was little medication available, little electrical power assuming the outside generators were operational, no protection from drug addicts seeking drugs, no operational equipment, few beds, jammed emergency rooms, and angry personnel and patients. Aid from any government source was slow to materialize. When the director of Ochsner Clinic in New Orleans was asked what government had contributed to the efforts of the clinic including pay for the personnel the answer was, "Nothing. We have asked and asked [the authorities] for fair compensation, and perhaps we will get it eventually, but we cannot go on indefinitely providing uncompensated care."[22]

Two outpatient clinics served the disenfranchised populations of New Orleans and personnel had to create new ways to deliver community-based care.[23] Charity Hospital's HIV Outpatient (HOP) Clinic responded to Hurricane Katrina by reconstituting itself with a much smaller staff. In the Algiers neighborhood of New Orleans across the Mississippi River, a new free clinic dubbed the Common Ground Health Clinic drew volunteer medical professionals from around the country. Getting into the city was a major effort because many were trying to get out and debris including trees, abandoned vehicles, parts of buildings and their roofs were everywhere. The airport was virtually closed as were the major highways. In the early days after Katrina, these clinics coalesced around the neediest populations. The reconstitution of the HOP clinic was driven by the urgent need to restore antiviral treatment for patients with human "immunodeficiency virus (HIV) infection in order to avert virologic resistance and disease progression," says Berggren. Many patients left medications behind as they attempted their escape from the city and its suburbs; others rationed pills. Approximately 40 of Ochsner Hospital's 600 physicians and 1,500 of its 7,400 other employees resigned after Katrina. Similar to the police department, approximately 250 officers out of 1,700 including the chief of police left the city or were not accounted for.[24] However, many of us who lived through Katrina heard numbers of fleeing officers as high as 600 officers and as many as one-half of the medical staff in hospitals left the city, too.

Obviously, precautions and some help came months and in several cases years after Katrina, reports The National Association of County and City Health Officials.[25] What happened after the storm particularly in New Orleans was disgraceful, largely preventable, nourished through federal and local governmental inadequacies, and sustained by an elitist agenda; it is unclear if the Power Elite agenda was intentional, but dying and missing men, women, and children matter little compared to intentions.

Investigation of Medical Practitioners

According to an investigation by the state's attorney general, a physician and two nurses "pretended that maybe they were God" and put to death four patients using a lethal injection of drugs, after determining that the four were either too ill or too incapacitated to be transported.[26] Certainty, it is more likely that the numbers of "put to death" patients topped over a hundred souls.

After a black-out, when a hospital staff including physicians and nurses learn that all power from the backup generators is about to stop, what's their plan? "That's when the very first tough ethical decision arose ... which was: Who are you going to save first if you know that you may be hours away from all power going out?"[27] At Memorial Hospital in New Orleans, the physicians decided that the babies would be saved first, and the intensive care unit patients, whose lives really depended on electricity. "They also decided at that point who would go last, and that was patients who had do not resuscitate orders" an indicator of the costs of the investigation is in the millions, a confidential source suggests. Had government provided the necessary services, would the medical practitioners behave in the manner in which they had, might be a worthy question. From my perspective, how do we really know what person occupied what bed with what condition? A government report a month after Katrina reads: "Disaster Medical Assistance Teams (DMATs) are teams of physicians, nurses and other medical professionals who provide medical care. FEMA reports that it deployed all of the nation's more than 50 DMATs in the initial response to Hurricane Katrina. At least one team was deployed to the New Orleans Superdome shelter. Louis Armstrong International Airport outside New Orleans served as a temporary field hospital for hurricane victims as they were evacuated from the city. DMAT members from a dozen teams deployed at the airport reported overwhelming numbers of patients, some of whom could not be saved under the austere conditions they faced. "Teams fanned out across the affected Gulf Coast, doing what they could to accommodate victims of the hurricane which, by some reports, also robbed the region of 6,000 hospital beds."[28]

Immediate Government Response to NO Police Officers and Others

The federal and local government had almost immediate reactions toward New Orleans Police Department (NOPD) NO officers, Jefferson Country deputies, and rescue providers; some were arrested, prosecuted, convicted of crimes; many of those officers and rescue workers were eventually released (after a loss of their jobs, reputations, and futures), and some retried. At least forty officers and deputies have yet to be found, but that's another story.

During Katrina's cleanup, officers and most rescue providers had no communicational systems with decision makers or top command; they had no operational vehicles, no gas, and no jails to hold violators or homes to hold people who lost their homes. Officers of the NOPD and law enforcement throughout the storm path not only lacked adequate technical tools of communication, transportation, and shelter, they also experienced great sacrifices to remain at work during a storm that affected them and their family members on a personal level.[29] From my personal experience, some officers commandeered vehicles at car dealerships and stole gasoline to patrol the streets and to transport the dead and injured; many officers violated Mayor Ray Nagin's orders to stop helping Katrina victims.[30] Imagine the frustration of officers and rescue workers who were ordered to quite helping others?

Some officers broke into retail business to dispose of weapons that those businesses showcased. Some officers fired at gang members after being attacked while other officers fired at violators engaged in heinous crimes including the sexual assault of children. The infrastructure of the NOPD was directly hit as eight police stations were flooded, police were left without sufficient supplies, and temporary headquarters had to be improvised.[31] There was no chain-of-command for several weeks after Katrina (see professionalism recommendations in Chapter 11), thus officers and rescue providers were left on their own; making their own decisions, and no matter the quality of decision, many were federally prosecuted and indicted. In response to the lack of effective policing, residents became themselves involved in rescue efforts, using boats to help people who were trapped on their roofs and providing what little medical attention they could. There was a long-standing distrust towards the NOPD which additionally contributed to the law enforcement breakdown during Katrina as deficiencies in police legitimacy hindered cooperation with residents.[32] One estimate is that the federal government indicted twenty-one New Orleans police officers (NOPD) and nine Jefferson Parish deputies for dubious actions despite their good deeds.[9] Once a handful of NO officers were detained and questioned by federal authorities before prosecution, other NO officers backed out of sight; some, however, continued to aid people in need. Action taken by federal authorities to question police officers added to the discontent in the city and added fire to gangbangers and angry citizens who opposed the cops.

Also from what the literature tells me is that approximately ninety-seven officers, deputies, relief workers, emergency care responders, and healthcare practitioners were exposed to infectious pathogens including MRSA, communicable diseases, and foodborne illnesses during Katrina (that we know of).[33, 10] How many military personnel were infected will never be known; a VA nurse at Alexandria Hospital in Pineville, Louisiana, says in confidence: "We had those young men sleeping on the floors in the chapel, visitor areas, and food areas because we had no more beds. Supplies were scare; doctors had decisions to make. Some of us made their decisions for them."

The Aftermath of Katrina

The Congressional Research Service presented the US Congress with a report a month after Hurricane Katrina which says: "The logistical hurdles posed by Hurricane Katrina have been formidable. Communications were knocked out in hard-hit areas, which compromised the

Igor Zh./Shutterstock, Inc.

[9] For example, less than a week after Katrina had made landfall (in August 2005), police shot and killed two unarmed individuals and wounded four others on the Danziger Bridge. Five former officers cooperated with a Justice Department investigation and pleaded guilty to engaging in a cover-up to make the shootings appear justified. After a jury convicted five other former officers in 2011, their attorneys argued that prosecutors' online comments and leaks to news organizations were part of a "secret public relations campaign" that deprived their clients of a fair trial. The officers will receive a new trial. (Source: Associated Press in New Orleans (2013, September 17). "New Orleans Police Officers Jailed Over Katrina Shootings To Get New Trial." The Guardian. Retrieved April 25, 2014: http://www.theguardian.com/world/2013/sep/17/new-orleans-police-officers-katrina-trial. My thoughts of this matter include the idea that the feds vigorously prosecuted those Danziger Bridge officers, but never once prosecuted the federal government politicians responsible for the flooding on New Orleans or the despicable care and treatment of Katrina's victims.

[10] A growing number of disease-causing organisms, also known as pathogens, are resistant to one or more antimicrobial drugs. A wide range of pathogens—including the bacteria that cause tuberculosis, the viruses that cause influenza, the parasites that cause malaria, and the fungi that cause yeast infections—are becoming resistant to the antimicrobial agents used for treatment. *Source:* Centers for Disease Control and Prevention. Retrieved September 4, 2014: http://www.cdc.gov/drugresistance/diseasesconnectedar.html

process of assessing and prioritizing needs. Physical access was blocked in some areas, and civil disorder was a problem in some others. Each kept responders from delivering aid. In some cases, victims were isolated without water and medicines, and hospitals that had not been evacuated were unable to sustain operations. Each circumstance required the emergency evacuation of critically ill patients to a triage center, which then itself became overwhelmed. Federal, state, and local governments, businesses and corporations, the faith community, and other volunteers all pitched in to speed relief to Katrina's victims, but keeping all of it coordinated remains a challenge."[34]

Nowhere in that government report does it explain the real tragedies that occurred during Katrina which include two thousand decomposed dead bodies laid in make-shift morgues, many of the dead unrecognizable, 700 persons are still (as of August 2014) missing, 400 corpses still remain unidentified, $150 billion in property damages and economic loss, 90,000 square miles were impacted. Also, family pets by the thousands were lost; think of all the lost photo albums of children's lives, personal belongings, and vehicles; self-esteem hit basement levels; and finally it should be acknowledged that inmates locked down in hundred-year-old jails, nursing home patients, and handicapped adults and children without support systems, drowned or were simply abandoned.[11] The floodwaters in and around New Orleans were laced with chemicals, snakes, human excrement, and the bloated bodies of humans, animals of many descriptions, and pets; many of those bodies were prisoners, patients in long-term care facilities, and victims of previous homicides buried in swampland graves of Louisiana; (See *Wicked Women: A Journey of Super Predators* for details about burying corpses in the wetlands) their leftover parts were results of creatures who roam those wetlands—scavengers if you will;[36] black and brown people went out every day to save family members left behind, shredded, and discarded.[37] According to a confidential account by NOPD officers during discussions on protecting the NO population in violation of the mayor's orders, the officers say they raided what they thought was a gang outpost in an Allegers' neighborhood apartment complex. "We felt like vigilantes because of (Mayor) Nagin's orders," one of the officers adds. There was no electricity so everything inside the building was dark. "It felt like one of those bad dreams." To their surprise, a naked little girl was bound and gagged to a broken toilet; as the officer shined his flashlight on her battered body, "We saw movement." Once outside, the officers realized that the movement was caused by maggots. It was hard to tell how long she had been dead, but she had recently been violated. "Maybe it's good she was dead because we couldn't get medical help for her if she was alive." The officers had no place to put the individuals arrested because jails were under water and there were no jailers in sight. They cuffed four of the gang members inside an abandoned car and the remaining two (both females) were cuffed to officers during their sweeps of the rest of Allegers. At a makeshift police headquarters they cuffed the females to chairs. The thinking was that these females, who were approximately seventeen years of age, would become victims themselves if cuffed inside a vehicle.

There is more that government reports avoided in their presentation to Congress through the Sarah Lister report:[38] sexual predators were swapping like zombies upon unprotected children in hospitals and detention facilities, gang members waging bitter war against what was left of law enforcement in the Gulf coast including New Orleans, and the mentally ill, junkies, and resentful youth had few boundaries or obstacles to guide their conduct. The petulant odor of moisture, death, and government inefficacy continues to linger in the memory of most Katrina survivors as do the memories of a resilient population, awesome criminal justice and healthcare providers, and of course, amazing cheeseburgers. Disasters two and three are in Chapter 2.

[11] Inmates in Templeman III, one of several buildings in the Orleans Parish Prison compound, reported that there were no correctional officers in the building, which held more than 600 inmates. These inmates, including some who were locked in ground-floor cells, were not evacuated until four days after floodwaters in the jail had reached chest-level. Some inmates reported that they saw bodies floating in the floodwaters as they were evacuated from the prison. The number of deaths is unknown. Inmates broke jail windows to let air in. They also set fire to blankets and shirts and hung them out of the windows to let people know they were still in the facility.
Source: Corinne Carey (2005, September 22). New Orleans: Prisoners Abandoned to Floodwaters: Officers Deserted a Jail Building, Leaving Inmates Locked in Cells. US Program: Human Rights Watch. Retrieved August 28, 2014: http://www.hrw.org/news/2005/09/21/new-orleans-prisoners-abandoned-floodwaters

Summary

The chapter opens with a discussion about a first and last lecture to university students who were about to experience a catastrophic event, Hurricane Katrina at the Gulf Coast. Through the lessons of history, the students were potentially prepared to effectively move forward and survive the impending storm as evidenced by accomplishment to complete their research course and graduate. Most of the population moved above the storm and most often without government support but rather the support of religious and nonprofit organizations and caring companies.

Blundering and unprepared federal and local government gave rise to the flooding of New Orleans, unnecessary hardships, redundant dictates, and medical emergencies, all which pushed individuals to make decisions they were not comfortable or prepared to make such as who should receive medical treatment or be arrested and who shouldn't receive treatment.

Name: ____________________ Date: ____________ School Identification Number: ________

STUDENT WORKSHEETS

Chapter 1 Disaster Comes in Threes

Define the following key terms from Chapter 1, and in your answer, show the page number where you found the definition. Provide an example for each key term.

1. Agents of Compliance

2. Federal Emergency Management Agency (FEMA)

3. Lessons of History

4. Power Elite

5. National Hurricane Center

6. Scholarly Work

7. Twin Moral Impulses

Name: ______________________________ Date: ____________ School Identification Number: ______

STUDENT WORKSHEETS

Chapter 1 Disaster Comes in Threes

Discuss and demonstrate in your own words that you comprehend the following learning objectives in this chapter.

1. Understand the role history and learning play in a healthy society and to the quality of life experiences and opportunities of an individual.

2. Identify the "players" in the justice community and their collaborative partners; explain in what way each can contribute to public safety, social order, and equality.

3. Comprehend the significance of political priorities toward public safety using the example of the New Orleans' Levees.

4. Describe in what way dying alone can be a powerful symbol of social abandonment and failure.

Name: ______________________________ Date: ____________ School Identification Number: ______

STUDENT WORKSHEETS

Chapter 1 Disaster Comes in Threes *(Continued)*

5. Identify and explain the relevance of the Power Elite in the discussions about Katrina strategies.

6. Describe policing strategy outcomes among Katrina victims. In what way do you see those strategies as appropriate or inappropriate? What would you have done differently if you were a police officer in New Orleans during the hurricane?

7. Describe some of the treatment outcomes among Katrina victims. In what way do you see treatment decisions as appropriate or inappropriate? What would you have done differently if you were a physician or a nurse in New Orleans during the hurricane?

8. Explain the ideas connected to "The Emperor's New Clothes" and how it applies to welfare recipients and welfare workers.

9. Describe some of the government's role among Katrina victims during the hurricane. If you were in charge, what would you have done differently and why?

CHAPTER 1 ENDNOTES

1. Fox Facts: Hurricane Katrina Damage (2006, August 29). Retrieved April 27, 2014: http://www.foxnews.com/story/2006/08/29/fox-facts-hurricane-katrina-damage/
2. William H. McNeill (1985). Why Study History? *American Historical Association*. Retrieved April 28, 2014: http://www.historians.org/about-aha-and-membership/aha-history-and-archives/archives/why-study-history-%281985%29
3. Hurricane Katrina Timeline (2005). National Geographic News. Retrieved April 23, 2014: http://news.nationalgeographic.com/news/2005/09/0914_050914_katrina_timeline_2.html

   Kristin A. Bates and Richelle S. Swan (2007). *Through the Eye of Katrina.* Durham, NC: Carolina Academic Press.
4. FOX Facts: Hurricane Katrina Damage (2006, August 29). Retrieved April 27, 2014: http://www.foxnews.com/story/2006/08/29/fox-facts-hurricane-katrina-damage/
5. History.com (2014). *Hurricane Katrina*. Retrieved April 23, 2014: http://www.history.com/topics/hurricane-katrina

   Also see, National Hurricane Center (2011). The Deadliest, Costliest, And Most Intense United States Tropical Cyclones From 1851 To 2010. Retrieved September 15, 2014: http://www.nhc.noaa.gov/dcmi.shtml Page 5.
6. JD Rogers (2006). Development of the New Orleans Flood Protection System prior to Hurricane Katrina Journal Of Geotechnical And Geoenvironmental Engineering. Retrieved August 30, 2014: http://web.mst.edu/~rogersda/levees/History%20New%20Orleans%20Flood%20Control-Rogers.pdf
7. US Coast Guard (2013). Hurricane Katrina. Retrieved April 26, 2014: http://www.uscg.mil/history/katrina/katrinaindex.asp
8. Dennis J. Stevens (2014). Failure of the American Prison Complex: Let's Abolish It. Iowa: Kendall Hunt. Page 136.
9. Catherine Kingfisher (1996–2011). *Women in the American Welfare Trap*. Philadelphia, PA: University of Pennsylvania Press. Page 16–18 and 131–134.
10. Loïc Wacquant (2009). Punishing the Poor: The Neoliberal Government of Social Insecurity. Durham, NC: Duke University Press. Also see, William Domhoff (2013). Wealth, Income, and Power. Who Rules America. Retrieved April 29, 2014: http://www2.ucsc.edu/whorulesamerica/power/wealth.html
11. Damon Centola, Robb Willer, and Michael Macy (2005). Model of Self-Enforcing Norms. *American Journal of Sociology*, 110(4): 1009–1040.
12. Peter Dreier (2006). Katrina: A Political Disaster. *National Housing Institute*, 145. Retrieved April 29, 2014: http://nhi.org/online/issues/145/politicaldisaster.html
13. Kristin A. Bates and Richelle S. Swan (2007). *Through the Eye of Katrina.* Durham, NC: Carolina Academic Press.
14. Anne M. Arlinghaus (2006). Religion, Rhetoric, and Social Change After Hurricane Katrina. *Vanderbilt Undergraduate Research Journal,* 2(1). Retrieved December 3, 2014: http://ejournals.library.vanderbilt.edu/index.php/vurj/article/viewFile/2750/1163

15. Eric Klinenberg (2013). Dying Alone: The Social Production of Urban Isolation. In Peter Conrad and Valerie Leiter (eds.) *The Sociology of Health and Illness: Critical Perspectives*. New York: Worth. Pages 102–116.
16. Peter Dreier (2006).
17. Ibid.
18. Eric Klinenberg (2013). Page 104. Also see, Jan Gurley, Nancy Lum, Merle Sande, Bernard Lo, and Mitchell Katz (1996). Person Found in the Homes Helpless or Dead. *New England Journal of Medicine*, 334: 1710–1716.
19. Eric Lipton(2006). White House Knew of Levee's Failure on Night of the Storm. New York Times. Retrieved May 12, 2014: http://www.nytimes.com/2006/02/10/politics/10katrina.html?pagewanted=all&_r=0
20. Hurricane Katrina Timeline (2005). Page 2.
21. Ruth E. Berggren and Tyler J. Curiel (2006). After the Storm—Health Care Infrastructure in Post-Katrina New Orleans. *New England Journal of Medicine*, 354: 1549–1552. DOI: 10.1056/NEJMp068039
22. Ibid.
23. Ruth E. Berggren (2006). Perspective: Adaptations. New England Journal of Medicine, 354(4):1550–1551.
24. Mathieu Deflem and Suzanne Sutphin (2009). Policing Katrina: Managing Law Enforcement in New Orleans. *Policing* 3(1):41–49. Also see Benjamin Sims (2007). The Day After the Hurricane: Infrastructure, Order, and the New Orleans Police Department's Response to Hurricane Katrina. *Social Studies of Science*, 37(1): 111–118. Retrieved April 27, 2014: http://cretscmhd.psych.ucla.edu/nola/volunteer/EmpiricalStudies/The%20day%20after%20the%20hurricane%20-%20infrastructure,%20order,%20and%20the%20new%20orleans%20police%20departments%20response%20to%20hurricane%20katrina.pdf
25. Program Details. National Association of County and City Health Officials. Retrieved April 25, 2014: http://www.naccho.org/topics/modelpractices/database/practice.cfm?PracticeID=320
26. Associated Press (2006, July 19). Physician, Nurses Accused of Giving Patients Deadly Injections After Hurricane Katrina. *Fox News.com*. Retrieved December 3, 2014: http://www.foxnews.com/story/2006/07/19/doctor-nurses-accused-giving-patients-deadly-injections-after-hurricane-katrina/
27. Sheri Fink (2013). *Five Days at Memorial: Life and Death in a Storm-Ravaged Hospital*. New York: Crown. Pages 3–6.
28. Sarah A Lister (2005, September 5). Hurricane Katrina: The Public Health and Medical Response. CRS Report for Congress. Retrieved August 25, 2014: http://fpc.state.gov/documents/organization/54255.pdf Page 13.
29. Mathieu Deflem and Suzanne Sutphin (2009). Policing Katrina: Managing Law Enforcement in New Orleans. *Policing* 3(1):41–49.
30. Peter Dreier (2006).
31. Mathieu Deflem and Suzanne Sutphin (2009).
32. Ibid.
33. Benjamin Sims (2007).
34. Sarah A Lister (2005, September 5). Page 1.
35. History.com (2014). Hurricane Katrina Facts. Retrieved April 27, 2014: http://www.history.com/topics/hurricane-katrina

36. Shana Agid (2007). Locked and Loaded: The Prison Industrial Complex and the Response to Hurricane Katrina. In Kristin A. Bates and Richelle S. Swan (Eds.) *Through the Eye of Katrina: Social Justice in the United States*. (Pages 55–72). Durham, North Carolina: Carolina Academic Press.

37. Walidah Imarisha (2005). Readings by & for Anti-Racist Educators and Organizers Legacies: Racism and Resistance in New Orleans Before and After Katrina. Retrieved April 26, 2014: http://katrinareader.org/sites/katrinareader.org/files/legaciesprint-tluhtd.html

38. Sarah A Lister (2005, September 5). Page 3.

Alexander Trinitatov/Shutterstock, Inc.

Some Might Question God's Existence In A Virtues Nation When Quality Healthcare and Social Justice Does Not Prevail

CHAPTER 2

Lessons Learned: Disasters Two and Three

Learning Objectives

After you read this chapter, you will be better prepared to:

- Characterize the significance of medical expense versus quality medical treatment and its relationship to public health.
- Identify the three components that give rise to resilient mutated strains of multidrug resistant bacteria and tuberculosis-causing mycobacteria which have evolved and flourished.
- Explain hospital associated infections and the outcome from those infections.
- Explain in what way a description of government as a sprawling massive enterprise can intensify inequality among specific groups of individuals in a democratic nation.
- Explain what the social consequences might be in relationship to bacteria resistant to antibiotics.
- Characterize what is meant by the thought that medical science and public health practices, because of their success, have led to complacency and bureaucratic indifference.
- Apply to real world (college students') experiences how the author might connect the phrase, "Nothing is as it seems." In what way do you agree or disagree that this is a helpful perspective in understanding real world events.
- Explain the 'head fake' strategy and apply it to this chapter.
- Describe the second and third disasters linked to this chapter.

Key Terms

Antimicrobial Resistant
Bacteria Resistant to Antibiotics
Biocultural Era
Colonization
Ebola
Evolution of Deadly Pathogens
Hospital Associated Infections
Infectious Pathogens
K.pneumoniae or *E.coli*
Lessons of History
Methicillin-Resistant Staphylococcus Aureus (MRSA)
Prisoner Associated Infections
Power Elite
Rule of Law
Social Justice
Sprawling Massive Enterprise
The Institute for Advanced Study
Thomas Theorem
Twin Moral Impulses

Words of Wisdom

Injustice anywhere is a threat to justice everywhere.

Martin Luther King, Jr.

Introduction

You might say that the focus of this book is how infectious disease affects the occupational performance of criminal justice, firefighters, and healthcare personnel in America. This chapter describes lessons learned from Hurricane Katrina (see Chapter 1) and it describes America's second disaster: the invasion of antimicrobial infectious pathogens including MRSA. The third disaster is characterized featuring the inability of first-responders to combat this new invasion. When you finish reading this chapter, you might come away with the idea that we learned little about providing services and treatment from Hurricane Katrina. Yet, we have learned about the injustice or lack of social justice in New Orleans during the Katrina experience which is consistent with the idea advanced by Dr. Martin Luther King, Jr. (above).

America Is Engaged in Another Disaster of Our Own Design

Igor Zh./Shutterstock, Inc.

America is engaged in another disaster which shows no mercy, and this one was made in the USA.

It seems, the federal government (in particular the US Food and Drug Administration) and their profiteer collaborators remain apathetic to the outcomes or at least to the outcomes of those individuals getting hit the hardest;[1] this thought is similar to the disenfranchised population of New Orleans, Louisiana, (NOLA) and all the individuals who engaged those populations during Hurricane Katrina such as criminal justice (primarily law enforcement and corrections) professionals and their collaborators (firefighters, hospital systems, physicians, nurses, and healthcare personnel).

Specifically, infectious pathogens resistant to antibiotics such as Methicillin-Resistant Staphylococcus Aureus (MRSA) and other deadly diseases represent a clear and present danger in a nation with the highest medical costs and oddly, the highest incarceration rates in the world.[2]

Yet, American healthcare expenditures purchase inferior healthcare in comparison to other nations.[3] For instance, the World Health Organization (WHO)[1] explains that Americans spent more on healthcare per capita ($8,608) and more on healthcare as a percentage of gross domestic product (18 percent or $2.7 trillion in 2011) than any other country.[4]

Once drug therapies or vaccine-induced immunities are arrested, you might say, or controlled, microbes evolve and find their way comfortably into new hosts such as prisoners because as a group they tend to be more vulnerable to disease than others and engage justice personnel more often than other groups, too; resilient mutates strains of multidrug resistant bacteria and tuberculosis-causing mycobacteria have evolved and flourished, in part through three components:[5]

- An Ignorance of the Need to Complete a Prescribed Course of Antibiotics
- By the Overuse of Antibiotics

[1] WHO is the directing and coordinating authority for health within the United Nations system. It is responsible for providing leadership on global health matters, shaping the health research agenda, setting norms and standards, articulating evidence-based policy options, providing technical support to countries and monitoring and assessing health trends. In the twenty-first century, health is a shared responsibility, involving equitable access to essential care and collective defense against transnational threats. See Chapter 2 for more details.

Gil C/Shutterstock, Inc.

About WHO

- And by Abuse of Antimicrobial (Destroying or Inhibiting the Growth of Microorganisms and Especially Pathogenic Microorganisms) Drugs

Bacteria have been evolving to resist the drugs designed to kill them since the first antibiotics were discovered.[6,2] US overuse of antibiotics in farming, prescription drugs, and antibacterial soaps have supercharged the process. A study found methicillin-resistant Staphylococcus aureus (MRSA) on three out of three planes tested for the 'super bug.' In commercial airliners, for instance, MRSA was found in highest concentrations on the flip-down tray table in front of each seat, with 60 percent of tray tables testing positive.[7] MRSA can be isolated from many different environments so it was not surprising to find it on the commercial airliners, in the grocery store, and in church where you pray. The public is bombarded with advertisements about the use of biocides in the home. Fact is, the overuse of sanitizers or biocides creates a "false sense of security," says one expert;[8] the thought is that widespread use of sanitizers will reduce the organism load which in turn will reduce the chance of acquiring infectious disease; yet, the literature does not back up this perspective what so ever unless there are new products developed.

[2] Antibiotics were used to treat serious infections in the 1940s; they have saved millions of lives and transformed modern medicine. In the last seventy years, bacteria have demonstrated the ability to mutate and "become resistant to every antibiotic drug developed. Any instance where antibiotics are used exerts more biological pressure on bacteria, consequently promoting development of resistance. The more antibiotics used—the more quickly bacteria develop resistance."

Source: Charles Moore (2013, November 26). Antimicrobial Resistance Caused By Over-Use And Abuse of Antibiotics Could Set Disease Control Back A Century. BioNews Texas. Retrieved September 22, 2014: http://bionews-tx.com/news/

The Centers of Disease Control and Prevention's (CDC) say that infectious pathogens are common in hospitals and in community settings.

Law enforcement officers, corrections officers, firefighters, and EMT/paramedics are on the front lines of infectious and "deadly bacteria and viruses every time they go to work."[9] For details, see Chapter 5 for correctional personnel, Chapter 6 for law enforcement officers, and Chapter 7 for firefighters and EMT/paramedics.

Katherine Welles/Shutterstock, Inc.

The US Centers for Disease Control and Prevention headquarters. The CDC is the national public health institute of the United States. Dekalb County, Georgia

Early Results of This New Disaster

Alice Park says that "we've come to assume that just about any bug we're saddled from strep to staph can be wiped out with a quick round of antibiotics."[10] In a comprehensive analysis of 5,810 hospitals nationwide, an estimated 103,000 individuals died in a single year from hospital infections (that's 101,000 more than Hurricane Katrina), and 75 percent of those deaths were preventable (also similar to Hurricane Katrina).[11]

Deaths linked to hospital infections represent the fourth leading cause of mortality among Americans, behind heart disease, cancer, and strokes.[12] In the US, roughly 2 million people every year get infections that cannot be treated with antibiotics, and 23,000 of them die.[13] There are more deaths and suffering of others linked to transmission of disease from hospitals.

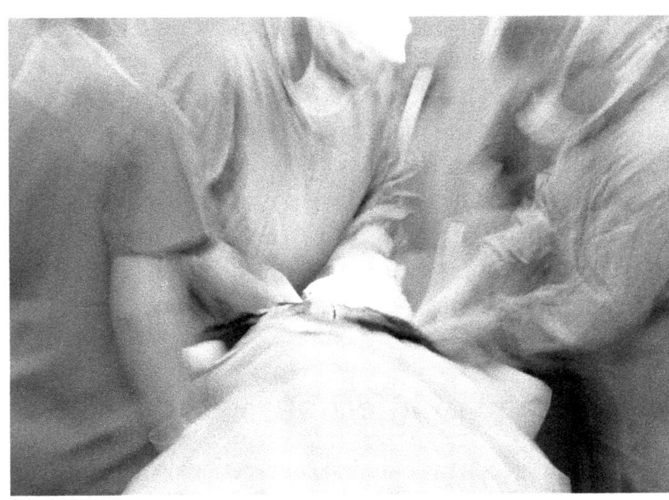

VILevi/Shutterstock, Inc.

The CDC Multistate Point-Prevalence Survey of Health Care Associated Infections used 2011 data from 183 US hospitals to estimate the burden of a wide range of infections in hospital patients. That year, about 721,800 infections occurred in 648,000 hospital patients (see Chapter 8 for more details).[14] About 75,000 patients with healthcare associated (that is patients contracted the infection after their hospital admission; later I use the term patient associated infection when discussing disease transmission from patients or constituents to healthcare and justice professionals) infections died during their hospitalizations. The most common healthcare associated infections were pneumonia (22 percent), surgical site infections (22 percent), gastrointestinal infections (17 percent), urinary tract infections (13 percent), and bloodstream infections (10 percent).

Colonization

Prisoners are a high risk group for contacting MRSA infections and other deadly pathogens.[15] For example, in 2002, Los Angeles County jail had 921 MRSA infections among prisoners, and in the first six months of 2003 there were 776 cases. The number of MRSA cases in Texas state prisons from January 1996 to July 2002 was 10,942, with three prisoner deaths linked to MRSA. The Federal Bureau of Prisons (BOP) estimates that 10–30 percent of their prisoners are colonized with Staphylococcus aureus in their noses or breaks in their skin, and many of those prisoners are further colonized with MRSA.[16] Colonization refers to persons who are more likely to develop staphylococcal infections, says BOP officials; however, many colonized persons remain asymptomatic and never become ill (that is, they become carriers or hosts and rarely show any indicators of disease or infection). Staphylococcal colonization occurs more commonly in injection drug users, persons with diabetes, hemodialysis patients, persons with acquired immunodeficiency syndrome (AIDS), surgical patients, and previously hospitalized patients.[17] A carrier including both criminal justice and healthcare professionals, and prisoners may transmit the organism to others. Colonization can persist for days to years, with "resolution influenced by the immune response to the organism, competition at the site from other organisms and, sometimes, use of antimicrobials."[18] One of the important issues about colonization is that many justice and healthcare providers never come forward about host or carrier status for various reasons as you will learn in Chapter 9 (among nurses), and Chapter 11.

What Powers the New Disaster?

For Hurricane Katrina, atmospheric and warm sea-surface conditions were conducive to that cyclone's rapid intensification, reports the National Climatic Data Center.[19] Similarly, the rapid intensification and spread of infectious diseases and other deadly pathogens in the US finds its atmosphere and warm sea-surface from the American prison complex. Jails and prisons annually crank out close to eight million angry men and women who anticipate committing a worse crime than the conviction that brought them to prison or jail depending on how long they were locked up, reports both the literature (scholarly research) and recidivism reports.[20] For example, an estimated two-thirds (68 percent) of 405,000 prisoners released in thirty states in 2005 were arrested for a new crime within three years of release from prison, and three-quarters (77 percent) were arrested within five years, government statistics show (the revolving door of justice).[21] It is the lower social economic class that interacts with the justice community most often; they are individuals whom experience poor health and inadequate healthcare before and during confinement in jail and prison (see Chapter 5 for more details).[22] If prisoners (which also includes inmates or those jailed) have not been exposed to MRSA and other deadly pathogens before confinement, prisons are reservoirs for infectious pathogens including Mycobacterium tuberculosis (TB), HIV/Aids, and hepatitis; they also represent agents of antisocial conduct, desperation, and violence for the sake of violence. We could say 'prisoner associated infection' if it helps better understand the relationship between prisoners and everyone they come in contact with while incarcerated or once released.

Transmission of Infectious Pathogens Including MRSA

A primary mode of transmission of infectious pathogens is person-to-person via contaminated hands.[23] MRSA in particular may also be transmitted by sharing towels, personal hygiene items, and athletic equipment; through close contact sports; and by sharing tattoo or injection drug use equipment.[24] Persons with MRSA pneumonia who are in close contact with others can potentially transmit MRSA by coughing up large droplets of infectious particles that can contaminate the environment of others. Persons with asymptomatic MRSA nasal carriage can also transmit MRSA, especially when symptomatic from a viral upper respiratory infection. MRSA can also cause a toxin mediated, food-borne gastroenteritis. For more details on disease transmission see Chapter 4; for right now what you need to know about disease transmission:**[3]** At the end of the day the black sheep or superbugs are multiplying and are more powerful than any individual, any organization, and any prescription drug available.

The Black Sheep

The deadly bacteria are called carbapenem-resistant Enterobacteriaceae or CRE. They're black sheep in a big herd of nearly ubiquitous existing everywhere germs that include common organisms inhabiting everybody's gut, such as the familiar Escherichia coli or E. coli. Now, "The cat's out of the bag," says Dr. Leonard Mermel of Brown University Medical School. "It's spreading," and he implies that it's out of control.[25] CDC officials are asking hospitals, intensive healthcare, and prisons to be alert of this strain of drug-resistant bacteria and chemically enhanced viruses. Other forms of CRE have been reported in those facilities with increasing frequency.**[4]**

As these organisms become increasingly prevalent, "Treatment of healthcare–associated infections most likely will become more difficult or even impossible," assert Mitchell Schwaber and Yehuda Carmeli at Israel's National Center for Infection Control.[26] One implication of Schwaber and Carmeli's postulation is that as these pathogens become widespread, extensively resistant Enterobacteriaceae will "make the hospital environment unsafe even to the general population."

Patch and Pray Healthcare

We can't "patch and pray" the levees of healthcare which hold back floodwaters of deadly pathogens that circumvent normal host defenses. To protect us, most of us rely on the effectiveness of medical science, our own intelligence which includes knowledge (thus sources including this book), and public health systems.**[5]** Yet, medical science and public health practices, "because of their success, have led to complacency and bureaucratic indifference and have helped to create the real biological peril in which we find ourselves. We live in a world in which new human pathogens emerge and old infectious diseases once thought conquered can resurface with a vengeance," explains Steven M. Wolinsky.[27] We can no longer control infectious diseases because they have, through

[3] Disease transmission requires the presence of an infectious agent, exposure to that agent, and a susceptible host. What are the routes of pathogen exposure?

- Inhalation
- Contact with blood or other body fluids
- Ingestion
- Fecal-oral
- An intermediate carrier (such as a tick)

Source: International Association of Fire Fighters (2014). Infection. Retrieved June 25, 2014: http://www.iaff.org/et/jobaid/InfDis/whnjs.htm

[4] A growing number of disease-causing organisms, also known as pathogens, are resistant to one or more antimicrobial drugs. A wide range of pathogens—including the bacteria that cause tuberculosis, the viruses that cause influenza, the parasites that cause malaria, and the fungi that cause yeast infections—are becoming resistant to the antimicrobial agents used for treatment.
Source: Centers for Disease Control and Prevention (2013). Diseases/Pathogens Associated with Antimicrobial Resistance. Retrieved July 26, 2014: http://www.cdc.gov/drugresistance/DiseasesConnectedAR.html

[5] World Health Organization (WHO)
Superbugs are now present in every corner of the planet. In some countries, about 50 percent of people infected with K.pneumoniae (Klebsiella pneumonia) or E.coli (Escherichia) coli bacteria won't respond to the most powerful antibiotics.
K.pneumoniae Kleb·si·el·la pneu·mo·ni·ae (kleb-sē-el'ă nū-mō'nē-ē)
A bacterial species found in soil and water, on grain, and in the intestinal tract of humans and other animals; it also occurs in association with several pathologic conditions, urinary tract infections, sputum, feces, and metritis in mares; capsular types 1, 2, and 3 of this organism may be causative agents in pneumonia; commonly associated with lobar pneumonia among hospitalized patients. Source: Medical Dictionary for the Health Professions and Nursing. TheFreeDictionary.com
Escherichia /Esch·e·rich·ia/ (esh″ĕ-rik′e-ah) Escherichia co′li a species constituting the greater part of the normal intestinal flora of humans and other animals; it is a frequent cause of urinary tract infections and epidemic diarrheal disease, especially in children. Source: Dorland's Medical Dictionary for Health Consumers. TheFreeDictionary.com

an evolutionary process, become resistant to antibiotics.[28] One result is that "with no new drugs, physicians are forced to increase the number of prescriptions of currently licensed drugs, which in turn, will result in more resistance to antibiotics," writes David Gilbertin the foreword of *Rising Plague*.[29]

We cannot entirely stop the spread of infectious diseases and other deadly pathogens which is a complicated discussion because:[30]

- Of an Increase In Antibiotic Resistance
- The Reluctance of Pharmaceutical Companies to Produce a Stable Supply of Drugs to Counter Anti-Resistance "Bugs"
- The Startling Priorities of Government to Aid Healthcare Corporations to Further Their Profits Margins (Explained Later) as Opposed to Supporting Public Health Agencies

Similar to crime, we can't stop it—crime (including pathogens) has been with mankind since we have been on this planet no matter what we do; fact is that criminals play "a normal role in social life"; crime is an indicator of a healthy society; the best we can hope for is to control crime, advises Emile Durkheim.[31] Concerning superbugs, experts say, America is not meeting the challenge to control them and they are not part of a healthy society.[32] Maybe they are part of a healthy elite social class and the Power Elite because many of those individuals and the corporations they control prosper from the madness of superbugs, injuries, and death, it could be argued (see Chapter 4 for details). Antibiotic resistance, infectious disease, or superbugs including MRSA and Ebola, however, provide huge benefits such as financial gains;[6] they have become powerful and undisputed methods of control of one social class over other social classes;[33] these benefits are similar to the benefits of crime and punishment.[34]

Disease Transmission Linked to Prison Populations

In what way are infectious diseases, prison populations, and public service personnel linked? Three ways: first, despite progress, gaps still remain in US and state preparedness to deal with the infectious disease outbreak.[35] Most states need to make improvements to better protect residents against infectious disease outbreaks and ready their communities for public health disasters. Most states have yet to maintain or increase public health funding levels. Two-thirds of states have decreased their public health funding. Recall during Hurricane Katrina, physicians and nurses were forced to make decisions about whom they might treat and whom they might not treat because of a lack of medical supplies and a loss of electricity (see Chapter 9 for additional details about hospitals, physicians, and nurses). The CDC reports that as December 10, 2014 the US rates 7.4 out of 10 (a 'C' grade) in preparedness for natural disasters, terrorism, and disease pandemics.[7]

Second: the link between infectious disease and prison relates to the notion that members of the lower social economic class (as opposed to the Power Elites) most often intersect with the justice community and their collaborative partners, and that those individuals generally experience poor healthcare. There is evidence that the eight million released prisoners and inmates are hosts of deadly pathogens and infectious diseases; also all eight million of them interact with criminal justice personnel at all levels.[36] It should be noted that a high percentile of those confined interact with healthcare personnel, too. For that reason, the prison industrial complex represents a catalyst of the infectious pathogens invasion.

[6] Ebola virus disease is a rare and deadly viral illness which is reportable to the National Notifiable Disease Surveillance System (NNDSS) in all US states and territories. Early recognition of Ebola is critical for infection control. If a diagnosis of Ebola is being considered, the patient must be isolated in a single room with a private bathroom for twenty-one days. Healthcare personnel should follow standard, contact, and droplet precautions, including the use of appropriate personal protective equipment (PPE). Infection control personnel should be contacted immediately.
Source: Centers for Disease Control (2014). Retrieved December 3, 2014: http://www.cdc.gov/vhf/ebola/hcp/case-definition.html

[7] Centers for Disease Control (2014). Retrieved December 10, 2014: http://www.cdc.gov/media/releases/2014/a1209-security-preparedness.html

Third: Despite the fact that criminal justice personnel and their collaborative partners commonly deal with safety and health threats (e.g., exposure to blood-borne pathogens, assault, highly stressful encounters), and on-the-job medical claims cost agencies precious human and financial resources, occupational health and safety programs have not traditionally been a focus within the justice community field in the US.[37] During the 2009 H1N1 pandemic, infectious diseases and other health threats continued to emerge, leaving many public service personnel unprepared and unprotected.[8]

Early Reports of Infectious Pathogens

Concerning infectious pathogens in general: it's only been a few years since two patients at a Rhode Island hospital tested positive for bacteria containing New Delhi metallo-beta-lactamase (NDM),[9] an enzyme that causes bacteria to be resistant to antibiotics.[38] [10] The Centers for Disease Control and Prevention (CDC; cdc.gov) applauded the hospital's staff for their professional response to the pathogen[11] and biologically enhanced germs (superbugs) that are resistant to antibiotic chemistry.[39] [12]When NDM was first identified in 2008, it was thought to be limited to healthcare settings in India, Pakistan, and Vietnam. NDM spread globally in a short period of time. The rapidly growing number of antimicrobial resistant pathogens coincides with a lean pipeline of new drugs to treat infections. The number of therapeutic options available to combat drug-resistant germs has dwindled, and few therapeutic options are being developed. Federal officials at CDC and everyone else who understands the scope of this enormous threat are plagued because response from healthcare enterprises, including pharmaceutical companies, is not expeditiously moving forward toward the development and distribution of products and practices to remedy the spread of pathogens and superbugs.

Social Justice and Public Health

The ethics of justice in a democratic nation mean that each person in society ought to receive her or his due and that "the burdens and benefits of society should be fairly and equitably distributed."[40] (For more details see Chapter 4.) Our public ethics, however, do not seem to fit our public problems especially when it comes to healthcare (more on this thought in Chapter 4). For right now what you need to know is that the relationship between government and big business, in particular healthcare and pharmaceutical industries (detailed in Chapter 4), suggests that persons of color who are also poor, similar to many of Katrina's victims, are 'disposable' (see Chapter 1 for details). In what way are disposable

[8] Orlando, Florida, Police Officer Christopher Seggi learned the hard way just how easy it is to acquire MRSA when he responded to a "routine" suspect transport in December 2006. Seggi noticed what appeared to be spider bites on the suspect's leg. He transported the suspect to the Orange County Correctional Facility and transferred custody without incident. Seggi returned to his cruiser and attempted to clean its backseat with a traditional "spray and wipe" cleaning method. There were no indications of infectious contaminants anywhere in the vehicle. The officer leaned on the backseat where the suspect had been restrained and was wearing his standard department-issued uniform, including long pants. Several days after the incident, the Orlando officer noticed what appeared to be a spider bite on his right knee. Thinking it was an insect bite, he disregarded it and went about his daily life. He went home to his wife, commuted in his personal vehicle, had dinner with family and friends, and traveled on an airplane.

While sitting in roll call, a safety bulletin on MRSA was circulated among officers. As Seggi read the bulletin, he went through the symptom checklist. It was a match which his physician confirmed. Seggi had contracted an infection from MRSA. Because of Seggi's contacts with so many people at work, your guess is as good as mine as to how many others were infected by this suspect. (Source: Jason Schneider (2007)). MRSA Infections: Tougher Than Kevlar. COPS. Retrieved April 29, 2014: http://www.officer.com/article/10249515/mrsa-infections-tougher-tha-kevlar

[9] NDM is transferred easily to other types of gram–negative bacteria and encodes multiple resistance genes in the new bacteria, "rendering them impervious to antibacterial drugs," reports Robyn Correll Carlyle.

[10] Agent that destroys bacteria.

[11] Agents of disease (e.g., a bacterium or a virus).

[12] Viruses are the smallest and simplest life form known. They are 10 to 100 times smaller than bacteria. The biggest difference between viruses and bacteria is that viruses must have a living host—like a plant or animal—to multiply and antibiotic chemistry cannot kill them, while most bacteria can grow on nonliving surfaces.

populations guided toward quality healthcare?[13] What happened to Katrina's (and society's) victims is a disgrace to the American ideals of social justice.[41] That disgrace can be felt by all the defenders of democracy: the young men and women who gave their lives and their limbs keeping freedom—free including those questionable wars in Vietnam, Afghanistan, Iraq, and those individuals in all the jurisdictions represented by criminal justice personnel and their partners across the country.

One perspective of social justice includes the idea that justice is a core value of public health in that public health stresses the fair disbursement of common advantages and the sharing of common burdens.[42] Social justice captures the twin moral impulses that animate public health:

- to advance human well-being by improving health
- to do so particularly by focusing on the needs of the most disadvantaged.

[13] In bioethics, discussions of justice have tended to focus on questions of fairness in access to healthcare: is there a right to medical treatment, and how should priorities be set when medical resources are scarce. But healthcare is only one of many factors that determine the extent to which people live healthy lives, and fairness is not the only consideration in determining whether a health policy is just.

Source: Madison Powers and Ruth Faden (2008). *Social Justice: The Moral Foundations of Public Health and Health Policy.* New York: Oxford University Press.

In bioethics, discussions of justice have tended to focus on questions of fairness in access to healthcare: is there a right to medical treatment, and how should priorities be set when medical resources are scarce. But healthcare is only one of many factors that determine the extent to which people live healthy lives, and fairness is not the only consideration in determining whether a health policy is just.[43]

The struggle for social justice in relationship to healthcare among lower economic segments of our society is a struggle for democracy and equality.[44] The role of social and economic injustices are root causes of the uneven distribution of disease across population groups linked to class, race, and gender. Think of it this way: there is a strong relationship between social and economic inequities and healthcare inequities. As infectious outbreaks occur or another disaster such as Hurricane Katrina, or for that matter after a bioweapon attack (see Chapter 10), it is the poor who are hurt the hardest. They have few options. Recall from Chapter 1 that the poor were imprisoned in New Orleans during Hurricane Katrina and the rest of us had the funds and networks to make decisions despite the fact that it was the same hurricane that affected us all.

"Getting tough on crime" as defined by government (which are political agendas and largely politicians are under the thumb of healthcare and pharmaceutical industries) justifies more prisoners, particularly from the lower social classes. More prisoners means more infectious disease because they are the most vulnerable; once an individual is confined healthcare practices are less than adequate, studies show;[45] additionally more prisoners means higher recidivism rates and more future criminals; but, it also means more law-abiding individuals interacting with hosts of infectious diseases.

As concluded in my last textbook, *The Failure of the American Prison Complex: Let's Abolish It*, the justice community has become a sprawling massive enterprise. Policing and incarceration has evolved a sociopolitical mythology that applies regardless of law or method. Governmental policy, regulations, and practices, all defined by government, take precedent over the US Constitutional rights of individuals whom government is sworn to equally protect and serve. Be mindful that the US Constitution and its Amendments were designed to regulate government.[46] Think about early American history: recall the primary reason the US Constitution was crafted—to control government not people.

Finally, one more point worth thinking about relates to the above thought about Constitutional rights. In my father's day and among ignorant twenty-first-century intellectuals, the innocuous phrase 'social justice' is some kind of a code for communism or modern leftist rhetoric for them.[47] I have always lectured my students, "open your mind, before you open your mouth." Good advice, I think. Social justice means to promote a just society by challenging injustice and valuing diversity.[48] It exists when "all people share a common humanity and therefore have a right to equitable treatment, support for their human rights, and a fair allocation of community resources," explains Matthew Robinson.[49] This thought reminds me of the movie, *A Few Good Men*. Dated, (1992; starring Tom Cruise, Demi Moore, and Jack Nicholson), and is worthy of your time. Kaffee (Cruise) is a military attorney defending two US Marines indicted for murder; their defense is that they were acting under 'Code Red' orders issued by Colonel Jessep (Nicholson). You might recall the famous conversation between Kaffee and Jessep:

Kaffee: Colonel Jessep, did you order the Code Red?

Judge Randolph: You don't have to answer that question!

Jessep: I'll answer the question! [to Kaffee]

Jessep: You want answers?

Kaffee: I think I'm entitled to.

Jessep: You want answers?

Kaffee: I want the truth!

Jessep: You can't handle the truth!

When the guilty verdict was read in court the conversation between Downey, a slow thinking white marine, and Galloway, a very precise black marine, went like this:

Downey: I don't understand... Colonel Jessup said he ordered the Code Red.

(Downey then looks to Galloway for leadership and guidance, I thought.)

Galloway: I know but...

Downey: Colonel Jessup said he ordered the Code Red! What did we do wrong?

Galloway: It's not that simple...

Downey: What did we do wrong? We did nothing wrong!

Galloway: Yeah we did. We were supposed to fight for people who couldn't fight for themselves. We were supposed to fight for Willy (the murdered Marine).

When this author talks about social justice, it means we should legally and morally defend those who can't defend themselves, asking and taking nothing in return.

Infectious Pathogens and Occupational Public Service Performance

The Occupational Safety and Health Administration (OSHA)[50] and the Center for Disease Control and Prevention (CDC)[51] are concerned with personnel in high-risk occupations and their ability to provide quality care and services to the American public in high-risk environments—environments that jeopardize their own health, the health of their families, and their communities because of the daily routines of their occupations. For example, the risk of becoming infected with blood-borne pathogens (e.g., hepatitis B, hepatitis C, HIV) during surgery, from victims of crime and others, is a real risk for healthcare providers.[52] Emergency room healthcare providers aiding victims of sexual assault including children have the potential of exposure to infectious diseases including sexually transmitted infections (STIs) especially Chlamydia trachomatis (CT), Neisseria gonorrhea (NG), and cytomegalovirus (CMV).[53] Sexually abused children go to school and interact with teachers, counselors, and other children. One study shows that up to 30 percent of sexually assaulted victims become carriers of STIs and other diseases.[54] Also, four New York City police officers have contracted the deadly HIV virus in the line of duty and were granted disability pensions, reports John Marzulli.[55] Receiving benefits for on-the-job infections is a rare occurrence among police officers, unlike firefighters (see Chapter 7, and recommendations in Chapter 11).

Today's officers are offered immunization with drugs like GlaxoSmithKline Twinrix for Hepatitis A and B;[56] education in the prevention of and protection from exposure to blood-borne pathogens and tuberculosis; personal protective equipment; training in search techniques that use a baton or the blade of the hand; and post-exposure counseling and medical care. There are now laws that require the source to provide a blood sample on request or through a court order. That won't help much during an arrest of a frisky suspect. Finally, today's officers have available an abundance of reassuring statistics that detail exposure rates and the rarity of exposure converting to a disease. Yet, officers and others are not immune and drugs they may take to arrest infectious diseases are inadequate.

In fact, it has been suggested that the American prison complex is the unwilling catalyst for the deadly super bug epidemic (see Chapter 5 for more details).[57] However, compliance to scrambled government regulation to battle meager healthcare and the public health mission is the driving force to corruption and fraud among public care providers especially law enforcement officers and healthcare practitioners including physicians.

Nothing Is as It Seems: Thomas Theorem

We cherish the myth that infectious pathogens have faded from existence because of America's political arrogance, because of advanced technology, and because our personal ideals that we are the most advanced society ever; even our god is superior to all other gods. For more information see the report from Jennifer Yang on New Antibiotics.[58] **14** That is what we thought also around a hundred years ago when we ended the "war to end all wars" (World War I). And the arrogance continued through two great global epidemics of that era, typhus and type A influenza pandemic each killing 20 million people or more; one of the early sites for the virus was the Portsmouth naval brig, and later at least 500 prisoners at San Quentin contracted influenza.[59] At its height, one-half of the prisoners in the California prison were ill and most assuredly a high percentile of correctional personnel.

14 New Antibiotics

The number of new antibiotics being developed is "alarmingly low," says the Infectious Diseases Society of America, reports Jennifer Yang. Many companies have stopped developing antibiotics altogether. Only five major pharmaceutical companies—albeit five of the biggest—GlaxoSmithKline, Novartis, AstraZeneca, Merck, and Pfizer, had active antibacterial discovery programs in 2008.

Since 1998, only four antibiotics have been developed by the world's eleven largest drug companies. For gram–negative superbugs, there were only seven antibiotics in an advanced stage of development in early 2013 and one of those companies filed for bankruptcy. Add to that the thought that only two new antibiotics were approved by the Food and Drug Administration (FDA) in the US since 2009. The experts are saying that a massive problem is on the horizon, and the challenge is that "nobody knows how to fix it," Yang reports.

There are scholars, including this writer, advancing the idea that an evolution of culture through time and space has to do with the evolution of the human species both physiologically and psychologically through quality of life experiences and technological (supposedly) achievement;[60] simultaneously and without human consent, as humans evolve, cultural including religious, occupational, and crime and punishment 'truths' evolve, too. As those beliefs become socially institutionalized (to make something a normal, accepted part of a social system or organization) through cultural social structures, standards of truth, and truth itself (however you wish to define truth) also evolve sometimes for the better and sometimes for the worse. A part of this thought can be explained through dynamic feedback over time between biological and cultural changes. Consider the following 'truths': the world is round; God is in the heavens; infectious diseases can be eradicated; capital punishment and war (which could be one in the same) are necessary; justice is blind; education and training about infectious pathogens and MRSA moves a healthcare provider toward superior performance of victims of exposure.

Is the world really a circle; does God only live above us; infectious diseases are not controlled; is there really a difference between killing people on the battlefield versus on the mean streets of any American city at the hand of local law enforcement or lethal court ordered elimination of a criminal (criminals were the witches in Salem, Native Americans, and Jews in Europe, too); justice is defined by those in power and that isn't you or me.

Finally, just because you learn about a topic such as disease transmission prevention as a nurse or a physician, similar to any university student (or a professor), does not automatically translate to agreement; learning things does not automatically mean that you'll use the information for the benefit of all, or that you will utilize your training in an appropriate way. Human beings do not necessarily make decisions based on education and training. Consider how healthcare providers, law enforcement officers, and priests (for those of us from Boston) might be responsible for errors in judgment affecting his or her professional conduct which may alter the life chances of others.[15]

How true is truth? This idea reminds me of a sociological perspective presented by Peter L. Berger in 1963.[61] [16] He clarifies, "Nothing is as it seems." As a criminologist and sociology professor, I know that one of the most difficult jobs of any teacher is to confront and train students to think in terms of reality versus the way they would like the world or an event to be. Once we inch through the social layers of reality, well—Berger's analogy is similar to peeling an onion, and we all know what happens when we peel an onion. Isn't that what happened as you learn about Hurricane Katrina? Seems students knew of its arrival days and in most cases a week before it arrived. Learning the lessons of Katrina can pave the way for all those obstacles and catastrophic events our society, you and me will—but 'will' is hardly accurate—'must' face today and every day after tomorrow to graduate, to find jobs, to make choices about your lifestyle, your intimate other, and how to raise your children if you have them. But do not think that everything will remain the same—your world will change, with or without your consent.

That said, a scholar implies that since mankind's existence on the planet because we both adapt and manipulate our natural environment, new and resurgent infectious diseases have always been along for the ride and have done the same thing. Public health is our salvation—our god! Chapter 3 will provide details about the public health enterprise in the US and how it relates to both the general population and the criminal justice enterprise and their collaborative partners.

Even today, we're under the impression that we're safe from HIV Aids or at least the stigma of it or so we're led to believe by a pharmaceutical monopoly; they define its creation, clarify its components, decide on its treatment, and control the medication sources, research, and limitations. Would any highly profitable enterprise snuff its cash cow—the plague?

Neutralizing the Plague

Aiding illiterate and poor children toward quality lifestyle opportunities isn't as profitable as the Prison Industrial Complex. Conversely, neutralizing the plague isn't as profitable as more hospital patients. According to the Commonwealth Fund, US customers spent more on healthcare per capita ($8,608) and more on healthcare ($2.7 trillion in 2011) as a percentage of US GDP (Gross Domestic Product, almost 18 percent) than any other customer on the planet other than four other nations.[62] For example, Kaiser State Health Facts (2013) reports that average cost per night in an American hospital is:[63]

- State/local government hospitals—$1,625
- Nonprofit hospitals—$2,025
- For-profit hospitals—$1,629

Commonwealth Fund ranks the United States last in the quality of healthcare among similar countries, and healthcare costs the most. More specifically, recently I experienced a one-night stay at a local hospital for a medication mix-up

[15] Who to Blame for Errors in the Medical World?

When a jetliner crashes, it makes headlines. There is an investigation, and the tragedy often yields important lessons. Most often, the industry learns from their mistakes. The world of medicine is far deadlier: "Medical mistakes kill enough people each week to fill four jumbo jets." But they go unnoticed, and rarely are things learned from those mishaps. "The same preventable mistakes are made over and over again, and patients are left in the dark about which hospitals have significantly better (or worse) safety records than their peers."

Source: Marty Makary (2012, September 21). How to Stop Hospitals From Killing Us. Retrieved September 24, 2014: http://online.wsj.com/news/articles/SB10000872396390444620104578008263334441352

[16] To improve quality of life choices, change the way you want to see the world to what is real; we create our own social reality. Each of us see the same event, yet interpret that event differently based on our expectations, culture, and experiences. Thomas Theorem: a fundamental principle of sociology is that if we define situations as real, they are real in their consequences. Source: WI Thomas and Dorothy Swaine Thomas (1928). The Child in America. New York: Little Brown Press. For instance, if you're a Muslim who believes that Allah loves martyrs, you act as though Allah loves martyrs, and you're willing to commit suicide because what you believe is "real" to you. When I act on what I believe to be true, others react to my actions, and our whole situation and perceptions of the situation are different from what they might be if we considered other alternatives. For instance, if you believe a rapist who claims he has a knife is telling the truth, your actions are as bound by that belief as they would be if he really did have a knife. It isn't what he has, what matters is do you believe him?

that provided stroke characteristics. After a series of tests and finding nothing wrong with me, a physician released me. My bill—$21,235.00; a high school friend and colleague suffered a heart attack and stayed in a Florida hospital for six nights—$230,000. However, there are other reasons why American ingenuity hasn't resolved the superbug epidemic.

Other Reasons for Not Resolving the Superbug Epidemic

MRSA continues to be a major cause of community-acquired antibiotic resistant infections, reports researchers from Infectious Diseases Society of America.[64] In the Infectious Diseases article, "Bad bugs, no drugs: no ESKAPE! An update . . . " it was noticed that companies in the late 1980s and early 1990s recognized the threat of MRSA, starting in 2000 new anti-MRSA drugs were developed similar to what Americans are experiencing about Ebola in 2014 (as I am developing this book).

However, the Alliance for the Prudent Use of Antibiotics says that the more antibiotics are used, the more likely MRSA and other deathly pathogens will become immune to resistance.[65,17] As resistance builds, there is no turning back. In their abstract the following is emphasized:

> Infections now occur that are resistant to all current antibacterial options. Although the IDSA (Infectious Diseases Society of America) is encouraged by the prospect of success for some agents currently in preclinical development, there is an urgent, immediate need for new agents with activity against these pan-resistant organisms. There is no evidence that this need will be met in the foreseeable future. Furthermore, we remain concerned that the infrastructure for discovering and developing new antibacterials continues to stagnate, thereby risking the future pipeline of antibacterial drugs.

[17] Antibiotic resistance occurs when an antibiotic has lost its ability to effectively control or kill bacterial growth; in other words, the bacteria are "resistant" and continue to multiply in the presence of therapeutic levels of an antibiotic. Some bacteria are naturally resistant to certain types of antibiotics. However, bacteria may also become resistant in two ways: (1) by a genetic mutation or (2) by acquiring resistance from another bacterium.

There are other reasons for the delay in remedies. One is scientific. "The low-hanging fruit has been picked," says Brad Spellberg in an earlier report by the Infectious Diseases Society of America.[66]

Spellberg adds, "But the concept that we've exhausted the pantry is ridiculous. Now we have to dig deeper, think harder and more cleverly." Adding to the grim picture, a comprehensive study of antibiotic development, covering innovative, small firms, as well as pharma giants, found in 2008 that only 15 antibiotics of 167 under development had a new mechanism of action with the potential to meet the challenge of multidrug resistance. Most of those were in the early phases of development.

Antibiotics are also cheap compared to other drugs.[67] The current healthcare system accepts the $50,000 price tag on cancer drugs that might provide a few weeks but not the "$5,000 for a course of antibiotics that might save their lives."[68]

What Causes Antibiotic Resistance?

Since the discovery of penicillin, antibiotics and antimicrobial drugs have been widely used. Taking an antibiotic can kill bacteria, but a few bacteria survive.[69] Those surviving bacteria are resistant to future antibiotics. They multiply and are in a process of evolution.[70] Every antibiotic we consume creates more drug-resistant bacteria. Societal factors also contribute to the drug-resistant bacteria such as inappropriate use of antibiotics (such as treating a cold, earaches, flu, and other infections that clear up on their own) can contribute to the growing number of antibiotic-resistant bacteria in our bodies. Also, not taking doses as prescribed can also contribute to the emergence of antibiotic-resistant bacteria.

Antibacterial agents are commonly found in cleaners, soaps, detergents, hand lotions, toothbrushes, and sometimes even plastic containers and mattresses. The widespread use of antibacterial products helps to produce resistant bacteria.

Another cause for concern is the use of antibiotics in livestock and agriculture which are often supplied with levels of antibiotics over long periods of time, and this is believed to promote the survival of antibacterial-resistant bacteria.[71] More than half of the antibiotics produced in the US are used for agricultural purposes.[72] There is some concern that these resistant bacteria can be transferred to humans through direct contact with animals or through consumption of their meat.

Arno Karlen writes that pathogens have evolved along with human beings. Karlen clarifies that deadly pathogens and human beings have engaged in a "dance of mutual adaptation we carry on with microbial fellow travelers."[73] One concern about Ebola from my perspective relates to its ability to evolve and become immune to drug treatment. Karlen says we are slow to accept the idea that we live in a new biocultural era. I take biocultural era to mean an era when human lives are increasingly measured and weighed in relation to the medical and scientific ideals; that is, notions of what is "normal" have changed drastically, explains Lennard J. Davis in his latest book, *The End of Normal Identity in a Biocultural Era.*[74]

Midst of a Deadly Infectious Pathogens Invasion

So here we are in the midst of a deadly pathogen assault. We acted and some say unnecessarily in Korea, Vietnam, Afghanistan, and Iraq;[75] American military is on alert over the Ukraine and Syria. It's time to take care of real business at home. Yet, the geniuses of the US and their sophisticated technology situated at The Institute for Advanced Study at 1 Einstein Drive, Princeton, New Jersey (no connection to Princeton University) are jacked-up toward launching millions of iPhones into the galaxy as a way of communicating with other solar systems.[76] Remedies toward preparedness and follow-through to aid people who potentially are exposed and die from infectious pathogens are not on the agenda or as profitable as developing a series of videos of shrimp running on tiny treadmills or examining extracted DNA from the teeth of skeletons in cemeteries to map the migration of European people or a war for that matter. As time permits, take a look at The Institute for Advanced Study at http://www.ias.edu/ to determine the relevance of such an expensive organization in light of mass incarceration of the poor and illiteracy in the US. Fact is, we build jails and prisons based on the number of poor minority readers in third grade, sources reveal.

Both the federal and state governments use a technique similar to "head-fake" expressed by Randy Pausch in *The Last Lecture*;[77] in sports, you learn to move your head in one direction throwing off your opponents while your feet are moving in the opposite direction. "It's like a magician using misdirection," Pausch writes. For more details on head-fake see Chapter 11. We neglect today's problems so tomorrow's society can run alongside shrimp on a tiny treadmill, that's what the geniuses at the $680 million endowed "Institute" imply and forget history!

Katherine Welles/Shutterstock, Inc.

Who Protects the Protectors of Liberty?

Ideas Inspiring This Book

The struggle to keep those brave (CJ personnel and their collaborative colleagues) individuals who defend the rule of law (such as the US Constitution) and democracy is related to public health purgatives.[18] Who protects the protectors? Law enforcement and correctional officers, firefighters, and healthcare providers including physicians and nurses are exposed daily to deadly pathways affecting their ability to practice their "craft." In my research for this book, few scholarly works are available about disease transmission other than blogs, sensationalized media reports, and Wikipedia type sources. I found numerous articles and books on police officer stress and alcoholism, correctional officer addiction and brutality, physician and healthcare misdiagnosis and Medicare fraud, and hospital expenses and death from MRSA and other deadly pathogens. But, little is available from reliable and scholarly work on infectious control other than washing your hands. It is hoped that this book will fill the gap in the literature and aid our due process protectors to remain free from contagion. Hopefully this work will also aid those defending liberty, the US Constitution, and the American dream to be able to better identify the culprits who orchestrated this epidemic including their goals, reasoning, and methods. Successful nations tend to learn from previous mistakes that became transparent disasters and obstacles that cross the paths of those nations and our individual lives. All of the above ideas inspiring this book have an intellectual tone to them—the real driving force is that 90 percent of those students enrolled in my research methods course in the Fall 2005, completed that course before the New Year 2006, once an abandoned hospital in Gulfport, Mississippi, was tied together for Southern Miss students. My classroom was in the old morgue and small red lights on the walls flashed every so often for no apparent reason. That May 2006 they graduated; needless to say I was a very proud professor during that ceremony, and a few tears rolled down my cheeks. Talk about overcoming obstacles! Anything is possible if you (or a society) want something bad enough. Most of my friends know that when an approaching storm is predicted and warm rainwater jumps off my face, I light up like a Christmas tree and dance in the rain, barefooted. My thoughts respectfully fly back to those incredible students, those committed justice professionals and their collaborative partners, and those amazing cheeseburgers from the Gulf Coast. Talk about a perfect storm! Chapter 3 describes the public health enterprise in America.

[18] The rule of law requires government to exercise its power in accordance with well-established and clearly written rules, regulations, and legal principles. Under the rule of law, no person may be prosecuted for conduct that is not punishable by law. For example, the due process clause of the Fifth and Fourteenth Amendments requires that statutory provisions be sufficiently definite to prevent arbitrary or discriminatory enforcement by a prosecutor (prosecutors are law enforcement officers). Prosecutors do not hold unfettered discretion to prosecute over a law that is so vague or of such broad applicability that evenhanded administration is not possible (see arbitrary government regulation discussions in Chapters 4–10). For example, a Florida law that prohibited Vagrancy was held void for vagueness because it was so generally worded that it encouraged erratic prosecutions and made possible the punishment of normally innocuous behavior (Papachristou v. City of Jacksonville, 405 U.S. 156, 92 S. Ct. 839, 31 L. Ed. 2d 110 [1972]). The rule of law also requires the government to exercise its authority under the law. This requirement is sometimes explained with the phrase "no one is above the law."
Sources: TheFreeDictionary.com and The American Bar Association.

Summary

This chapter talks about disasters two and three; deadly infectious pathogens and MRSA invasion and no remedies to resolve the invasion. Bottom line is that political arrogance or what can be called incompetence, technological accomplishment, or perhaps it's really complacence, intellectual reason, or maybe it could be good old American greed through healthcare and pharmaceutical enterprises.

Through the statistics provided it is clear that infectious diseases are out of control because they have, through an evolutionary process, become resistant to antibiotics. Also, the discussion is a complicated discussion because of an increase in antibiotic resistance, the reluctance of pharmaceutical companies to produce a stable supply of drugs to counter anti-resistance "bugs," and the startling priorities of government to aid healthcare corporations to further their profits margins.

There is a struggle to protect those brave individuals in criminal justice and healthcare who defend liberty and keep democracy safe. It asks the question, who protects the protectors? Equally important is that spread of MRSA and other deadly pathogens and their consequences are played among the disenfranchised populations of America than other groups.

Name: ______________________________ Date: ____________ School Identification Number: _______

STUDENT WORKSHEETS

Chapter 2 Lessons Learned: Disasters Two and Three

Define the following key terms from Chapter 2, and in your answer, show the page number where you found the definition. Provide an example for each key term.

1. Antimicrobial Resistant

2. Bacteria Resistant to Antibiotics

3. Biocultural Era

4. Colonization

5. Ebola

6. Evolution of Deadly Pathogens

7. Hospital Associated Infections

8. Infectious Pathogens

9. *K.pneumoniae* or *E.coli*

Name: ______________________________ Date: ______________ School Identification Number: ________

10. Lessons of History

11. Methicillin-Resistant Staphylococcus Aureus (MRSA)

12. Power Elite

13. Prisoner Associated Infections

14. Rule of Law

15. Social Justice

16. Sprawling Massive Enterprise

17. The Institute for Advanced Study

18. Thomas Theorem

19. Twin Moral Impulses

Name: ______________________________ Date: ____________ School Identification Number: ______

STUDENT WORKSHEETS

Chapter 2 Lessons Learned: Disasters Two and Three

Discuss and demonstrate in your own words that you comprehend the following learning objectives in this chapter.

1. Explain in what way a description of government as a sprawling massive enterprise can intensify inequality among specific groups of individuals in a democratic nation.

2. Explain what the social consequences might be in relationship to bacteria resistant to antibiotics.

3. Characterize is meant by the thought that medical science and public health practices because of their success, have led to complacency and bureaucratic indifference.

4. Apply to real world (college students') experiences how the author might connect the phase, "Nothing is as it seems." In what way do you agree or disagree that this is a helpful perspective in understanding real world events?

5. Explain the 'head fake' strategy and apply it to this chapter.

6. Describe the second and third disasters linked to this chapter.

CHAPTER 2 ENDNOTES

1. Dennis J. Stevens (2014). *Failure of the American Prison Complex: Let's Abolish it.* Dubuque, Iowa: Kendall Hunt. Page 348.
2. John Maki (2013, April 1). Let's Talk About Prison Health Care. Huff Post Chicago. Retrieved May 24, 2014: http://www.huffingtonpost.com/john-maki/lets-talk-about-prison-health-care_b_2975923.html
3. Gerard F. Anderson, Amber Willink, and Robin Osborn (2013). Reevaluating "Made in America"—Two Cost-Containment Ideas from Abroad. *New England Journal of Medicine*, 368(24):2247–49. Retrieved April 24, 2014: http://www.nejm.org/doi/full/10.1056/NEJMp1302140. Also see, Benjamin Sims (2007).
4. World Health Organization (WHO) (2013). Countries: United States. Retrieved April 24, 2014: http://www.who.int/countries/usa/en/
5. Brad Spellberg (2009). *Rising Plague: The Global Threat from Deadly Bacteria and our Dwindling Arsenal to Fight Them*. Amherst, New York: Prometheus Books.
6. Alice Park (2014, May 19). Man vs. Microbe: We're Losing the Battle Against Bacteria. Can We Win The War? Time, 183(19): 20.
7. Rachel Barclay (2014, May 24). The Real (and Disgusting) Health Dangers of Air Travel. *Healthline News.* Retrieved May 24, 2014: http://www.healthline.com/health-news/real-airplane-health-dangers-052414
8. AP Fraise (2002). Biocide Abuse and Antimicrobial Resistance—a Cause for Concern? Journal of Antimicrobial Chemotherapy, 49: 11–12.
9. Jason Schneider (2007). MRSA Infections: Tougher Than Kevlar. *Law Enforcement Technology,* 34(9): 18–23.
10. Alice Park (2014).
11. Michael J. Berens, and Ken Armstrong (2009, June 1). Killer Germ: Drug-Resistant Bug Kills More U.S. Patients Annually Than AIDS. *IRE Journal. Associated Press*. Retrieved April 24, 2014: http://www.ire.org/publications/ire-journal/search-journal-archives/?q=AIDS
12. ABC: Good Morning America (2012, July 24). Are Hospitals Spreading Germs to Patients? Retrieved May 14, 2014: http://abcnews.go.com/GMA/story?id=125911&page=1#.UbDNnm7D9uE
13. Alice Park (2014).
14. CDC Media Relations (2014, March 26). Despite Progress, Ongoing Efforts Needed To Combat Infections Impacting Hospital Patients. National and State Data Detail Threat Of Healthcare-Associated Infections And Opportunities For Further Improvements. Retrieved July 11, 2014: http://www.cdc.gov/media/releases/2014/p0326-hospital-patients.html
15. R. Klevens, M. Morrison, J. Nadle, S. Petit, K. Gershman, S. Ray, L. Harrison, R. Lynfield, G. Dumyati, J. Townes, A. Craig, E. Zell, G. Fosheim, L. McDougal, R. Carey, and S. Fridkin (2007). Invasive Methicillin-Resistant Staphylococcus Aureus Infections in the United States. *Journal of the American Medical Association*, 298(15), 1763–1771.
16. Federal Bureau of Prisons (2012). Management of Methicillin Resistant Staphylococcus Aureus (MRSA) Infections: Federal Bureau of Prisons, Clinical Practice Guidelines. Retrieved May 12, 2014: http://www.bop.gov/resources/pdfs/mrsa.pdf

17. Joan Robinson (2004). Colonization And Infection Of The Respiratory Tract: What Do We Know? *Paediatrics and Child Health*, 9(1): 21–24.

18. Ibid.

19. National Climatic Data Center (2005, December 29). Hurricane Katrina: National Oceanic and Atmospheric Administration Retrieved April 26, 2014: http://www.ncdc.noaa.gov/extremeevents/specialreports/Hurricane-Katrina.pdf

20. Dennis J. Stevens (2009). CSI Effect, Prosecutors, and Wrongful Convictions. *Criminal Law Bulletin*, 45(4), 591–612. Also see Dennis J. Stevens (2006). *Community Corrections: An Applied Approach*. Upper Saddle River, NJ: Pearson Prentice Hall. Pages 124–125. Also, Dennis J. Stevens (1998d). The Impact of Time-Served and Regime on Prisoners' Anticipation of Crime: Female Prisonization Effects. *The Howard Journal of Criminal Justice*, 37(2), 188–205.

21. Bureau of Justice Statistics (2014). 3 in 4 Former Prisoners in 30 States Arrested Within 5 Years of Release: Press Release. Retrieved April 24, 2014: http://www.bjs.gov/content/pub/press/rprts05p0510pr.cfm

22. Dennis J. Stevens (2014).

23. Federal Bureau of Prisons (2012). Page 2.

24. Esther Calbo, Núria Freixas, Mariona Xercavins, Montserrat Riera, Carmen Nicolás, Olga Monistrol, Maria del mar Solé, M. Rosa Sala, Jordi Vila, and Javier Garau1 (2011). Foodborne Nosocomial Outbreak of SHV1 and CTX-M-15–producing Klebsiella pneumoniae: Epidemiology and Control. *Clinical Infectious Disease*, 52 (6): 743–749.

25. Richard Knox (2012). Drug-Resistant Germ in Rhode Island Hospital Raises Worries. NPR Health. Retrieved May 24, 2014: http://www.npr.org/blogs/health/2012/06/22/155589409/drug-resistant-germ-in-rhode-island-hospital-raises-worries

26. Mitchell Schwaber and Yehuda Carmeli (2008). Carbapenem-resistant Enterobacteriaceae: a potential threat. *Journal of the American Medical Association*, 300(24): 2913.

27. Steven M. Wolinsky (2000). In Laurie Garrett's *Betrayal of Trust: The Collapse of Global Public Health*. New York: Hyperion. Page xil.

28. Arno Karlen (1995). *Man and Microbes: Disease and Plagues in History and Modern Times*. New York: Touchstone. Page 16.

29. Brad Spellberg (2009). *Rising Plague: The Global Threat from Deadly Bacteria and our Dwindling Arsenal to Fight Them*. Amherst, New York: Prometheus Books.

30. Dennis J. Stevens (2014). Pages 352–354.

31. Durkheim, Emile (1982). *The Rules of Sociological Method*, Translated by W.D. Halls, Edited by Steven Lukes. New York: The Free Press. Pages 102–103. Originally published in 1895.

32. Laurie Garrett (2000). *Betrayal of Trust: The Collapse of Global Public Health*. New York: Hyperion.

33. William Domhoff (2013); Laurie Garrett (2000); Walidah Imarisha (2005); Brad Spellberg (2009); Also see, Karl Marx (1978). The Eighteenth Brumaire of Louis Bonaparte. In Die Revolution. *The Marx Engels Reader* (R.C. Tucker, Trans., pages. 594–617). New York, NY: Norton. (Original work published 1852).

34. Dennis J. Stevens (2014). Pages 3–5.

35. Natalie McGill (2014). Despite Progress, Gaps Still Remain in US Preparedness: Many States Fail on Outbreak Indicators. *The Nation's Health*, 44(1), 1–18.

36. Dennis J. Stevens (2014).

37. Office of Community Oriented Policing Services (2012). Safety and Health Information and Education for Law Enforcement Departments. Washington, DC: US Department of Justice. Retrieved April 29, 2014: http://www.cops.usdoj.gov/Publications/03128445_Safety_Health_Information.pdf

38. Robyn Correll Carlyle (2012, June 27). Superbug Found in US Hospital. Outbreak News. Retrieved May 24, 2014: http://healthmap.org/site/diseasedaily/article/new-superbug-found-us-hospital-62712#sthash.eq9Yk179.dpuf

39. Richard Knox (2012). Drug-Resistant Germ in Rhode Island Hospital Raises Worries. NPR Health. Retrieved May 24, 2014: http://www.npr.org/blogs/health/2012/06/22/155589409/drug-resistant-germ-in-rhode-island-hospital-raises-worries

40. Dan E. Beauchamp (2013). Public Health and Social Justice. In Martine T. Donohoe (Ed.) Public Health and Social Justice, (Pages 11–19). San Francisco: Jossey-Bass.

41. Jay Arena (2014, February 18). Justice in New Orleans?: The Real Crimes of Former Mayor Ray Nagin and the Entire Ruling Class. *Black Agenda Report*. Retrieved April 29, 2014: http://www.blackagendareport.com/content/justice-new-orleans-real-crimes-former-mayor-ray-nagin-and-entire-ruling-class

42. Lawrence O. Gostin and Madison Powers (2006). What Does Social Justice Require For The Public's Health? Public Health Ethics And Policy Imperatives. *Health Affairs*, 25(4), 1053–1069.

43. Madison Powers and Ruth Faden (2008). *Social Justice: The Moral Foundations of Public Health and Health Policy*. New York: Oxford University Press. Also see, Norman Daniels (2008). *Just Health: Meeting Health Needs Fairly*. Boston: Cambridge University Press.

    Madison Powers and Ruth R. Faden (2000). Inequalities in Health, Inequalities in Health Care: Four Generations of Discussion About Justice and Cost-Effectiveness Analysis. *Kennedy Institute of Ethics Journal* 10 (2):109–127.

44. Martin T. Donohoe (2013). In Martine T. Donohoe (Ed.) *Public Health and Social Justice,* (Pages xi–xvii). San Francisco: Jossey-Bass.

45. Dennis J. Stevens (2014). Pages 348–351.

46. Wolfgram, Ann F. (2005). Population, Resources & Environment: A Survey of the Debate. The Heritage Foundation. Retrieved December 3, 2014: http://arts-sciences.cua.edu/econ/faculty/aguirre/resenv.htm

47. Michelle Malkin (2014). When Social Justice is a Code. Retrieved September 15, 2014: http://michellemalkin.com/2010/04/16/when-social-justice-is-a-code-phrase. Also see, Barry Loberfeld (2004, February 27). Social Justice: Code for Communism. FrontPageMagazine.com. Retrieved September 15, 2014: http://www.discoverthenetworks.org/guides/Z-Social%20Justice-Code%20for%20Communism.htm

48. Matthew Robinson (2013). What is Social Justice. Appalachian State University. Retrieved September 15, 2014: http://gjs.appstate.edu/social-justice-and-human-rights/what-social-justice

49. Matthew Robinson (2013).

50. United States Department of Labor (2007). Guidance on Preparing Workplaces for an Influenza Pandemic, OSHA 3327-02N 2007. Retrieved April 25, 2014: https://www.osha.gov/Publications/influenza_pandemic.html

51. Center for Disease Control and Prevention (CDC). Retrieved April 26, 2014: http://www.cdc.gov/

52. B. Stringer, C. Infante-Rivard, and J. Hanley (2001). Quantifying and Reducing The Risk of Bloodborne Pathogen Exposure. *AORN Journal*, 73(6):1135–1140.

53. S. Jo, J. Shin, K.J. Song, J.J. Kim, K.R. Hwang, and H. Bhally (2011). Prevalence and Correlated Factors of Sexually Transmitted Diseases—Chlamydia, Neisseria, Cytomegalovirus—in Female Rape Victims. *The Journal of Sexual Medicine*, 8(8), 2317–2326. Also see, C.M. Beck-Sagué and F. Solomon (1999). Sexually Transmitted Diseases in Abused Children and Adolescent and Adult Victims of Rape: Review of Selected Literature. *Clinical Infectious Diseases*, 28(1), 74–83.

54. S.K. Schwarcz and W.L. Whittington (1990). Sexual Assault and Sexually Transmitted Diseases: Detection And Management in Adults and Children. *Review of Infectious Disease*, 12(6), 682–690.

    C.M. Beck-Sagué and F. Solomon (1999). Sexually Transmitted Diseases in Abused Children and Adolescent and Adult Victims of Rape: Review of Selected Literature. *Clinical Infectious Diseases*, 28(1), 74–83.

55. John Marzulli (2008, October 2). Four Cops Got HIV On Job: Ruling. *Daily News*. Retrieved April 25, 2014: http://www.nydailynews.com/news/cops-hiv-job-ruling-article-1.300312

    Read more: http://www.nydailynews.com/news/cops-hiv-job-ruling-article-1.300312#ixzz2zviOI1E5

56. GlaxoSmithKline Twinrix ® [Hepatitis A Vaccine (Inactivated) and Hepatitis B (Recombinant) Vaccine]. It is the only hepatitis A and hepatitis B combination vaccine available in the US, and is available on a dosing schedule at 0, 7, 21–30 days, followed by a booster dose at 12 months.

    "Hepatitis A and hepatitis B are serious liver diseases which can be prevented through vaccination," stated travel medicine specialist Bradley A. Connor, M.D., Past President, International Society of Travel Medicine and a principal study investigator. "Twinrix's new accelerated dosing schedule offers an option that could benefit individuals such as those preparing to travel internationally to high-risk areas. It may also benefit emergency first care responders, especially those deploying to disaster areas overseas, as well as others at risk for hepatitis, such as people with sexually transmitted diseases and those who are HIV positive." Source: GSK (2013, August). FDA approves accelerated dosing schedule for GlaxoSmithKline's Twinrix. Retrieved April 25, 2014: http://www.gsk.com/media/press-releases/2007/fda-approves-accelerated-dosing-schedule-for-glaxosmithklines-twinrix.html

57. Dennis J. Stevens (2014). Page 349.

58. Jennifer Yang (2013, April 19). Superbug Drug Fight in Danger with Just Four Pharmaceutical Firms Left Making Antibiotics. The Star.com World. Retrieved May 28, 2014: http://www.thestar.com/news/world/2013/04/19/nightmare_bacteria_outstripping_development_of_effective_drugs_were_all_at_risk.html

59. LL Stanley (1919, May 9). Influenza at San Quentin Prison, California. Page 996. Retrieved May 30, 2014: https://archive.org/details/jstor-4575142

60. R Jurmain, L Kilgore, W Trevathan, and RL Ciochan (2012). Introduction to Physical Anthropology, 13th Edition. Belmont, CA: Wadsworth Cengage.

61. Peter L. Berger (1963). *An Invitation to Sociology: A Humanistic Approach*. NY: Anchor. Page 63.

62. Commonwealth Fund (2014). Retrieved December 4, 2014: http://www.commonwealthfund.org/Topics/Health-Policy-Reform.aspx http://www.commonwealthfund.org/Topics/Health-Policy-Reform.aspx????

63. Kaiser State Health Facts (2014). Retrieved December 4, 2014: http://kff.org/statedata/

64. HW Boucher, GH Talbot, JS Bradley, JE Edwards, D Gilbert, LB Rice, M Scheld, B Spellberg and J Bartlett (2009). Bad Bugs, No Drugs: No ESKAPE! An Update From The Infectious Diseases Society Of America. Journal of Clinical Infectious Diseases, 48(1):1–12.

65. Alliance for Human Research Protection (2012, October 7). America's Healthcare Crisis-Part V-FDA Complicit in Crimes. Retrieved December 4, 2014: http://www.ahrp.org/cms/content/view/874/9/

66. Brad Spellberg (2009). *Rising Plague*. Amherst, New York: Prometheus Books. Pages 36–38.

67. Jennifer Yang (2003).

68. Jennifer Yang (2013, April 19). Superbug Drug Fight in Danger with Just Four Pharmaceutical Firms Left Making Antibiotics. The Star.com World. Retrieved May 28, 2014: http://www.thestar.com/news/world/2013/04/19/nightmare_bacteria_outstripping_development_of_effective_drugs_were_all_at_risk.html

69. Janet Pheonix, Rachel Hampton, and Sarah Miller (2010). Antibiotic-Resistant Infections, MRSA, and C-Diff. National Center for Health Research. Retrieved June 1, 2014: http://center4research.org/medical-care-for-adults/infections-antibiotics-mrsa/antibiotic-resistant-infections-and-mrsa/

70. Arno Karlen (1995). Man and Microbes: Disease and Plagues in History and Modern Times. New York: Touchstone. Page 1.

71. Mayo Clinic (2014). Nutrition and Healthy Eating. Mayo Foundation for Medical Education and Research (MFMER). Retrieved December 3, 2014: http://www.mayoclinic.org/healthy-living/nutrition-and-healthy-eating/in-depth/free-range/art-20049386

72. National Institute of Allergy and Infectious Diseases (2014). Antimicrobial (Drug) Resistance. Retrieved June 1, 2014: http://www.niaid.nih.gov/topics/antimicrobialresistance/understanding/pages/causes.aspx

73. Arno Karlen (1995). *Man and Microbes: Disease and Plagues in History and Modern Times*. New York: Touchstone. Page 1.

74. Lennard J. Davis (2014). *The End of Normal Identity in a Biocultural Era.* Ann Arbor, MI: University of Michigan Press.

75. Peter Kirstein (2014). Why Iraq, Like Vietnam, Is Immoral and Unnecessary. *History News Network*. George Mason University. Retrieved April 29, 2014: http://hnn.us/article/10422

76. Eliza Gray (2013, July 22). The Original Genius Bar: With money tight for scientific research, the Institute for Advanced Study offers big brains a priceless draw: freedom. *Time*, 38–43. Retrieved April 28, 2014: http://content.time.com/time/magazine/article/0,9171,2147285,00.html

77. Randy Pausch (2008). *The Last Lecture*. New York: Hyperion Books. Page 39.

Ribah/Shutterstock, Inc.

CHAPTER 3

Essentials of Public Health

Learning Objectives

After you read this chapter, you will be better prepared to:

- From the author's viewpoint, explain the core components of this chapter, and the reason the author was inspired to write it. In what way do you agree or disagree with the author's position?
- Describe the tasks of public health professionals and clinicians and contrast the two professions. In what way are they similar and in what way do they differ?
- Characterize the Affordable Care Act and identify its advantages and disadvantages to the American public and to corporate America. In what way do you agree or disagree with the Affordable Care Act? State your reasons for your position.
- Characterize the medical model of health, and define and characterize the pathophysiologic reductionist approach and the holistic approach. Which do you prefer and why?
- Explain public health intervention strategies and connect each strategy to reductionism or holism philosophies of medicine.
- Explain government's necessity and role with public health. In what way do you agree or disagree with the author?
- Identify the four local models of public health organizations, and explain some of their activities or objectives. Generally, in what way might local public health organizations differ from federal public health organizations and in what way do public health organizations differ from medical clinics?
- Characterize the US Department of Health and Human Services and identify four agencies under their authority; define the primary function of each of those agencies.

Key Terms

Affordable Care Act
Biostatistics
Centers of Disease Control and Prevention
Disease Transmission
Environments (Natural and Physical)
Epidemiology
Food and Drug Administration
Holistic Medicine
Medical Clinic
Pathophysiologic
Prevention
Public Health (PH)
Reductionism in Medicine
US Department of Health and Human Services
Welfare State

Words of Wisdom

> Every single dollar spent lobbying a legislator on behalf of oil and gas is a toxic dollar that undermines public health and safety laws that protect Americans. That's contamination of the political system.
>
> Josh Fox

Introduction

The historical, present, and possibly future vision of public health systems and their personnel are engaged in a great societal endeavor to create "the circumstances that make health possible."[1] The knowledge base, skills, and authority including the chain-of-command varies widely among public health agencies which can encompass many professions and organizations are endowed with different resources, priorities, and jurisdictions; most often public health entities are under government control or directives. By examining those differences, we can better understand the commonalities among public health organizations and their accomplishments. At the conclusion of this chapter you will know more about public health agencies and their organizational structure, issues, and outcomes; you will examine specific systems and organizations and you will also have an opportunity to enhance your knowledge about various aspects of public health by reviewing the Appendixes described below.

Before getting started in the mission of public health, in the back of this chapter are four appendixes offering useful information. Take a look when time permits.

- Appendix 1: Universities with Public Health Undergraduate and Graduate Degrees
- Appendix 2: US Government Health Agencies, Descriptions of Services, and Website Addresses
- Appendix 3: Public Health Website Links
- Appendix 4: Disciplines of Public Health

Enhancing Our Knowledge about Public Health (PH)

To have a better understanding of public health it should be recognized that death, disability, and illness are collective (social) problems, and all persons are entitled to equal protection and opportunities in a democratic nation.[2] Yet, at the end of the day, America's public health expenditures, resources, and policies are inadequate; for example, the 2010 Gulf oil spill continues to bring misery and suffering to the communities along the Gulf Coast.[3]

Also MRSA and other deadly pathogens have evolved beyond the control of chemical antibodies.[4] One explanation in keeping with Josh Fox's above Words of Wisdom, is that American public health organizations are politically contaminated. Policy, for instance,is ruled more by politics than morality or reason.[5]

Remnants of Gulf Oil Spill

Scratchy Understanding of Public Health

Many of us might have a scratchy understanding about public health for good reason. Its history, presence, and future are profoundly different as are public health entities, agencies, and organizations. Public health workers in the US are at a distance from the early days of confronting "singular health threats such as polio, cholera, and tuberculosis. Modern public health professionals try to prevent problems from happening or re-occurring by implementing educational programs, developing policies, administering services, regulating health systems and some health professions, and conducting research, in contrast to clinical professionals, such as physicians and nurses, who focus primarily on treating individuals after they become sick or injured."[6] One such example, Alivio Medical Center, a medical clinic, is provided in this chapter for your review (see below for details).

Public health will always have a role in investigating, treating, and protecting people from disease; a new era is quickly emerging in which works such as *Criminal Justice and Public Health: MRSA and Other Deadly Pathogens* play a role promoting the idea that public health must focus their unique skill sets and tasks on the social conditions (social class, see Chapter 4 for details; recall the consequences of poverty in New Orleans when Hurricane Katrina arrived) and environment (see below, physical and natural) that help determine who will be healthy and live long and who will struggle with disability and illness and will die early.[1] This idea finds congruence with perspectives of the American Public Health Association.[7] Intrinsic to these thoughts underscores the basic premise that public health activity is aimed at the community as a whole rather than at an individual (more details below). The Affordable Care Act has greatly influenced public health agendas.

The Affordable Care Act

The Affordable Care Act, or Obama Care, was signed into law by President Obama in 2010,[2] and encourages the public health field to redefine itself and showcase the power of prevention. For example, as more people gain insurance coverage, public health agencies might consider restructuring and rethinking their role in providing clinical services. The Affordable Care Act also authorized the Prevention and Public Health Fund and Community Transformation Grants (PPHFCT) which offers an unprecedented investment in preventing disease and protecting against emergencies. There is a lot of discussion about the quality of the Affordable Care Act. Three qualities or advantages according to Kimberly Amadeo are:[8]

- The Act was designed to reduce overall healthcare costs by making services available to the 32 million who currently can't get insurance. They often use an emergency room at a hospital as their primary care physician, increasing costs for everyone. This started in 2014.

[1] Entities Comprising the Public Health Infrastructure
- About 3,000 county and city health departments and local boards of health
- 59 state, territorial, and island nation health departments
- Various US Public Health Service agencies in the US Department of Health and Human Services (HHS)
- Tribal health agencies, coordinated at HHS by the Indian Health Service
- More than 160,000 public and private laboratories
- Hospitals and other private sector healthcare providers
- Volunteer organizations, such as the American Red Cross, American Diabetes Association, American Cancer Society, and others

Source: Sarah A Lister (2005). An Overview of the US Public Health System in the Context of Emergency Preparedness, Congressional Research Service. CRS Report for Congress. Retrieved September 19, 2014: http://fas.org/sgp/crs/homesec/RL31719.pdf

[2] The Affordable Care Act for 2014: New Consumer Protections
- Prohibiting Discrimination Due to Pre-Existing Conditions or Gender. The law implements strong reforms that prohibit insurance companies from refusing to sell coverage or renew policies because of an individual's pre-existing conditions. Also, in the individual and small group market, the law eliminates the ability of insurance companies to charge higher rates due to gender or health status. Effective January 1, 2014. Learn more about protecting Americans with pre-existing conditions.
- Eliminating Annual Limits on Insurance Coverage. The law prohibits new plans and existing group plans from imposing annual dollar limits on the amount of coverage an individual may receive.
- Ensuring Coverage for Individuals Participating in Clinical Trials. Insurers will be prohibited from dropping or limiting coverage because an individual chooses to participate in a clinical trial. Applies to all clinical trials that treat cancer or other life-threatening diseases. Effective January 1, 2014.

Source: US Department of Health and Human Services. HHS. Healthcare. Retrieved May 2, 2014: http://www.hhs.gov/healthcare/facts/timeline/timeline-text.html

- It requires that all plans cover ten essential health benefits. Preventive services are free, which lowers healthcare costs by treating diseases before they reach an expensive crisis.
- For people who can't afford health insurance, the Federal government will pay the states to add them to Medicaid. The income requirement is expanded up to 133 percent of the Federal poverty level—roughly $31,000 for a family of four.

And three disadvantages of the Affordable Healthcare Act according to Kimberly Amadeo are:

- There are 30.1 million people who currently buy their own private health insurance. Many of them have had their plans cancelled by their insurance company because the plan doesn't meet the ten essential health benefits. Their costs for replacement insurance is higher because it provides services, like maternity care, that many of them don't need. (Source: Factcheck.org, The Keep Your Plan Promise, June 28, 2012)
- Between 3–5 million people could lose their company-sponsored healthcare plans. Many businesses will find it more cost-effective to pay the penalty and let their employees purchase their own insurance plans on the exchanges. Other small businesses might find they can get a better plan through the state-run exchanges. (*Source:* CBO, The Effects of the Affordable Care Act on Employment-Based Health Insurance, March 15, 2012)
- Increased coverage may actually raise overall healthcare costs in the short-term. That's because many people will receive preventive care and testing. These additional tests, such as cancer screening and cholesterol tests, will lead to higher medical spending. (Source: CBO, 2009 Study on Preventive Healthcare, August 7, 2009)

In 2014, 54 percent of Americans oppose the Act, and many groups work to repeal Obamacare, reports Amadeo. The Heritage Foundation's analysis by three researchers: Nina Owcharenko, Robert E. Moffit, and Curtis Dubay suggest:[9]

- The new law transfers vast powers to Washington bureaucrats who will control the dollars and decisions that should be in the hands of individual patients and their families, says Owcharenko.
- The individual mandate is an intrusion into personal liberty, argues Moffit.
- Tax increases in the new healthcare law will impede an already stagnant economic recovery, claims Dubay.

Also, there are organizations such as religious groups that ignore the contraception Obamacare mandates and bypass nearly all the hallmark provisions of Obamacare. For example, Samaritan Ministries, and other 'health sharing' groups like it, cater to a small-but-growing group of Americans who have chosen to opt out of the Affordable Care Act. [10,3]

Whatever your opinion is about The Affordable Healthcare Act, it is a policy aiding individuals who otherwise would not have insurance coverage. It also fits into the framework of the mission of public health.

[3] The medical director and vice president of Christian Care Ministries says that "the biggest thing to understand" (about religious health share organizations) is these groups do not provide insurance. Instead, they "facilitate the direct sharing of medical cost between people of like beliefs." Because of this distinction, the Alliance for Health Care Sharing Ministries successfully lobbied Congress for a religious exemption in 2009. This allows medical sharing groups to provide a form of coverage but dodge the deluge of Obamacare regulations governing the insurance industry. About 300,000 Americans are under the health share umbra of health share. Source: Philip Wegmann (2014, August 7) (see Endnote).

Starting Point

The first issue this writer should mention is that often university students (and the public for that matter) get confused about public health (PH); the thinking goes that PH is a branch of the medical community which it is not, although many medical models seem to dictate PH policy[11] (see the discussion below on reduction versus holistic medicine). Nor is PH a part of medical jurisprudence (law and local ordinances) linked to medical and surgical application. What you should take away from this chapter is a little bit about medicine and a better understanding of the agendas, policy, and outcomes of PH organizations even to the point of being able to identify PH agencies in your community. Let's start to better understand the business of PH by answering the question: what is medical model of health?

Medical Model of Health: Reductionist and Holistic Approaches

The World Health Organization (WHO, see Chapter 2 for more details) defines health in general as "a state of complete physical, mental and social well-being and not merely the absence of disease or infirmity."[12] The medical model dominates American PH efforts which focus largely on disease and injury and their outcomes; it is built upon a pathophysiologic[4] reductionist approach,[5] as opposed to a holistic approach. Deep understanding of basic biology and a robust market for investments in technological innovations has led to extraordinary medical advances in diagnostics, pharmaceuticals, devices, and procedures, which now typify American technology-intensive medical care system.[13] For instance, the leading causes of death are traditionally categorized by organ or by disease type: diseases of the heart, cancer, or pneumonia. The medical care system intrinsically focuses on individuals while PH focus is on groups, communities, and the nation. Even when focused on prevention for risk factor reduction and delivery of clinical preventive services (e.g., hypertension screening, mammography, and immunization), the primary goal is reduction in adverse outcomes of diseases. Another example of a reduction strategy might be to provide dialysis to enable necessary functions to occur bypassing dysfunctional systems.

Reductionism, as a guiding principle, is helpful and useful in medicine. The problem with reductionism stems not from its use but from the "wrongful assumption that it is the only solution. Reductionism becomes less effective when the act of dividing a problem into its parts leads to loss of important information about the whole."[14]

On the plus side, reductionism has given rise to an extraordinary understanding of our bodies and how they work. It has enabled development of technological aids that have incalculable value. Reductionism, however, leads to dissatisfaction in biomedical ideals, which in turn leads practitioners to move toward alternative, holistic modalities.[15, 6]

Holism can be defined as "the ability to use a biopsychosocial model taking into account cultural and existential dimensions—that everything affects health."[16] Holism can be viewed as the opposite of reductionism, say other researchers, and they add that "reductionism pervades the medical sciences and affects the way we diagnose, treat, and prevent diseases . . . there are limits to reductionism, and an alternative explanation must be sought to complement it."[17] For example, one physician uses holistic as guide to evaluate patient health. [18] This physician looks at day-to-day lifestyle choices and emotional support systems and evaluates how those choices and systems impact health. The mind is connected to the physical well-being of the body. Because of reductionism there is misgiving of western medicine as "too chemical" and of alternative medicine as "too herbal." Another example to help understand holistic versus reductionist practices in medicine can be seen through the experiences of Dr. Ralph at UCLA: "I see holism as . . . what is going on for that patient not just physically, but emotionally . . . you know so it's body, mind, spirit . . . the big thing for me is how are they sleeping, how are they in terms of support from around them, how are they eating . . . and that all acts, the symptoms are telling me that."[19]

[4] What is Pathophysiology? It is a deranged function in an individual or an organ due to a disease. For example, a pathophysiologic alteration is a change in function as distinguished from a structural defect.
Source: MedicineNet Retrieved May 18, 2014: http://www.medterms.com/script/main/art.asp?articlekey=10691

[5] Medicine is following a philosophy of 'reductionism': deconstructing a complex process into its component parts to enable better comprehension. Source: http://qjmed.oxfordjournals.org/content/103/9/721.long. Reductionism simply means treating a piece of a system, rather than the whole. We can remove a heart and replace it.
Source: UCLA Health. (See Endnote). An extreme example might relate to the idea of treating cancer cells as opposed to treating the entire body to fight cancer cells.

[6] Holistic medicine is defined in different ways. In general, it focuses on how the physical, mental, emotional, and spiritual elements of a person are interconnected to maintain health. When one part is not working well, it is believed to affect the whole person. Holistic approaches focus on the whole person rather than just on the illness or part of the body that is not healthy.
Source: American Cancer Society (2013, January 16). http://www.cancer.org/

Also here's how one nurse describes holistic medicine: Holistic nursing is defined as "all nursing practice that has healing the whole person as its goal." . . . "Integral health is the process through which nurses reshape basic assumptions and world-views about well-being and see death as a natural process of living."[20] Integral and holistic nursing serves bio-psycho-social-spiritual dimensions of individuals in caring, healing, and holism in healthcare.

The ideals of reductionism are guidelines for public health organizations, and I think with an understanding of reductionism versus holism you can better pursue a definition of public health.

What Is Public Health (PH)?

In a word, the Institute of Medicine's Committee for the Study of the Future of Public Health and The American Public Health Association's (APHA) clarify that PH is "prevention";[21] the APHA adds:

- Public health is the practice of preventing disease and promoting good health within groups of people, from small communities to entire countries
- Public health is policy development and population health surveillance

In 1988, the Institute of Medicine's Committee for the Study of the Future of Public Health[22] offered their broad mission of PH:**7**

On one hand, PH is "taken for granted because of the safe water, substantial protections against formerly epidemic diseases . . ." And on the other hand, "despite general complacency that the PH job is done, public concern is mounting over new health problems: toxic substances in air, water, and food . . ."[23] Finding a reasonable balance is challenging.**8**

Public health professionals rely on policy and research strategies to understand issues such as infant mortality, chronic disease, and infectious disease in particular populations. For example, the Center of Disease Control and Prevention (CDC) reports that each year, of the 2.5 million deaths recorded by National Vital Statistics,[24] nearly 900,000 Americans die prematurely from the five leading causes of death (explained below)—yet 20 percent to 40 percent of the deaths from each cause could be prevented.[25]

7 Broad Mission of PH is to fulfill "society's interest in assuring conditions in which people can be healthy. This requires that continuing and emerging threats to the health of the public be successfully countered."

8 Top 10 Public Health Achievements

- Vaccination
- Motor-Vehicle Safety
- Safer Workplaces
- Control of Infectious Diseases
- Decline in Deaths from Coronary Heart Disease and Stroke
- Safer and Healthier Foods
- Healthier Mothers and Babies
- Family Planning
- Fluoridation of Drinking Water
- Recognition of Tobacco Use as a Health Hazard

Source: Centers for Disease Control and Prevention (1999). Morbidity and Mortality Weekly Report. Retrieved May 28, 2014: http://www.cdc.gov/MMWR/preview/mmwrhtml/00056796.htm

Five Leading Causes of Death

The five leading causes of death in the US are heart disease, cancer, chronic lower respiratory diseases, stroke, and unintentional injuries (depending on age). Together they accounted for 63 percent of all US deaths in 2010, with rates for each cause varying greatly from state to state, age group to age group, race to race, and gender to gender. One study from the Centers for Disease Control and Prevention (CDC) (see Figure 3.1) suggests that, if all states had the lowest death rate observed for each cause, preventable deaths would consist of:

- 34 percent of premature deaths from heart diseases, prolonging about 92,000 lives
- 21 percent of premature cancer deaths, prolonging about 84,500 lives
- 39 percent of premature deaths from chronic lower respiratory diseases, prolonging about 29,000 lives
- 33 percent of premature stroke deaths, prolonging about 17,000 lives
- 39 percent of premature deaths from unintentional injuries, prolonging about 37,000 lives

Also, the National Vital Statistics report that age and method of death are different; for instance, aged 10–24, almost 41 percent of those deaths are unintentional accidents, 15 percent suicides and another 15 percent are from homicide, or approximately 71 percent of the deaths have little to do with disease. In the age group 45 to 64, cancer and heart disease account for 63 percent of the deaths.

Figure 1 Source: Centers for Disease Control and Prevention

Source: Centers for Disease Control and Prevention

Figure 3.1

The Role of Public Health

Public Health (PH) is a science on to itself with its own set of laws and regulations enacted by local governments and the federal government (more about this later). Locally, county (yes, you're correct—in Louisiana they have parishes, see Chapter 1) and city PH agencies are the most common agencies (details below). PH is also both a responsibility and an asset of any community, organization, and the nation. The legitimacy of a government can be best determined by a healthy population, and healthy populations tend to comply more often with legal, moral, and ethical perspectives or social order than less healthy populations.[26] Major improvements in society's health thereby enhancing social order can arise from controlling communicable diseases, eradicating environmental hazards, improving people's diets and enhancing the availability and quality of effective healthcare.[27] The work of PH is a societal effort with a societal benefit. PH takes the view held by many professions and societies throughout human history that healthy people are more productive and creative, and these attributes create a strong society.[28] Healthy people lead to better societies. For the welfare of the society, as a whole, it is better for people to be healthy than sick. There will be less dependence, less lost time from productive work, a greater pool of productive workers, soldiers, parents, and others needed to accomplish society's goals.[29,9]

[9] A system whereby the government undertakes to protect the health and well-being of its citizens, especially those in financial or social need, by means of grants, pensions, and other benefits. The foundations for the modern welfare state in the US were laid by the New Deal programs of President Franklin D. Roosevelt.
• a country practicing a welfare state system.
Source: google.com

Public Health Intervention Strategies

The fields of preventive medicine and PH share the objectives of promoting general health, preventing specific diseases, and applying the concepts and techniques of epidemiology toward these goals.[30] One way of thinking about PH is to consider three intervention strategies:

- Primary Intervention: seeks to avoid the occurrence of an illness or injury by preventing exposure to risk factors; for example, immunization and encouraging people to protect themselves from the sun's ultraviolet rays to prevent skin cancer.[31] At the level of primary prevention, an array of integrative modalities can be effective in health promotion, including lifestyle counseling, dietary guidance, stress mitigation techniques, interventions to improve sleep quality, and use of nutriceuticals and herbal supplements for health promotion.[32]
- Secondary Intervention: the event has occurred. The goal is to minimize the severity of its health consequences, but before the person notices that anything is wrong. A doctor checking for suspicious skin growths is an example of secondary prevention of skin cancer.[33] Find and treat disease early. In many cases, the disease can be cured. Also included at secondary intervention is stress management and nutritional supplementation which can reduce risk factors for chronic disease.[34]
- Tertiary Intervention: minimize disability by providing medical care and rehabilitation services. At the level of tertiary prevention, the full range of CAM modalities pertains to such goals as pain management, symptom

control, stress relief, disease management, and risk reduction.[35] The CDC says that the goals of tertiary prevention are:

- prevent damage and pain from the disease
- slow down the disease
- prevent the disease from causing other problems (or complications)
- give better care to people with the disease
- make people with the disease healthy again and able to do what they used to do

Developing better treatments for melanoma is an example of tertiary prevention. Examples include better surgeries, new medicines. Another way of thinking about intervention is to consider that illness or injury is the result of a chain of causation involving an agent, a host, and the environment. This is the traditional approach when thinking of infectious diseases:

- Agent: some virus or bacterium
- Host: susceptible human being
- Environment: means of transmission by which the agent reaches the host (example: air, water, food, human behavior, etc.)

Example: suicide among young people; the host are young people, agent can mean a gun, environment can include the social environment (family, school, media, etc.).

Idea Inspiring This Chapter

In Chapter 1, the discussion about social justice embraces the idea that justice is a core value of PH in that PH stresses the fair disbursement of common advantages and the sharing of common burdens. This thought reminds me that whatever quality of health standards I experience or chose to experience, others in my community and in the nation experience fewer opportunities to chose or even experience largely because of his or her social position (social class) and his or her health.[36] Social class and health are connected variables, make no mistake about it. Good health is like armor to knights in merry old England, it helps a knight to stay alive during combat. Imagine how much easier it is to earn a college degree if you're healthy versus not healthy. Imagine the difficulty in pursuing an intimate or a partner if you're ill or even raising your children by yourself and working, too. You also read in Chapter 1 that a disproportionate number of lower social class members, especially those who never left their homes, had few if any social relationships, died alone, more often than others. It could be implied that those individuals did not desire to be rescued and what of their health? Death under those circumstances are a powerful symbol of social abandonment and failure.

My reasons for writing this chapter is to better understand how public health works with the realization that a modern democratic nation and its politics must always search for the common good and justice. Justice means equal opportunities and protection which includes public health.

Yet, I wonder; if PH organizations are managed, connected, or directed by governmental bodies, in what way can justice be linked to prevention for all or is it politics as usual? How do I feel about that? I want to change it. Education and unbiased knowledge is one way "up and out." But there a few alternatives if your health is poor.

From Justice to Prevention

The level of societal health is linked through social justice that can be understood as an outcome of professional activities, regulated by government, and as a resource for individuals and society.[37] But it can also be understood in terms of political agendas as many of us witnessed during the sign-up for the Omaha Care in 2014. Yet, critics can say that now individuals will be chemically medicalized into "healthy patients," subjected to routine control check-ups, preventive medication, indications to lead healthy lifestyle and show correct comportment.[10,38] PH prevention can be considered an individual responsibility aimed at avoiding risk and preventing disease, argues Kottow. Elitists can adapt their lifestyles and incur the extra expense of having routine check-ups, including high-tech procedures, going to spas and gym workouts, and buying expensive pharmacological stabilizers. Recall in Chapter 1 that I was able to afford the high price of airline tickets for my daughter's departure from New Orleans before Katrina. It was estimated that 100,000 people were trapped in the city because of their economic and health circumstance.[39] Also, if risk is internalized, there is no major pressure to publicly intervene in social and environmental health-threatening conditions. Accordingly, international organizations have given up on major ecological interventions, now proclaiming "adaptation and mitigation" policies which are not far from a conservative business as usual attitude.

Access to health is considered a critical right of citizenship and an integral component of modern welfare societies.[40] There is an increasing awareness of the many social determinants of health which hinder or enable citizens to live a healthy life—and at the same time there is a growing understanding that health is a co-produced good and a shared responsibility of all parts of society: the citizens, the state, and the private sector.[11] Because of the increasing awareness of the determinants of PH, a review of the annual spending might help in a better understanding of the score of PH.

Government's Annual Public Health Spending

One estimate for annual spending on social security, Medicare, Medicaid, and other healthcare costs in 2014 is $2.54 trillion.[41] This total does not subtract the amount paid in during the year from those sources.[12] Some say that there is too much waste and inappropriate spending in the discretionary budget.

The Public's Health Spending

Additionally, it is helpful to know that the world's eleven largest drug companies made a net profit of $711.4 billion from 2003 to 2012.[42] Six of these companies are headquartered in the United Sates: Johnson & Johnson, Pfizer, Abbot Laboratories, Merck, Bristol-Myers Squibb, and Eli Lilly. In 2012 alone, the top eleven companies earned nearly $85 billion in net profits. According to IMS Health, a worldwide leader in healthcare research, the global market for pharmaceuticals is expected to top $1 trillion in sales by 2014. Despite expiring patents on blockbuster drugs and a wave of new regulation from the Affordable Care Act that will cost drug makers, the pharmaceutical industry will reap between "$10 billion and $35 billion in additional profits over the next decade," one source tells us.[43]

[10] Typical multiple-choice exam question: Who might financially gain the most from a chemically medicalized healthy patient?

a. Legislatures
b. Local government
c. Medical doctors
d. Pharmaceutical Industries (revenue $610 billion in 2012)
e. Prescription Drug Industries

Answer both d. and e.

[11] The Institute of Medicine (IOM) suggests that the public health system is not solely responsible for assuring the conditions of population health. The community, health-care delivery system, employers and business, the media, academia, and governmental public health infrastructure all play an important role. Several other factors beyond the control of these entities also affect population health. These include:

- Broad social, economic, cultural, health, and environmental policies and conditions at the global, national, state, and local levels;
- Characteristics and conditions of life and work, including education, socioeconomic status, psychosocial factors, public health services, and health care services;
- Social, family, and community networks;
- Behavioral factors; and
- Innate individual traits such as age, sex, and race.

In research regarding the actual causes of death in the US in 1990 and 2000, behavior and social factors such as tobacco use, poor diet/physical inactivity, and alcohol consumption were among the leading causes of death.

Source: Karen Shore (2007). *Understanding the United States Public Health System.* California Public Health Forum. Retrieved May 29, 2014: http://www.cahpf.org/GoDocUserFiles/207.CHI%20Brief%20United%20States.pdf

[12] For instance, the Social Security Administration reports an estimated $744 million in receipts and $680 million in expenditures for 2013. Source: Social Security Administration. Old-Age and Survivors Insurance Trust Fund, 1937–2013. Retrieved May 16, 2014: http://www.socialsecurity.gov/OACT/STATS/table4a1.html

Necessity of Government

One way to describe the necessity of American government is visible through the words of President Thomas Jefferson (third President of US) at his first inaugural address, March 1, 1801.[13]

Four years earlier, George Washington had turned over the presidency to his Vice President, John Adams. But Jefferson's inauguration was the first time in American history—if not the world's—that the reins of political power were peacefully transferred from one party to its political rivals as a result of popular election.[44] The significance of this event—and its contemporary lessons—cannot be overstated. Matthew Spalding writes for the Heritage Foundation that Jefferson points out that good government is "limited government and that limited government encourages civic happiness."[14] One way to take President Jefferson's words is to say that a constitutional government would aid in the quality of life choices of its constituents and provide due process of the law, equally, for all—social justice (see Chapter 2 for details). Life choice opportunities would include a healthy population. Little question that the societal factors that affect the health of a population is government and how the population shares its resources; "sharing determines the caring."[45] Even so, President Jefferson strongly favored a constitutional government empowered with specific responsibilities. My analysis of Jefferson's statement is that he is strongly implying that government is legally obliged to protect health and guide behavior furthering their individual financial support and their privacy which in turn enhances social order and legitimacy of government. The President seems to reject broad government intervention by limiting government in the lives and business of its constituents. Jefferson's most fundamental political belief was an "absolute acquiescence in the decisions of the majority."[46] He held a deep optimism in the ability of Americans to reason things out for themselves. Jefferson believed that the will of the people, expressed through elections, provides the most appropriate guidance for directing the republic's course. Jefferson also felt that the central government should be "rigorously frugal and simple." Frankly, safeguarding fundamental social change and dealing with present-day reality "is better cultivated through democratic consensus," some argue[47] (see Chapter 11 for more details about this statement).

[13] "A wise and frugal government, which shall restrain men from injuring one another, which shall leave them otherwise free to regulate their own pursuits of industry and improvement, and shall not take from the mouth of labor the bread it has earned. This is the sum of good government, and this is necessary to close the circle of our felicities."

[14] **About The Heritage Foundation**
The Heritage Foundation is the nation's most broadly supported public policy research institute, with hundreds of thousands of individual, foundation, and corporate donors. Heritage, founded in February 1973, has a staff of 275 and an annual expense budget of $82.4 million.

Our mission is to formulate and promote conservative public policies based on the principles of free enterprise, limited government, individual freedom, traditional American values, and a strong national defense.

Law and Obligation of Government toward Public Health and Public Safety

Lawrence Ogalthorpe Gostin characterizes the government's public health law as the study of the "legal powers and duties of the state to assure the conditions for the people to be healthy (e.g., to identify, prevent, and ameliorate risks to health in the population) and the limitations on the power of the state to constrain the autonomy, privacy, liberty, proprietary, or other legally protected interests of individuals for the protection or promotion of community health."[48] Implicit in this characterization of public health law are five components worth acknowledging:

- Government has a legal responsibility of PH activities (in Chapter 5 you will learn that government "must" provide healthcare to individuals under custodial supervision)
- Populations: government focuses on the health of the population not the individual
- Relationships: PH focuses on the relationship between population and the state and the individual/s who place the community at risk

- Services: PH deals with the provision of population-based services grounded on the scientific methodologies of PH which include biostatistics[15] and epidemiology[16]
- Coercion: PH authorities possess the power to coerce individuals and businesses for the protection of the community, rather than relying on a near universal ethic of voluntarism.

The Constitution, Government, and Public Health

The state is "an organization with a comparative advantage in violence, extending over a geographic area whose boundaries are determined by its power to tax constituents," says Douglas North, 1993 Nobel laureate in economics.[49] Government's responsibility and role are determined by law; the ultimate authority that allows the laws to be written is the Constitution. The Tenth Amendment: "The powers not delegated to the United States by the Constitution . . . are reserved to the states respectively." The US Constitution does not specifically mention health, but it does include among the fundamental purposes of government, the promotion of general welfare. One outcome of the Constitution, is that the primary responsibility of PH are the states. But the federal role in public health is not negligible. Many nongovernmental organizations play an important role in PH, through educational programs and lobbying. Government involvement in US healthcare system; Federal and local governments accounted for 45 percent of all healthcare expenditures in 2002. In 1929, the share was only 14 percent. However, nonprofit organizations independent of government control two-thirds of hospitals and 80 percent of clinics in the US (see Chapter 9 for the number of deaths in hospitals from infectious pathogens).

The National Association of County and City Health Officials (NACCHO)

Nearly every community in the US is served by a local health department (LHD). NACCHO, a private nonprofit organization, is the only national association which serves those departments, and its national headquarters is in Washington, DC. Over 1,450 LHDs are members of NACCHO; there are also an estimated 10,000 individual members. LHDs are the local stewards of PH in that they ensure the safety of the drinking water, the food served and sold in

[15] **What is Biostatistics?**
Biostatistics is the branch of statistics responsible for the proper interpretation of scientific data generated in the biology, PH, and other health sciences (i.e., the biomedical sciences). In these sciences, subjects (patients, mice, cells, etc.) exhibit considerable variation in their response to stimuli. This variation may be due to different treatments or it may be due to chance, measurement error, or other characteristics of the individual subjects. Biostatistics is particularly concerned with disentangling these different sources of variation. It seeks to distinguish between correlation and causation, and to make valid inferences from known samples about the populations from which they were drawn. Estimating the number of deaths from gun violence or looking at trends in drunk driving injuries by using math and science is the study of biostatistics. Source: Vanderbilt University, School of Medicine (2014). Retrieved May 4, 2014: https://medschool.vanderbilt.edu/biostatistics/content/what-biostatistics

[16] **What is Epidemiology**
When food poisoning or an influenza outbreak attacks a community, the "disease detectives" or epidemiologists are asked to investigate the cause of disease and control its spread. Epidemiologists do fieldwork to determine what causes disease or injury, what the risks are, who is at risk, and how to prevent further incidences. They spot and understand the demographic and social trends that influence disease and injury and evaluate new treatments. The initial discovery and containment of an outbreak, such as West Nile virus, often comes from epidemiologists. Some of the most important health-related discoveries in history are associated with epidemiology including the landmark 1964 Surgeon General's report on smoking tobacco stating its harmful effects. Biostatistics are often used in tandem with epidemiology. Source: What is PH (2014). http://www.whatispublichealth.org/what/

Epidemiology is considered a basic science of PH. Epidemiology is: (a) a quantitative discipline built on a working knowledge of probability, statistics, and sound research methods; (b) a method of causal reasoning based on developing and testing hypotheses pertaining to occurrence and prevention of morbidity and mortality; and (c) a tool for PH action to promote and protect the public's health based on science, causal reasoning, and a dose of practical common sense. Epidemiology is the study of the distribution and determinants of health-related states or events in specified populations, and the application of this study to the control of health problems. (Source: University of Alabama at Birmingham, School of PH. Retrieved May 4, 2014: http://www.soph.uab.edu/epi/academics/studenthandbook/what/ The last sentence (word for word) of UAB's definition is actually taken from the Centers of Disease Control and Prevention (CDC). Retrieved December 3, 2014: http://www.cdc.gov/reproductivehealth/epiglossary/glossary.htm

retail establishments, and monitor the air. LHDs develop and advance policies and promote conditions that make good health the default option. In addition, LHDs perform the following functions:

- Help create and maintain conditions in communities that support healthier choices such as diet, exercise, and tobacco control.
- Lead efforts that prevent and reduce the effects of chronic disease such as diabetes and cancer.
- Detect and stop epidemics of disease like the measles, tuberculosis, and food-borne illness and deadly pathogens.
- Protect and improve the health of communities through evidence-based (empirical methods of scientific methods of discovery—a process most university students learn in a research methods course) and activities.

NACCHO attempts to empower LHDs toward quality services to their communities by making information, practical field-tested tools, and innovative model practices accessible. NACCHO provides a website presenting information about the Affordable Healthcare Act (discussed below) community needs assessment tools, and PH infrastructure and systems to help LHD become certified agencies. See NACCHO's website at http://www.naccho.org/

Local Health Departments (LHD)

The responsibilities of local PH departments vary depending on many factors which can include resources, history, jurisdiction, and policy.

Described below are five different models of LHD and a list of their services to the communities they serve. One reason these models are offered is because you need to have a basic understanding of LHDs and how they function. What will become clear is that all of them are managed by public executives, staffed by public personnel who receive their paychecks and directives from government bodies at some level or another. Sometimes, private consultants or subcontracted personnel are involved with LHDs, but they too follow governmental policy and dictates. If you think you see a link between LHD and agents of compliance (as dicussed in Chapter 1), you're right. Even in PH, compliance requirements complicate and alter the performance of PH organizations. In an attempt to learn a little about PH organizations, five models and a federal PH agency are discussed.

Mecklenburg County Health Department (MCHD): Charlotte, North Carolina[50]

MCHD's website shows eighty-seven services they provide the county; everything from adult day health, birth and death certificates, child day care licensing and registration, flu shots, medical records, PH laboratory, public swimming pools permitting and sanitation, restaurant/food service permitting and sanitation, school health and safe routes to school, vaccination schedule, and wastewater treatment to name a few. MCHD, similar to most LHD, provides information such as:

Maternal, Child, and Infant Health

- In 2012, there were 13,848 births in Mecklenburg County; one of every five babies is born to a Hispanic mother.
- Almost 33 percent of births from 2008 through 2012 were delivered by Caesarean section.

Sexual Behavior

- In 2011, 50 percent of Mecklenburg high school students reported ever having sex and 35 percent reported having sexual intercourse with one or more partners in the past three months. Among those who had sex in the past three months about 61 percent reported using condoms and 26 percent reported drinking alcohol or using drugs before last sexual intercourse.

- In 2011, Mecklenburg County reported 246.7 cases of Gonorrhea per 100,000 population compared to 179.9 for North Carolina.
- In 2011, nearly 34 percent of Mecklenburg high school students reported having had at least one drink of alcohol and 16 percent reported binge drinking (five or more drinks in several hours) within the past month; 8 percent reported driving a car after they had been drinking. Almost 28 percent reported using marijuana one or more times during their life, up from 21 percent reported in 2009, an increase of 33 percent.

Methods of Preventing Chronic Disease and Disability

- Increase opportunities for physical activity through safe communities, greenways, parks and playgrounds, physical education and recess, sidewalks and bike lanes, and community connectivity.
- Improve access to healthy foods and food choices through community and school gardens.
- SNAP benefits accepted by farmer's markets, attracting full-service grocery stores to healthy school lunch and vending machine choices

It should be easy to see how health information can be used to enhance public health through PH agencies across the country. Even in developing nations, as an example, health workers are starved of the information that is the lifeblood of effective healthcare.[51] As a direct result, their patients suffer and die. In the words of the late James Grant, former executive director of Unicef, "The most urgent task before us is to get medical and health knowledge to those most in need of that knowledge."[52] Providing access to reliable health information for health workers in developing countries and in advanced nations is potentially the single most cost effective and achievable strategy for sustainable improvement in healthcare. Providing health information was not a priority during Hurricane Katrina as discussed in Chapter 1 other than receiving tetanus vaccines (which was appreciated); if it had been, maybe 2,000 people would not necessarily be the number of dead as a result of the blundering government and maybe it would have spared the suffering of a several thousand individuals who took ill. "The extension to all peoples of the benefits of medical, psychological and related knowledge is essential to the fullest attainment of health," says the World Health Organization.[53]

Multnomah County Health and Human Services (MCHHS): Portland, Oregon

MCHHS is committed to fostering a thriving business climate in Multnomah County, Oregon. The agency pursues that goal by coordinating public/private economic development efforts through the newly reorganized public/private Greater Portland Inc.

- Health Inspections and Licensing
- Smoke-Free Workplace
- Pest Prevention and Control
- Food Handler Program
- Food Service Operator Resources
- Workforce Development and Training
- Restaurant Inspections

All licensed food service establishments in Multnomah County receive two routine, unannounced inspections each year. Inspectors check for factors that could lead to food-borne illness including the manner in which foods are received and stored; how food is processed and cooked; and what cooling, holding, and reheating temperatures are used. Practices not in compliance with state laws are reported as violations. A placard visible at the restaurant's entrance indicates whether a facility passed its last inspection.

If critical violations are found that cannot be corrected at the time of the inspection, the restaurant is given fourteen days to make the correction. To provide further information about PH agencies, job opportunities at MCHHS follow:

Job Opportunities with MCHHS (as of 5/7/2014)

Corrections Clinical Lead Provider	$11,147.78 to $17,836.44	Monthly
Dentist Limited Practice Pediatrics	$93,060.72 to $148,897.44	Yearly
Environmental Health Director	$5,928.18 to $8,892.38	Monthly
Manager	$5,540.40 to $8,310.56	Monthly
Nurse Practitioner	$7,048.74 to $9,103.68	Monthly
On Call Dental Hygienist	$29.02 to $35.73	Hourly
On Call Dentist	$44.57 to $71.31	Hourly
Pharmacy & Lab Services Director	$8,375.52 to $13,400.80	Monthly
Psychiatric Nurse Practitioner	$7,048.74 to $9,103.68	Monthly

Source: MCHHS: http://agency.governmentjobs.com

Massachusetts Department of Public Health (DPH)

The Massachusetts Department of Public Health (DPH, http://www.mass.gov/eohhs/) is mandated by state law to "maintain, protect, and improve the health and wellbeing of the people" of Massachusetts. (Note: it does not say citizens only). To do this, DHP is divided into a central office in Boston, five district health offices, and four PH hospitals located throughout the state (but it's really a commonwealth not a state), and the State Laboratory Institute. Major health related offices within DPH are: family and community health, substance abuse services, HIV/Aids, environmental health, communicable diseases, health statistics, hospitals, and health quality systems. Several management, planning, and legal affairs offices are also a part of the DPH organization. A number of toll-free numbers for Massachusetts are operated by programs of the DPH. Unlike other states, the Commonwealth of Massachusetts operates a single PH agency.

Massachusetts' arbovirus surveillance of mosquitoes is a strategy performed by DPH in addition to all the activities mentioned about MCHD (Charlotte) and MCHHS (Portland). DPH has a website (http://westnile.ashtonweb.com/index2.asp) that provides county by county health data and about mosquitoes.

Ohio Department of Health (ODH)

Ohio operates a PH agency which partners (unlike Massachusetts) with 125 local health departments throughout the state which serve the citizens of Ohio (see ODH's website at http://www.odh.ohio.gov/localhealthdistricts/lhdmain.aspx). The PH system in Ohio is comprised of the ODH, local PH departments, and other partners such as healthcare providers and PH associations that work together to promote and protect the health of Ohioans.

In Ohio, local health departments, such as school districts, maintain independent governance, but often work together, along with the state and federal PH agencies. Depending on the type of health district (county or city jurisdiction MAP) funding comes from the support of their community through levies, city general operating funds, contracts, county government, and/or what is known as "inside millage."

To Profile Local Health Departments Here Are a Few Highlights as Reported for 2013:

- 37 city health departments
- 88 combined/general health districts
- 23 counties with more than 1 health department
- 61 cities contract for PH services with local health departments
- 4,789 full-time equivalent staff (FTEs) total
- Core Staff Include:
  - 956 Nurses
  - 726 Sanitarians
  - 156 Health Educators
  - 57 Epidemiologists

From the information from all four models described above (Mecklenburg County Health Department (MCHD), Charlotte, North Carolina; Multnomah County Health and Human Services (MCHH), Portland, Oregon; Massachusetts Department of PH (DPH); and Ohio (state) Department of Health (ODH), it is clear that each jurisdiction has their own model of public health. No single model fits all even across the country. However, PH is different from medical clinics; there are numerous private and public entities which are medical clinics across the country.[17] One example of a clinic was developed by Carmen Velasquez in Chicago.

[17] A Medical Clinic: A facility often associated with a hospital or medical school that is devoted to the diagnosis and care of outpatients.
Source: TheFreeDictionary.com

Alivio Medical Center

It was 1987 and Carmen Velasquez saw that Chicago's Pilsen (predominately Mexican) neighborhood needed a community health center.[54] Many families were uninsured or undocumented or faced language barriers and were not receiving any healthcare. Velasquez says there was a clinic in the area but many people who needed care were put on a six- to eight-month waiting list. The staff was not Spanish speakers nor bilingual. "So I decided to do something about it," Velasquez says. She and her partners secured almost a million dollar grant from the Chicago Community Trust for operations. For a location, another $2.2 million was raised for land and a building. The PH agency grew by 2009 with three locations and another is scheduled to open in 2015. Approximately 27,000 patients are serviced by these free clinics each year. Velasquez has received numerous awards for her tireless advocacy and the governor of Illinois proclaimed October 2 as "Carmen Velasquez Day" throughout the state. After a long career, Velasquez gained valuable insights about how to get things done. "First, you have to have the passion and that fire in your belly to go after something," she says. "Second, you can't let anybody drive your car. I knew where I wanted to go, and I knew also where I didn't want to be taken." Thanks to the Velasquez's of the world, thousands of people have access to affordable, respectful healthcare. Source: Anastasia Busiek, Editor (2014). The Magazine of Loyola University of Chicago. Page 22. And another reason this writer is proud of his alma mater.

Public Health agencies regardless of its jurisdiction, can partner with the federal Department of Health and Human Services and federal jurisdiction often overlaps LHD which tends to create problems and confusion for consumers, organizations attempting to comply with both agencies, and other public (such as the criminal justice community) entities partnering or collaborating with healthcare (hospitals, clinics, providers, and clinicians) providers. But then too, as Velasquez experienced above, grant money helps develop community healthcare facilities.

US Department of Health and Human Services (HHS)

The federal government has approximately twenty-three agencies that are under the authority of the Department of Health and Human Services (2013 budget $941 billion, more details below),[55] of which the Centers for Disease Control and Prevention (2013 budget $11.2 billion)[56] and Food and Drug Administration (2013 requested budget $4.5 billion)[57] are among the most prominent (see Appendix 1 at back of chapter for details and websites). There are approximately 77,000 employees working for this agency.

HHS is the US government's principal agency for protecting the health of all Americans and providing essential human services, especially for those who are least able to help themselves. HHS is headed by the Secretary who is the chief managing officer for a family of agencies, including eleven operating divisions, ten regional offices, as well as the Office of the Secretary. Secretary Kathleen Sebelius reports that "our good is for all Americans to live healthier, more prosperous, and more productive lives." The new HHS secretary Sylvia Burwell was sworn in June 2014; she is committed to the mission of ensuring that every American has access to the building blocks of healthy and productive lives.

Secretary Burwell has called for the Department to operate under three guiding tenets: to deliver results on a wide range of complex issues; to strengthen the relationships that drive progress; and to build strong teams with the talent and focus needed to deliver impact for the American people.[58]

The mission of the HHS is to help provide the building blocks that Americans need to live healthy, successful lives.[59] HHS reports that they fulfill that mission "every day by providing millions of children, families, and seniors with access to high-quality healthcare, by helping people find jobs and parents find affordable child care, by keeping the food on Americans' shelves safe and infectious diseases at bay, and by pushing the boundaries of how we diagnose and treat disease."[18]

[18] Apply to Work at HHS

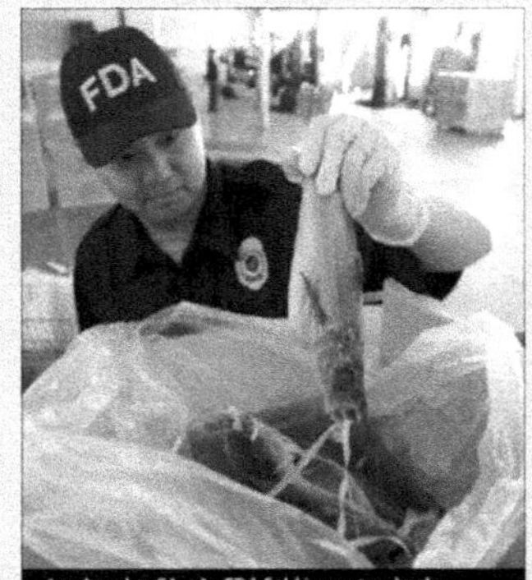

Los Angeles, CA – An FDA field inspector checks imported seafood for signs of contamination or spoilage, and prepares samples for laboratory analysis.

Source: HHS http://www.hhs.gov/careers/where/index.html

HHS is responsible for administering a wide variety of health and human services and conducting life-saving research for the nation (see careers at http://www.hhs.gov/careers/where/index.html). HHS manages over 300 programs that enhance the health and well-being of others. HHS's Headquarters, the Hubert Humphrey Building is located in Washington, DC. HHS also conducts work within its ten regional offices located throughout the United States. Here's an example of open opportunities as of May 6, 2014, at HHS's Headquarters: PH Advisor, International PH Analyst, and Paralegal Specialist.

HHS Branch Opportunities at Food and Drug Administration (FDA): Food and Drug Administration (FDA)

The Food and Drug Administration is headquartered in Rockville, MD, and sample opportunities include Attorney, Chemist, and Consumer Safety Officer. The mission of the FDA is to rigorously assure the safety, efficacy, and security of human and veterinary drugs, biological products, medical devices, and the safety and security of our nation's food supply, cosmetics, and products that emit radiation.

HHS Branch Opportunities at Centers for Disease Control (CDC)

The Centers for Disease Control is headquartered in Atlanta, GA, and sample opportunities include behavioral Scientists, Biologists, and Medical Officers. The mission of CDC is collaboration to create the expertise, information, and tools that people and communities need to protect their health—through health promotion, prevention of disease, injury, and disability, and preparedness for new health threats. CDC strengthens existing PH infrastructure while working with partners throughout the nation and the world.

HHC Management Challenges According to HHC[60]

Below I've listed their top five challenges. Go to their website for more.

- Management Challenge 1: Overseeing the Health Insurance Marketplaces
- Management Challenge 2: Transitioning to Value-Based Payments for Healthcare
- Management Challenge 3: Ensuring Appropriate Use of Prescription Drugs in Medicare and Medicaid

- Management Challenge 4: Protecting the Integrity of an Expanding Medicaid Program[61]
- Management Challenge 5: Fighting Fraud and Waste in Medicare Parts A & B

Be sure to check Chapter 8 for details about HHS's joint task force with the Department of Justice as they fight Medicare fraud through investigation and prosecution of hospitals, physicians, and surgeons.

Ethical Principles of Public Health

The American Public Health Association (APHA) provides twelve ethical principles for PH organizations of which three are provided below:[62]

1. PH should address principally the fundamental causes of disease and requirements for health, aiming to prevent adverse health outcomes.
2. PH should achieve community health in a way that respects the rights of individuals in the community.
3. PH policies, programs, and priorities should be developed and evaluated through processes that ensure an opportunity for input from community members.

Check APHA's website (apha.org) to view all of their ethical principles. Chapter 3 is about public health and society.

Summary

Public health is tasked with providing the circumstances that make health possible; yet, it will be argued in preceding chapters that criminal justice professionals and their collaborative partners are at risk of contagion and death from deadly pathogens more than other professions. Nonetheless, it was recognized that death, disability, and illness are collective (social) problems, and all persons in a democratic nation are entitled to equal protection and opportunities. This book and the American Public Health Association are in agreement with the idea that social class and environment play a role in public health. Public Health's focus is on an entire or specific population rather than at an individual. One result of those thoughts is the Affordable Care Act which encourages the Public Health field to redefine itself and showcase the power of prevention.

The medical model dominates American public health efforts; it focuses on disease and injury and their outcomes; it is built upon a pathophysiologic reductionist approach as opposed to a holism approach. This philosophy represents a core issue of public health along with social relationships including social class and natural and built environments (see Chapter 9 for more details). The mission of public health is prevention of disease through health surveillance and other strategies such as primary, secondary, and tertiary. The central idea inspiring this chapter and Chapter 4 to be written has to do with the link between social class and healthcare, and the search for the common good and justice. A point made several times is that most public health agencies are government operated or controlled suggesting that politics is alive and well in Public Health policy. Four models of local PH organizations and one private local agency were offered followed by a discussion of federal agencies. The challenges and ethics of public health agencies were detailed. Chapter 4 is about public health agencies and society.

Name: ______________________________ Date: ______________ School Identification Number: ________

STUDENT WORKSHEETS

Chapter 3 Essentials of Public Health

Define the following key terms from Chapter 3, and in your answer, show the page number where you found the definition. Provide an example for each key term.

1. Affordable Care Act

2. Biostatistics

3. Centers of Disease Control and Prevention

4. Disease Transmission

5. Environments (Natural and Physical)

6. Epidemiology

7. Food and Drug Administration

8. Holistic Medicine

9. Medical Clinic

10. Pathophysiologic

11. Prevention

12. Public Health (PH)

13. Reductionism in Medicine

14. US Department of Health and Human Services

15. Welfare State

Name: ______________________________ Date: ____________ School Identification Number: ______

STUDENT WORKSHEETS

Chapter 3 Essentials of Public Health

Discuss and demonstrate in your own words that you comprehend the following learning objectives in this chapter.

1. From the author's viewpoint, explain the core components of this chapter, and the reason the author was inspired to write it. In what way do you agree or disagree with the author's position?
2. Describe the tasks of public health professionals and clinicians and contrast the two professions. In what way are they similar and in what way do they differ?
3. Characterize the Affordable Care Act and identify its advantages and disadvantages to the American public and to corporate America. In what way do you agree or disagree with the Affordable Care Act and state your reasons for your position?
4. Characterize the medical model of health, and define and characterize the pathophysiologic reductionist approach and the holistic approach. Which do you prefer and why?
5. Explain public health intervention strategies and connect each strategy to reductionism or holism philosophies of medicine.
6. Explain government's necessity and role with public health. In what way do you agree or disagree with the author?
7. Identify the four local models of public health organizations, and explain some of their activities or objectives. Generally, in what way might local public health organizations differ from federal public health organizations and in what way do public health organizations differ from medical clinics?
8. Characterize the US Department of Health and Human Services and identify four agencies under their authority; define the primary function of each of those agencies.

APPENDIX 1

Universities with PH Undergraduate and Graduate Degrees

There are many accredited (if an institution is not accredited, while it's probably an awesome school, but don't waste your time)[19] universities that offer undergraduate and graduate degrees in PH. I've listed only fifteen, but there are more, which includes the universities' websites at the Council of Education for PH (CEPH). See their website http://ceph.org/accredited/

Boston University School of PH 715 Albany St. Boston, MA 02118 (617) 638-4640 Dean: Robert F. Meenan, MD, MPH, MBA	**Armstrong Atlantic State University** MPH Program in Community Health Education Department of Health Sciences 11935 Abercorn St. Savannah, GA 31419-1997 (912) 344-2780 Chair: James 'Sandy' A. Streater, Jr, MEd, EdD, CHES	**Northeastern University** Master of PH Program in Urban Health Bouve College of Health Sciences 316K Robinson Hall Boston, MA 02115-5000 (617) 373-7729 Interim Director: Irina Todorova, PhD
New York University Master of PH Program Global Institute of PH 240 Greene Street, 2nd Floor New York, NY 10003 (212) 992-6741 Director: James Macinko	**University of Maryland** School of PH 2242 SPH Building College Park, MD 20742 (301) 405-2438 Dean: Jane E. Clark, PhD	**University of Georgia College of PH** N130 Paul D. Coverdell Center Athens, GA 30602-7396 (706) 542-0939 Dean: Phillip L. Williams

[19] Council on Education for PH (CEPH) accreditation serves multiple purposes for different constituents. In general, specialized accreditation attests to the quality of an educational program that prepares for entry into a recognized profession. Following are the top five reasons why an institution should be accredited by CEPH:

- For the public, accreditation promotes the health, safety, and welfare of society by assuring competent PH professionals.
- For prospective students and their parents, accreditation serves a consumer protection purpose. It provides assurance that the school or program has been evaluated and has met accepted standards established by and with the profession.
- For prospective employers, it provides assurance that the curriculum covers essential skills and knowledge needed for today's jobs.
- For graduates, it promotes professional mobility and enhances employment opportunities in positions that base eligibility upon graduation from an accredited school or program.
- For PH workers, it involves practitioners in the establishment of standards and assures that educational requirements reflect the current training needs of the profession.

Source: Council on Education for PH (http://ceph.org/) and American PH Association

Brown University MPH Program PH Program Box G-S121 Providence, RI 02912 (401) 863-2059 Director: Patrick M. Vivier, MD, PhD (6/1/2002) 12/31/2014	**University of New England** Graduate Programs in PH College of Osteopathic Medicine 716 Stevens Avenue Portland, ME 04103-2670 (207) 221-4464 Director: Denise Bisaillon, EdD	**California State University, Long Beach** MPH and MS Programs in Community Health Education College of Health & Human Services 1250 Bellflower Blvd. Long Beach, CA 90840 (562) 985-4057 Interim Graduate Program Director: Toni Espinoza-Ferrel, BS, MPH
University of North Carolina at Charlotte PH Programs Department of PH Sciences College of Health and Human Services 9201 University City Boulevard, CHHS 427D Charlotte, NC 28223-0001 (704) 687-8742 Chair: Gary S. Silverman, DEnv	**University of North Florida** Master of PH Program Brooks College of Health Department of PH 1 UNF Drive Jacksonville, FL 32224 (904) 620-1427 Associate Professor: Michele Johnson Moore, PhD	**University of Pennsylvania** Graduate Program in PH Studies 417 Anatomy-Chemistry Building 3620 Hamilton Walk Philadelphia, PA 19104-6110 (215) 573-0917 Director: Jennifer Pinto-Martin, PhD, MPH
University of Alabama at Birmingham School of PH 1530 3rd Ave., South RPHB 140G Birmingham, AL 35294-0022 (205) 975-7742 Dean: Max Michael, MD	**Tulane University** School of PH and Tropical Medicine 1440 Canal St., Suite 2430 New Orleans, LA 70112 (504) 988-5397 Interim Dean: LuAnn E. White, PhD, DABT	**University of Texas Health Science Center at Houston** School of PH 1200 Herman Pressler Houston, TX 77030 (713) 500-9050 Dean: Roberta B. Ness, MD, MPH

APPENDIX 2

US Government Health Agencies, Description of Services, and Website Addresses[63]

Administration for Children and Families

The Administration for Children and Families (ACF) is a federal agency funding state, territory, local, and tribal organizations to provide family assistance (welfare), child support, child care, Head Start, child welfare, and other programs relating to children and families.
www.acf.hhs.gov/

Agency for Healthcare Research and Quality

The mission of the Agency for Healthcare Research and Quality (AHRQ) is to improve the quality, safety, efficiency, and effectiveness of healthcare for all Americans.
www.ahrq.gov/

Agency for Toxic Substances and Disease Registry

The Agency for Toxic Substances and Disease Registry (ATSDR) serves the public by using the best science, taking responsive PH actions, and providing trusted health information to prevent harmful exposures and disease related to toxic substances.
www.atsdr.cdc.gov/

Centers for Disease Control and Prevention

The mission of the Centers for Disease Control and Prevention (CDC) is to promote health and quality of life by preventing and controlling disease, injury, and disability.
www.cdc.gov/

Cooperative State Research Education and Extension Service

The Cooperative State Research, Education, and Extension Service (CSREES) is an agency within the U.S. Department of Agriculture (USDA) that combined the USDA's Cooperative State Research Service (CSRS) and Extension Service (ES) into a single agency.
www.csrees.usda.gov

Department of Health and Human Services

The Department of Health and Human Services (HHS) is the United States government's principal agency for protecting the health of all Americans and providing essential human services, especially for those who are least able to help themselves.
www.hhs.gov

Environmental Protection Agency

The mission of the Environmental Protection Agency (EPA) is to protect human health and the environment. Since 1970, EPA has been working for a cleaner, healthier environment for the American people.
www.epa.gov/

Food and Drug Administration

The Food and Drug Administration (FDA) is responsible for protecting the PH by assuring the safety, efficacy, and security of human and veterinary drugs, biological products, medical devices, our nation's food supply, cosmetics, and products that emit radiation, while advancing the public's health by helping to speed innovations that make medicines and foods more effective, safer, and more affordable; and helping the public get the accurate, science-based information they need to use medicines and foods to improve their health.
www.fda.gov

General Accounting Office

The General Accounting Office (GAO) supports the Congress in meeting its constitutional responsibilities and helps improve the performance and ensure the accountability of the federal government for the benefit of the American people. GAO's work includes oversight of federal programs; insight into ways to make government more efficient, effective, ethical and equitable; and foresight of long-term trends and challenges.
www.gao.gov/

Government Printing Office

Government Printing Office (GPO) is the Federal Government's primary centralized resource for gathering, cataloging, producing, providing, authenticating, and preserving published information in all its forms.
www.access.gpo.gov/

Centers for Medicare and Medicaid Services

Centers for Medicare and Medicaid Services (CMS) aims to ensure effective, up-to-date healthcare coverage and to promote quality care for beneficiaries.
www.cms.hhs.gov

Health Resources and Services Administration

The Health Resources and Services Administration (HRSA), is the primary Federal agency for improving access to healthcare services for people who are uninsured, isolated, or medically vulnerable.
www.hrsa.gov

Indian Health Service

The Indian Health Service (IHS) works to raise the physical, mental, social, and spiritual health of American Indians and Alaska Natives to the highest level. Its goal is to assure that comprehensive, culturally acceptable personal and PH services are available and accessible to American Indian and Alaska Native people.
www.ihs.gov

Library of Congress

The Library of Congress is the nation's oldest federal cultural institution and serves as the research arm of Congress. The Library's mission is to make its resources available and useful to the Congress and the American people and to sustain and preserve a universal collection of knowledge and creativity for future generations.
http://www.loc.gov/index.html

National Highway Traffic Safety Administration

National Highway Traffic Safety Administration's (NHTSA) mission is to save lives, prevent injuries, and reduce economic costs due to road traffic crashes, through education, research, safety standards, and enforcement activity.
www.nhtsa.dot.gov

National Institutes of Health

The mission of the National Institutes of Health (NIH) is science in pursuit of fundamental knowledge about the nature and behavior of living systems and the application of that knowledge to extend healthy life and reduce the burdens of illness and disability.
www.nih.gov

National Library of Medicine

The National Library of Medicine (NLM), on the campus of the National Institutes of Health, is the world's largest medical library. The Library collects materials and provides information and research services in all areas of biomedicine and healthcare.
www.nlm.nih.gov

National Office of PH Genomics

The National Office of PH Genomics (NOPHG) promotes the integration of genomics into PH research, policy, and practice in order to improve the lives and health of all people. PH Genomics is an emerging field that assesses the impact of genes and their interaction with behavior, diet, and the environment on population health.
www.cdc.gov/genomics

Occupational Safety and Health Administration

Occupational Safety and Health Administration's (OSHA) mission is to assure the safety and health of America's workers by setting and enforcing standards; providing training, outreach, and education; establishing partnerships; and encouraging continual improvement in workplace safety and health.
www.osha.gov

Ounce of Prevention

The Ounce of Prevention campaign aims to equip health educators and consumers with information as well as practical and useful tips on preventing infectious diseases.
www.cdc.gov/ounceofprevention

Substance Abuse and Mental Health Services Administration

The Substance Abuse and Mental Health Services Administration (SAMHSA) has sharply focused its mission on building resilience and facilitating recovery for people with or at risk for mental or substance use disorders.
www.samhsa.gov/

USDA Office of PH and Science

The USDA Office of PH and Science (OPHS) provides expert scientific analysis, advice, data, and recommendations on all matters involving PH and science that are of concern to the Food Safety Inspection Services (FSIS).
http://www.fsis.usda.gov/wps/portal/informational/about-fsis/key-contacts/ophs/ophs

US PH Service Commissioned Corps

The mission of the US PH Service Commissioned Corps is to protect, promote, and advance the health and safety of our Nation.
www.usphs.gov

APPENDIX 3

PH Website Links

APHA is proud of its participation in Partners in Information Access for the PH Workforce; a collaborative project to provide PH professionals with timely, convenient access to information resources to help them improve the health of the American public. Go to APHA's website for links: http://www.apha.org/about/Public+Health+Links/

APPENDIX 4

Disciplines of PH

PH is concerned with limiting health disparities and a large part of PH is the fight for healthcare equity, quality, and accessibility. The field of PH encompasses many academic disciplines; however, PH is mainly composed of the following core areas:

- Behavioral Science/Health Education
- Biostatistics
- Emergency Medical Services
- Environmental Health
- Epidemiology
- Health Services Administration/Management
- International/Global Health
- Maternal and Child Health
- Nutrition
- PH Laboratory Practice
- PH Policy
- PH Practice

CHAPTER 3 ENDNOTES

1. Raymond Goldsteen, Karen Goldsteen, and David Graham (2010). *Introduction to Public Health*. New York: Springer Publishing. Page 2.
2. Dan E. Beauchamp (2013). PH and Social Justice. In Martine T. Donohoe (Ed.) *PH and Social Justice*, (pages 11–19). San Francisco: Jossey-Bass.
3. Smithsonian (2014). Gulf Oil Spill. Retrieved May 21, 2014: http://ocean.si.edu/gulf-oil-spill
4. Brad Spellberg (2009). *Rising Plague: The Global Threat from Deadly Bacteria and our Dwindling Arsenal to Fight Them*. Amherst, New York: Prometheus. Pages 11–12.
5. Laurie Garrett (2000). *Betrayal of Trust: The Collapse of Global Public Health.* New York: Hyperion. Pages 2–4.
6. What is PH (2014). Retrieved May 19, 2014: http://www.whatispublichealth.org/what/
7. American Public Health Association (2013, November). Innovating, Learning & Moving Public Health Forward. A Forum Co-hosted by the American Public Health Association and the Robert Wood Johnson Foundation. Retrieved December 5, 2014: https://www.apha.org/~/media/files/pdf/fact%20sheets/2013 aphareport6192014.ashx
8. Kimberly Amadeo (2014). Obamacare Pros and Cons: Detailed Advantages and Disadvantages of the Affordable Care Act. About.com US Economy. Retrieved May 2, 2014: http://useconomy.about.com/od/health carereform/a/Obamacare-Pros-And-Cons.htm
9. The Heritage Foundation. The Case Against Obamacare: Healthcare Policy Series for the 112th Congress. Retrieved May 2, 2014: http://www.heritage.org/research/projects/the-case-against-obamacare
10. Philip Wegmann (2014, August 7). How These Religious People Found a Way to Opt Out of Obamacare. *The Daily Signal.* Retrieved August 7, 2014: http://dailysignal.com/2014/08/07/religious-people-found-way-opt-obamacare/?utm_source=heritagefoundation&utm_medium=email&utm_campaign=morningbell&mkt_tok=3RkMMJWWfF9wsRonuKjAZKXonjHpfsX56OgtUKW%2FlMI%2F0ER3fOvrPUfGjI4AScVjI%2BSLDwEYGJlv6SgFQrLBMa1ozrgOWxU%3D
11. Lawrence Ogalthorpe Gostin (2000). *Public Health Law: Power, Duty, Restraint*. Berkley, CA: University of California Press. Page 3.
12. Preamble to the Constitution of the World Health Organization as adopted by the International Health Conference, New York, 19–22 June 1946; signed on 22 July 1946 by the representatives of 61 States (Official Records of the World Health Organization, no. 2, p. 100) and entered into force on 7 April 1948.
13. Hayley A. Lawrence (2014). Holism vs. Reductionism: Comparing the Fundamentals of Conventional and Alternative Medicinal Modalities. *Explore IM.* Retrieved May 20, 2014: http://exploreim.ucla.edu/education/holism-vs-reductionism-comparing-the-fundamentals-of-conventional-and-alternative-medicinal-modalities/
14. Andrew C Ahn, Muneesh Tewari, Chi-Sang Poon, and Russell S Phillips (2006). The Clinical Applications of a Systems Approach. PLoS Med, 3(7): e209. Retrieved September 16, 2014: http://www.plosmedicine.org/article/info%3Adoi%2F10.1371%2Fjournal.pmed.0030209
15. Hayley A. Lawrence (2014).
16. Joshua Freeman (2005). Towards a Definition of Holism. *British Journal of General Practice*, 55(511):154–155.
17. Andrew C. Ahn, Muneesh Tewari, Chi-Sang Poon, and Russell S. Phillips (2006). The Limits of Reductionism in Medicine: Could Systems Biology Offer an Alternative? PLoS Medicine, 3(6):709–713.
18. Cited in Hayley A. Lawrence (2014).

19. Education (2014). Holism vs. Reductionism: Comparing the Fundamentals of Conventional and Alternative Medicinal Modalities. UCLA Center for East West Medicine. Retrieved August 27, 2014: http://exploreim.ucla.edu/education/holism-vs-reductionism-comparing-the-fundamentals-of-conventional-and-alternative-medicinal-modalities/
20. Barbara Montgomery Dossey and Lynn Keegan (2012). *Holistic Nursing: A Handbook for Practice.* Boston: Jones and Bartlett. Pages 5, 8, and 14.
21. American Public Health Association (APHA). What is Public Health? Washington, DC: Retrieved December 4, 2014: https://www.apha.org/what-is-public-health
22. The Future of PH (1988). Institute of Medicine's Committee for the Study of the Future of PH. Page 19. Washington, DC: National Academy Press.
23. Ibid. Page 138.
24. National Vital Statistics Reports (2013). Deaths: Leading Causes for 2010, 62(6): 1–97. Retrieved December 5, 2014: http://www.cdc.gov/nchs/data/nvsr/nvsr62/nvsr62_06.pdf
25. Centers for Disease Control and Prevention (CDC) (2014). Press Release: Up To 40 percent of Annual Deaths from Each of Five Leading US Causes are Preventable. Atlanta, GA: Department of Health and Human Services. Retrieved May 2, 2014: http://www.cdc.gov/media/releases/2014/p0501-preventable-deaths.html
26. Don Nutbeam (2006). Using Theory to Guide Changing Communities and Organizations. In Maggie Davies and Wendy Macdowall (2006). *Health Promotion Theory.* (Pages 37–46). Berkshire, England: Open University Press. Retrieved December 5, 2014: http://www.sanjeshp.ir/phd/phd_91/Pages/Refrences/health%20education%20and%20promotion/[Maggie_Davies,_Wendy_Macdowall]_Health_Promotion_(BookFi.or.pdf
27. Maggie Davies and Wendy Macdowall (2006).
28. Raymond Goldsteen, Karen Goldsteen, and David Graham (2010). *Introduction to Public Health.* New York: Springer Publishing. Page 7.
29. Raymond Goldsteen, Karen Goldsteen, and David Graham (2010). Page 8.
30. David L. Katz and Ather Ali (2009). Preventive Medicine, Integrative Medicine and the Health Of The Public. *Integrative Medicine and the Health of the Public.* Retrieved May 16, 2014: http://www.iom.edu/~/media/Files/Activity%20Files/Quality/IntegrativeMed/Preventive%20Medicine%20Integrative%20Medicine%20and%20the%20Health%20of%20the%20Public.pdf
31. Center for Disease Control and Prevention (CDC) (2014). Module 13: Levels of Disease Prevention. Retrieved December 5, 2014: http://www.cdc.gov/brfss/
32. David L. Katz and Ather Ali (2009).
33. CDC (2014). Module 13.
34. David L. Katz and Ather Ali (2009).
35. Ibid.
36. Lawrence O. Gostin and Madison Powers (2006). What Does Social Justice Require for the Public's Health? Public Health Ethics and Policy Imperatives. *Health Affairs*, 25(4), 1053–1069.
37. Ilona Kickbusch, Daniela Maag, and Hans Saan (2005). Partnerships for Health Enabling Healthy Choices in Modern Health Societies. Background Paper for Parallel Forum at European Health Forum Badgastein. Retrieved May 17, 2014: http://old.ilonakickbusch.com/health-literacy/Gastein_2005.pdf
38. Miguel Kottow (2012). PH Transitions and the "New Public Health." SpringerBriefs in PH, 1: 23–31.
39. Kurt Mutchler (2014). Hurricane Katrina Then and Now: Lifting the Fog of Memory. National Geographic Magazine. Retrieved December 3, 2014: http://proof.nationalgeographic.com/2014/08/27/hurricane-katrina-then-and-now-lifting-the-fog-of-memory/
40. Ilona Kickbusch, Daniela Maag, and Hans Saan (2005).

41. The Heritage Foundation (2014). Entitlement Program Spending Is Massive. Retrieved May 16, 2014: http://www.heritage.org/federalbudget/spending-cuts
42. Big Pharma (2014). *Drug Watch*. Retrieved May 20, 2014: http://www.drugwatch.com/manufacturer/
43. Forbes (2013, May 25). Obamacare Will Bring Drug Industry $35 Billion in Profits. Retrieved May 20, 2014: http://www.forbes.com/sites/brucejapsen/2013/05/25/obamacare-will-bring-drug-industry-35-billion-in-profits/
44. Matthew Spalding (2001). Thomas Jefferson Still Lives. *The Heritage Foundation*. Retrieved May 14, 2014: http://www.heritage.org/research/reports/2001/02/thomas-jefferson-still-lives
45. A Mahat, SA Bezruchka, V Gonzales, FA Connell (2013). Assessment Of Graduate Public Health Education In Nepal And Perceived Needs Of Faculty And Students. *Human Resource Health*, 11(1):11–16.
46. US History (2014). Jeffersonian Ideology. US history.org. Retrieved September 19, 2014: http://www.ushistory.org/us/20b.asp
47. Ryan T Anderson (2014, September 4, 2014). Federal Judge: U.S. Constitution Doesn't Require Redefinition of Marriage. The Daily Signal. Retrieved September 4, 2014: http://dailysignal.com
48. Lawrence Ogalthorpe Gostin (2000). Public Health Law: Power, Duty, Restraint. Berkley, CA: University of California Press. Page 4.
49. William Roberts Clark, Matt Golder, and Sona N Golder (2013). *Principles of Comparative Politics*. Thousand Oaks, CA: Sage. Page 90.
50. The Mecklenburg County Health Department (MCHD): Charlotte, North Carolina. Retrieved May 6, 2014: http://charmeck.org/mecklenburg/county/HealthDepartment/Pages/ServiceFinder.aspx
51. N. Pakenham-Walsh, C. Priestly, and R. Smith (1997). Meeting The Information Needs of Health Workers in Developing Countries. British Medical Journal, 314(90): 7074–7078.
52. Ibid.
53. World Health Organization. (2005).Constitution of The World Health Organization. Retrieved May 14, 2014: http://apps.who.int/gb/bd/PDF/bd47/EN/constitution-en.pdf/ Page 1.
54. Anastasia Busiek, Editor (2014). The Magazine of Loyola University of Chicago. Page 22.
55. Department of Health and Human Services (2014). *Fiscal Year 2013 Budget in Brief*. Retrieved May 5, 2014: https://wayback.archive-it.org/3920/20131028130024/http://www.hhs.gov/budget/fy2013/budget-brief-fy2013.pdf/ Page 1.
56. Ibid. Page 27. Budget includes funds for Agency for Toxic Substances and Disease Registry.
57. Ibid. Page 14.
58. Department of Health and Human Services (2014). Security of HHS. Retrieved August 5, 2014: http://www.hhs.gov/secretary/about/index.html
59. Department of Health and Human Services (2014). Secretary Kathleen Sebelius. Our Vision. Retrieved May 6, 2014: http://www.hhs.gov/secretary/about/vision.html
60. Department of Health and Human Services (2014). Managing Challenges. Washington, DC: Office of Inspector General. Retrieved May 5, 2014: http://oig.hhs.gov/reports-and-publications/top-challenges/2013/challenge01.asp
61. See the Medicaid Fraud Unit for US Department of Health and Human Services. Retrieved December 5, 2014: http://oig.hhs.gov/fraud/medicaid-fraud-control-units-mfcu/index.asp
62. American Public Health Association (2014). Principles of Ethical Practice of Public Health. Retrieved December 5, 2014: http://www.aphaportal.org/misc/ajphethicspolicy07.pdf
63. American Public Health Association. US Government Health Agencies. Retrieved December 5, 2014: https://www.apha.org/~/media/files/pdf/fact%20sheets/healthinallpoliciesguide169pages.ashx

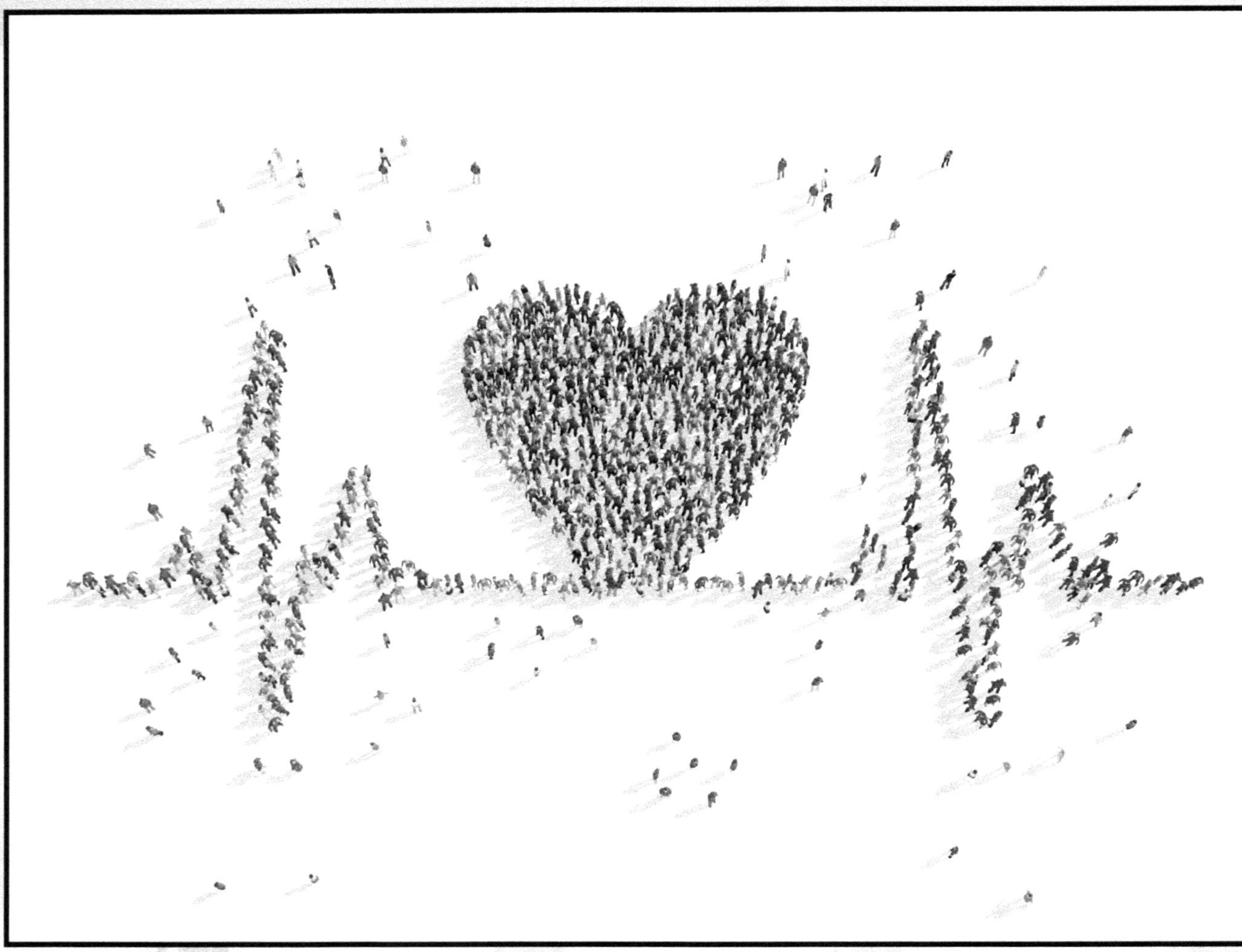

tai11/Shutterstock, Inc.

CHAPTER 4

Public Healthcare and Society

Learning Objectives

After you read this chapter, you will be better prepared to:

- Characterize the public health controversies or issues and explain why one of the issues is the most important issue in this controversy.
- Describe the relationship between social class and public health. Utilize an example from Hurricane Katrina and the Chicago heat wave from Chapter 1.
- Characterize the social class perspective in this chapter, and apply those characteristics to your community or neighborhood. In what way does this perspective help you better understand your neighborhood?
- Clarify conflict theory, its process, and its outcomes using social hierarchy in your example.
- What is the most important perspective about public health that you learned, and in what way might it make a difference in your life to have learned this information?

Key Terms

Bureaucracy
Conflict Theory
Exploitation
Passive Obedience
Power Elite
Social Class
Social Hierarchy
Upper Social Class

Words of Wisdom

The art of medicine consists of amusing the patient while nature cures the disease.

Voltaire

Introduction

Chapter 3 describes the mission of public health as the fulfillment of "society's interest in assuring conditions in which people can be healthy. This requires that continuing and emerging threats to the health of the public be successfully countered."[1] Those conditions it is argued depend in part on the effectiveness of the criminal justice community (law enforcement, courts, and corrections) and their collaborative partners (firefighters, healthcare personnel, and practitioners including physicians and nurses; each described in the chapters ahead).

It is theorized that the criminal justice community and their collaborative partners run a high risk of contagion, injury, and death from their at risk environments where they perform the majority of their services (see Chapter 5 through Chapter 10 for specifics); those at risk environments linked with the 'agents of compliance ' (detailed in Chapter 1, and 5 through Chapter 11) hinder the quality of their performance.[2] This chapter focuses on public health and social class. Reasonably, given that individuals of the lower social economic class most often intersect with the justice community and their partners, and lower social class individuals generally experience poor healthcare, and expose criminal justice and healthcare personnel in at risk environments to infectious pathogens and MRSA. What about the future concerning Ebola? Is that virus likely to become an issue among justice and healthcare personnel? Yet, begging an answer to a serious question: why would individuals in one social class experience different public healthcare and treatment than members of other social classes in a democratic nation cored in equality? Recall from Chapter 2 that when we discuss Hurricane Katrina care and treatment, we must talk about social justice, social hierarchies—the haves and the have nots. There is plenty of controversy surrounding public health so let's get into it.

Public Health Controversy

We've learned that the primary mission of public health (PH) is prevention. Yet, there are several issues about prevention that are worth acknowledging. A huge controversy seems to relate to reductionism versus holistic (described in Chapter 3). In addition, there are seven core issues about public health (PH) that seem to be hotly debated including PH as a method of social control, natural and built environments, and issues of social class (see Chapter 2 for details); but other perspectives require attention, too, such as:

- Individual Freedom or Liberty
- Economic Impact of PH Measures
- Intervention Strategy Agreement
- Public Health Official's Behavior
- Moral and Religious Oppositions
- People Can Be Healthy
- Proactive Versus Curative

Individual Freedom or Liberty

A question that arises is to what extent can and should the government restrict individual freedom for the purposes of improving the community's health?[3] (Recall from Chapter 2 that the CDC says that if a diagnosis of Ebola is being considered, the patient will be isolated in a single room for twenty-one days. Also, see Chapter 10 for restrictions to liberty during terrorist attacks). Individual liberty issues can include the notion that many oppose being told, ordered, or directed through policy as to what to do, even to protect their own health. PH directives include expansive strategies such as seat belt laws (keep in mind that seat belt laws also provide law enforcement with another tool to stop your vehicle) and at other times PH can be restrictive such as age to smoke and to buy alcohol and legal marijuana; wonder how this will play out—can persons smoke legal marijuana instead of cigarettes at local movie theaters and bars?

The Economic Impact of PH Measures

The FDA has the power to control goods including drugs; local PH agencies have power over retailers and services such as restaurants through licensing and inspections (go back to the list of local PH agencies and review their licensing and inspection prerogatives in Chapter 3). Industries often resist PH measures. Those who pay are not the ones who benefit from PH measures. Examples: Milk pasteurization, tobacco industry, pharmaceutical companies, Brazilian state, and the Amazonian rainforest, etc.

Intervention Strategy Agreement

Other controversies have to do with concerns about intervention (discussed below) strategies as discussed above. PH interventions have propensity to be embroiled in controversies over this concern.[4] There are PH debates about the science of myth of climate change and solar influences on climate change,[5] or Avian flu-culling birds—PH versus livelihood issues,[6] or latest H1N1 pandemic—if it was a pharma industry influenced scare.[7] Controversies are intrinsic apparently to PH issues similar to other disciplines such as psychology, political science, and sociology. For example, a room full of psychologists could never agree on the psychological profile of Sigmund Freud.[1]

Additionally, in PH similar to other disciplines, interventions, and definitions, communities are the targeted groups, and because of sociological and economic dynamics that are inherent in any target communities, somewhere someone is bound to be affected directly or indirectly.[8]

[1] One perspective among many criminal justice professionals is that there is no right or wrong; it all depends on "how" it is argued. Outcomes depend on how the evidence is presented. Think of a trial of a violent defendant who is really guilty of murder and is found not guilty as an example.

Behavior of Public Health Officials

Sometimes, PH directors engage in controversial performance.[9] For example, after controversial sermons, Pasadena officials placed Dr. Eric Walsh the PH director of Pasadena, California, on paid leave. City officials discovered online videos of Walsh criticizing homosexuality, calling the founder of Islam a Satanist, and calling evolution a "religion of Satan."

Moral and Religious Oppositions

Promoting condoms to prevent AIDS is one way of promoting immoral behavior—or is it? Alcohol is prohibited in some countries for religious reason: is religious intervention in PH good if it saves lives but severely restricts individual freedom? What rules the day—individual desires, government rules, or religious guidelines?

People Can Be Healthy

The mission states that PH's goal is that "people can be healthy." Health is not guaranteed. Health is a possibility, although through PH's actions there is an attempt at a highly probable outcome or so it's hoped. One reality is that not everyone will be healthy even if each one exists in health-producing conditions.[10] Rather, PH creates conditions in which people can be healthy. Whether any single individual is healthy will vary. Healthcare clinicians believe in the obligation of their practitioners to care for all people in need of their services. Yet, they accept the fallibility of their professions; not every patient will be "cured" regardless of the effort expended by the practitioner to bring about this outcome. Some individuals care less about their health than their own indulgence. For example, cigarettes, alcohol and drugs, and making choices about lifestyles, occupations, and partners that clearly place them at risk.

The classic and defining PH strategy is to prevent poor health by "assuring conditions in which people can be healthy." Other than for immunization, the major focus of the healthcare system's primary prevention activities is on the behavioral determinants of health, rather than structural or policy factors.[11]

Proactive versus Curative

Public health is proactive, rather than curative: Do not wait until people get sick and then treat them, rather, create conditions in which they can be healthy. The success of PH is measured by the health of the populations living in the "treated" circumstances. What is entailed in "assuring conditions in which people can be healthy"? In the answer to this question lies the source of the varied interests, knowledge, and skills that differentiate PH professionals from each other.

Public Health, Monopoly, and Methods of Social Control

Public health (PH) is "always committed to changing social aspects of life—from sanitary to housing to working conditions—and often used the arm of the state (i.e., through laws and legal power) to gain its ends (i.e., quarantines, vaccination)."[12] Indisputable and moral decisions are made by allegedly impartial experts.[13] Fact is, most PH professionals have little training in PH or advanced education for that matter, a committee representing the Institute of Medicine of the National Academies reports.[14] This thought of little training and so on for PH professionals was visible during Hurricane Katrina (see Chapter 1). To reverse the above situation (see below for more PH problems) is almost impossible; when PH executives place community members and the profession at risk there are few options; even retaining expensive legal aid guarantees little in the form of a reversal. Similar to the American prison industrial complex, PH has become a sprawling, massive enterprise (there's too much money at stake, see Chapter 2 for details).

> Public health agencies define their own rules, investigate their violations, enforce decisions and policy, and punish violators without due process indicating that their monopoly on medicine and PH takes precedence over constitutional liberties.
>
> *Source:* Dennis J. Stevens (2014). *Failure of the American Prison Complex: Let's Abolish It.* Iowa: Kendall Hunt.

On the other hand, maybe PH agencies are over-burdened and have become an iron cage for their personnel as Max Weber would explain it.[15] Weber writes that possibly modernized society is nothing more than a "polar night of icy darkness," a highly rational and bureaucratically[2] organized social order, an "iron cage in which people are trapped" and depersonalized.[16]

This thought should not come as a surprise to most of us who have dealt with government agencies. For instance, drivers' license and auto license plates requirements: long lines, no deviations from the posted rules, and complaining about anything means dealing with bitter words from the people who work in those offices. Or getting justice in public university: I recall a student who enrolled in two social problems cources from me, over a three-semester span: each course had a different book, different syllabus, different requirements, and yet the administration said SOL (sorry about your luck), and charged the student for both classes ($1,100) but refused to provide credit hours for both classes. The administration and staff responded similar to hitting a brick wall, no one attempted to help the student other than myself. I sent an email stating that the two courses were completely different and asked why the university's computer or the sociology advisement center didn't catch the alleged duplication?

Bureaucratic organizations set the rules toward social order and the consequences for not following those rules. They demand passive obedience: unquestioning obedience to authority or faith in authority.[17]

[2] Bureaucracy is a system of government in which most of the important decisions are made by state officials rather than by elected representatives. Source: OxfordDictionary.com. According to Max Weber in his book Economy and Society, bureaucracy is a particular type of administrative structure developed through rational-legal authority. Bureaucratic structures evolved from traditional structures with the following changes:

1. Division of labor; jurisdictional areas are clearly specified, activities are distributed as official duties.
2. Organization follows hierarchical principle—subordinates follow orders or superiors.
3. Internal, abstract rules govern decisions and actions. Rules are stable, exhaustive, and can be learned. Decisions are recorded in permanent files.
4. Means of production or administration belong to bureaucracy or office. Personal property separated from office property.
5. Officials are selected on basis of technical qualifications, appointed not elected, and compensated by salary.
6. Employment by the organization is a career. The official is a full-time employee and looks forward to a life-long career. After a trial period they get tenure of position and are protected from arbitrary dismissal.

Fact is, most federal and state agencies including the Food and Drug Administration, the US Department of Health and Human Services, Federal Emergency Management Agency, and federal law enforcement agencies including the Department of Justice (i.e.; DEA, FBI, Marshalls) are so impersonal and 'fixed' in the way they provide services that it is a wonder that they are thriving in their turf war with state agencies and able to operate above the law of the land. Make no mistake, however, healing centers are also very bureaucratic organizations comprised of hieratical managers, divisions of labor, and so on.[3]

[3] "The general spirit of bureaucracy is secret, mystery, safeguarded inside itself by hierarchy and outside by its nature as a closed corporation. . . . it's knowledge is therefore authority . . . passive obedience . . . bureaucracy is a circle from which no one can escape." Source: Karl Marx (2000). Karl Marx: Selected Writings. NY: Oxford Press. Pages 36–37.

For example, a local police officer can be sued by anyone for civil liabilities (denial of due process rights, see Chapter 6 for details); not true for federal agents.

James Q. Wilson explains it this way: the management of government agencies is powerfully constrained by limitation on the ability of managers to buy and sell product or to hire and fire personnel.[18] Laws and regulations limit how individuals can be hired, greatly reducing the chances of firing anyone, and managers are surrounded with countless rules about fairness and procedure. Compliance with every one of the countless rules is the way to keep your job. Wilson suggests that many federal and state employees work at their own pace, it's because they can't be fired.

Wilson attempts to explain bureaucratic behavior on the "bottom" of the bureaucracy—those who do the work, beginning with a contrast of similar institutions (armies, prisons, and schools) that have succeeded and failed; a position clarified in my last book, *The Failure of the American Prison Complex: Let's Abandon It*.[19] Wilson suggests that neither the liberal view (more money, new programs) or the conservative ideology (smaller government) provides a single answer. Policy, rules, and regulation are developed by those with little or no understanding of its implementation. In addition, Jeffrey Kraus from Wagner College at Staten Island, New York, (who evaluated Wilson's book)[20] writes that Wilson implies that government bureaucracy can be made "efficient" by giving bureaucrats more incentives and flexibility, a strategy, Wilson concludes, that conflicts with our political culture. Here's the bottom line, if Wilson is correct, yet I'm sure there are some exceptions, imagine what that might mean about PH personnel and the way they conduct business. If getting the impression that bureaucratic organizations are alien to a democratic process, you are correct.

One last thought about bureaucratic organizations. In the chapters ahead describing correctional officers (Chapter 5), law enforcement officers (Chapter 6), and firefighters (Chapter 7), it becomes clear that those agencies are operated through a bureaucratic organization as described above. Surprisingly enough as you read Chapter 8 (healthcare) and Chapter 9 (Hospitals, Physicians, and Nurses) you could easily envision bureaucratic characteristics within the organizations that employ healthcare workers particularly organizational policy and policy that relates to compliance regulations. Fact is, you will note that the 'agents of compliance' among all the personnel discussed in this book are similar (see each chapter for specifics) and generalized for you in Chapter 11. What you need to know right now is that the agents of compliance influence the quality of performance or lack of performance among criminal justice, firefighters, and healthcare providers.

Public Health and Medicaid Issues

Ellen O'Brien reports that one of the most persistent questions in US PH policy concerns is the mix of personal and public responsibility for long-term care.[21] Nearly half of the nation's nursing home bill was paid by Medicaid in 2003, while just over a quarter was paid out-of-pocket, and less than 10 percent was covered by private insurance. Medicaid provides assistance to the poor, and to those who are impoverished by high medical and long-term care spending. To be eligible for Medicaid assistance with the costs of nursing home care, individuals must have limited assets, and must contribute all of their available income toward the cost of that care. An individual must reduce his or her countable assets to $2,000 or less and contribute all of their monthly income with the exception of $30 for personal needs. O'Brien says that the law (developed by the Department of Health and Human Services) contend that "impoverished is a fallacy. Most affluent people—and even millionaires—transfer their assets to qualify for public subsidies intended for the poor." She says they "hire estate-planning lawyers and artificially impoverish themselves" in order to qualify for public assistance. O'Brien concludes that something needs to be done about abuses of the Medicaid eligibility rules.

The studies reviewed in her work do not support the claim that asset transfers are widespread or costly to Medicaid, or that restricting Medicaid eligibility would substantially increase savings or purchases of private long-term care insurance. While some seniors might be tempted to make large financial gifts to their children or grandchildren in order to hasten qualification for Medicaid, doing so within the five years prior to applying for the program could disqualify them from receiving its benefits.[22] Before applying for Medicaid, seniors who own their home also need to consider the fate of the property. Under federal law, a home is exempt from the asset limits described above, but if the owner dies while receiving Medicaid nursing home benefits, the government can take the house. Families that want to avoid losing a treasured home, therefore, might choose to forgo Medicaid, especially if the applicant's life expectancy is short and relatives have the means to pay anticipated costs out of pocket.

A senior may be able to keep his or her home in the family either by adding a child's name to the deed at least five years before applying for Medicaid (as if they know when they will require specific care), or by setting up an asset-protection trust before applying.[23] This type of trust enables a person or couple to transfer some type of property, such as a home or cash-like assets, to another person to hold and manage for their benefit, says Gabriel Heiser, a Nashville-based lawyer specializing in nursing home law and author of *How to Protect Your Family's Assets from Devastating Nursing Home Costs: Medicaid Secrets*. "This is not a do-it-yourself project, however," he says. He recommends hiring a lawyer to help with the process. But living with the experiences of nursing homes, it's a damn if you do and damn if you don't position. James Q. Wilson's (see above for details) description of government workers fits Medicaid workers both state and federal. Dealing with those employees to protect my mother's financial interest and health benefits was like dealing with a university student who neither speaks English or cares to learn English enrolled in a research methods course.[24]

Costs of Nursing Homes

Because of government (both federal and state) regulations of nursing homes (and hospitals and other healthcare facilities) across the country, compliance with federal and state regulations drives up the costs of their services.[25] For example, see the 715-page document entitled "Title 42 Public Health of the US Rules, Regulations, and Certifications."[26] However, another possible explanation is that some proprietary homes take excessive profit to the detriment of care quality.[27]

In 2012, a private room cost an average of $248 daily, or more than $90,500 annually, according to a 2012 survey by MetLife.[28] A semi-private room ran $222 daily, or more than $81,000 per year. And the average nursing home stay is 835 days, or more than two years, according to the government's latest National Nursing Home Survey. Of course, these costs might be evaluated in relationship to services provided. For instance, you learned in Chapter 1 that the US has one of the highest hospital costs in the world but the quality just is not there in comparison to other countries. One study of 525 nursing homes in New York weighing costs and quality suggests problems or as the authors imply, opportunities to enhance services.[29, 4]

[4] The AARP suggests that in ten years, assisted living facilities will double. For example, where my mother resides in a assisted living home, annual costs will exceed $120,000 a year.
Source: AARP (2014). Retrieved December 10, 2014: http://www.aarp.org/relationships/caregiving-resource-center/LTCC/

Natural and Built Physical Environments

Physical environment includes both the natural and built environments. The natural environment is defined by the features of an area that includes topography, weather, soil, water, animal life, and other such attributes; and the built environment is defined by the structures that people have created for housing, commerce, transportation, government, recreation, and so forth.[30] Health threats arise from both the physical and built environments. Common health threats related to the natural environment include weather-related disasters such as tornados, hurricanes, and earthquakes, as well as exposure to infectious disease agents that are endemic in a region.

Another large body of research on the social environment and health focuses on social integration, social networks, and social support. It is widely recognized that social relationships and affiliation have powerful effects on physical and mental health.[31]

A classic public health model that uses the ecological approach for understanding and preventing disease is the epidemiological triangle with its agent-host-environment triad used to better understand disease transmission.[5] The epidemiological triangle was developed and is used to understand infectious disease transmission and to provide a model for preventing transmission, and thus, infectious disease outbreaks. The three points of the triangle are the agent, host, and environment. The agent is the microbial organism that causes the infectious disease—virus, bacteria, protozoa, or fungus; the host is the organism that harbors the agent; and the environmental aspects included in an epidemiological triangle are those factors that facilitate transmission of the agent to the host. These could be aspects of the natural environment, the built environment, or the social environment. Time is considered in the triangle as the period between exposure to the agent and when illness occurs; the period that it takes to recover from illness; or the period it takes an outbreak to subside.[6]

Clearly, the environment can be the total of factors that enable the agent to penetrate and infect the host. The environmental factors specified in the model can include, depending upon the disease itself, an array of social and physical attributes that permit the agent to penetrate and infect the host. For example, the external environment is the sum total of influences that are not part of the host and comprises physical, climatologic, biologic, social, and economic components.[32] The physical environment includes weather, temperature, humidity, geologic formations, and similar physical dimensions.

Contrasted with the physical environment is the social environment, which includes social class (discussed below) and represents the totality of the behavioral, personality, attitudinal, and cultural characteristics of a group of people.[33] Both these facets of the external environment have an impact on agents of disease and potential hosts because the environment may either enhance or diminish the survival of disease agents and may serve to bring agent and host into contact.

One of the major issues in developing PH models is where to place the emphasis and, thus, where to intervene to improve health? Is it at the individual level or at the environmental level? This issue is at the heart of PH practice or reduction (detailed above). Therefore, in the simplest conceptualization of prevention strategies, we have two choices: We can focus our efforts on changing individual behavior directly or on changing the environment in which individual behavior occurs, however, going to the root of the problem apparently is not an option because of the nuances of social class.

Social Class

America is a socially stratified nation made up of social layers of groups of individuals. These social layers tend to be linked to individuals with similar access to power, wealth, prestige, and characteristics consistent with the social group (see Chapter 2).[34] Social class is characterized through numerous variables such as: education,

[5] **What is Disease Transmission?**
The primary routes of infectious disease transmission in US healthcare settings are contact, droplet, and airborne. Contact transmission can be sub-divided into direct and indirect contact. Direct contact transmission involves the transfer of infectious agents to a susceptible individual through physical contact with an infected individual (e.g., direct skin-to-skin contact). Indirect contact transmission occurs when infectious agents are transferred to a susceptible individual when the individual makes physical contact with contaminated items and surfaces (e.g., door knobs, patient-care instruments or equipment, bed rails, examination table). Source: Occupational Safety & Health Administration (2014). Safety and Health Needs. Retrieved July 9, 2014: https://www.osha.gov/SLTC/healthcarefacilities/infectious_diseases.html

[6] Prevention measures are those that disrupt the relationship between at least two of the factors in the triangle of disease transmission—agent, host, and environment. For example, four of the leading causes of death in the world are chronic obstructive pulmonary disease, acute respiratory tract infections, lung cancer, and tuberculosis. A fifth, asthma, causes global morbidity. A greater effect is needed to introduce new therapies and reduce the disease burden for these illnesses. Four external and modifiable drivers are responsible for a substantial percentage of the disease burden represented by the major lung diseases: tobacco, outdoor air pollution, household air pollution, and occupational exposures to lung toxins. Pressures for economic development and lax regulation are contributing to the continued proliferation of these drivers. Public health approaches to the most common lung diseases could have a huge impact on reducing morbidity and mortality. For instance, increased advocacy from and mobilization of civil society will bring attention to the drivers of lung diseases. The World Health Organization should negotiate accords similar to the Framework Convention on Tobacco Control to address air pollution and occupational exposures. Large increases in funding by both private and public organizations are needed to identify technologies that will reduce health risks while allowing populations to enjoy the benefits of economic development. This paradigm focuses on public health more than on individual medical treatment and has a greater chance of reduction in the burden of lung disease. Source: Neil W. Schluger and Ram Koppaka (2014). Lung Disease in a Global Context. A Call for Public Health Action. *Annals of the American Thoracic Society*, 11(3): 407–416.

family, income, networks, power, occupation, region of residence, wealth, among others. [7] For instance, advanced education is often prized among the middle class but not necessarily among the lower class.

For example, several studies show that up to 20 percent of corporate directors who sit on two or more corporate boards, and are called the "inner circle" of the corporate directorate, unite 80–90 percent of the largest corporations in the United States into a well-connected "corporate community."[35] Other studies show that disenfranchised poverty and illiterate social class individuals tend to make up 60 percent of those incarcerated.[36]

Social class can mean a set of intermarrying and interacting families who see each other as equals, share a common style of life, and have a common viewpoint on the world, explains William G. Domhoff.[37]

Members of the elite upper class, for instance, live in exclusive suburban neighborhoods, expensive downtown condominiums, and country estates. Their lifestyles are everybody else's goals. Adult members of the upper class socialize in expensive country clubs, downtown luncheon clubs, hunting clubs, and garden clubs. Young women of the upper class are "introduced" to high society each year through an elaborate series of debutante teas, parties, and balls. Women of the upper class gain experience as "volunteers" through a nationwide organization known as the Junior League, and then go on to serve as directors of cultural organizations, family service associations, and hospitals and healthcare clinics.[38]

In the US, the upper class or elites probably make up only a few tenths of one percent of the population and are the directors of corporate America: .0.05 percent to .001 percent of the population influence policy in corporations and banks, nonprofit organizations, and the government including the military; here's where it gets tricky.[8] The Power Elite can be described as the elite of the elite upper social class.[9] Not all members of the elite social class in America are members of the Power Elite, in C Wright Mills' explanation. Bottom line: the elite social class consists of approximately 35,000 individuals who control the US economy including public health strategies and organizations through the Power Elites (also discussed in Chapter 11), it could be argued.[10]

[7] We generally think of elite or upper class, middle class, and lower or working class. Think of class in the sense of a social hierarchy. That does not mean the people in one social class are better than people in another class such as being a parent, a student, or as a member of a profession. Social class relates to status which is an important social construct because the positions we occupy lead to the roles we play. *Source:* John Carl (2013). Think Sociology. NY: Pearson. Page 65–67.

[8] The top one percent of households in the US own 35 percent of all privately held stock, 64 percent of all financial securities, and 62 percent of all business equity. The top ten percent own up to 94 percent of stocks, bonds, trust funds, and business equity, and almost 80 percent of non-home real estate. Since financial wealth describes the control of income-producing assets, it can be argued that 10 percent of the American population control the US economy. Source G. William Domhoff (2013). *The Triumph of the Corporate Rich Who Rules America.* NY: McGraw-Hill.

[9] The Power Elite: the governing elite in the US draws its selective members from three areas: (1) the highest political leaders including the president and a handful of key cabinet members and close advisers; (2) major corporate owners and directors; and (3) high-ranking military officers. Source: C. Wright Mills (1956). The Power Elite. New York: Oxford University Press.

[10] **An Example of a Power Elite Representative:**
Henry A. McKinnell, Jr. Ph.D.; he retired as chairman and CEO of Pfizer Inc, the world's largest research-based pharmaceutical company in 2006. He joined Pfizer in 1971 in Tokyo. Over the years, he held positions of increasing responsibility around the world, including service as president of Pfizer Asia, based in Hong Kong. He also served as Pfizer's country manager–Iran/Afghanistan. In 1984 Hank relocated to New York, where he served as vice president–strategic planning, chief financial officer, president–Pfizer medical device group, president–Pfizer pharmaceuticals group, president and chief operating officer, president and chief executive officer from January 2001 to May 2001, and as chairman and chief executive officer, from May 2001 to August 2006, and chairman to December 2006.
Hank is a member of the Boards of Directors of Pfizer Inc, Moody's Corporation, and ExxonMobil Corporation. Hank is a member of the Academic Alliance and chairman of the Academic Alliance Foundation, which supports infectious diseases prevention, care, and treatment in Sub-Sahara Africa. He is also vice chairman of the World Economic Forum and member of the WEF Foundation Board of Trustees, and chairman of the Connecticut Science Center. Hank is Chairman Emeritus of the Business Roundtable, an association of 170 CEOs of America's largest companies, the Pharmaceutical Research Manufacturers Association, the Food and Drug Law Institute, and the Medical Device Manufacturers Association. Hank is a member of the Massachusetts Institute of Technology (MIT) Corporation, and has served on the President's Advisory Council on HIV/AIDS. He is also a director of the Medal of Honor Foundation, the Business Council, the Royal Shakespeare Company of America, the Japan Society, and a member of the Stanford University Graduate School of Business Advisory Council. He is a member of the Boards of Trustees of the Memorial-Sloan Kettering Cancer Center, the New York City Public Library, and the New York City Police Foundation.

Hank holds a Bachelor's Degree in business from the University of British Columbia, and M.B.A. and Ph.D. degrees from the Stanford University Graduate School of Business.

As suggested in the Introduction of this chapter, one sociological and reasonable explanation for the continual exploitation of the socioeconomic lower class by the Power Elite can be translated to wealth and power, ignorance and arrogance.[39,11] Wealth and power are clear categories, yet ignorance and arrogance require a little discussion. Many wealthy people are indeed ignorant but many in the lower class are also ignorant. Ignorant means "lacking knowledge or awareness in general, uneducated or unsophisticated, and discourteous."[40] Many of the "old money" people I know have little managerial skills and know little about the "day to day" business decisions made by their representatives, managers and lawyers, and so on. Others don't care what decisions are made. Conversely many in the lower class lack the understanding of how exploitation works, and rather than overcoming their ignorance through education, fight it without realizing that a fight or violence is what those "in charge" expect from individuals they subjugate—"build more prisons for the dummies." Violence demonstrated by member of the lower class justifies harsh criminal justice strategies which includes long prison sentences. As Jeffrey Reiman and Paul Leighton explain it, the rich get richer and the poor get prison.[41]

Andre Lorde advises that learning how to take our social differences and make them strengths is advantageous toward individual success.[42] But she clarifies, and rightfully so, that "for the master's tools will never dismantle the master's house. They may allow us temporarily to beat him at his own game, but they will never enable us to bring about genuine change. And this fact is only threatening to those women who still define the master's house as their only source of support." Education and knowledge are the "way up and out" regardless of your gender, age, race, or social class. One way to describe Lorde's perspective is through conflict theory.

[11] Wealth and power are clear categories, some of us have both and some have one or the other. Some of us have an enormous amount of both. Who has predominant power in the US? From 1776 to today, one answer is those who have the wealth control income-producing land and businesses and have power. George Washington was one of the biggest landowners of his day and presidents in the nineteenth century were close to the railroad interests; the Bush family has oil and other natural resources, agribusiness, and finance. In twenty-first-century America, the politicians and big money people have controlling interests in banks, corporations, agribusinesses, and "big real estate developers, working separately on most policy issues, but in combination on important general issues—such as taxes, opposition to labor unions, and trade agreements with other countries—set the rules within which policy battles are waged." Source G. William Domhoff (2014). *The Class-Domination Theory of Power*. Retrieved May 21, 2014: http://www2.ucsc.edu/whorulesamerica/power/class_domination.html

Social Hierarchy

The knowledge that in the US a socioeconomic gradient or differences in measures of social hierarchy is a property of populations, not individuals, is a foundation to build a strong PH agenda.[43] Sometimes it doesn't matter what intellect, ambition, or motivation an individual or a group of individuals possess, quality of life opportunities including healthcare prerogatives are more likely available to upper social class persons than lower class persons, the literature and government statistics confirm.[44]

As is obvious from Chapter 1 in the accounts during Hurricane Katina and the brief discussion of the deaths in Chicago during the heat wave, there is strong evidence supporting a connection between social hierarchy and health and how you die. In fact, writes Stephen Bezruchka, "In essentially all developed and middle income countries, societies with a greater hierarchy tend to be less healthy than those with a smaller gap between social and economic classes."[45] Fundamentally, at the core of this perspective, if you believe it to be true and the evidence says it's more true than not, the primary determinants of disease are economic and social; therefore, remedies must also be economic and social (explained later is one sociological explanation which is conflict theory). One place to start is from justice to prevention.

Conflict Theory

Lorde's perspective (above) is consistent with Karl Marx's notion that if one group has more bargaining power and resources than another group, the group with the most bargaining power and resources wins.[46] It doesn't matter if the group with the least resources are right or wrong—they lose: if not today then tomorrow or in another way that each group member expects.

The lower class would not enhance their bargaining power even if they use the tools of their master such as education, political office, or corporate status because the essence or value of those tools will no longer hold their significance and further exploitation is probable, explains Lorde. For example, electing a black man to the Presidency of the United States has not significantly changed shades of discrimination or the rate of black incarceration because some believe that America had few choices but to elect President Obama to show we're not prejudiced or because of "guilt."[47] Unfortunately, blacks and brown who succeed are looked upon as part of affirmative action of sorts; that's not only a white perspective, it's a black and brown perspective, too. Also, wealthy and powerful blacks easily operate within the elite social class, but always work hard to pick the right schools, right neighbors, and right churches for fear not to be labeled ghetto trash.[48] This phenomenon is similar to any other poor person including immigrants, disabled, elderly, and so on.

On the other hand, young, poor, illiterate black and brown men are imprisoned more often (per capita) than other young, poor, and illiterate persons. To really understand how the prison complex continues its exploitation even after President Obama took office, we need to locate the prison industrial complex within the framework of the big picture. If the prison industrial complex is merely a tool of government, and government is a tool of the ruling class or as Marx puts it, government is a committee of the "Bourgeoisie" then a common enemy is required to make it all function and to justify its own existence.

Using Karl Marx and Friedrich Engels theoretical framework of Conflict Theory, according to my interpretation, is one way to better understand the above perspective:[49,12]

- social classes always engage in a struggle over resources
- winners are the social class with the most resources
- the class that wins the struggle exploits the losers in numerous ways

Think of it this way: the haves (elites) and the have nots (you and me). Exploitation of the losers is in the form of untrue ideas about the losers; for example, when I ask my students about poor people I often hear; "They like it." I'd respond with, "What study supports that perspective? Most of you are poor—do you like being poor? Do you like being dependent on parents, part-time underpaid jobs, and student loans?" Every sign of physical health and mental competence favors individuals who are not poor or have low socioeconomic status (SES). What is said about the poor and some often believe it themselves, that the "material disadvantages of lower SES are primarily responsible for these inequalities, either directly or by inducing psychosocial harm."[50] Theories cannot explain, however, "why the relation between SES and health outcomes (knowledge, behavior, morbidity, and mortality) is not only remarkably general across time, place, disease, and kind of health system but also so finely graded up the entire SES continuum," explains Linda S. Gottfredson.

Exploitation is also in the form of criminalization of the poor (especially if an individual is unhealthy) and their subsequent mass incarceration. Prisoners look forward to prison, is part of the exploitation and untruths created to justify their return to prison. Nonetheless, the function of the judicial system is to protect the property of the elite social class in America, who represent the controllers and owners of production or the bourgeoisie.[51] If those under the supervision of corrections represent primarily (SES) lower class America, does that mean that only lower class inhabitants commit crime? Here's what the research shows: it is more likely that social class is the strongest predictor as to whether an individual will be identified, apprehended, indicted, convicted, and incarcerated.[52,13]

[12] If this is your first read of Karl Marx, consider that he is one of the most influential philosophers and economists of the past century. Set aside any political thoughts concerning his work and focus on his theoretical perspectives which help explain social events and circumstance linked to the larger economic sector. In fact, because of the global economic downturn, Mark's theoretical perspectives are welcomed worldwide into economic discussions and his book on the Communist Manifesto is the second largest seller in the world. Source: Guy Haselmann, (2014, January 3). U.S. Rates Strategy: A Look at 2014 and Beyond. Retrieved December 3, 2014: http://www.integratedmgt.com/2010/wp-content/uploads/2014/02/2014-and-Beyond.pdf

[13] Criminal apprehension, prosecution, convictions and subsequent imprisonment have little to do with whether a person committed a crime or not; it all depends on how good he or she fits the profile. Source: Dennis J. Stevens (2011). *Media and Criminal Justice: The CSI Effect*. Boston: Jones and Bartlett. Page 12.

Chapters Ahead

Public health is tasked with providing the circumstances that make good health possible; yet, it will be argued in preceding chapters that criminal justice professionals and their collaborative partners are at risk from the high-risk environments where they are employed; they are also vulnerable to disease transmission from the individuals whom they are providing services, a lack of pharmaceutical antimicrobial products to meet the evolution of deadly infectious pathogens including MRSA, organizational policy and politics, and government regulation which hinders their performance (see Chapter 10 for details). Chapter 5 discusses the notion that the majority of prisoners representing the lower class continue to have inferior healthcare; once released, the chapter will argue that the prison industrial complex is the catalyst of this deadly invasion and prisoners are the hosts or carriers of MRSA and other deadly pathogens.

Summary

It is recognized that death, disability, and illness are collective (social) problems, and all persons in a democratic nation are entitled to equal protection under the law; however, members of the lower social class interact more often with justice personnel than members of other social classes. Because of their poor health, which reflects public health issues of the lower social class, it becomes clear that public health guidance is not necessarily equally provided to all American residents and visitors.

The public health controversies or issues were detailed early in the chapter. Bureaucracy, among other observations within government, was an answer to the ineffective government policy toward the lower social class. For PH to be effective, physical environments and social relationships must be part of the equation. One explanation for the exploitation of lower classes included Conflict Theory.

Name: ______________________________ Date: ____________ School Identification Number: ________

STUDENT WORKSHEETS

Chapter 4 Public Healthcare and Society

Define the following key terms from Chapter 4, and in your answer, show the page number where you found the definition. Provide an example for each key term.

1. Bureaucracy

2. Conflict Theory

3. Exploitation

4. Passive Obedience

5. Power Elite

6. Social Class

7. Social Hierarchy

8. Upper Social Class

Name: ______________________________ Date: ______________ School Identification Number: ________

STUDENT WORKSHEETS

Chapter 4 Public Healthcare and Society

Discuss and demonstrate in your own words that you comprehend the following learning objectives in this chapter.

1. Characterize the public health controversies or issues and explain why one of the issues is the most important issue in this controversy.
2. Describe the relationship between social class and public health. Utilize an example from Hurricane Katrina and the Chicago heat wave from Chapter 1.
3. Characterize the social class perspective in this chapter, and apply those characteristics to your community or neighborhood. In what way does this perspective help you better understand your neighborhood?
4. Clarify conflict theory, its process, and its outcomes using social hierarchy in your example.
5. What is the most important perspective about public health that you learned, and in what way might it make a difference in your life to have learned this information?

CHAPTER 4 ENDNOTES

1. The Future of Public Health (1988). Institute of Medicine's Committee for the Study of the Future of PH. Page 19. Washington, DC: National Academy Press.
2. Occupational Safety and Health Administration (OSHA) (2014). Infectious Diseases. Washington, DC: US Department of Labor. Retrieved May 21, 2014: https://www.osha.gov/SLTC/healthcarefacilities/infectious_diseases.html/ Also see, Center for Disease Control and Prevention (CDC) (2014). Selected Category: Emergency Response/Public Sector. Atlanta, GA: US Department of Health and Human Services. Retrieved May 21, 2014: http://blogs.cdc.gov/niosh-science-blog/category/emergency-response/
3. Dan E. Beauchamp (1985). The Neglected Tradition of Public Health. *The Hastings Center Report*, 15(6): 28–36.
4. Rajan R Patil (2011). PH Controversies: Common Characteristics. *Journal of Global Infectious Disease*, 3(1): 97–98.
5. CM Ammann, F. Joos, D.S. Schimel, B.L. Otto-Bliesner, and R.A. Tomas (2007). Solar influence on climate during the past millennium: results from transient simulations with the NCAR Climate System Model. Proceeding from National Academy of Science, USA, 104(10):3713–8. Also see, C.F. Keller (2007). Global Warming 2007. An Update To Global Warming: The Balance Of Evidence And Its Policy Implications. A Review of The Current State-Of-The-Controversy. *Scientific World Journal*, 7:381–394.
6. David E Swayne (2008). Avian Influenza. Epidemiology of Avian Influenza in Agricultural and Other Man-Made Systems. In David E. Swayne (Editor), *Avian Influenza*. (Pages 59–67). Ames, Iowa: Blackwell. Also see, C.W. Beard (2002). Avian Influenza Debate Continues. *Journal of American Veterinarian Medical Association*, 221:1546.
7. M. Girard (2010). More Queries about H1N1 Scandal. *British Medical Journal*, 341:c3716.
8. Rajan R Patil (2011).
9. Frank Shyong (2014, May 14). Pasadena PH Director Resigns After Controversial Sermons. *Los Angeles Times*. Retrieved May 16, 2014: http://www.latimes.com/local/lanow/la-me-ln-pasadena-health-director-resign-20140514-story.html
10. Raymond Goldsteen, Karen Goldsteen, and David Graham (2010).
11. RG Evans and GL Stoddart (2003). Consuming Research, Producing Policy? *American Journal of Public Health* 93(3): 371–379.
12. Irving Kenneth Zola (2013). Medicine as an Institution of Social Control. In Peter Conrad and Valerie Leiter, *The Sociology of Health & Illness: Critical Perspectives, 9th edition*. New York: Worth Publishers. (Pages 497–506). Page 497.
13. Ibid.
14. Kristine Gebbie, Linda Rosenstock, and Lyla M. Hernandez (Editors) (2014). Who Will Keep the PH Healthy? Educating PH Professionals for the 21st Century: Committee on Educating PH Professionals for the 21st Century. Board on Health Promotion and Disease Prevention. Institute of Medicine of the National Academies. Washington, DC: The National Academies Press.
15. Dennis J. Stevens (2014). *The Failure of the American Prison Complex: Let's Abolish It.* Dubuque, Iowa: Kendall Hunt.

16. Max Weber (1978). Guenther Roth and Claus Wittich (Editors). *Wirtschaft und Gesellschaft (Economy and Society).* Berkeley: University of California Press. Originally published in 1920. Pages 958–980. Also see, Max Weber (1958). *The Protestant Ethic and the Spirit of Capitalism.* New York: Scribner's Press. Originally published in 1904. Pages 47–78.
17. Karl Marx (2000). *Karl Marx: Selected Writings.* NY: Oxford Press. Page 36–37.
18. James Q. Wilson (1989). *Bureaucracy: What Government Agencies Do and Why They Do It.* New York: Basic Books.
19. Dennis J. Stevens (2014).
20. See Amazon.com: James Q. Wilson (1989). *Bureaucracy: What Government Agencies Do and Why They Do It* (Basic Books Classics). Retrieved May 15, 2014: http://www.amazon.com/Bureaucracy-Government-Agencies-Basic-Classics/dp/product-description/0465007856
21. Ellen O'Brien (2005, May). Medicaid's Coverage of Nursing Home Costs: Asset Shelter For The Wealthy Or Essential Safety Net? *Issue Brief. Long Term Care Financing Project.* Washington, DC: Georgetown University. Retrieved May 5, 2014: http://ltc.georgetown.edu/pdfs/nursinghomecosts.pdf
22. Emily Mullin (2013, February 26). How To Pay For Nursing Home Costs: Medicare, Medicaid, And Other Resources Can Help Minimize The Cost Of Long-Term Care. *US News and World Report.* Retrieved May 5, 2014: http://health.usnews.com/health-news/best-nursing-homes/articles/2013/02/26/how-to-pay-for-nursing-home-costs
23. Ibid.
24. PSYC 2103. Research Methodology. (3) (W) Prerequisites: Psychology major; and PSYC 1101, PSYC 2101, and STAT 1220, STAT 1221, or STAT 1222, all with grades of C or above within two attempts. Hands-on experience with experimental, observational, and correlational methods of psychological research. Communicating research results using APA Style is a major component of the course. Emphasis on methodology rather than content and applicability of methods to current topics in psychology. A grade of C or above must be earned within two attempts to continue in the psychology major. Source: UNCC, Department of Psychology. Retrieved May 14, 2014: http://catalog.uncc.edu/undergraduate-catalogs/current/course-descriptions/PSYC
25. Dana B Mukamel, Yue Li, Charlene Harrington, William D. Spector, David L. Weimer, Lauren Bailey Less (2011). Does State Regulation of Quality Impose Costs on Nursing Homes? *Medical Care*, 49(6):529–534.
26. Subchapter G—Standards And Certification (2012, January 3). Washington, DC: US Government. Retrieved May 20, 2014: http://www.gpo.gov/fdsys/pkg/CFR-2011-title42-vol5/pdf/CFR-2011-title42-vol5-chapIV.pdf
27. Ciaran O'Neill, Charlene Harrington, Martin Kitchener, Debra Saliba (2003). Quality of Care in Nursing Homes: An Analysis of Relationships Among Profit, Quality, and Ownership. Medical Care, 41(12): 1318–1330.
28. Emily Mullin (2013, February 26).
29. Dana Mukamel and William D. Spector (2000). Nursing Home Costs and Risk-Adjusted Outcome Measures of Quality. *Medical Care*, 38(1): 78–89.
30. Raymond Goldsteen, Karen Goldsteen, and David Graham (2010). Page 40.
31. L.F. Berkman, T. Glass, I. Brissette, and T.E. Seeman (2000). From Social Integration to Health: Durkheim In The New Millennium. *Social Science and Medicine*, 51(6):843–57.
32. Robert H. Friis and Thomas Sellers (2010). *Epidemiology For Public Health Practice Paperback.* Sudsbury, MA: Jones and Bartlett.

33. Raymond Goldsteen, Karen Goldsteen, and David Graham (2010). page 41.
34. John Carl (2013). *Think Sociology.* NY: Pearson. Page 65–67.
35. William Domhoff (2013). *The Triumph of the Corporate Rich Who Rules America.* NY: McGraw-Hill.
36. Bureau of Justice Statistics (2012). Correctional Populations in the United States, 2011. US Department of Justice: Washington, DC. Retrieved May 24, 2013: http://www.bjs.gov/index.cfm?ty=pbdetail&iid=4537
37. William Domhoff (2013).
38. John Carl (2013). Also see, William Domhoff (2013). *The Triumph of the Corporate Rich Who Rules America.* NY: McGraw-Hill.
39. Jeffrey Reiman and Paul Leighton (2012). *Rich Get Richer and the Poor Get Prison, The Plus MySearchLab with eText*—Access Card Package (10th Edition). Upper Saddle River, NJ: Pearson.
40. Dictionary.com (2014, May 21). Retrieved May 21, 2014: http://dictionary.reference.com/browse/ignorant
41. Jeffrey Reiman and Paul Leighton (2012).
42. Andre Lorde (1984). The Master's Tools Will Never Dismantle the Master's House. In *Sister Outsider: Essays and Speeches*. Berkeley, CA: Crossing Press. (Pages 110–114).
43. Stephen Bezruchka (2013). Promoting Public Understanding of Population Health. In Martin T. Donohoe (ed.) *PH and Social Justice*. (Pages 493–507). San Francisco: Jossey Bass.
44. Stephen Bezruchka (2013); Cohen, Thomas H. & Tracey Kyckelhahn (2010). Felony Defendants in 75 Large Urban Counties: State Court Processing Statistics, 2006. Washington, DC: US Department of Justice. Bureau of Justice Statistics. NCJ 228944. Retrieved May 18, 2014: http://bjs.gov/content/pub/pdf/fdluc06.pdf/ Also see, Dennis J. Stevens (2014).
45. Stephen Bezruchka (2013). Page 493–494.
46. Marx Karl (1978). The Eighteenth Brumaire of Louis Bonaparte. Die Revolution. *The Marx Engels Reader.* (Pages 594–617). Robert C. Tucker, Translator. New York: Norton. Originally published 1852.
47. Nassim Nicholas Taleb (2010). *The Black Swan: Second Edition: The Impact of the Highly Improbable Fragility.* New York: Random House. Also see Andrew Hacker (2010). *Two Nations: Black and White, Separate, Hostile, Unequal.* New York: Simon and Schuster. Page 4.
48. Nassim Nicholas Taleb (2010). Pages 30–33.
49. Karl Marx and Friedrich Engels (1978). Manifesto of the Communist Party. *The Marx-Engels Reader.* (Pages 473–484). Robert C. Tucker, Translator. NY: Norton. Originally published in 1848. Also see, Marx Karl (1978). The Eighteenth Brumaire of Louis Bonaparte. Die Revolution. *The Marx Engels Reader.* (Pages 594–617). Robert C. Tucker, Translator. New York: Norton. Originally published 1852.
50. Linda S. Gottfredson (2004). Intelligence: Is It the Epidemiologists' Elusive "Fundamental Cause" of Social Class Inequalities in Health? *Journal of Personality and Social Psychology*, 86(1): 174–199.
51. William G. Domhoff (2013). Wealth, Income, and Power. Who Rules America. Retrieved May 15, 2014: http://www2.ucsc.edu/whorulesamerica/power/wealth.html
52. Jon B. Gould and Stephen D. Mastrofski (2004). Suspect Searches: Assessing Police Behavior under the Constitution. *Criminology and Public Policy* 3: 316–362. Also see, Dennis J. Stevens (2014). and Jim Bueermann (2012). Being Smart on Crime With Evidence-Based Policing. Washington, DC: National Institute of Justice, NCJ 237723.

Andreas Gradin/Shutterstock, Inc.

CHAPTER 5

Prisoners, Correctional Personnel, and Compliance Issues

Learning Objectives

After you read this chapter, you will be better prepared to:

- Identify the theory of the chapter in relationship to the prison industrial complex; in what way does it make sense and in what way doesn't it make sense to you?
- Identify several of the points made concerning prisoners becoming unwilling carriers or hosts of infectious pathogens which represents a clear and present danger. Which point carries the most weight toward this danger and why?
- Discuss the particulars about the recidivism rates presented and explain in what way several of those points further the theory you identified above.
- Identify and explain the points presented indicating why healthcare during confinement is inadequate and futile.
- Explain why the practices of confinement are to maximize custody and control in an attempt to maximize public safety as opposed to minimizing the transmission of infectious pathogens or to efficiently deliver healthcare. In what way do you agree or disagree with each point?
- Identify the principal risk factors in correctional facilities and the Standards of Care suggested by the American Bar Association. In what way might those Standards address those principal factors?
- Describe the effects on imprisonment upon female offenders especially segregation and its outcomes.
- Discuss the impact of prisoner healthcare upon correctional personnel.
- Discuss the impact of black prisoners coming home on their personal relationships.
- Explain in what way communities are impacted by the release of prisoners, and how can those affects be altered?
- Comprehend the effects of a political contradiction on mass incarceration and its outcomes. In what way does this make sense to you or in what way does it not make sense?

Key Terms

Applied Sociologists
Catalyst
Colonization
Contagion
Evidence Base Corrections
Formal and Informal Organizations
Indefensible Behavior
Infectious Pathogens and MRSA (IPM)
Mass Incarceration
Prison Industrial Complex (PIC)
Socially Approved Rhetoric
Standard of Care
Tautology

Words of Wisdom

There's no one place a virus goes to die—but that doesn't make its demise any less a public health victory. Throughout human history, viral diseases have had their way with us, and for just as long, we have hunted them down and done our best to wipe them out.

Jeffrey Kluger[1]

Introduction

We are in the midst of a lethal invasion by deadly pathogens including MRSA and Ebola as advanced in Chapters 1, 2 and 3; the evidence, both scholarly and governmental statistics in this chapter (Chapter 5),[2] suggest that the Prison Industrial Complex (PIC) explained below is the catalyst of this lethal invasion and that released prisoners (from prisons) and inmates (from jails) consisting of both male and female, adults and juveniles, are carriers or hosts of infectious pathogens;[3] those individuals hold a similar socioeconomic status (SES) or social economic class; that is, they tend to be financially poor (but not necessarily morally bankrupt), unemployed or underpaid, hold little education, have poor health, and lack healthcare when they were in the general population;[4,1] prisoners and inmates (the term 'prisoners' will include inmates which is usually used to describe jailed individuals) have a high vulnerability to infection once incarcerated;[2] and because prisoners are regularly exposed to infectious pathogens and MRSA (IPM) and in the future possibly Ebola become the unwilling carriers or hosts of IPM, contagion potential exists among custodians, volunteers, and visitors and the communities they are released to;[3] a clear and present danger exists to everyone who crosses their path: on a city bus, at the movie theater, or at a shopping mall and everywhere in-between.[4] This clear and present danger is complicated by:

- A widening of the lower social class which now includes members of the former middle class because of the economic downswing in the American economy.[5]
- The monopoly and enlargement of economic sectors dominated by the Power Elites (see Chapter 2).[6]
- Huge institutional release of prisoners, most whose healthcare was poorly assessed and inadequately treated.[7]

[1] Sophisticated data tell us that poverty and illiteracy are pathways to prison; if you can't read in fourth grade, and you're poor, black, or brown, your chances of going to prison are 1 in 15. Many states and municipalities plan the number of new prison and jail facilities guided by the low level literacy scores of elementary students. Through the "school prison pipeline," the future of prisons looks bright.
Source: Kathleen Cushman (2005). *Sent to the Principle*. New York: New Generation Press. Also see Dennis J. Stevens (2014). *The Failure of the American Prison Complex: Let's Abolish It*. Iowa: Kendall Hunt. Pages 237–241.

[2] **American Public Health Association (APHA)**
Prisoners disproportionately suffer from substance abuse problems, mental illnesses, chronic diseases, and communicable diseases such as HIV/AIDS, hepatitis B, hepatitis C, and tuberculosis. Within prisons the rate of hepatitis C ranges from 15 percent to 40 percent, while the rate is 2 percent in the general population. The rate of confirmed AIDS cases in the prison population is four times that of the overall population. Source: APHA (2003). Standards for Health Services in Correctional Institutions, 3rd edition. For more information, see their website at apha.org

[3] Many of the situations that place correctional officers at risk happen as the result of the violent behavior of the prisoners, a group with a high prevalence of infection because of past and present high risk behavior. Studies of four prison populations in the US revealed that approximately half of the prisoners had serological evidence of previous hepatitis B infection with 1.3% to 8.0% of the study population who were carriers. Source: US Department of Labor. Section 9. Summary and Explanation of the Standard. Occupational Safety & Health Administration (OSHA).

[4] **Contagion:** the transmission of a disease by direct or indirect contact. Source: Medical Merriam-Webster.com Retrieved December 4, 2014: http://www.merriam-webster.com/browse/medical/a.htm When this author writes about the plague of prisons, I mean everyone which includes the general public, criminal justice personnel (the three C's—cops, courts, and correctional personnel), and their collaborative partners (correctional personnel, firefighters, healthcare practitioners including physicians, emergency medical technicians, and emergency room personnel, as described in previous chapters).

- An alarming increase in antibiotic resistance (see Chapter 2 and 3) from the infections.[8]
- A reluctance of pharmaceutical companies to produce or market a stable supply of drugs to counter anti-resistance "superbugs" (see Chapter 1 and 2).
- The failures of the prison complex including correctional private healthcare providers (see below).
- Culture clash: prisoners are the effects of enforced residence, custody officers are the effects of employment. This clash negatively impacts prisoners and officers and their families, their circle of friends, and their communities.[9]
- Huge number of correctional (430,000 as of 2003)[10] personnel, especially retention or turnover of correctional personnel—average annually around 16 percent of staff leave[11] as compared to 3.2% across all jobs.[12]
- A tautology (explained later) exists: the law is the law (because it's the law)! Which allows government, as motivated by the Power Elite, to continually exploit its constituents in the name of justice; this thought might include terrorism and medical isolation strategies (see Chapter 4 and 9).

DevonSun/Shutterstock, Inc.

Additionally, most prison (federal, state, local, and private) systems are unable to meet their legal healthcare obligations, explain several researchers;[13] consequently, the public, correctional personnel, and American communities will inevitably pay a higher price when prisoners are released (about 8 million annually of which 600,000 are from prisons) with increased transmissions of IPM and higher recidivism rates.[5] These thoughts can become extremely complicated should Ebola find its way into prison and jail systems in the US. There have been many reported cases of two or three members of the same family coming down with MRSA and folliculitis only to discover that a family member is incarcerated and often visited.[6] However, be clear that some experts summarized some of the literature on prison effects stating: "the evidence indicates that imprisonment is not generally or uniformly devastating . . . Imprisonment, in and of itself, does not seem inevitably to damage individuals."[14] Before we jump into the chapter, there are four appendixes at the end of this chapter: my bias, principles governing healthcare, how to prevent infection, and facts about female prisoners.

[5] Recidivism: rearrested and reconvicted. **Recidivism Rates in US**

- About two-thirds (68%) of released prisoners were arrested for a new crime within 3 years, and three-quarters (77%) were arrested within 5 years.
- Within 5 years of release, 82% of property offenders were arrested for a new crime, compared to 77% of drug offenders, 74% of public order offenders, and 71% of violent offenders.
- More than a third (37%) of all prisoners who were arrested within 5 years of release were arrested within the first 6 months after release, with more than half (57%) arrested by the end of the first year.
- Two in five (42%) released prisoners were either not arrested or arrested once in the 5 years after their release.
- A sixth (16%) of released prisoners were responsible for almost half (48%) of the nearly 1.2 million arrests that occurred in the 5-year follow-up period.
- An estimated 11% of released prisoners were arrested in a state other than the one that released them during the 5-year follow-up period.
- Within 5 years of release, 84% of inmates who were age 24 or younger at release were arrested, compared to 79% of inmates ages 25 to 39 and 69% of those age 40 or older.

Source: Alexia D. Cooper, Matthew R. Durose and Howard N. Snyder (2014). Prisoners Released in 30 States in 2005: Patterns from 2005 to 2010. Washington, DC: Bureau of Justice Statistics. NCJ 244205. Retrieved June 3, 2014: http://www.bjs.gov/index.cfm?ty=pbdetail&iid=4986/ Note: percentages rounded; prisoners in the above case refers only to prisoners released from prison not necessarily jail.

[6] Folliculitis occurs when hair follicles become infected, often with Staphylococcus aureus or other bacteria. Certain variations of folliculitis are also known as hot tub folliculitis and barber's itch. Severe infections can cause permanent hair loss and scarring, and even mild folliculitis can be uncomfortable and embarrassing. Source: Mayo Clinic http://www.mayoclinic.org/diseases-conditions/folliculitis/basics/definition/CON-20025909

Chapter's Theory

At the heart of this chapter is the prison industrial complex (PIC);[7]

> Theory of this Chapter: Prison Industrial Complex (PIC) is the catalyst of a deadly infectious pathogens and MRSA (IPM) invasion through those individuals under their care, custody, and employment.

My theory finds congruence with research which suggests the effects of place or neighborhood—locations where individuals reside, shop, recreate, and work—have been widely studied as sources of environmental influences on individual behaviors, exposures, and physiology, including public health intervention initiatives.[15]

> However, despite modern prisons' strong influence on the transmission and clinical outcomes of infectious diseases, custodial authorities and public health officials in many countries have yet to implement credible interventions to minimize the adverse impacts prison settings exert on the epidemiology of communicable diseases—particularly with respect to inmates. Among many vulnerable populations, prisons are evolving as one of the social institutions that determine their health status and health outcomes.[16]

And be mindful that if prisoners are affected, then so too are the people who work there, visit there, and volunteer there, but to a less extent assuming their health and healthcare does not place them at risk.[8]

Objectives of This Chapter

The objectives of this chapter is twofold: to share knowledge about the documented exploitation through mass incarceration of the disenfranchised or marginalized lower class;[9] and second to document the plague developed and disseminated by the prison industrial complex through the collateral damage from the war on drugs, the criminalization of poverty, and rapid growth of a sprawling enterprise whereby government policy as motivated by the Power Elite take precedent over Constitutional law.[17] The "law is the law" which is defined by a formal (detailed later) government; but how government enforces, punishes through mass incarceration is informal in nature and outweighs the constitutional rights of any individual. See Appendix 1: My Bias Linked to Crime and Punishment.

For example, a physician-epidemiologist with a specialty in family and social medicine,[18] followed Dr. John Snow's example;[10] he mapped the very beginning of the AIDS epidemic in the South Bronx and discovered that the maps he produced "charting poverty, poor education, crime, and deaths due to drug overdose [were] almost identical to the AIDS maps." Drug users share needles and syringes. Needle-sharing turned out to be the "AIDS pump" in the Bronx. Many drug users have served time in prison and in jail. This thought helps formulate additional liabilities of prisoner personnel and for that matter the vulnerability of prisoners, too.

[7] Prison Industrial Complex (PIC) refers to a term used to describe the overlapping interests of government and industry that use surveillance, policing, and imprisonment as solutions to what are, in actuality, economic, social, and political "problems." *Source:* Rachel Herzing (2005). What is the Prison Industrial Complex? Political Research Associates. Retrieved May 27, 2014: http://www.publiceye.org/defendingjustice/overview/herzing_PIC.html

[8] My reasoning is this: poor children who have little choice but to live among poor families in poor neighborhoods; they attend poor schools which are a catalyst to law enforcement intrusion which ultimately leads to incarceration of those children or as they age up. Being poor and illiterate are not the only component of incarceration; there also exists a school-to-prison pipeline.

- 85 percent of all juveniles who interface with the juvenile court system are functionally illiterate.
- More than 60 percent of all prison prisoners are functionally illiterate.
- Illiteracy and crime are closely related. The Department of Justice states that the link between academic failure and delinquency, violence, and crime is welded to reading failure.

Source: Dennis J. Stevens (2014). *Failure of the American Prison Complex: Let's Abolish It.* Dubuque, Iowa: Kendall Hunt. Page 239.

[9] Mass imprisonment implies not just rising numbers of prisoners, but also the concentration of social and health effects of imprisonment on whole population subgroups such as young African Americans and Latinos living in neighborhoods of concentrated disadvantage. *Source:* Oxford Bibliographies (2014).

[10] Dr. John Snow first traced an outbreak of cholera to a water pump in the Soho district of London in 1854, the field of epidemiology was born.

Correctional Personnel Compliance Issues

A fundamental principle and legal responsibility of jails and prisons is custody and public safety by carrying out the punishment of the courts among other missions.[19] Because most of those confined represent the lower social economic class, they share another similarity—bad health and low immunity.**[11]** This principle, responsibility, and bad health of the individuals supervised by correctional personnel carry an inherent consequence: occupational risks or what I call, agents of compliance to correctional personnel, prison and jail volunteers, and visitors which include the following categories that can occur at different times, under different circumstances, and with different intensities (see Chapter 11 for generalized version of liability):

- Prisoner Associated Infections
- Organizational System Policy and Politics (often based on US Supreme Court decisions; the law impacts correctional policy;[20] and political ideas about punishment—get tough on crime sanctions; one reason for off-the-wall politics is that there is little if any political accountability)[21]
- Government (State and Federal) Compliance Regulation which is often complex and often written in ambiguous legal language[22]

These agents of compliance tend to hamper correctional personnel performance particularly in light of the fact that pharmaceutical companies are reluctant to produce or market a stable supply of drugs to counter anti-resistance "superbugs." Similar to crime, if it is controlled or reduced through prevention strategies, revenues into the justice system would be greatly reduced. Conversely, to cure or control infectious pathogens through counter anti-resistance products and the healthcare market would be would be financially impacted.[23]

[11] **What is low immune function?**
Low immune function refers to an underactive and poor performing immune system. The immune system's prime function is to protect the body against infection and the development of cancer. Support and enhancement of the immune system is perhaps the most important step in achieving resistance to disease and reducing susceptibility to colds, flus, and cancer. Supporting the immune system involves a health-promoting lifestyle, stress management, exercise, diet, and the appropriate use of nutritional supplements and herbal medicines.
Source: Dr.Murray.com

[12] "Recognizing that prisons disproportionately confine sick people, with mental illness, substance abuse, HIV disease among other illnesses; and that prisoners are subject to further morbidity and mortality in these institutions due to lack of access and/or resources for health care, overcrowding, violence, emotional deprivation, and suicide . . . [the American Public Health Association] condemns the social practice of mass imprisonment."

Old News

None of the evidence above is news. When I started teaching and led group encounters at Stateville Penitentiary near Chicago in 1988 (while in grad school), it was clear from my observations and the books I read that mass incarceration held a different purpose and produced outcomes other than reducing crime. You might want to browse through those books which are considered classics:

- John Irwin's 1980, *Prisons in Turmoil*
- Gresham M. Sykes' 1966, *The Society of Captives*
- James B. Jacobs' 1978, *Stateville: The Penitentiary in Mass Society*

Many of my scholarly studies at the time and over the next twenty-five years are consistent with The American Public Health Association's position on prisons: [24,**12**]

My point is that little has changed for the better within the PIC over the years or even over a generation. PIC should carry the great burden of healthcare including assessment and treatment of substance abusers. Also little has changed among individuals suffering from serious mental illness to lesser forms of mental illness.[25] There have been some advances made particularly with female healthcare related to pregnant prisoners, but those advances are isolated suggesting that pregnant prisoners continue to remain at risk once arriving at a penitentiary.

The odd part is that most university students reading this textbook were born somewhere around the date of the American Public Health Association's conclusion and those students know that in twenty plus years many changes have occurred; but, PIC has moved slowly toward evidence-based-corrections consequently ignoring the scholarly work conducted by researchers all concluding similar findings and recommendations . . . PIC has failed.[13] That is not to say that the courageous, respectful, and compassionate correctional personnel have failed—it is to say that the PIC has failed its personnel, prisoners, and the nation. In my terms, it has outsourced itself to a level of organizational incompetence.

> [13] **What is Evidence Based Corrections?**
> Abstract
> Relatively few policy decisions regarding corrections use scientific evidence to assist in making informed decisions. This article (see below) emphasizes the importance of using evidence-based corrections if we are to be successful in reducing crime in the community. As an example of how scientific information can be used to make decisions, an assessment technique designed by University of Maryland researchers is used to assess the effectiveness of correctional strategies, interventions, and programs. This technique uses a two-step procedure for drawing conclusions about what works in crime prevention. Studies within each area (e.g., drug treatment, cognitive skills programs, educational programs) are assessed for scientific rigor. The scientific rigor score and the direction and significance of the results are used to draw conclusions about what works, what doesn't, what is promising, and what we don't know.
> *Source:* Doris Layton MacKenzie (2000). Evidence-Based Corrections: Identifying What Works. *Crime & Delinquency*, 46(4): 457–471.

Correctional Statistics

Year ending in 2012, adult correctional authorities supervised an estimated 7 million individuals (or 1 of every 34 American adults), reports the Bureau of Justice Statistics (BJS).[26] Each year, almost 700,000 prisoners arrive at prison (state or federal managed) and about the same number are released.[27] An estimated 13 million arrive at jails (county or municipally managed) while an estimated 7 million are released. The expenditures for state prisons were $40,413,017,000 for 2006.[28] Preliminary data from the Census Bureau's annual State Government Finance Census indicate states spent $48.5 billion on corrections in 2010, about 6% less than in 2009.[29] As a side note, states spent $571.3 billion on education in 2010 and $462.7 billion on public welfare.

The average state correctional expenditure per prisoner was $28,323 in 2010, although a quarter of states spent $40,175 or more, BJS explains. However, these expenditures in 2014 have grown to an estimated $32,000 as an average while some states spend as much as $85,000 on special prisoners such as those on death row or locked down in protective cells.

Some states shell out more money from its general fund for the prison system than the higher education system.[30] For example, since 1980, higher education spending in California has decreased by 13 percent in inflation adjusted dollars, "whereas spending on California's prisons and associated correctional programs has skyrocketed by 436 percent," reports Huff Post.[31]

Standard of Care

The principal risk factors in correctional facilities among offenders are proximity, high-risk sexual behavior, and injection drug use which often cause needlesticks (see below for details).[32] Based on the type of disease transmissions and epidemics reported in the literature, four diseases in particular are targeted for preventive measures: tuberculosis, human immunodeficiency virus, hepatitis, and sexually transmitted diseases. Knowledge of risk factors helps define effective preventive measures along five themes of action: information and education, screening, limiting harm from risk behavior by distributing condoms and exchanging syringes, treatment, and vaccinations.

The American Bar Association in their Standards on Treatment of Prisoners states that correctional authorities should provide prisoners with humane and healthful living conditions;[33] safety from harm, including protection from punitive or excessive force and protection from abuse by other prisoners and staff; and necessary healthcare (see Appendix 2: Standard 23-6.1 General Principles Governing Healthcare).

Another organization, the National Commission on Correctional Healthcare brags about their accreditation and the number of representatives in other organizations, but to learn about their standards you have to spend $129.00 minimum for their book on the topic, and as expected they "sell" accreditation to professionals and organizations. Sounds like a cool but suspect gig (see their website at http://www.ncchc.org).

Nonetheless, prison healthcare has reached such low levels of effectiveness that federal class action lawsuits and privatization of prison healthcare have produced major changes including mandated prison healthcare among confinement organizations. Another way of enhancing healthcare is discussed in the conclusion of this chapter.

Healthcare for Prisoners

Disease prevention education, vaccination where appropriate, and disease surveillance are basic public health tools that can be used in the correctional setting with public health goals in mind.[34] But when you think of prisoners forget your stereotypes; think about the kind of person most likely to be incarcerated. Generally, prisoners under remand of a state correctional system "come from indigent areas, are not well-educated and lead extremely unhealthy lifestyles. Current treatment costs provided by corrections healthcare systems are expensive and continue to rise."[35] Healthcare in confinement facilities is inadequate and futile because of:[36]

- a lack of quality personnel and system resources
- the at-risk vulnerability of the individual prisoners
- custody regulations, public attitudes, and official policy
- political bullying and arrogance toward DOC administration

One researcher asks: Why should public funds pay for prisoner healthcare when law-abiding residents pay their own way?[37] Another researcher makes the point that such a dichotomy is morally intolerable and that all US residents (citizens and noncitizens alike) should also be assured healthcare.[38] At this writing, healthcare is not available for everyone (see Chapter 2's discussion about Affordable Health Care). Nonetheless, there are legal, ethical, social, and public health reasons why prisoners, as wards of the state, must be supplied healthcare.[39] For example, in *Estelle v. Gamble* (USC, 1976), the Supreme Court held that deprivation of healthcare constituted cruel and unusual punishment, a violation of the Eighth Amendment to the Constitution.[40]

This interpretation created a de facto right to healthcare for individuals in jail as a pretrial detainee and those convicted of a crime in prison or jail. *Estelle v. Gamble* (USC, 1976) also pushes the envelope in the sense of "deliberate indifference," a legal definition that prohibits ignoring the plight of prisoners who need care. In legal terms, "deliberate indifference" mandates a provision for all confined individual persons to medical care and a professional medical opinion.[41] Correctional authorities and healthcare professionals who infringe this right do so at their peril and may be prosecuted in federal or state courts.[42]

Denying Healthcare

Should a correctional system actually deny or offer poor-quality healthcare, a prisoner would have few alternatives, despite the law mentioned above. In the past two decades, a substantial number of prisons and jails have decreed that prisoners must pay at least part of the bill for their medical services. However, over one-half of the prison populations were unemployed prior to imprisonment and well over three-quarters of female prisoners were also unemployed lacking health insurance or funds to pay for healthcare services..[43] Another new process is to transfer elderly prisoners to private nursing homes and hospices facilities in order to financially cover those prisoners under federal Medicaid.[44]

Remember that a vast majority of prisoners return to society. Proper care helps to preserve their physical function, which makes it possible for former prisoners to reintegrate into their communities and to embark on productive activities rather than becoming a burden to the state. For example, hypertension and diabetes treatment are known to prevent strokes, heart attacks, and other sequelae that would burden society with

14 Sequelae is a pathology, an abnormal condition resulting from a previous disease, therapeutic intervention, injury, or trauma; such as paralysis after poliomyelitis, deafness after treatment with an ototoxic drug, or scar formation after a laceration. *Source:* Dictionary of Modern Medicine, Retrieved December 4, 2014: http://medical-dictionary.thefreedictionary.com/sequelae.

long-term care of disabled persons.[14] It is in the society's best interest that released prisoners be free of disabling diseases. Public health reasons for providing care to prisoners are so strong that many view correctional medicine and public health medicine as essentially two approaches to the same problem.[45] Prisoners include a larger share of risk-taking individuals than a similar sampling of free persons. Statistics show that they have a larger proportion of the health problems associated with risk taking—hepatitis B and C,[46] HIV (there are no vaccines to prevent),[15] TB, and syphilis, to name a few.[47]

Correctional facilities are critical settings for the efficient delivery of prevention and treatment interventions, but healthcare is not adequately provided for most prisoners.[48,16]

Healthcare interventions stand to benefit from healthy prisoners and correctional personnel, their families, and the PH of the communities to which prisoners return and where officers reside. If IPM are to be eradicated, or controlled, it makes sense that PH managers implement prevention strategies in the prisons and jails, where large numbers of infected individuals are incarcerated for a long period of time or even a few days. Most prisoners pass through jails on their way to prison and connect with jail personnel and individuals temporarily confined. In one study, for example, the epidemiology reporting prison-level risk factors for Staphylococcus aureus colonization and infection in New York State Prisons included the proportion of prisoners with drug offenses, the length of prisoner stay, and the jail from which prisoners originated.[49]

[17]In a study on North Carolina prisoners, it was discovered that prison drug dealers were linked not by gangs, but by former juvenile detention centers attended by the prisoners.[50]

Correctional Dilemma

Prisoners, and it would stand to reason that correctional personnel, face constant exposure to pathogenic organisms, infection, and disease.[51] However, the practices of confinement are to maximize custody and control as opposed to minimizing the transmission of IPM or to efficiently deliver healthcare because of:[52]

- Overcrowding (caused by better law enforcement apprehension strategies, more laws mandating sentences, i.e., drug possession, mandatory sentencing polices, i.e., Three Strikes, and harsher sentences)[53]
- Inadequate Assessments Testing, and Treatment Healthcare (medical, dental, and mental)
- Bans on Prevention Items and Services Such as Soap, Water, Clean Laundry (see Appendix 3: How to Prevent Infection)
- Insufficient Infection-Control Expertise
- The Graying of Prisoners
- Lack of Condoms and Sterile Needles
- Longer Prison Sentences

[15] Centers for Disease Control and Prevention report that half of gay and bisexual men diagnosed with HIV are not receiving care and treatment for their infection. HIV treatment can suppress the amount of virus in the body to a level low enough to dramatically improve a person's own health and to greatly reduce their risk of transmitting HIV to others. Yet fewer than half of men who have sex with men (MSM) diagnosed with HIV have achieved viral suppression. Up to 19% of those infected are not aware of the condition. Men who have sex with men represent approximately 2% of the American population but account for 63% of new HIV infections.
Source: CDC (2014, September 26). *Morbidity and Mortality Weekly Report* (MMWR), 63(38).

[16] Prisons are usually under state jurisdiction and tend to house prisoners with long prison sentences or those evaluated as a threat to the institution, other prisoners, and personnel. There are approximately 1,500 prisons in the US including federal prison facilities. Jails are usually under county or parish jurisdiction such as a sheriff, and house inmates for short periods, while awaiting adjudication, or in the process of being transferred to state or federal facilities. Because of prison overcrowding, states transfer prisoners based on their conviction record to local jails to serve the balance of their sentence. If a heinous criminal was convicted of drug possession, he or she could be transferred locally and engage in a work program at your local restaurant. There are approximately 3,600 jails in the US. For example, The Broward Sheriff's Office maintains five jails: the Main Jail, the North Broward Bureau, the Joseph V. Conte Facility, Paul Rein Detention Facility, and the Stockade Facility. The number of beds in the entire system is nearly 4,800.
Source: Broward, Florida Sheriff's Office Retrieved December 4, 2014: http://www.sheriff.org/about_bso/dodcc/jails/mainjail.cfm

[17] Colonization implies that the patient has a sufficiently high concentration of organisms at a site that they can be detected, yet the organism is causing no signs or symptoms.
Source: Joan Robinson (2004). Colonization And Infection Of The Respiratory Tract: What Do We Know? Paediatrics and Child Health, 9(1): 21–24.

- Bureaucracy (see Chapters 4 and 11 for details)
- Frequent Transfers of Prisoners
- Early Releases (good time or parole)
- Confidential Policies
- Lockdown Procedures
- High Pervasiveness of Mental Illness[18]
- High Pervasiveness of Substance Abuse[19]
- Rising Healthcare Costs
- Recidivism[54] (see details on recidivism in this chapter)

Confinement resources are spent on custody issues and technology that deals with control. For example, New Jersey Department of Corrections is responsible for managing more than $880 million and employing nearly 10,000 persons, including 6,500 in custody positions to supervise approximately 27,000 prisoners.[55] Another example is the Illinois Department of Corrections (IDOC) which reported that its prisons spend an estimated 98 percent of their allotted resources on basic operations of prisons; that means that less than 2 percent of their correctional resources are available for initiatives such as disease control and rehabilitation.[56]

Budget Issues or Something Else

The reality is, says the Vera Institute, the IDOC, similar to most local, state, and federal confinement systems across America, lack approval not funds from policymakers to spend on healthcare, disease control, and for that matter—rehabilitation.[57] Faced with the mass incarceration problems mentioned above, policymakers wrestle with enormous budgetary dilemmas. Legislators and corrections officials attempt to manage this continuing trend by exploring different policy options and sharing innovative solutions.[58] Yet, a major debate of policymakers usually has to do with those who deserve assistance and those who do not deserve assistance.[59,20]

Prisoners out-of-state as part of a jail or prison space rental initiative are rarely evaluated by the landlord state, my experience tells me. When those prisoners are returned to the original state where they were convicted, it's unlikely that any healthcare evaluation or assessment or treatment is conducted. The entire idea of mental or physical health evaluation or assessment of is out of sorts with custody training, control strategies, and mission of the department of corrections.

[18] Mental illness estimates are 706,000 in state prisons, 79,000 in federal prisons, and 480,000 in jails, 2006. Also, people with mental illnesses are overrepresented in probation and parole populations at estimated rates ranging from two to four times the general population.
Source: National Institute of Corrections. http://nicic.gov/mentalillness

[19] Of all prisoners in 2006, 85 percent were substance-involved; 1.5 million prisoners met the America Psychological Association's DSM-IV of the medical criteria for substance abuse or addiction. Another 458,000 had not met the strict DSM-IV criteria but had histories of substance abuse and were under the influence of alcohol or other drugs at the time of their crime, committed their offense to get money to buy drugs, were incarcerated for an alcohol or drug law violation, or shared some combination of these characteristics. Substances were involved in:
—78% of violent crimes
—83% of property crimes
—77% of public order, immigration or weapons offenses, and probation/parole violations
Alcohol was implicated in the incarceration of more than half of all inmates in America; illicit drugs were implicated in three-fourths of incarcerations. Source: Columbia University (2014). Substance Abuse. Retrieved June 4, 2014: http://www.casacolumbia.org/addiction-research/reports/substance-abuse-prison-system-2010

[20] **The 'Deserving' Versus The 'Undeserving'**
The question of who is deserving of government subsidies and how much they should get is a fundamental issue underlying the allocation of resources. Whether we admit it or not, health services and coverage for vulnerable populations such as . . . prisoners, homeless people, and substance abusers are balanced against more popular priorities such as tax relief, economic development, education, highway improvements, and pre-school and child care . . . whether the population and health condition in question is "deserving" or "undeserving" of support and care quickly becomes a key, although usually unspoken, point in the debate. (The relevant issues are) divided into three categories: (1) those with healthcare problems that are the equivalent of an "act of God," such as most forms of cancer, premature birth, mental retardation, and, to some extent, age (children and the elderly); (2) those with health care problems that are viewed as being their own fault, resulting from behavior that could be reversed if they only were to make better choices, such as the overweight or obese, substance abusers, prisoners, the homeless, single mothers, illegal aliens, the HIV-infected, and the poor; and (3) the offspring of parents who made "bad" choices, such as illegal immigrants, . . . or substance abusers. (The first group is) . . . deserving; the second, clearly "undeserving"; and the third, the children of the undeserving, occupying a middle ground. (That translates to prisoners as undeserving). This writer does not necessarily agree with these deserving and undeserving descriptions. The US Constitution is a leveling devise—or should be.

Prisoner Exposure to Infectious Pathogens

Compared with the general public, new prisoners have an "increased prevalence of human immunodeficiency virus infection, hepatitis B virus infection, hepatitis C virus infection, syphilis, gonorrhea, chlamydia, and Mycobacterium tuberculosis (TB) infection," researchers report.[60] While confined, many prisoners are exposed to MRSA and other infections with airborne organisms, and influenza virus, and varicella-zoster virus.

These findings are consistent with the federal agency, The Centers for Disease Control and Prevention (CDC) (discussed in Chapter 2); CDC says that prisoners (which can mean correctional personnel and visitors, as well as the police officers who will rearrest (recidivism) those prisoners once released; it's a round-robin effect) are at risk for the acquisition of blood-borne pathogens, sexually transmitted diseases, and bacterial pathogens such as CRE.[61] Both CRE and MRSA are resistant to all commonly prescribed beta-lactam antibiotics. As you can imagine, prisoners interact and breathe the same air along with countless millions of correctional personnel and volunteers, visitors, and other prisoners. This perspective should come as no surprise because the hospitals across the country have similar problems with IPM.[62] MRSA deaths in hospitals and nursing homes are doubling each year, and in an earlier year when MRSA was recognized as an agent of death, an estimated 19,000 died after being infected.

The number of deaths from Enterocolitis due to Clostridium difficile (C. difficile) has increased dramatically in recent years, from 793 deaths in 1999 to 7,298 deaths in 2006 in hospitals (see Chapter 2 for more details about hospitals). Enterocolitis due to Clostridium difficile is an inflammation of the intestines that is dominantly associated with antibiotic use and can be passed from person to person and it's out of control (webmd.com). Diarrhea is a major cause of morbidity (diseased state) and mortality in infants and children worldwide.[63]

Acknowledging that these facts exist is one thing; connecting them to prisoners is another. The question begging an answer is how many prisoners pass through hospitals and how many patients and staff pass through prisons?[64,21]

21 It is estimated that up to a quarter of the individuals with HIV in the US previously passed through a correctional facility; and 29 to 43 percent of all those infected with the hepatitis C virus and 40 percent of all those who contacted TB also previously passed through a correctional facility the year of their diagnosis. Conversely, governments generally must provide prisoners healthcare. Medicaid can't be used, except when prisoners are hospitalized off-site 24 hours or longer. This way a state or county can pass on costs for such things as heart surgery or a stay in a psychiatric facility.
Sources: See Endnote

22 At least six states and counties from Maryland to Oregon are getting prisoners coverage under Obamacare and its expansion of Medicaid. The fledgling movement would shift to the federal government some of the more than $6.5 billion in annual state costs for treating prisoners. Proponents say it also will make recidivism rarer, because prisoners released with coverage are more likely to get treatment for mental illness, substance abuse, and other conditions that can lead them to crime free decisions. Intrinsic in this thought is the the notion that most individuals consciously place themselves in a scenario providing opportunity and decide on committing the crime: opportunity and motive are at the core of American criminal law.
Source: See Endnote

Prison Systems and Human Immunodeficiency Virus (HIV)

The magnitude and the scope of healthcare problems posed by male and female prisoners seropositive for HIV are enormous. According to one study, female prisoners represent a higher percentile of prisoners exposed to HIV because a high proportion of prisoners are intravenous drug users who often have not received appropriate healthcare or HIV-directed services prior to incarceration.[65] Researchers are finding more and more detainees (illegals) with HIV than expected; in fact up to 30 percent of detainees have been assessed with HIV.[66, 22]

Jails and HIV

Researchers advise that more than 750,000 individuals are held in the nation's jails each day, but over 9 million pass through jails each year.[67] The high turnover presents both opportunities and challenges in providing HIV testing in jails and linking HIV-infected prisoners to services during incarceration and after release. Helping high-risk individuals in jails learn their HIV status and linking them to care is an important public health opportunity.

Prison Systems and Tuberculosis (TB)

American prisoners (jail and prison) are a high-risk population for TB control efforts, including treatment for latent (the term used here is different from the term that will be used in Chapter 4 and Chapter 5; here it refers to Pathology and means 'of an infectious agent or disease in a hidden phase or dormant') tuberculosis infection (LTBI).[68] Completion of therapy after prisoner release is poor, too.**[23]** Researchers reviewed 210,976 TB cases in the United States, of which 4 percent (all percentages rounded) or 7,820 prisoners with TB were reported from correctional systems.[69] Federal and state prison case rates were 29 and 24 cases per 100,000 prisoners, respectively, which were considerably higher than those in a free population (7 per 100,000 people). Prisoners with TB were more likely to have at least one TB risk factor compared with nonprisoners (60 vs. 42 percent, respectively) and to receive directly observed therapy (65 vs. 41 percent, respectively); however, they were less likely to complete treatment (77 vs. 89 percent, respectively). Among prisoners, 59 percent completed treatment within 12 months compared with 73 percent of nonprisoners. In conclusion, the researchers report that TB case rates in prison systems remain higher than in the general population. Prisoners with TB are less likely than nonprisoners to complete treatment.

23 Similar to many professionals who work in prisons, my experiences of keeping myself healthy was a constant process even to the point of never allowing a prisoner to look me in the eyes because TB is an airborne disease. That was hard to do especially among female prisoners who were always more aggressive than male prisoners as a group. "Mycobacterium tuberculosis is transmitted in airborne particles called droplet nuclei that are expelled when persons with pulmonary or laryngeal TB cough, sneeze, shout, or sing," reports Wisconsin Department of Health Services. *See* their website at: http://www.dhs.wisconsin.gov/communicable/InfectionControl/TB.htm

Another study documented the change in TB prevalence in the San Francisco City and County Jail.[70] The findings show that despite a continuing decline in TB in the US, jails remain a high-risk setting for the identification of active LTBI. Prevalence of active TB was 72 per 100,000 jail population for 1998. In 1998 one-third of active TB cases were found through jail screening. Latinos represented an estimated 20 percent of those booked and 43 percent of those Latinos had LTBI. Follow-up studies showed little change.[71] Prisoners with TB are less likely than nonprisoners to complete treatment probably because of poor healthcare procedures.[72]

Female Prisoner Healthcare

The scholarly literature informs us that many female prisoner issues include sexual assault (rape) and misconduct against them, prison sentencing, medical neglect, discrimination, lack of privacy, and contraband initiatives.[73] Organizations, too, such as Amnesty International, The Pennsylvania Prison Society, and the John Howard Society (which are organizations that pride themselves on protecting prisoner rights) attempt to emphasize various female prisoner concerns.

The primary healthcare issues confronting females in prison, in particular, are mental health, substance abuse, and communicable diseases. Also, individually, many females are denied access or visitation to their children by the prison administration as part of disciplinary sanctions, department of youth services, or the families of the men whom they were convicted of murdering.[74] Women prisoners have needs which are distinct from male prisoners.[75] Health promotion in prisons and the health of the community outside prisons are connected. Most female prisoners are mothers and some are grandmothers. To better understand this perspective, the Bureau of Justice Statistics estimates that 62 percent of female and 45 percent of male prisoners had minor children prior to their incarceration;[76] these percent estimates number almost 1.7 million minor children have a mother or father in prison.

In the US, female prisoners can mean juveniles—children and adult female prisoners experience harsh prison treatment.[77] Prison practices toward females in custody are devalued even less than females in the American society.[78] Female prisoners are viewed as "fallen women," regardless of their conviction crime, and therefore whatever treatment or destruction those prisoners encounter by correctional staff or other prisoners is justified. For example, when females including girls are moved to SEG (see below for details) for mental health or disciplinary reasons, they are strip searched. With four or more correctional officers present, the prisoner must: take off all her clothes, lift her breasts and, if large, her stomach, turn around, bend over, spread her buttocks with her hands and cough, and stand up and face the wall. If the woman is menstruating, she must remove her tampon or pad and hand it to a correctional officer. She must open herself for inspection. If she is pregnant, she must open herself enough to determine if she is hiding contraband. An officer with a video camera stands a few feet away and records the entire strip search. This officer is almost always male.[79]

You know why, too. It is part of the accepted perspective about females which is best explained by the famous actress, Bette Davis: "When a man gives his opinion, he's a man. When a woman gives her opinion, she's a bitch. Bitches don't change, so harsh punishment is justified. You know how the thinking goes..." For Facts About Female Prisoners see Appendix 4: Facts About Female Prisoners.

Females in Jail

In the last decade, the number of women in US jails has increased at an annual average of 7 percent. These women typically suffer from untreated, serious health problems.[80] This participatory research project explored health problems and healthcare from the perspective of women incarcerated in a county detention facility located in the western US. The findings revealed that females in jail suffer from physical, mental, and iatrogenic health problems. Barriers to care included concerns about privacy and dignity as well as waiting time for treatment, co-payments, and concealing problems in order to obtain work opportunities.

The American Jail Association (AJA) provides ten facts about females in jails, and this writer found the three provided as the most interesting. Feel free to browse AJA's website for more details (Go to Google.com and type American Jail Association female prisoners).

- Women pose a lower public safety risk than men. Women typically enter the criminal justice system for nonviolent crimes that are often drug- and/or property-related. Within correctional facility settings, incidents of violence and aggression committed by incarcerated women are extremely low. Women released from incarceration have lower recidivism rates than their male counterparts; this holds true for rearrests, reconvictions, and returns to correctional facilities with or without new sentences.
- Women's engagement in criminal behavior is often related to their connections with others. Relationships with children, family, and others are often paramount for women. Their exposure to dysfunctional and abusive relationships throughout their lives can elevate their risk for future victimization and the perpetration of violence—and their often unhealthy relationships (with men or others) can lead to their own involvement in crime and criminal justice.[24]
- The cost of overly involving women in criminal justice is high. Given what we now know about women—their low risk, parental responsibilities, and significant needs (mental and physical health, histories of trauma, substance abuse, financial, etc.)—and some of the strategies we can employ to improve their outcomes, it is difficult to reconcile that 60 percent of women released from incarceration are re-arrested and nearly a third are returned to confinement. Most instances of these are for technical violations rather than new crimes, and they often stem from unmet "survival needs," such as difficulty meeting financial obligations, lower employment skills, or the inability to secure safe housing.

> **24** The fact that women engaged in criminal behavior is often related to their connections with others reminds me of a quote about females and healthcare that I think you'll find interesting:
>
> "The greatest public health threat for many American women is the men they live with."
>
> *– Anne Quindlen*

Female Solitary Confinement or SEG and Healthcare

My own studies demonstrate that a huge gap in the scholarly literature exists about female prisoners, particularly females locked down in solitary confinement or what is commonly called segregation (SEG) or "the hole" and healthcare.[81] My observations in women's facilities were consistent with what I knew about women in American society—they are second to men. Other than the few female predators that I have written about in *Wicked Women: A Journey of Super Predators* (2014) and of all females incarcerated, perhaps an estimated 10 percent are hardened violators and the characteristics of most incarcerated females are similar to male prisoners: poor, unemployed, illiterate, and with little formal education, but unlike males, females are usually apprehended and convicted of crimes connected to others—like their abusers (see above).[25]

The reason there is a discussion about female SEG is because the final experience for most females in SEG regardless of age, health (mental or psychical), condition (unconscious, asleep, or recovering from surgery or an accident), is sexual assault and a lack of healthcare.[82]

SEG is a specific area or group of cells within a prison and local jail where prisoners and detainees are held in isolation from the general confined population.[83] Specifically, SEG is the placement of a local, state, or federal prisoner or detainee into a space isolated from other prisoners, usually as a form of discipline, protection, or prevention.[84] Prisoners are "written up" for various disciplinary reasons such as fighting or wandering into "out of bounds" or restrictive areas. Prisoners and detainees including juveniles can be disciplined for unruly or disorderly behavior implying that unruly or disorderly conduct determinate at the discretion of individual custody personnel.[85]

[25] Around 90 percent of most females in prison, regardless of their age were raped, robbed, and beaten most of their life by fathers, husbands, brothers, and caretakers. My thoughts are consistent with scholars who explain that the experiences of most female prisoners are linked with histories of abuse that manifest themselves into high levels of drug addiction and are compounded by the effects of imprisonment, particularly solitary confinement.
Source: Julian Ford, Robert L. Trestman, Fred Osher, Jack E. Scott, Henry J. Steadman, and Pamela Clark Robbins (2009). Mental Health Screens For Corrections. National Institute of Justice. Retrieved June 2, 2014: https://www.ncjrs.gov/pdffiles1/nij/216152.pdf

Sometimes, custody officers might be compelled to write a prisoner up (because of the number of write-ups, the seriousness of the offense, or the breach of a restricted area). Other times, SEG can be a sanction related to the protection practices of a prisoner from other prisoners (celebrity, cop, or child killer) or it can be sanctioned as a method of preventing a prisoner from attacking others including correctional personnel, correctional volunteers, and correctional property. In both cases, protection or prevention rationales, although prisoners can request SEG for personal reasons (which can or cannot be approved), SEG is often used as protection or prevention tool without the consent of the prisoner.[86]

Some prisoners "act out" or become highly aggressive toward others or even aggressive toward their own body. One rationale of SEG is to protect prisoners, staff and volunteers, and correctional property. How this protection occurs is unclear.[87] At the core of this rationale is the "rotten apple" theory which implies that isolating or removing the "bad apple" (i.e., the most violent or vulnerable prisoners) helps prevent other prisoners from committing assaults and infractions. Nonetheless, most detention facilities have SEG wings (often an isolated structure away from other prison activities) or a few single cells used for the purpose of isolating prisoners for disciplinary, protection, or prevention solutions. That is, a prison within a prison. Female prison facilities similar to male facilities have SEG wings or cells.

Mandated Prison Healthcare: California

When the standards of care mentioned above are not met and individuals file lawsuits against state prison healthcare, sometimes those suits lead to mandated healthcare providers such as the State of California. In Marciano Plata et al. (Plaintiffs) versus Arnold Schwarzenegger et al. (defendants) the US District Court ordered on October 3, 2005, that the court supports its earlier decision to establish a Receivership to take control of the delivery of medical services to California state prisoners confined by the California Department of Corrections and Rehabilitation ("CDCR") (see CDOC website at http://www.cphcs.ca.gov/faq.aspx).

This mandated order was unprecedented in size and scope nationwide. The responsibility of the Receiver (California in this case) is to bring prison medical care to constitutional standards, but no predetermined time frame was established for the Receivership to return the healthcare to state control. Some estimates are up to ten years to get the system up to constitutional muster. Mental health, dental, substance abuse, and treatment or juvenile health in California prisons is not included in the Receivership. Some eighty-seven California state and federal court cases later at an estimated public expense of $21.4 million, little has changed based on the June 2013 case (Marciano Plata, et al., [Plaintiffs] v. Edmund G. Brown, Jr., et al., [defendants]). Just months prior to this June case, the defendants objected to the Receiver's statements that "[o]vercrowding and its consequences are and have been a chronic, widespread and continuing problem for almost twenty years" and "there is no persuasive evidence that a constitutional level of medical care has been achieved." In May 2011, the US Supreme Court affirmed a lower court order that California release some 46,000 prisoners because of the inhuman conditions under which they were being held. In the Court's words, "A prison that deprives prisoners of basic sustenance, including adequate medical care, is incompatible with the concept of human dignity and has no place in a civilized society."[88]

Criticism of Mandated Healthcare

Mandated prison healthcare is a charade and is documented in *Failure of the American Prison Complex: Let's Abolish It* (pages 364–367); the day-to-day is different than mandates similar to the directives and policies before the mandate. Officially, one thing is said—unofficially something else happens. Why? I call it Socially Approved Rhetoric inspired by C. Wright Mills some seventy years ago.[89] I put a different spin on it but here's how it works.[26]

There were regulations, constitutional laws, and compassionate souls directing practice and obligations of healthcare in prisons prior to the mandates. What incentives were and are now in place to assure that the individuals involved in prison healthcare will change? Court rulings? Even prison time for violators of mandates? How many corrupt cops, medical doctors, and politicians are now in prison? When the FBI records are reviewed at http://www.fbi.gov/e-mail-updates (you can get their weekly cases by plugging in) website, of 475 cases from January 2012 through June 4, 2014, an estimated ninety-seven were indictments of judges, local officials (policymakers), law enforcement, and correctional officers by the US Department of Justice.

[26] **Socially Approved Rhetoric**—Mills urged us to see motives not as inner dispositions that cause action but rather as rhetorical constructs that define action with respect to particular social context. Motives used to explain someone's behavior or action after the behavior occurred might be a distance from the motives before the behavior. Explaining after an occurrence might be a devise to gain favor with whoever is listening or asking a question. "Why did you abuse that child?" Answer: Because when I was a child, I was abused. Turn it upside down. The PIC officially claims this or that, fully knowing that that is what people want to hear (socially approved) and based on approval ratings (not verifiable facts), the PIC is doing something completely different. Sort of like the old bait and switch of an American president who said that Iraq developed mass weapons of destruction when in fact, they had not developed those weapons. Based on the information, America invaded Iraq. It was a devise, a ploy, an excuse to win support of the American people to wage war.
Source: Martin Halpern (2003). Congress Should Censure President Bush. History Network. Retrieved June 2, 2014: http://hnn.us/article/18195

Private Healthcare in Prisons

About twenty years ago, prison privatization was seen as a way to provide good healthcare for prisoners at a reasonable cost.[90] Many prison officials joined a growing number of states that hired private healthcare companies. But the results of that trend have been mixed. See what you think from a few of the typical cases presented below.

Florida Private Healthcare

Florida's twenty-six state prisons are now under a healthcare umbra, although there were many hot debates in the state legislature.[91] Corizon (discussed below) is the private prison healthcare provider awarded the contract despite the bad publicity about Corizon's fine of $1.2 million after causing a prisoner to suffer partial paralysis. The Florida Department of Corrections contracted out of $353.8 million for healthcare, which could potentially save the state $51 million.

In 2012, Corizon projected that it would maintain "between 97 [percent] and 99 percent" of current staff at the subject prisons in Florida. It's too soon to tell how Corizon will do at the job at this writing. But previous experiences imply that it's over for those state employees regardless what FDOC Teamsters Local 2011 (corrections' personnel union) is telling them. New employees will be "mandated" to join the Teamsters union—like it or not.

Mississippi Department of Corrections (MDOC)

Mississippi Department of Corrections contracts with Wexford Health Services, Inc., headquartered in Green Tree, Pennsylvania. Wexford provides medical services to prisoners at state-operated facilities. Each privately operated facility has its own contracted medical services provider. Wexford was awarded the $95 million MDOC contract in 2006. Previously, MDOC contracted with Correctional Medical Services (CMS), headquartered in Creve Coeur, Missouri.

Maine Department of Corrections

Maine Department of Corrections has 2,100 state prisoners and Cumberland County Jail prisoners are provided with a private healthcare provider and thus far few complications have emerged. Some states report significant cost savings through privatization, while others report that private contractors cut too many corners and even go bankrupt, leaving public officials with the bills.

Crisis with Private Healthcare Providers

There are few different outcomes between public and private healthcare providers. The private companies have a better public relations department, so they offer a higher quality of socially approved rhetoric. Nonetheless, the legislature of the State of Illinois gave Wexford Health Services, a private prison healthcare company, a $115 million a year, 10-year contract to provide healthcare services to an estimated 50,000 prisoners in twenty-six adult prisons, the annual (total) prison expense of which is about $1.4 billion. After two years in operation, it has been learned that neither the IDOC nor the state legislature audited Wexford performance before or during their operations.[92] A study by John Maki, Executive Director of the John Howard Association in Chicago (see Chapter 2 for details), says he hears a lot of complaints from prisoners about the healthcare. "I don't think we fully know what we're getting for this contract. Again, I think it's just good government, you got to show me. We need an account of how this money is being spent."

Maki reports that he received an e-mailed statement from a spokeswoman for IDOC, which says, "The department monitors Wexford through a comprehensive and continuous quality improvement process." Over the course of weeks, IDOC refused to provide someone who could explain exactly what's involved in that quality improvement process.

These facts have profound and underexamined implications for state and local budgets, public safety, and civic health. In its January 2013 Quarterly Report, IDOC reported that it housed almost 50 percent more prisoners than it was designed to hold. Many minimum- and medium-security facilities housed more than 100 percent beyond their design capacity.

Final Analysis of Healthcare Providers

In a final analysis of prison healthcare one study pretty well sums it up by saying that in a review of state prison programs and research in healthcare related issues important to these prisoners' successful transitions to the community, the researchers find that, in general, such services are currently inadequate regardless if healthcare services are provided by public or private entities.[93] Healthcare services in prison and jail go beyond clinical practitioners and include prison-based nursing services which are also "seriously neglected and woefully lacking in structure and resources."[94] Building sustainable group capacity into prison-based healthcare, through developing social interaction, cohesion, participation, and political action can benefit prisoners, correctional personnel, and the communities where prisoners are returned to and where correctional personnel currently reside. Go to Appendix 3 to see how to prevent infections and why prisoners cannot protect themselves.

Effects of Prisoner Health on Correctional Personnel

You've read since the beginning of this chapter that prisoners are vulnerable to IPM, and contagion can happen through casual contact between individuals, shared surfaces, and even personal items, such as towels and linens. Factors associated with the spread of MRSA for example, include: close skin-to-skin contact, openings in the skin, contaminated items and surfaces, crowded living conditions, and poor hygiene.[95]

Prisoners are at a high risk of contracting IPM, so too are correctional personnel, visitors, volunteers, and subcontractors such as private healthcare personnel, teachers, and group leaders.[96] If incarceration reduces life span for prisoners, is there a relationship between length of correctional employment and life span among correctional personnel?[97] Each additional year incarcerated for prisoners produces an estimated 16 percent increase in the odds of death, which translates to a 2-year decline in life expectancy for each year served in prison. It is interesting to note that military personnel and correctional personnel have similar at-risk levels of contacting IPM.[98]

One of the challenges that correctional administrators realize is that when correctional professionals are healthier, they are less likely to be cynical, angry, and disgruntled, the all-to-typical outlook that many correctional professionals particularly correctional custody officers share.[99] When custody officers are happy and healthy, employees stay in their jobs and work hard to advance and further the mission of their employer. When they're unhappy, personnel quit or become complacent about the job or become angry. Stress from the job ranks high among most custody officers.

Occupational Stress

Among custody officers, similar to police officers, occupational stress from a health perspective tops the list; but a lot of stress producers can often be resolved.[100] Like police officers, one important source of correctional officer stress is the work environment; that is, with overcrowded prisons, the safety of correctional personnel is always at-risk.[101] Other environmental stressors for correctional personnel include:[102]

- prisoner assaults or critical incidents
- interactions with prisoners
- conflicts with co-workers, especially the administration
- conflicts with correctional policy

My experience tells me that, similar to law enforcement officers' occupational stress, often violators or offenders behave in unpredictable ways with the intention of igniting the fuse of justice professionals. Just as street-smart thugs know how to "rattle the cage of police officers," prisoners know how to manipulate their custodians into stressful moments which pushes an inexperienced or hot-tempered officer to act in an unprofessional manner including indefensible (not justifiable; inexcusable) behavior; prisoners have all day to talk and think about their custodians;[103] unprofessional behavior provides the offender and his or her colleagues with an open door to a lawsuit against the officer, their training instructors, and the facility or department, and winning.

Sometimes my experience tells me that custody officers who disagree with correctional policy will allow inappropriate prisoner and sometimes correctional officer behavior to occur so that policy can be tested in court and reversed.

One way to relieve occupational stress visited upon custody officers is to change policy, if possible. Another way is to look the other way when officers engage in certain conduct that might compromise policy. Let me explain, applied sociologists understand that there exists in every organization a formal world and an informal world.[27]

The future of correctional officer health programs should include the development of services designed to reduce officer stress and combat those accompanying physical, emotional, and administrative consequences, but also to improve their physical and emotional wellness.[104] The establishment of wellness or fitness programs designed to promote exercise, nutrition, and emotional health of employees is increasing due to spiraling healthcare costs employers pay for sick leave, disability, lower levels of productivity, lawsuits, corrupt personnel, and employee turnover, and laziness not to mention accidents such as needlesticks.

Needlesticks

There is a gap in the literature on blood-borne pathogen risk among correctional healthcare workers even though the prevalence of blood-borne infections, including hepatitis B virus (HBV), among prisoners is high.[105] One study, conducted in three state correctional healthcare facilities, found that 64 percent of those workers received primary hepatitis B (HB) vaccine series. Vaccination rates varied by state and by job category. Parenteral exposures were not uncommon among all healthcare workers; 9 percent of clinicians and 2 percent of nonclinical staff reported one or more needlesticks in the six-month period prior to the study. One recommendation made by the researchers, given the potential risk of exposure to HBV, universal vaccination should be encouraged and should include those nonclinicians with job duties that may involve potential exposure to blood/body fluids. One-third of new infections among New York State prison employees were due to occupational exposure.[106]

[27] The Differences Between Formal and Informal Organizations and Applied Sociologists Formal organizations are groups created for a certain purpose and built for maximum efficiency. Authority in formal organizations such as a prison or a police department is impersonal, and rules, regulations, and laws are written, chain of command is clearly defined, division of labor is absolute, and individuals perform according to their status. Formal organizations are comparatively more inflexible. It is not easy to bring change. Informal organizations are flexible. There is no rigidity here. Changes can be brought forth easily. It requires only the change in attitudes of the members. Informal organizations consist of face-to-face decisions and personal relationships rather than status relationships. Source John Carl (2011). Think Sociology. Boston: Pearson. Page 111.
Applied Sociologist (AS): is a term that describes practitioners who use sociological theories and methods outside of academic settings with the aim to 'produce positive social change through active intervention.' *Source:* J.G. Bruhn (1999). Introductory Statement: Philosophy and Future Direction, *Sociological Practice* 1(1): (1–2).
In what way does a particular theory work in real time? Most AS might agree with Carl but add that formal organizations are indeed formal—rules and so on; but then informal social relationships work simultaneously with the formal relationships. In a university classroom, for example, professors establish syllabi—the rules. Late students will lose one toenail after the second absence. Yet, students are late three times and the prof shrugs her shoulders—"okay, next time," she says with a smile to the late student. Prisons have rules which often include consequences, but many times personnel look the other way for many reasons: they disagree with the policy, they like the 'violator' or need the 'violator's' toward order, the consequences for the offense is not rational or reasonable, or the officer is just lazy and doesn't like intervening.

Hepatitis B (HBV)

Hepatitis B is a liver disease caused by the hepatitis B virus. As many as 1.25 million people living in the US have hepatitis B virus (HBV);[107] intrinsic to the large numbers of people infected with HBV, think in terms of the number of released prisoners coming home to American communities (more later on 'coming home'). Not all people who are infected with HBV look or feel sick; they can have the virus and not have symptoms or know they are sick. HBV can be either acute or chronic.

- Acute HBV infection is a short-term illness that occurs within the first six months after someone is exposed to the HBV. Acute infection can, but does not always, lead to chronic infection.
- Chronic HBV infection is a long-term illness that occurs when the HBV remains in a person's body.

Hepatitis B vaccination is the most effective measure to prevent (HBV) infection and its consequences; most firefighters are vaccinated against hepatitis B. The consequences of chronic HBV can include cirrhosis of the liver, liver cancer, liver failure, and death. In adults, ongoing HBV transmission occurs primarily among unvaccinated persons with behavioral risks for HBV transmission (e.g., heterosexuals with multiple sex partners, injection-drug users [IDUs], and men who have sex with men [MSM]) and among household contacts and sex partners of persons with chronic HBV infection.[108]

In settings in which a high proportion of adults have risks for HBV infection (e.g., sexually transmitted disease/human immunodeficiency virus testing and treatment facilities, drug-abuse treatment and prevention settings, healthcare settings targeting services to IDUs, healthcare settings targeting services to MSM, and correctional facilities). In other primary care and specialty medical settings in which adults at risk for HBV infection receive care, healthcare providers should inform all patients about the health benefits of vaccination, including risks for HBV infection and persons for whom vaccination is recommended, and vaccinate adults who report risks for HBV infection and any adults requesting protection from HBV infection. To promote vaccination in all settings, healthcare providers should implement standing orders to identify adults recommended for hepatitis B vaccination and administer vaccination as part of routine clinical services, not require acknowledgment of an HBV infection risk factor for adults to receive vaccine, and use available reimbursement mechanisms to remove financial barriers to hepatitis B vaccination.

HBV Disease Transmission

HBV is transmitted through percutaneous (puncture through the skin) or mucosal (direct contact with mucous membranes) exposure to infectious blood or body fluids.[109] Persons with chronic infection also serve as the main reservoir for continued HBV transmission. Although chronic infection is more likely to develop in persons infected as infants or young children, rates of new infection and acute disease are highest among adults.

During 1990–2005, incidence of acute hepatitis B in the United States declined 78 percent. The greatest decline (96 percent) occurred among children and adolescents, coincident with an increase in HBV vaccination coverage. This success can be attributed in part to the established infrastructure for vaccine delivery to children and to federal support for perinatal hepatitis B prevention programs.

Female Correctional Officers

A study of female correctional officers working in a large metropolitan jail confirms prior research.[110] Although most of the female officers in that study believed that men and women are equal, they tend to believe that men and women perform the job differently and that women are less likely to advance in management. Many of the jail officers were restricted from working with male prisoners, but in prisons that was not the case. The females in jail confirmed the existence of sexual harassment, but they tended to minimize it and to report it as less significant than gender harassment. Also, since most prisoners tend to be male, most prison and jail initiatives are male trait dominated leaving female prisoners, particularly their healthcare, less than inferior.[111] Female correctional officers fall within this category of inferior when it comes to promotion, fringe benefits, and healthcare. Similar to police officers, female correctional officers tend to be better educated than male officers and leave their jobs more often than males for greater opportunities, my experience tells me. Also, female officers tend to be more at ease with prisoners suggesting feelings of confidence in their abilities, whereas male officers, I noticed, tend to be more aggressive probably to cover their feelings of insecurity or to appear to be more "macho" among prisoners. I noticed similar responses among male and female law enforcement officers throughout my career and wrote about those findings in several studies after testing those perspectives.[112]

Correctional Officers' Health

During the week of May 23, 2006, some 1,300 prisoners and 14 correctional personnel in 11 California state prisons became sick from a pathogen known as campylobacter—a bacterium that is found in contaminated food or water.[113] Correctional and public health officials responded to the outbreak, and eventually the incident passed. No staff or prisoners died. Public health officials attributed the cause of the illness to bacteria in the milk supply. Such outbreaks regularly occur; for example on one occasion in 1996, 100 staff and prisoners within a juvenile hall became sick after eating a Thanksgiving meal;[114] in 1994 a Texas prison containing a population of mentally retarded prisoners experienced a large tuberculosis outbreak. Fifteen cases of tuberculosis were identified and more than 100 prisoners were infected. The culture-confirmed patients were infected with an identical strain of tuberculosis.

The prison followed standard tuberculosis infection control policies, but these controls were inadequate to prevent tuberculosis transmission in this special population. Tuberculosis transmission was associated with residing on the D Wing of the prison, attending school in Classroom A (eventually it was learned that the teacher was a host of TB), and working on the prison utility work crew.[115] Another incident occurred in the Pennsylvania prison system which experienced an outbreak of TB that infected several hundred prisoners.[116] The conditions within jails or prisons—close confinement of prisoners who may have suppressed immune systems—are ideal for the transmission of IPM. One might speculate that the public health officials in California took a deep breath of relief that the recent illness was not severe acute respiratory syndrome (SARS) or the H5N1 avian bird flu that have very high rates of mortality. A virulent strain of influenza could move through a prison system in a short period of time.[117]

Many jails and prisons have avoided the misfortune of advanced contagion among prisoners and correctional staff, thanks to the efforts of efficient and professional correctional administrators such as my old boss, Dr. Don Cabana (Superintendent of the Mississippi Department of Corrections and former department chair, University of Southern Mississippi). Also because of efficient custody and medical care staff (including infection-control nurses who work within larger prison systems), and sheriffs and jail managers who have worked with their intellect and humanity and not their political careers and followed advice from public health officials and their mentors to maintain control have reduced contagion.

Correctional administrators have to overcome a number of challenges including the temptation to serve their masters yet to provide healthcare within prisons. The testimony of one professional to the Commission on Safety and Abuse in America's Prisons outlined seven factors in 2005 that were responsible for a lack of appropriate medical care:[118]

- Healthcare is Not a Priority
- Lack of Medical Autonomy
- Lack of Appropriate Funding and Resources
- Lack of Qualified Staff
- Lack of Adequate Space
- Attitude of Medical Staff
- Overcrowding

The first issue shapes all the others. One reality is that correctional healthcare has become a birth to death enterprise; correctional administrators struggle with the best and legal manner to respond to infants born in custody, or what action to take when an elderly prisoner is dying—do they return them to the community on a compassionate release, confine them in a hospice, or let them die in a prison hospital unit? Which action is the most appropriate, the most legal, and the one they can get away with to keep their job, some might ask. In many confinement facilities, observers comment that "in California, where control of healthcare in state prisons has been ceded to a federal judge, one prisoner was dying needlessly from medical malpractice or neglect every six to seven days as recently as October 2005."[119] If this statistic is an accurate representation of the national landscape, many more prisoners will die from factors such as benign neglect, medical misadventure.[120]

Conclusions about Healthy Correctional Personnel

Prominent scholars contend that much of what has been done in corrections for both prisoners and personnel in the past several decades is based on "quackery," and that rehabilitative, educational, and vocational programs have often been delivered on the basis of questionable theories of crime.[121]

Happy Correctional Officers

When correctional officers are relaxed and physically fit, they are better able to cope with their jobs and bring the organization closer to their goals.[122] Comfortable officers are less likely to be cynical, angry, and hostile to the prisoners, their colleagues, or visitors. When officers are healthier, they are likely to provide better supervision, and this may reduce prisoner-on-prisoner violence, as well as other disruptive behaviors. As a result, the correctional health status of officers and prisoners are inextricably intertwined. A growing number of correctional agencies have recognized that developing stress reduction and health promotion programs for personnel—and their families—is a sound investment for the agency.

Healthier officers may be less likely to quit, which increases the seniority on a shift, and reduces prisoner misconduct. Less employee turnover is also cost-effective, as agencies can divert more resources into rehabilitation, rather than constantly recruiting and training new officers. Higher levels of physical and psychological fitness may enhance the immune systems of these officers and reduce the likelihood of contracting illness or disease.

Ultimately, a career correctional officer will spend over ten years behind bars—measured in eight- or twelve-hour shifts. Jails and prisons that provide supportive counseling, critical incident debriefing, stress reduction, and health promotion programs for their employees will benefit in cost savings, the officers will have a happier disposition, and the prisoners will have one less challenge.

Unhealthy Communities

The PIC exasperates criminally violent behavior, gives rise to unhealthy communities, and weakens the democratic process through a system of oppression by denying inalienable rights of a targeted group of individuals and anybody it touches. How many prisoner lives are destroyed by the justice process and how many more lives are forever tainted through mass incarceration techniques established by government?

Punitive methods of control do not serve the greater good nor do they foster healthy communities or individual recovery. There are over 200,000 (convicted) sex violators residing in American communities who are on parole or probation, and each year we've learned that a huge number of prisoners return to their communities, where previous former prisoners live. "Unfortunate collateral consequences" arise in those communities such as child abuse, family violence, the spread of IPM, homelessness, and community disorganization.[123]

Consequently, community cohesion is unstable, employment prospects and economic well-being are rare, there are no opportunities to join in the democratic process, family stability and childhood development are stifled, and mental and physical healthcare are inadequate.[124]

Convicted offenders especially sex offenders on probation, parole, and on sex registrars along with the thousands of returning ex-prisoners, their families, and their victims impact the health of community members and the health of the community itself. There are "tipping points" beyond which communities can no longer favorably influence righteous community member behavior.[125] Attitudes, behavior, and violent lessons learned in prison and violent lessons learned by victims are transmitted to a free society. Previously accepted social values and norms change, disorder and incivility increase, outmigration follows, and crime and violence increase.

Moral authority becomes vested in "street-smart" young men for whom drugs and crime are a way of life.[126] This phenomenon can impact the socialization and safety of young people, the power of prison sentences to deter, and the future trajectory of crime rates and crime victimization but most of all, the health of the community and its community members are at-risk.[127]

Real-life social community networks can shape every aspect of each community member's routine: how they feel, whom they marry, whether they fall ill, how much money they make, and whether they vote. Behavioral outcomes and attitudes of each community member are often shaped by their neighbors and often their neighbors are simply anonymous community members residing and working in the neighborhood.[128]

Sociologists conceptualize the collective civic value of social networks which includes the influence, social resources, and social solidarity (social cohesion or glue) within a community as social capital. Those networks include the social bonding of similar community members and the bridging between diverse community members. Bonding and bridging are linked to socially accepted values and norms or social reciprocity.[129] A compelling argument is that communities are governed by what can be called the Three Degrees Rule. Each community member influences and in turn is influenced by other community members up to three degrees removed from each of them, many of whom are unknown individuals.

When government perceives a community as marginal in terms of social class, community members and their community at-large are subjected to political disenfranchise, fewer municipal amenities, more street potholes, an abundance of slum building owners, and boarded up buildings that house thugs.[130] Marginal community members also experience greater intrusion by the police in their private lives because those members both individually and collectively possess few social networks which include political clout or protection.

HIV

The majority of persons who enter a correctional facility today will return home in the near future. In keeping with that thought, Michele Goodwin shows a direct correlation between prison and HIV among incarcerated (males) and their heterosexual (females) intimate others.[131]

More than one million individuals are living with HIV and more than half a million have died from AIDS since the beginning (1981) of the epidemic. HIV, similar to chronic Hepatitis C, epidemic in and out of prisons is out of control.[132] Although initially branded as a gay, white male disease in the US, the face of HIV/AIDS has extensively changed since the first description of an opportunistic infection, Pneumocystis carinii pneumonia afflicting five males in Los Angeles, was reported by the CDC in 1981.[133]

African American Women

African American women, who make up around 12 percent of the female population, now account for two-thirds of new HIV infections. HIV is now the leading cause of death for African American women aged 25 to 34 years, and the third leading cause of death for African American women 35 to 44 years of age. "The majority of these women represent a changing face for the HIV/AIDS epidemic in the US, infection resulting from contact with their African American male partners unduly and often unknowingly infected with HIV," argues Michele Goodwin at the University of Maryland.[134] The data are consistent with other researchers who studied the effectiveness of an HIV Prevention Program for low-income women of color visiting their incarcerated partners. Intervention participants also were more likely to be tested for HIV, to have partners who got tested, and to talk with their partners about significantly more HIV-related topics.[135]

Because of the war on drugs and mandatory sentencing laws, empirical data suggest that draconian sentencing guidelines linked to crack and cocaine disproportionately impacts arrests, prosecutions, sentencing, and incarceration.

The bottom line is a gross disparity in who is incarcerated in US prisons; more black men than any other group.[136] For example, the collateral effects include African American men suffering and dying disproportionately from HIV/AIDS—and infecting their heterosexual female partners as mentioned above. Prison sex and prison rape results in the transmission of sexual diseases and HIV/AIDS.

Also, prisoners with HIV suffer from the same mental health disorders as uninfected prisoners but are additionally subject to mental health problems uniquely related to their HIV infection.[137] Other research shows that incarceration has been identified as a key variable to be addressed in halting the HIV epidemic among African Americans.[138]

Catalysts of Infectious Pathogen Epidemic and Violence

After everything you've read above it should come as little surprise that released prisoners are catalysts of the IPM epidemic which includes unhealthy communities. It is unlikely that anyone wants to consider jails and prisons as a catalyst of IPM because that thinking challenges American healthcare ingenuity and political responsibility to do the right thing.[28] One reason for this lack of concern might be a locked-stepped idea that a critical assessment of confinement as a device of immense collateral damage is a political contradiction; confinement was originally designed to diminish cruel and unusual punishment of previous centuries. In a sense, a tautology is one way to justify the political contradictions engrained in PIC strategies, to proclaim that prison responds to wicked violators because violators are wicked; the law is the law because it's the law.[29] One researcher passionately argues that imprisonment—originally conceived as a response to the crimes of individuals—

[28] Catalyst: an agent that provokes or speeds significant change or action, http://www.merriam-webster.com/dictionary/catalyst

[29] The statement the "law is the law" can be described as tautology in logic which suggests that the conclusion of a theory makes explicit what is implicit in the premise of the theory. Thus, "law" is defined through itself. The existence of the law is explained through its parts, and its parts are explained as the whole. Can you see how race, age and socioeconomic class relates to a tautology?
Source: George Ritzer and Douglas J. Goodman (2004). *Sociological Theory, 6th ed.* New York: McGraw Hill. Page 541.

has become mass incarceration: a destabilizing force, a plague upon our body politic that undermines families and communities, damaging the very social structures that prevent crime.[139]

Today, it is clear that confinement produces angry and violent men and women who, prior to entering those systems, were convicted of nonviolent crimes such as drug possession convictions among others which constitute over a third of all new arrivals into the system, and over fifty percent of incoming federal prisoners in 2014.[140] Another reason not to consider jail and prisons as watering holes of IPM relates to a lack of quality care among prisoners which in and by itself suggests that confinement policy and practice produce serious civil rights' violations. There are huge incentives for government to exaggerate the quality of healthcare provided.

More reasons are provided below and almost all of those answers relate to the perspective of financial profit or what some might call "American Greed." Once we entertain the consequences of a huge number of prisoners released each year who were the breathing hosts of deadly pathogens, transferable diseases, and contagious parasites, maybe our perspective would change.[141] For example, Eric Pan and colleagues report Staphylococcus aureus clinical isolates obtained from patients who were prisoners of the San Francisco County jail system showed an increase in the prevalence of methicillin-resistant Staphylococcus aureus (MRSA) from 29 percent, in 1997, to 74 percent, in 2002;[142] 91 percent of the MRSA isolates carried staphylococcal chromosomal cassette mec (SCCmec) type IV.

Free people can, in a small way, alter the growth of pathogens and infections, and wash a cup, our hands, and clean ourselves after a restroom stop; prisoners have few alternatives toward health and prevention which includes what they eat, who breathes on them and why, or who they sleep next to or with for some prisoners. The women at MCI Framingham, a prison near Boston provided six sheets of TP twice a day, as I recall.

What you need to know right now, are three more things:

- First: When elected officials mandate harsher sentences, their intent is to be tough on crime or save taxpayer money, not to fill prisons with prisoners who are at-risk mentally and physically prior to confinement such as the elderly, special needs, mentally ill, substance abuse offenders among others, all with expensive healthcare needs. As a result, prison healthcare systems across the country are never meaningfully taken into account when elected officials determine the laws, policies, and funding that govern the PIC.
- When new measures such as zero tolerance police strategies in an effort to make some community's "feel" safer, it can even be argued that there is some increased safety for the public while more and more individuals are confined. "Sadly, this approach proved disastrous when prison capacity ran out and prisoners were released early. The fundamental failing of policy has been the lack of a firm focus on reform and rehabilitation, so that most" individuals continue to commit more crimes against more victims once they are released back onto the streets.[143]
- Are hospital pathogens and infections a by-product of prisons or are the promoters of prison pathogens and superbugs a product of healthcare inadequacies? Regardless of your answer, it's clear that at the end of the day the black sheep or superbugs are multiplying and are more powerful than any individual or any organization.

Summary

In the midst of a lethal invasion of deadly pathogens and a lack of resources to combat them this chapter suggests that the Prison Industrial Complex is the catalyst of this invasion through released prisoners. Prisoners hold a similar socioeconomic status (SES) and a similar high vulnerability to infection. Thus, the clear and present danger of IPM control is complicated and several additional explanations are advanced. It is theorized that PIC is the catalyst of this deadly invasion through prisoners.

The objective of the chapter is to share knowledge about the exploitation through mass incarceration and to document the plague developed and disseminated by the PIC through the collateral damage from the war on drugs, the criminalization of poverty, and rapid growth of the sprawling enterprise whereby government goals take precedent over Constitutional law.

According to the ABA's Standard of Care suggestions, the risk factors in correctional facilities among offenders are proximity, high-risk sexual behavior, and injection drug use which often cause needlesticks. Healthcare is inadequate and futile because of a lack of quality personnel and system resources, the at-risk vulnerability of the individual prisoners, custody regulations, public attitudes, and official policy, and political bullying and arrogance toward DOC administration. Healthcare interventions stand to benefit from healthy prisoners and correctional personnel, their families, and the PH of the communities to which prisoners return and where personnel reside. Prisoners and correctional personnel face constant exposure to pathogenic organisms, infection, and disease. The practices of confinement are to maximize custody and control in an attempt to maximize public safety as opposed to minimizing the transmission of IPM or to efficiently deliver healthcare because of overcrowding among other reasons. Female prisoner issues include sexual assault (rape) and misconduct against them, prison sentencing, medical neglect, discrimination, lack of privacy, and contraband initiatives. Also, private healthcare does not offer better service than public providers.

Correctional personnel are faced with similar problems as prisoners. Female correctional personnel experience more difficulties with administration policy because they are usually better educated than traditional personnel. When prisoners return to communities, those communities are at risk from health issues and violence issues. For example, moral authority becomes vested in "street-smart" young men for whom drugs and crime are a way of life.

Name: ______________________________ Date: ____________ School Identification Number: ______

STUDENT WORKSHEETS

Chapter 5 Prisoners, Correctional Personnel, and Compliance Issues

Define the following key terms from Chapter 5, and in your answer, show the page number where you found the definition. Provide an example for each key term.

1. Applied Sociologists

2. Catalyst

3. Colonization

4. Culture Clash

5. Contagion

6. Evidence Based Corrections

7. Formal and Informal Organizations

8. Indefensible Behavior

9. Infectious Pathogens and MRSA (IPM)

10. Mass Incarceration

11. Prison Industrial Complex (PIC)

12. Socially Approved Rhetoric

13. Standard of Care

14. Tautology

Name: ______________________________ Date: ______________ School Identification Number: ________

STUDENT WORKSHEETS

Chapter 5 Prisoners, Correctional Personnel, and Compliance Issues

Discuss and demonstrate in your own words that you comprehend the following learning objectives in this chapter.

1. Identify the theory of the chapter in relationship to the prison industrial complex; in what way does it make sense and in what way doesn't it make sense to you?
2. Identify several of the points made concerning prisoners becoming unwilling carriers or hosts of IPM which represents a clear and present danger. Which point carries the most weight toward this danger and why?
3. Discuss the particulars about the recidivism rates presented and explain in what way several of those points further the theory you identified above.
4. Identify and explain the points presented indicating why healthcare during confinement is inadequate and futile.
5. Explain why the practices of confinement are to maximize custody and control in an attempt to maximize public safety as opposed to minimizing the transmission of IPM or to efficiently deliver healthcare. In what way do you agree or disagree with each point?
6. Identify the principal risk factors in correctional facilities and the Standards of Care suggested by the American Bar Association. In what way might those Standards address those principal factors?
7. Describe the effects on imprisonment upon female offenders especially segregation and its outcomes.
8. Discuss the impact of prisoner healthcare upon correctional personnel.
9. Discuss the impact of black prisoners coming home on their personal relationships.
10. Explain in what way communities are impacted by the release of prisoners, and how can those effects be altered?
11. Comprehend the effects of a political contradiction on mass incarceration and its outcomes. In what way does this make sense to you or in what way does it not make sense?

APPENDIX 1

My Bias Linked to Crime and Punishment

I feel that writers of scholarly work have a moral obligation to offer his or her position on the topics they write about for the benefit of their readers, in particular to aid their students. One objective would be for a reader and student to develop his or her own informed decision about what he or she reads.

My health at my present "near death" status according to my students is far better than the twenty-two-year-old prisoners I taught and counseled at Stateville Penitentiary near Chicago, and much better than the forty-year-olds in my groups at Attica in Upstate New York. Why? Because I have choices similar to most 'free individuals' and members of educated middle class America. Choices about what I eat, how long I sleep, whom I associate with, how to keep myself physically clean, and how much exercise to engage in at safe environments. I choose what stresses me and what doesn't—other than long, ridiculous red lights on highways, outrageous cable bills, and an iPhone that I can't decipher, and a frustration to find a parking place when I'm late for class at school.

But, I've always felt good about myself; I observed and wrote at length about young men and women in group classes at the penitentiaries who hated themselves but their "fronts" were that of happy, hard people. In my observations, there were people I considered hurting but chose not to do so. Their individual choice! Violent prisoners choose differently—they act upon their impulse without concern for the consequences to their victims or themselves or their own family members and friends. For instance, often youngsters will commit crimes of sexual violence without concerning themselves with the consequences their own family members will confront if he or she is apprehended. Their choices brought them to prison once they caught the justice system's attention which may or may not have been through their behavior. They should be punished. My thoughts are that around 75 to 80 percent of those incarcerated in American prisons don't belong there such as drug possession and addicts, the mentally ill, nonviolent offenders, and all the women who stood up to the men who beat the crap out of them every day of their married life; yet, then too all the proud young men who stood on a street corner when the wrong cops came their way. In *Failure of the American Prison Complex: Let's Abolish It*, I outline a systematic method of reducing the prison population. We must find solutions to enable offenders particularly nonviolent offenders to pay back, to rectify, to give back to society, maybe within certain limits on their movement. As a noble Rabbi adds in *Failure*, "But the idea to throw people away as so much human garbage is unconscionable for the Jewish people." And it should be that way for American people, too. See page 410 in *Failure*.

As a youngster, I was an aggressor—not that I was abused—I was the abuser. I messed with the system and anybody in my way in whatever manner brought me closer to whatever goal I had in my head which never was to be compromised. All I will admit is that violence of all varieties was known to me. I am not compulsive; rather I calculate my actions and assess my targets, and then at the right moment—it's a go. The forest preserve across the street from my childhood home was often raised in fire, I recall at age five; homes in the swank neighborhood nearby were often burglarized but little was missing, I noticed at age 10; and many young friends by age 12 ignored their own principles to amuse me. As with most violent young men (and women, see *Wicked Women: A Journey of Super Predators*) from upper middle class families, prison and punishment were never a deterrent to my behavior. What was a deterrent to violence as an adult, is that I accepted what had been taught to me about compassion, empathy, and respect particularly for God and country. People don't always respond to learning right away—some take more time than others. I'm a slow learner. I'm a slow learner about things of that variety. Nonetheless, positive values taught and exercised through quality care providers or hopefully parents to very young children have huge dividends for those youngsters and society and their "almost" victims. I can still see my grandmother's (Victoria) lips moving as she told me about how animals die helplessly in forest fires. Violence will never leave my hand, I will admit to you—unless you mess with my children, then all bets are off.

APPENDIX 2

Standard 23-6.1 General Principles Governing Healthcare

Standards of Treatment for Prisoners
American Bar Association
Correctional authorities should ensure that:

- a qualified healthcare professional is designated the responsible health authority for each facility, to oversee and direct the provision of healthcare in that facility;
- prisoners are provided necessary healthcare, including preventive, routine, urgent, and emergency care;
- such care is consistent with community healthcare standards, including standards relating to privacy except as otherwise specified in these Standards;
- special healthcare protocols are used, when appropriate, for female prisoners, prisoners who have physical or mental disabilities, and prisoners who are under the age of eighteen or geriatric; and
- healthcare that is necessary during the period of imprisonment is provided regardless of a prisoner's ability to pay, the size of the correctional facility, or the duration of the prisoner's incarceration.
- Prisoners should not be charged fees for necessary healthcare.
- Dental care should be provided to treat prisoners' dental pain, eliminate dental pathology, and preserve and restore prisoners' ability to chew. Consistent with Standard 23-2.5, routine preventive dental care and education about oral healthcare should be provided to those prisoners whose confinement may exceed one year.
- Prisoners should be provided timely access to appropriately trained and licensed healthcare staff in a safe and sanitary setting designed and equipped for diagnosis or treatment.
- Healthcare should be based on the clinical judgments of qualified healthcare professionals, not on non-medical considerations such as cost and convenience. Clinical decisions should be the sole province of the responsible healthcare professionals, and should not be countermanded by non-medical staff. Work assignments, housing placements, and diets for each prisoner should be consistent with any healthcare treatment plan developed for that prisoner.
- Prisoners should be provided basic educational materials relating to disease prevention, good health, hygiene, and proper usage of medication.

APPENDIX 3

How to Prevent Infection

Listed below are the best methods to prevent infection as recommended by the University of Chicago Medicine.[144] As you read through the list below, think about ways correctional personnel could perform any of these activities, let alone prisoners.

- The best way to prevent staph or MRSA infections is to practice good hygiene.
- Keep your hands clean by washing regularly with soap and water or using an alcohol-based hand sanitizer. (Soap, and alcohol-based hand sanitizers are contraband by most Department of Corrections across the US.)
- Limit your use of antibacterial products in your home. Instead of using antibacterial cleaners, use an alcohol-based cleaner. Use soap instead of antibacterial hand wash.
- Keep cuts and wounds covered with a bandage until they are completely healed. (Bandages are contraband in most prison systems.)
- Avoid contact with other people's wounds or bandages. (Easier said than done; if you're correctional personnel do you stop a fight between prisoners?)
- Avoid sharing personal items such as towels, sheets, razors, clothing, and athletic equipment. (Do prisoners have choices?)
- Washing clothing and linens regularly with hot water and dry them in a hot dryer; wash athletic clothing after every use. (Not likely)
- Non-washable athletic equipment (e.g., head gear) should be wiped down with a phenol or chlorine-based wipe such as liquid Lysol after each use. (Phenol or chlorine wipes are contraband.)
- Avoid sharing lip balms, lotions, or any other cosmetics. (Fat chance)
- Eat organic meat, which comes from livestock that have not ingested antibiotics. (Prisoners have no input into selection process of food.)

APPENDIX 4

Facts About Female Prisoners

The American Jail Association says that there are nine facts about female prisoners that are relevant to an understanding of female prisoners in American prisons.[145]

- Women pose a lower public safety risk than men. Women typically enter the criminal justice system for nonviolent crimes that are often drug- and/or property-related.
- Women's pathways to criminal justice are different than men's. Women entering jails are much more likely to have experienced poverty, intimate partner violence, sexual abuse, and/or other forms of victimization often linked to their offending behavior.
- Women's engagement in criminal behavior is often related to their connections with others. Relationships with children, family, and others are often paramount for women.
- Women entering jails and prisons often report histories of victimization and trauma and continue to be vulnerable to victimization within correctional settings.
- Correctional policies and practices have largely been developed through the lens of managing men, not women. Generally, policies and practices in jails (and prisons) do not reflect an understanding of the risk and needs of female offenders because much of the empirical research originally focused on male offenders.
- Jail and prison classification systems can result in unreliable custody designations and overclassification of female prisoners. Most jail classification systems have not been normed and validated specifically for women; yet they are often used to guide key housing and security decisions.
- Gender-informed risk assessment tools can more accurately identify women's risk and needs. Emerging research suggests that women have different risk factors than do men.
- Women are more likely to respond favorably when jail staff members adhere to evidence-based, gender-responsive principles. Because of their overwhelming needs, transition and reentry of incarcerated females can be especially challenging for women, particularly with the understanding that most female prisoners are mothers of young children.
- The cost of overly involving women in criminal justice is high. Given what we now know about women—their low risk, parental responsibilities, and significant needs (mental and physical health, histories of trauma, substance abuse, financial, etc.)—and some of the strategies we can employ to improve their outcomes, it is difficult to reconcile that 60 percent of women released from incarceration are rearrested and nearly a third are returned to confinement.

CHAPTER 5 ENDNOTES

1. Jeffrey Kluger is a senior writer at TIME Magazine and author of several books on science topics, such as *Simplexity; Splendid Solution: Jonas Salk and the Conquest of Polio; Journey Beyond Selene;* and *Lost Moon: The Perilous Voyage of Apollo 13.*
2. Dennis J. Stevens (2014). *Failure of the American Prison Complex: Let's Abolish It.* Dubuque, Iowa: Kendall Hunt. Also see, Bureau of Justice Statistics (2014). Correctional Populations in the United States, 2012. NCJ 243936. Washington, DC: Department of Justice. Retrieved May 25, 2014: http://www.bjs.gov/index.cfm?ty=pbdetail&iid=4843
3. Angela Davis (1997). *The Prison Industrial Complex.* CA: AK Press. Also see, Rachel Herzing (2005). What is the Prison Industrial Complex? Political Research Associates. Retrieved December 3, 2014: http://www.publiceye.org/defendingjustice/overview/herzing_pic.html
4. Bureau of Justice Statistics (2014). Correctional Populations in the United States, 2012. NCJ 243936. Washington, DC: Department of Justice. Retrieved May 25, 2014: http://www.bjs.gov/index.cfm?ty=pbdetail&iid=4843
5. Ulrich Witt (2013). The Crisis Behind the Crisis. *Environmental Innovation and Societal Transitions*, 6: 120–122.
6. Guy Haselmann (2014, January 3). U.S. Rates Strategy: A Look at 2014 and Beyond. Retrieved December 3, 2014: http://www.integratedmgt.com/2010/wp-content/uploads/2014/02/2014-and-Beyond.pdf
7. Robert Greifinger (2010). *Public Health Behind Bars: From Prisons to Communities.* New York, NY: Springer-Verlag. Pages 103–126. Also see, Dennis J. Stevens (2014). *The Failure of the American Prison Complex: Let's Abolish it.* Dubuque, Iowa: Kendall Hunt. Pages 347–366.
8. Alice Park (2014, May 19). Man vs. Microbe: We're Losing the Battle Against Bacteria. Can We Win The War? *Time,* 183(19): 20.
9. Melanie Jordan (2011). The Prison Setting as a Place of Enforced Residence, Its Mental Health Effects, and The Mental Healthcare Implications. *Health & Place,* 17(5): 1061–1066.
10. Sourcebook of Criminal Justice Statistics (2014). Employees of Federal, State, Local, and Private Adult Correctional Facilities. Table 1.104 Retrieved June 2, 2014: http://www.albany.edu/sourcebook/pdf/t1104.pdf
11. Correctional Officers: Strategies to Improve Retention, 2nd edition (2010). Centerville, UT: MTC Institute. Retrieved December 3, 2014: https://www.mtctrains.com/sites/default/files/CO%20Retention%202010.pdf
12. Bureau of Labor Statistics (2014). Job Openings and Occupational Turnover. Retrieved June 2, 2014: http://www.bls.gov/jlt/home.htm
13. Allen Beck (2013). PREA Data Collection Activities, 2013. Washington, DC, Bureau of Justice Statistics. Retrieved May 24, 2014: http://www.bjs.gov/index.cfm?ty=pbdetail&iid=4637. Also see, Joseph E. Paris (2008). Why Prisoners Deserve Health Care. *Virtual Mentor*, 10(2): 113–115. Retrieved May 24, 2014: http://virtualmentor.ama-assn.org/2008/02/msoc1-0802.html. Also see, Erica S. Pan, Binh A. Diep, Heather A. Carleton, Edwin D. Charlebois, George F. Sensabaugh, Barbara L. Haller, and Françoise Perdreau Remington (2003). Increasing Prevalence of Methicillin-Resistant Staphylococcus aureus Infection in California Jails. *Clinical Infectious Diseases*, 37(10): 1384–1388. Also see, Dennis J. Stevens (2014). Page 351.
14. Frank J. Porporino (1990). Differences in Response to Long-Term Imprisonment: Implications for the Management of Long-Term Offenders. *Prison Journal*, 80: 35–36.
15. Niyi Awofeso (2010). Prisons as Social Determinants of Hepatitis C Virus and Tuberculosis Infections. *Public Health Reports*, 125(4): 25–33. Retrieved June 3, 2014: http://www.ncbi.nlm.nih.gov/pmc/articles/PMC2882972/
16. Niyi Awofeso (2010).

17. Dennis J. Stevens (2014).
18. Ernest Drucker (2013). *A Plague of Prisons: The Epidemiology of Mass Incarceration in America*. New York: New Press.
19. Clair A Cripe, Michael G Pearlman, and Daryl Kosiak (2013). *Legal Aspects of Corrections Management*. Boston: Jones and Bartlett. Pages 26, 91.
20. Ibid. Page XV.
21. Harlan Yu and David G Robinson (2012). The New Ambiguity of 'Open Government.' UCLA Law Review Discourse, 178. Retrieved September 8, 2014: http://www.uclalawreview.org/pdf/discourse/59-11.pdf/ Page 208.
22. Davis D Breaux and Annie I Anton (2008). Analyzing Regulatory Rules for Privacy and Security Requirements. IEEE Transactions on Software Engineering, 34(1). Retrieved September 8, 2014: https://www.cs.cmu.edu/~breaux/publications/tdbreaux-tse08.pdf
23. Robert J. Guidos (2011). Combating Antimicrobial Resistance: Policy Recommendations to Save Lives. *Clinical Infectious Disease*, 52(5): 397–428.
24. Alan Berkman (1995). Prison Health: The Breaking Point. *American Journal of Public Health*, 85(12), 1607–1618.
25. A Frasera, A Gathererb, and P Haytonc (2009). Mental Health in Prisons: Great Difficulties But Are There Opportunities? *Public Health*, 123(6): 410–414.
26. Bureau of Justice Statistics (BJS, 2013). Correctional Populations in the United States, 2012. US Department of Justice: Washington, DC. Retrieved May 27, 2014: http://www.bjs.gov/content/pub/pdf/cpus12.pdf
27. BJS (2013).
28. Sourcebook of Criminal Justice Statistics (2010). Direct Expenditures For Correctional Activities Of State Governments And Percent. Table 1.9. Retrieved December 3, 2014: http://www.albany.edu/sourcebook/pdf/t192010.pdf
29. Tracey Kyckelhahn (2012, December 10). State Corrections Expenditures, FY 1982–2010. Bureau of Justice Statistics. NCJ 239672. Washington, DC: Department of Justice. Retrieved May 27, 2014: http://www.bjs.gov/index.cfm?ty=pbdetail&iid=4556
30. Huff Post (2012, September 6). California Spending More On Prisons Than Colleges, Report Says. Retrieved May 27, 2014: http://www.huffingtonpost.com/2012/09/06/california-prisons-colleges_n_1863101.html
31. Aaron Sankin (2012, September 8) California Spending More on Prisons Than Colleges. *Huff Post*. Retrieved December 4, 2014: http://www.huffingtonpost.com/2012/09/06/california-prisons-colleges_n_1863101.html
32. G. Niveau (2006). Prevention of Infectious Disease Transmission in Correctional Settings: A Review. *Public Health*, 120(1): 33–41.
33. American Bar Association (2010). *Standards of Treatment for Prisoners*. Retrieved May 29, 2014: http://www.americanbar.org/publications/criminal_justice_section_archive/crimjust_standards_treatmentprisoners.html
34. G. Niveau (2006).
35. Chad Kinsella (2004). Corrections Health Care Costs. Trends Alert: Critical Information for State Decision-Makers. The Council of State Governments. Retrieved May 27, 2014: http://www.prisonpolicy.org/scans/csg/Corrections+Health+Care+Costs+1-21-04.pdf
36. Allen Beck (2013). Also see, Joseph E. Paris (2008). Dennis J. Stevens (2014).
37. Chancellor and Secretary of State for Justice (2010). Breaking the Cycle: Effective Punishment, Rehabilitation and Sentencing of Offenders. Retrieved May 27, 2014: http://webarchive.nationalarchives.gov.uk/20120119200607/http:/www.justice.gov.uk/consultations/docs/breaking-the-cycle.pdf
38. Joseph E. Paris (2008).
39. Ibid.

40. William J. Rold (2006). Legal Considerations in the Delivery of Health Care Services in Prisons and Jails. In M. Puisis (Ed.), *Clinical Practice in Correctional Medicine* (2nd ed., Pages 520–528). Philadelphia, PA: Mosby-Elsevier.
41. Joseph E. Paris (2008).
42. National Commission on Correctional Health Care (2014). *Standards for Health Services in Prisons*. Chicago, IL: National Commission on Correctional Health Care.
43. Bureau of Justice Statistics (2014). Correctional Populations in the United States, 2012. NCJ 243936. Washington, DC: Department of Justice. Retrieved May 25, 2014: http://www.bjs.gov/index.cfm?ty=pbdetail&iid=4843
44. Chris Kardish (2014, February 27). States Look to Nursing Homes to Lower Prison Health Care Costs. Governing. Retrieved June 1, 2014: http://www.governing.com/news/headlines/gov-states-look-to-nursing-homes-to-lower-prison-health-care-costs.html
45. Robert Greifinger (2010). *Public Health Behind Bars: From Prisons to Communities.* New York, NY: Springer-Verlag. Pages 103–126.
46. Correctional Officers and Blood-Borne Viruses (2013). The Australasian Society for HIV Medicine (ASHM). Retrieved June 3, 2014: http://www.ashm.org.au/images/Publications/Booklets/CorrOffiBBV2013_WEB.pdf
47. Robert Greifinger (2010). Pages 174–211.
48. Theodore Hammett, Mary P. Harmon, and William Rhodes (2002). The Burden of Infectious Disease Among Inmates of And Releases From US Correctional Facilities. *American Journal of Public Health*, 92, 1789–1794.
49. Franklin D. Lowy, Allison E. Aiello, Meera Bhat, Vicki D. Johnson-Lawrence, Mei-Ho Lee, Earl Burrell, Lester N. Wright, Glenny Vasquez and Elaine L. Larson (2007). Staphylococcus aureus Colonization and Infection in New York State Prisons. *The Journal of Infectious Diseases*, 196(6): 911–918.
50. Dennis J. Stevens (1997). Origins And Effects Of Prison Drug Gangs In North Carolina. *Journal of Gang Research*, 4(4): 23–35.
51. Joseph A. Bick (2007). Infection Control in Jails and Prisons. *Clinical Infectious Diseases: Healthcare Epidemiology*, 45: 1047–1055.
52. Joseph A. Bick (2007).
53. David Ingram (2013, November 5). Even with Changes, US Prisons Might Stay Overcrowded: Report. *Reuters*. Retrieved June 4, 2014: http://www.reuters.com/article/2013/11/05/us-usa-prisons-idUSBRE9A405120131105
54. Bureau of Justice Statistics (2014). 3 in 4 Former Prisoners in 30 States Arrested Within 5 Years of Release: Press Release. Retrieved April 24, 2014: http://www.bjs.gov/content/pub/press/rprts05p0510pr.cfm
55. Department of Corrections: State of New Jersey (2014). Retrieved May 27, 2014: http://www.state.nj.us/corrections/pages/about_us/Mission_Statement.html
56. John Maki (2013, April 1). Let's Talk About Prison Health Care. *Huff Post Chicago*. Retrieved May 24, 2014: http://www.huffingtonpost.com/john-maki/lets-talk-about-prison-health-care_b_2975923.html
57. Vera Institute of Justice (2013). The Price of Prisons in Illinois. Retrieved May 27, 2014: www.vera.org/files/price-of-prisons-illinois-fact-sheet.pdf
58. Chad Kinsella (2004). Corrections Health Care Costs. Trends Alert: Critical Information for State Decision-Makers. The Council of State Governments. Retrieved May 27, 2014: http://www.prisonpolicy.org/scans/csg/Corrections+Health+Care+Costs+1-21-04.pdf
59. Christine C. Ferguson (2014). Barriers to Serving the Vulnerable: Thoughts Of A Former Public Official. Health Affairs. Retrieved May 27, 2014: http://content.healthaffairs.org/content/26/5/1358.full
60. JA Bick (2007). Also see, Theodore Hammett, Mary P. Harmon, and William Rhodes (2002).
61. Centers for Disease Control and Prevention (2014). Retrieved May 24, 2014: http://www.cdc.gov/

62. MZ David, S Medvedev, SF Hohmann, B Ewigman, and RS Daum (2012). Increasing Burden of Methicillin-Resistant Staphylococcus aureus Hospitalizations at US Academic Medical Centers, 2003–2008. *Infection Control and Hospital Epidemiology*, 33:8.
63. L K Pickering (2004). Antimicrobial resistance among enteric pathogens: National Immunization Program. *Seminar in Pediatrics Infectious Diseases*, 15(2), 71–77.
64. Theodore Hammett, Mary P. Harmon, and William Rhodes (2002). Mark Niquette (2014, February 6). Also, Anne C. Spaulding, B. Stephenson, G. Macalino, W. Ruby, J. G. Clarke, and T.P. Flanigan (2002). Human Immunodeficiency Virus in Correctional Facilities. *Clinical Infectious Diseases,* 35(3):305–312.
65. Peters S. Dixon, Timothy P. Flanigan, Barbara A. DeBuono, Jeffrey J. Laurie, Mary Lou De Ciantis, John Hoy, Michael Stein, H. Denman Scott, and Charles C.J. Carpenter (1993). Infection With The Human Immunodeficiency Virus In Prisoners: Meeting The Health Care Challenge. *The American Journal of Medicine*, 95(6): 629–635.
66. Michelle Van Handel, John F. Beltrami, Robin J. MacGowan, Craig B. Borkowf, and Andrew D. Margolis (2012). Newly Identified HIV Infections in Correctional Facilities, United States, 2007. *American Journal of Public Health*, 102(2): 201–204. Also for footnote see, Mark Niquette (2014, February 6). Jails Enroll Inmates in Obamacare to Pass Hospital Costs to U.S. Bloomberg News. Retrieved June 5, 2014: http://www.bloomberg.com/news/2014-02-06/jails-enroll-inmates-in-obamacare-to-pass-hospital-costs-to-u-s-.html
67. Anne C. Spaulding, Kimberly R. Jacob Arriola, Kevin L. Ramos, Theodore Hammett, Sofia Kennedy, Giulia Norton, and Melinda Tinsley (2007). Enhancing Linkages to HIV Primary Care in Jail Settings: Report on a Consultants' Meeting. *Journal of Correctional Health Care*, 13(2): 98–128.
68. Mary Castle White, Jacqueline Peterson Tulsky, CJ Portillo, E. Menendez, E. Cruz, and Joe Goldenson (2001). Tuberculosis Prevalence in an Urban Jail: 1994 and 1998. *International Journal of Tuberculosis and Lung Disease*, 5(5), 400–404.
69. Jessica R. MacNeil, Mark N. Lobato, and Marisa Moore (2005). An Unanswered Health Disparity: Tuberculosis Among Correctional Inmates, 1993 Through 2003. *American Journal of Public Health*, 95(10): 1800–1805.
70. Mary Castle White, Jacqueline Peterson Tulsky, CJ Portillo, E. Menendez, E. Cruz, and Joe Goldenson (2001).
71. Mary Castle White, Jacqueline Peterson Tulsky, E. Menendez, Joe Goldenson, and L.M. Kawamura (2005). Incidence of TB in Inmates with Latent TB Infection: 5-Year Follow-Up. *American Journal of Preventive Medicine*, 29(4): 295–301.
72. Jessica R. MacNeil, Mark N. Lobato, and Marisa Moore (2005).
73. Dennis J. Stevens (2014). Page 186.
74. Dennis J. Stevens (1999). Interviews with Women Convicted of Murder: Battered Women Syndrome Revisited. International Review of Victimology, 6(2), 117–135.
75. Roger Watsona, Anne Stimpsona, and Tony Hostickb (2004). Prison Health Care: A Review of the Literature. *International Journal of Nursing Studies*, 41(2): 119–128.
76. Bureau of Justice Statistics (2008). Parents in Prison and Their Minor Children. 2007. Washington, DC: U.S. Department of Justice. Office of Justice Programs. NCJ 222984. Retrieved June 2, 2014: http://bjs.ojp.usdoj.gov/index.cfm?ty=pbdetail&iid=823
77. M. K. Papen (2011). Senate Memorial 40; 50TH LEGISLATURE—State of New Mexico. Retrieved June 4, 2014: http://www.nmlegis.gov/sessions/11%20regular/memorials/senate/SM040.html
78. A. Davis, A. De-Groot, and C. Shaylor (1998). Symposium: Women in prison. *New England Journal on Criminal & Civil Confinement*, 24(2): 339–453.
79. Victoria Law (2013).
80. Diane C. Hatton, Dorothy Kleffel, and Anastasia A. Fisher (2006). Prisoners' Perspectives of Health Problems and Healthcare in a US Women's Jail. *Women & Health*, 44(1): 119–136.

81. Dennis J. Stevens (2015). Women in Solitary Confinement: Health and Recidivism. *Modern American Prisons*, Stephen Richards (Ed). Southern Illinois University Press. Forth coming [Chapter]
82. Dennis J. Stevens (2015). Dennis J. Stevens (2014). Also see, Victoria Law (2013, December 12). Women in Solitary Confinement: Sent to Solitary for Reporting Sexual Assault. *Solitary Watch: News From a Nation in Lockdown*. Retrieved June 5, 2014: http://solitarywatch.com/2013/12/12/women-solitary-confinement-sent-solitary-reporting-sexual-assault/
83. Encyclopedia of Prisons and Correctional Facilities (2005). Los Angeles: Sage Publications.
84. Dennis J. Stevens (2014). Women in Solitary Confinement: Health and Recidivism. (Editor, Stephen Richards) Modern American Prisons. Southern Illinois University Press. (Pages 147–161).
85. D.A Fraser, V.R. Mosley, W.C. Thornion, P.H. Belknap, and R.A. Rogers (1984). Recent Legal Developments. Criminal Justice Review, 9(1): 47–52.
86. Dennis J. Stevens (2003). *Applied Community Policing in the 21st Century*. Boston: Allyn Bacon.
87. Daniel P. Mears (2013). Supermax Prisons. Criminology & Public Policy. doi: 10.1111/1745-9133.12031
88. George J. Annas (2012). America's Plague of Incarceration. *The Lancet*, 379(9814): 401–402.
89. C. Wright Mills (1940). Situated Actions and Vocabularies of Motive. *American Sociological Review*, 5(6): 904–913.
90. Ryan Keith (2001, March). What Kind Of Services Should The State Provide For Inmates? And What Can The State Afford? Illinois Isn't The Only State Wrestling With This Dilemma. Retrieved May 24, 2014: http://www.lib.niu.edu/2001/ii010323.html
91. Billy Manes (2013, June 12). Happytown: Private Health Care for Florida Prisons. *Orlando Weekly*. Retrieved May 29, 2014: http://orlandoweekly.com/news/happytown-private-health-care-for-florida-prisons-1.1503723
92. "Illinois Never" (2012). Did Their Homework. Wbez.org/news. Retrieved May 30, 2014: http://www.wbez.org/news/illinois-signed-14-billion-prison-contract-without-doing-homework-102873
93. Theodore M. Hammett, Cheryl Roberts, Sofia Kennedy (2001). Health-Related Issues in Prisoner Reentry. *Crime & Delinquency,* 47(3): 390–409.
94. Dean Whitehead (2006). The Health Promoting Prison (HPP) and Its Imperative for Nursing. *International Journal of Nursing Studies,* 43(1): 123–131.
95. Jason Schneider (2007). MRSA Infections: Tougher Than Kevlar. Law Enforcement Technology, 34(9): 18–23.
96. Allison E Aiello, Franklin D Lowy, Lester N Wright, and Elaine L Larson (2006). Meticillin-resistant Staphylococcus aureus among US Prisoners And Military Personnel: Review And Recommendations For Future Studies. *The Lancet Infectious Diseases*, 6(6): 335–341.
97. Evelyn J. Patterson (2013). The Dose–Response of Time Served in Prison on Mortality: New York State, 1989–2003. *American Journal of Public Health,* 103(3): 523–528.
98. Allison E Aiello, et al. (2006).
99. Amanda Mathias Humphrey (2008). Doing Time Together: Correctional Officer Health. Rick Ruddell and Mark Tomta (Editors) Issues in Corrections. Richmond, VA: New Gate Press. Pages 227–243.
100. Dennis J. Stevens (2007). *Police Officer Stress: Sources and Solutions*. Upper Saddle River, NJ: Pearson. Page 77–81.
101. Matthew Harwood (2009, July 21). Panel: Prison Overcrowding Jeopardizes Guard and Inmate Safety. Security Management. Retrieved June 4, 2014: http://www.securitymanagement.com/news/panel-prison-overcrowding-jeopardizes-guard-and-inmate-safety-005904
102. Peter Finn (2000). *Addressing Correctional Officer Stress: Programs and Strategies*. Washington, DC: U. S. Department of Justice.
103. Stanton Samenow (2010). The Myth of the Out of Character Crime. New York: CreateSpace.
104. Peter Finn (2000). *Addressing Correctional Officer Stress: Programs and Strategies.* NCJ 183474. National Institute of Justice. Retrieved May 31, 2014: https://www.ncjrs.gov/pdffiles1/nij/183474.pdf

105. Robyn R.M. Gershon, Clifford Mitchell, Martin F. Sherman, David Vlahov, Mary Kathleen Lears, Sarah Felknor, and Rebecca A. Lubelczyk (2005). Hepatitis B Vaccination In Correctional Health Care Workers. *American Journal of Infection Control*, 33(9): 510–518.
106. K Steenland, A J Levine, K Sieber, P Schulte, and D Aziz (1997). Incidence of Tuberculosis Infection Among New York State Prison Employees. *American Journal of Public Health*, 87(12): 2012–2014.
107. Alabama Department of Public Health (2014). Hepatitis B. Bureau of Communicable Disease. Retrieved June 30, 2014: http://www.adph.org/hepatitis/index.asp?id=6096
108. Eric E. Mast, Cindy M. Weinbaum, Anthony E. Fiore, Miriam J. Alter, Beth P. Bell, Lyn Finelli, Lance E. Rodewald, John M. Douglas, Jr., Robert S. Janssen, and John W. Ward (2006, December 8). A Comprehensive Immunization Strategy to Eliminate Transmission of Hepatitis B Virus Infection in the United States. Morbidity and Mortality Weekly Report (MMWR), 55. Centers for Disease Control and Prevention. Retrieved June 25, 2014: http://www.cdc.gov/mmwr/pdf/rr/rr5516.pdf
109. Eric E. Mast, Cindy M. Weinbaum, Anthony E. Fiore, Miriam J. Alter, Beth P. Bell, Lyn Finelli, Lance E. Rodewald, John M. Douglas, Jr., Robert S. Janssen, and John W. Ward (2006, December 8).
110. Joanne Belknap (1991; 2008). Women in Conflict: An Analysis of Women Correctional Officers. *Women and Criminal Justice*, 2(2): 89–115.
111. B.J. van den Bergha, L.F. Møllera, and P. Haytonb (2010). Women's Health In Prisons: It Is Time To Correct Gender Insensitivity And Social Injustice. *Public Health,* 124(11): 632–634.
112. Dennis J. Stevens (2009). *Introduction to Policing in America*. Boston: Jones & Bartlett. Also see, Dennis J. Stevens (2008). *Police Officer Stress: Sources and Solutions*. Upper Saddle River, NJ: Prentice Hall.
113. Rick Ruddell and Mark Tomita (2008). Opportunities for Change in Correctional Health. In Ruddell and Tomita (Ed.) *Issues Correctional Health.* (Pages 243–263). Richmond, Kentucky: Newgate Press.
114. Arit I. Parikh, Michele T. Jay, Diamond Kassam, Terry Kociemba, Bobbe Dworkis, Pamela D. Bradley, and Kenneth Takata (1997). Clostridium Perfringens Outbreak at a Juvenile Detention Facility Linked to a Thanksgiving Holiday Meal. *Western Journal of Medicine*, 166:417–419.
115. D. Bergmire-Sweat, B.J. Barnett, S.L. Harris, J.P. Taylor, G.H. Mazurek, and V. Reddy (1996). Tuberculosis Outbreak in a Texas prison, 1994. *Epidemiology and Infection*, 117:485–492.
116. Austin et al. v. Pennsylvania Department of Corrections. 1995 WL 65458. Retrieved December 3, 2014: http://www.state.nj.us/corrections/pages/about_us/Mission_Statement.html. Also see, Rick Ruddell and Mark Tomita (2008). Page 243.
117. Rachel D. Schwartz (2006). Pandemic Flu Preparedness and Response in Corrections Facilities. *Infectious Diseases in Corrections Report 9*(10): 1, 3–4.
118. Rick Ruddell and Mark Tomita (2008). Page 244.
119. John J. Gibbons and Nicholas de B. Katzenbach (2006). *Confronting Confinement: A Report of the Commission on Safety and Abuse in American Prisons*. New York: Vera Institute of Justice. Page 38. Retrieved May 31, 2014: http://www.vera.org/sites/default/files/resources/downloads/Confronting_Confinement.pdf
120. Rick Ruddell and Mark Tomita (2008). Page 246.
121. Edward J. Latessa, Francis T. Cullen, and Paul Gendreau (2002). Beyond Correctional Quackery—Professionalism and the Possibility of Effective Treatment. *Federal Probation,* 66:43–59.
122. Rick Ruddell and Mark Tomita (2008). Page 246.
123. Joan Petersilia (2009). *When Prisoners Come Home: Parole and Prisoner Reentry: Parole and Prisoner.* Oxford, UK: Oxford University Press.
124. Dennis J. Stevens (2014). Page 401.
125. N. Christakis and J. Fowler (2009). *Connected: The Surprising Power of Our Social Networks and How They Shape Our Lives.* New York: Little, Brown and Company.

126. Joan Petersilia (2001). When Prisoners Return to Communities: Political, Economic, and Social Consequences. *Federal Probation*, 65(3): 3–9.
127. C.F. Hairston (2001). Prisoners and families: Parenting issues during Incarceration. From Prison to Home: The Effect of Incarceration and Reentry on Children, Families, and Communities. Retrieved June 2, 2014: http://aspe.hhs.gov/hsp/prison2home02/Hairston.htm#Conclusions
128. R.J. Sampson, J.D. Morenoff, T. Gannon-Rowley (2002). Assessing "Neighborhood Effects": Social Processes and New Directions in Research. *Annual Review of Sociology*, 28: 443–478.
129. T. Claridge (2004), Social Capital and Natural Resource Management. Unpublished Thesis, University of Queensland, Brisbane, Australia.
130. Janice E. Perlman (1976). *The Myth of Marginality: Urban Poverty and Politics in Rio de Janeiro*. Berkeley: University of California Press.
131. Michele Goodwin (2013, March 29). Panel 1: AIDS/HIV. Presentations at the University of Maryland, Carey Law School. *Switch Point Stories*. Retrieved May 29, 2014: http://digitalcommons.law.umaryland.edu/switch/2013/mar29/7/
132. S.A. Allen, A. Osei, L. Taylor, A. Cabral, Anne Spaulding, and J.D. Rich (2003). Treatment of Chronic Hepatitis C in a State Correctional Facility. Annals of Internal Medicine, 138(3):187–90. Also see, Anne C. Spaulding, C.M. Weinbaum, DT-Y. Lau, R. Sterling, L.B. Seeff, H.S. Margolis, and J.H. Hoofnagle (2006). A Framework for Management of Hepatitis C in Prisons. *Annals of Internal Medicine*, 144:762–769.
133. Centers for Disease Control and Prevention (2014). A Timeline of AIDS. Retrieved May 29, 2014: http://aids.gov/hiv-aids-basics/hiv-aids-101/aids-timeline/embed.html
134. Michele Goodwin (2013, March 29).
135. Olga Grinstead Reznick, Megan Comfort, Kathleen McCarney, and Torsten B. Neilands (2011). The Effectiveness of an HIV Prevention Program for Women Visiting Their Incarcerated Partners: The Home Project. AIDS Behavior, (2): 365–375. Retrieved May 29, 2014: http://www.ncbi.nlm.nih.gov/pmc/articles/PMC3032899/
136. Michele Goodwin (2013, March 29); Dennis J. Stevens (2014); Samuel Walker (2001). *Sense and Nonsense about Crime and Drugs*. Belmont, CA: Wadsworth
137. C. Mayer (1995). HIV-Infected Prisoners: What Mental Health Services Are Constitutionally Mandated? *Journal of Psychiatry & Law*, 23(4): 517–553.
138. Olga Grinstead, Meagan Comfort, Kathleen McCartney, K. Koester, and T. Neilands (2008). Bringing It Home: Design And Implementation of an HIV/STD Intervention For Women Visiting Incarcerated Men. *Aids Education and Prevention*, 20(4): 285–300.
139. Ernest Drucker (2013). *A Plague of Prisons: The Epidemiology of Mass Incarceration in America*. New York: New Press.
140. Dennis J. Stevens (2014). Page 395.
141. Allen Beck (2013). Also see, Joseph E. Paris (2008). Why Prisoners Deserve Health Care. *Virtual Mentor*, 10(2): 113–115. Retrieved May 24, 2014: http://virtualmentor.ama-assn.org/2008/02/msoc1-0802.html
142. Erica S. Pan, et al. (2003).
143. Chancellor and Secretary of State for Justice (2010). Breaking the Cycle: Effective Punishment, Rehabilitation and Sentencing of Offenders. Retrieved May 27, 2014: http://webarchive.nationalarchives.gov.uk/20120119200607/http:/www.justice.gov.uk/consultations/docs/breaking-the-cycle.pdf page 1.
144. University of Chicago Medicine (2014). MRSA Research Center. Retrieved June 1, 2014: http://mrsa-research-center.bsd.uchicago.edu/patients_families/faq.html
145. American Jail Association (AJA) (2014). Retrieved June 2, 2014: https://members.aja.org/About/StatisticsOfNote.aspx

David Bailey /Shutterstock, Inc.

CHAPTER 6

Law Enforcement Officers and Compliance Issues

Learning Objectives

After you read this chapter, you will be better prepared to:

- Explain the daily health experiences of most law enforcement occupations compared with other occupations.
- Identify the agents of compliance which impact law enforcement performance.
- Describe the role of police officers in relationship to anarchy and government corruption.
- Identify the key elements linked to the mission of law enforcement and explain which of those elements might be of the utmost importance to the department; in what way would those elements impact the public the most.
- Identify the mission of law enforcement components and relate those components to officer gender. In what way would the typical male or female officer be prepared to address each component while engaged in a police action or a 911 call?
- Identify the five assumptions about local law enforcement in America and explain in what way one of the five might impact the positive healthcare of police officers the most.
- Discuss the perspective about law enforcement's use of force policy and explain in what way those policies appear to be advantageous or disadvantageous to officers and to the American public.
- Articulate the way social environments affect police officer exposure to deadly pathogens.
- Explain how the following comment lends itself to officer health issues including exposure to infectious diseases: the law on the books is not "what law is."
- Describe in what way police legitimacy relates to law and order and officer health issues.
- Characterize the relevance of drug syringe sticks in relationship to police officers and methods on reducing syringe sticks.
- Describe the consequences to officers arising from hazardous chemical spills.
- Explain the hazards to police officers of clandestine methamphetamine (clan meth) laboratories.
- Describe some of the methods of prevention of disease among police officers. In what way could some of those recommendations be put into operation?
- Characterize the police officer subculture, and explain how it impacts exposure to deadly pathogens and healthcare of officers. How can the subculture be reduced, and what consequences might follow if it were reduced?

Key Terms

Cardiovascular Disease (CVD)
Clan Meth
Crime Displacement
Culture
Disease Transmission
Fragmented
Latent and Manifest Function
Judiciously
Police Subculture
Social Environments
Stop and Frisk Policy
Syringe Stick Injuries
Sworn Officers
Title 42 USC, Section 1983
Terry Stops
Zero Tolerance

Words of Wisdom

It's about time law enforcement got as organized as organized crime.

Rudolph Giuliani

Introduction

Law enforcement practitioners have an increased incidence of health problems including exposure to infectious disease and MRSA (IPM) because of their at-risk occupational environments and because of compliance issues.[1] In the future, the risk to Ebola is also likely. As described in Chapter 1 and Chapter 5, police officers are similar to correctional officers affected by the agents of compliance.[1] As an occupational group, local law enforcement officers have greater morbidity and mortality rates than the general public.[2] For example, police officers have one of the poorest cardiovascular disease (CVD) health profiles of any occupation.[2] Women officers in particular are more vulnerable to CVD than male officers.[3] Overall, the occupational fatality rate of law enforcement personnel is up to five times greater than the national average.[4] Officers have higher levels of non-traditional CVD risk factors, too.[5,3] Previous epidemiological research indicates that police officers, similar to correctional officers as discussed in the previous chapter, have an elevated risk of death relative to the overall general population.[6] Because many readers have little formal knowledge about law enforcement, healthcare issues and basic occupational descriptions of officers and their jobs are discussed. However, when we discuss infection potentials:[7,4]

From a healthcare perspective, cardio-metabolic studies have estimated the cost of in-service related disease among local police officers to be between $400,000 and $750,000; in-service disease accounts for up to 50 percent of early retirements, and accounts for up to 60 percent of police absenteeism.[8]

[1] The Agents of Law Enforcement Compliance: suspects (police only call suspects perpetrators on television), Violator, and Victim Associated Infections Organizational System Policy and Politics Government (State and Federal) Compliance Regulation

[2] Local law enforcement officer is an employee of a local law enforcement agency who is an officer sworn to carry out law enforcement duties. Examples of this class are sheriffs, deputy sheriffs, chiefs of police, city police officers, and sworn personnel of law enforcement subunits of port and transit authorities. For national level general data, this class includes campus police officers employed by local city and community college districts. Private campus police are excluded. Source: Bureau of Justice Statistics (2014). http://www.bjs.gov/

[3] The majority of CVD is caused by risk factors that can be controlled, treated, or modified, such as high blood pressure, cholesterol, overweight/obesity, tobacco use, lack of physical activity, and diabetes. There are also some major CVD risk factors that cannot be controlled.

In terms of attributable deaths, the leading CVD risk factor is raised blood pressure (to which 13 percent of global deaths is attributed), followed by tobacco use (9 percent), raised blood glucose (6 percent), physical inactivity (6 percent) and overweight and obesity (5 percent). *Source:* World Heart Federation see WHF's website at http://www.world-heart-federation.org/press/fact-sheets/cardiovascular-disease-risk-factors/

[4] Disease transmission requires the presence of an infectious agent, exposure to that agent, and a susceptible host.

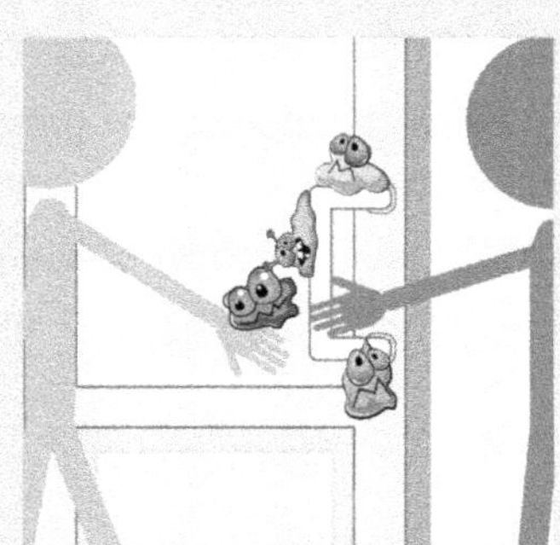

Mjak/Shutterstock, Inc.

To better understand the daily health experiences of most officers, nearly one-half (47 percent) of officers work a non-day shift compared to 9 percent of US workers.[9] The percent of officers with depression is nearly double (12 percent vs. 7 percent) of other occupations, and officers are nearly four times more likely to sleep less than six hours in a twenty-four-hour period than the general population (33 percent vs. 8 percent). A higher percentage of officers are obese (41 percent vs. 32 percent), have the metabolic syndrome (27 percent vs. 19 percent), and have higher mean serum total cholesterol levels (201 mg/dL vs. 193 mg/dL) than comparison employed populations.

Frances L Fruit/Shutterstock, Inc.

Female officers face unique stressors as a result of working in a male dominated occupation including work factors, such as the 'perception' of inadequate physical ability, administrative and general public sexual harassment and discrimination. Nonwork stressors might include expected and actual family responsibilities such as child and elder care particularly if parent/s reside in assisted living arrangements.[10] However, female officers are better educated when hired by most departments and are, indeed, women. Research shows that women officers talk to each other, explain exposure risk to each other, explain prevention, seek professional (both physiological and psychological) help, and emotionally support other women officers in meaningful ways which implies that they handle stress better as a group than male officers, my own research suggests.[11]

Just for the record, female officers tend to be better equipped to deal with many street situations because they do not necessarily represent a threat to suspects and are more likely to be respected more often than male officers to suspects and by the audience observing a police-citizen encounter.[12] Also there is a tendency for female officers to assess the encounter in greater detail than male officers, seeking solutions in keeping with their training and bringing justice to the suspect more often than to their personal ideas of justice.[5]

Nonetheless, there are a variety of ways in which police potentially come in contact with blood-borne diseases; the most dramatic of which are assaults by criminals wielding weapons; providing safety to individuals who are infected prior to becoming a victim; and victims infected by criminals with blood-borne diseases would also qualify for disease transference; also transference can come to officers providing comfort to victims of traffic accidents and catastrophic events such as the officers aiding Hurricane Katrina victims discussed in Chapter 1.[13] Frequently, violators are also drug users who are one of the largest populations of individuals infected by AIDS and Hepatitis B virus (see Chapter 2 for more details).[14] It is not uncommon for officers to sustain cuts and abrasions in the course of struggles and to come in contact with a criminal's or a victim's blood and bodily products including dealing with dead bodies (more detail later). To better understand police and infectious pathogens and MRSA (IPM), it would be helpful to understand their role in America, to review a police agency's fundamental principles and to review the statistics linked to law enforcement and officers before talking about specific healthcare issues.

[5] There are few reliable studies on female officers. I selected the one below to fill the gap. It is reported that female managers in corporate America score higher in the following categories than male managers.

- Persuasive Motivation
- Assertiveness
- Willingness to Risk
- Empathy
- Flexibility
- Sociability
- Team Building
- Leadership Styles of Problem Solving and Decision-Making

Women leaders are more persuasive, assertive, and willing to take more risks than male leaders
Syda Productions/Shutterstock, Inc.

Source: Caliper (2014). Qualities that Distinguish Women Leaders. Retrieved June 21, 2014: https://www.calipercorp.com/portfolio/the-qualities-that-distinguish-women-leaders/

The Role of Police

The fact is that many nations, and civilizations for that matter, would experience less anarchy and government corruption if the human rights of their populations were safeguarded through professional law enforcement initiatives through healthy sworn police officers.[15, 6] This compelling argument is evidenced among Americans who enjoy a steady rise in their quality of life experiences; social mobility in the US is probably in the top percentile of all countries particularly through advanced education—education is the way up and out of poverty.[16, 7] Yet, many (particularly nonpractitioner academics) argue that the police represent tiny empires all of their own and that police corruption is everywhere.[17] Recall from Chapter 1 the litigation and damaging descriptions brought against New Orleans' (NOLO) law enforcement personnel, most of whom put their own lives and families on hold to provide safety to others; but to this day, no federal personnel or politicians have been indicted for the injustices suffered by the victims of political neglect and incompetence after Hurricane Katrina.[8] To this day, ancient Roman bridges are admired and continue to be in use. It is implied that after Roman bridge builders laid the last brick, they stood under the bridge while Roman legions crossed above the bridge.[18] Talk about accountability.

Nonetheless, the personal healthcare of many officers is usually hidden from outside view because of government compliance regulations about privacy and because of the police subculture (more later) whereby police officers are swayed and manipulated to minimize preventive healthcare practices and remedies in keeping with an Alpha-male perspective.[19]

Guaranteeing human rights, especially due process mandates, in a constitutional society is what is expected from local law enforcement while providing initiatives of public safety.[20] When local (excludes federal officers) police officers violate the due process

[6] Sworn officers are persons formally authorized to make arrests while acting within the scope of explicit legal authority. Source: Bureau of Justice Statistics (2014). http://www.bjs.gov/ In clearer terms, sworn officers are sworn by the state regardless where they work in the state; they are employed to conduct lawful arrests and under certain circumstance have the authority to use force, even lethal force, in conducting an arrest. For example, North Carolina Law (Chapter 14, Article 14) reports that a qualified sworn law enforcement officer is a law enforcement officer employed by a local, state, campus, or company police agency in North Carolina who satisfies all of the following:

- The individual is authorized by the agency to carry a handgun in the course of duty.
- The individual is not the subject of a disciplinary action by the agency that prevents the carrying of a handgun.
- The individual meets the requirements established by the agency regarding handguns.

[7] By providing high quality education for all students, we can leverage opportunity, if we know how to focus our efforts. The good news is that we do know how. See endnote for source.

[8] "In the '90s, we had officers arrested and prosecuted and [who] went to jail for rapes, for arson, kidnappings, killings, drugs, bank robberies," said Mary Howell, a local attorney who has represented victims of police abuse for more than thirty years. After a string of police atrocities in the '90s—which sent two officers to death row for capital murder—the Justice Department came to town to clean up the force. Prosecutors stayed from 1996 to 2004, at which time most people thought the problems had been solved. Then came Katrina, during which there were many instances of police bravery, but also more misconduct. It became apparent, to the advocates of federal oversight that the eight-year effort did little to alter police corruption.

Source: John Burnett (2011, August 18). Verdict In Katrina Shooting Buoys Police Reform. NPR News. Retrieved June 16, 2014: http://www.npr.org/2011/08/18/139668648/verdict-in-katrina-shooting-buoys-police-reform. Note: The above perspective is not shared by everyone similar to the tragic incident and results stemming from Ferguson, Missouri, where some blame the police. Some imply police power is out of control suggesting a closer look in lethal force police protocols which is always a good idea, but what about the behavior and consequences of individuals who violate the laws and values of society? That great contributor to quality of life opportunities, Dr. Martin Luther King, Jr., clarified that nonviolence is a powerful and just weapon. It is a weapon unique in history, which cuts without wounding and ennobles the man who wields it. It is a sword that heals. With that said, judging from all the looting and disruption across the country after Ferguson, it might appear to some observers that thugs control the streets in the name of justice. My intent is to offer another perspective in keeping with my occupation as a professor and researcher as opposed to taking a position.

Posted Saturday, February 16th, 2013 NOLA Defender (http://www.noladefender.com/category/tags/doj)

The gloves have come off in the City's dispute with the feds over reforming the NOPD. Since reneging on its earlier support for the NOPD consent decree, the City has had plenty to say about the feds and their agreements. On Friday, it was the feds' turn to defend themselves from claims that the agreement designed to implement close to 500 reforms at the New Orleans Police Department was untenable. In a motion so long that it required a separate motion to let the judge know how long it was going to be, the feds issued a harsh rebuke to the City's claims, calling the Landrieu administration "cynical" and egregious distorters, among other things.

rights of individuals, those individuals have a right to file a federal lawsuit against officers, the department, and the training instructors under Title 42 USC, Section 1983.[9] Influencing police decision-making processes is a signpost of democratic policing as is accountability.[21]

Police officers are accountable to the communities they serve, the taxpayers who pay the bills, and the legal order governing their authority. In this regard, if officers are unhealthy, stressed, or poorly hired, in what way can officers bring his or her agency (the mission local law enforcement agencies follow and the ideas of the American Bar Association are also shown) closer to its moral and legal responsibilities?[10]

Mission of Local Law Enforcement

The key elements linked to the mission of law enforcement follow; experts tend to rank these elements in the order below linked to both law enforcement and their constituents:

- Reducing danger[22] (as opposed to escalating danger)
- Delivering quality police services designed toward public safety and to reduce crime through police presents, investigations, and arrests of suspects.[23]
- Limiting the fear of crime[24] (Often the fear of crime can push people into behavior that creates a greater danger than previously experienced—law-abiding people buy guns and use them.)[25]
- Enhancing constituent quality of life experiences[26]
- Defending the due process guarantees in the rule of law[27]
- Being accountable to the people, the department, and the state[28]

Use of Force

There is a volume of research analyzing police use of force including deadly force.[29] In one study of 1,220 arrests from Phoenix, Arizona, the strongest predictors of police use of force are length of time the officer was employed, suspect's race, chemical impairment, an attempt to flee, and possession of a weapon.

In another study, police use of force was used in 306 (7 percent) cases of individuals who had mental disorders out of 4,267 encounters between 1995 and 2008.[30] Violators who were perceived to have mental illness were more likely to threaten or use weapons on police and to have weapons used or threatened against them by police, as compared to those individuals who were not perceived to have a mental disorder.

[9] Title 42 USC, Section 1983: Every person who, under color of any statute, ordinance, regulation, custom, or usage, of any State or Territory or the District of Columbia, subjects, or causes to be subjected, any citizen of the United States or other person within the jurisdiction thereof to the deprivation of any rights, privileges, or immunities secured by the Constitution and laws, shall be liable to the party injured in an action at law, suit in equity, or other proper proceeding for redress, except that in any action brought against a judicial officer for an act or omission taken in such officer's judicial capacity, injunctive relief shall not be granted unless a declaratory decree was violated or declaratory relief was unavailable.

Source: Findlaw.com Retrieved June 9, 2014: http://codes.lp.findlaw.com/uscode/42/21/I/1983#sthash.Riw6d3T6.dpuf

[10] **American Bar Association's Standard 1-2.2. Major Current Responsibilities of Police**

In assessing appropriate objectives and priorities for police service, local communities should initially recognize that most police agencies are currently given responsibility, by design or default, to:

- Identify Criminal Offenders And Criminal Activity And, Where Appropriate, To Apprehend Offenders And Participate In Subsequent Court Proceedings
- Reduce The Opportunities For The Commission of Some Crimes Through Preventive Patrol And Other Measures
- Aid Individuals Who Are In Danger of Physical Harm
- Protect Constitutional Guarantees
- Facilitate The Movement of People And Vehicles
- Assist Those Who Cannot Care For Themselves
- Resolve Conflict
- Identify Problems That Are Potentially Serious Law Enforcement or Governmental Problems
- Create And Maintain A Feeling of Security In The Community
- Promote And Preserve Civil Order
- Provide Other Services On An Emergency Basis

ABA's Website Retrieved June 12, 2014: http://www.americanbar.org/publications/criminal_justice_section_archive/crimjust_standards_urbanpolice.html

The less lethal coercive power granted to police officers is not without its restrictions.[11] Such limitations are delineated per the United States Supreme Court, via *Graham v. Connor*, applying the broad standard of objective reasonableness.[31] A far more salient operational guide to assessing what is objectively reasonable rests within departmental use-of-force policy, which like other police policies can vary widely from jurisdiction to jurisdiction. At best, research has noted that many agencies tend to instruct officers via a force continuum, although the nature (i.e., various designs, levels, and ordering of force tactics, and appropriate force relative to citizen resistance) of such policies are relatively unknown.

Marsan/Shutterstock, Inc.

Based on a national survey of policing agencies, departments utilize a use-of-force continuum. However, there is no commonly accepted use-of-force continuum used by enforcement practitioners.

In a study of 3,230 sworn personnel in thirty departments, use of force abuse was evaluated.[32] Officers rated that abuse was used depending on the seriousness of an excessive force violation, their support for discipline, and their willingness to report such misconduct. Novice officers, highly experienced veterans, and supervisory personnel were more likely than officers with moderate levels of experience to view excessive force as serious and worthy of more severe discipline. Very often, when situations come to public attention through sensational media reporting such as the Ferguson tragedy, things heat up. For instance, one headline read, Since Ferguson, police have killed more than a dozen teenagers, half of them black. Some did nothing more than carry a BB gun. (see The Daily Beast 11/25/2014 at dailybeast.com). When you read the article it becomes clear that those killed were not in Ferguson, but across the country. Everybody loves to hammer cops but when someone breaks into your house or steels your kitty, you call 9-1-1. Most officers do the right thing and help people get through their day to day as safely as possible.

[11] *Graham v. Connor* 490 US 386, 109 S. Ct. 1865, 104 L. Ed. 2d 443—Supreme Court, 1989—

What constitutional standard governs a free citizen's claim that law enforcement used excessive force in the course of making an arrest, investigatory stop, or other "seizure." The US Supreme Court held that such claims are properly analyzed under the Fourth Amendment's "objective reasonableness" standard, rather than under a substantive due process standard. In this action under 42 USC § 1983, petitioner Dethorne Graham recovered damages for injuries allegedly sustained when law enforcement officers used physical force against him during the course of an investigatory stop in Charlotte, North Carolina. For more information on Fourth Amendment Rights, see fourthamendment.com/ccl.php

[12] Police officers similar to correctional personnel in Chapter 3 don't choose their "clients" or violators.

Five Assumptions about Local Law Enforcement in America

Five assumptions that require acknowledgment about local law enforcement will aid in a better understanding of social control issues and disease transmission (explained later) to officers. The five fundamental assumptions below follow in no particular order, are not observable or salient issues at all times, and may impact the estimated 1,700 local law enforcement agencies consisting of approximately 700,000 sworn officers in different ways at different times.[33]

- The police are considered as a class of authorities facing the problem of managing divergent expectations of conduct. Democracy's ideological conflict between the norms governing the work of maintaining order and the principle of accountability to the rule of law and the people complicate authority.[12] Local police officers "are expected to be (at the same time) a rule enforcer, parent, friend, social worker, street fighter, sharpshooter, and officer of the law"[34] and defender of the rights of others.

- The police cannot nor should they attempt to control crime alone.[35] Officers cannot nor should they attempt to provide their own well-being which includes preventive and ongoing healthcare.[36] Fact is, the police do not control the mean streets of America. It's all in the numbers—an estimated 700,000 cops versus 318 million residents[37] ratio 1 cop for every approximately 450 residents.
- Officers and police agencies are not equal because each officer and each agency is unique; each is affected differently by events and circumstances that shape the response of the officers, the agencies, and the policy and regulations; but exposure to health risks and quality healthcare are another matter.[38] Yet, officers should accept the responsibility and consequences of their own conduct and their own healthcare (including negligence or substitutes for poor health such as alcohol, drugs, and sexual misconduct) rather than pointing blame elsewhere. This thought includes the police organizational structure—it too must own up to its responsibilities of providing officers with quality healthcare and training linked to healthcare that enables officers to effectively provide quality social order initiatives in line with the rule of law.[39]
- Among police officers, the risks of the streets are less traumatic than the organizational factors they face, which includes policy developed by non-police professionals (academics who have no justice experience in particular), top-down bureaucratic practices (federal government intervention where their agenda has nothing to do with law enforcement but is engaged in a turf war), and policy initiatives linked to strategies developed as a law enforcement response to the war on crime, drugs, and terrorism (also designed by nonpracticing academics and politicians).[40]
- Local Law Enforcement Agencies Are:
  - Fragmented (existing or functioning as though broken into separate parts: source thefreedictionary.com; Note—broken does not mean busted or out of commission)[13]
  - Lack Cooperation Between Other Government Agencies and Police Agencies; for example, strategies of reform in municipalities require the cooperation of many service agencies; often the heads of those bureaucracies do not fully understand they are partners in their city's program, not victims of empire building by the police.[41] Also, some police departments do not trust other departments with investigative information.[42] Finally, police departments do not necessarily report arrests or certain police strategies to federal enforcement agencies such as the Uniform Crime Report (therefore use UCR reports as a guide not an absolute). More details, see fbi.gov and click on ucr
  - Duplication of Police Services Between Agencies[43]
  - Many Inconsistent Standards and Regulations;[44] for example, in North Carolina breaking and entering (B&E) into an unoccupied home is second degree BE which can be a Class 1 misdemeanor, if occupied then it's first degree B&E which can carry prison time (source: NC General Status: 14.3 and 14.7).
  - Promotion process is not necessarily linked to official performance appraisal methods; administrators and supervisors tend to use subjective approaches to measure performance such as favoritism, coercion, and ability to assimilate into the police subculture.[45]

> [13] Fragmented Police Agencies Have a Purpose—Separation of Powers implied in the US Constitution. Separation prevents concentration of power (seen as the root of tyranny) and provides each branch with weapons to fight off encroachment by the other two branches. As James Madison argued in the Federalist Papers (No. 51), "Ambition must be made to counteract ambition." Clearly, our system of separated powers is not designed to maximize efficiency; it is designed to maximize freedom.
>
> *Source:* Doug Linder (2014). Separation of Powers. University of Missouri KC. Retrieved June 12, 2014: http://law2.umkc.edu/faculty/projects/ftrials/conlaw/separationofpowers.htm

Social control through local law enforcement must negotiate the maintenance of order and the quality of that order through the rule of law that a given system is capable of sustaining the procedures appropriate to the achievement of such order.[46] Achieving order with unhealthy or high death rate potentials represent other issues particularly when those issues are linked to the social environment.

A Word about Social Environments

Actually, you have been reading about social environments through the last three chapters in roundabout ways. Now it's time to take a look at the social environment because it tells us what to expect and how to act. A relevant factor that clearly shapes our behavior and concepts of human life and behavior at the university, downtown, and on the highways is the rule of law.[47] Imagine what the quality of life experiences would be without the rule of law (Constitution) and without professional (healthy) personnel to enforce those laws in a professional manner? The law is all that stands between social order and anarchy.

Africa Studio/Shutterstock, Inc.

You have read above that across the US, there is no single standard relative to "no knock" entrances to your home causing conflict and death of homeowners and police officers; likewise, there is no single standard on policies linked to the use of deadly force. Community disturbances resulting from the police use of excessive or deadly force continue to plague many American communities.[48]

Under the color of law, as they say, or sworn (explained above) law enforcement officers have the legal responsibility to interact with you, to stop you, to conduct a probable cause arrest, and to use lethal force when necessary. Officers do not have the legal authority to revise the Constitution and to develop the laws and the law makers do not have the authority to enforce the laws; this thought lends itself to the idea of a separation of powers.[49]

In America's social environments, the rules of engagement among sworn officers seems complicated; yet, most of us fail to acknowledge the basic legal and moral responsibilities of a sworn officer within the framework of the rule of law: 14

- Detainment
- Use of deadly force

When you add good health to the officer's and agency's responsibilities, another image might materialize.15

14 American society expects that a person with the legal right to detain and to use lethal force must be also mentally competent and physically healthy.

Joe Belanger/Shutterstock, Inc.

15 Is there a single standard for the health of police officers or even policy protecting officers from villains, let alone deadly infectious pathogens or does that go along with the job?

Our social environment is understood within the contents of our culture comprised of community, religion, social networks, families, history, and occupation among others. Lives of people individually are governed by religious, political, economic, and organizational rules—formal and informal (explained in Chapter 3) which reflect societal norms (written rules and laws), values (what is understood as good, right, and fair; i.e., the value of an education is a way up and out of poverty), and beliefs (opinions) of their particular social context.

If police policies on health, gunning down an alleged violator, or following through on a "no knock" warrant are inconsistent, inappropriate, or just wrong—who guards the guardians?[50] This question was asked within a police misconduct paradigm some twenty years ago; but in the twenty-first century we need to reframe this thought in terms of protecting our cops—not handcuffing them in the performance of their jobs.

Occupational Death Rate among Workers

One study shows that over a three-year period (2000–2002) the US workforce has an estimated occupational death of rate of forty-one workers per million workers.[51] Fishermen and construction workers, for example, have the highest occupational fatality (>1,000 deaths per million workers annually). Members of the military (361–671 per million), police and related protective service workers (108 per million), and firefighters (93 per million) also have markedly elevated rates. Lawyers (7–14 per million) and waiters (5 per million) have relatively low rates of occupational death. The fundamental ethic of healthcare is that sick persons must receive care (but we don't always know who they are).[52] This premise carries an implicit latent (unexpected) consequence:[16] an occupational risk to law enforcement officers who respond to contagious patients by chance because of accidents (victims are saved and comforted), by strategy because of crowd control (constituents are subdued or adverted away from an at-risk scenario), or by obligation because of "stops" or arrests of violators who are restrained and processed into the justice system.[17] It would be appropriate to discuss the number of officers assaulted or killed in the line of duty.

Officers Assaulted and Murdered

According to the Federal Bureau of Investigation (FBI), the following information concerns duly sworn city, university and college, county, state, and tribal law enforcement officers who were assaulted in the line of duty in 2012 and who met certain other criteria.[53] Note that the overview below does not include the number of officers whose health was comprised by violators; my experience tells me that sometimes violators have the intent of contaminating officers (and correctional personnel) with whatever infection they have at the moment.

[16] Latent function: Present but not visible; the unrecognized or unintended (unexpected) consequence of a social process as opposed to a manifest function which is intentional (expected) consequences of a social process.

Source: Open Education Sociology Dictionary. Retrieved June 9, 2014: http://sociologydictionary.org/

[17] Among police officers, "stops" are referred to as "Terry stops." A "Terry Stop" is a stop of a person by law enforcement officers based upon "reasonable suspicion" that a person may have been engaged in criminal activity, whereas an arrest requires "probable cause" that a suspect committed a criminal offense. The name comes from the standards established in *Terry v. Ohio*, 1968. The issue in the case was whether police should be able to detain a person and subject him to a limited search for weapons without probable cause for arrest. The Court held that police may conduct a limited search of a person for weapons that could endanger the officer or those nearby, even in the absence of probable cause for arrest and any weapons seized may be introduced in evidence.

Source: USLegal.com. Retrieved June 9, 2014: http://definitions.uslegal.com/t/terry-stop/

Overview:

- In 2012, the FBI collected assault data from 11,759 law enforcement agencies that employed 520,047 officers. These officers provided service to more than 247 million persons, or 78.9 percent of the nation's population.
- Law enforcement agencies reported that 52,901 officers were assaulted while performing their duties in 2012.
- The rate of officer assaults in 2012 was 10.2 per 100 sworn officers.

The following information concerns duly sworn city, university and college, county, state, tribal, and federal law enforcement officers who died in 2012 as a result of felonious incidents in the line of duty.[54] The law enforcement officers included in this report also met additional criteria (e.g., they had full arrest powers; they ordinarily wore/carried a badge and a firearm).

Overview:

- In 2012, 48 law enforcement officers died from injuries incurred in the line of duty during felonious incidents.
- Of the officers feloniously killed, 21 were employed by city police departments, including 6 who were members of law enforcement agencies in cities with 250,000 or more inhabitants.
- Line-of-duty deaths occurred in 26 states, Puerto Rico, and the U.S. Virgin Islands.
- By region, 22 officers were feloniously killed in the South, 8 officers in the West, 6 officers in the Midwest, and 6 officers in the Northeast. Six officers were feloniously killed in U.S. territories; 5 in Puerto Rico and 1 in the U.S. Virgin Islands.

For example, on June 8, 2014, two Las Vegas police officers (Alyn Beck 41 and Igor Soldo 31, both of whom were husbands and fathers) were having lunch at a pizza buffet in an aging strip mall about five miles northeast of the Las Vegas Strip when the Millers fatally shot them.[55] The killers, Jerad and Amanda Miller (husband and wife), left a neighbor's apartment where they had been staying around 4:30 p.m. and walked with backpacks to the strip mall, about five miles away.

The officers were sitting in a booth when Jerad Miller fatally shot Officer Soldo in the back of his head. As his partner tried to react, Miller shot him once in the throat. Amanda Miller opened fire on Officer Beck several times. Police believe that while the Millers wanted to target police, the choice of Soldo and Beck was random.

Pulling the mortally wounded officers from the booth, the Millers took the guns and ammunition of the officers and placed a yellow Gadsden flag featuring the phrase "Don't tread on me" and a swastika on Beck's body. The flag, with its roots in the American Revolution, is a symbol for anti-government groups. Police said they believe the swastika was intended to paint police as Nazis, not necessarily an expression of the Millers' own white supremacist views.

Three thousand uniformed officers joined in the funeral procession for Officer Igor Soldo on June 11, 2014.[56] Soldo joined the Las Vegas Police Department in 2006 after moving with his family from war-torn Bosnia when he was 13. He graduated from the University of Nebraska-Lincoln, and worked as a correctional officer at a Lincoln jail until he got his job with the LVPD.

Local Law Enforcement Statistics

Local police departments make up more than two-thirds of the 18,000 state and local law enforcement agencies in the United States.[57] A local police department is a general purpose law enforcement agency, other than a sheriff's office, that is operated by a unit of local government such as a town, city, township, or county. Tribal police are classified as local police in Bureau of Justice Statistics (BJS) data collections.

BJS Bureau of Justice Statistics

Included below are some of the summary findings that may catch your interest based on the 2008 Census of State and Local Law Enforcement Agencies (CSLLEA) and the 2007 Law Enforcement Management and Administrative Statistics (LEMAS) survey.

- 12,501 local police departments with the equivalent of at least one full-time officer were operating in the US (not including the sheriffs' offices).
- Local police departments had about 593,000 full-time employees, including 461,000 sworn officers.
- Municipal and township police departments employed an average of 2.3 full-time officers per 1,000 residents. (What is the ratio of officers per residents in your hometown?)
- About half of local police departments employed fewer than ten sworn personnel, and about three-fourths served a population of less than 10,000.

- In 2007, about 1 in 8 local police officers were women, compared to 1 in 13 in 1987.
- About 1 in 4 officers were members of a racial or ethnic minority in 2007, compared to 1 in 6 officers in 1987.
- In 2007, local police recruits were required to complete an average of 1,370 training hours.
- Average starting salaries for entry-level local police officers in 2007 ranged from $26,600 per year in the smallest jurisdictions to $49,500 in the largest. Overall, the average starting salary earned by entry-level officers was about $40,500.
- Overall, local police operating costs for fiscal year 2007 were $116,500 per sworn officer and $260 per resident.

Also, as of September 2007, an estimated 3,000 sheriffs' offices performed law enforcement functions. Nationally, sheriffs' offices employ about 369,000 sworn and civilian personnel and operate at a cost of roughly $30 billion.[58]

Some sheriff's offices perform all of the local law enforcement in the community such as serve warrants, operate jails, protect courts and sometimes the fire department, too. For example, Charlotte Mecklenburg Police Department (Charlotte, NC) does it all except the fire department; the Broward Sheriff's Office (Florida) does it all: law enforcement, courts, jails, and fire fighters.[59]

Despite the Rule of Law

When an officer arrests a violator, the explanation by many (nonpracticing justice professionals) academic scholars and the court recognize that the law on the books is not "what law is."[60] For that matter, it is generally agreed that police work is what the police say it is.[61] Said another way, there exists compelling evidence that police policy and crime control imagery are distinctively different than the operational realities of policing, police practice, and how others view the police. These differences or inconsistencies significantly influence an officer's compliance with policy and laws when delivering routine police services. For example, in some jurisdictions where a mandatory arrest policy is linked to all domestic violence calls, officers responding to calls do not always conduct an arrest even when the evidence (and policy) says they should. In many states, a mandatory arrest policy is in place generally for a domestic violence response. Another example is found among officers conducting searches among drug suspects. Nearly two-thirds of the officers in a study conducted unconstitutional searches of suspects linked to a war of drug initiative, and surprisingly, the courts challenged none of those searches.[62] Police performance tends to produce huge social costs when police performance does not match policy or violates the due process rights of suspects. Continuing along this line of reasoning, many officers view the justice system as too lenient because of a revolving door justice (same suspects apprehended, same criminals returned to the streets) which diminishes the occupational status and social worth of police officers regardless of how many constituents they help or how many bad guys they arrest. Among those costs, the self-image of an officer and the legitimacy of law enforcement are both challenged.[63] No wonder so many officers attempt to assimilate (integrate, do their best to be accepted) into their police subculture regardless of their decisions and their health. Yet, unhealthy officers detract from the legitimacy of law enforcement and eventually provide poor police services to the community and at an extreme—an innocent person is injured and dies. For instance, the Boston Police Department "accepts full responsibility" for the death of Victoria Snelgrove, a twenty-one-year-old journalism student at Emerson College, who was killed by a police projectile fired to disperse crowds celebrating the Boston Red Sox victory over the New York Yankees.[64] Some ninety minutes after the Red Sox celebrated on the infield at Yankee Stadium, an estimated 80,000 jubilant and mostly young fans converged on Kenmore Square in Boston. Accounts report that the officer immediately fired his gun leveled at Victoria Snelgrove's head. The officer fired two rounds in extremely quick succession, and the girl immediately dropped. All her friends were around her.[65] They were screaming.

Another report suggests that Officer Rochefort Milien had little training on how to use his weapon and had earlier observed the most senior commander on the scene "repeatedly firing indiscriminately."[66] The Bureau of Internal Investigations at the Boston PD sustained three charges of unreasonable judgment, and one charge of excessive force against Officer Milien who agreed to accept a ninety-day suspension over the death of Victoria Snelgrove.[67] What is not commonly known is that Officer Milien was in poor health; earlier that day he phoned his precinct sergeant saying he couldn't come to work because of a "strange skin rash on . . . face and hands," but was told he had to because of the Yankee vs. Sox game "or else," a confidential police officer and former student informant advised this writer.

Legitimacy of Law Enforcement

For policing in a democratic society to be effective, it must be considered legitimate by the vast majority of the people.[68] Police must be seen as having the "right" to exercise force. Frankly, if a police agency does not have legitimacy, then it must operate by the use of brute force.[69] The public will perceive the police as professional and comply with their directives when the police utilize their legally mandated prerogative such as discretion and use of force as objectively as circumstances permit.

Police agencies must be perceived as performing "judiciously" during public intrusions.[18] Policy versus practice issues are widened by how the media reports the police effort and how the public responds to those reports such as the Victoria Snelgrove death discussed above. Is the media changing the police officer reality? Similar to most criminal justice professors, students often proclaim that they want to be a crime scene investigator (CSI) or a police detective solving old homicide cases. I tell them to go to Hollywood and audition because real cops and detectives engage in different activities than those shown by the popular television performances. In fact, I wrote a book on that topic—*Media and Criminal Justice: CSI Effect* a few years ago which most students in a criminology classroom enjoy. I do enjoy television particularly police performances. However, one concern is the amount of harm fostered by the entertainment media to both law enforcement officers and the public. Television performances and movies are actually educating criminals and encourages others to commit crime.

[18] Judiciously: Sensible and wise. Showing wisdom, good sense, or discretion, often with the underlying aim of avoiding trouble or waste.

Centered in this thought, it could be argued that the self-image of an officer is usually developed somewhere between media portrayals and how the public views those portrayals. The public who encounter an officer on the street, reinforce the media's perspective with an end result which challenges both the self-image an officer holds and the legitimacy of law enforcement as an institution. A qualified source informs us that a "sharp contrast between the crime-fighting imagery of the police and the peacekeeping reality of police activities was one of the first and most important findings of the flood of police research that began in the 1960s."[70]

As an officer better understands what style of performance is expected from him and her as a peacekeeper, the notion of violence seems entirely out of place or vice versa. Fact is that the expectations held by policymakers, interest groups, and the public are at the core of police legitimacy and that legitimacy provides the police with the power (and budget) to exercise crime control tactics, police stress control options, and police healthcare expectations. The public and many government agencies including the judiciary frequently challenge the legitimacy of police authority, which has become a major problem in the twenty-first century. A number of individuals challenge the authority of an officer even during a routine interaction. How well does an officer's self-image hold up to these legitimacy discrepancies and in what way do these discrepancies affect the performance of an officer?[71] One answer could be that the police redefine a rationale about their experiences and their health which are closer to media accounts than what their job actually is and their health condition. What the "job" produces for most law enforcement officers other than the satisfaction of helping others and putting away the bad guy, is that health is an occupational hazard for law enforcement of all ranks. "The effects of stress—low morale, high turnover, absenteeism, and early death . . . exact a high cost from officers, their families, and their agencies."[72]

Nonetheless, another piece of the professional status puzzle is that police professionals do not control police policy yet are given the responsibility of management and setting day-to-day directives to mirror policy.[73] Relevant to this discussion is the compelling argument which reveals that police policy, in a democratic society, rightfully belongs outside the control of those who perform a police function. For example, a study shows that policing is being reconstructed worldwide. Its distinguishing features are:

- The separation of those who authorize policing from those who do it (see above for details).
- The transference of both functions away from government.

Because police have a monopoly on the use of force and detainment power, if they developed the laws linked to use of force and detainment, what could be expected from their performance? If the police developed the rules, in what way would police performance help public safety and human rights? To understand what is happening to policing, it is essential to distinguish the way in which policing is authorized from the way in which it is provided; does this idea hold for health risks and healthcare among police officers?

Simply put, the community will support the police when the community feels police mirror their own ideals. The greater the legitimacy of a police agency, the fewer the violators and the less coercion of force required by the agency toward social order. How the police do their job, or their style, is far more relevant to matters of their professionalism than apprehending bad guys. In a "how" perspective the words "healthy" are strongly implied; unhealthy police add to the lack of legitimacy of a department which in turn refers to the level of citizen compliance to mandates, regulations, and laws.

Imbalance

Another way to look at the policy versus practice issue is to say that an inconsistency or imbalance exists in the policing profession—an imbalance between mandates, regulations, and laws including expectations of police behavior and the passion of officers to serve and protect. This disparity between dictates and ideals can produce more stress and less healthcare application among officers than dealing with even some of the worst problems on America's mean streets. Caution: it is possible that the disparity between organizational policy and officer practices will well be the best model of a police organization.

Nonetheless, legitimacy of police practice depends upon the finesse, manners, and health demonstrated by an officer when he or she intrudes in the daily life of his or her constituents; the health of an officer is noticeable by observers in the field and in my opinion, has much to do with whether an individual will follow the directive of an officer or compliance of regulation. It makes sense that the more professionalism and good health demonstrated by an officer, the more likely it is that the public accepts police intrusion as legitimate. But, the professionalism of police officers is seriously flawed. When the flaw is unmasked, the self-imagine of most cops (and consequently quality police service) is affected in ways too numerous to describe.[19]

Imagine how an officer feels when she or he discovers the realities of the street are different from their previous expectations during the early months of his or her career. Many officers cling to the police subculture for respect and approval which might mean more than doing the right thing despite syringe sticks, hazardous chemical exposures, and all the health hazards law enforcement officers may experience in the daily routine of his or her job.

Syringe Sticks

Police initiatives, particularly to comply with policy such as the war on drugs, sometimes apply zero tolerance strategies.[74, 20] Whether it works or not is not necessarily the focus of this section; however, Federal Judge Shira A. Scheindlin ruled that the New York Police Department engaged in rampant unconstitutional and racially biased policing through its controversial stop-and-frisk policy (or zero tolerance).[75]

[19] My argument is one to consider: that is, because many law enforcement agencies follow low standards, particularly educational standards, in the hiring process, most recruits are coming from a lower class background as opposed to a middle class background which also means healthier experiences. A GED, a valid driver's license, and 21 years of age just doesn't cut it, but then the pay and community respect isn't there either.

[20] Zero tolerance policing can be defined in a number of ways. The most publicized approach involves strict, non-discretionary enforcement of laws regardless of the circumstances or the minor nature of the offence. Stop and Frisk policies used at random. Advocates of zero tolerance stress that while it does involve 'positive action' by the police, it does not necessarily equate to automatic arrest for trivial offenses. Advocates of zero tolerance claim that it reduces both minor and major crime, that it reduces the fear of crime in the community, and increases confidence in the police. On the other hand, critics dispute the link between zero tolerance and crime reduction, suggesting that other reforms in policing, as well as social and demographic factors contributed to recent declines in crime rates. *Source:* see endnote Jayne Marshall.

Other times, officers stop individuals whom an officer might suspect of criminal violations for one reason or another and sometimes the officer conducts a search of the suspect.[21]

Staying on point, when officers search individuals sometimes they are careless or distracted, pricking themselves (needlestick injuries) happens often with the syringe or needle of a drug user who might be infected.[22] For example, Rockland, Massachusetts, (near Boston) police officer Thomas MacDonald was pricked by a syringe as he patted down William Naumenko, 20, of Hull, MA, in the Hingham County courthouse bathroom.[76] Naumenko's sister had told police that she feared her brother was shooting heroin in the bathroom and MacDonald went to check on him.

In another example, the injury was tiny. But for Officer Anthony Martinez of Lower Allen Township, who had patted down Michael Merza, the needlestick could be life-changing.[77] Whether the convicted drug abuser is found guilty of aggravated assault in the Cumberland County, Pennsylvania, case could boil down to whether he thought the uncapped hypodermic needle in his pocket could be considered a weapon. After Merza was taken into custody, they learned that Merza, whom they described as a known drug user, had "a deadly communicable disease." Now, Martinez might have been exposed to the disease.

Following up on Merza's case, Merza was found not guilty in poking Officer Martinez with a needle during his arrest.[78] During the trial, the prosecution (First Assistant District Attorney Jaime Keating) attempted to prove that Merza had malicious intent when he did not tell Martinez about the needle with Hepatitis C in his pocket. The opening statement by the prosecutor was: "It is one of every police officer's worst nightmares."

[21] There is no proof that the zero-tolerance policing adopted by New York City and other cities in the 1990s had anything to do with the decline in violent crime. Crime also dropped in jurisdictions that did not use the approach. Millions of people have been arrested under the policy for minor violations such as possession of small amounts of marijuana. And one thing is beyond dispute: this arrest-first policy has filled the courts to bursting with first-time, minor offenders who do not belong there and wreaked havoc with people's lives. Even when cases are dismissed, people can be shadowed for years by error-ridden criminal records.

Source: Brent Staples (2012, April 28). The Human Cost of 'Zero Tolerance.' New York Times. Retrieved June 18, 2014: http://www.nytimes.com/2012/04/29/opinion/sunday/the-cost-of-zero-tolerance.html?_r=0

[22] *Syringe Stick Injuries:* syringe or needlestick injuries are wounds made by a sudden prick from sharp pointed objects such as needles. These injuries make a small puncture (hole) on the skin. They usually happen on the finger, but may also happen on the hand, arm, or foot. They may cause bleeding, pain, and swelling on the wound site. Needlestick injuries usually happen to healthcare workers in hospitals, clinics, and labs. They may also happen at home or in the community, where needles are not properly disposed of.

Source: Drugs.com http://www.drugs.com/cg/needle-stick-injuries.html

Reducing Syringe Sticks

One answer to reducing syringe sticks would be quality training, but a comprehensive approach to reducing HIV transmission among injecting drug users (IDUs) would relate to the removal of legal barriers to syringe access.[79] Legal barriers include both "law on the books" and "law on the streets," as previously discussed which is the actual daily routine practice of law enforcement officers. Changes in syringe and drug control policy can be ineffective in reducing such barriers if police continue to treat syringe possession as a crime or evidence of criminal activity.

Numerous scientific studies demonstrate that syringe exchange programs (SEPs) can play an important role in reducing HIV and viral hepatitis infection and advancing public safety, including the safety of law enforcement officials.[80] Federal law has prohibited the use of federal funds for SEPs. Since the ban was lifted in 2009, several state and local health authorities have sought funds for SEPs as part of a broader approach to preventing HIV infections. Injection drug users (IDUs) account for approximately 19 percent of all infections (209,000 cases) and 12 percent of all new HIV infections in 2006. Research tells us that SEPs are an effective public health approach to reducing the spread of HIV/AIDS and other blood-borne diseases such as hepatitis.[81] Research also says that SEPs promote public health and safety by taking syringes off the streets and protecting police officers from needlestick injuries. Studies have also shown that SEPs do not increase crime or drug use and provide a gateway to drug treatment and HIV prevention services.[82] For example:

- A study of police officers in Rhode Island found that nearly 30 percent had been stuck by a needle at one point in their careers, with more than 27 percent experiencing two or more needlestick injuries.[83]

- A 2009 study concludes that SEPs reduce needlestick injuries among police officers and help lower the number of contaminated syringes in communities.[84]
- A study of Connecticut police officers found that needlestick injuries were reduced by two-thirds after implementing SEPs.[85]
- "SEPs take dirty needles off the streets and increase the safety of our police officers. Indeed, these programs have decreased needlestick injuries to police by 66 percent." Bob Scott, former Captain, Sheriff's Office, Macon County, NC. February 2011[86]
- A Baltimore study demonstrated that SEPs helped to reduce the number of improperly discarded syringes by almost 50 percent.
- SEPs do not encourage the initiation of drug use nor do they increase the frequency of drug use among current users.[87]

The presence of SEPs in communities does not expand drug-related networks or increase crime rates. Research shows that neighborhoods in Baltimore with SEPs experienced an 11 percent decrease in break-ins and burglaries, whereas areas of the city without SEPs experienced an 8 percent increase in crime.[88] Another study conducted in Baltimore demonstrated that the number of arrests did not increase after the establishment of SEPs. Finally, in this regard, a study concludes that SEP participants are five times more likely to enter a drug treatment program than non-participants.[89]

Just for the record, another example in an effort to dismantle the open drug market and improve public order, a large-scale police initiative named the Citywide Enforcement Team (CET), began in Vancouver in spring of 2003.[90] An evaluation was conducted on both the CET's impact upon drug consumption and access to sterile syringes and health services among injection drug users (IDUs). The researchers learned that concerning drug use patterns, intensified police presence prompted 'rushed' injections, injecting in riskier environments, discouraged safer injection practices, and increased unsafe disposal of syringes. Service providers indicated that the CET negatively impacted contact between health services and IDUs, as outreach was compromised due to the displacement of IDUs. Police activities also negatively influenced IDUs' access to syringes and their willingness to carry syringes, and syringe confiscation was reported. The intensification of police activities led to less drug activity in the area so drug users moved to another location in the city—or crime displacement.[23] How many officers were caught off guard and stuck with a syringe will never really come to light; a confidential police informant (one reason I used the above study was because I knew a former student on the Vancouver PD) indicated that a lot of the chatter in the locker room was that divorces or separations were huge because the partners of officers refused intimacy until officers were tested for HIV and hepatitis. Some officers felt that being tested implied that they did not trust their sergeants whom they depended upon for promotions and "sweet assignments."

[23] Displacement: crime will simply relocate to other times and places since the "root causes" of crime were not addressed. *Source:* Rob T. Guerette (2009). Analyzing Crime Displacement and Diffusion. Center for Problem-Oriented Policing. University at Albany. Retrieved June 18, 2014: http://www.popcenter.org/tools/displacement/print/

A study explored the ramifications of a police drug crackdown on drug injectors' ability to practice harm reduction during "crackdown initiatives" in New York City.[91] Analysis suggests that particular crackdown tactics, notably frequent police searches of participants' bodies and elevated surveillance of the precinct's public spaces, reconfigured participants' experiences of their bodies and the public spaces comprising the precinct in ways that adversely affected their capacity to engage in harm reduction. Frequent police searches, for example, discouraged participants from carrying the injection equipment they needed to ensure that they could inject with a sterile syringe. Constant monitoring of local public spaces made it difficult for homeless women and men to inject safely.

Hazardous Chemical Exposures

While on the job, officers are often exposed to chemical hazards.[92] Chemical hazards are classified as solids, liquids, or gases that enter the body through inhalation (the most common), ingestion (often food contamination), or absorption. Depending on the nature of the substance, the magnitude of the exposure, and the length of time of the exposure will determine the outcome of the effect. Researchers in one study report that hyperinsulinemia was associated with increased all-cause and cardiovascular mortality in police officers independent of other risk factors, although these associations weakened with the lengthening of the follow-up period. The association of insulin with noncardiovascular mortality was U-shaped.[93] Cancer is the eventual outcome routinely experienced by officers from chemical exposures.[94] This outcome is consistent with several mortality studies.[95] Lung disease, cardiovascular abnormalities, skin rashes, and blood-related diseases are other prevalent diseases associated with chemical exposure. Airborne particles (dusts, mists, and fumes) can be absorbed easily and often without the immediate knowledge of the victim.

Biological hazards include infectious microorganisms, plant or animal toxins, and animals or the pets of victims at crime scenes. Biological hazards can cause viral hepatitis, cause allergic reactions such as those linked to molds, deplete oxygen, or produce toxic gases.

Hazardous Materials

The potential for officers to be exposed to hazardous materials is significant; investigating traffic accidents can be a source of exposure. Also, more than 4 billion tons of chemicals are transported yearly by surface, air, and water routes; nearly one million individuals are directly involved in the transportation process. When accidents occur, law enforcement officers are usually the first responders. To clarify the magnitude of this issue, the Agency for Toxic Substances Disease Registry developed the Hazardous Substances Emergency Events Surveillance (HSEES) system. Fifteen state health departments participate in HSEES through cooperative agreements.[96]

What HSEES system information has shown:

- Approximately 9,000 hazardous substance releases occur annually in the fifteen reporting states.
- Releases at facilities account for up to 75 percent, and transportation-associated releases account for up to 30 percent of reported events.
- Most releases occur on weekdays between 6 a.m. and 6 p.m.
- Releases tend to increase in spring and summer.
- Equipment failure and human error cause most releases at facilities.
- Human error and equipment failure cause most releases during transport.
- More than 90 percent of events involve the release or threatened release of only one hazardous substance.
- Releases of hazardous substances most often injure employees, followed by the general public and—less frequently—first responders and schoolchildren.
- Respiratory irritation and eye irritation are the most commonly reported symptom or injury.
- Approximately 50 percent of people who reported developing symptoms or injuries from a HSEES event are treated at a hospital and released.

Clandestine Methamphetamine Labs

Hazards imposed by raids on clandestine methamphetamine (clan meth) laboratories are a huge issue among law enforcement officers including federal officers, too.[24] For example, the El Paso Intelligence Center (EPIC) reports 11,210 meth seizures year ending 2012 across the US.[97] An estimate in officers might suggest 6 officers minimum per raid or 67,260; what we don't know is how many of these officers participated in more than one raid. According to information learned from a tri-county drug task force member in North Carolina, and a former student, is three raids a year; therefore, approximately 22,420 law enforcement officers participated in clan meth raids in 2012 across the

[24] Meth is a Schedule II controlled substance; it's a powerful central nervous system stimulant and is more potent than amphetamines. It has legitimate medical uses for treating some illnesses such as narcolepsy, yet it remains a lethal and unpredictable drug when abused.
Source: G. Hargreaves (2000, April). Clandestine Drug Labs. The FBI Law Enforcement Bulletin, 64(4): 1.

country. Caution: the above are estimates and not reliable because what we also don't know is the actual number of clan raids because many departments don't necessarily report their drug activities unless the department is part of a tri-county taskforce or the taskforce is operating on federal grant money. The EPIC explains further that Kentucky police raided 1,585 clan meth labs in 2012, but the Indiana State Police raided 1,700 meth labs in 2013.[98] Each and every time a clan meth lab is raided, law enforcement personnel are at risk.[99]

Exposed officers to active lab activities have a seven- to fifteen-fold greater risk of becoming ill during response activities as compared to exposures to setup, in-transit, and former labs.[100] Those officers also have a greater chance to physical hazards such as spills, fires, explosions, and uncontrolled reactions. Carpeting, wallboard, ceiling tile, and fabric can absorb spilled or vaporized chemicals. Furniture and drapes can become contaminated. For example, in Wisconsin, a meth lab was discovered in Grant County by the Southwestern Wisconsin Meth Task Force.[101] While no responders were injured the local hazmat team dressed in protective clothing and looked through the country house for hazards that needed to be contained.

Dale A Stork/Shutterstock, Inc.

It was discovered that many chemicals were on-site and the operator had been "cooking" the drugs in nearly every room and the basement of the residence. The site was so contaminated from chemical residue that it had to be razed.

Different Way to Manufacture Meth 2014

Just when law enforcement's experiences linked to clan labs has been enhanced and perfected, like everything else, a new method to produce the product has been learned.[102] The Violent Crime Drug Task Force in Tulsa County seized five pounds of crystal meth made in a conversion meth lab in which "only a partial step in the manufacturing process is carried out and/or raw or unrefined drug precursors are chemically altered into a new chemical that is used on the street as the final product," Maj. Shannon Clark says. "It's a new way to develop methamphetamine." And added that "It's a quick way."

Deputies serving a search warrant at an auto sales business discovered the lab and immediately noticed that what they had found was not consistent with the one-pot, or shake-and-bake labs to which they're accustomed. The deputies say that they had never seen this type of lab before adding that "the drug crystallized on the investigators' gloves as they seized the various components." It was learned that a Dallas tri-county drug unit in the same time frame had a similar experience. More than likely, by the time this book is in press (June 2015) clan labs across the country will manufacture their product in a similar fashion.

Clan Lab Raids Can Lead to Dead Officers and Lawsuits

Police across Texas often violate the Constitution and put the lives of both officers and civilians at risk by entering homes unannounced.[103] There is a widespread problem of officers bursting into homes because many law enforcement bodies do not have written rules specifying when enforcement officers must first knock.

"Not having a solid policy in place exposes the police and people in the house to personal danger and sets the police up for liability in a federal lawsuit," says the Texas Police Chief's Association (TCRP) Director Jim Harrington. For example, a man suspected of growing marijuana fatally shot a Burleson County sergeant investigator who entered his home unannounced near Houston as part of a team executing a search warrant for drugs. A grand jury dropped a murder charge against the shooter, but indicted him for alleged marijuana possession while possessing a deadly weapon, the Bryan Eagle reported.

"It is a natural inclination to protect one's home at night when unidentified individuals suddenly burst through the front door," the (TCRP) says accompanying the "Police Overuse of No-Knock Entries" report. The lack of formal rules allegedly gives officers too much discretion and makes it easy to violate Fourth Amendment protections.

Police forcing their way into residences without first identifying themselves entered the spotlight after a controversial 2009 search by police. Officers entered the home of two women; the women were handcuffed and interrogated for an hour. The women filed a federal lawsuit and though their case was first dismissed, the U.S. Fifth Circuit Court of Appeals ruled police violated their Constitutional rights.

Dead Bodies

Law enforcement officers are often exposed to dead bodies at crime scenes, accidents, suicides. All dead bodies are potentially infectious, although most organisms in the dead body are unlikely to infect healthy persons.[104] However, what about those individuals who died but had infectious diseases prior to their death? To minimize the risks of transmission of known and also unsuspected infectious diseases dead bodies should be handled in such a way that the body fluids and tissues are away from an officer's touch. Staff training is highly recommended and only highly trained officers should service dead bodies. This information above is well and good but it doesn't happen that way. Many times officers are involved in situations that occur momentarily and other times officers are involved with dead bodies through natural disasters. Relying on their training is essential towards public safety and the well being of officers.

Dead Bodies after Natural Disasters

Following natural disasters, there is often concern that the bodies of victims can cause epidemics amongst surviving populations.[105] Sometimes these thoughts lead to inappropriate burial of the dead without proper identification of the victims. There are risks of infection from dead bodies after a natural disaster occurs such as Hurricane Katrina as discussed in Chapter 1. Many problems arise from handling, isolating those bodies, and disposing of those bodies.

Disease Transmission

Requires the presence of an infectious agent, exposure to that agent, and a susceptible host as mentioned in Chapter 2. These elements are considered to characterize the infectious disease risk from dead bodies.[106] However, victims of natural disasters usually die from trauma and are unlikely to have acute or "epidemic-causing" infections. This indicates that the risk that dead bodies pose for the public is extremely small. However, persons who are involved in close contact with the dead—such as police officers, military personnel, rescue workers, volunteers, and others—may be exposed to chronic infectious hazards, including hepatitis B virus, hepatitis C virus, HIV, enteric pathogens, and Mycobacterium tuberculosis. Suitable precautions for these persons include training, use of body bags and disposable gloves, good hygiene practice, and vaccination for hepatitis B and tuberculosis.

Disposal of bodies should respect local custom and practice where possible. There is little evidence of microbiological contamination of groundwater from burial.[107]

After the Meth Raid

After law enforcement raid and shut down a clan meth lab, there remains danger to those contracted to clean the premises.[108] Meth stays in the walls for up to a year, experts say. Building service contractors, maid services, and carpet cleaners hired to clean a structure after a meth lab raid have been exposed to meth and the chemical to produce meth. It is a highly specialized field of cleaning. There are no written standards for those companies or one right way of doing the job, consequently there are numerous accidents. Special remediation efforts are necessary after a team completes its work, such as testing the quality of indoor air, dictates part of the procedure.

Tuberculosis (TB)

TB is a disease caused by a bacterium called Mycobacterium tuberculosis (TB).[109] The bacteria usually attack the lungs, but TB bacteria can attack any part of the body such as the kidney, spine, and brain. If not treated properly, TB

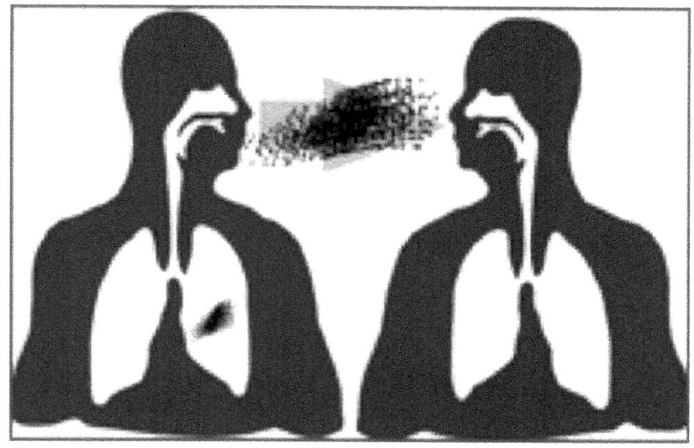
Source: CDC

disease can be fatal. TB is spread through the air from one person to another. The bacteria are put into the air when a person with TB disease of the lungs or throat coughs, sneezes, speaks, or sings. People nearby may breathe in these bacteria and become infected: recall disease transmission: it requires the presence of an infectious agent, exposure to that agent, and a susceptible host.

For example, when a police officer breathes in TB bacteria when aiding an injured person perhaps in a car wreck, the bacteria can settle in the lungs and begin to grow. From there, they can move through the blood to other parts of the body, such as the kidney, spine, and brain. As though fighting crime and dangerous felons is not enough, the LAPD is being confronted with another dangerous threat: the recent outbreak of tuberculosis.[110]

Scientists from the Center for Disease Control and Prevention (CDC) have been dispatched to the Los Angeles area to collaborate with the LAPD and public health officials to contain the highly contagious disease and to stop it from spreading. This particular strain is unique to the Los Angeles area. Statistics indicate that nearly eighty cases of tuberculosis have been reported since 2007. The majority of those cases are among people who live in the Skid Row area. Health officials have estimated that approximately 4,600 people are at risk of contracting TB, due to their exposure to the disease. Police officers have been instructed not to confront the homeless in particular because of this threat. Similar to most airborne viruses, prevention remains the key strategy for reducing CHD mortality.

Evidence Room Contamination

When the employees at a police department in Kentucky expressed concern about potential exposures and health effects when working in the evidence vault used to store drug evidence, their agency contacted the National Institute for Occupational Safety and Health (NIOSH) to request a Health Hazard Evaluation (HHE).[111] Drugs in the vault included marijuana, cocaine, methamphetamine, heroin, and oxycodone.

Prior to the NIOSH HHE, police department employees filed a complaint with the Kentucky Labor Cabinet, Occupational Safety and Health Program. An industrial hygienist from this program performed air sampling for mold outdoors and indoors in the drug vault. Compared to the outdoor air sample, the indoor air sample had similar (or lower) levels of Aspergillus mold. However, the indoor air sample had much higher levels of Chaetomium mold that typically grows in soil or decaying plant matter (for example, on the roots of marijuana plants).

Identified in the drug vault were terpenes—chemicals produced by plants such as marijuana that contribute to their taste and smell. Drug particles present a potential health risk to the employees because of their known physiological and neurological effects at high doses. We know less about the health effects from low-level exposures to illicit drugs over extended periods of time. Employees reported nonspecific health symptoms, most commonly upper-respiratory symptoms, headaches, eye irritation, and skin rash.

Some of the more notable recommendations for Drug Evidence Rooms from NIOSH include:

- Dispose of drugs frequently to reduce the amount of material.
- Dry marijuana and other plant-based drugs prior to storage.
- Replace the organic vapor and particulate filters in the drying chamber according to the manufacturer's guidelines, or more frequently if odors are detected in the drying chamber exhaust.
- After drying plant-based drugs, store them in sealed plastic bags.
- Maintain a relative humidity level of 30–50% to minimize mold growth.

Traffic Particles

Exposure to traffic particles is associated with an increase in the occurrence of acute myocardial infarction (AMI). A heart attack (also called an acute myocardial infarction or AMI) occurs when the arteries that supply oxygen and nutrients to the heart become blocked and the blood supply is slowed or stopped. The result is that the part of the heart muscle that is fed by the blocked arteries may be damaged or destroyed.[112] What is being said is that police officers (and people in general), especially those in or near cities, tend to be vulnerable to air pollution more often than officers in noncity environments.[113]

This thought is consistent with other researchers who offer a similar conclusion.[114] Another study shows that for specifically healthy young men in-vehicle (North Carolina State Troopers) experiences with air fine particulate matter (PM2.5) may cause physiological changes that involve inflammation, coagulation, and cardiac rhythm.[115] Researchers explain that more knowledge is needed on the effects in other organ systems if we are to identify and characterize the most effective and efficient means for reducing the still considerable adverse health impacts of ambient air PM.[116]

Benzene is an organic air pollutant. HHC classifies benzene as a human carcinogen.[117] Benzene is emitted into urban air supplies from motorized vehicles. Police officers directing traffic and riding in police vehicles during their entire shift especially those officers in urban environments are highly exposed to traffic pollutants; this thought suggests that these officers are exposed to traffic pollutants more often than others. Excessive or prolonged exposure could have a possible carcinogenic affect.[118]

Traffic Radar

All radar devices emit nonionizing radiation in the region of the electromagnetic spectrum referred to as microwave radiation.[119] Traffic radar devices are manufactured to emit one of three nonionizing frequencies: 10.525 gigahertz (GHz) in early radar devices, these devices also came to be known as X-band radars; after 1975, 24.15 GHz were designed which lies in the portion of the spectrum known as K-band in devices, and 33.4 to 36.0 GHz after 1990 is what is known as the Ka-band.

Traffic radar devices operate in a Doppler mode, meaning that they use the Doppler effect of a frequency shift in the signal reflected from a moving target vehicle to detect the speed of the vehicle. As Doppler radars these devices emit what is known as continuous-wave (CW) radiation. Theoretical approaches to biochemical mechanisms of tumor induction initiated by high frequency fields assume that proteins charge by heat shock may work as tumor promoters.[120] However, police officers experience few occupational exposures that might increase their cancer risk, and the few studies reported to date have generally reported no increase in cancer rates.[121] There are two reasons why I am addressing traffic speed radar: many officers have suggested that radar devices particularly handheld devices emanate microwaves linked somehow to cancer; it has been implied by scholars that radar can be a trigger in the development of cancer; the National Institute for Occupational Safety and Health (NIOSH) reported that exposure to emissions from police radar might increase the risk of leukemia and testicular, brain, eye, and skin cancers.[122]

Prevention from Disease

Each year, 5,000 to 6,000 workers in the United States die from acute traumatic occupational injuries. However, most hazards can be anticipated and prevented. One book, *Preventing Occupational Disease and Injury,* provides information to assist in assessing the potential for disease or injury, recognizing occupational diseases and injuries such as brain cancer, sick building syndrome and asthma, evaluating relevant data and designing and implementing control measures.

"Occupational safety and health education must extend to the general public, with basic concepts of prevention of occupational diseases and injuries introduced as elements of primary and secondary education," explains James A. Merchant, dean of the College of Public Health at the University of Iowa.[123]

Prevention from disease among law enforcement officers depends on four fundamental tasks:[124]

- Anticipation: of the potential for disease or injury.
- Recognition: of occupational disease and injury. Ongoing gatherings, analysis, and dissemination of data on the occurrence of disease and injury in law enforcement. Recognition can rely on existing data sources such as death causes, workers' compensation, or health records.
- Evaluation: for helping to determine if a causal relationship exists. Basic parameters of relevance when measuring exposure to chemical and physical hazards are concentration or intensity of exposure. Additionally, it is necessary to look at health outcomes associated with hazards.
- Control: the precautionary principle of the public health is to prevent illness and injury even in the absence of thoroughly documented hazards.

Spray Device

The latest weapon carried by Sanford, Florida, police officers does not fire bullets and would not do much damage if they hit you with it.[125] But the device officers in Sanford carry in their shirt pocket sprays a mist that might protect the officers in the event they are exposed to harmful bacteria or viral germs. The devices, which are slightly larger than a marker pen, spray a mist that protects against pathogens the officers might come in contact with, from being exposed to blood from an injured person to being spit in the face by a prisoner. Departments should look into reliable ways of aiding officers similar to firefighter organizations who stand on the front line of the well being of firefighters (see Chapter 7).

Police Subculture

Culture is a shared lifestyle; it has its own set of values, norms, and expectations for its members. In this sense, culture is a signifying system which represents a "whole way of life of a social group or whole society."[126] Occupational subcultures (individuals belong to a larger culture outside of work and an occupational culture or subculture) can be explained as one way in which occupational members cope with their working environment.[127] Since most members of a subculture share similar values, norms, and expectations, it could be said that within every organization, such as a police department, there may be more than one subcultural group; for example, traffic officers and commanders. To better understand this concept, culture is a learned lifestyle and a subculture suggests that many individuals share both the culture at-large and many also share in a learned lifestyle from the workplace, where we attend school, church, and at play. Members assimilate into subcultures in a similar way that they did their best to become a member of the larger societal culture perhaps where they live such as the south (i.e., they say "y'all" if they want to fit in) or the north. Police researchers have long speculated on the importance that culture plays in the everyday functioning of officers.[128] Earlier it was suggested that police officers tend to guide their individual healthcare requirements in order to satisfy their police subculture.

Therefore, a culture and a subculture are man-made aspects of social organization, and its influence can operate invisibly at deeper, almost mythic, or subconscious level. Some authors write entire books on culture and subcultural development, but what you need to know about a police subculture is that the occupation of policing develops its own way of doing business. For instance, it has its own terms and jargon which are used on a daily basis. Terms are used, for instance, to make verbal and radio communications easily understood and quick. Policing, as an occupation, has often been described as hours of boredom, followed by minutes of sheer terror. In any occupation where such extremes exist, it is necessary to have cultural characteristics which reinforce the collective and impersonal nature of the work.[129] In part, this working personality develops its own customs, laws, morality, and language or esoteric terms to communicate with each other and to control situations.[130]

Officers band together to make sense of their experiences and to protect themselves from the uncertainties of the job, which includes the organizational structure and their supervisors. A police subculture enables a wide variety of police activities on the job and off the job. It links together the experiences of officers in order to:

- make sense of those experiences
- to provide justification to continue police work
- to help an officer balance the inconsistencies of the organization and the job[131]

Some refer to police culture as the thin blue line, but in essence, it is a shared lifestyle which also provides a support group for its members which the police organization has little, if any, control. One result of a subculture whether it's a subculture of children, cops, or community members is that peer pressure plays a significant role in influencing the performance of its participants. Also it is not a far reach to describe peer pressure as part of any cultural perspective because groups depending on many variables take on expectations and rules of its own. The police culture (similar to most subcultures) members encourage and justify attitudes and performance. Therefore, finding a balance between policy and practice can be justified by a police subculture.

Research confirms that well entranced officers in a police subculture regard the police organization and their superiors as "bullshit."[132] Therefore it is safe to say that a police subculture aids officers toward finding a balance when dealing with (real or imagined) inconsistencies of their police experiences. Health issues fall into a "sissy" or "no-tell" model among most street cops and most public service workers including correctional officers discussed in the last chapter and firefighters in the next chapter. Even in surveys, cops (corrections officers and firefighters) practice a "no-tell" about their health. For example, in a survey consisting of almost 3,000 public service workers about occupational exposures (OEs) and risk of hepatitis B virus (HBV) infection, almost 7 percent reported infection through syringe stick, cut with a contaminated object, mucous membrane exposure to blood, and being bitten by a human.[133] The rate of OE varied by occupation in this order: police officers, corrections officers, sheriff officers, and firefighters. In a final analysis, based on survey data, the researchers say that HBV infection prevalence is comparable to the overall US prevalence and did not vary by occupation. HBV infection was not associated with any OEs, but is associated with older age, being nonwhite, and a previous history of a sexually transmitted disease (each of these variables are not necessarily linked to the police subculture as strongly as other variables; old personnel don't care, and being nonwhite with a history of STD can make you an outsider). Their conclusion: "This study demonstrated that although OEs are not uncommon among PSWs, HBV infection was more likely to be associated with nonoccupational risk factors."

The truth of the matter is far different. "Most of the police Brian knew with more than 10 years of (police) service were dealing with some kind of medical or psychological issue."[134] Also consider all of the evidence reported above about disease transmission.

The police subculture also helps officers rationalize and justify their attitudes and behavior, on the job and at home, even when those attitudes and activities are inappropriate or unlawful.[25] At its extreme, a police subculture can widen the "us" (officers) and "them" (management and even citizen) gap. However, it could be speculated that if a police organization enhanced its professional standing and controlled its inconsistencies by reducing or controlling its bureaucratic foundations that the influence of the police subculture would be doomed or at least weakened.[135]

[25] You might say that officers 'redefine' accounts of their activities in keeping with compliance issues in order raise above any possible litigation or harassment from suspects. (See Chapter 5 and 11 for more details). Redefining accounts can for some officers open the door for corruption. However, most officers move toward justice by 'redefining' an account in order for a prosecutor to 'charge' and convict a defendant and to help the victims of crime or accidents. Chapter 11 talks about professionalization of officers in order to officers to perform their jobs at quality levels. Source: Dennis J Stevens (2008). Police Officer Stress: Sources and Solutions. Upper Saddle River, NJ: Pearson. Page 365, 370.

Changing Police Subculture

Greater attention must focus on the various causes and impacts of occupational stress and mental anguish among officers, as well as how these relate to the law enforcement subculture.[136, 26]

On the other hand, researchers suggest something we already know—policing is a high-stress occupation in which exposure to potentially traumatic events is common, and resistance, resilience (bouncing back), and recovery from exposure to potentially traumatic events are essential to maintaining the health and effectiveness of police officers.[137] Therefore, one assumption that can be drawn is that manipulating or eliminating the police subculture could further the risks of officers; without a support system how much longer would it take talented men and women to perform his or her job? It takes one corrupt cop to make an entire department look bad; if management changes up the biggest threat—them and ridiculous redundant policy maybe officers would have a better chance of keeping themselves orientated in an appropriate manner. In a study of 319 Boston police officers (233 males and 86 females), 63 percent reported that supervisors employ intimidation methods to keep them controlled and a similar response was about the objectivity and professionalism of supervisors.[138] Then, too, hire right from the get-go which means worthy pay, benefits, and training. See Chapter 10 for more recommendations on how to resolve many of the issues confronting law enforcement officers.

[26] **Law Enforcement Subculture**
Law enforcement's common but dangerous subculture poses one of the most significant risks to the health and wellness of its personnel. This subculture leads officers to feel that they need to act as though they can handle anything; it emphasizes individual strength and independence, which encourages personnel to maintain a façade of invincibility. Out of fear that they will appear weak, police officers generally do not encourage each other to talk about their problems. They may cry at the funerals of their fallen warriors, but they usually avoid talking about their deepest wounds or fears. Law enforcement personnel represent the "good guys," yet many officers seem to forget or ignore their own humanity.
Source: see endnote Mark Malmin (2012, April).

Summary

Law enforcement practitioners have an increased incidence of health problems including exposure to infectious disease and MRSA (IPM) because of their at-risk occupational environments and because of the police subculture. Female officers face unique stressors as a result of working in a male dominated occupation including work factors, such as perception of inadequate physical ability, sexual harassment, and discrimination. However, female officers seek professional help both physiological and psychological, and emotionally support other women officers in meaningful ways which implies that they handle stress better as a group than male officers. Just for the record, female officers tend to be better equipped to deal with many street situations because they do not necessarily represent a threat to suspects or the audience observing the encounter.

Sworn officers were defined leading to a discussion on the idea that in criminal justice there are no right or wrong answers—everything depends on how the evidence is presented. The key elements linked to the mission of law enforcement were detailed such as reducing danger (as opposed to escalating danger).

Five assumptions about the police organizations were acknowledged as were social control issues and disease transmission to officers.

The social environment was characterized as shaping our behavior and concepts of human life, and it was pointed out that the rule of law is all that stands between us and anarchy. Statistics were provided about the numbers of officers assaulted and murdered.

Officer liability linked to syringe sticks, hazardous chemical exposures, hazardous materials, clandestine methamphetamine labs, dead bodies, TB, evidence room contamination, traffic particles, and radar were offered. Finally, a discussion about police subcultures was offered providing a student with a pretty good idea as to how it works and the consequences of eliminating police subcultures.

Name: ______________________________ Date: ____________ School Identification Number: ______

STUDENT WORKSHEETS

Chapter 6 Law Enforcement Officers and Compliance Issues

Define the following key terms from Chapter 6, and in your answer, show the page number where you found the definition. Provide an example for each key term.

1. Cardiovascular Disease (CVD)

2. Clan Meth

3. Crime Displacement

4. Culture

5. Disease Transmission

6. Fragmented

7. Latent and Manifest Function

8. Judiciously

9. Police Subculture

Name: ______________________ Date: ____________ School Identification Number: ________

10. Social Environments

11. Stop and Frisk Policy

12. Syringe Stick Injuries

13. Sworn Officers

14. Title 42 USC, Section 1983

15. Terry Stops

16. Zero Tolerance

Name: ________________________ Date: ____________ School Identification Number: ________

STUDENT WORKSHEETS

Chapter 6 Law Enforcement Officers and Compliance Issues

Discuss and demonstrate in your own words that you comprehend the following learning objectives in this chapter.

1. Explain the daily health experiences of most law enforcement occupations compared with other occupations.
2. Identify the agents of compliance which impact law enforcement performance.
3. Describe the role of police officers in relationship to anarchy and government corruption.
4. Identify the key elements linked to the mission of law enforcement and explain which of those elements might be of the utmost importance to the department; in what way would those elements impact the public the most.
5. Identify the mission of law enforcement components and relate those components to officer gender. In what way would the typical male or female officer be prepared to address each component while engaged in a police action or a 911 call?
6. Identify the five assumptions about local law enforcement in America and explain in what way one of the five might impact the positive healthcare of police officers the most.
7. Discuss the perspective about law enforcement's use of force policy and explain in what way those policies appear to be advantageous or disadvantageous to officers and to the American public.
8. Articulate the way social environments affect police officer exposure to deadly pathogens.
9. Explain how the following comment lends itself to officer health issues including exposure to infectious diseases: the law on the books is not "what law is."
10. Describe in what way police legitimacy relates to law and order and officer health issues.
11. Characterize the relevance of drug syringe sticks in relationship to police officers and methods on reducing syringe sticks.
12. Describe the consequences to officers arising from hazardous chemical skills.
13. Explain the hazards to police officers of clandestine methamphetamine (clan meth) laboratories.
14. Describe some of the methods of prevention of disease among police officers. In what way could some of those recommendations be put into operation?
15. Characterize the police officer subculture, and explain how it impacts exposure to deadly pathogens and healthcare of officers; how can the subculture be reduced, and what consequences might follow if it were reduced?

CHAPTER 6 ENDNOTES

1. John M. Violanti (2014). *Dying for the Job: Police Work Exposure and Health*. Springfield, Illinois: Charles C. Thomas Publisher. Page 3. Also see, Dennis J. Stevens (2008). *Police Officer Stress: Sources and Solutions*. Upper Saddle River, New Jersey: Pearson. Page 4.
2. Tara A. Hartley, Cecil M. Burchfiel, Desta Fekedulegn, Michael E. Andrew, and John M. Violanti (2011). Health Disparities In Police Officers: Comparisons To The U.S. General Population. International Journal Emergency Mental Health, 13(4): 211–220. Also see, Tara A. Hartley, Desta Fekedulegn, Cecil M. Burchfiel, Anna Mnatsakanova, Michael A. Andrew, and John M. Violanti (2014). Health Disparities Among Police Officers. In John M. Violanti (Ed.) *Dying for the Job: Police Work Exposure and Health*. (Pages 21–40). Springfield, Illinois: Charles C. Thomas Publisher.
3. Tara A. Hartley, Anna Mnatsakanova, Cecil M. Burchfiel, and John M. Violanti (2014). Stressors and Associated Health Effects for Women Police Officers. In John M. Violanti (Ed.) *Dying for the Job: Police Work Exposure and Health*. (Pages 93–108). Springfield, Illinois: Charles C. Thomas Publisher.
4. Franklin H. Zimmerman (2014). Cardiovascular Risk in Law Enforcement. In John M. Violanti (Ed.) *Dying for the Job: Police Work Exposure and Health*. (Pages 41–51). Springfield, Illinois: Charles C. Thomas Publisher.
5. Michael Wirth, John E. Vena, and James Burch (2014). Risk of Cancer Incidence and Cancer Mortality among Police Officers. In John M. Violanti (Ed.) *Dying for the Job: Police Work Exposure and Health*. (Pages 57–73). Springfield, Illinois: Charles C. Thomas Publisher.
6. John M. Violanti, Desta Fekedulegn, Tara A. Hartley, Michael E. Andrew, JK Gu, and Cecil M. Burchfiel (2013). Life Expectancy In Police Officers: A Comparison With The U.S. General Population. *International Journal of Emergency Mental Health*, 15(4):217–228.
7. Oliver Morgan (2004). Infectious Disease Risks From Dead Bodies Following Natural Disasters. Rev Panam Salud Publica, *American Journal of Public Health*, 15(5):307–312.
8. John M. Violanti (2014). Page 3.
9. Tara A. Hartley, Cecil M. Burchfiel, Desta Fekedulegn, Michael E. Andrew, and John M. Violanti (2011).
10. Tara A. Hartley, Anna Mnatsakanova, Cecil M. Burchfiel, and John M. Violanti (2014). Stressors and Associated Health Effects for Women Police Officers. In John M. Violanti (Ed.) *Dying for the Job: Police Work Exposure and Health*. (Pages 93–108). Springfield, Illinois: Charles C. Thomas Publisher.
11. Dennis J. Stevens (2008). *Police Officer Stress: Sources and Solutions*. Upper Saddle River, New Jersey: Pearson. Pages 184–189.
12. Joanne Belknap (2014). *The Invisible Woman: Gender, Crime, and Justice*. Belmont, CA: Wadsworth Contemporary Issues. Page 491.
13. Explanation of the Standard (1992). Occupational Exposure to Bloodborne Pathogens. Washington, DC: US Department of Labor. Section 9—IX. Summary and Explanation of the Standard. Retrieved June 11, 2014: https://www.osha.gov/pls/oshaweb/owadisp.show_document?p_table=PREAMBLES&p_id=811
14. John M. Violanti (2014).
15. Dennis J. Stevens (2008). Page 2. Also see, Chief Charles H. Ramsey (2002). Preparing the Community For Community Policing: The Next Step In Advancing Community Policing. In Dennis J. Stevens (Ed.), *Policing and Community Partnerships*. Upper Saddle River, NJ: Prentice Hall. Pages 29–44.
16. María "Cuca" Robledo Montecel (2013). Education as Pathway Out of Poverty. Intercultural Development Research Association. Retrieved June 16, 2014: http://www.idra.org/IDRA_Newsletter/January_2013_Fair_Funding/Education_as_Pathway_Out_of_Poverty/#sthash.O5omyxAl.dpuf
17. John P. Crank (2004). Understanding Police Culture, 2nd edition. Cincinnati: Anderson. Pages 110–111.
18. Ancient Roman Bridges (N.D.). Retrieved June 17, 2014: http://www.mariamilani.com/ancient_rome/Ancient_Roman_Bridges.htm

19. Mark H. Chae and Douglas J. Boyle (2013). Police Suicide: Prevalence, Risk, and Protective Factors. Policing: *An International Journal of Police Strategies and Management,* 36(1): 90–118.
20. Dennis J. Stevens (2002). Civil Liabilities And Arrest Decisions. In Jeffery T. Walker, *Policing and the Law.* (Pages 53–71). Upper Saddle River, NJ: Prentice Hall.
21. Jerome H. Skolnick (1999, August). Ideas on American Policing: On Democratic Policing. *Police Foundation.* Page 8. Retrieved online June 10, 2014: http://www.policefoundation.org/content/democratic-policing
22. Sam Walker and Charles Katz (2011). *The Police in America, 4th edition.* New York: McGraw Hill.
23. William C. Dement (2004, April 23). Stanford University Center of Excellence. For The Diagnosis and Treatment of Sleep Disorders. 4th Annual FOCUS Conference on Respiratory Care and Sleep Medicine. Baltimore, Maryland.
24. Dennis J. Stevens (2003). *Applied Community Policing in the 21st Century.* Boston: Pearson Education. Page 38.
25. Dennis J. Stevens (1997). Urban Communities And Homicide: Why American Blacks Resort To Murder. *Policing and Society*, 8: 253–267.
26. Sam Walker and Charles Katz (2011).
27. American Bar Association (2014).
28. Dennis J. Stevens (2009). *An Introduction to American Policing.* Boston: Jones and Bartlett Publishers. Page 335.
29. Charles Crawford, and Ronald Burns (1998). Predictors of the Police Use of Force: The Application of a Continuum Perspective in Phoenix. *Police Quarterly,* 1(4): 41–63.
30. Dragana Kesic, Stuart D.M. Thomas, and James R.P. Ogloff (2013). Use of Nonfatal Force on and by Persons With Apparent Mental Disorder in Encounters With Police. *Criminal Justice and Behavior*, 40: 321–337.
31. William Terrill and Eugene A. Paoline (2013). Examining Less Lethal Force Policy and the Force Continuum: Results From a National Use-of-Force Study. *Police Quarterly*, 16: 38–65.
32. Anthony J. Micuccia and Ian M. Gommeb (2005). American Police and Subcultural Support for the Use of Excessive Force. *Journal of Criminal Justice,* 33(5): 487–500.
33. Bureau of Justice Statistics (2014). Local Police. Retrieved June 12, 2014: http://www.bjs.gov/index.cfm?ty=tp&tid=71
34. Jerome H. Skolnick (2011). Justice Without Trial: Law Enforcement in Democratic Society, 4th edition. New Orleans, Louisiana: Quid Pro, LLC. Page 4.
35. William Bratton (1999, February 28). Dispelling New York's Greatest Fear. *New York Times*, Section 4, page 19. Also see, Ronald D. Hunter (1994). Who Guards The Guardians? Managerial Misconduct In Policing. In Thomas Barker and David L. Carter (Eds.), *Police Deviance,* 3rd ed., (Pages 169–184). Cincinnati: Anderson.
36. John P. Crank (2004). *Understanding Police Culture*, 2nd edition. Cincinnati: Anderson. Pages 110–111.
37. US Census. Retrieved June 18, 2014: http://www.census.gov/topics/population.html
38. Robert A. Brown, Kenneth J. Novak, and James Frank (2009). Identifying Variation In Police Officer Behavior Between Juveniles and Adults. *Journal of Criminal Justice*, 37: 200–208.
39. Samuel Walker and Charles Katz (2012). *The Police in America. An Introduction*, 8th Edition. New York: McGraw Hill.
40. Dennis J. Stevens (2008). *Police Officer Stress: Sources and Solutions*. Upper Saddle River, NJ: Pearson. Page 10. Also, see Dennis J. Stevens (2004). Origins Of Police Officers' Stress Before And After 911. *Police Journal,* 77(2), 145–173. Dennis J. Stevens (2005). Police Officer Stress And Occupational Stressors: Before And After 911. In Heith Copes (Ed.), *Policing and Stress*, (1–15), Upper Saddle River, NJ: Prentice Hall. Dennis J. Stevens (1999). Stress and the American Police Officer. *Police Journal*, 72(3), 247–259. Dennis J. Stevens (1998). What Do Officers Really Think About Their Job. *The Journal*, 51(1), 60–62.
41. Wesley G. Skogan (2008). Why Reforms Fail. *Policing and Society: An International Journal of Research and Policy*, 18(1): 23–34.
42. Samuel Walker (2007). Police Accountability: Current Issues and Research Needs. Paper presented at the National Institute of Justice (NIJ) Policing Research Workshop: Planning for the Future, Washington, DC. Retrieved June 14, 2014: https://www.ncjrs.gov/pdffiles1/nij/grants/218583.pdf

43. David H. Bayley and Clifford D. Shearing (2001, July). The New Structure Of The Police: Description, Conceptualization, And Research Agenda. Washington, DC: US Department of Justice. Office of Justice Programs. NCJ 187083.
44. Damian Warburton (2004). Drawing The Thin Blue Line: The Reality Of Who Controls The Police. *Police Journal*, 77(2): 135–144.
45. J.B. Stinchcomb (2004). Searching For Stress In All The Wrong Places: Combating Chronic Organizational Stressors In Policing. *Police Practice and Research,* 5: 259–277.
46. Jerome H. Skolnick (2011). Page 208. http://books.google.com/books?hl=en&lr=&id=4IHWq5A31IoC&oi=fnd&pg=PT19&dq=%E2%80%A2+The+police+cannot+nor+should+they+attempt+to+control+crime+or+police+healthcare+alone.+In+a+democratic+society,+the+public+has+a+responsibility+to+govern+themselves.+&ots=YzySgGw2Yy&sig=5QocLBjP4iPaIAqsYWncHT-V1iE#v=onepage&q&f=false
47. Raymond L. Goldsteen, Karen Goldsteen, and David G. Graham (2011). *Introduction to Public Health.* New York: Springer Publishing. Page 14.
48. Community Relations Service (1999). Police Use Of Excessive Force A Conciliation Handbook For The Police And The Community. Washington, DC: U.S. Department of Justice. Retrieved June 16, 2014: http://www.justice.gov/archive/crs/pubs/pdexcess.pdf
49. David H. Bayley and Clifford D. Shearing (2001, July).
50. Ronald D. Hunter (1994). Who Guards The Guardians? Managerial Misconduct In Policing. In Thomas Barker and David L. Carter (Eds.), *Police Deviance*, 3rd ed., (Pages 169–184). Cincinnati: Anderson.
51. Kent A. Sepkowitz and Leon Eisenberg (2005). Occupational Deaths among Healthcare Workers. *Emerging Infectious Diseases*, 11(7). Centers for Disease Control and Prevention. Retrieved May 14, 2014: http://wwwnc.cdc.gov/eid/article/11/7/pdfs/04-1038.pdf
52. A. Zuger and SH Miles (1987). Physicians, AIDS, and Occupational Risk. Historic Traditions and Ethical Obligations. *Journal of the American Medical Association*, 258:1924–1928.
53. FBI (2014). Uniform Crime Reports. http://www.fbi.gov/about-us/cjis/ucr/leoka/2012/officers-assaulted/assaults_topic_page_-2012
54. FBI (2014). Officers Feloniously Killed. Uniform Crime Reports. Retrieved June 12, 2014: http://www.fbi.gov/about-us/cjis/ucr/leoka/2012/officers-feloniously-killed/felonious_topic_page_-2012
55. Michelle Rindels and Justin Pritchard (2014, June 9). Police: Vegas Cop Killers Had Anti-Government View. *PoliceOne.com*. Retrieved June 13, 2014: http://www.policeone.com/police-heroes/articles/7269559-Details-emerge-in-deadly-ambush-on-Las-Vegas-cops/?utm_source=newsletter&utm_medium=email&utm_campaign=featuredNews&nlid=7265060
56. Ken Ritter and Michelle Rindels (2014, June 12). Slain Vegas Officer Mourned By 3K Cops At Funeral. Associated Press. Retrieved June 14, 2014: http://www.policeone.com/news_internal.asp?view=7284070
57. Bureau of Justice Statistics (2014). Local Police. Washington, DC: US Department of Justice. Retrieved June 10, 2014: http://www.bjs.gov/index.cfm?ty=tp&tid=71
58. Andrea M. Burch (2012). Sheriffs' Offices, 2007—Statistical Tables. Washington, DC: Bureau of Justice Statistics. US Department of Justice. Retrieved June 10, 2014: http://www.bjs.gov/content/pub/pdf/so07st.pdf
59. Broward County Sheriff's Officer (2014). Retrieved June 18, 2014: http://www.sheriff.org/about_bso/dle/districts/
60. Jon B. Gould and Stephen D. Mastrofski (2004). Suspect searches: Assessing police behavior under the U.S. Constitution. Criminology & Public Policy, 3(3), 315–362.
61. Cheryl Maxson, Karen Henningan, and David C. Sloane (2002, October 24). Not just a popularity contest: Factors that influence public opinion of the police. NCJRS. Washington, DC: U.S. Department of Justice, Office of Justice Programs.
62. Sam Walker (2001). Broken windows and fractured history. In Roger G. Dunham and Geoffrey P. Alpert (Eds.), Critical issues in policing: Contemporary readings, 4th ed. (Pages 480–493). Prospect Heights, IL: Waveland Press.

63. Eve Buzawa and C. Buzawa (1996). Domestic violence: The criminal justice response. Thousand Oaks, CA: Sage Publications. Also see Eve Buzawa, Gerald T. Hotaling, and Andrew Klein (2000, March). Response to domestic violence in a pro-active court setting—final report. NCJRS. Washington, DC: U.S. Department of Justice, Office of Justice Programs.
64. CNN News (2004, October 22). Boston Police Accept 'Full Responsibility' In Death Of Red Sox Fan: Woman Killed By Projectile Fired To Disperse Crowds. Retrieved June 18, 2014: http://www.cnn.com/2004/US/10/22/fan.death/ Friday, October 22, 2004 Posted: 3:54 AM EDT (0754 GMT)
65. Thomas Farragher and David Abel (2004, October 22). Postgame Police Projectile Kills an Emerson Student. Boston.com. Retrieved June 18, 2014: http://www.boston.com/sports/baseball/redsox/articles/2004/10/22/postgame_police_projectile_kills_an_emerson_student/?page=full
66. Associated Press (2006). Report: Police Errors Cited Student's Death; Discipline Possible. Retrieved June 18, 2014: http://usatoday30.usatoday.com/sports/baseball/al/redsox/2005-05-25-student-death-world-series_x.htm
67. City of Boston (2005, September 16). Boston Police Announce Disciplinary Findings. Retrieved June 18, 2014: http://www.cityofboston.gov/news/Default.aspx?id=2819
68. Damian Warburton (2004). Drawing The Thin Blue Line: The Reality Of Who Controls The Police. Police Journal, 77(2), 135–144.
69. Norm Stamper (2005). Breaking Rank: A Top Cop's Expose Of The Dark Side Of American Policing. New York: Nation Books.
70. Sam Walker (2001). Broken windows and fractured history. In Roger G. Dunham and Geoffrey P. Alpert (Eds.), Critical issues in policing: Contemporary readings, 4th ed. (Pages 480–493). Prospect Heights, IL: Waveland Press.
71. For instance, while writing this paragraph for another book (*Police Officer Stress*) in April 23, 2005, a Salem police officer who was also a student of the writer was on an extra detail controlling traffic while a roadway was being repaired. A motorist refused to obey the officer's directions and decided to drive through the uniformed officer sending him to the hospital in serious condition. It is unlikely the officer will be able to report to duty for a year or more. Unusual? Go back and look at the number of officers assaulted and killed which will confirm the idea that many officers are disrespected daily.
72. National Institute of Justice (2004, February). National Institute of Justice 2001 Annual Report. NIJ 195076. Washington, DC: U.S. Department of Justice. Office of Justice Programs. Retrieved December 5, 2014: https://www.ncjrs.gov/pdffiles1/nij/195076.pdf
73. Andrew Cohen (2003, March 3). Justices get tough on crime. CBSNews.com. Court Watch. Retrieved June 18, 2014: http://www.cbsnews.com/stories/2003/03/05/news/opinion/courtwatch/main542892.shtml
Also see, Christopher S. Koper (2002, March). Federal legislation and gun markets: How much have recent reforms of the federal firearms licensing system reduced criminal gun suppliers. *Criminology and Public Opinion,* 1(2), 151–178.
74. Jayne Marshall (1999, March). Zero Tolerance Policing. Retrieved June 18, 2014: http://www.ocsar.sa.gov.au/docs/information_bulletins/IB9.pdf
75. Evan Goldstein (2013, August 13). NYPD's Stop-and-Frisk Policy Ruled Unconstitutional. Drug Policy Alliance. Retrieved June 18, 2014: http://www.drugpolicy.org/blog/nypds-stop-and-frisk-policy-ruled-unconstitutional
76. Maribeth Conway (2010, July 27). Rockland Cop Pricked With Needle In Hingham District Court Bathroom. Retrieved June 18, 2014: http://www.enterprisenews.com/x466685563/Rockland-cop-stabbed-with-needle-at-Hingham-District-Court?template=printart
77. Dan Miller (2012, April 29). Lower Allen Township Police Officer Might Have Gotten 'Deadly Communicable Disease' After Pricking Finger On Suspect's Uncapped Needle. *The Patriot-News.* Retrieved June 18, 2014: http://www.pennlive.com/midstate/index.ssf/2012/04/lower_allen_township_police_of.html
78. Andrew Carr (2012, June 25). Man In Needle Case Found Not Guilty On Assault Charges. *The Sentinel Newspaper.* Retrieved June 19, 2014: http://cumberlink.com/news/local/crime-and-courts/trial-continues-for-man-accused-of-sticking-police-officer-with/article_c9182fec-bf3c-11e1-bb63-001a4bcf887a.html

79. Leo Beletskya, Grace E. Macalinob, and Scott Burrisc (2005). Attitudes of Police Officers Towards Syringe Access, Occupational Needle-Sticks, And Drug Use: A Qualitative Study Of One City Police Department In The United States. *International Journal of Drug Policy*, 16(4): 267–274.
80. The Foundation for AIDS Research (2011, May). Public Safety, Law Enforcement, and Syringe Exchange. Retrieved June 18, 2014: http://www.amfar.org/uploadedFiles/amfarorg/Around_the_World/TREAT_Asia/factsheetJan2010.pdf
81. A. Wodak and A. Cooney (2006). Do Needle Syringe Programs Reduce HIV Infection Among Injecting Drug Users: A Comprehensive Review Of The International Evidence. Substance Use and Misuse, 41(6): 777–813. Also see, Institute of Medicine (2006). Preventing HIV Infection Among Injecting Drug Users in High-Risk Countries. An Assessment of the Evidence. Washington, DC: National Academies Press.
82. Holly Hagan, James P McGough, Hanne Thiede, Sharon Hopkins, Jeffrey Duchin, and E. Russell Alexander (2000). Reduced Injection Frequency And Increased Entry And Retention In Drug Treatment Associated With Needle-Exchange Participation In Seattle Drug Injections. *Journal of Substance Abuse Treatment*, 19(3): 247–250.
83. J. Lorentz, J. Hill, and B. Samini (2000). Occupational Needle Stick Injuries in a Metropolitan Police Force. *American Journal of Preventive Medicine*, 18:146–150.
84. S.W. McCampbell and P.N. Rubin (2000). A Needle Exchange Program: What's In It for Police? *Police Executive Research Forum*, 14(10). Also see, C.S. Davis, and L. Beletsky (2009). Bundling Occupational Safety With Harm Reduction Information As A Feasible Method For Improving Police Receptiveness To Syringe Access Programs: Evidence From Three U.S. Cities. Harm Reduction Journal, 6:16.
85. S.L. Groseclose, B. Weinstein, T.S. Jones, L.A. Valleroy, L.J. Fehrs, and W.J. Kassler (1995). Impact Of Increased Legal Access To Needles And Syringes On Practices Of Injecting-Drug Users And Police Officers—Connecticut, 1992–1993. *Journal of Acquired Immune Deficiency Syndromes & Human Retrovirology*, 10(1):82–89.
86. The Foundation for AIDS Research (2011, May). Public Safety, Law Enforcement, and Syringe Exchange. Retrieved June 18, 2014: http://www.amfar.org/uploadedFiles/amfarorg/Around_the_World/TREAT_Asia/factsheetJan2010.pdf
87. Institute of Medicine (2006). *Preventing HIV Infection Among Injecting Drug Users in High-Risk Countries: An Assessment of the Evidence.* Washington, DC: National Academies Press.
88. The Foundation for AIDS Research (2011, May).
89. Holly Hagan, James P McGough, Hanne Thiede, Sharon Hopkins, Jeffrey Duchin, and E. Russell Alexander (2000). Reduced Injection Frequency And Increased Entry And Retention In Drug Treatment Associated With Needle-Exchange Participation In Seattle Drug Injections. *Journal of Substance Abuse Treatment,* 19(3): 247–250.
90. Will Smalla, Thomas Kerrc, John Charettea, Martin T. Schechterb, and Patricia M. Spittalb (2006). Impacts of Intensified Police Activity On Injection Drug Users: Evidence From An Ethnographic Investigation: Cities And Drugs: Responding To Drugs In The City of Vancouver, Canada. *International Journal of Drug Policy*, 17(2): 85–95.
91. Hannah Coopera, Lisa Mooreb, Sofia Gruskinc, and Nancy Kriegerd (2005). The Impact of A Police Drug Crackdown On Drug Injectors' Ability To Practice Harm Reduction: A Qualitative Study. Social Science & Medicine, 61 (3): 673–684.
92. John M. Violanti (2014).
93. Marja Pyorala, Heikki Miettinen, Markku Laakso, and Kalevi Pyorala (2000). Plasma Insulin and All-Cause, Cardiovascular, and Noncardiovascular Mortality: The 22-year Follow-Up Results of the Helsinki Policemen Study. *Diabetes Care,* 23(8): 10
94. Michael Wirth, John E. Vena, and James Burch (2014). Risk of Cancer Incidence and Cancer Mortality among Police Officers. In John M. Violanti (2014).
95. John M. Violanti (2014).
96. Centers for Disease Control and Prevention (2014). Fact Sheet: Hazardous Substances Emergency Events Surveillance System. Retrieved June 20, 2014: http://emergency.cdc.gov/surveillance/hsees.asp

97. El Paso Intelligence Center (2013). National Seizure System (NSS). Washington, DC: US Department of Justice. Retrieved June 15, 2014: http://www.justice.gov/dea/resource-center/meth-lab-maps.shtml
98. Indiana State Police (2014). Statistics for Clandestine Labs in Indiana. Retrieved June 15, 2014: http://www.in.gov/meth/2330.htm
99. J. Arballo (2008, May 16). The Police: Many Blame Health Problems on Years of Busting Meth Labs. Retrieved June 15, 2014: http://www.pe.com/reports/2008/methlegacy/stories/PE_News_Local_D_methutah18.1660026.html
Also see, L. Bruck (2007, September 2). Methamphetamine: Recipe for Disaster. Retrieved June 15, 2014: http://ehstoday.com/fire_emergencyresponse/ehs_imp_72459/
100. John M. Violanti (2014). Page 5.
101. David F. Peterson (ND). Hazardous Materials—Clandestine Drug Labs. Firehouse.com Retrieved June 24, 2014: http://www.health.state.mn.us/divs/eh/meth/lab/dpeterson.pdf
102. Amanda Bland (2014, April 12). Tulsa County Sheriff's Deputies Uncovered A Type Of Methamphetamine Lab New To Northeastern Oklahoma During A Raid Friday. *Tulsa World*. Retrieved June 15, 2014: http://www.tulsaworld.com/news/crimewatch/new-type-of-meth-lab-raided-in-tulsa-man-jailed/article_5bf71c0c-a421-562e-b628-2d5d536ae5f6.html?mode=print
103. Michael McLaughlin (2014, June 15). Texas Police 'No-Knock' Raids Often Violate Constitution And Risk Lives: Rights Group. *Huffington Post*. Retrieved June 15, 2014: http://www.huffingtonpost.com/2014/06/09/andrea-mears-hitting-man-drone-beach_n_5472709.html
104. John M. Violanti (2014). Page 9.
105. John M Violanti (2014). *Dying for the Job: Police Work Exposure and Health*. Springfield, Illinois: Charles C Thomas Publisher. Pages 8.
106. Oliver Morgan (2004). Infectious Disease Risks From Dead Bodies Following Natural Disasters. *Rev Panam Salud Publica, American Journal of Public Health*, 15(5):307–312.
107. L. Bruck (2007, September 2). Methamphetamine: Recipe for Disaster. Retrieved June 15, 2014: http://ehstoday.com/fire_emergencyresponse/ehs_imp_72459/
108. Jeff Cross (2004, January 21), Danger to Cleaning Pros Lurks in Meth Lab Sites. Cleanfax.com Retrieved June 15, 2014: http://www.cleanfax.com/articles/danger-to-cleaning-pros-lurks-in-meth-lab-sites
109. Centers for Disease Control and Prevention (2014). TB. Retrieved June 18, 2014: http://www.cdc.gov/tb/
110. Christal Sizemore (2013, March 4). LAPD Has More Worries than Just Guns and Criminals. *Law Enforcement Today*. Retrieved June 10, 2014: http://www.lawenforcementtoday.com/2013/03/04/lapd-has-more-worries-than-just-guns-and-criminals/#sthash.uhTTlJmf.dpuf
111. Kenneth W. Fent, Srinivas Durgam, Christine West, and John D. Gibbi (2008). Police Officers' Chemical Exposures in a Drug Vault. *Evidence Magazine*. Retrieved June 12, 2014: http://www.evidencemagazine.com/index.php?option=com_content&task=view&id=798
112. University of Michigan (2014). Heart Attack (Acute Myocardial Infarction—AMI). Retrieved June 18, 2014: http://www.uofmhealth.org/quality-safety/heart-attack
113. C. Tonne, J. Yanosky, A. Gryparis, S. Melly, M. Mittleman, R. Goldberg, S. von Klot, and J. Schwartz (2009). Traffic Particles And Occurrence Of Acute Myocardial Infarction: A Case-Control Analysis. *Occupational and Environmental Medicine*, 66(12): 797–804.
114. T. Lanki, J. Pekkanen, P. Aalto, R. Elosua, N. Berglind, D. D'Ippoliti, M. Kulmala, F. Nyberg, A. Peters, S. Picciotto, et al. (2006). Associations of Traffic Related Air Pollutants With Hospitalization for First Acute Myocardial Infarction: The HEAPSS Study. *Occupational and Environmental Medicine*, 63(12): 844–51.
115. M. Riediker, W.E. Cascio, T.R. Griggs, M.C. Herbst, P.A. Bromber, L. Neas, R.W. Williams, and R.B. Delvin (2004). Particulate Matter Exposure in Cars is Associated with Cardiovascular Effects in Healthy Young Men. *American Journal of Respiratory Critical Care Medicine*, 169: 934–940.
116. M. Lippmann (2014). Toxicological And Epidemiological Studies Of Cardiovascular Effects Of Ambient Air Fine Particulate Matter (PM2.5) And Its Chemical Components: Coherence And Public Health Implications. *Critical Reviews in Toxicology*, 44(4): 299–347.

117. John Violanti (2014). Page 9.
118. John Violanti (2014). Page 9.
119. Murray M. Finkelstein (1998). Cancer Incidence Among Ontario Police Officers. *American Journal of Industrial Medicine,* 34: 157–162.
120. B.D. Hardin (1992). Testimony. In *The Effects of Traffic Radar Guns on Law Enforcement Officers.* Hearing before the Ad Hoc Subcommittee on Consumer and Environmental Issues of the Committee on Governmental Affairs, United States Senate, August 10, 1992. Also see, John Violanti (2014), page 11.
121. Murray M. Finkelstein (1998). Cancer Incidence Among Ontario Police Officers. *American Journal of Industrial Medicine*, 34: 157–162.
122. W.G Lotz, R.A. Rinsky, and R.D. Edwards (1995). Occupational Exposure of Police Officers to Microwave Radiation from Traffic Radar Devices. National Technical Information Service Publication PB95-261350. Cincinnati, Ohio: NIOSH.
123. James A. Merchant and Luz Maritza (2012). *Preventing Occupational Disease and Injury, 2nd edition.* In press.
124. Barry S. Levy, Gregory R. Wagner, Kathleen M. Rest, and James L. Weeks (2005). *Preventing Occupational Disease and Injury,* 2nd edition. Washington, DC: American Public Health Association. Also see, John M. Violanti (2014). Page 4.
125. Gary Taylor (2009, November 4). Fla. Cops Have A New Weapon To Fight Germs. *Orlando Sentinel.* Retrieved June 13, 2014: http://www.policeone.com/police-products/infection-control/articles/1961964-Fla-cops-have-a-new-weapon-to-fight-germs/
126. Robin Williams (1981). *Culture*. London: Collins.
127. Eugene A. Paoline III (2003). Taking Stock: Toward a Richer Understanding of Police Culture. *Journal of Criminal Justice,* 31(3): 199–214.
128. Eugene A. Paoline III (2003).
129. SJ Harrison (1998). Police Organizational Culture: Using Ingrained Values To Build Positive Organizational Improvement. Journal of Public Administration and Management: An Interactive Journal, 3 (2), 17–24.
130. William A. Westley (1970). *Violence And The Police: A Sociological Study Of Law, Custom, and Morality.* Cambridge, MA: MIT Press. Also John P. Crank (2004). Pages 25, 182.
131. John P. Crank (2004). Page 3. Also see, Wayne W. Bennett and Karen M. Hess (2004). Pages 263–264.
132. Neal Trautman (2004). Corruption to Increase Dramatically. National Institute of Ethics. Retrieved June 20, 2014: http://connect.lawofficer.com/profile/NealETrautman
133. Francisco M. Averhoff, Linda A. Moyer, Bradley A. Woodruff, Adeline M. Deladisma, Joni Nunnery, Miriam J. Alter, and Harold S. Margolis (2002). Occupational Exposures and Risk of Hepatitis B Virus Infection Among Public Safety Workers. *Journal of Occupational & Environmental Medicine*, 44(6): 591–596.
134. Erika Hayasaki (2014, March 14). Life of a Police Officer: Medically and Psychologically Ruinous. The Atlantic. Retrieved June 20, 2014: http://www.theatlantic.com/health/archive/2014/03/life-of-a-police-officer-medically-and-psychologically-ruinous/284324/
135. Dennis J. Stevens (2008). Page 116.
136. Mark Maimin (2012, April). Changing Police Subculture. FBI Law Enforcement Bulletin. Retrieved June 20, 2014: http://www.fbi.gov/stats-services/publications/law-enforcement-bulletin/april-2012/changing-police-subculture
137. Michael E. Andrew, Janie L. Howsare, Tara A. Hartley, Erin M. McCanlies, Cecil M. Burchfiel, and John M. Violanti (2014). Protective Attributes: Resilience in Policing. In John M. Violanti (Ed.) (2014). (Pages 145–151).
138. Dennis J. Stevens (2006) Police Apprehension of Sexual Offenders and Sexual Assault Conviction Levels: Why Conviction Levels are Low in Boston. *Police Journal*, 79(2), 125–154.

Digital Storm/Shutterstock, Inc.

CHAPTER 7

Firefighters, Emergency Medical Technicians, and Compliance Issues

Learning Objectives

After you read this chapter, you will be better prepared to:

- Identify some of the challenging experiences of firefighters and Emergency Medical Technicians. In what way could some of those consequences have been avoided?
- Comprehend active shooter encounters and how the fire and police departments are developing new responses toward those encounters. In what way do you agree or disagree that the new model will aid firefighters and Emergency Medical Technicians to stay safe?
- Explain firefighter encounters with natural and manmade disasters and some of the consequences of those encounters to firefighters and Emergency Medical Technicians.
- Define Coronary Heart Disease (CHD), characterize its risk factors and its effect upon firefighters, and describe ways to alter this leading cause of in-duty death.
- Describe the relationship between fine particles and respiratory experiences for firefighters.
- Understand the dynamics of fire smoke and its consequences to firefighters.
- Characterize presumption law rationale and its politics; describe its influence upon firefighters and public funds. In what way do you agree or disagree with presumption laws?
- Detail some of the inconsistent evidence not necessarily supporting presumption laws.
- Describe some of the evidence supporting presumption laws.
- Identify and detail the prevention techniques recommended by NIOSH. Add other recommendations to the list that you think would be effective in saving firefighter lives.
- Characterize the healthy worker effect (HWE) and its influence on research outcomes as those outcomes might affect presumption law politics.
- Explain the author's final thoughts about firefighters and Emergency Medical Technicians and describe in what way you agree or disagree with those thoughts.

Key Terms

Active Shooter
Active Shooter Response
Arena of Violence
Automated External Defibrilator (AED)
Coronary Heart Disease
Emergency Medical Services (EMS)
Emergency Medical Technician (EMT)
Fire Suppression
Health Worker Survivor Effect (HWE)
Particulate Matter (PM)
Presumption Laws
Soft Posting Policy
Workmen's Compensation

Words of Wisdom

If the facts don't fit the theory, change the facts.

Albert Einstein

Introduction

Firefighters and Emergency Medical Technicians (EMT) personnel experience many unexpected issues in their daily routine on their occupation.

For example, in Missouri, a fast moving fire with several explosions caused by a faulty electrical strip killed three children and injured three others.[1] A meth lab was discovered in a back room of the home. Sometimes they encounter unexpected health issues, too. For example, an EMT was exposed to the secretions of Streptococcus pyogenes (S.pyogenes) from an infected child while providing CPR; the firefighter developed an infection of the hand and subsequent febrile illness with hypotension, erythematous rash, renal failure, and hypocalcemia (more later).[2]

In another case, a 47-year-old male firefighter collapsed after performing strenuous physical activity at the site of a trench rescue. Despite cardiopulmonary resuscitation (CPR) and advanced life support (ALS) administered by crew members, ambulance service personnel, and at the hospital's emergency department, the firefighter died.[3] Another example relates to a 50-year-old male volunteer Fire Chief responding to a medical call with his fire department, then responding alone to a separate incident involving a carbon monoxide alarm at a private residence.[4] The Chief found no carbon monoxide. Later, still alone the Chief called his wife and described symptoms of heart attack. She called 911 while the Chief retrieved an oxygen cylinder and a non-rebreather mask from the fire department's engine parked in the station's apparatus bay. The Chief was self-administering 100 percent oxygen when a certified emergency medical technician arrived. The Chief lost consciousness, CPR was initiated, but the EMT did not have an automated external defibrillator (AED);[1] the Chief died. An autopsy revealed arteriosclerosis, with 95 percent occlusion of the left main coronary artery and 90 percent occlusion of the right coronary artery.[2]

[1] An automated external defibrillator (AED) is a portable device that checks the heart rhythm. If needed, it can send an electric shock to the heart to try to restore a normal rhythm. AEDs are used to treat sudden cardiac arrest (SCA). SCA is a condition in which the heart suddenly and unexpectedly stops beating.

[2] Rapid access to an AED is probably the single most important determinant of outcome for an out-of-hospital cardiac arrest with ventricular fibrillation.

Source: NIOSH Alert (2007). US Department of Health and Human Services. See endnote.

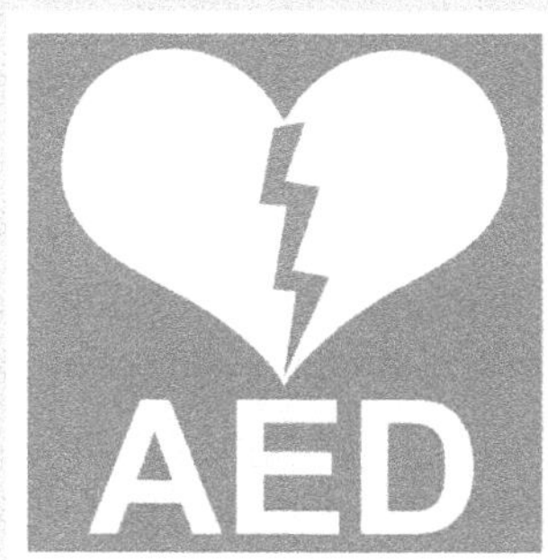

Semmick Photo/Shutterstock, Inc.

A 21-year-old firefighter died, another firefighter was overcome by heat stroke, and two others by heat exhaustion during the construction of a fire line during a small wildland fire which occurred in an area of steep slopes in southern California. The firefighters were in training all morning and went into action that afternoon.[5]

One last example; Saturday, June 21, 2014, in Washington, DC, firefighters from Truck 13 (Engine 10, Firehouse) were on the scene of a crash when a gunman opened fire.[6] The crash suspect returned to the scene and opened fire in a crowd of witnesses and the firefighters; no one was hit. Police did not return fire. DC has a "soft postings" policy. That is, firefighters have been ordered to leave their firehouse most nights and park their truck on the street for four hours at the highest high-crime corners throughout DC as they wait for fire and EMT calls.[3] Firefighters see soft posting as a form of punishment.

"It's got to be retaliation (by city administrators)," says Ed Lehan, a sergeant who works on Truck 13 at Engine 10. "We don't have any protection. We don't have bulletproof vests."[7]

After reading the above, you too might think that firefighters and EMT are pushed and regulated into many challenging experiences sometimes without their knowledge and sometimes without appropriate training or backup. Firefighters must rely on their training, co-workers, and supervisors; also they rely on powerful and professional organizations that represent them such as the International Association of Fire Fighters (IAFF) among others.[4]

Firefighters are also exposed in encounters with the agents of infection through disease transmission when responding to active shooter responses, natural and manmade disasters, and dead bodies. Firefighters, through daily circumstance of their daily occupational routines, also experience high rates of occupational fatalities and injuries as compared with other occupations other than law enforcement and correctional personnel which are detailed below.

Presumption laws to protect firefighters were developed to aid them when their work experiences affect their health which reduces the quality of their performance (see Appendix 1 for Employment Profile of Firefighters and Appendix 2 for Employment Profile of Emergency Medical Technicians (EMT); included is a discussion on the difference between EMT and emergency medical services personnel); yet some experts imply firefighters experience similar health issues as the general public and it follows that the benefits of presumption laws may be incongruous with their findings (detailed later).

Active Shooter Response

Unnoticed in the twentieth century yet becoming normative in the twenty-first century are police and firefighters training together as teams to aid victims during mass shootings by an active shooter.[5] Most fire department policies call for firefighters to "stand by," a new model engagement is on the horizon.

[3] **Washington, D.C., firefighters forced to shoulder more responsibilities**
Government officials in Washington, D.C., faced a storm of criticism after ordering local fire departments to help deter crime. While still expected to respond to emergency calls, these firefighters were forced out of the firehouse during overnight hours — a "soft post"— and positioned at key intersections throughout the city. The intent of the directive is to provide a visible reminder that first responders are in the area and can react quickly to any kind of public safety problem.

Source: Envisage Technologies (2014, February 18). Retrieved July 2, 2014: http://www.envisagenow.com/soft-posting-responsibilities-put-firefighters-at-risk/#sthash.9IQJZuVf.dpuf

[4] The International Association of Firefighters (IAFF) is a labor union representing professional firefighters in the United States and Canada. The IAFF was formed in 1918 and is affiliated with the AFL-CIO in the United States and the Canadian Labour Congress in Canada. The IAFF is headquartered in Washington, D.C., and has some 300,000 members in more than 3,200 locals and affiliates in every U.S. state and in Canada.

[5] **Profile of an Active Shooter**
An Active Shooter is an individual actively engaged in killing or attempting to kill people in a confined and populated area; in most cases, active shooters use firearms(s) and there is no pattern or method to their selection of victims.

tkemot/Shutterstock, Inc.

Active shooter situations are unpredictable and evolve quickly. Typically, the immediate deployment of law enforcement is required to stop the shooting and mitigate harm to victims. Because active shooter situations are often over within ten to fifteen minutes, before law enforcement arrives on the scene, individuals must be prepared both mentally and physically to deal with an active shooter situation. See Chapter 6 on dead bodies and circumstances on handling dead bodies.

Source: The Department of Homeland Security (DHS). Active Shooter Profile. Retrieved June 28, 2014: http://www.dhs.gov/sites/default/files/publications/active_shooter_educational_booklet_508.pdf

An unhappy employee disables the sprinkler system in his four-story office building.[8] During business hours, he secretly chains most of the stairwell doors closed on each floor. He retrieves gasoline that he stored in a utility closet (kept in cleaning agent bottles, so as not to attract notice) and pours it onto desks and chairs. He ignites the gasoline, knowing that the fire alarm activation will recall the elevators to the main floor. He shoots his co-workers who attempt to stop him.

As the fire continues to grow the world watches the smoke and some employees jump out of windows on live television, everyone asks a similar question: Why aren't firefighters making rescues? Fire and EMT personnel are on "stand-by" two blocks away, waiting for law enforcement to neutralize the active shooter and declare the scene safe.

Fire service policy is consistent with violent individuals who adapt new tactics.[9] Although the policy of "standing by" until the scene is safe, this policy has been effective at most violent incidents for firefighters, but necessarily helpful to victims.

Today, whether we describe a concept as a police escort, as force protection, or as Rescue Task Forces (the term used by Arlington County, Va., Fire Chief Jim Schwartz), the application is straightforward: law enforcement officers surround a small team of firefighters, EMTs, and medics. However, there are other models that are in the works such as active shooter preparedness.

Active Shooter Preparedness

Another plausible perspective other than surrounding firefighters is to train cops and firefighters together, or what is called active shooter preparedness. One reason this perspective might be relevant to your understanding of firefighters is that firefighters encounter (not to their choosing) victims, crime scenes, and violent people including the police. With this new model of response, firefighters are put into an arena of active violence which will impact their time to assess disease transmission potentials and the safety of victims including the perpetrators of the violence whom all take a priority over the personal safety of the firefighter. Recall from the active shooter description that there is no pattern or method to the selection of victims by an active shooter, and these events by their very nature are unpredictable and evolve quickly, advises DHS. Acknowledging that most firefighters similar to most law enforcement officers are highly inspired to help others, something I learned while engaged in field research, assessments, and hiring committees among criminal justice personnel over the years.

The Department of Homeland Security (DHS) aims to enhance preparedness through a "whole community" approach by providing training, products, and resources to a broad range of stakeholders on issues such as active shooter awareness, incident response, and workplace violence.[10] DHS offers free courses, materials, and workshops to better prepare firefighters to deal with an active shooter situation and to raise awareness of behaviors that represent pre-incident indicators and characteristics of active shooters.

Milwaukee

For example, moving in a diamond formation, police officers with drawn weapons and firefighters swept through the halls of Milwaukee middle school during a training exercise.[11] The scene was an active-shooter drill, part of a collaborative training effort between the Milwaukee fire and police departments that is unprecedented in the city. "We are a team," police Lt. James Mac Gillis explains to firefighters and officers.[12] "No teammate gets left behind. The Police Department's primary mission is to protect the team, and the Fire Department's mission is to treat the casualties."

St. Louis

More than 1,800 police and firefighters in St. Louis, Missouri, have participated in the Multiple Attack Counter Terror Action Capabilities, or MACTAC, training program aimed at preparing them and workers for a deadly mass shooting or terrorist attack.[13]

Denver

Hundreds of police, firemen, and paramedics gathered in Denver for training in rescuing injured people from mass shootings while an active shooter continues his or her shooting spree.[14] The various agencies used lessons learned from past mass shootings to find ways to rescue injured people during a gunfight.

"In general, fire department policies didn't allow them (firefighters or EMT) to go into an active shooter situation," Kellar says and adds, "The law enforcement would go after the shooter and bypass the injured." This policy has changed as you noticed from the above discussion. First responders know speed makes the difference between life and death for victims. The chances for survival increase the sooner a victim reaches a trauma center.

Firefighters and emergency medical technician response (EMT) through policy have changed slowly, but policy is changing. Firefighters and paramedics no longer are waiting for police officers to deem an area safe before treating the injured resulting often in their own victimization.

How police departments respond to shooting scenes has also evolved, from the first on-scene officers waiting for a critical incident or SWAT team to the officers pursuing an active shooter.[15]

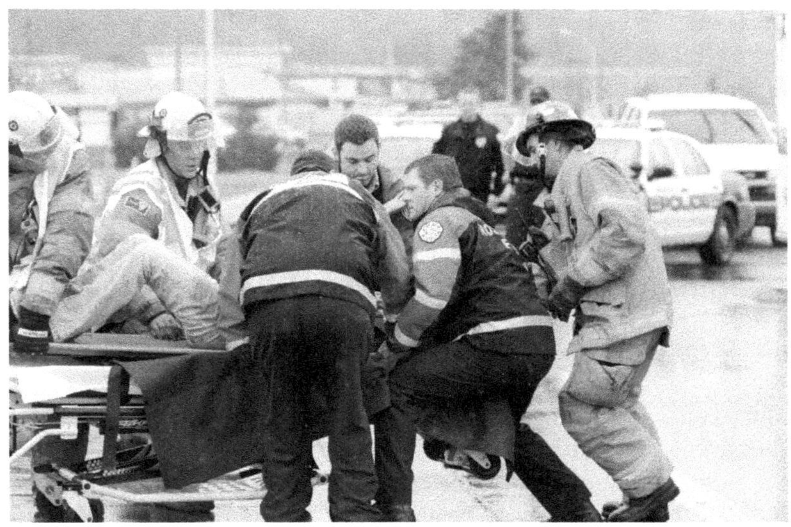

TFoxFoto/Shutterstock, Inc.

Response time is essential as you can imagine when it comes to a gunfight for victims or vehicle accident victims. A victim can bleed out from a gunshot wound in five to six minutes, and as an example, the Milwaukee Fire Department has extensive experience treating gunshot victims with a record of saving about 93 percent of those patients in 2011.

Duel training has many benefits to communities; some wish to push training into a combined single agency consisting of police and firefighters or public safety officers (PSO). Although a full discussion of PSO is beyond the scope of this chapter what you need to know right now is that both the International Association of Fire Fighters (IAFF) and the International Association of Fire Chiefs (IAFC) report that:[16,6]

Firefighters and Natural Disasters

Victims of natural disasters such as Hurricane Katrina as discussed in Chapter 1, according to scholars who lack practical experience, report that those victims usually die from trauma and are unlikely to have acute or "epidemic-causing" infections.[17] Those well intended scholars go on to suggest that first responders such as police, but equally likely firefighters and EMT personnel, share little risk with dead bodies from natural disasters because those dead bodies pose little if any threat. Yet, persons who are involved in close contact with the dead may be exposed to chronic infectious hazards, including hepatitis B virus, hepatitis C virus, HIV, enteric pathogens, and Mycobacterium tuberculosis, those scholars suggest.[18] Precautions include training, use of body bags and disposable gloves, good hygiene practice, and vaccination for hepatitis B and tuberculosis. Disposal of bodies should respect local

[6] Combining roles of the firefighters and police officers is a concept that challenges and undermines the career firefighter's role as a guardian of public safety. It also replaces the function and unit of a fire department that can rapidly assess and respond to many hazards . . . (these combined roles are) unacceptable for the fireground, urgent care and other situations where citizen and public-safety personnel's lives are dependent on rapid intervention. *Source:* see endnote IAFF and IAFC.

custom and practice where possible. When there are large numbers of victims, burial is likely to be the most appropriate method of disposal. There is little evidence of microbiological contamination of groundwater from burial.

Yet, caution is strongly advised because it was clearly implied from Hurricane Katrina's experiences (see Chapter 1) that many of the dead were prisoners, patients in long-term care facilities, and victims of previous homicides buried in swampland graves of Louisiana; their leftover parts were results of creatures who roam those wetlands—scavengers if you will.[19]

World Trade Center

The attack on the World Trade Center (WTC) on 9/11/2001 produced a massive dust cloud with acute exposure; the rubble pile burned over three months and exposed more than 300,000 residents, first responders including police, firefighters, and EMT, and rescue workers.[20] Most of those first responders experienced significant respiratory symptoms characterized by cough, dyspnea (shortness of breath), gastroesophageal reflux (food and liquid in stomach leak backward from stomach into the esophagus—the tube from the mouth to the stomach), and nasal stuffiness. Among those complaining of respiratory symptoms and normal spirometry (measuring of breath), almost half had abnormalities detected with impedance oscillometry consistent with distal airways' disease. Also, acute eosinophilic pneumonia (inflammatory condition of the esophagus) is a rare consequence of acute high dust exposure. World Trade Center dust consists of large particle-size silicates, but fly ash and asbestos fibers may be found in bronchoalveolar lavage cells.[21]

Leading Cause of Line-of-Duty Death among Firefighters

The leading cause of line-of-duty death among firefighters is sudden cardiac (pertaining to the heart) events stimulated through some level of coronary heart disease (CHD, discussed below).[22] These sudden cardiac events account for approximately 45 percent of all firefighter duty-related fatalities, and most of those firefighters dying from sudden cardiac events had CHD. Nonetheless, strenuous physical activity, emotional stress, and environmental pollutants all strain the cardiovascular system, and each can increase the risk of sudden cardiac events in susceptible (CHD prone or actual) individuals. Sudden cardiac death is more likely to occur during or shortly after emergency duties such as fire suppression, despite the fact that these duties comprise a relatively small proportion of firefighters' annual duties. Some experts are saying that firefighters are dying on the job from 'preventable cardiovascular conditions' (details below).[23]

> What you need to know right now is that a leading contributing factor to firefighter injury and death is lack of fitness.[24]

Therefore, the Fire Service Joint Labor Management Wellness-Fitness Initiative (WFI) was set a focus on providing fitness assessments to all fire service personnel.[7]

Here's how it works in the body: platelets (spiky cells found in the blood which are essential for health) play a critical role in the formation of an occlusive thrombus (stationary blood clot among the wall of a blood vessel) during an ischemic (local deficiency of blood supply) event. One study tested the effect of firefighting training among firefighters. As expected, performing any firefighting activity including training exercises results in significant increases in heart rate (75 beats per minute) and core temperature (0.7°C; the average normal human core temperature is around 98.2°F or 36.8°C, plus or minus 1.3°F (0.7 C) when taken orally), and significant changes in blood chemistry values. The most important finding is that even eighteen minutes of simulated firefighting triggered a 24 percent increase in platelet number and a significant increase in platelet aggregability. One implication is that short bouts of firefighting training can increase thrombotic (intravascular coagulation of the blood in any part of the circulatory system, as in the heart, arteries, veins, or capillaries) among healthy firefighters. So you can imagine the results of unhealthy firefighters. However, the literature reminds us that health among firefighters should be the first priority of all departments because health impacts heart disease.[25]

[7] Again it is union representation developing programs for firefighters. This wellness fitness initiative is sponsored by the International Association of Firefighters. For more details see: http://www.iaff.org/HS/Well/index.htm

Coronary Heart Disease (CHD) and Firefighters

Alan Bailey/Shutterstock, Inc.

Coronary Heart Disease (CHD) sometimes called coronary artery disease (CAD) accounts for the deaths discussed above and many others among firefighters while on duty and probably other justice personnel and individuals in extremely high to extremely low physical performance type occupations.[26, 8]

Because of the relevance in the relationship between CHD and firefighters, I thought it helpful to discuss CHD in a little more detail. Fact is, certain emergency firefighting duties are associated with a risk of death from coronary heart disease that is markedly higher than the risk associated with nonemergency duties. Fire suppression was associated with the highest risk, which was approximately 10 to 100 times as high as that for nonemergency duties (more details later).

Beyond all of the normal Coronary Artery Disease (CAD) risk factors: hypertension, hip-waist ratio, insulin resistance, age, physical inactivity, and high ratio of triglycerides to HDL cholesterol, it seems that exposure to carbon monoxide, hydrogen cyanide, and particulate matter in smoke further increase the likelihood of on-duty deaths.[27]

Coronary artery disease among firefighters is due to a combination of personal and workplace factors.[9] The personal factors are well-known: age, gender, family history, diabetes mellitus, hypertension, smoking, high blood cholesterol, obesity, and lack of exercise.[28] Not as widely known, however, is that firefighters have exposures to workplace factors that are associated with adverse cardiovascular outcomes such as fire smoke which is a complex mixture of heated gases, vapors, and particulate matter. The composition of the smoke is determined not only by the fuel source, but also by fire conditions (e.g., oxygen availability, temperature, etc.).[29] While hundreds of decomposition products are found, two of the more common and well-known gases with cardiovascular effects are carbon monoxide and hydrogen cyanide.

Mayo Clinic says that because coronary artery disease often develops over decades, it can go unnoticed until an individual has a heart attack. Mayo advises prevention has to do with a healthy lifestyle and a physically fit body; of course, you've heard this before.

Carbon Monoxide

Recall the fire chief above who died suddenly. Best bet—it was probably the carbon monoxide that triggered his heart attack, but he was in poor health. Carbon monoxide, a by-product of incomplete combustion, is present in virtually all fire environments. A number of studies have quantified a firefighter's exposure during various phases of fire suppression.[30] High concentrations of carbon monoxide have been documented not only during knockdown (to reduce the flame or heat on the more vigorously burning parts of a fire edge), but also during overhaul (most of the time, the hardest work comes after the fire. Overhaul. That's when you get the most dirty . . . and break the most stuff) when firefighters frequently remove their self-contained breathing apparatus (SCBA) (hint: the breathing apparatus stays on). If inhaled, carbon monoxide disrupts the blood's transport of, and intracellular use of, oxygen. The

[8] **Heart Disease** is a broad term used to describe a range of diseases that affect your heart. The various diseases that fall under the umbrella of heart disease include diseases of your blood vessels, such as coronary artery disease; heart rhythm problems (arrhythmias); heart infections; and heart defects you're born with (congenital heart defects). The term "heart disease" is often used interchangeably with "cardiovascular disease." Cardiovascular disease generally refers to conditions that involve narrowed or blocked blood vessels that can lead to a heart attack, chest pain (angina), or stroke. Other heart conditions, such as infections and conditions that affect your heart's muscle, valves, or beating rhythm, also are considered forms of heart disease.
Source: Mayo Clinic. http://www.mayoclinic.org/diseases-conditions/heart-disease/basics/definition/con-20034056

[9] **Coronary Artery Disease:** Coronary artery disease develops when your coronary arteries—the major blood vessels that supply your heart with blood, oxygen and nutrients—become damaged or diseased. Cholesterol-containing deposits (plaque) in your arteries and inflammation are usually to blame for coronary artery disease.
Source: Mayo Clinic. Retrieved June 27, 2014: http://www.mayoclinic.org/diseases-conditions/coronary-artery-disease/basics/definition/con-20032038

resulting hypoxia (deficiency in the amount of oxygen reaching the tissues) can cause myocardial infarction (pertaining to the muscular tissue of the heart).

Association between Fine Particles and Respiratory/Cardiovascular

There are a number of health-related concerns linked to firefighters' exposure to smoke particulates during fire suppression operations.[10] In 2010, the International Association of Firefighters (IAFF) and a federal agency, the US Fire Administration (USFA) jointly published a study focusing on respiratory diseases among firefighters.[31] The study reports that among firefighters respiratory disease is the result of "a career of responding to fires and hazardous materials' incidents; it is caused by breathing toxic smoke, fumes, biological agents, and particulate matter on the job." The study says that firefighters are at-risk of exposure to agents that cause respiratory disease. A number of exposures at fire scenarios are common combustion products that present respiratory disease hazards and include: acrylonitrile, asbestos, arsenic, benzene, benzo(a)pyrene and other polycyclic hydrocarbons (PAHs), cadmium, chlorophenols, chromium, diesel fumes, carbon monoxide, dioxins, ethylene oxide, formaldehyde, orthotoluide, polychlorinated biphenyls, and vinyl chloride.[32] Firefighters are also routinely exposed to respirable (small enough to be inhaled) particulate matter of liquids, hydrocarbons, soot, diesel fumes, dusts, acids from aerosols, and smoke. Health effects are produced by the particulates themselves, and by certain chemicals adsorbed into the particulates. The mixture of hazardous chemicals is different at every fire and the synergistic effects of these substances are largely unknown.

Other studies suggest particulate matter, as a component of air pollution, has adverse cardiovascular effects.[33] For example, long-term repeated exposure to elevated concentrations of particulate matter has been associated with cardiovascular mortality and the initiation /progression of atherosclerosis. In addition, short-term exposure to fine particulates has been associated with triggering heart attacks, particularly among firefighters with preexisting heart disease.

Particulate matter (PM) has been linked to a range of serious respiratory and cardiovascular health problems.[34] The key effects associated with exposure to ambient PM matter include: premature mortality, aggravation of respiratory and cardiovascular disease (as indicated by increased hospital admissions and emergency room visits, school absences, work loss days, and restricted activity days), aggravated asthma, acute respiratory symptoms, chronic bronchitis, decreased lung function, and increased risk of myocardial infarction.

Recent epidemiologic[11] studies estimate that exposures to PM may result in tens of thousands of excess deaths per year, and many more cases of illness among the US population and firefighters.[35] For example, long-term repeated exposure to elevated concentrations of PM matter has been associated with cardiovascular mortality and the initiation/progression of atherosclerosis. In addition, short-term exposure to fine particulates has been associated with triggering heart attacks, particularly among people with pre-existing heart disease.

[10] Fire Suppression is the marked reduction of the rate of heat release of a fire and the prevention of its regrowth by means of direct and sufficient application of water through the fire plume to the burning fuel surface.

ID1974/Shutterstock, Inc.

Source: McGraw-Hill Dictionary of Architecture and Construction. Retrieved June 27, 2014: http://encyclopedia2.thefreedictionary.com/Fire+suppression.

[11] Epidemiologic: branch of medicine that deals with the study of causes, distribution, and control of disease populations.

Increased Heart Rates and Heavy Physical Exertion

A significant portion of the firefighter's daily routine is spent at rest or doing light work around the fire station; similar to police and correctional officers who go from boring surveillance to huge excitement in a heartbeat. The fire station's alarm sounds at any time, and firefighters are expected to deploy rapidly to the incident scene. Firefighters react to these emergency calls with an increase in their heart rates, probably due to a surge in sympathetic nervous system activity (e.g., the flight or fight response). The increase in heart rate frequently persists through the course of fire suppression activities; a finding not surprising given the heavy physical demands of structural firefighting.[36]

The pattern of sedentary periods interrupted by catecholamine surges and heavy physical exertion has been suspected to put firefighters at increased risk for acute heart attacks. Recall the consequences of training presented earlier upon firefighters. Epidemiologic studies in the general population report that heavy physical exertion sometimes immediately precedes and triggers the onset of acute heart attacks and sudden cardiac death.

Heat Stress and Heat Illnesses

Heat stress and heat illnesses are well recognized hazards of firefighting. Fire suppression can increase body temperature resulting in sweating and fluid loss, which can cause serum electrolyte changes, lower stroke volume (the volume of blood pushed during each contraction of the heart), or lower cardiac output.[37] Heat stroke has been reported to increase the risk of myocardial ischemia, arrhythmias, and conduction abnormalities.[38]

Heat can also increase the risk of injuries in workers as it can produce sweaty palms, fogged-up safety glasses, and dizziness. Burns may also occur as a result of accidental contact with hot surfaces or steam.[39] Recall the young firefighter in the introduction who died and the others who were exposed to heat stress during the construction of a fire line during a wildland fire in the steep slopes of southern California. Of the crew interviewed by the employer, 80 percent had symptoms of heat illness. The young man who died had been ill the day prior to the incident. The ambient temperature at the time of the incident was 98°F and the relative humidity was approximately 30 percent. Investigators concluded that in order to prevent future occurrences, fire agencies should:[4]

- Require supervisors to regularly monitor firefighters, using generally accepted methods, during periods of high heat stress.
- Assure firefighters' workloads are appropriate for their level of acclimatization.
- Assure firefighters' workloads are appropriate for ambient weather conditions and clothing.

Workers at greater risk of heat stress include those who are sixty-five years of age or older, are overweight, have heart disease or high blood pressure, or take medications that may be affected by extreme heat.[12]

[12] Heat stroke is the most serious heat-related disorder. It occurs when the body becomes unable to control its temperature: the body's temperature rises rapidly, the sweating mechanism fails, and the body is unable to cool down. When heat stroke occurs, the body temperature can rise to 106°F or higher within ten to fifteen minutes. Heat stroke can cause death or permanent disability if emergency treatment is not given. Source: Centers for Disease Control and Prevention (2013). Workplace Safety and Health Topics. Heat Stress. Retrieved June 30, 2014: http://www.cdc.gov/niosh/topics/heatstress

[13] **Sounds of the City**

For reference, here are some familiar sounds and their decibel levels:

Whisper	30 dB*
Normal Conversation/Laughter	50–65 dB
Vacuum Cleaner at 10 feet	70 dB
Washing Machine/Dishwasher	78 dB
Midtown Manhattan Traffic Noise	70–85 dB
Motorcycle	88 dB
Lawnmower	85–90 dB
Train	100 dB
Jackhammer/Power Saw	110 dB
Thunderclap	120 dB
Stereo/Boom Box	110–120 dB
Nearby Jet Takeoff	130 dB

Sound levels vary greatly depending on your distance from the noise source.

*dB= decibels, the units for measuring sound.

[14] Decibels are the universal units of sound measurement. Decibels are measured using a meter that registers sound pressure and displays these readings on a scale. City meters are highly sensitive and undergo frequent calibration to ensure accurate readings. Some leeway is given to account for the sensitivity of the meters.

Source: New York City Department of Environmental Protection (2007). Bureau of Environmental Compliance. Retrieved June 30, 2014: http://www.nyc.gov/html/doh/downloads/pdf/epi/noise_code.pdf

Noise Exposure

Firefighters' noise exposures are obvious: sirens, air horns, diesel engines, and the roar of a large structure fire itself.[13] During emergency operations, sound levels exceeding 120 decibels have been measured.[14] Studies of community and occupational groups find a link between noise exposure and hypertension, and possibly a link with ischemic heart disease.[41]

It is important to note that firefighters' noise exposure (short duration, high intensity) differs from that studied in community and in other occupational groups [lower intensity for a longer duration (e.g., full-shift)]. Yet, given the extent of the noise-induced hearing loss found in firefighters, it is plausible that noise exposure increases the risk of hypertension and possibly ischemic heart disease among firefighters.

Streptococcus Pyogenes (Strep Throat) and Firefighters

Cases of a toxic shock-like syndrome have been reported in association with Streptococcus pyogenes (S. pyogenes—strep throat) infection. For example, in a case of a firefighter, mentioned in the Introduction of this chapter, exposed during attempted CPR to the secretions of a S. pyogenes-infected child, the firefighter developed an infection of the hand and subsequent febrile illness with hypotension, erythematous rash, renal failure, and hypocalcemia.[42] Bacterial isolates of blood and cerebrospinal fluid from the deceased child were identical in type and exotoxin production with isolates grown from the hand wound of the firefighter. Additionally, an evaluation of the relative importance of host and pathogen factors on the survival rates of patients with invasive S. pyogenes infection found a number of clinical and demographic factors to be associated with risk for death.[43] Of the 3,422 case-patients with severe S. pyogenes infection, almost 700 (20 percent) of those individuals died within thirty days after their evaluation for the above study began. Analysis of the cause of death includes: increasing age, diagnosis of necrotizing fasciitis (Flesh-Eating Bacteria, source webmd.com) or pneumonia, and underlying malignancy. Of those patents that died seven days after a diagnosis of severe S. pyogenes infection includes infectious and parasitic diseases, neoplasms, and diseases of the blood and blood forming organs.

Statistics of Fatalities and Injuries among Firefighters

The International Association of Firefighters (IAFF) reports that 1 in 50 firefighters are exposed to infectious diseases in the line of duty.[44,15] One estimate of fatalities per 100,000 firefighters is 16.5 (police 14.2) and a national average of 5.0 was consistent during the same time period.[45] The estimated rate of 12.7 fatalities per 100,000 (EMT) workers annually is also higher than the national average.[46]

However, Census of Fatal Occupational Injuries reports that the number of fatal work injuries among protective service occupations decreased 21 percent in 2012 to 224 fatalities—reaching the lowest count since the occupational series began in 2003.[47] The decline was led by lower numbers of fatal injuries to police and sheriff's patrol officers, which dropped 20 percent to 104 (includes homicide of officers presented in Chapter 3) in 2012 to continue a two-year downward trend. Fatal injuries to both security guards and firefighters reached series' lows with 48 and 17 fatalities, respectively.

Recall from Chapter 3 that syringe (needle) sticks for police were reduced when needle exchange programs were in place. You might like what Charles Aughenbaugh, Jr., President of the New Jersey Deputy Fire Chiefs Association says about needle exchange programs: "In the cities that have adopted needle exchange programs, there is a dramatic reduction in needle sticks to firefighters who crawl on their hands and knees through smoke-filled rooms to search for victims."[48]

[15] And their average pay is around $25,000. Details on EMT later.

Source: Bureau of Labor Statistics. (2014). Retrieved June 27, 2014: http://www.bls.gov/oes/current/oes533011.htm

Disease Transmission Data: The breakdown goes like this (of the 1 in 50): 5 percent were exposed to hepatitis B, over 10 percent were exposed to hepatitis C, 9 percent were exposed to human immunodeficiency virus, less than 1 percent were exposed to hepatitis A, almost 30 percent were exposed to tuberculosis, 11 percent were exposed to meningitis, 16 percent to blood/bodily fluids, and 19 percent were exposed to some other communicable disease, the IAFF reports.

The Census of Fatal Occupational Injuries database documented 91 EMT provider occupational fatalities.[49] The National EMT Memorial Service database contained 70 fatalities, and the Fatality Analysis Reporting System identified 8 ground-transportation EMT occupational fatalities. There was also wide variation in fatality counts by cause of injury.

Researchers estimate that there were at least 67 ground transportation-related fatalities, 19 air ambulance crash fatalities, 13 deaths resulting from cardiovascular incidents, 10 homicides, and 5 other causes, resulting in 114 EMT worker fatalities during a 6-year period.[50] One conclusion of the researchers is that occupational fatality rate for EMT workers exceeds that of the general population and is comparable with that of other emergency public service workers.

Slips, Trips, and Falls

Firefighters and EMT infrequently (but they do) experience physical slips, trips, and falls. The physical factors that may be related to slip-, trip-, or fall-related accidents are summarized by their intrinsic (balance, age, experience, muscular strength and fitness, body mass, fatigue) and extrinsic (equipment, reduced vision, surface condition, heat) nature.[51] Homeland Security advises that between 2006 and 2008, an estimated 81,070 firefighter injuries occurred annually. Of this number, 39,715 occurred on the fireground and 4,880 occurred while responding/returning from an incident.[52]

- The majority of fire-related firefighter injuries (87 percent) occur in structure fires. In addition, on average, structure fires have more injuries per fire than nonstructure fires.
- Thirty-eight percent of all fire-related firefighter injuries resulted in lost work time.
- Firefighter injury fires are more prevalent in July (10 percent) and peak between the hours of 2 and 5 p.m.
- Overexertion/strain is the cause of 25 percent of fire-related firefighter injuries.
- More than half of firefighter injuries (62 percent) result in no lost work time.

The medical and indirect costs of occupational injuries and illnesses are sizable, at least as large as the cost of cancer (see Chapter 1 for details).[53] Workers' compensation covers less than 25 percent of these costs, so all members of society share the burden. The contributions of job-related injuries and illnesses to the overall cost of medical care and ill health are greater than generally assumed.

Presumption Laws

The idea of providing financial assistance through state wage compensation (WC) benefits for firefighters has been around since the 1970s; however, an increasing number of states have proposed and enacted laws mandating that firefighters diagnosed with certain diseases be "presumed to have contracted such diseases while in the course of employment."[54] (Note: See Appendix 3 for a Summary of State Presumption Disability Laws.) Typically, when an employee is diagnosed with a disease or injury, the employee must prove that the disease or injury was a result of the employment in order to receive workers' compensation benefits. If, however, a statutory presumption of compensability exists then the employee's injury or disease is presumed to be a result of the employment. Currently, forty-two states have firefighter presumption laws of some type although the laws and its limitations are continually in flex probably because no one figured on the scope, payout, and legislative (lobby) power and determination of the organizations backing firefighters in particular such as IAPF and IC among others. During the 2013 legislative session, twenty-eight states attempted to introduce or revise occupational disease laws regarding firefighters. By facilitating benefits to firefighters and police who may develop cancers or heart disease related to employment, law makers acknowledge the unique exposures for the people who protect us. From my perspective, it appears that because of the strength of unions representing firefighters that more pay and benefits are assigned to them than law enforcement and correctional officers.

Presumption Law Rationale

In our technological and scholarly age we are increasingly dependent on having professionally drawn data to aid in informed policymaking decisions. In fact, report some scholars, there is good reason to worry about the old adage that "if it is not counted it didn't happen." This concern has encouraged the need to improve occupational health surveillance and entitlements.[55] Fundamental to effective occupational health surveillance and entitlements among firefighters and EMT in particular are *presumption laws*.

In a typical state workers' compensation case, the employee seeking to show work causation of an alleged injury bears the burden of proof.[56] Legislatures, however, can alter this arrangement by shifting or reversing the burden of proof, so that the responding employer bears the burden of showing lack of causation. The typical method of achieving this goal is by erecting a "presumption" of causation.[16] The injured worker, though bearing some burden to show that he is injured or diseased, and disabled, enters the courtroom with the law presuming the fact that the malady complained of arose in the court of employment and is medically related thereto.

Often, the burden of proof is on an employee to show that the "cause" of his or her illness or disability is directly derived from job performance in line with training and job regulations, unless a presumption position is in place. Public servants unable to perform his or her occupational responsibilities at the level expected because of health reasons encountered through the job might file for workers compensation or other forms of financial assistance and get it. With a typical public claim—a slip, fall, or car accident—the employee must prove that the injury was job-related. But in a claim based on a "presumption," the government has the burden of proving that the job did not cause the outcome or disease.[57]

> [16] Legal Definition of Presumption: A conclusion made as to the existence or nonexistence of a fact that must be drawn from other evidence that is admitted and proven to be true.
> *Source:* free legal dictionary.com/

Presumption statutes shift the 'burden of proof' from the claimant to the employer. For example, the state has the burden to prove that an employee did not get the virus (or whatever) at work, and if the state fails to carry out its burden, then the claimant shall be rewarded with compensation as prescribed.

The chain of causality seem vague: for public safety employees, any heart ailment caused by illness is compensable, unless the employer can trace the exposure to specific, non-work conditions.[58] Where the cause/exposure is unknown—as in most cases—there can be no outcome other than the awarding of benefits.

Recently, government officials have been complaining that they rarely win presumption cases, even to the point of presenting evidence that the worker's smoking, obesity, or family history were causal factors. The vagueness of it all has proven to be quite challenging due to significant data limitations and conflicting published studies on the link between certain occupational diseases and the firefighting profession. Also, firefighters are primarily employed by state municipalities and political subdivisions which are often self-insured entities. The self-insured market is not required to report data to outside organizations or the public for that matter. So what is known is merely 'an approximation of truth.'

Baltimore and Presumption Laws

The Chesapeake Employers' Insurance Company, which handles workers' compensation for the state of Maryland and many municipalities, paid out $10 million for all police and fire presumption claims since fiscal 2009 to 2014.[59] Mounting a legal challenge is difficult, even if a firefighter with lung disease was a heavy smoker for years an expert says. In Baltimore, presumption claims from firefighters and police have cost the city, on average, about $500,000 a year since 2009. The city is self-insured, meaning taxpayers cover all such costs.

California and Presumption Laws

The California state legislature recognized the significant health hazards to all firefighters. The following laws have been implemented under the aggressive sponsorship and lobbying by CPF.[60] These laws are intended to protect the rights and benefits of firefighters who become ill as a result of occupational exposures to hazards and the daily stress of the job. The optimum protection for all firefighters is active participation in an individual wellness and fitness plan, regular medical check-ups, the appropriate use of all personal protective equipment and on-scene safety precautions.

- Labor Code Section (Workers' Compensation in California)[61]
- Labor Code §3211.5 Presumption for Bio-Chemical Exposures (effective January 1, 2003)
- Labor Code §3212. Heart, Hernia, and Pneumonia Presumption (amended January 1, 2002)
- Labor Code §3212.1 Cancer Presumption (amended January 2012)
- Labor Code §3212.6 Tuberculosis Presumption (amended January 1, 2002)
- Labor Code §3212.8 Blood-Borne Infectious Disease and Methicillin-Resistant Staphylococcus
- Aureus (MRSA) Presumption (amended January 1, 2009)
- Labor Code §3212.85 Presumption for Bio-Chemical Exposures (effective January 1, 2003)
- Labor Code §3212.9 Meningitis Presumption (amended January 1, 2002)

Pennsylvania and Presumption Laws

In 2011, Pennsylvania lawmakers approved Act 46 of 2011—the Firefighter Cancer Presumption Law—which designates cancer as an occupational disease for firefighters and enables them to receive workers' compensation benefits if they develop cancer and can establish exposure to certain carcinogens at fire or hazmat incidents during their careers.[62] The new law provides broad mandates. According to the Pennsylvania Firefighter Cancer Coalition:

- The law applies to any cancer. Firefighters who have served four or more years will be entitled to a presumption that their cancer is job-related, similar to the process used when firefighters suffer from lung cancer, heart disease, or more recently, Hepatitis C.
- Firefighter cancer claims may be brought on behalf of any active or retired, career or volunteer firefighter who is being treated or has been treated for cancer, regardless of when the cancer was diagnosed or treated. [17]
- The law extends the period for filing claims to 600 weeks after separation from service. Firefighters who separated as long ago as January 2000 may be entitled to benefits.
- Firefighter cancer claims may also be brought on behalf of surviving family members of firefighters who died as a result of cancer. To qualify for benefits, surviving spouses or dependent children must file a claim within three years of the firefighter's death.
- Volunteer firefighters must participate in PennFIRS reporting to make a cancer claim, and must have passed a physical exam before their service that did not reveal the presence of cancer.
- Benefits may include retroactive and prospective salary and benefits, medical care for cancer treatment, and reimbursement for medical costs.

[17] Insurers are pulling workers' compensation coverage from cash-strapped municipalities in response to a 2011 law linking firefighting with increased cancer risks. Dubbed the Firefighters Cancer Presumption Act, Act 46 of 2011 recognizes every form of cancer found in a firefighter as a work-related illness. The onus to prove otherwise is on the municipality. Before the law, a claim could be filed going back 300 weeks. The law doubled that to 600 weeks. Anticipating an onslaught of claims, insurers are pulling out, including MRM Trust, which provided Clarks Summits' volunteer firefighters with workers' compensation, Borough Manager Virginia Kehoe said. "They were anticipating so many claims," Ms. Kehoe said. The borough turned to the State Workers' Insurance Fund and is now paying roughly $19,000 a year. Before Act 46, the borough was paying $14,000 a year. Source: Joseph Kohut (2013, April 29). State Law Leads To Workers' Comp Drops For NEPA Firefighters. TheTimes-Tribune.com. Retrieved June 26, 2014: http://thetimes-tribune.com/news/state-law-leads-to-workers-comp-drops-for-nepa-firefighters-1.1481071

British Columbia (BC), Canada, and Presumption Laws

To demonstrate that the US is not alone with presumption laws, under the Workers' Compensation Act in British Columbia, Canada, when a firefighter who was regularly exposed to the hazards of a fire scene contracts a prescribed occupational disease, the disease is presumed to be due to the nature of the worker's employment as a firefighter.[63] The Firefighters' Occupational Disease Regulation lists the following nine cancers as prescribed occupational diseases that are causally related to the occupation of firefighting:

- Primary leukemia
- Primary non-Hodgkin's lymphoma
- Primary bladder cancer
- Primary site brain cancer
- Primary colorectal cancer
- Primary kidney cancer
- Primary lung cancer
- Primary testicular cancer
- Primary ureter cancer

The Politics of Presumption Laws

In practice, presumption laws may create more problems than they solve. For insurance carriers it could set a precedence for other compensation groups; for the courts particularly courts sitting in judgment municipalities and counties that were WC self insured more litigation,[18] and for the stressed taxpayers who ultimately foot the bills, cases of questionable compensability can be shocking: the firefighter with lung cancer who smokes two packs a day, the obese police officer with heart disease, and the corrections officer with a flu-caused heart problem.[64]

For most personnel, the answer would be different. For the public safety employees covered by presumption laws, compensability is a given. Their safety net is woven of much finer cloth than that which protects most public employees.[19]

[18] Many municipalities and counties across the US were WC self-insured. Because of the presumption laws and rising benefits, those public entities wished to pull out of the WC business. When they did, lawsuits were filed; look over this suit from the Court of Appeals of New York. The defendants were the Village of Ilion et al., and the Plaintiffs, Village of Herkimer, Appellant, v. County of Herkimer, & c., Respondent, et al., Defendants. No. 80 Decided: May 1, 2014.

The primary issue in this breach of contract action is whether a municipality's liability upon withdrawing from a county self-insurance fund should have been discounted to present value. Under the circumstances presented, we hold that the withdrawal fee reflected benefits to be paid in the future and therefore should have been discounted to its current value as of the date it was due. Read more at http://caselaw.findlaw.com/ny-court-of-appeals/1665013.html

[19] Jimmy Walters worked for the Florida Department of Corrections. In December 2009, he came down with a cold, but continued to work for a week. He suffered from chills and nausea on his days off and then experienced chest pain. He went to a hospital, where he was treated for "heart symptoms" and subsequently diagnosed with myopericarditis and cardiomyopathy. He was hospitalized for several days. He filed a workers' comp claim, under Sec 112.18, the "firefighter's presumption" which creates a rebuttable presumption of occupational causation for disabling heart disease.

For most workers, there would be no conceivable issue of compensability for flu-caused heart problems, but most workers do not work in the public safety arena and most workers are not protected by presumption laws. The facts of the case were not in dispute: there was a direct causal relationship between Walters' stomach flu and subsequent heart problems.
Source: Jon Coppelman (2012, October 22). Presumption Laws: Wide Open Door to Benefits. Workers' Comp Insider. Retrieved June 25, 2014: http://www.workerscompinsider.com/2012/10/presumption-law.html

Dmitry Natashin/Shutterstock, Inc.

Inconsistent Evidence and Presumption Laws

The risk of infection with blood-borne pathogens such as hepatitis B virus (HBV) among public safety workers such as firefighter and EMT personnel is considered a high risk. Yet, in a study of almost 600 firefighters, only forty-six (8 percent) had past or current HBV virus infection.[65] Employees reporting blood contact with skin had been infected more often than employees without this exposure (11 percent vs. 6 percent). Prevalence of infection did not differ by age, years on the job, or job duties. The adjusted prevalence of hepatitis B virus infection among male employees (5 percent) was not significantly different than the prevalence in American men (7 percent). Although the overall risk of hepatitis B virus infection is not greater among fire department employees than the general population, blood contact with skin may elevate this risk.

In another study firefighters and EMT personnel have the potential for occupational exposures to blood, which increases their risk for occupational blood-borne infection. Researchers reviewed the literature of occupational blood exposures, the seroprevalence (the development of detectable specific antibodies to microorganisms in the blood serum as a result of infection or immunization) of blood-borne pathogens among these workers, and the seroprevalence (the number of persons in a population who test positive for a specific disease based on serology—blood serum—specimens) of blood-borne pathogens among the patients they serve.[66] Despite the expected findings, firefighters and EMT personnel do not have an elevated seroprevalence of hepatitis C virus compared with the general population.[67]

Although the nature of firefighting and EMT service intersects with seemingly health hazards, previous mortality and morbidity studies of those occupations have produced inconsistent evidence for an increased risk of mortality from cardiovascular disease, respiratory disease, cancer, and accidents.[68]

Mortality experiences since 1915 were examined in 5,655 Boston firefighters, comprising all male members of the city fire department with three or more years of service. The observed cause of death as stated on the death certificates of 2,470 deceased firefighters is compared with the numbers expected, based on rates for the male population of Massachusetts, and with the US. Among all firefighters, deaths from all causes were 91 percent of expected deaths. The standardized mortality ratio (SMR) was markedly reduced (less than 50) for infectious disease, diabetes, rheumatic heart disease, chronic nephritis, blood diseases, and suicide. The SMR was 86 for cardiovascular deaths, 83 for neoplastic deaths, and 93 for respiratory deaths. The SMR for accidents was 135 for active firefighters.

The results suggest that the survival experience of firefighters is strongly influenced by strict entry selection procedures, ethnic derivation, and sociocultural attributes of membership. While excessive morbidity has been demonstrated in firefighters, "there does not appear to be a strong association between occupation and cause-specific mortality," the researchers conclude.[69]

Other research supports the above conclusion. For example: [70]

- In 2009, a study on cancer among firefighters published by the National League of Cities (NLC) found that "there is a lack of substantive scientific evidence currently available to confirm or deny linkages between firefighting and an elevated incidence of cancer."[71]

The National Institute for Occupational Safety and Health (NIOSH) reports that despite its use of weaker standards for determining strength of association, the NIOSH study finds only "small to moderate increases in risk for several cancer sites and for all cancers combined, stemming mostly from excess malignancies of the respiratory, digestive, and urinary systems."[72]

Other evidence comes from the National Council on Compensation Insurance, Inc.'s (NCCI)—White Paper on Firefighter Presumptive Coverage (this organization might have a financial interest in presenting the evidence below).[73]

In many states, workers' compensation (WC) benefits for firefighters have been expanded, says NCCI, in order to account for the potential increased risk inherent in the nature of employment for firefighters. NCCI receives requests to estimate the probable cost impacts and potential consequences to WC system of such legislative changes. The NCCI notes that firefighters are the primary group they are discussing but realize the other public service personnel might be included.

Preventing On-Duty Cardiovascular Deaths

The National Institute for Occupational Safety and Health (NIOSH) reports that many on-duty cardiovascular deaths among firefighters can be prevented.[74] To reduce these deaths, NIOSH recommends that fire departments and firefighters:

- follow established medical screening guidelines
- adopt risk reduction measures during firefighting operations
- develop and participate in comprehensive wellness/fitness programs

Over twenty-five published studies examine the link between heart disease and firefighters or mortality literature in the last fifteen years. Conclusions of those studies are conflicting to say the least (e.g., some studies support the relationship of heart disease and firefighters, while others do not). In the late 1990s a reviewer of the firefighter mortality literature reports that "Sudden death, myocardial infarction, or fatal arrhythmia occurring on or soon after near-maximal stress of the job are likely to be [work] related…"[75] It may be relevant to acknowledge that similar to all scientific method studies, limitations do exist, but the framework is far superior to personal opinion because those studies can be replicated and hopefully similar results will come forth.[76]

But there are some serious concerns about the studies which are inconsistent with presumption laws.[77]

The Healthy Worker Effect (HWE)

The healthy worker effect (HWE) is a scholarly preference in health studies that are believed to have strongly affected the validity of previous cohort (group) mortality studies on the link between firefighting and heart disease and for that matter, studies evaluating the at-risk situations of many occupational groups including the police (Chapter 4), correctional personnel (Chapter 3), and healthcare professionals (Chapter 6). Think of it this way, one of the criterion for employment is a very positive health report.[20] There is a strong, healthy hired effect among firefighters, owing particularly to the recruitment of, for example, nondiabetic candidates.[78]

In previous studies in which the reported standardized mortality ratios for diabetes among firefighters are much less than unity, generally around 0.3 to 0.5, because diabetes is known to increase the risk of heart disease, a deficit of diabetes among firefighters is expected to lead to a deficit of heart injury and disease. This would make the cohort mortality studies incapable of detecting any increase in risk of heart injury and disease among firefighters. There is also a strong healthy worker survivor effect (another component of the HWE) among firefighters. In addition, heart disease is a classic example of the HWE because heart disease is chronic and its risk factors can be identified in the hiring selection process. It is believed that:

- a major problem of previous studies on firefighting and heart disease is their failure to recognize the importance of the HWE when interpreting their results
- a technique to re-assess results in light of the HWE is urgently needed.

[20] Firefighting is physically challenging as well. Applicants should be in excellent physical shape and should continue an exercise program to improve strength, flexibility, endurance, and agility. If applicants are in less than excellent physical condition, get a physician's clearance and begin immediately to improve. Source: Commonwealth of Massachusetts. Becoming a Firefighter. Public Safety. Retrieved June 28, 2014: http://www.mass.gov/eopss/agencies/dfs/dfs2/mfa-trng/becoming-a-firefighter.html

This above study addresses the generally accepted principles relating to HWE, including its definition and sources, and proposes a technique for reassessing the literature in light of the HWE. The model technique developed by the researcher was applied to carefully re-assess 23 studies that provided direct evidence for the relationship between firefighting and heart disease. Before the re-assessment, 7 of the 23 studies showed positive evidence and 16 showed no evidence. After the re-assessment, 11 studies showed positive evidence and 12 showed no evidence. Based on the results of the reassessment of the 23 studies, the researchers conclude that there is:

- strong evidence of an increased risk of death overall from heart disease among firefighters;
- insufficient evidence, even after considering the HWE, that there is an increased risk of death from aortic aneurysm among firefighters;
- insufficient evidence, even after considering the HWE, for a relationship between firefighting and any heart disease subtype, such as acute myocardial infarction.

One strong likelihood supporting the above perspective relates to hiring requirements. Recruits have largely better health than those not selected for the job and often better health than the general population to whom the workers are compared. For example, before placement, firefighter candidates are screened for many cardiovascular conditions and risk factors (e.g., diabetes and hypertension). This leads to a strong healthy hired effect, one component of the HWE.

Final Thoughts

I admit that objectivity is far more challenging than subjectivity (opinion) because it's easier, the results sound good, and those results would conform more often to the perspectives of some of my colleagues which would enhance my credibility and in turn enhance my friends at Facebook and my contacts at Linkin. But alas, I would love to write fiction and make more money. Nonetheless, researchers have frequently, even inadvertently, introduced errors while collecting, analyzing, and storing data of all types.[79] Such errors may lead to serious misinterpretations by both the original researcher and subsequent investigators; it would also open the doors to misconduct and behavior unbecoming of firefighters and their collaborative partners in law enforcement, the courts including prosecutors, corrections, and healthcare.

Only true experiments offer definitive evidence for causal inferences, but the fact of the matter is that not all activities, circumstance, or outcomes including psychological or behavioral interventions are readily amenable to experiments.[80] Some things cannot be measured. The above thought falls right into Einstein's admirable thought that "everything that can be counted does not necessarily count; everything that counts cannot necessarily be counted."

Researchers present causal inferences in relationship to presumption laws suggesting that firefighters and their partners experience similar health exposure risk as the general population; those researchers go so far as to imply that firefighters and their partners should not receive board sweeping benefits such as those covered under presumption laws. From my perspective, I ask: how likely is that I, as part of the general public and a university professor face similar health risks and personal safety as would a patrol officer, a firefighter, or a correctional officer? Assuming there are no other options, how likely is it that I will intentionally enter a student's dorm and put out a fire or deal directly with a terrorist, an active shooter, or someone bleeding in a car wreck?

In the scientific method of discovery, a procedure is in place regarding the problem formulation, methodology including the sample (if used) or instruments used, reliability, and validity.[81] Most of us tend to say that the "literature" is more reliable than opinion. I might agree but how do experienced and knowledgeable researchers decide which groups or which sample are more valid than another sample to observe in a study? The questions are about how we select choice-unobservable assumptions and how valid are those choices? Whether causal inferences or conclusions are reached by "smart psychologists observing people's smiles, smart neuroscientists observing fMRI data, smart empiricists observing happiness survey data, or smart economic theorists introspecting about which assumption about well-being seem attractive, these conclusion are reached based on something beyond observed choices and the rationality hypothesis."[82] Being objective or unbiased implies that we make professional decisions as opposed to subjective opinions. As Max Weber implied some time ago, to understand a fisherman, you have to walk in his shoes.[83,21] Walking in a fisherman's shoes, however, also means that you are trying to become a fisherman. When I assess police policy, do I wear a police uniform? Would the very individuals I am attempting to assess know that I am not a cop? Do I wear similar shoes as an extremely violent offender in a maximum custody penitentiary when evaluating his or her dangerousness to society? For me when observing, instructing, or leading a group encounter comprised of prisoners as a criminologist, my perspectives and focus are different from an attorney, psychologist, correctional officer, counselor, sociologist and so on. Each of us would bring his or her training and theoretical perspectives to the table and to his or her conclusions even if framed in similar evidence; each of us have a different emphasis or focus based on our own formal training and level of education; finally based on the university and the department where he or she completed our formal education would also impact our conclusions. For example, most of my graduate school professors had a University of Chicago state-of-mind about the social world and made reference to the exploitation of the masses on a daily basis in their classrooms. If you read any of the work or listened to my lectures, you probably heard the name of Karl Marx five million times. As objective as I am, the truth of the matter is that no one is unbiased particularly those of us with a lot of education.

I agree that official policies, strategies, and outcomes provided by the justice community are best served through evidence-managed or data-driven analysis, a product of the Scientific Methods of Discovery. I agree that to enhance firefighters (and criminal justice personnel and their collaborative partners) and to secure the democratic process, the firefighting community must utilize the best objective empirical studies to design, evaluate, and redesign public policy, but with the understanding that those empirical studies are biased.[84]

In a final analysis, some researchers neglect strategic characteristics of their samples; researchers with little practical experience in criminal justice or firefighting develop systematic and causal inferences or conclusions based on excellent textbook theory. Yes, there is a "but"; but this thought moves me back to the Words of Wisdom at the beginning of the chapter: "If the facts don't fit the theory, change the facts"—Albert Einstein. If this sounds to realistic for you, recall that earlier in this chapter and in Chapter 1 4, 5, 6, and 11 that officers redefine accounts to fit compliance regulations and to move toward a criminal charge and ultimately a conviction of a suspect. But also, to deter any litigation potentials linked to compliance issues. Yes, to redefine can open the doors to corruption but also to public safety. I get the impression that researchers and other professionals might unintentionally do exactly that. When evidence from a study, a crime scene, a corporate report, a medical or psychological evaluation, or a prosecutor's case does not support the theory or hypothesis as expected, tinker with the evidence and make it fit (their own agenda). For example, I can see a correlation between the scholarly inconsistences linked to firefighters and infectious exposures and some scholarly inconsistences linked to crime and punishment; for example, "It is frequently claimed that low

[21] Max Weber and Verstehen

Why do people act differently in each of their social groups? How have social groups, formal organizations, and society as a whole changed with time? These are questions that Max Weber, one of the founding fathers of sociology, would ask. He thought of sociology as a science of social action. Weber believed that understanding why people do the things they do is the basic building block of sociology, a concept he termed Verstehen (A German word that means to understand in a deep way. Source: Open Sociology Dictionary. Retrieved July 3, 2014: http://sociologydictionary.org/verstehen/) He believed that sociologists should not just study a group of people but also try to gain an empathetic understanding for the individuals in that group.

"Put yourself in his shoes" or "walk a mile in each other's shoes." This common sentiment illustrates what Verstehen is all about: gaining an understanding of social action from the insider's point of view in order to better understand the interactions within a group and the group's purpose. This, in turn, helps to explain how groups of people make sense of the world around them, how they fit into society as a whole, and how they've helped society evolve over time.

Source: Erin Long Crowell, see endnote. (2014). Max Weber and Verstehen. Retrieved July 3, 2014: http://education-portal.com/academy/lesson/bureaucracy-definition-characteristics-meaning.html#lesson

literacy is related to unemployment, a lack of aspirations, poor physical and mental health, and/or great deprivation, which can lead to crime."[85] That makes sense. Easy to connect low literacy and lack of wealth, too. Yet, affluent and often educated defendants tend to be released despite guilt particularly if they're white; conversely, poor and often illiterate defendants tend to be convicted despite innocence particularly if they're black or brown. There is a strong relationship between poverty, illiteracy, and criminal convictions (please note the word convictions) including high rates of wrongful convictions among poor illiterate and largely black and brown populations in the US.[86] For instance, government statistics report that in 2011, 70 percent of all new arrivals into prisons for violent crime convictions were black or brown as opposed to whites who numerically dominate the American population. Additionally, in death penalty jurisdictions, overzealous prosecutors can easily distort a criminal investigation to the extent that an innocent defendant can be pressured into offering erroneous testimony through the threat of facing the death penalty regardless of innocence or their race.[87]

The above thoughts are consistent with a prominent scholar's perspective that history is written by the privileged; history includes research, and in this sense, if the privileged are elegant theorists who articulate the professional standards of research and suggest that the general public's health risk is similar to firefighters and their collaborative partners then it is easy to venture that theory is actually that—theory as opposed to reality.[88] Perhaps a reason that firefighters reply on strong bargaining tools such as firefighter unions to serve and protect them (a position not as pervasive among law enforcement officers or correctional personnel) might be related to all those researchers who preach that the world is flat. In a final analysis, in keeping with the Constitutional spirit of the US, if the states are the laboratories of democracy then it is up to each state to enact its presumption laws in accordance with the wishes of the public since it's their dime or their property that burns faster depending on the motivation and skill of the firefighters.

In part, there is a coexistence of two contradictory sides (i.e., good and evil, life and death, freedom and law enforcement, war and peace, positive and negative poles, fire and water; each are as inseparable as they are opposed), their conflict, and their fusion develops into a new category; a matrix if you will. Karl Marx's perspectives imply that the world and everything in it is in a state of evolution. Everything is the same, but it's not. For instance, "every organic being . . . every moment it assimilates matter supplied from without, and gets rid of other matter; every moment some cells of its body die and other build themselves anew; in a longer or shorter time the matter of it is completely renewed and is replaced by other molecules of matter, so that every organic being is always itself and yet something other than itself."[89] Firefighting is also in a state of evolution if Marx thinkers are correct. But to become more productive, firefighters require similar protections that they professionally provide the rest of us against destruction. Similar to law enforcement, I don't think it prudent to consider the alternatives.

Summary

Several examples were provided suggesting that firefighters and emergency medical technicians (EMT) personnel experience many unexpected issues in their daily routine on their occupation. Becoming normative in the twenty-first century are police and firefighters training together as teams to aid victims in various circumstance. Yet it is reported that this training places firefighters into an arena of violence which will impact their time to assess disease transmission potentials and the safety of victims including the perpetrators of the violence whom take priority over the personal safety of the firefighter.

Victims of natural disasters such as Hurricane Katrina and disasters such as the World Trade Center, according to scholars, report that those victims usually die from trauma and are unlikely to have acute or "epidemic-causing" infections.

The leading cause of line-of-duty death among firefighters is sudden cardiac events stimulated through some level of coronary heart disease. However, there are a number of health related concerns linked to firefighters' exposure to smoke particulates during fire suppression operations. Also, two organizations jointly published a study focusing on respiratory diseases among firefighters. The study reports that among firefighters respiratory disease is the result of "a career of responding to fires and hazardous materials incidents; it is caused by breathing toxic smoke, fumes, biological agents . . ."

A significant portion of the firefighters' daily routine is spent at rest or doing light work around the fire station; similar to police and correctional officers who go from boring surveillance to huge excitement in a heartbeat, firefighters react to these emergency calls with an increase in their heart rates, probably due to a surge in sympathetic nervous system activity.

Heat stress and heat illnesses are well recognized hazards of firefighting. Fire suppression can increase body temperature resulting in sweating and fluid loss, which can cause serum electrolyte changes, lower stroke volume, or lower cardiac output. Heat stroke has been reported to increase the risk of myocardial ischemia, arrhythmias, and conduction abnormalities.

Studies of community and occupational groups find a link between noise exposure and hypertension, and possibly a link with ischemic heart disease. Cases of a toxic shock-like syndrome have been reported in association with Streptococcus pyogenes infection. One organization reports that 1 in 50 firefighters are exposed to infectious diseases in the line of duty. One estimate of fatalities per 100,000 firefighters is 16.5 and an estimated rate of 12.7 fatalities per 100,000 (EMT) workers annually, both are higher than the national average.

The idea of providing financial assistance through state wage compensation (WC) benefits for firefighters has been around since the 1970s; an increasing number of states have proposed and enacted laws mandating that firefighters diagnosed with certain diseases be "presumed to have contracted such diseases while in the course of employment." Fundamental to effective occupational health surveillance and entitlements among firefighters and EMT in particular are presumption laws.

In practice, presumption laws may create more problems than they solve, some argue, such as insurance carriers and municipalities, and counties that are self-insured.

Inconsistent evidence suggests that blood-borne pathogens such as hepatitis B virus (HBV) and other infectious pathogen exposures among firefighters is not significantly different than the general public. Some organizations say that many on-duty cardiovascular deaths among firefighters can be prevented.

The healthy worker effect (HWE) is a scholarly preference in health studies that are believed to have strongly affected the validity of previous cohort mortality studies on the link between firefighting and heart disease and for that matter, studies evaluating the at-risk situations of many occupational groups.

In a final analysis, I admit that objectivity is far more challenging than subjectivity because it's easier, the results sound good, and it conforms more often the perspectives of my colleagues. Yet, researchers have frequently, even inadvertently, introduced errors while collecting, analyzing, and storing data of all types. Such errors may lead to serious misinterpretations by both the original researcher and subsequent investigators; it would also open the doors to misconduct and behavior unbecoming of firefighters and their collaborative partners in law enforcement, the courts including prosecutors, corrections, and healthcare. It all comes down to—do we put out our own fires or do we let trained professionals do it for us.

Name: ________________________________ Date: ______________ School Identification Number: ______

STUDENT WORKSHEETS

Chapter 7
Firefighters, Emergency Medical Technicians, and Compliance Issues

Define the following key terms from Chapter 7, and in your answer, show the page number where you found the definition. Provide an example for each key term.

1. Active Shooter

2. Active Shooter Response

3. Arena of Violence

4. Automated External Defibrillator (AED)

5. Coronary Heart Disease

6. Fire Suppression

7. Emergency Medical Services (EMS)

Name: ______________________________ Date: ______________ School Identification Number: ________

8. Emergency Medical Technician (EMT)

9. Healthy Worker Survivor Effect (HWE)

10. Particulate Matter (PM)

11. Presumption Laws

12. Preventable Cardiovascular Deaths

13. Soft Posting Policy

14. Workman's Compensation

Name: ______________________________ Date: ____________ School Identification Number: ______

STUDENT WORKSHEETS

Chapter 7
Firefighters, Emergency Medical Technicians, and Compliance Issues

Discuss and demonstrate in your own words that you comprehend the following learning objectives in this chapter.

1. Identify some of the challenging experiences of firefighters and Emergency Medical Technicians. In what way could some of those consequences been avoided?

2. Comprehend active shooter encounters and how the fire and police departments are developing new responses toward those encounters. In what way do you agree or disagree that the new model will aid firefighters and Emergency Medical Technicians to stay safe?

3. Explain firefighter encounters with natural and manmade disasters and some of the consequences of those encounters to firefighters and Emergency Medical Technicians.

4. Define Coronary Heart Disease (CHD), characterize its risk factors, and its effect upon firefighters, and describe ways to alter this leading cause of in-duty death.

5. Describe the relationship between fine particles and respiratory experiences for firefighters.

6. Understand the dynamics of fire smoke and its consequences to firefighters.

7. Characterize presumption law rationale and its politics; describe its influence upon firefighters and public funds. In what way do you agree or disagree with presumption laws?

8. Detail some of the inconsistent evidence not necessarily supporting presumption laws.

9. Describe some of the evidence supporting presumption laws.

10. Identify and detail the prevention techniques recommended by NIOSH. Add to their list other recommendations that you think would be effective in saving firefighter lives.

11. Characterize the healthy worker effect (HWE) and its influence on research outcomes as those outcomes might affect presumption law politics.

12. Explain the author's final thoughts about firefighters and Emergency Medical Technicians and describe in what way you agree or disagree with those thoughts.

APPENDIX 1

Employment Profile of Firefighters

The duties of firefighters include fire prevention, emergency medical service, hazardous material response, search and rescue, and disaster assistance. Firefighters are:

- Trained in fire suppression
- Have the legal authority and responsibility to engage in fire suppression
- Are employed by a fire department of a municipality, county, fire district, or state
- Are engaged in the prevention, control, and extinguishment of fires or response to emergency situations

Also, as of May 2013 there were 302,870 full-time firefighters in the US.

- **Pay:** Median pay for firefighters is estimated at $48,270 per year or $23.21 per hour. Entry level qualifications are high school completion.
- **Job Outlook:** Employment of firefighters is projected to grow 7 percent from 2012 to 2022, slower than the average for all occupations. Physically fit applicants with high test scores and paramedic training should have the best job prospects. Of interest: California has 28,990 firefighters who earn an average of $34.44 per hour or $71,630 for the year. Florida has 23,750 firefighters who earn an average of $24.81 per hour or $51,610. New Jersey, New York, and California firefighters earn over $70,000 per year. Yet, San Francisco-San Mateo-Redwood City, CA, Metropolitan Division pays their firefighters $90,140. Pay sometimes doesn't mean a thing when an active shooter has his sight on you.

Source: US Department of Labor (2011). Fact Sheet 8: Law Enforcement and Fire Protection. Under the Fair Labor Standard Act (FLSA).

APPENDIX 2

Employment Profile of Emergency Medical Technicians (EMT)

The Bureau of Labor Statistics explains that emergency medical technicians (EMTs) and paramedics care for the sick or injured in emergency medical settings. People's lives often depend on their quick reaction and competent care. EMTs and paramedics respond to emergency calls, performing medical services and transporting patients to medical facilities. Most of the approximate 240,000 EMTs and paramedics work full-time. EMTs and paramedics experience a much larger than average number of work-related injuries or illnesses.

- **Entry Level:** All emergency medical technicians (EMTs) and paramedics must complete a postsecondary educational program. All states require EMTs and paramedics to be licensed; requirements vary by state.
- **Pay:** The median annual wage for emergency medical technicians (EMTs) and paramedics was $31,020 or $14.91 an hour in May 2012.
- **Job Outlook:** Employment of emergency medical technicians (EMTs) and paramedics is projected to grow 23 percent from 2012 to 2022, much faster than the average for all occupations.

Differences between EMT and EMS

There is some confusion in terms: EMT is not necessarily an EMS or emergency medical services person. Emergency medical technicians (EMTs) and paramedics care for the sick or injured in emergency medical settings and are usually certified to provide those medical services (more later on EMT's profile). An EMS usually drives an ambulance or assists an ambulance driver in transporting sick, injured, or convalescent persons. They also assist in lifting or moving patients. There are about 18,000 of EMS employed full-time. Source: US Department of Labor.

APPENDIX 3

State Presumptive Disability Laws

The following states have presumptive disability laws primarily for firefighters which recognize that firefighters are at increased risk for certain illnesses. The laws create a presumption that the specified diseases are job-related. Because the laws vary greatly from state to state, readers should use the links to review the specific state laws to determine the law's application.

Code Part: WC =Workman's Comp, RS = Retirement/Pension System,
GP = General Provisions

State	Heart Disease	Lung Disease	Cancer	Infectious Diseases	Code Part
Alabama	Y	Y	Y	Y	GP
Alaska	Y	Y	Y		WC
Arizona			Y	Y	WC
Arkansas					
California	Y		Y	Y	WC/RS
Colorado			Y	Y	WC
Connecticut	Y		Y	Y	WC
Delaware					
Florida	Y			Y	GP
Georgia	Y	Y			RS
Hawaii	Y	Y			RS
Idaho	Y	Y		Y	WC
Illinois	Y	Y	Y	Y	RS
Indiana	Y	Y	Y		GP
Iowa	Y	Y	Y	Y	RS
Kansas	Y	Y	Y		RS
Kentucky					
Louisiana	Y	Y	Y	Y	GP
Maine	Y	Y	Y	Y	WC
Maryland	Y	Y	Y		WC
Massachusetts	Y	Y	Y		RS
Michigan	Y	Y			WC

State	Heart Disease	Lung Disease	Cancer	Infectious Diseases	Code Part
Minnesota	Y		Y	Y	WC
Mississippi					
Missouri	Y	Y	Y		RS
Montana					
Nebraska	Y	Y	Y	Y	GP
Nevada	Y	Y	Y	Y	GP
New Hampshire	Y	Y	Y		WC
New Jersey					
New Mexico	Y		Y	Y	WC
New York			Y	Y	RS
North Carolina					
North Dakota	Y	Y	Y	Y	GP
Ohio	Y	Y			WC
Oklahoma	Y	Y	Y	Y	RS
Oregon	Y	Y	Y		WC
Pennsylvania			Y	Y	WC
Rhode Island		Y	Y	Y	GP
South Carolina	Y	Y			WC
South Dakota	Y	Y	Y		RS
Tennessee	Y	Y	Y		GP
Texas	Y	Y	Y	Y	GP
Utah	Y	Y		Y	WC
Vermont	Y		Y		WC
Virginia	Y	Y	Y	Y	WC
Washington	Y	Y	Y	Y	WC
West Virginia	Y	Y			WC
Wisconsin	Y	Y	Y	Y	GP
Wyoming					
Totals	37	32	33	25	WC=20 RS=10 GP=10

- Washington and Wyoming covers police officers

Source: International Association of Firefighters. Retrieved June 25, 2014: https://www.iaff.org/hs/phi/docs/PresumptiveDisabilityChart.pdf

CHAPTER 7 ENDNOTES

1. David F. Peterson (ND). Hazardous Materials—Clandestine Drug Labs. Firehouse.com. Retrieved June 24, 2014: http://www.health.state.mn.us/divs/eh/meth/lab/dpeterson.pdf
2. Respiratory Diseases and the Fire Service (2010). The Catalyst. JOIFF. Retrieved June 25, 2014: http://www.joiff.com/catalyst/Oct10.pdf
3. NIOSH Alert (2007). Preventing Fire Fighter Fatalities Due to Heart Attacks and Other Sudden Cardiovascular Events. US Department of Health and Human Services. Centers for Disease Control and Prevention. Page 8. Retrieved June 26, 2014: http://www.cdc.gov/niosh/docket/archive/pdfs/NIOSH-199/0199-060107-alert.pdf
4. NIOSH Alert (2007). Page 9.
5. Centers for Disease Control and Prevention (2013). Workplace Safety and Health Topics. Heat Stress. Retrieved June 30, 2014: http://www.cdc.gov/niosh/face/stateface/ca/97ca010.html
6. Firefighter Close Calls (2014). Firefighter Under Fire In Washington DC...As In Shots Fired At The Firefighters. Retrieved June 28, 2014: http://www.firefighterclosecalls.com/
7. Amy Brittain (2014, March 1). In The D.C. Fire Department, A Cold War Simmers Between The Chief And The Rank And File. *The Washington Post.* Retrieved June 28, 2014: http://www.washingtonpost.com/investigations/in-the-dc-fire-department-a-cold-war-simmers-between-the-chief-and-the-rank-and-file/2014/03/01/3e757d4e-9b55-11e3-9080-5d1d87a6d793_story.html
8. Paul A. Atwater (2013, January 28). The Fire Service's Role in Active-Shooter Situations. *Firefighternation.* Retrieved June 28, 2014: http://www.firefighternation.com/article/strategy-and-tactics/fire-service-s-role-active-shooter-situations
9. Newman S. "Braving the Swarm: Lowering Anticipated Group Bias in Integrated Fire/Police Units Facing Paramilitary Terrorism." Master's thesis, Naval Postgraduate School, March 2011.
10. US Department of Homeland Security (DHS). Retrieved June 28, 2014: http://www.dhs.gov/active-shooter-preparedness
11. Ashley Luthern (2014, April 8). Police, Firefighters Train As Teams To Aid Victims During Mass Shootings. *Milwaukee, Wisconsin Journal Sentinel.* Retrieved June 29, 2014: http://www.jsonline.com/news/crime/police-firefighters-train-as-teams-to-aid-victims-during-mass-shootings-b99242339z1-254381051.html
12. Ibid.
13. Joel Currier (2014, April 21). Police, Firefighters Train for Mass Shooting in St. Louis County. *St. Louis Post-Dispatch.* Retrieved June 28, 2014: http://www.stltoday.com/news/local/crime-and-courts/police-firefighters-train-for-mass-shooting-in-st-louis-county/article_043d04f2-b1c4-57f7-ad57-db46cec25a05.html
14. Noelle Phillips (2014, May 29). Cops, Fireman, EMS Train For Mass Shootings At Old Denver Hospital. *The Denver Post.* Retrieved June 28, 2014: http://www.denverpost.com/news/ci_25860173/cops-fireman-ems-train-mass-shootings-at-old
15. Ashley Luthern (2014, April 8).
16. International Association of Fire Fighters (IAFF) and the International Association of Fire Chiefs (IAFC) (ND). Police and Fire Consolidation. Retrieved June 29, 2014: http://www.iaff.org/09News/PDFs/PSO Systems.pdf

17. Oliver Morgan (2004). Infectious Disease Risks From Dead Bodies Following Natural Disasters. Rev Panam Salud Publica, American Journal of Public Health, 15(5):307–312.

18. Ibid.

19. Shana Agid (2007). Locked and Loaded: The Prison Industrial Complex and the Response to Hurricane Katrina. In Kristin A. Bates and Richelle S. Swan (Eds.) *Through the Eye of Katrina: Social Justice in the United States.* (Pages 55–72.) Durham, North Carolina: Carolina Academic Press.

    Also see, Walidah Imarisha (2005). *Readings by & for Anti-Racist Educators and Organizers Legacies: Racism and Resistance in New Orleans Before and After Katrina.* Retrieved April 26, 2014: http://katrinareader.org/sites/katrinareader.org/files/legaciesprint-tluhtd.html

20. William N. Rom, Joan Reibman, Linda Rogers, Michael D. Weiden, Beno Oppenheimer, Kenneth Berger, Roberta Goldring, Denise Harrison, and David Prezant (2010). *Emerging Exposures and Respiratory Health. Proceedings of the American Thoracic Society,* 7(2): 142–145.

21. William N. Rom, Michael Weiden, Roberto Garcia, Ting An Yie, Pratan Vathesatogkit, Doris B. Tse, Georgeann McGuinness, Victor Roggli, and David Prezant (2002). Acute Eosinophilic Pneumonia in a New York City Firefighter Exposed to World Trade Center Dust. *American Journal of Respiratory and Critical Care Medicine,* 166(6): 797–800.

22. Denise L. Smith, Steven J. Petruzzello, Eric Goldstein, Uzma Ahmad, Krishnarao Tangella, Gregory G. Freund, and Gavin P. Horn (2011). Effect of Live-Fire Training Drills on Firefighters' Platelet Number and Function. *Focus on Firefighter Physiology,* 15(2): 233–239.

23. NIOSH Alert (2007).

24. Denise L. Smith, David A. Barr, and Stefanos N. Kales (2013). Extreme Sacrifice: Sudden Cardiac Death in the US Fire Service. *Extreme Physiology & Medicine*, 2(6). Retrieved June 30, 2014: http://www.ncbi.nlm.nih.gov/pmc/articles/PMC3710100/

25. Rachel E. Klaren, Gavin P. Horn, Bo Fernhall, and Robert W. Motl (2014). Accuracy of the VO2 peak Prediction Equation in Firefighters. *Journal of Occupational Medicine and Toxicology,* 9(17). Retrieved June 29, 2014: http://www.ncbi.nlm.nih.gov/pmc/articles/PMC4016782/

26. Stefanos N. Kales, Elpidoforos S. Soteriades, Costas A. Christophi, and David C. Christiani (2007). Emergency Duties and Deaths from Heart Disease among Firefighters in the United States. *New England Journal of Medicine*, 356:1207–1215.

27. Fit For Duty (2014). Retrieved June 27, 2014: http://www.fitforduty.org/?p=89

28. Denise L. Smith, David A. Barr, and Stefanos N. Kales (2013).

29. St. Paul Fire Foundation (2010). Cardiac and Cardiovascular. Retrieved June 27, 2014: http://www.stpaulfirefoundation.org/?zone=/unionactive/view_article.cfm&HomeID=182884&page=Firefighter20Health2026 20Wellness

30. NIOSH Alert (2007). Page 4.

31. Respiratory Diseases and the Fire Service (2010). The Catalyst. JOIFF. Retrieved June 25, 2014: http://www.joiff.com/catalyst/Oct10.pdf

32. Ibid.

33. Centers for Disease Control and Prevention (2013).

34. US Environmental Protection Agency (2014). Particulate Matter. Retrieved June 27, 2014: http://epa.gov/ncer/science/pm/

35. Ibid.

36. Tee L. Guidotti (1995). Occupational Mortality Among Firefighters: Assessing The Association. *Journal of Occupational Environmental Medicine*, 37:1348–1356. Also see, D.L. Smith, S.J. Petruzzello, and T.S. Manning (2001). The Effect of Strenuous Live-Fire Drills on Cardiovascular and Psychological Responses of Recruit Firefighters. *Ergonomics*, 44: 244–254.

37. Government of the District of Columbia (2007). Fire and Emergency Medical Services Department. Retrieved June 29, 2014: http://www.iafc.org/files/safetywkplanlocalex_dc2008_044memorandumrubinfiresafetyweekjune.pdf

38. NIOSH Alert (2007).

39. Centers for Disease Control and Prevention (2013).

40. Ibid.

41. NIOSH Alert (2007).

42. Terence D Valenzuela, Thomas M Hooton, Edward L Kaplan, and Patrick Schlievert (1991). Transmission Of 'Toxic Strep' Syndrome From An Infected Child To A Firefighter During CPR. *Annals of Emergency Medicine,* 20(1): Pages 90–92.

43. Theresa L. Lamagni, Shona Neal, Catherine Keshishian, David Powell, Nicola Potz, Richard Pebody, Robert George, Georgia Duckworth, Jaana Vuopio-Varkila, and Androulla Efstratiou (2009). Predictors of Death after Severe Streptococcus pyogenes Infection. *Emerging Infectious Diseases*, 15(8). Retrieved June 23, 2014: http://wwwnc.cdc.gov/eid/article/15/8/pdfs/09-0264.pdf

44. The International Association of Firefighters (2014). Infectious Diseases. Retrieved June 23, 2014: http://www.iaff.org/et/jobaid/InfDis/whnjs.htm

45. Raphael M. Barishansky and Matthew R. Streger (2003). Occupational Fatalities in Emergency Medical Technicians. *Annals of Emergency Medicine,* 42(1): 160–164.

46. Ibid.

47. Census of Fatal Occupational Injuries (2013). US Department of Labor. Retrieved June 23, 2014: http://www.bls.gov/news.release/archives/cfoi_08222013.htm

48. The Foundation for AIDS Research (2011, May). Public Safety, Law Enforcement, and Syringe Exchange. Retrieved June 18, 2014: http://www.amfar.org/uploadedFiles/amfarorg/Around_the_World/TREAT_Asia/factsheetJan2010.pdf

49. Raphael M. Barishansky and Matthew R. Streger (2003).

50. Brian J. Maguire, Katherine L. Hunting, and Nadine R. Levick (2002). Occupational Fatalities In Emergency Medical Technicians: A Hidden Crisis. *Annals of Emergency Medicine*, 40(6): 625–632.

51. Pui W. Kong, Joe Suyama, David Hostler. (2013) A Review Of Risk Factors Of Accidental Slips, Trips, And Falls Among Firefighters. *Safety Science,* 60, 203–209.

52. US Department of Homeland Security (2011). FEMA. Fire-Related Firefighter Injuries Reported to NFIRS. Topical Fire Report Series, 11(7). Retrieved June 28, 2014: http://www.usfa.fema.gov/downloads/pdf/statistics/v11i7.pdf

53. J. Paul Leigh (2011). Economic Burden of Occupational Injury And Illness In The United States. Milbank Quarterly, 89(4):728–72.

54. NCCI White Paper On Firefighter Presumptive Coverage (2014). National Council on Compensation Insurance, Inc. Retrieved June 26, 2014: http://kslegislature.org/li/b2013_14/committees/ctte_s_cmrce_1/documents/testimony/20140218_07.pdf

55. David H. Wegman and Christer Hogstedt (2014). If It's Not Counted It Didn't Happen! *Occupational Environment Medicine*, 71(7):457–458.

56. David B. Torrey (2014). National Association Of Workers' Compensation Judiciary Firefighter Cancer Presumption Statutes In Workers' Compensation And Related Laws: An Introduction And A Statutory/Regulatory/Case Law Table. Retrieved June 24, 2014: http://www.nawcj.org/Images/archives/Comparative_Law/NAWCJ%20FIREFIGHTER%20PRESUMPTIONS%20Essay%20Table%202013.pdf

57. Scott Calvert and Luke Broadwater (2014, February 22). New Firefighter Benefits Stoke Workers' Comp Debate. *The Baltimore Sun*. Retrieved June 24, 2014: http://articles.baltimoresun.com/2014-02-22/news/bs-md-workers-comp-presumptions-20140222_1_cancers-maryland-law-compensation

58. Jon Coppelman (2012, October 22). Presumption Laws: Wide Open Door to Benefits. *Workers' Comp Insider.* Retrieved June 25, 2014: http://www.workerscompinsider.com/2012/10/presumption-law.html

59. Scott Calvert and Luke Broadwater (2014, February 22).

60. California Professional Firefighters (2014). Public Safety Presumptions. Retrieved June 24, 2014: http://www.cpf.org/go/cpf/health-and-safety/firefighter-presumptions/

61. Ibid.

62. Joan E. Collier (2012, November 19). Pennsylvania's Firefighter Cancer Presumption Law: A Second Look. *Workers Compensation Institute.* Retrieved June 26, 2014: https://www.wci360.com/blog/pennsylvanias-firefighter-cancer-presumption-law-a-second-look

63. Susan Hynes (2011). Cancers Presumed To Be Caused By Exposures In Firefighting. *BC Medical Journal*, 53(4): 197–204.

64. Jon Coppelman (2012, October 22).

65. Bradley A. Woodruff, Linda Moyer, Kathleen M. O'Rourke, and Harold Margolis (1993). Blood Exposure and the Risk of Hepatitis B Virus Infection in Firefighters. *Journal of Occupational Medicine,* 35(10): 1058–1065.

66. Winifred L. Boal, Thomas Hales, and Clara Sue Ross (2005). Blood-Borne Pathogens among Firefighters and Emergency Medical Technicians. Prehospital Emergency Care, 9(2): 236–247. http://informahealthcare.com/doi/abs/10.1080/10903120590924915

67. Eric E. Mast, Cindy M. Weinbaum, Anthony E. Fiore, Miriam J. Alter, Beth P. Bell, Lyn Finelli, Lance E. Rodewald, John M. Douglas, Jr., Robert S. Janssen, and John W. Ward (2006, December 8). A Comprehensive Immunization Strategy to Eliminate Transmission of Hepatitis B Virus Infection in the United States. *Morbidity and Mortality Weekly Report (MMWR),* 55. Centers for Disease Control and Prevention. Retrieved June 25, 2014: http://www.cdc.gov/mmwr/pdf/rr/rr5516.pdf

68. A.W. Musk, R.R. Monson, J.M. Peters, and R.K. Peters (1978). Mortality among Boston firefighters, 1915–1975. *British Journal of Industrial Medicine*, 35:104–108.

69. Ibid.

70. Claire Reiss (2013, November 14). NIOSH Publishes Study of Cancer Among Firefighters. *National League of Cities Risk Information Sharing Consortium.* Retrieved June 26, 2014: http://www.nlc.org/Documents/NLC-RISC/NIOSH%20Study%20Analysis%20FINAL%2011-25-2013%20.pdf

71. National League of Cities (2009). Assessing State Firefighter Cancer Presumptions Laws and Current Firefighter Cancer Research. Retrieved December 5, 2014: https://www.iafc.org/files/safety_ReviewFindings NLCreportOnCancerRiskInFirefighters.pdf

72. NIOSH Alert (2007). Page 1.

73. NCCI White Paper On Firefighter Presumptive Coverage (2014). National Council on Compensation Insurance, Inc.

74. NIOSH Alert (2007). Page 1.

75. Tee L. Guidotti (1995). Occupational Mortality Among Firefighters: Assessing The Association. *Journal of Occupational Environmental Medicine*, 37:1348–1356.

76. Dennis J. Stevens (2000). *Measuring Performance: A Guide to Evaluative Research*. Authors Choice. Pages 6–8. Also see Dennis J. Stevens (2014). *The Failure of the American Prison Complex: Let's Abolish it*. Iowa: Kendall Hunt Publishing. Pages 61–67.

77. Thomas Hales (2009). Cause for Concern Fire & Life Safety Section. Reducing Firefighter Deaths and Injuries: Changes in Concept, Policy, and Practice. International Association of Chiefs of Firefighters. Retrieved June 27, 2014: http://www.riskinstitute.org/peri/images/file/S908-D9-Hales.pdf

78. B.C. Choi (2000). A Technique to Reassess Epidemiologic Evidence in Light of the Healthy Worker Effect: The Case Of Firefighting And Heart Disease. *Journal of Occupational Environmental Medicine*, 42(10):1021–1034.

79. Patricia C. Smith, Karen A. Budzeika, Neville A. Edwards, Steven M. Johnson, and Linda N. Bearse (1986). Guidelines For Clean Data: Detection Of Common Mistakes. *Journal of Applied Psychology*, 71(3), 457–460. Also see, Glen Walters and Gregory Crawford (2013). In and Out of Prison: Do Importation Factors Predict All Forms of Misconduct or Just the More Serious Ones? *Journal of Criminal Justice*, 41(6): 407–413.

80. Bruce Thompson, Karen E. Diamond, Robin McWilliam, Patricia Snyder, and Scott W. Snyder (2005). Evaluating the Quality of Evidence from Correlational Research for Evidence-Based Practice. *Exceptional Children*, 71(2): 181–194.

81. Mark Dantzker and Ronald Hunter (2011). Research Methods for Criminology and Criminal Justice. Boston: Jones and Bartlett. Also see, Samuel Walker (2001). Sense and Nonsense about Crime and Drugs. Belmont, CA: Wadsworth.

82. Botond Koszegi and Matthew Rabin (2007). Mistakes in Choice-Based Welfare Analysis. *The American Economic Review*, 97(2). Retrieved July 2, 2014: http://www.jstor.org/discover/10.2307/30034498?uid=2&uid=4&sid=21104243596187

83. Erin Long Crowell (2014). Max Weber and Verstehen. *Education Portal*. Retrieved July 3, 2014: http://education-portal.com/academy/lesson/bureaucracy-definition-characteristics-meaning.html#lesson

84. Mark Dantzker and Ronald Hunter (2011). *Research Methods for Criminology and Criminal Justice*. Boston: Jones and Bartlett. Also see, Samuel Walker (2001). *Sense and Nonsense about Crime and Drugs*. Belmont, CA: Wadsworth.

85. Christina Clark and George Dugdale (2008). Literacy Changes Lives: The Role of Literacy in Offending Behaviour. National Literacy Trust. Retrieved July 7, 2014: http://www.literacytrust.org.uk/assets/0000/0422/Literacy_changes_lives__prisons.pdf

86. Bureau of Justice Statistics (2013). Corrections Populations. Retrieved July 7, 2014: http://www.bjs.gov/content/pub/pdf/p12tar9112.pdf

87. Dennis J. Stevens (2011). *The Media and Criminal Justice: CSI Effect*. Boston: Jones and Bartlett. Page 230.

88. Randall G. Shelden (2008). *Controlling The Dangerous Classes: A Critical Introduction To The History Of Criminal Justice* (2nd ed.), Boston: Allyn & Bacon. C. Hensley, and R. Tewksbury (2005). Wardens' Perceptions of Prison Rape. *Prison Journal*, 85(2): 186–197.

89. Friedrich Engels (1978/1892). Socialism: Utopian and Scientific. Robert C. Tucker (Editor) Marx-Engels Reader. (Pages 683–718). New York: Norton. Page 696.

spotmatik/Shutterstock, Inc.

CHAPTER 8

Healthcare Personnel and Compliance Issues

Learning Objectives

After you read this chapter, you will be better prepared to:

- Identify the fundamental principle and legal responsibility of healthcare personnel and the consequences of those principles and responsibilities.
- Identify the agents of compliance that affect the professional performance of healthcare personnel.
- Explain the reasoning why the author is using 'patient associated infections' as opposed to the common term of 'hospital associated infections' used in the healthcare literature.
- Characterize the realities of patient associated infections.
- Articulate the characteristics of the four primary issues related to disease transmission at healing centers.
- Explain ambulatory care and provide examples of their operations. In what way do they exasperate patient associated infections?
- Discuss hospitals and identify in what way they exasperate patient associated infections? What might be some of the answers as to why patient associated infections have yet to be controlled?
- Characterize the role of nurses and explain their relationship to patients and to the healthcare profession. Discuss the role conflict between nurses and physicians.
- Describe the primary issues of the author concerning this chapter.
- Identify the final thoughts of the author and explain in what way you agree or disagree with them. Which of those final thoughts do you consider to be the most imperative issue affecting patient associated infections and the well-being of healthcare personnel? Why?

Key Terms

Ambulatory and Acute Care
Agents of Compliance
Antimicrobial-Resistant Infections
Bloodstream Infection (BSI)
Carriage
Colonization (medical term)
Contact Network Epidemiology
Disease Management Protocols
Healing Centers
Healthcare Personnel
Nosocomial
Patient Associated Infections
Practice Based Discipline
Occupational Acquired Diseases

Words of Wisdom

In theory, there is no difference between theory and practice.
But, in practice, there is.

Jan L.A. van de Snepscheut and/or Yogi Berra

Introduction

A fundamental principle and legal responsibility of healthcare is that sick, injured, and contagious individuals receive care and treatment.[1] This principle and responsibility carry an inherent consequence:[2] an occupational risk to disease transmission from patients under their treatment, care, and observation; at the core of this argument is the reluctance of pharmaceutical enterprises has yet to develop effective antimicrobial products to meet the evolution of deadly infectious pathogens including MRSA; what I call the agents of compliance among healthcare personnel is the focus of this chapter.[3] Specifically:

- Patient Associated Infections (PAI) [1]
- Organizational Healthcare System Policy (i.e., the subordination of personnel through a bureaucratic structure that demands passive obedience particularly nurses) and Politics
- Government (State and Federal) Compliance Regulation: little evidence exists that government regulations are cored in Constitutional guarantees including due process. An exception can include Title 42, USC Section 1983 depending on how you interpret it. see Chapter 6.

These agents of compliance hamper healthcare personnel to perform at reasonable and expected levels of their profession (see previous chapters and Chapter 11 for the generalized model of agents of compliance that influence the conduct of other professionals). Public service personnel including emergency managers often focus on complying with governmental and administrative regulations ignoring compassion, reason and the Constitutional guarantees among victims and their properties.[2] For example, although clandestine, or illegal, drug laboratories are not a new hazard to the response community, an oven exploded as two people were using acetone, hydrochloric acid, and sodium hydroxide to make meth in an apartment laboratory. One person received chemical burns and was taken to a hospital where three unknowing hospital employees were also exposed.[4] Hospital personnel began vomiting and became incapacitated. Additionally, three ambulance personnel and two police officers received eye irritation and respiratory distress from their exposures. All of the infected personnel in this example were obliged by law and policy to process the victims in the manner described above. Imagine the person in the exposition had been infected with Ebola or some other lethal infectious disease and it was in the incubation period? Before you say impossible, recall the past perceptions of contracting HIV/Aids. The truth of the matter is that clinical latent infection of HIV typically lasts eight to 10 years after contact.[5]

The delivery of healthcare services (e.g., treatment and care) often requires healthcare systems (the organization) to employ and manage a variety of personnel engaged in: building maintenance, clinical laboratories, chiropractors, dental hygienists and dentists, emergency department professionals, first responders, food service, housekeeping, mortuary personnel, registered nurses including licensed practical nurses, physicians, security and administrative personnel, social service therapists, and technicians (there are probably more but this list will do for now).[3] Occupational descriptions within a system can depend on its:

[1] Most often the healthcare literature refers to 'healthcare associated infections' or hospital associated infection to describe disease transmission among patients; patients are admitted to healthcare facilities or centers based on an assumption that they are not carriers of infection or once treated, are not vulnerable to infection. The problem with those assumptions is that most patients are rarely tested for infection including those visiting emergency departments, ambulatory or acute care centers, and outpatient centers. Also, technology must provide processes and pharmaceutical products that control infectious transmission and the pathogens themselves. Easier said than done! Others suggest that since the writer is not a medical or chemist expert that he has few contributions about solutions to infectious transmission and control. Yet the above thoughts are consistent with medical and chemist experts (see this chapter for resources) confirming Einstein's thought that we cannot solve our problems with the same thinking we used when we created them.

[2] Carol W. Lewis and Stuart C. Gilman (2011). The Ethics Challenge in Public Service: A Problem-Solving Guide. San Francisco: Jossey-Bass. Pages 1–6.

[3] Healthcare is the fastest-growing sector of the US economy, employing over 18 million workers. Women represent nearly 80 percent of the healthcare work force. There are approximately 3 million registered or licensed practical nurses.

Source: CDC http://www.cdc.gov/niosh/topics/healthcare/

- Legal and Organizational Mission and Responsibilities
- Size (From A Single Physician to a Huge System with 75,000 Employees)
- Managing Directors Who Develop Policy

There are a variety of descriptions of healthcare centers so to reduce conflict this author refers to all of them as 'healing centers'; this chapter will specifically highlight ambulatory and acute care, emergency departments (ED), hospitals, and manual therapy centers.

It would be helpful to acknowledge that infection rates and categories of infection of personnel (and patient) vulnerability to disease transmission varies from healing center to healing center including similar centers in the same healthcare system.[6] Because of the wide scope of organizational policy and government mandates of healthcare systems, each healing center including official descriptions of those centers, vary from system to system, too. What is in common among healing centers are the agents of compliance described above; hopefully, you have become accustomed with agents of compliance in most of the preceeding chapters because criminal justice personnel (including firefighters) similar to healthcare personnel operate in similar at-risk environments which are managed through a similar bureaucratic organization complete with a hierarchy of command, division of labor, and policy that sets the rules toward social order and the consequences for not following those rules (see Chapter 4 for a discussion on bureaucracy).

Under the federal system of government, each state regulates their healthcare practices; the federal government mandates further regulation to healthcare systems, and offers financial assistance to those healthcare systems in compliance with state and federal mandates.[7] One way to look at this perceptive is that the federal government bribes state government into conforming to US regulations. Many systems are enhancing their staff to include infection prevention managers. For example, see Appendix 1 for a Job Listing: RN I/ Infection Preventionist at Levine Cancer Institute. (Of course, without technological advancements on medical processes to control disease transmission and pharmaceutical products to control infections what does it matter?)

The diversity among healthcare personnel, the diversity of their workplaces, the diversity of deadly infections, and resistance of deadly infections to antibiotic products make occupational exposure a serious struggle, to say the least. It should be easy to understand that healthcare professionals are occupationally exposed to a variety of infectious diseases and injuries during the performance of their duties.[8] Often, the realities of patient associated infection and healthcare or healing center associated infections are hard to separate; yet, the consequences among most infectious recipients is consistent, regardless of the method of disease transmission or the source of an infection.

[4] With all of the resources available in America including wealth, technology, and knowledge disease transmission cannot be stopped or even controlled. Source: Steven M. Wolinsky see endnote

snapgalleria/Shutterstock, Inc.

[5] Surveys were conducted in 183 hospitals. Of 11,282 patients, 452 had 1 or more HCAI. Of 504 such infections, the most common types were pneumonia, surgical-site infections, and gastrointestinal infections. Clostridium difficile was the most commonly reported pathogen producing 12 percent of HCAI. Device-associated infections (i.e., central-catheter-associated bloodstream infection, catheter-associated urinary tract infection, and ventilator-associated pneumonia), which have traditionally been the focus of programs to prevent HCAI, accounted for over one-fourth of such infections. It was estimated that there were 648,000 patients with 721,800 HCAI in US acute care hospitals in 2011.
Source: See endnote

The Reality of Patient Associated Infections

Patient associated infections such as methicillin-resistant staphylococcus aureus (MRSA), methicillin-susceptible staphylococcus aureus (MSSA), and Vancomycin-resistant enterococcus (VRE) among other pathogens originate across a wide range of clinical conditions and are hosted by a wide variety of patients including long-term patients and outpatients. Patient associated infections produce unnecessary suffering and premature death among personnel including their family members and friends and other patients.[4]

The Centers for Disease Control and Prevention (CDC) estimate the annual death rate for healthcare personnel from occupational events is higher than the general population (details later).[5] Researchers report as of 2014 that "no single US surveillance (monitoring) system can provide estimates of the burden of all types of healthcare associated infections across acute care patient populations." Because healthcare personnel similar to correctional personnel (Chapter 4), law enforcement officers (Chapter 5), and firefighters (Chapter 6) are directly engaged with patients, prisoners, violators, and victims whose health history is often unknown, it is more likely that personnel are exposed to deadly pathogens more often than the individuals they engage.[9]

One reality of infection transmission in healthcare centers is that prevention, surveillance, and control are an impossible challenge.[10]

Another reality is that all facilities at every level do not necessarily comply with infectious prevention regulation regardless of the origin of those regulations (city, corporation, federal, organizational, religious, or state). My experience tells me which is congruent with researchers.[11] The perspective of this writer is congruent with the CDC and rings true with healthcare-associated infections or disease transmission at emergency departments, ambulatory and acute care centers (detailed below), hospitals and among registered nurses in particular (see Chapter 8 for physicians and surgeons), and manual therapists. [12]

Disease Transmission in Healing Centers

There are four primary interrelated issues linked to disease transmission at healing centers:

- Disease transmission is linked with invasive procedures and devices which can promote microorganisms.[13] For example, "indwelling urinary catheters are the most common cause of urinary tract infections, and bloodstream infections are often associated with vascular access devices."[14]
- Resilient mutated strains of multidrug resistant bacteria and virus have evolved and flourished in part through abuse of antimicrobial drugs;[15] stemming from the alleged success of healing centers to contain infections (through underreporting for instance), complacency and government bureaucratic indifference has occurred (and as mentioned previously in Chapter 2).[16] Finally, new antibiotic development has not kept pace with the emergence of antibiotic-resistant pathogens *leaving healthcare personnel and their patients with outcomes beyond their control.*[17]
- Prevention, training, and incentives to control disease transmission are not a priority in healthcare systems for various reasons including financial losses. For example, traditional infection control policies have focused on engineering controls, specific protocols, and personal protective equipment.[18] Variations in organizational and individual factors explain much of the variations in self-protective behavior in healthcare settings.
- 2011 data from 183 US hospitals shows that about 721,800 infections occurred in 648,000 hospital patients.[19] About 75,000 patients with healthcare-associated infections died during their hospitalizations. The most common healthcare-associated infections were pneumonia (22 percent), surgical site infections (22 percent), gastrointestinal infections (17 percent), urinary tract infections (13 percent), and bloodstream infections (10 percent).

Individuals on the front line of most epidemics and infections are healthcare personnel. For example, during a severe acute respiratory syndrome (SARS) epidemic, healthcare professionals were affected. According to the World Health Organization (WHO), 8,098 cases occurred during the outbreak, and 774 (9.6 percent) persons died. Healthcare personnel accounted for 1,707 (21 percent) of those infected (no data exists on the number of healthcare professionals who died).[20] Also, WHO reports that the death toll from the outbreak of Ebola during the summer of 2014 in Guinea, Liberia, Nigeria, and Sierra Leone rose to 729.[21] One implication from the news reports (which this writer cannot reliably document), almost one-third of those who died from Ebola were employed in a healthcare role. There is no known cure for Ebola.

Primary Routes of Infectious Disease Transmission

The primary routes of infectious disease transmission at healing centers and across the globe are:

- Contact
- Droplet

Contact can be direct and indirect contact. Direct contact transmission involves the transfer of infectious agents to a susceptible individual through physical contact with an infected individual (e.g., direct skin-to-skin contact). For example, disease transmission (see Chapter 2 for details) among healthcare professionals to patients can include dental hygienists. Researchers describe an investigation of a dental hygienist who developed active pulmonary tuberculosis (TB); the hygienist worked for several months while infected in the state of Washington.[22] Many of her clients, once tested, were infected with TB. (Don't let this account of a dental hygienist keep you away from your dentist, but there is nothing wrong in asking about the steps taken concerning prevention of disease transmission.)

Indirect contact transmission occurs when infectious agents are transferred through physical contact with contaminated items and surfaces (e.g., door knobs, patient-care instruments or equipment, bedrails, examination table).

Droplets containing infectious agents such as MRSA and VRE are generated when an infected person coughs, sneezes, or talks—the disease is airborne.[23] Also disease can be transmitted through certain medical procedures such as suctioning or endotracheal intubation (medical procedure in which a tube is placed into windpipe through mouth or nose).

Emergency department personnel tend to encounter sick, injured, and contagious persons in the daily routines of their job.

Emergency Departments (ED), Disease Transmission, Professionals, and Patients

It makes sense that patients visiting emergency departments (ED) represent a cross-section of an entire (municipality, county, region, or for that manner nation) area's population and values of infections such as HIV seroprevalence (the overall occurrence of a disease within a defined population at one time, as measured by blood tests); and accordingly ED studies are often used to assess the general trends of decease transmission surveillance (the healthcare literature uses the term 'surveillance'; in the terms of the writer, it's 'investigation') across the US and in other countries.[24]

An early study estimated the pervasiveness of human immunodeficiency virus (HIV) and bloodstream infection (BSI) among ED patients and ED professionals (EDP) including volunteers.[25] Three pairs of inner-city and suburban hospital ED in high AIDS incidence areas were evaluated. In both inner-city and suburban ED patient HIV seroprevalence varies with patient demographics and clinical presentation; EDW were unaware of the infection status of most HIV-positive patients; this perspective has not changed much by 2014.[26] However, the risk to an EDP of occupationally acquiring HIV infection varies by ED location and the nature and frequency of BC; this risk can be reduced by adherence to universal precautions, experts say (see details in the Final Thoughts section of this chapter).[6]

Researchers performed a systematic review of the ED literature to assess the appropriateness of routine HIV screening to ED patients.[27] The researchers strongly recommend the HIV screening to high-risk patients (i.e., those with identifiable risk factors) or high-risk populations (i.e., those

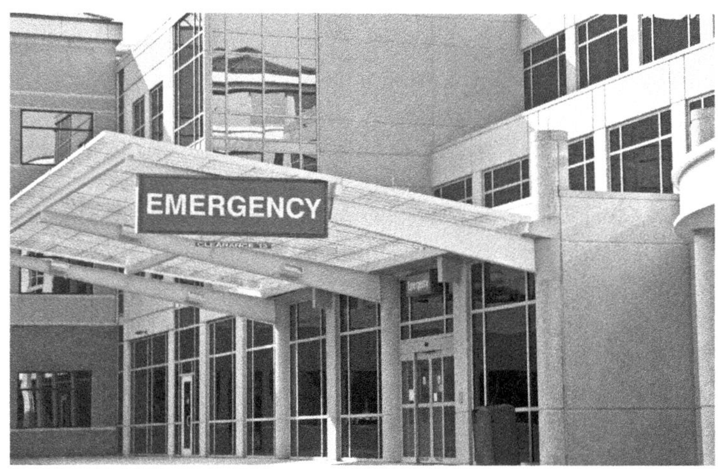

Mark Winfrey/Shutterstock, Inc.

[6] **Emergency Department Visits**

- Number of visits: 129.8 million
- Number of injury-related visits: 37.9 million
- Number of visits per 100 persons: 42.8
- Percent of visits with patient seen in fewer than 15 minutes: 25.1%
- Percent of visits resulting in hospital admission: 13.3%
- Percent of visits resulting in transfer to a different (psychiatric or other) hospital: 2.1%
- Wait time: 15 minutes or less 25%; 59 minutes or less 66%
- Payment made with private insurance 37%
- No insurance or self pay 16%

Source: National Hospital Ambulatory Medical Care Survey: 2010 Emergency Department Summary Tables. http://www.cdc.gov/nchs/data/ahcd/nhamcs_emergency/2010_ed_web_tables.pdf

where HIV seroprevelance is at least 1 percent). Most of the individuals requesting emergency department services are never screened.

Of the 7,109 eligible patients at an urban ED, almost 90 percent of them agreed to be HIV tested.[28] Fifty-seven of those tested were diagnosed as HIV-positive patients. Each of the infected patients had low CD4 cells or T-cells counts which are the "generals" of the human immune system. These cells send signals to activate your body's immune response when they detect "intruders," like viruses or bacteria.[29] The US has the technology to test large segments of the population.

Emergency Departments (ED) and Adolescents

Adolescents are at risk for developing a variety of sexually transmitted infections for many reasons. Of 71 million adolescents who visited American ED over a seven-year period, almost 1.2 million had a sexually transmitted infection.[30] Mean age was 17.1 years, and over 90 percent were female patients. Overall, 80 percent of those patients diagnosed with a sexually transmitted infection were treated (received antibiotics or were admitted to the hospital); 91 percent of the patients had pelvic inflammatory disease. Finally, HIV testing is rarely accomplished among the 71 million adolescent patients who visited ED for healthcare, report researchers.[31] And when visitors arrive at ED units, it is the healthcare professional who engages with them.

Ambulatory Care and Acute Care Centers

Traditional healthcare providers or clinical models continue to evolve within the framework of the overall healthcare system. Yet of late, there appears to be massive change occurring in healthcare systems which aside from technology and federal lawsuits toward compliance (see Chapter 8 for details), they provide a new service model of healthcare delivery: Ambulatory care.[32, 7] Depending on your definition, some refer to ambulatory care as an outpatient facility, an acute care or rehabilitation center, medicine specialties clinic, neurology center, chiropractor clinic, or an orthopedic clinic among other descriptions.[8]

Many healthcare provider systems discovered an optimal way to improve treatment of patients originally with problem wounds; one method was to create an independent multidisciplinary wound-healing center as an outpatient clinic, as well as an inpatient ward.[33] An integrated wound-healing department concept was thought to be the new standard in wound healing containing both an outpatient clinic and inpatient ward, employing full-time personnel, allowing for the development of all features vital for optimal wound treatment. The initial results demonstrated that healing centers resulted in improved rates of providing care and treatment; they were also financially successful adding an incentive to provide more centers outside the hospital walls; the growth of detached centers from hospitals can also be seen in the growth of emergency departments or Urgent Care type centers currently established throughout many cities and rural areas in America.

[6] Ambulatory care: Medical care provided on an outpatient basis, including diagnosis, observation, treatment, and rehabilitation services.
Source: MedicineNet.com (Dictionary)
Note: there are numerous definitions for ambulatory care that I found at Google
[7] A Working Definition of Ambulatory Care: while I found numerous definitions and conflicting descriptions for the term ambulatory care, "healing centers" add clarity to its function. These healing centers are expected to increase as a percentage of total healthcare volume with impatient care continues to decline.

Evolution of Healthcare Providers

Corporate medical practice, a market economy, and a consumer culture are transforming healthcare. The service relationships of physician and surgeons, treatment and care, testing and evaluations have become commodities.[34]

Healthcare systems directed by disease management protocols (to improve outcomes, reduce costs, and standardize care), provides programmed service commodities. In addition, medical-surgical specialties, now "packaged" for the care of body parts and conditions (as Breast, Stroke, Obesity, Aneurysm Centers), are also commercialized. The healthy body is a business, yet it is evident that medicated or pharmaceutical cures are not a priority; sick patients produce a greater profit than cured patients. The realization of commercialized medicine seems to be counter to the mission of healthcare and to the moral perspectives of a democratic society. That is, health has to do with social standing. The poor die sooner than those with wealth.

Nonetheless, there is some consistency in university medical healthcare institutions but variation in descriptions about ambulatory care; also, a quick glance at their university medical and ambulatory curriculums, numerous differences quickly emerged.

Adam Vilimek/Shutterstock, Inc.

Increases Represent Healthcare Revenue

Virginia Commonwealth University (VCU) Ambulatory Care

VCU Ambulatory Care's website first shows a magnificent glassed building and the figure below suggesting numerous services available.

Ambulatory Care Center		Nelson Clinic	
Floor 07—Ambulatory Surgery	BRIDGE	Floor 07—ENT Dental Medicine Clinic Oral Surgery Family Medicine	
Floor 06—Harold F. Young Neurosurgical Center PM&R		Floor 06—OT/PT Hand Center Women's Health	
Floor 05—Adult Neurology Neurophysiology Lab		Floor 05—ENT Dermatology	
Floor 04—Internal Medicine Specialties Medical Specialties Clinic		Floor 04—Ophthalmology Clinic	
Floor 03—General Surgery Orthopedics Vascular Lab		Floor 03—Urology Mammo-Breast Imaging Audiology	
Floor 02—Primary Care Clinics		Floor 02—Ambulatory Psychiatry Ped. Oncology Clinic	Bridge to Gateway
Floor 01—Ambulatory Care Center Pharmacy		Floor 01—Ambulatory Care Administration Pediatric Pulmonary	
Floor Basement—Radiology–CT–ACC Radiology–MRI–ACC			

Source: Virginia Commonwealth University (VCU) Ambulatory Care. http://www.vcuhealth.org/?id=149&sid=1

University of North Carolina (UNC) Ambulatory Care

A UNC healthcare publication states:

> UNC Health Care extends beyond Chapel Hill and into the greater Triangle area through its network of primary care and specialty physician practices located in Orange, Wake, Durham, Chatham, and Lee counties. These offices, in addition to the UNC Family Medicine Center and Ambulatory Care Center, provide the basic health care outpatient services most families need, in convenient neighborhood locations. Over 800,000 people are cared for at UNC practices and clinics each year.

Source: University of North Carolina Ambulatory Care. https://www.unchealthcare.org/site/aboutus

University of California Los Angeles (UCLA) Ambulatory Care

A UCLA publication advises:

> **Outpatient Clinics:** With over 100 different outpatient specialty clinics and nursing areas in the UCLA Health System, the opportunities for nursing practice are almost endless. These clinics provide a comprehensive array of treatments and clinical centers, addressing topics from Internal Medicine, Vascular, Cardiology, Transplant, Oncology, Neurology, Heart Failure, Dermatology, AIDS, Neurosciences, Women's Health, Geriatrics, and Plastic Surgery. The clinics provide dozens of treatments such as Outpatient Surgery, Interventional Radiology, Chemotherapy and Radiation, Nuclear Medicine, Hemepharesis, and Eye Care.

Source: University of California Los Angeles (UCLA) Ambulatory Care. http://nursing.uclahealth.org/body.cfm?id=50

Levine Cancer Institute, Charlotte, North Carolina

A number of healthcare provider systems including hospital organizations operate or lease healing centers which can include check-up sites, treatment delivery, ambulatory and acute care, urgent care (similar to emergency departments but outside a hospital structure) at numerous locations in various parts of the country. For example, in Charlotte, North Carolina, the Levine Cancer Institute and its financial partner "is a cancer institute without walls. It is connecting to Carolinas HealthCare System's network of cancer care programs throughout the Carolinas to provide patients greater access to cancer specialists, treatment, clinical trials and support services, wherever they live. The Institute functions as a series of integrated cancer programs, distributing high-quality cancer care system-wide . . . provide a full spectrum of healthcare and wellness programs . . . Its network of more than 900 care locations includes academic medical centers, fourteen owned hospitals, twenty-six leased or managed hospitals, healthcare pavilions, physician practices, destination centers, surgical and rehabilitation centers, home health agencies, nursing homes, and hospice and palliative care. Altogether, Levine operates 7,460 licensed beds and employs more than 60,000 people. Additionally, Levine operates thirteen cancer care locations and performs the latest clinical research.

Levine Cancer Institute and Carolina Health Care recognize that they must successfully transform healthcare in an environment that "is increasingly shifting provider incentives from volume to quality, service, and efficiency will require the system to integrate our capabilities."[35] With all of the above it seems awkward to talk in terms of ambulatory care yet in an attempt to characterize healthcare organizations, it is clear that healthcare delivery is constantly in a state of change. Levine recognizes those changes and implies that it develop ambulatory care units for asthma, diabetes, heart failure, and vascular disease. However, they also operate numerous other sites dedicated to chemotherapy and other forms of treatment. Levine's financial report shows a net revenue for 2012 of close to $7 billion; $228 million as a cost of financial assistance to individuals without insurance; and the total value of uncompensated care and other community benefits during 2012 was $1.25 billion.

Differences between healthcare organizations, particularly teaching institutions might have to do with findings from the American Academy of Ambulatory Care Nursing (AAACN).[36] The AAACN describes the ambulatory setting as an important sector of the healthcare system, uniquely structured to meet the increasingly complex needs of patients and communities. An AAACN committee suggests that organizations develop and operate educational and training programs for registered nurse residency programs to address the:

- "education-to-practice" gap and increased risk for errors in ambulatory centers
- high turnover of new graduates in the first year of practice in ambulatory centers
- and because of the increasing complexity of patient care within all practice settings in ambulatory centers.

The education to practice gap and increased risk for errors is cored in the idea that residencies for new registered nurse graduates are considered an important way to bridge the gap between education and practice. This education to practice gap has the ring of my experiences with higher education which is in a state of shock because of the online programs and the idea of filling college sits no matter the consequence. For example, recently I was offered a university professor's position with a nationally known educational institution that has an open door policy for all new students regardless of their academic achievements; there's more. The open door policy excluded any mental (no entering exams or previous grades from secondary schools or other colleges) or physical capability to succeed in a classroom or just life (or the ability to turn in projects when those projects are due or to demonstrate some respect for the opinions of their classmates, let alone their professors).

Diseases that are considered "Acute Care" and chronic disease are largely addressed with ambulatory care type processes and facilities similar to Levine Cancer Institute mentioned above. A focus on wellness of individuals has become the new emphasis in addressing the long-term nature and lifestyle related issues surrounding the health of a patient.

Given the changes in healthcare policy, diseases affecting the population, and economic factors, ambulatory care centers of the future will be reflections of all the issues as a physical response.

The occurrence and undesirable complications from hospital associated infections has been recognized in the literature for the last several decades; and those occurrences continue to rise at "an alarming rate" among patients and healthcare professionals.[37] Originally hospital associated infections referred to those infections associated with admission in an acute-care hospital (formerly called a nosocomial infection), but the term now applies to infections acquired in the continuum of settings where persons receive healthcare provided by healthcare professionals including long-term care, home care, and ambulatory care facilities.

Hospitals and Disease Transmission

The CDC advises that on any given day, approximately one in twenty-five US patients has at least one infection contracted during the course of their hospital care.[38] Those totals add up to about 722,000 infections in 2011.[9]

Healthcare professionals are always vulnerable to attack by transient microorganisms from intact patient skin and from environmental surfaces.[39] Although the amount of contamination is not quantified and the exact incidence is not apparent, it happens more than expected; otherwise, deathly pathogens transmission and its remedies would control if not entirely eliminate healthcare associated infections.

[8] The CDC Multistate Point-Prevalence Survey of Health Care-Associated Infections, published in New England Journal of Medicine, used 2011 data from 183 US hospitals to estimate the burden of a wide range of infections in hospital patients. That year, about 721,800 infections occurred in 648,000 hospital patients. About 75,000 patients with healthcare-associated infections died during their hospitalizations. The most common healthcare-associated infections were pneumonia (22 percent), surgical site infections (22 percent), gastrointestinal infections (17 percent), urinary tract infections (13 percent), and bloodstream infections (10 percent).

The most common germs causing healthcare-associated infections were C. difficile (12 percent), Staphylococcus aureus, including MRSA (11 percent), Klebsiella (10 percent), E. coli (9 percent), Enterococcus (9 percent), and Pseudomonas (7 percent). Klebsiella and E. coli are members of the Enterobacteriaceae bacteria family, which has become increasingly resistant to last-resort antibiotics known as carbapenems.

Source: CDC Media Relations.

Gloves and gowns of healthcare professionals frequently become contaminated with MRSA and Vancomycin-Resistant Enterococci (VRE) during the routine care of patients, and particularly during care of the patient's respiratory tract and any associated indwelling devices.[40,10] Fact is, limited therapeutic options exist for the treatment of vancomycin-resistant Enterococcus (VRE) bacteremia, say the experts.[41]

As part of a larger infection control strategy, including high-compliance hand disinfection, healing centers attempt to provide a useful barrier to transmitting antibiotic-resistant organisms among patients in an inpatient setting.[11] Also, vaccination of healthcare professionals is associated with a substantial decrease in mortality among patients. Yet, virus studies show no associated decrease in reduction in many infectious transmissions including non-fatal influenza infection in patients despite all the vaccinations.[42]

Disease transmission in healing centers happens in a number of ways: here's one of those ways. Four patients acquired MRSA during their inpatient stay on the cardiac surgery unit.[43] All four patients and one healthcare professional were found to be carrying an identical epidemic strain. No other members of staff were found to be colonized with MRSA.[12] It was concluded that the colonized healthcare professional is the source of the outbreak. It stands to reason that if five individuals were colonized with MRSA, other healthcare professionals were also exposed to MRSA, too. Also, we know that MRSA is a frequent cause of surgical site infection, but point-source outbreaks are rarely recognized.[44] The report of transmission of viruses, such as human immunodeficiency virus (HIV), hepatitis B virus (HBV), and hepatitis C virus (HCV), from healthcare professionals to patients has alarmed public opinion with potential repercussions on health organization.[45] Findings in a study show that healthcare professionals perceive personal and familial health risks from their exposure to emerging acute respiratory infectious diseases, but the majority of those healthcare professionals apparently (or that is what researchers conclude) accept the risks.[46] Of course, should healthcare professionals study closely disease transmission they will discover (if they haven't already) that even simple processes such as aerosol generating procedures (AGPs) expose healthcare professionals to pathogens causing acute respiratory infections (ARIs)?[47]

Yet, the real inquiry is where had infected healthcare professionals contacted diseases in the first place?

[10] What is Vancomycin-Resistant Enterococci (VRE)?
Enterococci are bacteria that are normally present in the human intestines and in the female genital tract and are often found in the environment. These bacteria can sometimes cause infections. Vancomycin is an antibiotic that is used to treat some drug-resistant infections caused by enterococci. In some instances, enterococci have become resistant to this drug and thus are called vancomycin-resistant enterococci (VRE). Most VRE infections occur in hospitals.

Source: CDC. Retrieved July 8, 2014: http://www.cdc.gov/hai/organisms/vre/vre.html

[11] Are certain people at risk of getting VRE?
The following persons are at increased risk of becoming infected with VRE:

- People who have been previously treated with the antibiotic vancomycin or other antibiotics for long periods of time.
- People who are hospitalized, particularly when they receive antibiotic treatment for long periods of time.
- People with weakened immune systems such as patients in intensive care units, or in cancer or transplant wards.
- People who have undergone surgical procedures such as abdominal or chest surgery.
- People with medical devices that stay in for some time such as urinary catheters or central intravenous (IV) catheters.
- People who are colonized with VRE.

Source: CDC. Retrieved July 8, 2014: http://www.cdc.gov/hai/organisms/vre/vre.html

[12] Which person is a MRSA host?

wavebreakmedia/Shutterstock, Inc.

Colonization implies that the patient has a sufficiently high concentration of organisms at a site that they can be detected, yet the organism is causing no signs or symptoms. Source: Joan Robinson (2004). Colonization And Infection Of The Respiratory Tract: What Do We Know? Paediatrics and Child Health, 9(1): 21–24. Another definition: Colonization occurs when a microorganism is found on or in a person without causing a disease.

Source: medical-dictionary.thefreedictionary.com/colonize

Registered Nurses and Disease Transmission

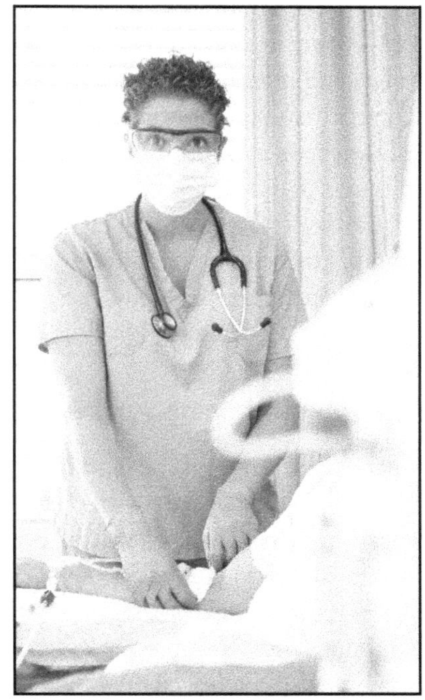

Tyler Olson/Shutterstock, Inc.

Contacts with potentially infectious patients make registered nurses (RN) a higher risk than the general population or, for that matter, other healthcare professionals and staff.[48,13] During an influenza pandemic, illness among RN might result in hospital professionals, physicians, and RN. RN report a median of 40 contacts (85 percent work-related) as compared to general occupational professionals who report 12 contacts (33 percent work-related). For RN, 51 percent of work-related contacts were with patients (74 percent involving skin-to-skin contact, and 63 percent lasted <15 minutes); 40 percent were with staff members. Although RN have a high frequency of close contact with patients, their time dedicated to each patient is limited.[14] What researchers speculate is that healthcare professionals especially RN are major reservoirs of MRSA and other deathly pathogens.[49]

Researchers suggest that the risk for infectious diseases by airborne transmission is greater among RN than the general population because of frequent and intensive contacts among RN with potentially infected patients.[50] The working conditions of RN (and probably hospital, clinic, and ambulatory and acute care personnel) are risk factors for patient associated infections, healthcare associated infections, and occupational injuries.[51] Future outbreaks of emerging infections are dependent on the staffing shortages and working conditions especially of RN in healthcare facilities.

In addition, RN high proportion of work-related skin-to-skin contact highlights the potential for fecal–oral transmission of disease (e.g., norovirus infection). RN can spread infection from infected patients to the general population.[52]

Discovering reliable data about RN and disease transmission is challenging;[53] perhaps the following confidential e-mail from a nurse can help us better understand the challenge: "I worked with a friend that had MRSA. She was not only not allowed to work, but was also denied workman's comp. She was told that there was no way to "prove" that she received it at the hospital, vs. out in the community. Hospitals are not willing to risk the liability of a patient that tests positive for MRSA, and claiming they got it from their nurse." In some countries, such as Germany, although MRSA and other deadly pathogens are an occupationally acquired infection among healthcare personnel, authorities do not report it.[54] (That's not to say that in the US we report everything—see details about statistics above.) Estimates of patient and healthcare associated infection from the worldwide literature vary widely depending on the country, hospital specialty, and setting (endemic, non-endemic, or outbreak).[55] The role of healthcare personnel as hosts of MRSA is not well understood, researchers advise (which also adds to the challenge of finding reliable data and data about patient associated infection).[56]

[13] The practice of nursing is a scientific process founded on a professional body of knowledge. It is a learned profession based on an understanding of the human condition across the lifespan and the relationship of a client with others and within the environment. The practice of nursing is an art dedicated to caring and to assisting clients by providing sustained, vigilant, and continuous care to those acutely or chronically ill.

Source: North Carolina Board of Nursing. Retrieved July 20, 2014: http://www.ncbon.com/dcp/i/nursing-practice-registered-nurse

[14] **Work Environment of RN**

RN work in hospitals, physicians' offices, home healthcare services, and nursing care facilities. Others work in correctional facilities, schools, or serve in the military.

How to Become a Registered Nurse

RN usually take one of three education paths: a bachelor's degree in nursing, an associate's degree in nursing, or a diploma from an approved nursing program. RN must be state licensed.

Source: US Department of Labor. Occupational Outlook Handbook. Registered Nurses. Retrieved July 10, 2014: http://www.bls.gov/ooh/healthcare/registered-nurses.htm

Contact Network Epidemiology

An approach to modeling the spread of infectious diseases that explicitly considers patterns of person-to-person contacts within a community.[57] Contacts can be asymmetric, with a person more likely to infect one of their contacts than to become infected by that contact. This is true for some sexually transmitted diseases that are more easily caught by women than men during heterosexual encounters; and for severe infectious diseases that cause an average person to seek medical attention and thereby potentially infect healthcare personnel who would not, in turn, have an opportunity to infect that average person. Researchers report that the probability of an epidemic and the expected fraction of a population infected during an epidemic can be different in semi-directed networks, in contrast to the routine assumption that these two quantities are equal. They acknowledge that these methods more accurately predict the vulnerability of healthcare personnel and the efficacy of various hospital-based containment strategies during outbreaks of severe respiratory diseases.

Staffing Patterns and Turnover

Staffing patterns and the working conditions among RN are risk factors for healthcare associated infections as well as occupational injuries and infections.[58] Staffing shortages, especially of RN, have been identified as one of the major factors expected to constrain hospitals' ability to deal with future outbreaks of emerging infections. These problems are compounded by a global nursing shortage.[15] What we do know about RN is that evidence shows that nurse staffing influences patient outcomes particularly the early death of patients.[59] RN turnover impacts the relationship between nursing leadership and quality of care particularly in long-term facilities;[60] it is likely that RN turnover in hospitals and clinics also impact nursing leadership and quality of care in those facilities and those systems.

A sufficient supply of nurses is critical in providing our nation's population with quality healthcare.[16]

Also, despite the widespread use of the hepatitis B vaccine (HBV), hepatitis B remains the most commonly transmitted blood-borne pathogen in almost any healthcare setting.[61] One implication of this finding is that hepatitis B is an infection spread by patients, not personnel, since most personnel are vaccinated similar to law enforcement and correctional officers as well as firefighters.

[15] **Occupational Employment and Wages: Registered Nurses May 2013**
Assess patient health problems and needs, develop and implement nursing care plans and maintain medical records. Administer nursing care to ill, injured, convalescent, or disabled patients. May advise patients on health maintenance and disease prevention or provide case management. Licensing or registration required; includes Clinical Nurse Specialists, but excludes Nurse Anesthetists, Nurse Midwives, and Nurse Professionals. There are approximately 2.7 million working registered nurses earning an average of $68,000 a year. Ten percent of all working nurses earn an average of $96,000 a year.
Source: US Department of Labor. Retrieved July 10, 2014: http://stats.bls.gov/oes/current/oes291141.htm

[16] American Nursing Association (ana.com) states that registered Nurses (RNs) and Advanced Practice Registered Nurses (APRNs) play an integral role in the delivery of primary care and help to bring the focus of our healthcare system back where it belongs—on the patient and the community. The current US nursing shortage is already having a detrimental impact on our healthcare system, and it is expected to grow to a 260,000-nurse shortfall by 2025. A shortage of this magnitude would be twice as large as any shortage experienced by this country since the 1960s. Cuts to nursing workforce development or Title VIII funding would be detrimental to the healthcare system and the patients we serve.

Manual Therapists and Disease Transmission

Manual (e.g., physical and occupational therapy, athletic training, chiropractic, osteopathy, massage, sports medicine) professionals work in environments where MRSA and other deathly pathogens are a common acquired infection.[62] A literature review was conducted about: microbiology, development of MRSA, risk factors for infection, clinical presentation, diagnostic tests, screening tests, reporting, treatment, prevention for patients and athletes, and prevention for healthcare professionals. A conclusion reached by researchers is that there exists a health risk in the community and to patients and athletes treated by manual therapists. Manual professionals among others including patients can play an essential role in recognizing MRSA infections and helping to control its transmission in the healthcare environment and the community.[63]

Healthcare Personnel Injury Statistics

OSHA reports approximately 3.8 million occupational injuries occurred in 2012 or 3.7 per 100,000.[64] Hospitals and nursing particularly in residential care facilities report approximately 430,000 injuries or almost double the 100,000 rate of the general workplaces.[17] Another indicator of the danger of healthcare personnel is the illness per 100,000 statistics that show an average of 3.4 for all professionals versus 4.5 for healthcare professionals in 2012.[65]

[17] Of 4,628 workers killed through injury on the job in 2012, or 3.4 per 100,000, 15 were in hospitals and 25 were among nurses or .07 healthcare professionals. Occupational Safety and Health Administration (OSHA) places all healthcare provider deaths into 1 of 6 distinct categories:

- Transportation Accidents
- Assaults and Violent Acts
- Contact with Objects and Equipment
- Falls
- Exposure to Harmful Substances or Environments
- Fires and Explosions

Source: US Department of Labor. Occupational Safety & Health Administration. Retrieved July 7, 2014: https://www.osha.gov/oshstats/commonstats.html

Healthcare Personnel and Occupational Death Statistics

Some scholars argue the occupational death rate for healthcare personnel is unknown and the number of events which are agents of those deaths are also unknown.[66] One reason for those unknowns is because deaths from occupationally acquired diseases are not routinely captured in any data bank. Also, there is no national agency that systematically tracks occupationally acquired infection leading to death. Additionally, this writer suggests some other reasons for those unknown outcomes including:

- Some professionals might not know they are infected (remember colonization which means a person can be infected without showing any signs of their infection, see Chapter 4).
- Some professionals might not report their condition because they might lose their job, clock time, or a promotion, while others might feel that their benefits or their financial situation cannot support treatment.
- Organizational policy hinders acknowledgment of infection or policy does police, and not provide a clear path of reporting. Healthcare organizations have much to lose if infection, treatment, and death among their personnel suddenly become news.
- Governmental compliance regulations and statistic takers are everywhere but nowhere. It is highly likely that most government reports are inaccurate and misleading.

Experiences with severe acute respiratory syndrome and the US smallpox vaccination program have demonstrated the vulnerability of healthcare professionals to occupationally acquired infectious diseases and deadly pathogens.[67] Researchers estimate healthcare professional occupational infection death rate at 17–57 per 1 million healthcare professionals in 2005. The US workforce rate per one million workers is 42.5; healthcare personnel have higher occupational death rates than sheet workers, bartenders, lawyers, and waiters. Chapter 6 describes firefighters who have a death rate at 93 per million, and Chapter 5 talks about law enforcement officers that have a death rate of 108 per million.

What is known about estimated healthcare personnel deaths from specific occupationally acquired infections includes the following:[68]

- Hepatitis B: in 1983, 10,000 healthcare professionals were infected with hepatitis B through occupational exposure. The natural history of hepatitis B infection indicates that chronic infection developed in 5–10 percent (500–1,000) of these persons. Although estimates vary, up to 25 percent (250 persons) of those with chronic infection will die from a hepatitis B–related complication.

- Hepatitis C: transmission from a hepatitis C–infected patient to a healthcare professional occurs in 1–3 percent of exposures. With an estimated 380,000 percutaneous injuries annually, 50–150 transmissions are expected. It is estimated that up to 5 percent of those infected, or 3–8 healthcare professionals annually, will die of liver disease.
- HIV Infection: as of 2005, 26 (46 percent) of 57 US healthcare professionals who have voluntarily reported, documented occupationally acquired HIV infection have progressed to AIDS, as have 121 (88 percent) of 138 healthcare professionals with possible occupational transmission. Twenty-four (42 percent) of 57 proven transmissions have occurred in nurses, 16 (28 percent) in clinical laboratory technicians, and 6 (11 percent) in nonsurgical physicians. Among the 138 persons with possible occupational acquisition, in addition to the occupations above, cases were noted among 12 emergency medical technicians (9 percent), 6 surgeons (4 percent), 15 health aide/attendants (11 percent), and 13 housekeepers and maintenance professionals (9 percent).
- Tuberculosis: Tuberculosis has long represented an occupational threat to healthcare professionals. This risk was evident during the late 1980s and early 1990s, when several outbreaks of tuberculosis (TB) and active drug-resistant diseases (see Chapter 1 for details) occurred in the US. Treatment for occupationally acquired resistant tuberculosis has resulted in death.

Expenditures versus Prevention

About fifteen years ago, The Institute of Medicine (IM) reports that adverse medical events result in an estimated $4.5–5.7 billion per year in additional costs for patient care.[69,18] The Institute suggests that ". . . errors are caused by faulty systems, processes, and conditions that lead people to make mistakes or fail to prevent them."[70] For more details see Chapter 8.

Another report provides a range of estimates for the annual direct hospital cost of treating healthcare associated infections in the US.[71] The overall annual direct medical costs of healthcare infection in US hospitals ranges from $28.4 to $33.8 billion (for hospital consumers) and $35.7 billion to $45 billion (for inpatient hospital services which would include outpatient and ambulatory and acute care). After adjusting for the range of effectiveness of possible infection control interventions, the benefits of prevention range from a low of $5.7 to $6.8 billion (20 percent of infections preventable, Consumer Price Index (CPI) for all urban consumers) to a high of $25.0 to $31.5 billion (70 percent of infections preventable, CPI for inpatient hospital services). Of course, reducing the suffering and premature death of healthcare personnel might be considered a benefit, too.

> **18** Medical errors can be defined as the failure of a planned action to be completed as intended or the use of a wrong plan to achieve an aim. Among the problems that commonly occur during the course of providing healthcare are adverse drug events and improper transfusions, surgical injuries and wrong-site surgery, suicides, restraint-related injuries or death, falls, burns, pressure ulcers, and mistaken patient identities. High error rates with serious consequences are most likely to occur in intensive care units, operating rooms, and emergency departments. Source: Institute of Medicine
>
> **19** What will become clear on the pages ahead is that deadly pathogens continue to evolve and to take control of our healing centers more rapidly than our technological evolution and our enterprising spirit to control those deadly pathogens.
>
> *Source:* Laurie Garrett (2000), *Betrayal of Trust.* New York: Hyperion.

Some Issues and Observations of the Writer

Frankly, there is an enormous amount of information in this chapter because of the nature and scope of this chapter—healthcare personnel and their vulnerability to infection and their underlying vulnerability to organizational demands and governmental compliance regulation;[19] intrinsic to this vulnerability among healthcare professionals and organizational deficiency is the irrationality of government bureaucracy (see Chapter 1 for more details), redundant compliance regulations, and management of governmental bureaucracies that possess the prodigy to define (and suspiciously enforce) the rules of the playing field; yet those same rule makers and enforcers possess little incentive to win and share anything other than their governance through their hands of their custodians, the American elitist social class—those who dictate terms and conditions to corporate America (see Chapter 1–6 for more details).

Keep Chapter Uncomplicated

This writer has attempted to make this chapter as uncomplicated as possible; yet, must acknowledge that in the healthcare literature, there is:

- Enormous repetition from scholarly study to scholarly study.
- Numerous ambiguous terms from one source to another. For instance, ambulatory care does not exist in one set of references, and when it is found it is defined differently from source to source.
- Similar to the study of criminology, in the mysteries of healthcare infections it seems everyone has an opinion and usually those opinions are often misguided. For that reason, the citations in this chapter are primarily from scholarly and government sources as opposed to news reports from sources such as CNNews and the New York Times; also, this writer stayed clear of Wikipedia and other suspect sources such as encyclopedias and undocumented blogs.
- Convoluted writing styles are pervasive in the healthcare literature: from a university student convoluted writing is one thing; from researchers through peer reviewed colleagues and their editors—all whom possess PhDs, JDs, or MDs, convoluted styles of writing are puzzling. For instance: "Cutaneous CAMRSA infection typically presents as an abscess, with or without surrounding cellulitis, in otherwise healthy participants of athletic activities who have or do not have MRSA-associated risk factors."[72] Yes, there are medical terms here, but still! Or check out this sentence: "Barring unprecedented growth in the nursing workforce or unforeseen new forces in health care that intervene to reduce burden of care in society, the numbers of nurses will not keep pace with the demand for services."[73]
- Some issues are overemphasized yet other relevant issues are often neglected: finding topics about patient death from healthcare or hospital associated infection is well represented (Google—7.3 million hits). Finding reliable sources about "patient associated infection," (Google—9 total) or healthcare organizational policy handicapping the prevention of disease transmission among healthcare personnel (Google—under 200).
- Rampant unnecessary plagiarism: when I typed the following sentence and other sentences into google—"The fundamental ethic of health care is that sick persons must receive care." I got 2,100 hits. I thought, well that's okay until I studied the hits and learned that this statement sometimes was represented almost word for word and other sources changed a word or two here or there; accompanying sentences in those article were almost similar and most lacked citations. As a researcher, this makes me uneasy because I am never sure where the data originated and when it was written. One answer might link to arrogant medical researchers who may feel that the process of real research does not apply to their studies nor is it imperative that they follow professional standards.
- Multiple researchers in almost every study: there were up to twenty-four individual researchers in a single healthcare study; look over the endnotes of this chapter and compare those endnote references to Chapters 2–5; one or two researchers can accomplish a huge amount of quality research without all of the coordinating and validating of his or her thoughts with so many others; think of Masters and Johnson or the Mayo Clinic evolved gradually from the frontier practice of Dr. William Worrall Mayo and his two sons, William J. and Charles H. Mayo. Huge numbers of researchers in a single study is uncommon in other disciplines; rest assured that an individual with numerous initials after his or her name will correct me and exquisitely explain in more repetitious, convoluted, and redundant nouns the merits of repetition, convolution, and redundancy. Einstein clarifies that "Everything should be made as simple as possible, but not simpler."

Finally in this regard you noticed the "Words of Wisdom" for this chapter: "In theory, there is no difference between theory and practice. But, in practice, there is." How do you theoretically explain the realities of unnecessary suffering and premature yet preventable death of patients and healthcare professionals to their children or to their parents?

Final Thoughts

Focusing on both Daniel Diekema (President of SHEA) and Tom Frieden (CDC Director) and their eye-opening conclusions that 2 million patients are exposed to healthcare associated infections; that 200 or more hospital patients die every day after being admitted to a hospital because of deadly pathogens and the medical world's powerlessness to treat those pathogens.[74] Focusing on the reality of these findings, three thoughts require acknowledgment:

- Hospital patients die because they have been admitted to a hospital for care regardless of their physical condition prior to their admission to the hospital.
- Negligence of the hospital organizational structure (whatever or however it is arranged) to protect patients, personnel, visitors, and volunteers.
- Failure on the part of the pharmaceutical industry to develop antibiotic products that can compete with the evolution of deadly pathogens (see Chapter 2 for details).

The information provided by Diekema and Frieden, the realities discussed above, and the findings throughout this chapter about emergency departments, ambulatory and acute care clinics, hospitals and nurses are disturbing to say the least. Yet, this writer must acknowledge that the statistics and conclusions are cored in what are 'reported' deaths linked to hospital associated infections and should be utilized as a guide. CDC cautions their own death estimates as limited in that "attributable mortality is often difficult to determine from a patient's records."[75] Even for experts, it can be problematic to determine whether patients die from their infection or from their co-morbidity. The CDC reports that the number of deaths that result from occupationally acquired infection particularly among healthcare professionals "is an educated guess at best."[76] Their ideas are consistent with the FBI's Uniform Crime Reports (UCR) and their own caution that the UCR should be used as a guide. Nonetheless, all HCAI and medical mistakes at American hospitals are estimated at 210,000 patient deaths a year, more than twice the number in a frequently quoted Institute of Medicine article.[77]

Then, too consider that medical practice, a market economy, government over-regulatory compliance mandates, and a consumer culture are persistently transforming healthcare expectations at such a rapid pace that experts have difficulty understanding those changes and predicting the outcomes.[78]

Twenty some years ago, patient safety studies revealed the most frequent types of adverse events impacting hospitalized patients were:

- Adverse Drug Events
- Nosocomial Infections (defined earlier as hospital acquired infection)
- Surgical Complications

Little has changed as evidenced by the above data and from the previous pages of this chapter.

More than half the MRSA cases reported in 2014 involve the most virulent form of the bacteria, bacterium with the USA300 genetic background. "But the incidence varied from 35 percent at one hospital to 80 percent at another," says Dr. Spellberg.[79] "All these differences in (percentile death) rates suggest that the epidemiology and other factors of antibiotic resistance vary greatly . . ." Carriage (meaning patients could pass the bacteria along to others, but were not necessarily sick with infection; hosts) among patients too, differ from facility to facility. For instance, one study reports carriage rates went from a high of 52 percent in one facility to a low of 7 percent in another.

"The high overall levels of MRSA are reason for concern," Huang says. "But the variation in rates between facilities may be good news because it suggests some facilities are finding effective ways to contain the bacteria."[80]

Interestingly enough, official reports also reveal that the percentile of infants with MRSA can vary from center to center with some centers reporting no cases at all.[81] All of the above data reveal that healthcare professionals are more often exposed to MRSA and other deadly pathogens at one healthcare center versus another healthcare center. Some answers below might help in a better understanding of this overall phenomenon.

Key Differences between Healthcare Centers

One key difference between healthcare centers (aside from glass, polished floors, and location) is the healthcare administration or those who control or significantly influence healthcare policy of that institution, center, or system; those in control tend to set the environmental issues in part through compliance policies (limiting litigation potentials from government, patients, and personnel) admission screening policy, hiring standards, and scheduling. Even emergency department professionals (EDP) are unaware of the infection status of most HIV-positive patients; this perspective has not changed much even with America's advanced technology and, what was it Diekema said—awareness. However, the risk to an EDP of occupationally acquiring HIV infection varies by the emergency department's location; also the nature and frequency of HCAI type infections suggest that emergency department policy has a significant effect on personnel and patient outcomes.

Experts agree that HCAI are considered an undesirable outcome; and despite the understanding that HCAI are preventable, they are considered an indicator of the quality of patient care, an adverse event, and are a patient safety issue, experts say.[82] Studies show that physician staffing is not associated with infectious risk in hospitals; so we really cannot blame physicians.[83] Bottom line . . . it effects the bottom line (profits and loss statements). More about this perspective in Chapter 11 Conclusions and Recommendations. But, let's stay on point.

Researchers agree that it is the critical care work environment (created by the organization) that influences the likelihood of infection more than healthcare professionals.[84] The literature suggests that critically ill patients are susceptible to healthcare associated infection because of their illnesses and the need for intravenous access and invasive monitoring. In healthcare (similar to every other enterprise including law enforcement, corrections, education, and Walmart), changing the behavior of personnel without changing underlying social structures or larger environmental determinants will provide few contributions toward behavioral change.[85] For example, when police officers become stressed to the point of post-traumatic stress disorder (PTSD) behavioral patterns (assuming you accept PTSD as a legitimate disorder), providing treatment is one thing; sending 'cured' officers back to the same environment that promoted PTSD is impractical. Treat the stress and change the stress triggers; for most cops, those triggers are administrative policies—environment! Be careful to read this with the intent of the author. By environment, I don't mean the social environment where an officer, physician, or firefighter performs his or has task but the organizational environment—the chain of command, the quality of administrators, and so on. Similar to drug rehabilitation—returning recovered addicts to the same community with the same friends and the same parties and the same sex partners is an easy transition back to addiction.

Whom to blame for the preventable suffering, premature deaths, and healthcare negligence including medical and surgical mistakes? **[20]** See Chapter 7 for more details on medical and surgical mistakes. Some experts imply that even among pregnant healthcare professionals that "since it is (first) the responsibility of the individual" (as opposed to the antenatal care provider and employer) to know of the risks and potential interventions both before and after exposure.[86] "If exposure occurs or if the HCP develops an infective illness," medical experts should be consulted as opposed to the organization taking the primary initiative toward recovery. Blame healthcare associated infection and disease transmission on the healthcare professional particularly registered nurses (RN) even those who aren't registered. RN have the most to lose and females are the easiest to put on the defensive end of a sexual political battle similar to female physicians, teachers, cops, or stay-at-home moms.

There is merit and profound reasoning for drawing upon the American cultural value system for an answer. Public men and private women or sexual politics take your pick.

[20] Events that should never occur in surgery ("never events") happen at least 4,000 times a year in the US. Over a twenty-year period, researchers found more than 9,744 paid malpractice claims cost over $1.3 billion.

Source: J Nordqvist (2012, December 22). Surgical Errors Occur More Than 4,000 Times A Year In The U.S. Medical News Today. Retrieved July 25, 2014: http://www.medicalnewstoday.com/articles/254426.php

Gender-Specific Policies

Program interventions are pervasive within the global healthcare system; often these interpersonal dimensions of healthcare professionals impact quality care among patients.[87] An explanation for the origin of gender inequalities is organizationally structural, as the labor market has been organized "on the pillars of a prevailing patriarchy and androcentrism."[88] For example:

> . . . interventions and their outcomes demonstrate (in this report) that integrating gender into reproductive health programmes does appear to have a positive impact on reproductive health outcomes, whether by exploiting, accommodating or transforming gender inequities.[89]

Gender inequality policies at the workplace can accommodate gender differences rather than challenge gender relations. But for right now, employed healthcare females in the US report:[90]

- less job security
- lower control or autonomy over their job responsibilities
- worse contractual working conditions
- poorer self-perceived physical and mental health than male healthcare professionals.

Conversely, employed healthcare males report a higher degree of physically demanding work, lower support, higher levels of effort-reward imbalance, higher job status, are more exposed to noise and work longer hours than females. This writer takes these findings to mean that a male in a female dominated occupation such as nursing would respond similarly as other female registered nurses. Also consider that regulation in all but ten states allow nurses to prescribe medication independently. That effectively ties the services of nurses to the services of physicians and reduces the ability of nurse to compete in the market with physicians (this regulation and similar authorizations and prohibitions continue to change).[91]

Consider female doctors.[92] The literature advises that women physicians' enthusiasm reflected in their confidence that they live in the best of all worlds, but she is still 'Emily ' (pretty, smart, yet emotional—gender inequality starts at birth with the name) in a man's job—and similar to registered nurses who are referred to as a midlevel provider (even though registered nurses engage with patients more than physicians) which used to be a woman's job until the medicine-men developed a (financial) monopoly of medicine and pushed women from those sacred positions. More startling data from Linda Brodsky, is that physicians are the professional group with the highest rate of suicide.[93] Studies show that female physicians are eight times more likely to commit suicide compared to their male colleagues (more about physicians in Chapter 7).

"The master's tools will never dismantle the master's house," Audre Lorde advises.[94] What Lorde means (I think) is that women can become a physician and abstractly "beat him at his own game, but they (the female physician) will never enable us to bring about genuine change. And this fact is only threatening to those women who still define the master's house as their only source of support" (and this writer adds—identity; if your master also represents who you are—there is no you). In what way would this perspective apply to President Barack Obama's administration? Relevant to an understanding of nurses and their compliance to male trait dominance, is the bureaucratic organizational structure in which they are employed (see Chapter 4 for more details on bureaucracies and Chapter 11 for some recommendations). The underlining principle of any bureaucratic organization is 'passive obedience' to the rules and regulations of the hierarchical organizational structure. Orders come top down, reports go up. This means—no questions: follow orders!

Occupational role model descriptions and responsibilities are tied to organizational role model expectations which are usually culturally bound as opposed to the individual, explains the Society of Human Resource Management.[95]

Once healthcare human resource professionals have devoted time and resources to compete for talent, the next step is to get new hires quickly up to speed. The best way to accomplish this task is through a socialization process of new personnel.[21] This process is not centered in the personnel but rather organizationally centered. By this the writer means, during the socialization encounter it is the organizational philosophy, policies, and expectations which are culturally bound and justify the organizational philosophy which is emphasized regardless of the rank, role, or ability of the personnel.[22] Personnel owe the company store, sort'a speak for the job and the training. Some of those company stores, such as Rush University Medical Center in Chicago, reported total assets of over $3 billion, $1.5 billion in net patient services, and $1.7 billion in payroll and benefits in 2013.[96] Incidentally, Rush is one of 35 hospitals across the US designated by the Centers for Disease Control and Prevention to treat Ebola.[97] These centers have been determined to be staffed, to be equipped and to have current capabilities, training and resources to provide the complex treatment necessary to care for a person with Ebola while minimizing risk to healthcare personnel. Widen the gap of gender bias through recruits. For example, 488 'student' future registered nurses completed questionnaires; results show that registered nurses at the hospitals and other facilities where the students interned did not provide good role models as opposed to teachers, supervisors, and administrators who have a direct impact on student graduation and employment outcomes.[98] Those results are not a surprise to researchers, particularly researchers who pay attention to research standards linked to their participants (students) and how they were asking the questions. It reminds me of what this writer calls the Francis D'Ambra Effect. Francis was the police chief of a small North Carolina city and a student of this writer; he was enrolled in a research methods class conducted at the North Carolina Justice Academy in Salemburg, NC. The chief appeared in class with results from his own study; he informed the class that almost every single participant in his study felt safe. He walked, in full uniform (stars, sunglasses, and a wide-jaw grin) from residence to residence with his police cruiser (tinted windows, an agents of antennae, and driven by one of his commanders) which followed the chief through the streets. The chief asked each resident if they felt safe in "his city and if you appreciate the job I and my officers are performing." We had a good laugh that day, but it took some time for him to unpuff his chest as he understood that his sample had few choices in their responses under the circumstances. He was not measuring what he thought he was measuring; this finding would, of course, affect the validity of his conclusion. He was "actually measuring how afraid the residents were of the police, would be my guess," advanced another student who was at the time a police chief of a larger NC community. Yes, I wrote about the Francis D'Ambra Effect and lecture on it to present day research methods students.[99]

Prior to the 1990s, nursing orientation programs were frequently based on "tradition, expert opinion, and intuition."[100] Improvements improved traditional values, expert opinion ideals, and specific intuition of those in charge. Many registered nurses continue to be exposed to old school (male dominated) orientation methods which I sense continues a good old boy system of dominance. Competency seems to mean: "Yes, I will be a good little girl, and you will hire me and reward me." In total, my explanation relates to a theory I studied as a graduate student at Loyola

[21] **Socialization**
Socialization is broadly defined as "a process in which an individual acquires the attitudes, behaviors and knowledge needed to successfully participate as an organizational member." Socialization is an ongoing process that sometimes lasts for a year. It represents a sense-making process that helps new hires adapt, form work relationships, and find their place in the organization.
Source: The Society of Human Resource Management see endnote

[22] **Profile of a Nursing University: Rush University Medical Center, Chicago**
The medical university at Rush-Presbyterian-St. Luke's Medical Center is one of the nation's top hospitals, according to U.S. News & World Report. Rush offers over seventy highly selective residency and fellowship programs in medical and surgical specialties and subspecialties: nursing, health sciences, and graduate. Rush University offers degrees in nursing, masters, and PhD in medicine and medicine related disciplines including biotechnology, biochemistry, and pharmacology. It is the twentieth largest private sector employer in Chicago with over 8,000 employees and a payroll of more than $500 million.
Source: Rush University of Chicago. Retrieved December 5, 2014: http://www.rush.edu/

University of Chicago—the theory of cognitive dissonance:[23] "If a person is induced to do or say something which is contrary to his private opinion, there will be a tendency for him (or her) to change his opinion so as to bring it into correspondence (I think the theorist means congruence or agreement) with what he (or she) has done or said."[101] The title of the article is very applicable to the argument: Cognitive Consequences of Forced Compliance. For instance, when a CDC team conducted onsite visits at each designated centers such as Rush Medical Center mentioned above to review all aspects of caring for a patient with Ebola, including staff training, infection control, personal protective equipment (PPE) use, and details such as handling and management of the trash from a patient's room was cognitive consequences of forced compliance in play for the personnel directed by the administration? The CDC Director Tom Frieden said that "These (designated) hospitals have worked hard to rigorously assess their capabilities and train their staff.[102] Trained the staff to answer the question appropriately or trained the staff to deal with Ebola or a little of both? Little says the same staff will be present or in the same job classification when Ebola hits.

The "get-in-and-do-it" focus has been based on task performance which has been described as the "orientation norm prior to the advent of registered nurse residency programs."[103] Researchers including this writer strongly recommend that a total redesign of traditional orientation methodology is necessary to build competence and confidence amongst new healthcare graduates.[104]

Occupational Conflict between Registered Nurses and Physicians

Another reason RN might not be able to successfully bridge the gap in healthcare associated infections and disease transmission is because of the occupational conflict between their job responsibilities (and knowledge some might add) and physicians. Professional relationships between registered nurses and physicians have often been described in terms of two models: interactions between two health professions, and one centered on the patriarchy of male physicians and the deference of female nurses (also see the above discussion about the organization and nurses).[105] The certification of nurses is through a state license process which defines an RN's responsibilities similar to physicians. An inquiry made by RN is typified in this question:[24]

A significant source of stress in nursing is conflict with physicians. There is evidence in the literature that different ways of resolving conflicts generate more or less stress for those involved; however, it is usually the RN striving to resolve the gap between RN authority and the authority of the physician rather than the other way around.[106] The nurse-doctor relationship is historically one of female nurse deference to male physician authority. When nurses and doctors are female, traditional power imbalances in their relationship diminish, suggesting that these imbalances are

[23] Cognitive dissonance is the mental conflict that people experience when they are presented with evidence that their beliefs or assumptions are wrong. Source: John Calverley (2011). When Bubbles Burst: Surviving the Financial Fallout. Nicholas Brealey Publishing. Page 211.

Leon Festinger started with a very simple proposition. If a person holds two cognitions that are psychologically inconsistent, he or she experiences Dissonance: a negative drive state (not unlike hunger or thirst). Because the experience of dissonance is unpleasant, the person will strive to reduce it—usually by struggling to find a way to change one or both cognitions to make them more consonant with one another. What Festinger achieved was the forging of a dynamic marriage between the cognitive (thinking) and the motivational.

Source: E. Aronson (1997) Back to the future: Retrospective review of Leon Festinger. A Theory of Cognitive Dissonance. *American Journal of Psychology*, 110(1): 121–137.

[24] Typical Inquiry made by RN: The physicians I work with tell me I can do whatever they tell me to do. Is that true? No. Both the RN and LPN have their own scope of practice. The nurse's practice is defined by the Nursing Practice Act (NPA), Rules, Level of Licensure, and Agency Policies. No one can expand the licensed nurse's scope beyond what the law has approved. Source: North Carolina Board of Nursing. Retrieved July 20, 2014: http://www.ncbon.com/dcp/i/nursing-practice-faq--nursing-practice

based as much on gender as on professional hierarchy.[107] See Chapter 9 for more details on physicians and hospitals. Also see Chapter 11 for professionalization of nurses as a social leveling devise.

What to Do about Hospital Infection?

Recall the firefighters in Chapter 7 who have strong unions and Presumption Laws to help them survive occupational health hazards. There is little question that registered nurses (and other occupations including law enforcement officers) must move in the direction of labor bargaining which is part of legislative rights enacted from the time of President Franklin D. Roosevelt's New Deal in the 1930s through the Kennedy and Johnson administrations of the 1960s.[108] Economic history in the US suggests that American economic decline which began in the latter 1990s when American unions were being forced out, in some cases prohibited in many organizations, and legislation favored corporate America particularly the companies that moved out of the US.

Equally important, many experts have characterized the Food and Drug Administration as having toughened regulation pertaining to "pharmaceutical makers in ways that lead to manufacturing line shutdowns and withdrawals from production."[109] A major consequence of those exaggerated regulations toward compliance creates dangerous shortages of off-patent drugs used in hospital and clinical settings including drugs that are important in chemotherapy, anesthesia, and infection control.

Summary

A fundamental principle of the healthcare profession is that sick, injured, and contagious individuals receive healthcare. There are occupational risks to healthcare personnel. Delivery of healthcare services requires a variety of occupational descriptions and diversity. Deadly pathogens have evolved more rapidly than our technological evolution and our enterprising spirit to control those deadly pathogens in healing centers.

The reality of infections is that they produce unnecessary suffering and premature preventable death among patients and healthcare personnel and their family members and friends. With all of America's resources including wealth, technology, and knowledge disease transmission cannot be stopped or even controlled.

There are three primary interrelated issues linked to infections, resilient mutated strains of multidrug resistant bacteria because of a lack of new antimicrobial products, prevention, training, and incentives to control disease transmission of deadly pathogens are not a priority in healthcare organizations.

Emergency departments are reviewed in relationship to HCAI and its impact upon patients and professionals; visits by adolescents are also discussed in relationship to sexually transmitted diseases. Several examples of ambulatory care providers are profiled, as well as hospitals and nurses. Conclusions include the CDC report on both healthcare associated infections (HCAI) and prevention; it reveals that declines have been noticed particularly from bloodstream infections (BSI) and surgical site infections. Yet experts contradict CDC's position that all is well.

In the final thoughts of this author, I point out that hospital patients die because they have been admitted to a hospital for care regardless of their physical condition prior to their admission to the hospital; also negligence of the hospital organizational structure exists to protect patients, personnel, visitors, and volunteers; and failure on the part of the pharmaceutical industry to develop antibiotic products that can compete with the evolution of deadly pathogens. However because of the impact of HCAI on healthcare professionals it is recommended that strong union representation should be considered similar to the firefighters discussed in Chapter 7.

Name: ______________________________ Date: ____________ School Identification Number: ______

STUDENT WORKSHEETS

Chapter 8 Healthcare Personnel and Compliance Issues

Define the following key terms from Chapter 8, and in your answer, show the page number where you found the definition. Provide an example for each key term.

1. Ambulatory and Acute Care

2. Agents of Compliance

3. Antimicrobial-Resistant Infections

4. Bloodstream Infection (BSI)

5. Carriage

6. Cognitive Dissonance

7. Colonization (medical term)

8. Contact Network Epidemiology

9. Disease Management Protocols

10. Healing Centers

11. Healthcare and Hospital Associated Infections (HCAI)

12. Healthcare Professionals (HCP)

13. Nosocomial

14. Practice Based Discipline

15. Occupational Acquired Diseases

16. Registered Nurse (RN)

Name: ______________________________ Date: ______________ School Identification Number: ________

STUDENT WORKSHEETS

Chapter 8 Healthcare Personnel and Compliance Issues

Discuss and demonstrate in your own words that you comprehend the following learning objectives in this chapter.

1. Identify the fundamental principle and legal responsibility of healthcare personnel and the consequences of those principles and responsibilities.
2. Identify the agents of compliance that affect the professional performance of healthcare personnel.
3. Explain the reasoning why the author is using 'patient associated infections' as opposed to the common term of 'hospital associated infections' used in the healthcare literature.
4. Characterize the realities of patient associated infections.
5. Articulate the characteristics of the four primary issues related to disease transmission at healing centers.
6. Explain ambulatory care and provide examples of their operations. In what way do they exasperate patient associated infections?
7. Discuss hospitals and identify in what way they exasperate patient associated infections? What might be some of the answers as to why patient associated infections have yet to be controlled?
8. Characterize the role of nurses and explain their relationship to patients and to the healthcare profession. Discuss the role conflict between nurses with physicians.
9. Describe the primary issues of the author concerning this chapter.
10. Identify the conclusions of this chapter and explain in what way you agree or disagree with those conclusions.
11. Identify the primary final thoughts of the author and explain in what way you agree or disagree with them. Which of those final thoughts do you consider to be the most imperative issue affecting patient associated infections and the well-being of healthcare personnel? Why?

APPENDIX 1

Job Listing: RN I/Infection Preventionist Levine Cancer Institute (28361)

Job Summary

Responsible for the day-to-day Infection Prevention program and activities for any designated healthcare facility, clinic and healthcare service throughout the continuum of care for the Carolinas Healthcare System.

Essential Functions

- Abstracts data from patient charts for surveillance and focus studies and generates healthcare associated infection statistics. Develops and pilots data collection tools. Utilizes several electronic systems to collect data.
- Reports routine and significant epidemiological findings from surveillance activities to department leadership and the Medical Director.
- Maintains accurate records of infections; compiles, analyzes and disseminates surveillance data. Collaborates with leadership and makes recommendations for improvements based on data analysis, reviews of current literature, comparisons of observed practices to professional standards or results of multidisciplinary conferences.
- Advocates for the patient, visitor and healthcare worker throughout the continuum of care; creates, implements and revises infection prevention policies.
- Assists with investigation and follow-up of healthcare workers and non-employees exposed to communicable diseases, and occupational exposures.
- Assists with investigation, and recommendations for corrective action related to healthcare facility construction and moisture management activities.
- Identifies unsafe infection control practices and hazards. Designs, implements and monitors alternative solutions to system-wide, departmental or unit problems.
- Is a resource person for infection prevention issues; may serve on committees or subcommittees such as Infection Prevention Committee, QSOC, EOC Committee, Performance Improvement Committee, Patient Safety Committee, or clinical value analysis teams.
- Collaborates with the Hospital Based Public Health Epidemiologist, Safety, Emergency and Infectious Disease Medicine in policy development, investigation, and recommendation for actions related to bioterrorism readiness, and community outbreak and control measures.

Physical Requirements

Works in an office and/or boardroom type setting. Surveillance work requires walking throughout the facility. Possible travel/driving to CHS facilities as required. May be prolonged periods of sitting at desk reviewing medical records, updating policies, planning educational program or utilizing a PC. Requires frequent contact with all levels of personnel. Intact sense of sight and hearing required.

Education, Experience and Certifications

Must speak and understand English fluently. Bachelors Degree in Nursing or healthcare related field preferred. Current NC license as a Registered Nurse required. Certification in Infection Control and Prevention (CIC) preferred. At least 2 years clinical experience as RN, preferably acute care required. Ability to identify and research problems required. Ability to analyze and interpret data and problem solve required. Excellent oral and written communication skills required. Intermediate to advanced computer skills required. Knowledge of Microbiology, biostatistics, and basic principles of hospital epidemiology preferred. Ability to produce epidemiological studies preferred. Ability to interpret fundamental bio-statistical information and computer generated.

CHAPTER 8 ENDNOTES

1. A Zuger and SH Miles (1987). Physicians, AIDS, and Occupational Risk. Historic Traditions and Ethical Obligations. *Journal of the American Medical Association*, 258:1924–1928.
2. Centers for Disease Control and Prevention (2005). Occupational Deaths among Healthcare Workers. *Emerging Infectious Diseases*, 11(7). Retrieved July 20, 2014: http://wwwnc.cdc.gov/eid/article/11/7/04-1038_article
3. Didier Pittet and Richard P Wenzel (1995). Nosocomial Bloodstream Infections: Secular Trends in Rates, Mortality, and Contribution to Total Hospital Deaths. *Archives of Internal Medicine*, 155(11):1177–1184.
4. David F. Peterson (ND). Hazardous Materials—Clandestine Drug Labs. Firehouse.com. Retrieved June 24, 2014: http://www.health.state.mn.us/divs/eh/meth/lab/dpeterson.pdf
5. Mayo Clinic (2014). Diseases and Conditions: HIV/Aids. Retrieved December 6, 2014: http://www.mayoclinic.org/diseases-conditions/hiv-aids/basics/symptoms/con-20013732
6. OSHA (2014). Safety and Health Topics. Infectious Diseases. US Department of Labor. Retrieved July 8, 2014: https://www.osha.gov/SLTC/healthcarefacilities/infectious_diseases.html
7. Deborah Haas-Wilson (1992). The Regulation of Health Care Professionals Other than Physicians. *Regulations.* Washington, DC: Cato Institute. Retrieved December 6, 2014: http://www.cato.org/sites/cato.org/files/serials/files/regulation/1992/10/reg15n4d.html
8. OSHA (2014).
9. RE Rothman, KS Ketlogetswe, T Dolan, PC Wyer, and GD Kelen (2003). Preventive Care In The Emergency Department: Should Emergency Departments Conduct Routine HIV Screening? A Systematic Review. *Academy Emergency Medicine,* 10(3):278–285.
10. Shelley S Magill, Jonathan R Edwards, Wendy Bamberg, Zintars G. Beldavs, Ghinwa Dumyati, Marion A. Kainer, Ruth Lynfield, Meghan Maloney, Laura McAllister-Hollod, Joelle Nadle, Susan M. Ray, Deborah L. Thompson, Lucy E. Wilson, and Scott K. Fridkin (2014). Emerging Infections Program Healthcare-Associated Infections and Antimicrobial Use Prevalence Survey Team. *New England Journal of Medicine*, 370(13): 1198–1208.
11. G Hawkins, S Stewart, O Blatchford, and J Reilly (2011). Should Healthcare Workers Be Screened Routinely For Meticillin-Resistant Staphylococcus Aureus? A Review Of The Evidence. *Journal of Hospital Infection,* 7(4):285–289.
12. Morbidity and Mortality Weekly Report (2009, March 19). Guidance for Control of Infections with Carbapenem-Resistant or Carbapenemase-Producing Enterobacteriaceae in Acute Care Facilities. Retrieved July 8, 2014: http://www.cdc.gov/mmwr/preview/mmwrhtml/mm5810a4.htm
13. HP Loveday, JA Wilson, RJ Pratt, M Golsorkhi, A Tingle, A Bak, J Browne, J Prieto, and M Wilcox (2014). Epic3: National Evidence-Based Guidelines for Preventing Healthcare-Associated Infections in NHS Hospitals in England. *Journal of Hospital Infection*, 86(1): S1–S70.
14. Infection Prevention and Control (2011). Infection: Prevention and Control of Healthcare-Associated Infections In Primary And Community Care (Partial Update Of NICE Clinical Guideline: NICE Guideline). London, England. Retrieved July 11, 2014: http://www.nice.org.uk/guidance/cg139/resources/infection-control-nice-guideline2

15. Steven M. Wolinsky (2000). In Laurie Garrett's *Betrayal of Trust: The Collapse of Global Public Health.* New York: Hyperion. Page xil. Also see, Arno Karlen (1995). *Man and Microbes: Disease and Plagues in History and Modern Times*. New York: Touchstone. Page 16. And, Brad Spellberg (2009). *Rising Plague: The Global Threat from Deadly Bacteria and our Dwindling Arsenal to Fight Them*. Amherst, New York: Prometheus Books.

16. Steven M Wolinsky (2000). In Laurie Garrett's *Betrayal of Trust: The Collapse of Global Public Health.* New York: Hyperion. Page xil.

17. Earl S. Ford, Wayne H. Giles, and William H. Dietz (2002). Prevalence of the Metabolic Syndrome Among US Adults: Findings From the Third National Health and Nutrition Examination Survey. *Journal of American Medical Association*, 287(3):356–359.

18. D Moore, B Gamage, E Bryce, R Copes, and A Yassi (2005). Protecting Health Care Workers From SARS And Other Respiratory Pathogens: Organizational And Individual Factors That Affect Adherence To Infection Control Guidelines. *American Journal on Infectious Control*, 33(2):88–96.

19. Centers for Disease Control and Prevention. Press Release. Despite Progress, Ongoing Efforts Needed to Combat Infections Impacting Hospital Patients. Retrieved July 31, 2014: http://www.cdc.gov/media/releases/2014/p0326-hospital-patients.html

20. Kent A. Sepkowitz and Leon Eisenberg (2005). Occupational Deaths among Healthcare Workers. Emerging Infectious Diseases, 11(7). *Centers for Disease Control and Prevention.* Retrieved July 8, 2014: http://wwwnc.cdc.gov/eid/article/11/7/pdfs/04-1038.pdf

21. Aljazeer Reports (2014, July 31). Ebola Forces State Emergency In Sierra Leone. Retrieved July 31, 2014: http://www.aljazeera.com/news/africa/2014/07/ebola-forces-sierra-leone-emergency-2014731132240772882.html

22. JL Merte, CM Kroll, AS Collins, and AL Melnick (2014). An Epidemiologic Investigation of Occupational Transmission of Mycobacterium Tuberculosis Infection to Dental Health Care Personnel: Infection Prevention and Control Implications. *Journal of the American Dental Association,* 145(5): 464–471.

23. OSHA (2014). Safety and Health Topics. Infectious Diseases. US Department of Labor. Retrieved July 8, 2014: https://www.osha.gov/SLTC/healthcarefacilities/infectious_diseases.html

24. OA Esan, AS Akanmu, and I Akinsete (2003). HIV Seroprevalence In Emergency Department Patients: Lagos University Teaching Hospital, Lagos, 1999. *The Nigerian Postgraduate Medical Journal*,10(2):71–75.

25. R Marcus, DH Culver, DM Bell, PU Srivastava, MH Mendelson, RJ Zalenski, B Farber, D Fligner, J Hassett, and TC Quinn (1993). Risk of Human Immunodeficiency Virus Infection Among Emergency Department Workers. *American Journal of Medicine*, 94(4):363–370.

26. Aids.gov. Retrieved July 10, 2014: http://www.aids.gov/hiv-aids-basics/just-diagnosed-with-hiv-aids/understand-your-test-results/cd4-count/ Also see CDC Media Relations (2014, March 26). Despite Progress, Ongoing Efforts Needed To Combat Infections Impacting Hospital Patients. National and State Data Detail Threat of Healthcare-Associated Infections and Opportunities for Further Improvements. Retrieved July 11, 2014: http://www.cdc.gov/media/releases/2014/p0326-hospital-patients.html

27. RE Rothman, KS Ketlogetswe, T Dolan, PC Wyer, and GD Kelen (2003). Preventive Care In The Emergency Department: Should Emergency Departments Conduct Routine HIV Screening? A Systematic Review. *Academy Emergency Medicine,* 10(3):278–285.

28. Yvette Calderon, Jason Leider, Susan Hailpern, Robert Chin, Reena Ghosh, Jade Fettig, Paul Gennis, Polly Bijur, and Laurie Bauman (2009). High-Volume Rapid HIV Testing in an Urban Emergency Department. *AIDS Patient Care STDS.* 23(9): 749–755. Retrieved July 10, 2014: http://www.ncbi.nlm.nih.gov/pmc/articles/PMC2859778/

29. Aids.gov. Retrieved July 10, 2014: http://www.aids.gov/hiv-aids-basics/just-diagnosed-with-hiv-aids/understand-your-test-results/cd4-count/

30. KR Beckmann, MD Melzer-Lange, and MH Gorelick (2004). Emergency Department Management of Sexually Transmitted Infections in US Adolescents: Results From The National Hospital Ambulatory Medical Care Survey. Annual Emergency Medicine, 43(3):333–338.

31. Ethan Cowan, Jason Leider, Lorena Velastegui, Juliana Wexler, Jennifer Velloza, and Yvette Calderon (2013). A Qualitative Assessment of Emergency Department Patients' Knowledge, Beliefs, Attitudes, and Acceptance towards Revised HIV Testing Strategies. *Academic Emergency Medicine*, 20(3): 287–294.

32. John Barker, Ed Pocock, and Charles Huber (ND). The Future of Ambulatory Care. Practicing Architecture. Retrieved July 13, 2014: http://www.aia.org/practicing/groups/kc/AIAB086508

33. Finn Gottrup (2004). A Specialized Wound-Healing Center Concept: Importance Of A Multidisciplinary Department Structure And Surgical Treatment Facilities In The Treatment Of Chronic Wounds. *The American Journal of Surgery*, 187(5): S38–S43.

34. JD Stoeckle (2000). From Service To Commodity: Corporization, Competition, Commodification, And Customer Culture Transforms Primary Care. *Croatian Medical Journal* 41(2):141–143.

35. 2013 Value Report (2014). Differentiable Care and Value Within One Integrated System. Retrieved July 24, 2014: http://www.carolinashealthcare.org/documents/chs/2013-value-report.pdf

36. American Academy of Ambulatory Care Nursing (2014). Ambulatory Registered Nurse Residency White Paper—The Need For An Ambulatory Nurse Residency Program. Pitman, NJ. Retrieved July 15, 2014: https://www.aaacn.org/sites/default/files/documents/white-paper-May2014.pdf

37. Amy S Collins (2008). Preventing Healthcare–Associated Infections. In Patient Safety and Quality: An Evidence-Based Handbook for Nurses; In RG Hughes (Ed); Agency for Healthcare Research and Quality: Rockville, MD, USA, 2008; Chapter 41, pp. 547–575. Retrieved July 11, 2014: http://www.ahrq.gov/professionals/clinicians-providers/resources/nursing/resources/nurseshdbk/CollinsA_PHCAI.pdf

38. CDC Media Relations (2014, March 26). Despite Progress, Ongoing Efforts Needed To Combat Infections Impacting Hospital Patients. National and State Data Detail Threat of Healthcare-Associated Infections And Opportunities For Further Improvements. Retrieved July 11, 2014: http://www.cdc.gov/media/releases/2014/p0326-hospital-patients.html

39. Mary Cipriano Silva and Ruth Ludwick (2006). Ethics Column "What Would You Do? Ethics and Infection Control." OJIN: The Online Journal of Issues in Nurses, 11(2). Retrieved July 11, 2014: http://www.nursingworld.org/MainMenuCategories/ANAMarketplace/ANAPeriodicals/OJIN/Columns/Ethics/DNPEthical.aspx

40. Graham M. Snyder, Kerri A. Thom, Jon P. Furuno, Eli N. Perencevich, Mary-Claire Roghmann, Sandra M. Strauss, Giora Netzer, and Anthony D. Harris (2008). Detection of Methicillin-Resistant Staphylococcus aureus and Vancomycin-Resistant Enterococci on the Gowns and Gloves of Healthcare Workers. Infection Control and Hospital Epidemiology, 29(7).

41. EP Balli, CA Venetis, S Miyakis (2014). Systematic Review And Meta-Analysis Of Linezolid Versus Daptomycin For Treatment Of Vancomycin-Resistant Enterococcal Bacteremia. *Antimicrobial Agents Chemotherapy*, 58(2):734–739.

42. William F Carman, Alexander G Elder, Lesley A Wallace, Karen McAulay, Andrew Walker, Gordon D Murray, and David J Stott (2000). Effects Of Influenza Vaccination Of Health-Care Workers On Mortality Of Elderly People In Long-Term Care: A Randomised Controlled Trial. The Lancet, 355(9198): 93–97.

43. C Haill, S Fletcher, R Archer, G Jones, M Jayarajah, J Frame, A Williams, AM Kearns, and PJ Jenks (2013). Prolonged Outbreak Of Meticillin-Resistant Staphylococcus Aureus In A Cardiac Surgery Unit Linked To A Single Colonized Healthcare Worker. *Journal of Hospital Infection*, 83(3): 219–225.

44. SA Crusz, C Yates, S Holden, A Kearns, and T Boswell (2014). Prolonged Outbreak Of Staphylococcus Aureus Surgical Site Infection Traced To A Healthcare Worker With Psoriasis. *Journal of Hospital Infections*, 86(10): 42–46.

45. V Puro, P Scognamiglio, and G Ippolito (2003). HIV, HBV, or HCV Transmission From Infected Health Care Workers To Patients. Medical Lav, 94(6): 556–68.

46. Y Koh, DG Hegney, and V Drury (2011). Comprehensive Systematic Review Of Healthcare Workers' Perceptions Of Risk And Use Of Coping Strategies Towards Emerging Respiratory Infectious Diseases. *International Journal of Evidence-Based Healthcare,* 9(4):403–419.

47. K Tran, K Cimon, M Severn, CL Pessoa-Silva, and J Conly (2012). Aerosol Generating Procedures and Risk of Transmission of Acute Respiratory Infections to Healthcare Workers: A Systematic Review. *PLOS-One*, 7(4): 357–397.

48. Helen Bernard, Richela Fischer, Rafael T. Mikolajczyk, Mirjam Kretzschmar, and Manfred Wildner (2009). Nurses' Contacts and Potential for Infectious Disease Transmission. *Emerging Infectious Diseases*, 15(9): 1438–1444.

49. G Omuse, S Kariuki, and G Revathi (2012). Unexpected Absence of Meticillin-Resistant Staphylococcus Aureus Nasal Carriage By Healthcare Workers In A Tertiary Hospital In Kenya. *Journal Hospital Infection*, 80(1):71–73.

50. Helen Bernard, Richela Fischer, Rafael T. Mikolajczyk, Mirjam Kretzschmar, and Manfred Wildner (2009).

51. Patricia W. Stone, Sean Clarke, Jeannie Cimiotti, and Rosaly Correa-de-Araujo (2004). Nurses' Working Conditions: Implications for Infectious Disease. Emerging Infectious Diseases. International Conference on Women and Infectious Diseases (ICWID) Retrieved July 12, 2014: http://wwwnc.cdc.gov/eid/article/10/11/04-0253_article

52. Helen Bernard, Richela Fischer, Rafael T. Mikolajczyk, Mirjam Kretzschmar, and Manfred Wildner (2009).

53. G Omuse, S Kariuki, and G Revathi (2012).

54. Frank Haamann, Madeleine Dulon, and Albert Nienhaus (2011). MRSA as an Occupational Disease: A Case Series. *International Archive of Occupational and Environmental Health*, 84(3): 259–266.

55. G Hawkins, S Stewart, O Blatchford, and J Reilly (2011). Should Healthcare Workers Be Screened Routinely For Meticillin-Resistant Staphylococcus Aureus? A Review Of The Evidence. *Journal of Hospital Infection*, 7(4):285–289.

56. Ibid.

57. LA Meyers, ME Newman, and B Pourbohloul (2006). Predicting Epidemics on Directed Contact Networks. *Journal of Theoretical Biology*, 240(3):400–418.

58. PW Stone, SP Clarke, J Cimiotti, and R Correa-de-Araujo (2004). Nurses' Working Conditions: Implications For Infectious Disease. *Emerging Infectious Diseases*, 10(11): 1984–1989.

59. SH Cho, JH Hwang, and J Kim (2008). Nurse Staffing and Patient Mortality In Intensive Care Units. *Nursing Research,* 57(5): 322–330.

60. S Zimmerman, AL Gruber-Baldini, JR Hebel, PD Sloane, and J Magaziner (2002). Nursing Home Facility Risk Factors for Infection and Hospitalization: Importance of Registered Nurse Turnover, Administration, and Social Factors. *Journal of the American Geriatrics Society*, 50: 1987–1995.

61. David K. Henderson, Louise Dembry, Neil O. Fishman, Christine Grady, Tammy Lundstrom, Tara N. Palmore, Kent A. Sepkowitz, and David J. Weber (2010). SHEA Guideline for Management of Healthcare Workers Who Are Infected with Hepatitis B Virus, Hepatitis C Virus, and/or Human Immunodeficiency Virus. Infection Control and Hospital Epidemiology, 31(3). Retrieved July 8, 2014: http://www.shea-online.org/Assets/files/guidelines/BBPathogen_GL.pdf

62. B Green, CD Johnson, JT Egan, M Rosenthal, EA Griffith, and MW Evans (2012). Detection of Methicillin-Resistant Staphylococcus aureus and Vancomycin-Resistant Enterococci on the Gowns and Gloves of Healthcare Workers. *Journal of Chiropractic Medicine*, 11(1): 64–76.

63. PR Cohen (2008). The Skin In The Gym: A Comprehensive Review Of The Cutaneous Manifestations Of Community-Acquired Methicillin-Resistant Staphylococcus Aureus Infection In Athletes. *Clinical Dermatology,* 26(1):16–26. Also see, PR Cohen (2007). Community-Acquired Methicillin-Resistant Staphylococcus Aureus Skin Infections: Implications For Patients And Professionals. *American Journal of Clinical Dermatology,* 8(5): 259–270.

64. OSHA. Economic News Release. Department of Labor, Bureau of Labor Statistics. Retrieved July 8, 2014: http://www.bls.gov/news.release/osh.t01.htm

65. Ibid.

66. OSHA (2014). Safety and Health Topics. Infectious Diseases. US Department of Labor. Retrieved July 8, 2014: https://www.osha.gov/SLTC/healthcarefacilities/infectious_diseases.html

67. Kent A Sepkowitz and Leon Eisenberg (2005). Occupational Deaths among Healthcare Workers. *Emerging Infectious Diseases*, 11(7): 1003–1008. Retrieved July 20, 2014: http://www.ncbi.nlm.nih.gov/pmc/articles/PMC3371777/pdf/

68. Ibid.

69. Amy S Collins (2008). Preventing Healthcare–Associated Infections. In Patient Safety and Quality: An Evidence-Based Handbook for Nurses; In RG Hughes (Ed); Agency for Healthcare Research and Quality: Rockville, MD, USA, 2008; Chapter 41, pp. 547–575. Retrieved July 11, 2014: http://www.ahrq.gov/professionals/clinicians-providers/resources/nursing/resources/nurseshdbk/CollinsA_PHCAI.pdf

70. Institute of Medicine (1999). To Err is Human: Building a Safer Health System. Retrieved July 24, 2014: http://www.iom.edu/~/media/Files/Report%20Files/1999/To-Err-is-Human/To%20Err%20is%20Human%201999%20%20report%20brief.pdf Page 2.

71. R Douglas Scott (2009). The Direct Medical Costs of Healthcare-Associated Infections In U.S. Hospitals And The Benefits Of Prevention. Centers for Disease Control and Prevention. Retrieved July 24, 2014: http://www.cdc.gov/HAI/pdfs/hai/Scott_CostPaper.pdf

72. PR Cohen (2005). Cutaneous Community-Acquired Methicillin-Resistant Staphylococcus Aureus Infection In Participants Of Athletic Activities. *South Medical Journal*, 98(6):596–602.

73. Patricia W. Stone, Sean Clarke, Jeannie Cimiotti, and Rosaly Correa-de-Araujo (2004).

74. CDC Media Relations (2014, March 26). Despite Progress, Ongoing Efforts Needed To Combat Infections Impacting Hospital Patients. National and State Data Detail Threat Of Healthcare-Associated Infections And Opportunities For Further Improvements. Retrieved July 11, 2014: http://www.cdc.gov/media/releases/2014/p0326-hospital-patients.html

75. Centers for Disease Control and Prevention (2007). Estimating Health Care-Associated Infections and Deaths in U.S. Hospitals, 2002. Retrieved July 20, 2014: http://www.cdc.gov/HAI/pdfs/hai/infections_deaths.pdf

76. Kent A. Sepkowitz and Leon Eisenberg (2005). Occupational Deaths among Healthcare Workers. Emerging Infectious Diseases, 11(7). Page 1006. Centers for Disease Control and Prevention. Retrieved July 8, 2014: http://wwwnc.cdc.gov/eid/article/11/7/pdfs/04-1038.pdf

77. Scientific American (2013, September 20). How Many Die from Medical Mistakes in U.S. Hospitals? Retrieved July 17, 2014: http://www.scientificamerican.com/article/how-many-die-from-medical-mistakes-in-us-hospitals/

78. JD Stoeckle (2000). From Service To Commodity: Corporization, Competition, Commodification, And Customer Culture Transforms Primary Care. *Croatian Medical Journal* 41(2):141–143.

79. Los Angeles Biomedical Research Institute at Harbor-UCLA Medical Center (LA BioMed). (2014, June 2). MRSA rates varied dramatically across geographic areas. *ScienceDaily*. Retrieved July 14, 2014: www.sciencedaily.com/releases/2014/06/140602104758.htm

80. Courtney Reynolds, Victor Quan, Diane Kim, Ellena Peterson, Julie Dunn, Matthew Whealon, Leah Terpstra, Hildy Meyers, Michele Cheung, Bruce Lee, and Susan S. Huang (2011). Methicillin-Resistant Staphylococcus aureus (MRSA) Carriage in 10 Nursing Homes in Orange County, California. *Infection Control and Hospital Epidemiology*, 32(1). Retrieved July 20, 2014: http://www.sciencedaily.com/releases/2010/12/101201162115.htm

81. AL Shane, NI Hansen, BJ Stoll, EF Bell, PJ Sánchez, S Shankaran, AR Laptook, A Das, MC Walsh, EC Hale, NS Newman, SJ Schrag, and RD Higgins (2012). Methicillin-Resistant and Susceptible Staphylococcus Aureus Bacteremia and Meningitis In Preterm Infants. Eunice Kennedy Shriver National Institute of Child Health And Human Development Neonatal Research Network. *Pediatrics*, 129(4): 914–922.

82. Amy S Collins (2008). Preventing Healthcare-Associated Infections. In Patient Safety and Quality: An Evidence-Based Handbook for Nurses; In RG Hughes (Ed); Agency for Healthcare Research and Quality: Rockville, MD, USA, 2008; Chapter 41, pp. 547–575. Retrieved July 11, 2014: http://www.ahrq.gov/professionals/clinicians-providers/resources/nursing/resources/nurseshdbk/CollinsA_PHCAI.pdf

83. Patricia W Stone, Monika Pogorzelska, Laureen Kunches, and Lisa R Hirschhorn (2008). Hospital Staffing and Health Care-Associated Infections: A Systematic Review of the Literature. *Clinical Infectious Diseases*, 47(7):937–944.

84. Deena Kelly, Ann Kutney-Lee, Eileen T Lake, and Linda H Aiken (2013).The Critical Care Work Environment and Nurse-Reported Health Care–Associated Infections. *American Journal of Critical Care,* 22(6): 482–488.

85. Lawrence W. Green and Marshall W. Kreuter (2005). *Health Program Planning: An Educational and Ecological Approach.* 4th edition. New York: McGraw Hill.

86. TL Chin, AP MacGowan, SK Jacobson, and M Donati (2014). Viral Infections in Pregnancy: Advice For Healthcare Workers. *Journal of Hospital Infection*, 87(1):11–24.

87. Veloshnee Govender and Loveday Penn-Kekana (2007). Gender Biases and Discrimination: a Review of Health Care Interpersonal Interactions. *Women and Gender Equity Knowledge Network*. Retrieved July 18, 2014: http://www.who.int/social_determinants/resources/gender_biases_and_discrimination_wgkn_2007.pdf/ Also see, Charlotte Feldman-Jacobs and Peju Olukoya (2006). A Summary of 'So What' Report. Population Reference Bureau for the Interagency Gender Working Group (IGWG) and World Health Organization (WHO). Retrieved July 18, 2014: http://www.prb.org/igwg_media/SowhatSummary_Eng.pdf

88. Javier Campos-Serna, Elena Ronda-Pérez, Lucia Artazcoz, Bente E Moen, and Fernando G Benavide (2013). Gender Inequalities In Occupational Health Related To The Unequal Distribution Of Working And Employment Conditions: A Systematic Review. *International Journal for Equity in Health,* 12: 57. Retrieved July 18, 2014: http://www.equityhealthj.com/content/pdf/1475-9276-12-57.pdf

89. Charlotte Feldman-Jacobs and Peju Olukoya (2006). A Summary of 'So What' Report. Population Reference Bureau for the Interagency Gender Working Group (IGWG) and World Health Organization (WHO). Retrieved July 18, 2014: http://www.prb.org/igwg_media/SowhatSummary_Eng.pdf/ Page 14.

90. Javier Campos-Serna, Elena Ronda-Pérez, Lucia Artazcoz, Bente E Moen, and Fernando G Benavide (2013).

91. Deborah Haas-Wilson (1992). The Regulation of Health Care Professionals Other than Physicians. Cato. Retrieved December 6, 2014: http://www.cato.org/sites/cato.org/files/serials/files/regulation/1992/10/reg15n4d.html

92. Regina Markell Morantz-Sanchez (2000). *Sympathy & Science: Women Physicians in American Medicine.* Chapel Hill, NC: University of North Carolina Press. Pages 2–5.

93. Linda Brodsky (2013, July 13). Suicide In Female Physicians: Recognize, Respond, Reconsider. Kenvinmd.com. Retrieved July 18, 2014: http://www.kevinmd.com/blog/2013/07/suicide-female-physicians-recognize-respond-reconsider.html

94. Audre Lorde (1983). The Master's Tools Will Never Dismantle the Master's House. Pages 94–101, in Cherrie Moraga and Gloria Anzaldua (Eds). *The Bridge Called My Back: Writings by Radical Women of Color*. New York: Kitchen Table Press.

95. Society of Human Resource Management (2006). Organizational Entry: Onboarding, Orientation and Socialization. Retrieved July 14, 2014: http://www.shrm.org/research/articles/articles/pages/organizationalentryonboarding,orientationandsocialization.aspx

96. Rush University Medical Center (2014). Retrieved July 26, 2014: http://www.rushu.rush.edu/servlet/Satellite?blobcol=urlfile&blobheader=application%2Fpdf&blobkey=id&blobnocache=true&blobtable=document&blobwhere=1320161092501&ssbinary=true

97. Rush Medical Center (2014). Retrieved December 6, 2014: http://www.rush.edu/news/look-inside-ebola-treatment-center

98. Nicholas Drey and Dinah Gould (2013). Student RN Experiences of Infection Prevention And Control During Clinical Placements. *American Journal of Infection Control*, 41(9): Pages 760–763.

99. Dennis J. Stevens (2000). *Measuring Performance: A Guide to Evaluative Research.* Authors Choice. Pages 45–47.

100. American Academy of Ambulatory Care Nursing (2014). Ambulatory Registered Nurse Residency White Paper—The Need For An Ambulatory Nurse Residency Program. Pitman, NJ. Retrieved July 15, 2014: https://www.aaacn.org/sites/default/files/documents/white-paper-May2014.pdf

101. Leon Festinger and James M. Carlsmith (1959). Cognitive Consequences of Forced Compliance. *The Journal of Abnormal and Social Psychology,* 58(2), 203–210.

102. Rush Medical Center (2014).

103. American Academy of Ambulatory Care Nursing (2014).

104. Benner P, Stephen M, Leonard V, Day L. Educating Nurses: A Call for Radical Transformation. San Francisco, CA: Jossey-Bass; 2010. Also see, Renee Twibell, Jeanne St. Pierre, Doreen Johnson, Deb Barton, Christine Davis, Michelle Kidd, and Gwendolyn Rook (2012). Why New Nurses Don't Stay and What the Evidence Says We Can Do About It. *American Nurse Today,* 7(6). Retrieved July 16, 2014: http://utahcnatraining.blogspot.com/2012/08/why-new-nurses-dont-stay-and-what.html

105. WG Rothstein and S Hannum (2007). Profession And Gender In Relationships Between Advanced Practice Nurses And Physicians. *Journal of Professional Nurses,* 23(4): 235–240.

106. Nili Tabak and Koprak Orit (2007). Relationship Between How Nurses Resolve Their Conflicts With Doctors, Their Stress And Job Satisfaction. *Journal of Nursing Management*, 15(3): 321–331.

107. Barbara Zelek and Susan P Phillips (2003). Gender and Power: Nurses and Doctors in Canada. *International Journal for Equality*, 2:1.

108. US Department of State (ND). US Economy Labor in America: The Worker's Role. Retrieved July 16, 2014: http://countrystudies.us/united-states/economy-9.htm

109. Walter Olson (2011). A Hospital Drug Shortage Made In Washington. Cato at Library. Retrieved July 25, 2014: http://www.cato.org/blog/hospital-drug-shortage-made-washington

karen roach/Shutterstock, Inc.

CHAPTER 9

Hospitals, Physicians, and Agents of Compliance

Learning Objectives

After you read this chapter, you will be better prepared to:

- Discuss the perspective that relates to hospital and physician performance and describe the various agents of compliance in this chapter.
- Identify the ways in which hospital systems can improve their efficiency.
- Explain the weakness and strength of vertical integration among hospital systems. In what way can vertical integration move a hospital system toward federal prosecution?
- Identify and discuss the products of commercialized healthcare providers.
- Explain the role of venture capital among physicians.
- Discuss physician medical errors and probable causes. In what way could disease transmission and patient associated infection be considered medical error?
- Identify the federal agencies involved in fraud investigations and the outcomes of those investigations.
- From all of the cases prosecuted in this chapter, which case sounds arbitrary or highly suspect to you and why?
- Describe the reasons that some experts think the criminal justice community should borrow the decision making processes of the medical community. In what way do you agree or disagree with that recommendation.
- Describe the final thoughts of the author about hospitals, physicians, and agents of compliance. Identify the prediction made and explain in what way you agree or disagree with that prediction.

Key Terms

American Hospital Association
Anomie
Capitalist Physicians
Evidence Based Medicine
Excluded from Medicare and Medicare Participation
Fear of Prosecution
Health Fraud Prevention and Enforcement Action Team (HEAT)
HMOs
Managed Care
Medical Errors
Medicare Fraud
'Never Events'
Physician Errors
Revolutionizing Instruments of Production
Surgeon Errors
Venture Capital
Vertical Integration

Words of Wisdom

The art of medicine consists of amusing the patient while nature cures the disease.

—Voltaire

Introduction

The highest hospital patient cost on the planet is at an American hospital; yet American hospitals and clinics kill more patients than other nations.[1] Statistically, three times as many people die every year because of medical errors and disease transmission in American hospitals as die on American highways—100,000 deaths[2] compared to an estimated 34,000.[3] Of this group, 80,000 die from patient associated infections (see Chapter 8 for more details); many of those deaths were preventable lest we forget the unnecessary suffering personnel and patients endured during recovery, if there was a recovery. Given the number of hospital admissions, 1 of every 361 people admitted to a hospital die because of medical errors or infection regardless of the reason a patient was admitted to a hospital, reports the American Hospital Association.**[1]** Based on the number of deaths, hospitals are more dangerous than American prisons.[4]

Despite the enormous revelation that hospitals are dangerous places, I am hesitant to offer the evidence produced from my research because I have no intention to shatter medical infallibility, which is a revered and necessary component of a strong and safe America similar to the criminal justice system and education despite their 'dark sides'.

The focus of this chapter is about hospitals, physicians, and surgeons and their collective and individual agents of compliance and helplessness to control disease transmission, marketplace demands and organizational policy, and government compliance regulation including the fear of prosecution.

Healthcare Providers and Agents of Compliance

American healthcare providers are the most commercialized and the most prosecuted through government compliance regulations in the world.**[2]** For instance, the Department of Justice reports that since its inception to prosecute, strike force operations in nine locations have

Luis Louro/Shutterstock, Inc.

1 The American Hospital Association reports that there are approximately 5,723 registered hospitals in the US as of 2014. Those hospitals house 920,829 hospital beds and have 36,156,245 yearly admissions. The total expenses for all US hospitals exceeds $829 billion a year. More than 1 in 10 Americans were admitted to a hospital last year.
Source: American Hospital Association. Facts. Retrieved August 6, 2014: http://www.aha.org/research/rc/stat-studies/fast-facts.shtml

2 For example, in Little Rock, Arkansas, a federal grand jury indicted Robert Barrow and Angela Barrow charging the husband and wife physician team with six counts of healthcare fraud. The indictment says that the doctors were affiliated with a local massage therapist, whose services were billed to health insurers as physical therapy, and with whom the doctors would split the proceeds. Related claims to Medicare and Arkansas Blue Cross and Blue Shield alone exceeded $1.2 million during the alleged fraud. If convicted, the Barrows face up to ten years' imprisonment on each of the six counts of healthcare fraud plus ten years' imprisonment for the overarching conspiracy.
Source: US Department of Justice (2014). Medicate Strike Force. http://www.justice.gov/opa/pr/2014/January/14-crm-082.html/

brought litigation against more than 1,500 defendants who collectively have falsely billed the Medicare program for more than $5 billion (from the perspective of federal investigators).[5]

Concerning commercialization, many private and public entrepreneurs are building large corporate systems to compete in the highly competitive world of managed care and treatment.[6] Certainly the ills of a competitive marketplace coupled with a fear of federal prosecution sets numerous organizational and personal agendas into motion; undeniably market discipline regulates every aspect of social life and the "regressive economic rationality that drives it" sacrifices public good, public values, and social responsibility of healthcare professionals including physicians and surgeons as will be clarified in the pages ahead.[7] Maybe commercialization and prosecution has something to do with the overall expense of American healthcare, especially hospital patient care. As you look through this chapter, judge for yourself.

Also, I view the realization of government prosecution as an out-of-control matrix of its own design that devours unprepared organizations such as healthcare systems and naive physicians who on one hand are in the business of making a difference to those who require their care and expertise; but does not matter how much of a difference they make to anyone or a community; what matters is how well they can protect themselves from government intrusion based on government standards and government enforcement; similar to crime and punishment and a position I clarified in the *Failure of the American Prison Complex: Let's Abolish It* one mission of government is that it remains a sprawling massive enterprise which tends to intensify inequality among specific groups of individuals in a democratic nation; while, at the same time, it creates a disposable society of goods, resources, and individuals; governmental policy, regulations, and practices, all defined by government, take precedent over the Constitutional rights of individuals including the poor and physicians and surgeons whom government is sworn to equally protect and serve. Where do the poor find medical attention when the only clinic in the area cannot meet federal standards or has been excluded from Medicate participation (details later)? Overall the issues of healthcare similar to police officers, teachers, and parents is not how well they perform as individuals or as part of the team, but how well insulated and knowledgeable they are when it comes to their collective and individual agents of compliance particularly in light of a lack of antibiotics:

- Patient Associated Infections
- Organizational System Policy and Politics
- Government (State and Federal) Compliance Regulation

The Institute of Medicine argues a similar position suggesting that "more commonly, errors are caused by faulty systems, processes, and conditions that lead people to make mistakes or fail to prevent them."[8] (More details in Explanations of Physician and Surgeon Error section).

Hospitals

Hospitals differ in size (beds and amenities), specialty (intensive care patient electronic monitoring units and cancer), and operating costs, so operational efficiency will differentiate successful hospital systems from those that fail (see details below of top five hospitals in the US).[9] There is no perfect hospital or perfect hospital model that can represent all hospitals. Nonetheless, operational efficiency will enhance the fiscal health of a hospital which is a topic well within the scope of this chapter as will become clear later in the chapter; what you need to know right now are ways hospital systems improve their efficiency:

- Adherence to Medical Standards
- Quantifying Care and Treatment Based on Evidence-Based Medicine (see below for details)
- Improving Patient Satisfaction Scores
- Updated IT Computer Systems

Hospitals, physicians, and surgeons are reliant on computer technology both with patient care and day-to-day operations; it is vital that IT systems help, not hinder, the commitment of a healing center and a healer.[3] Hospital systems have become commercialized and follow paths that lead those systems to financial independence; yet there are consequences for healthcare patients and personnel, some of which are unrelenting regardless of recovery attempts.

Hospital reform also includes connectivity (to other healthcare providers), electronic medical records, and transparency as commonplace practices.[4,10]

This could mean that in several years, and certainly before 2020, any person considering a hospital stay will simply go on-line to compare hospitals relative to infection rates, degrees of surgical success, and many other metrics.[11] Americans comparison shop, so comparing hospital services and costs is something Americans do well. Inevitably when we are able to do this, hospitals will be driven by quality, service, and cost—all of which will be necessary to compete.

Hospitals and Commercialization

What hospital systems (as opposed to an individual hospital) have entered is the place Americans, particularly conservative Americans, cherish: the open competitive market. In the open market, the end result is as always; there are winners and losers. Approximately one-third of the hospitals in operation presently in the US will not cross the 2020 finish line as winners.[12] Other experts agree that healthcare is facing an uncertain future given its commercialization, rising costs to patients, and the social media's lack of attention to disease transmission and death among personnel and patients. The more profitable hospitals, with California hospitals as an exception (see below for details), have a tight vertically integrated relationship with physicians— contractual or ownership of physician practices; vertically integrated systems tend to produce higher hospital prices and spending.[13,5]

mariakraynova/Shutterstock, Inc.

[3] At the core of these challenges are IT strategies and systems which cause financial repercussions and hospital mistakes. Ideally, computer technology and IT strategies should reduce operational inefficiencies; yet IT strategies and computer systems are often too complicated, time consuming, and are rarely integrated into the actual processes of the healing center; therefore healthcare personnel tend to ignore them. Often, patients wind up in the wrong beds, are discharged earlier or later than appropriate, and sometimes patients receive the wrong medication intended for another patient.

Also, hospitals cannot afford to waste the limited time of their physicians and nurses on IT frustrations. Slow log-in times, slow IT helpdesk response times, and other IT lag issues reduce the amount of patient-facing time for clinicians. For instance, one five-minute log-in lag per clinician per day in a 100-clinician hospital (with an estimated average salary of $90/hour) would cost a hospital more than $200,000 a year in lost patient-facing time.

Source: Terry Maher (ND). Discharge Focus Puts Hospital Capacity Issue to Bed. USC Consulting Group. Retrieved August 12, 2014: http://www.usccg.com/ref/pdfs/USCWhitepaperEDArticle.pdf

[4] Innovation in mobile communication technology has provided novel approaches to the delivery of healthcare and improvements in the speed and quality of routine medical communication. However, bacterial contamination of mobile communication devices (MCDs) are an important issue affecting the implementation of effective infection control measures. Also, 9–25 percent of MCDs are contaminated with pathogenic bacteria, researchers learned.

Source: see endnote RR Brady, J Verran, NN Damani, and AP Gibb (2009). Review of Mobile Communication Devices as Potential Reservoirs of Nosocomial Pathogens. *Journal of Hospital Infection*, 71(4): 295–300.

[5]Vertical Integration in healthcare systems relates to a "network of organizations that provides or arranges to provide a coordinated continuum of services to a defined community, and is held clinically and fiscally accountable for the outcomes and health status of those served."

Source: KJ Devers, SM Shortell, DA Anderson, JB Mitchell, and KL Morgan (1994). Implementing Organized Delivery Systems: An Integration Scorecard. *Health Care Management Review*, 19:7–20. Another perspective is from the Medical Dictionary for the Health Professions online: A system that provides primary care, specialty care, or hospitalization, as necessary, through interdisciplinary and specialty collaboration.

Vertical Integration

Vertical Integration ideally might reduce healthcare spending and it should enhance the quality of care and treatment by improving communication across healing centers; but, vertical integration can increase providers' market power and facilitate the payment of what are effectively kickbacks for inappropriate referrals as investigated by Federal Bureau of Investigation and Health Care Fraud Prevention and Enforcement Action Team (HEAT) (see below for details).[6] It is important to note that Federal Trade Commission's approval is not required for the formation of clinically integrated networks.[14]

According to DHG Healthcare, a healthcare consulting firm, clinical integration is not:[15]

- Simply physician employment
- Led solely by hospitals
- A reduction of choice or limiting services
- Only based on a new electronic medical records system
- Simply a mechanism to gain negotiating leverage over payers
- A stand-alone independent practice association/physician-hospital organization messenger contract model
- A return to capitation of the 1990s

On the other hand, clinical integration is:

- A network led by select employed and private practice physicians typically working with a hospital to improve quality and efficiency of care
- Increased coordination between providers, supported by reliable data, to improve outcomes and reduce waste
- A legal structure that allows members of the network to be financially rewarded for demonstrated performance
- A vehicle that allows the network to collectively negotiate contracts on behalf of its members
- A model that lays the foundation for the future realities of accountable care

Finally, a common argument raised about hospital commercialization is that hospitals that are freed from competitive pressures are able to offer more charity care to poor consumers because insured patients, particularly managed care and privately insured patients, cross-subsidize a hospital's charity care. When the argument that increased competition in the healthcare sector inhibits a healthcare system or individual hospital's ability to offer charity care was analyzed, researchers report little relationship between the absence of competition and the provision of charity care.[16]

[6] A vertical integrated healthcare system is broad-based and provides a full range of services, including ambulatory, acute, and non-acute institutional and residential care. Geographically the system should serve the needs of a defined population and reduce the gaps present in the healthcare system. There is the institutional view which focuses on clinical services and whereby the system is the center of the healthcare system. There is also a community view of vertical integrated healthcare systems whereby the system supports a wellness model that reflects community priorities and needs, in which access to appropriate care is an important issue. To achieve these goals, there must be a shared philosophy and vision throughout the organization. This mandates the involvement of healthcare personnel and patients, or a socialization process as discussed among nurses described in Chapter 8. There must be effective and accepted indicators to monitor both the process and outcome of care. It is important to measure consumer satisfaction, access to care, quality of care, and clinical outcomes. What vertical integration ultimately comes down to is that the healthcare system, in and by itself controls policy and enforcement, hiring and training of all personnel including physicians and surgeons. Everyone works for the healthcare system. *Source:* Douglas Sinclair (2001). Health Care Reform: The Effect of A Vertically Integrated Health System on Emergency Medicine. *Canadian Journal of Emergency Medicine*, 2(3):154–155.

Hospital Policy Differences

One study evaluated thirteen US metropolitan areas consisting of 590,000 workers and their dependents; what was concluded is that hospital prices for privately insured patients are much higher than Medicare payment rates and those prices vary widely across and within markets.[17] The variation in hospital and specialist physician prices within communities implies that some hospitals and some physicians have significant commercialized market power over patients and over any market competition; this power includes the capacity to command high prices and to some extent it also implies that those systems control wages. Despite the presence of a dominant insurer such as Blue Cross or Unitedhealth

Group in the areas tested, most of the hospitals command prices that were higher than Medicare, and some hospitals commanded prices that are twice what Medicare pays.[7] The price gap within markets is even greater for hospital outpatient care, with the highest-priced hospital typically paying nearly double the lowest-priced hospital.

There exists a wide variation in private insurer payment rates to hospitals and physicians across and within local markets; this finding implies that some providers have a significant competitive edge to negotiate higher-than-competitive prices, says the Center for Studying Health System Change (HSC).[18] In eight healthcare markets: Cleveland, Indianapolis, Los Angeles, Miami, Milwaukee, Richmond, San Francisco, and rural Wisconsin—the average inpatient hospital payment rates of four large national insurers ranged from 147 percent of Medicare in Miami to 210 percent in San Francisco. In extreme cases, some hospitals command almost five times what Medicare pays for inpatient services and more than seven times what Medicare pays for outpatient care. Variation within markets is affected too. For example, the hospital with prices at the 25th percentile of Los Angeles hospitals received 84 percent of Medicare rates for inpatient care, while the hospital with prices at the 75th percentile received over 100 percent more of Medicare rates. The highest-priced Los Angeles hospital with sizable inpatient claims received 418 percent of Medicare. While not as pronounced, significant variation in physician payment rates also exist across and within markets and by physician specialty.

[7] The largest 125 US health insurers collected some $713 billion in 2012 premiums. The top 25 accounted for nearly two-thirds of the total. The top five companies follow:

- Unitedhealth Group
- Wellpoint Inc. Group
- Kaiser Foundation Group
- Humana Group
- Aetna Group

Source: Evi Heilbrunn (2013, December 16). Top Health Insurance Companies. Best? Not Necessarily. But These Health Insurers Have The Biggest Market Share. US News and World Report. Retrieved August 6, 2014: http://health.usnews.com/health-news/health-insurance/articles/2013/12/16/top-health-insurance-companies

By contrast, California, which has a health insurance market that is dominated by for-profit health maintenance organizations (HMOs), reflects a wide variety of organizational approaches along a continuum that stretches from contractual networks to fully integrated systems.[19] If a trend is emerging in the early twenty-first century in California, it seems to favor less "vertical integration" and more reliance on "virtual integration" among physician groups, hospitals, and health plans.

A study evaluated 1,858 patients undergoing cardiac valve replacement surgery at 37 hospitals in 7 states for 2008.[20] The researcher reports that cardiac valve replacement surgery is an expensive but profitable procedure, with average cost and contribution margin per case of $38,667 for individuals with private insurance. Patients with Medicare pay an average of $30,986. Hospitals charge significantly higher prices and earn significantly higher contribution margins from private insurers than from Medicare for patients undergoing cardiac valve replacement. Thus, hospitals require methods through their own vertical integrated systems to maximize their income. For example, some systems pick and private insured patients for extended stays and surgery because they add to the profit statements at a greater rate than patients with Medicare. Hospital systems faced experiencing differences between Medicare payments versus the systems projected costs concentrate on patients or markets with private insurers, while hospitals in competitive markets, which there are few, focus their attention on cutting costs.[21]

Economic experts suggest that healthcare organizations must become digital to survive. Some critical questions must be asked and answered by the healthcare managers and officials such as what areas will require additional investment and growth—and what activities will we no longer be able to support?[22] As health systems take their giant steps toward preparing for financial independence, one perspective is certain: carefully analyzing the ways in which reform could affect an organization—and developing a comprehensive business development plan in response—is critical to the success and domination of a healthcare system.[23]

Relevance of Hospital Commercialization Descriptions

By this time you're probably wondering why all the descriptions about healthcare entrepreneurship, commercialization, and the economic fortitude or spirit of hospital systems and their resources are discussed in this chapter.

As long as physicians remain in solo practice and further their control over medicine (see HMOs and venture capital below) and hospitals remain acute care citadels in control of costs and hospital patients,[24] it is likely that hospital costs will continue to rise (and that healthcare providers will be under close observation by federal task force agencies). The principal focus and energy of healthcare systems are lock-stepped toward profit and loss statements; there is little wrong with the idea of making a profit if deadly pathogens and medical errors were controlled or at best minimized. Disease transmission through patient or hospital associated infection (or whatever term you wish to use; see Chapter 8 for more details) will also continue to rise in healing centers or all varieties including ambulatory centers, acute care units, outpatient centers, and emergency departments (see Chapter 8 for details) and among personnel and patients. The rise of deadly infections is persistent in healing centers regardless of the profitability or lack of it; the option is either hospitals police themselves (which is preferred), or socialized medicine (at least at the state level) should become law, or all physicians work for a healthcare system as opposed to being independent, or the other way around (physicians own and operate the hospital systems).[25] Obviously, hospitals cannot nor have they policed themselves, the evidence suggests. Rather, hospital systems are using their resources to build facilities and to buy equipment in order to attract patients and physicians "whom they woo intensively."[26]

What healing centers have done is linked not to infection control but sound capitalist ideologies (see the Final Thoughts section of this chapter for details); hospital systems are building contractual networks or buying medical networks of physician care and treatment centers, outpatient and acute care centers for the purpose of controlling physician costs and referrals.[27] Although most physicians are solo or linked to a few other physicians, there is a smaller number of very large and rapidly growing multispecialty physician groups which are often owned by hospitals, health plans, private equity firms, or other non-physician sponsors.[28] A final thought about the relationship of hospitals and capitalist enterprises, both patients and hospital enterprises constantly use the legal powers of the state and federal government to advance their own interests. Sometimes, physicians and surgeons are caught in the middle between patients and hospital systems (see Medicine and Human Error below) of a legal battle. Consider the enforcement and prosecution costs when thinking about hospital commercialization; could those resources be utilized in a more advantageous manner patricianly in the prevention and cures of infections?

Hospitals and Federal Prosecution

The previous chapter (Chapter 8) suggests similar agents of compliance among healthcare personnel and in that case, nurses. Hospitals (administrators and staff), physicians, and surgeons come under the cloak of out-of-control infections, politics and policy, and compliance regulation similar to ambulatory and acute care, emergency department, and other healthcare personnel (see Chapter 8). One difference might be that hospitals, physicians, and surgeons have more to lose than their health. For example, Saint Joseph London Hospital in Kentucky agreed to pay the US government $16.5 million to resolve civil allegations that it submitted false or fraudulent claims to the Medicare and Kentucky Medicaid programs for medically unnecessary heart procedures.[29] "We all rely on health care providers to make treatment decisions based on clinical, not financial, considerations," says the prosecuting government attorney. The government contends that several doctors working at the hospital performed numerous invasive cardiac procedures on Medicare and Medicaid patients who did not need them. The hospital then billed the federal programs for these unnecessary procedures, which include coronary stents, pacemakers, coronary artery bypass graft surgeries (CABGS), and diagnostic catheterizations.

The settlement to the US government was originally filed by three cardiologists who will share $2.5 million for their "whistleblower" action. Also, Dr. Sandesh Patil at Saint Joseph Hospital had performed medically unnecessary coronary stents; he pled guilty to a federal healthcare fraud offense and was sentenced to thirty months' imprisonment.

Largest Hospitals in the United States

The five largest hospitals in the United States are:[30]

1. New York-Presbyterian Hospital/Weill Cornell Medical Center (New York City)—2,236 beds. New York-Presbyterian/Weill Cornell is a major non-profit teaching hospital that offers a variety of services, including a renowned cancer program. The facility admits 48,000 emergency room patients every year and performs

38,500 inpatient and 39,400 outpatient surgeries, as well as 13,700 births. Emergency care is provided 24 hours a day, 7 days a week to adults and children in the level I trauma center, psychiatric emergency receiving center, and burn center for the city of New York. The hospital also features a high-risk neonatal transport service, where the hospital serves as an emergency transfer, receiving, and stabilization center.

2. Florida Hospital Orlando (Fla.)—1,972. Florida Hospital Orlando is a non-profit acute-care community hospital that serves over 32,000 inpatients and 53,000 outpatients annually. Serving as a major tertiary facility for much of the southeastern part of the United States, the hospital is part of the Florida Hospital system, a group of private hospitals operated by Adventist Health System. It contains nationally renowned institutes for cardiology, diabetes, orthopedics, and neuroscience. The hospital was founded in 1908 by leaders of the Adventist Church.
3. Jackson Memorial Hospital (Miami)—1,756. Jackson Memorial Hospital is a non-profit tertiary teaching hospital that first opened in 1918. The hospital works in conjunction with the University of Miami Miller School of Medicine to offer a wide variety of services, educational programs, a space for clinical research and health-related community services. The hospital is well-known for its Ryder Trauma Center, the only adult and pediatric level I trauma center in the Miami-Dade area. It also features a 66-bed neonatal intensive care unit, the largest unit in the state, and is the only Florida hospital to perform every kind of organ transplant.
4. University of Pittsburgh (Pa.) Medical Center Presbyterian—1,602. Founded in 1893, University of Pittsburgh Medical Center Presbyterian is a non-profit adult medical-surgical referral hospital with a strong emphasis on research. Closely connected to the University of Pittsburgh School of Medicine, the hospital is a recognized leader in cardiology and cardiothoracic surgery, trauma services, neurosurgery, and organ transplantation. The hospital handles over 30,000 emergency room admissions every year and performs 26,800 inpatient and 23,600 outpatient surgeries. UPMC Presbyterian is also designed as a level I regional resource trauma center. The hospital is divided into two buildings—UPMC Presbyterian and UPMC Montefiore—that are linked by a bridge.
5. Methodist Hospital (Indianapolis)—1,450. Methodist Hospital, which is part of Clarian Health, is the largest hospital in Indiana with one of the largest critical care departments and the largest neuroscience critical care unit in the country. The hospital also implemented the first and largest comprehensive intensive care patient electronic monitoring system in Central Indiana. As a hospital with one of the largest emergency departments in the country, almost 97,000 patients came through Methodist's ED in 2008. One-hundred-thirty beds are dedicated to the critical care unit. The hospital has established itself as a leader in the community by launching outreach initiatives, including the Indiana Poison Center, Indiana Mothers' Milk Bank, and ThinkFirst Shaken Baby Program.

Physicians

The number of physicians in the US has decreased since 1970; as of 2012, there were approximately 5.5 physicians per 100,000 of the population graduating medical school that year.[31] Number of graduating medical doctors has not changed much; the American population has increased.

The education of physicians in the US is lengthy and involves undergraduate education, medical school, and graduate medical education, says the AMA.[32] The term "graduate medical education" includes residency and fellowship training which takes a total of about twelve to fourteen years (depending on residency) of formal education including residency. Nonetheless, much of the recent work in tackling meticillin-resistant Staphylococcus aureus (MRSA) has focused on something as simple as hygiene in hospitals; yet, it is unclear how much physicians and nurses know about the treatment and management of patients who are colonized or infected with MRSA. In one study it was learned that many aspects of MRSA and its management was deficient among physicians and nurses.[33] It might be easy to conclude that of the many years of education and training, MRSA and other deadly pathogen control methods have not been a priority. Furthermore, although, exposure to blood-borne pathogens from sharps injuries continues to pose a significant risk to healthcare personnel including physicians and nurses, the actual number of injuries sustained remains unclear, primarily due to under-reporting.[34] One estimate puts the number of injuries at 4 percent of healthcare professionals. Physicians and nurses are the most at risk, the researchers learned.

Just to provide an idea about the number of visits to private physicians outside of the hospital, between 1989 and 1998 the number increased significantly from 677 million to 797 million, although the rate of visits per 100 population did not change significantly.[35] In dollars, between 1995 and 2003, average physician net income from the practice of medicine declined about 7 percent after adjusting for inflation.[36] This estimated decline in physicians' real income is in comparison to other professionals who earned an approximate 7 percent increase after adjusting for inflation during the same period. Among different types of physicians, primary care physicians fared the worst with a 10 percent decline in real income between 1995 and 2003, while surgeons' real income declined by an estimated 8 percent.

The US Department of Labor as of 2012 reports an average wage among physicians and surgeons is equal or greater than $187,200 per year or $90.00 per hour.[37, 8] Employment of physicians and surgeons is projected to grow 18 percent from 2012 to 2022, faster than the average for all occupations. Job growth will occur because of the continued expansion of healthcare-related industries.

Capitalist Physicians and Surgeons

In the mid-1970s, physicians started to invest in their own clinical laboratories (28% of all groups), radiology laboratories (32%), electrocardiological laboratories (32%), and audiology laboratories (16%).[38] Almost 40 percent of all independent physicians operate their own laboratories. The larger the group of physicians connected together in a doctors' office environment, the more likely it is that the group collectively own healthcare laboratories. For instance, 23 percent of three-physician groups and 78 percent of all physician groups own their own laboratories. Also, the larger the physician base, the greater the likelihood that they collectively own their own surgical suites.[39]

When discussing physicians and income, a brief discussion about abortion is warranted. For instance, in many jurisdictions that have a mental health indication for abortion, "it is often applied inconsistently and with a lack of transparency, causing unfair access to lawful services."[40] In jurisdictions where lawful abortion rules and regulations are applied inconsistently, physicians make decisions. In some cases, those decisions include the legal and human rights of the patients. In other jurisdictions that might not be the case. Some physicians charge "fees considerably in excess of those charged for similarly managed procedures, may be suspected of opportunistically serving exploitive, self-interested motivations rather than their patients' health interests,"[41] say some researchers.

[8] **What Physicians and Surgeons Do**
Physicians and surgeons diagnose and treat injuries or illnesses. Physicians examine patients; take medical histories; prescribe medications; and order, perform, and interpret diagnostic tests. They counsel patients on diet, hygiene, and preventive healthcare. Surgeons operate on patients to treat injuries, such as broken bones; diseases, such as cancerous tumors; and deformities, such as cleft palates.
Source: US Department of Labor (2014). Physicians and Surgeons. Retrieved August 9, 2014: http://www.bls.gov/ooh/healthcare/physicians-and-surgeons.htm

[9] Venture capital defined: Money made available for investment in innovative enterprises or research, especially in high technology, in which both the risk of loss and the potential for profit may be considerable. Source: TheFreeDictionary.com. A private equity transaction in an existing company or start-up involves an entrepreneur, their staff, and financial investors. The financiers invest equity, becoming shareholders in the company. The main opportunities for physicians desiring exposure to venture capital come indirectly (through the company being funded) or directly (through the venture capital investor). Source: Fred Dotzler (2001). See endnote.

Physicians, Surgeons, and Venture Capital

Some consulting firms loan money to organizations and individuals such as physicians who specialize in biotechnology, pharmaceuticals, medical devices and equipment, drug delivery, healthcare services, and healthcare data and information.[42] Those consulting firms push the idea that physicians (and hospital systems) can enhance organizational and individual experiences (and income) by raising capital for a start-up of a new venture.[9]

Venture capital is also called risk capital and is fueled by the vision of the heyday of the late 1990s: private companies moving rapidly from inception to IPO (initial public offering), with millionaires being created on a weekly basis.[43] The industry at least as it pertains to healthcare has cooled, some experts say, but venture capital is still one of the best means for promising young medtech/pharma/biotech/ or medical services companies to finance their product creation and pathways to market.

Venture Capital Is Not Without Its Ills

The medical industry is struggling to adapt to what appears to be a thriftier healthcare system;[44] one reporter refers to a "venture-capital drought" in certain financial areas of investment. For example, investments in the medical-device and equipment industry fell in 2013 to $2.14 billion, down more than 40 percent from 2007. Venture money received by the biotechnology sector declined 28 percent over the same period, while software startups recorded a 75 percent increase.

Success of Venture Capital

Another reporter suggests that because of Obamacare (Affordable Care Act, see Chapter 2 for details) the healthcare industry will completely change for a profit.[45] "This is the greatest opportunity I've seen in my lifetime. It's the first time we are seeing really fundamental changes happen. And there's a lot of money that can be made as this chaos is sorted out," says a co-founder and managing member of a healthcare-focused venture capital firm. With trillions of dollars estimated to be spent, as the Affordable Care Act develops, there "are trillions more to be reallocated . . ."[46] The thinking is that healthcare providers will be forced to find new ways to manage patients and costs, experts say. One implication arising from these thoughts is that venture capitalist firms will risk huge funds on physicians and surgeons in their efforts to build their market positions and practices.

Examples of Venture Capital Firms for Physicians

A few examples of venture capital firms that financially aid physicians and surgeons follow:[47]

- *Accuitive Medical Ventures* is a $160 million fund that invests exclusively in early stage medical device technology opportunities nationwide. The group invests up to $10 million per company over the life of a deal.
- *Advent International* invests in companies at all stages of development, from emerging growth enterprises to large profitable businesses. The group can provide up to $200 million in equity for a single transaction and will consider a variety of investment structures, including minority equity positions, leveraged recapitalizations, and management buyouts. Current portfolio includes companies in the cardiovascular, orthopedic, imaging, and diagnostics fields.
- *Alpha Capital Partners* provides equity financing for promising growth businesses and buyouts or recapitalizations of established companies. Investment typically ranges from $500,000 to $4 million per enterprise, with concentration in the greater Midwest. The portfolio includes developers of automated immunoassay instruments, digital interconnect systems for medical imaging equipment, and surgical cable and instruments.
- *Hickory Venture Capital* provides long-term venture capital financing to small but rapidly growing private companies throughout the Southeast, Southwest, Mid-Atlantic, and Midwest. The firm typically invests $1 million to $2 million initially, and may fund up to $6 million over time. The group does not seek control, but instead backs strong management teams.
- *Norwest Venture Capital* commonly serves as one of the lead investors for its portfolio companies. Total investment in a company can range from $1.5 million to $20 million. The portfolio covers automated sample preparation, blood-gas sensing, minimally invasive surgery, and orthopedics.
- *TGap Venture Capital Fund* is a $20 million venture capital firm formed in 2002 with its headquarters in Kalamazoo, Michigan. The Fund invests in early stage medical devices, medical services, and IT technology companies. TGap's typical initial investment in a company is between $250,000 and $1,000,000, and is made as part of a larger financing in conjunction with other investors.

Physicians, Health Maintenance Organization Act (HMO), and Managed Care

The push of hospital systems into multifaceted business and both contractual and employment of physicians has led physicians to reorganize into larger units and networks of managed care that control costs and quality of services rendered.[48] Managed care can be defined as any arrangement for healthcare in which an organization, such as an "HMO, another type of doctor-hospital network, or an insurance company, acts as intermediate between the person seeking care and the physician."[49]

By 1976, there were 175 HMOs with 6 million members.[10] However, insurance carriers developed their own HMOs to compete with physicians. By 1987, there were 650 HMOs with about 29 million members. By 1990 there were forty-two national firms that enrolled one-half of all HMO members. Most of the new HMOs owned by physicians and insurance carriers alike consisted of networks of private physicians linked by part-time contracts rather than a staff of workers. Often physicians would extend their networks and financially gain from managed care, hospitals, and other healthcare systems.

Sometimes, physicians are prosecuted for decisions to engage with other networks and organizations. For example, Roland Borrasi MD, was convicted of Medicare fraud after he accepted a salary from a hospital in exchange for continually referring patients to the facility, a violation of 42 U.S.C. § 1320a-7b (see below for details).[50] Here are some of the facts of the case: Borrasi owned Integrated Health Centers in South Carolina, a corporate group of healthcare providers in Illinois. He worked primarily at nursing homes and hospitals. He received remuneration from a licensed inpatient psychiatric hospital in Illinois. Reimbursements from the Medicare federal health care program constituted the vast majority of payments received by the psychiatric hospital. Between 1999 and 2002, the government argues that Borrasi accepted bribes for an increasing stream of Medicare patient referrals. The government says that to conceal these (alleged) bribes, Borrasi was placed on the psychiatric hospital's payroll, given a false title (Service Medical Director), and job description. In December 2006, a grand jury returned an indictment against Borrasi charging him with one count of conspiracy to defraud the US government, and six counts of Medicare-related bribery in violation of *42 U.S.C. § 1320a-7b et seq.*[11] The jury's verdict was that Borrasi is guilty; the

[10] **Health maintenance organizations (HMO)** are defined as entities which provide basic health services to their enrollees, and, for an additional payment, supplemental 'health services. Prepaid enrollment fees for the basic and supplemental health' services must be fixed uniformly under a community rating system—without regard for the medical history of any individual or family. The basic health services that must be provided by the HMO to its enrollees are:

- physicians' services (including consultant and referral services by a physician)
- inpatient and outpatient hospital services
- medically necessary emergency health services
- short-term (not to exceed twenty visits) outpatient evaluative and crisis-intervention mental health services

Source: Health Maintenance Organization Act of 1973. http://www.ssa.gov/policy/docs/ssb/v37n3/v37n3p35.pdf

[11] **42 U.S.C. § 1320a-7b: (a) Making or causing to be made false statements or representations**

Whoever—

- knowingly and willfully makes or causes to be made any false statement or representation of a material fact in any application for any benefit or payment under a Federal health care program.
- at any time knowingly and willfully makes or causes to be made any false statement or representation of a material fact for use in determining rights to such benefit or payment,
- having knowledge of the occurrence of any event affecting: his initial or continued right to any such benefit or payment, or the initial or continued right to any such benefit or payment of any other individual in whose behalf he has applied for or is receiving such benefit or payment, conceals or fails to disclose such event with an intent fraudulently to secure such benefit or payment either in a greater amount or quantity than is due or when no such benefit or payment is authorized.
- having made application to receive any such benefit or payment for the use and benefit of another and having received it, knowingly and willfully converts such benefit or payment or any part thereof to a use other than for the use and benefit of such other person,
- presents or causes to be presented a claim for a physician's service for which payment may be made under a Federal health care program and knows that the individual who furnished the service was not licensed as a physician, or
- for a fee knowingly and willfully counsels or assists an individual to dispose of assets (including by any transfer in trust) in order for the individual to become eligible for medical assistance under a State plan under subchapter XIX of this chapter, if disposing of the assets results in the imposition of a period of ineligibility for such assistance under section 1396p (c) of this title.

Source: Cornell Law (2014). § 1320a–7b—Criminal penalties for acts involving Federal health care programs. http://www.law.cornell.edu/uscode/text/42/1320a-7b

court sentenced Borrasi to seventy-two months' imprisonment and two years' supervised release. Borrasi's position was that funds received were to compensate him for actual services rendered, but the government had another opinion and won. Even on appeal, Borrasi lost.

The HMOs and networking of physicians according to some experts does not mean that physicians are corporatized executives (or even that they know anything about business), although some can be considered managerial executives. For example, some venture capital firms are headed by physicians. One venture capital firm reports this about its CEO:[51] Ross Jaffe, MD specializes in early-stage investing in medical devices, bringing significant clinical insight to each venture. Ross co-founded Versant Ventures in 1999 after spending nine years at Brentwood Venture Capital where, as a general partner, he led investments in medical devices, drug delivery, and healthcare information systems companies . . . Ross completed his residency training in Internal Medicine/Primary Care at the University of California . . . remained a part-time physician there until 1995. Before and during medical school he was an Analyst for Lewin and Associates.

Physician Error

In a study of 500 hospital physicians who manage hospital patients, 40 percent report that at least once a month, they took on more patients than they could safely handle.[52] About a quarter of physicians report high workload prevents them from fully discussing treatment options with patients; and 22 percent report that they sometimes ordered unnecessary tests because they did not have enough time to examine the case of the patients. Also, it appears that monetary concerns may help explain the workloads, says a researcher at Johns Hopkins University School of Medicine in Baltimore.[53] However, the researchers also learned that physician errors in judgment were strongly associated with reports of inadequate supervision, indicating that systems failures contributed to at least a subset of the cognitive errors and most often those errors involved emergency surgical care.

Medicine and Human Error

One issue is that medical organizations through commercialized policy and government indifferent compliance regulations are bustling with obstacles that led to human error.[54] One medical professional wrote that physicians and surgeons learn on the job; they often improvise much of their technique and self-confidence. Medical experts say that medicine is fundamentally a human endeavor;[55] therefore, human error is inescapable. Adding to the issues of human error are the realities of the profession that is an enterprise of constantly changing knowledge, uncertain information, fallible individuals, and at the same time human lives are on the line. Also, one key challenge of infection control results from inappropriate patient-care practices. Improving practices frequently implies modifying behavior, and the behavior of physicians is the behavior modeled most often by other healthcare personnel including nurses.[56]

Surgeon Error

Studies show that up to two-thirds of hospital adverse incidents are attributable to surgical care.

More than one-half of adverse incidents are preventable.[57] Little question that the surgical management of disease is complicated and as every chapter in this book has brought evidence to, disease management is uncontrollable requiring many components toward recovery including pharmaceutical antibiotics which are not available. Following is a list of organizational and human factors that contribute to poor surgical outcomes:[58]

- Surgeon Inexperience
- Low Hospital Volume for an Operation
- Excessive Workload
- Fatigue (most surgeons are overworked with huge caseloads)[59]
- Poor Technology
- Insufficient Supervision of Trainees
- Inadequate Hospital Systems
- Poor Communication among Staff, Time of Day
- Bureaucracy or Administrative Failures

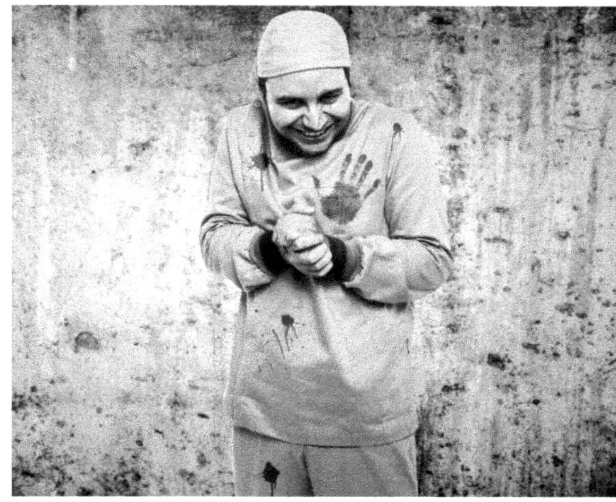

Minerva Studio/Shutterstock, Inc.

'Never Events'

The term "adverse event" describes harm to a patient as a result of medical care, such as infection associated with use of a catheter. The term "never events" refers to a specific list of serious events, such as surgery on the wrong patient, that the National Quality Forum (NQF) deemed "should never occur in a health care setting."[60] The Inspector General's team at DHS, estimated that:

- almost 14 percent of hospitalized Medicare beneficiaries experienced adverse events during their hospital stays.
- An additional 13.5 percent of Medicare beneficiaries experienced events during their hospital stays that resulted in temporary harm.
- Physician reviewers determined that 44 percent of adverse and temporary harm events were clearly or likely preventable.
- Hospital care associated with adverse and temporary harm events cost Medicare alone an estimated $324 million in October 2008.
- FY 2009 equates to $4.4 billion spent on care associated with events.

'Never Events' that should never occur in surgery happen at least 4,000 times a year in US hospitals.[61] One estimate from Johns Hopkins University researchers show that over 80,000 'never events' occurred between 1990 and 2010. They estimate that at least thirty-nine times a week a surgeon leaves foreign objects inside their patients, which includes towels or sponges. In addition surgeons performing the wrong surgery or operating on the wrong body part occurs around 20 times a week.

The frequency of preventable and lethal patient harms has increased from 1984 to 2002–2008, reports one researcher because of the:[62]

- increased complexity of medical practice and technology
- increased incidence of antibiotic-resistant bacteria
- overuse/misuse of medications
- aging population
- movement of the medical industry toward higher productivity and expensive technology, which encourages rapid patient flow and overuse of risky, invasive, revenue-generating procedure

Cost of Medical Errors

About fifteen years ago, The Institute of Medicine reported that adverse medical events in the US result in an estimated $4.5 to $5.7 billion per year in additional costs for national patient care.[63,12] The Institute states that "beyond their (medical errors) cost in human lives, preventable medical errors, exact other significant tolls. They have been estimated to result in total costs (including the expense of additional care necessitated by the errors, lost income and household productivity, and disability) of between $17 billion and $29 billion per year in hospitals nationwide."[64] Caution: the IM report does not mention patient associated infection, or MRSA or any other deathly pathogens.

[12] Medical errors can be defined as the failure of a planned action to be completed as intended or the use of a wrong plan to achieve an aim. Among the problems that commonly occur during the course of providing healthcare are adverse drug events and improper transfusions, surgical injuries and wrong-site surgery, suicides, restraint-related injuries or death, falls, burns, pressure ulcers, and mistaken patient identities. High error rates with serious consequences are most likely to occur in intensive care units, operating rooms, and emergency departments. Source: Institute of Medicine

Explanations of Physician and Surgeon Errors

When physicians and surgeons are responsible for medical errors even serious errors such as permanent disability and death, contrary to the premises of malpractice law, the vast majority of those errors are not solely the result of individual physician or surgeon failure.[65]

The vast majority of surgical errors involved contributions from more than one medical clinician; frequently, it is a chain of events spanning more than one phase of care that leads to a reportable error. For example, surgeons report that cognitive failures (e.g., of judgment or vigilance) play a role in more than half the error incidents; but those surgeons also report that systems factors such as system policy which may well encompass compliance issues contributed in 84 percent of these cases.[66] Are physicians who are learned men and women caught up in decisions influenced by government prosecution?

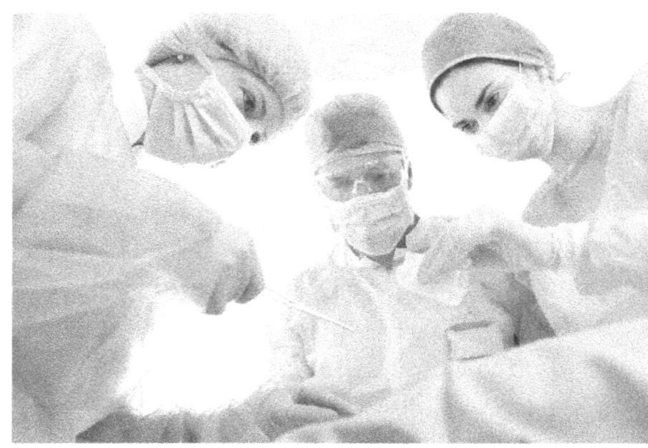

StockLite/Shutterstock, Inc.

Fear of Prosecution

When a physician or a nurse fears prosecution for righteous performance, is it possible that she or he would do the wrong thing to avoid prosecution? In an attempt to explain the fear of prosecution as a factor linked to suspect decisions made by hospital systems and physicians, perhaps a fear of crime perspective can shed some light. For instance, some scholars wonder why the public persists in believing that violent crime is a widespread national problem despite declining trends in crime and the fact that crime is concentrated in urban locations?[67] Those scholars proposed that Cultivation theory applies; this theory suggests that widespread fear of crime is fueled in part by heavy exposure to violent dramatic programming on prime-time television. They tested 2,300 Philadelphia residents; their results support Cultivation theory's predicted effects of television on the public. When individuals have a fear of crime for keeping the law, would she or he resort to illegal behavior?

Studies show that behavior is different when the fear of crime is present;[68] other studies add that perceptions of risk are explicably situated in an individual's understandings of the social and physical make-up of their neighborhood or, I will add, their occupational environment (similar to criminal justice personnel), as well as the agents of compliance and broader social attitudes and values.[69] Studies show that "the impact of fear of crime ranges from detrimental physiological changes to physiological reaction and behavioral adaptations."[70]

In my own study on why American blacks resort to murder, I learned that homicide was seen as an appropriate response in at-risk environments by law-abiding individuals who believed (via the media) that crime was pervasive in their community; they believed that if they did not buy a weapon and squeeze the trigger when they perceived an attack, they would be killed.[71] The risk of murder by a nonviolent person is worth the perceived gain. Before you say no, how would you explain nonviolent females who after years of punishment, kill their domestic violent abuser?[72] Or parents who kill the sexual violator of their child? Or the states that have shoot-first laws on the books. Is it true that most of us depending on our environment and our perceptions of the social facts, could resort to the worst crimes imaginable? Are physicians immune to decisions that other physicians might not make depending on their individual interpretation of the social facts? The fear of prosecution (civil liabilities USC Section 1983 of Title 42) even among police officers plays a role in whether the officer will conduct an arrest regardless of the crime.[73] Do physicians take their own lives despite The Hippocratic Oath he or she pledged to as part of graduation from medical school?[74]

Physician Depression and Suicide

Each year in the US, roughly 300 to 400 physicians die by suicide, but the statistics might be higher because of underreporting.[75]

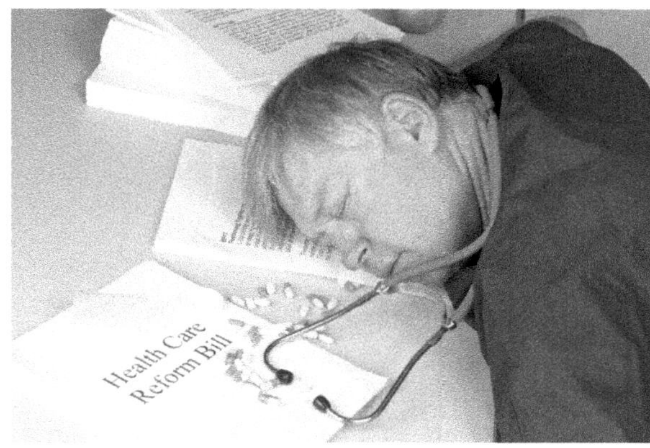

Joe Belanger/Shutterstock, Inc.

Depression is a major risk factor in physician suicide. Other factors include bipolar disorder and alcohol and substance abuse. Of interest, there is no evidence that work-related stressors are linked to elevated rates of suicide among physicians. Medical students have rates of depression 15 to 30 percent higher than the general population. Contributing to the higher suicide rate among physicians is their higher completion to attempt ratio, which may result from greater knowledge of lethality of drugs and easy access to means or in this writer's terms, more confidence that he or she can take charge of the situation. For instance, in my experiences with addiction among prisoners, there is a visible lack of self-respect but lots of confidence probably as a defense mechanism.

As previously mentioned in Chapter 8, suicide deaths among physicians are higher for female physicians than male physicians. But they are also 250 to 400 percent higher among female physicians when compared to females in other professions. Among male physicians, death by suicide is 70 percent higher when compared to males in other professions. Female physicians have a higher rate of major depression than age-matched women with doctorate degrees.

Becoming a physician has "become a miserable and humiliating undertaking."[76] Some physicians might feel that America has declared war on them—"and both physicians and patients are the losers." Medical students opt for high-paying specialties so they can retire as quickly as possible. Physician MBA programs—that promise a way into management—are flourishing. The website known as the Drop-Out-Club—which hooks doctors up with jobs at hedge funds and venture capital firms—has a solid following. In fact, physicians are so bummed out that 9 out of 10 doctors would discourage anyone from entering the profession.

Healthcare Fraud Prevention and Enforcement Action Team (HEAT)

Heat is a joint task force of the Department of Health and Human Services and the Department of Justice.[13] The Heat Task Force successes follow:[77]

- Between 2008 and 2011, HEAT actions led to a 75% increase in individuals charged with criminal health care fraud.

[13] **HEAT Task Force**
Health Care Fraud Prevention and Enforcement Action Team (HEAT)
In May 2009, the Department of Health and Human Services (HHS) and Department of Justice (DOJ) created the Health Care Fraud Prevention and Enforcement Action Team (HEAT). With its creation, the fight against Medicare fraud became a Cabinet-level priority. HEAT's work is directed by HHS Secretary Sylvia Mathews Burwell and Attorney General Eric Holder (as of June 2014).
HEAT's mission

- To gather resources across the government to help prevent waste, fraud, and abuse in the Medicare and Medicaid programs.
- To crack down on the people and organizations who abuse the system and cost Americans billions of dollars each year.
- To reduce health care costs and improve quality of care by preventing fraudsters from preying on people with Medicare and Medicaid

Source: Heat Task Force http://www.stopmedicarefraud.gov/aboutfraud/heattaskforce/index.html

- Since 2007, HEAT's Medicare Fraud Strike Force, a multi-agency group of investigators designed to fight Medicare fraud, has charged more than 1,400 defendants who collectively falsely billed the Medicare program more than $4.8 billion.
- In 2011, HEAT coordinated the largest-ever federal health care fraud takedown involving $530 million in fraudulent billing.

Expanding the Medicare Fraud Strike Force:

The joint DOJ-HHS Medicare Fraud Strike Force is a multi-agency team of federal, state, and local investigators designed to fight Medicare fraud. The Force uses Medicare data analysis techniques and an increased focus on community policing to combat fraud. The Medicare Fraud Strike Force has recently expanded to include nine cities:

- Baton Rouge, Louisiana
- Brooklyn, New York
- Chicago, Illinois
- Dallas, Texas
- Detroit, Michigan
- Houston, Texas
- Los Angeles, California
- Miami–Dade, Florida
- Tampa Bay, Florida

HEAT's Annual Report to Congress

The Fraud Prevention System (FPS) made significant progress using technology to "identify bad actors and take administrative action to protect the Medicare Trust Funds."[78] In the second implementation year, which aligned with Fiscal Year 2013, The Centers for Medicare & Medicaid Services (CMS) took administrative action against 938 providers and suppliers due to the FPS. For example, the FPS identified an aberrant provider that had a pattern of inappropriate billing. Investigators conducted an unannounced site visit, interviewed beneficiaries, and reviewed medical records. It was discovered that the provider was using unlicensed and unqualified individuals to provide care. CMS revoked the provider from Medicare, preventing future payments with the intent of protecting quality of care.

The FBI adds that rooting out healthcare fraud is central to the well-being of American citizens and their economy. Healthcare "fraud costs the country tens of billions of dollars a year. It's a rising threat, with national healthcare expenditures estimated to exceed $3 trillion in 2014 and spending continuing to outpace inflation."[79] The FBI aids our understanding of physicians and others who make decisions in keeping with economic gain as opposed to the health of his or her patients (yet, some of us might suggest stupidity, laziness, or convoluted administrative billing processes as likely sources of alleged fraud). Recent cases show that medical professionals continue, and "may be more willing, to risk patient harm in furtherance of their schemes."

Monetary Results of Federal Prosecution

During Fiscal Year (FY) 2013, the Federal government won or negotiated over $2.6 billion in healthcare fraud judgments and settlements, and it attained additional administrative impositions in healthcare fraud cases and proceedings. As a result of these efforts, as well as those of preceding years, in 2013, approximately $4.3 billion was deposited with the Department of the Treasury and the Centers for Medicare & Medicaid Services (CMS), transferred to other Federal agencies administering healthcare programs, or paid to private persons during the fiscal year. Of this $4.3 billion, the Medicare Trust Funds received transfers of approximately $2.85 billion during this period, and over $576 million in

Federal Medicaid money was similarly transferred separately to the Treasury as a result of these efforts. The HCFAC account has returned over $25.9 billion to the Medicare Trust Funds since the inception of the Program in 1997.

Enforcement Actions of Department of Justice

In 2013, the Department of Justice (DOJ) opened 1,013 new criminal healthcare fraud investigations involving a little under 2,000 potential defendants.[80] Federal prosecutors had 2,041 healthcare fraud criminal investigations pending, involving 3,535 potential defendants, and filed criminal charges in 480 cases involving 843 defendants. A total of 718 defendants were convicted of healthcare fraud-related crimes during the year.

Also in 2013, DOJ opened 1,083 new civil healthcare fraud investigations. In 2013, Federal Bureau of Investigation (FBI) healthcare fraud investigations resulted in the operational disruption of 425 criminal fraud organizations.

Sample of Healthcare Fraud Won the First Week in August 2014[81]

- McKesson Corporation has agreed to pay $18 million to resolve allegations that it improperly set temperature monitors used in shipping vaccines under its contract with the Centers for Disease Control and Prevention. McKesson is a pharmaceutical distributor with corporate headquarters in San Francisco.
- Four people involved in the operation of Advanced Family Medical Center and Watkins-Tsai Imaging in Coal Grove, Ohio, have pleaded guilty to conspiracy to commit healthcare fraud, admitting that they improperly charged government insurance programs for medically unnecessary procedures.
- The owner of Columbus-based Janis Home Health Care, Eric Isakov, 45, was sentenced to forty-two months in prison, followed by two years of supervised release, and ordered to pay restitution of $900,000 for defrauding the Medicare and Medicaid programs by paying kickbacks in the form of gift cards and videogame systems to people who would sign up with his company, and paying senior living centers for referrals.
- A disbarred Florida attorney was sentenced in federal court in Tampa, Florida, to serve seventy months in prison in connection with her role in a $28.3 million Medicare fraud scheme involving false claims for physical and occupational therapy services. Margarita Grishkoff, 60, of Charlotte, North Carolina, pleaded guilty earlier to conspiracy to commit healthcare fraud. In addition to serving a prison term of seventy months, Grishkoff was sentenced to serve three years of supervised release and ordered to pay $14,424,856 in restitution, jointly and severally with her co-conspirators.
- Atlanta—Tracey Cota and Gary Lang have pleaded guilty to conspiracy to violate the Anti-Kickback Statute by paying and receiving illegal remuneration in exchange for Medicaid patient referrals to hospitals in the Atlanta area and on Hilton Head Island, S.C.
- The City of New York has agreed to pay the United States $1.05 million to settle allegations that the New York City Human Resources Administration (HRA) violated the False Claims Act by causing various insurance companies (known as "managed care organizations" or "MCOs") to provide healthcare coverage to individuals that HRA knew, or should have known, were ineligible to receive Medicaid benefits through New York State's Medicaid program.
- The Justice Department announced that Community Health Systems Inc. (CHS), the nation's largest operator of acute care hospitals, has agreed to pay $98.15 million to resolve multiple lawsuits alleging that the company knowingly billed government healthcare programs for inpatient services that should have been billed as outpatient or observation services. The settlement also resolves allegations that one of the company's affiliated hospitals, Laredo Medical Center, improperly billed the Medicare program for certain inpatient procedures and for services rendered to patients referred in violation of the Physician Self-Referral Law, commonly known as the Stark Law. CHS is based in Franklin, Tennessee, and has 206 affiliated hospitals in 29 states.
- A federal jury in Los Angeles found that the former owner of a durable medical equipment (DME) supply company located in Carson, California, was guilty of healthcare fraud charges relating to a ten-year scheme in which Medicare was fraudulently billed more than $8 million for DME that was not medically necessary.

Federal Prosecution Concerns

Despite incidents of federal healthcare program fraud, the US Department of Justice and Health and Human Services have avoided shutting down hospital systems;[82] instead prosecutors have opted for less severe alternatives, or so they say. Criminal charges and mandatory exclusions from federal healthcare programs due to Medicare or Medicaid fraud are an organizational death sentence for hospitals and probably physician officers as well. There has recently been a shift in advancing more prosecution since 2012. Saint Joseph's mentioned above, Pacific Health Corporation and WakeMed Health and Hospitals were recently prosecuted. In addition, in researching FBI archives, it appears that forty-two physicians and several outpatient centers have been prosecuted or at least indicted from 2012 to 2014.

When hospitals are prosecuted for Medicare and Medicaid fraud, losing to federal government means that the hospital will be excluded for five years from Medicare and Medicaid participation.[83,14] Losing to the federal prosecution is costly and a death sentence; there is a ripple effect in the community that turns the situation fatal. "How do you fight the federal government in a federal court when they have unlimited resources including influence to win prosecution," a healthcare official reports in confidence to this writer. A point well taken! See below, their win rate is nine of ten cases prosecuted.

Some experts argue that criminal charges and Deferred Prosecution Agreements ("DPAs") for Medicare and Medicaid fraud are generally unnecessary because civil False Claims Act ("FCA") settlements and Corporate Integrity Agreements ("CIAs") "are better suited to deter, punish, and rehabilitate fraudulent conduct by hospitals."[84] Civil FCA settlements and CIAs are better alternatives to criminal charges and DPAs because they do not carry the same high risk of organizational demise and because those alternatives help to rehabilitate an organization while permitting it to continue in business, usually through a monitoring system.

However, the list of entities and individuals barred from participation in Medicare is "peppered with the names of home health agencies and DME companies that have been prosecuted criminally, convicted and mandatorily excluded.[85] US Department of Health and Human Services HHS and Office of Inspector General (OIG) excluded 3,214 individuals and entities. Among those excluded were 1,132 criminal convictions for crimes related to Medicare and Medicaid;[86] 311 convictions to other healthcare programs; 180 for patient abuse or neglect; and 1,324 as a result of licensure revocations.

In total (which includes the above 3,214 excluded individuals and entities), the US Department of Health and Human Services (HHS), Department of Justice (DOJ) including the Federal Bureau of Investigation (FBI), and the Centers for Medicare & Medicaid Services (CMS) Center for Program Integrity, has suspended enrollments of high-risk providers in five Strike force locations and have removed or excluded over 17,000 providers from the Medicare program since 2011.[87]

[14] The statutory authority for exclusion is found at 42 USC §1320a-7 et seq.
The law authorizes exclusion of entities and individuals from Medicare, Medicaid, and all other federal or federally funded health benefit programs.
The law authorizes two kinds of exclusions: mandatory and permissive. Exclusion is mandatory for four categories of criminal activity:

1. A conviction for program-related crimes.
2. A conviction relating to patient neglect or abuse.
3. A felony conviction relating to health care fraud involving a health care program operated or financed in whole or in part by any federal, state or local government agency. Crimes for which exclusion is mandatory under this category include: fraud, theft, embezzlement, breach of fiduciary responsibility, or "other financial misconduct." The mandatory exclusion penalty also applies to criminal violations of the False Claims Act, the Anti-Kickback Law, and other fraud and abuse laws.
4. A felony conviction related to controlled substances, i.e., a felony conviction relating to the unlawful manufacture, distribution, prescription, or dispensing of a controlled substance.

Source: Francis J. Serbaroli (2012). The Medicare and Medicaid Exclusion Penalty. New York Law Journal, 247(98). Also, 18 USC §287; 3. 42 USC §1320a-7b(b).

An Example of Exclusion

In The United States District Court For The Western District Of Tennessee Eastern Division (No. 01-1341), Frank R. Pennington, MD was denied his claim that a ten-year exclusion from Medicare, Medicaid, and all federal healthcare programs was inappropriate punishment for his actions. The suit reads in part: "facts in this matter are undisputed. Plaintiff was licensed to practice medicine and worked as a physician in the state of Tennessee. On June 9, 1998, Plaintiff was indicted in the United States District Court for the Western District of Tennessee on one count of unlawfully, wilfully, and knowingly possess[ing] with intent to distribute approximately 15.1 grams of cocaine base (crack cocaine), a controlled substance. On June 17, 1999, Plaintiff pled guilty to possession of less than five grams of cocaine base with intent to distribute in violation of 21 U.S.C. § 841(a)(1). Plaintiff was sentenced to a term of imprisonment of forty-seven months and a term of supervised release and was ordered to pay a fine in the amount of $75,000 in addition to a special assessment of $100. Based on Plaintiff's felony conviction, the Tennessee Board of Medical Examiners revoked Plaintiff's license to practice medicine on November 9, 1999."[88]

Decision Process of Physicians and Surgeons

How physicians reach decisions about medicine is a topic described by a medical physician himself in his book: *How Doctors Think.*[89] That author says that it is an agonized inquiry into the processes by which medical minds—brilliant, experienced, highly erudite medical minds—synthesize information and understand both illness and treatment. Most often, it is conveyed that physicians make appropriate decisions and sometimes they don't get it right at all. One medical expert says that "[m]ost errors are mistakes in thinking. And part of what causes these cognitive errors is our inner feelings, feelings we do not readily admit to and often don't realize."[90]

Attribution errors happen when a doctor's diagnostic cogitations are shaped by a particular stereotype. It can be negative: when five doctors fail to diagnose an endocrinologic tumor causing peculiar symptoms in "a persistently complaining, melodramatic menopausal woman who quite accurately describes herself as kooky." But positive feelings also get in the way; an emergency room physician misses unstable angina in a forest ranger because "the ranger's physique and chiseled features reminded him of a young Clint Eastwood—all strong associations with health and vigor." Other errors occur when a patient is irreversibly classified with a particular syndrome: "diagnosis momentum, like a boulder rolling down a mountain, gains enough force to crush anything in its way."

It should be acknowledged that medical specialization can confer a false sense of certainty, and can often lead to diagnostic and therapeutic errors.[91] Yet, many physicians, it should also be acknowledged, hold a dislike for compliance regulations and often ignore requirements to, for example, wash their hands.[92]

Decision-making processes for physicians and surgeons can often start at cost-effectiveness analysis (CEA) methodology for evaluating the tradeoffs between health benefits and costs.[93] For example, a surgeon decided to operate on a patient and during the process she finds disease; she might first attempt at a surgical cure; if patient survives surgery, the original surgery which was ignored is unsuccessful. Making the right decision is a key factor for less litigation than more litigation and physicians and surgeons consider litigation during the performance of their daily routines. "The ways of finding the right decision are as many as the number of people who have to make them."[94] New research and new techniques are continually changing (details below about healthcare changes and physician stress). However, finding a solution with the help of decision-trees starts by preparing a set of solved cases.[95]

In many situations, for instance, a missed diagnosis of leukemia is much more expensive in terms of loss of years of life than a diagnosis of pertussis (whooping cough).[96] The chance of error cannot be eliminated altogether but efforts can be made to make appropriate decisions. This can be accomplished by using a sufficiently valid test or by combination of tests where feasible. The fact, however, is that medical errors do occur.

The question is what type of error is more affordable considering the monetary cost, pain, and the risks involved. An approach can be evolved for each patient separately to minimize such costs.

Criminal Justice Decision Making versus Medical Decision Making Processes

Some scholars suggest because of the growth of the criminal justice system and despite increased government accountability that substantial gaps continue because there are gaps between ideal policing and actual police practice.[97] Some suggest that performance monitoring and evidence-based practices should be enhanced in policing, yet medicine seems to have its own issues that tend to deal with life and death more often. What was attempted in a scholarly study is to say that criminal justice should draw upon examples from medicine about decision making relative to performance because medicine has been "examined in more depth"; decision making in medicine has to do with a process to identify types of decision-making errors that can undermine effective practice and policy; decisions in medicine allegedly can illustrate how systemic factors influence everyday decision making; and finally, decisions in medicine draws attention to the benefits of decision making-focused monitoring and assessment. Yet, the evidence in this chapter suggests that perhaps medicine should reach out to criminal justice particularly evidence based policing to formulate more effective strategies to deal with organizational policy errors, the errors in physician and surgeon judgment, and the lack of pharmaceutical products to help control disease transmission and recovery. And perhaps both groups should follow the firefighters lead and allow collective bargaining through a strong union to protect them. In 1999, the always conservative American Medical Association (AMA) voted to support unionization of physicians. This move is so radically different from the AMA former position but because physicians feared their profession was not supporting them, physicians were at the top of the list above nurses dissatisfied with their jobs.[98] For instance, here is what one says about the profession: "I soon discovered how powerless doctors really are."[99] "Most of my patients' problems were rooted in social conditions that were outside my control. The best I could do was manage their symptoms." Recall from Chapter 2, the medical model dominates American public health efforts; it focuses on disease and injury and their outcomes; it is built upon a pathophysiologic reductionist approach as opposed to a holism (which includes environmental) approach.

Final Thoughts and Prediction

Former President Ronald Reagan said that America fought a war on poverty and poverty won. With 46 million Americans now counted as poor, it's tempting to think President Reagan may have been right.[100] Thus—individuals without healthcare insurance or with the wrong healthcare coverage such as Medicare, what happens to those individuals when it comes to the circumstance of health including healthcare prevention? Which hospital systems, which physicians, or which surgeons can be trusted to make the right choices for those who do not live the American dream? Public health remains a question of social justice.

It can be expressed that similar to Jean Jacques Rousseau's idea we're "forced to be free" and similar to Karl Marx's notion that a free society is chained by profiteers and targeted populations that are relentlessly expanding their markets and thus their choices of customers, clients, or patients. Clearly, Karl Marx's notion that if one group has more bargaining power than another group, and the groups are engaged in a debate, the group with the most resources wins. It does not matter if the group with the least resources is right or wrong—they lose (see Conflict Theory in Chapter 4).[101] The financial struggle between solo physicians and hospital systems is no contest! How many of the medical errors and patients who die in hospitals through infection and other deathly pathogens represent lower class Americans? There is no way to tell since data are not recorded. How convenient!

As healthcare systems expand their markets, prices, monopoly, and domination of healthcare and the personnel they employ, this pattern reminds this writer of Karl Marx's "materialist conception of history" thesis entitled *The German Ideology* written in 1845.[102] The ruling class consists of individuals who pretty well own the means of production, or in 2015 terms, the means of services and products such as healthcare and pharmaceutical enterprises. It is the elitist social class who decide what services, what products, what iPhones are relevant, and which ones are not.[103]

Close to the writer's finding in *The Failure of American Prison Complex: Let's Abandon It*, this question arose: why go to the root of the problem with offenders or in this case with patients when you can send them to prison and hospitals? In Marx's terms, the individuals who make the choices are comprised of "a committee of the bourgeoisie" (the ruling class who own the economy) for the proletarian (you and me).[15] "The bourgeoisie (elitist class of which some members are also members of the Power Elite, see Chapter 1–3 for details) cannot exist without constantly revolutionizing the instruments of production (including services). . . The need of constantly expanding market for its products chases the bourgeoisie over the whole surface of the globe," says Marx. Apparently, Marx is implying that producing cures from disease transmission espe-

[15] Bourgeoisie in Marx's (1883; 1978) terms means the social class of modern capitalists; owners of the means of social production and employers of wage-labor. Proletarians are modern wage-laborers; selling their labor to the bourgeoisie.

cially deadly pathogens is different from producing profits and his thoughts are relevant to antibiotics. Antibiotics in particular, have a poor return on investment because they are taken for a short period of time and cure their target disease, explains a Task Force of the Infectious Diseases Society of America. In contrast, drugs that treat chronic illness, such as high blood pressure, are taken daily for the rest of a patient's life. "Companies have figured out that they make a lot more money selling the latter drugs than they do selling antibiotics," says experts.[104] Obviously there remains a lack of incentive for companies to develop antibiotics. "Disease is the biggest money maker in our economy," says John H. Tobe, author of *I Found Shangri-La.*[16]

The notion of profit first and lives second is consistent with studies that show the US has the highest first-day infant mortality rate of any other country in the industrialized world, according to a report from Save the Children.[105]

Hospitals and Infant Mortality

Despite a healthcare system that outspends those in the rest of the world, statistics say that infants and mothers fare worse in the US than in many other industrialized nations.[106] The infant mortality rate in Canada is 25 percent lower than the US; the Japanese rate, more than 60 percent lower. The World Health Organization (WHO) ranks America behind forty-one other countries in preventing mothers from dying during childbirth.

The United States has a higher ratio of maternal deaths than at least forty other countries, even though Americans spend more per capita for maternity care than any other nation.[107] It is hard to understand why American hospitals have a high ratio of maternal deaths considering the technological advances and arrogance of many Americans who are under the impression that America is superior to all other nations in every way. It is expected that those death statistics would steadily improve not decline. But the rate of maternal deaths has risen over the last decade, and the number of premature and low-birthweight babies is higher than it was in the 1980s and 1990s. One reason is that mothers tend to be less healthy than in the past, "which contributes to a higher-risk pregnancy," says a medical expert.[108] Another reason appears to be that convenience in healthcare has grown to take priority over the best financial outcomes. Most healing centers have evolved into highly profitable labor-and-delivery machines, "operating according to its own timetable rather than the less predictable schedule of mothers and babies (and patients in general)."[109,17]

Many babies who die at birth were born too early, and others suffer infections or complications at birth. Many of those infants could be saved with fairly inexpensive medical interventions, Save the Children argues. The first day of life is the most dangerous day for mothers and babies, but expanding access to several products that cost under $6 each—bag-and-mask devices to help babies breathe, antiseptic to prevent umbilical cord infections, antibiotics to treat infections, and steroids to delay pre-term labor—could help save an estimated one million infants around the world. Save the Children isn't sure exactly why the United States has such a high rate of first-day infant mortality. But it is expected that the US healthcare philosophy of profit first has a lot to do with it.

[16] A prediction this writer makes based on the accounts and evidence in this chapter is that hospital systems will move their market shares and power to pharmaceutical empires including distribution outlets such as Walgreens but particularly online pharmaceutical direct sale enterprises. Eventually, those empires will include pharmaceutical research and product development. Which laws will prevent their domination in more markets linked to their healthcare delivery? There are laws against murder and conspiracy against other forms of violence and abuse but apparently hospitals cannot be held accountable for infectious transmission and medical error deaths or injury let alone be held accountable for the illness or death of their personnel through patient associated infection.

[17] Among a publicly insured Michigan Medicaid cohort, overall vaccination percentages with tetanus, diphtheria, and acellular pertussis (Tdap) vaccines were low for all pregnant women. Black, Asian, and Arab women were less likely to receive a Tdap vaccine compared to white women. Vaccinating pregnant women with tetanus, diphtheria, and acellular pertussis (Tdap) vaccines is an important strategy for providing passive immunity to infants, who are at highest risk of mortality and morbidity from pertussis. In another study, 14.3% of women received Tdap during pregnancy, with rates highest among whites and lowest among Arab women.

Source: Centers for Disease Control and Prevention (2014, September 24). Morbidity and Mortality Weekly Report. Retrieved September 26, 2014: http://www.cdc.gov/media/mmwrnews/2014/0925.html - C3

Summary

The highest hospital patient cost on the planet is at an American hospital, yet American hospitals and clinics kill more patients than other nations. High costs might relate to the fact that healthcare systems are commercialized and prosecuted through government compliance regulations. A point made is that it is not how well hospitals or physicians perform, but how well insulated and knowledgeable they are when it comes to their collective and individual agents of compliance to patient associated infections, organizational system policy, and government (state and federal) compliance regulation.

Methods to improve hospital efficiency are identified and commercialization of hospital systems is discussed. However, because of the competitive new market hospitals are entering, it is expected that up to one-third of them will not be in operation by 2020.

Vertical integration was described as one method to enhance quality of care and treatment; policy differences among hospital systems exist and can increase providers' market power and facilitate the payment of what are effectively kickbacks for inappropriate referrals.

The relevance of the commercialization of hospitals and physicians was explained and cored in the idea that profit rather than infection control and prevention are emphasized. The principal focus and energy of healthcare systems are lock-stepped toward profit and loss.

Capitalist physicians and surgeons were described as individuals who started in the 1970s and today almost 40 percent of all independent physicians operate their own laboratories. Venture capital plays a key role among physicians and hospitals seeking to expand their control and business. However physicians' and surgeons' errors were described along with their causes. Although monetary concerns may help explain the workloads, medicine and human errors are linked to hospital commercialism and government indifferent compliance regulations. Many of those errors similar to disease transmission are preventable.

The cost of medical errors to patients and healthcare providers was estimated at $4.5 to $5.7 billion per year in additional costs for national patient care. Then, too, there is the cost of human lives and suffering. Fraud investigation and enforcement taken by the Department of Justice, among other federal agencies is detailed. Some of the concerns linked to federal prosecution is that exclusion from medicate participation is more like a death sentence, probably the worst punishment federal agencies can hand down to hospitals because it amounts to a death sentence.

Despite incidents of federal healthcare system fraud, the US Department of Justice and Health and Human Services have tried to avoid shutting down hospital systems; however, criminal charges against physicians and mandatory exclusions for hospitals and outpatient centers from federal healthcare programs due to Medicare or Medicaid fraud are a death sentence for hospitals and probably physicians as well. There has recently been a shift in advancing more prosecution since 2012. Experts have suggested that criminal justice system decision making processes should reflect those processes of the medical community, but this chapter speaks otherwise. The final thoughts of the author are presented cored in the evidence of this chapter.

Name: ______________________________ Date: ______________ School Identification Number: ______

STUDENT WORKSHEETS

Chapter 9 Hospitals, Physicians, and Agents of Compliance

Define the following key terms from Chapter 9, and in your answer, show the page number where you found the definition. Provide an example for each key term.

1. American Hospital Association

2. Anomie

3. Capitalist Physicians

4. Evidence Based Medicine

5. Excluded from Medicare and Medicaid Participation

6. Fear of Prosecution

7. Healthcare Fraud Prevention and Enforcement Action Team (HEAT)

8. HMOs

9. Managed Care

Name: ____________________ Date: __________ School Identification Number: ______

10. Medical Errors

11. Medicare Fraud

12. 'Never Events'

13. Physician Errors

14. Revolutionizing Instruments of Production

15. Surgeon Errors

16. Venture Capital

17. Vertical Integration

Name: ______________________________ Date: ____________ School Identification Number: ______

STUDENT WORKSHEETS

Chapter 9 Hospitals, Physicians, and Agents of Compliance

Discuss and demonstrate in your own words that you comprehend the following learning objectives in this chapter.

1. Discuss the perspective that relates to hospital and physician performance and describe the agents of compliance in this chapter.
2. Identify the ways in which hospital systems can improve their efficiency.
3. Explain the weakness and strength of vertical integration among hospital systems. In what way can vertical integration move a hospital system toward federal prosecution?
4. Identify and discuss the products of commercialized healthcare providers.
5. Explain the role of venture capital among physicians.
6. Discuss physician medical errors and probable causes. In what way could disease transmission and patient associated infection be considered medical error?
7. Identify the federal agencies involved in fraud investigations and the outcomes of those investigations.
8. From all of the cases prosecuted in this chapter, which case sounds arbitrary or highly suspect to you and why?
9. Describe the reasons that some experts think the criminal justice community should borrow the decision making processes of the medical community. In what do you agree or disagree with that recommendation?
10. Describe the final thoughts of the author about hospitals, physicians, and agents of compliance. Identify the prediction made and explain in what way you agree or disagree with that prediction.

CHAPTER 9 ENDNOTES

1. Peter Pronovost and Edward Vohr (2010). *Safe Patients, Smart Hospitals: How One Doctor's Checklist Can Help Us Change Health Care from the Inside Out.* New York: Plum. Pages 4, 12–18.
2. David Houle and Jonathan Fleece (2012). Why One-Third Of Hospitals Will Close By 2020. *Consensus Medical Communication*. Retrieved August 5, 2014: http://www.kevinmd.com/blog/2012/03/onethird-hospitals-close-2020.html
3. NHTSA (2013). Highway Deaths. Retrieved August 5, 2014: http://www.nhtsa.gov/About+NHTSA/Press+Releases/NHTSA+Data+Confirms+Traffic+Fatalities+Increased+In+2012
4. American Hospital Association (2014). Facts on US Hospitals. Retrieved August 5, 2014: http://www.aha.org/research/rc/stat-studies/fast-facts.shtml
5. Department of Justice (2014). Medicare Fraud Strike Force Set Record Numbers for Health Care Fraud Prosecutions. Retrieved August 10, 2014: http://www.justice.gov/opa/pr/2014/August/14-civ-841.html
6. JC Robinson and LP Casalino (1996/2014). Vertical Integration and Organizational Networks in Health Care. *Health Affairs*, 15(1): 7–22. Retrieved August 6, 2014: http://content.healthaffairs.org/content/15/1/7.full.pdf
7. Henry A. Giroux (2013). (2013, February 27). The Disimagination Machine and the Pathologies of Power. Symploke, 21(1–2): 257–269. Retrieved August 10, 2014: http://truth-out.org/news/item/14814-the-politics-of-disimagination-and-the-pathologies-of-power
8. Institute of Medicine (1999). To Err is Human: Building a Safer Heath System. Retrieved July 24, 2014: http://www.iom.edu/~/media/Files/Report Files/1999/To-Err-is-Human/To Err is Human 1999 report brief.pdf
9. Scott Rupp (2013, November 18). Three Reasons Why IT Efficiency is Key to Your Hospital's Survival in the New Healthcare Economy. *Electronic Health Reporter*. Retrieved August 6, 2014: http://electronic healthreporter.com/three-reasons-why-it-efficiency-is-key-to-your-hospitals-survival-in-the-new-healthcare-economy/
10. RW Brady, J Verran, NN Damani, and AP Gibb (2009). Review of Mobile Communication Devices as Potential Reservoirs of Nosocomial Pathogens. *Journal of Hospital Infection,* 71(4): 295–300.
11. David Houle and Jonathan Fleece (2012).
12. Ibid.
13. Laurence C Baker, M Kate Bundorf, and Daniel P Kessler (2014). Vertical Integration: Hospital Ownership Of Physician Practices Is Associated With Higher Prices And Spending. *Health Affairs*, 33(5): 756–763.
14. Dani Gordon (2014, July 29). 12 Things Clinical Integration Is—And Is Not. *Becker's Hospital Review.* Retrieved August 6, 2014: http://www.beckershospitalreview.com/hospital-physician-relationships/12-things-clinical-integration-is-and-is-not.html
15. Ibid.

16. Competition Law and Policy (2013). Competition and Poverty Reduction 2013. Retrieved August 21, 2014: http://www.oecd.org/daf/competition/competition-and-poverty-reduction2013.pdf Pages 257–258.
17. C White, AM Bond, and JD Reschovsky (2013). High And Varying Prices For Privately Insured Patients Underscore Hospital Market Power. Research Brief, 27: 1–10.
18. PB Ginsburg (2010). Wide Variation In Hospital And Physician Payment Rates Evidence Of Provider Market Power. Research Brief, 16: 1–11.
19. JC Robinson and LP Casalino (1996/2014).
20. JC Robinson (2011). Variation In Hospital Costs, Payments, And Profitability For Cardiac Valve Replacement Surgery. *Health Service Research,* 46(1): 1928–1945.
21. J. Robinson (2011). Hospitals Respond To Medicare Payment Shortfalls By Both Shifting Costs And Cutting Them, Based on Market Concentration. *Health Affairs: Project Hope*, 30(7):1265–1271.
22. Steve Brown, Richard Lamming, John Bessant, and Peter Jones (2005). *Strategic Operations Management.* Boston: Elsevier. Butterworth Heinemann. Pages 1–3, 371–374.
23. Makani Themba-Nixon (2005). Helping Public Health Matter: Strategies for Building Public Awareness. NACCHO Exchange 4(2), 10–12.
24. JC Robinson and LP Casalino (1996/2014).
25. Dennis J. Stevens (2014). *Failure of the American Prison Complex: Let's Abolish It.* Iowa: Kendall Hunt. Pages 395, 409, 412.
26. Peter Conrad and Valerie Leiter (2013). *The Sociology of Health and Illness: Critical Perspectives.* New York: Worth Publishers. Page 267.
27. JC Robinson and LP Casalino (1996/2014).
28. Lawton R. Burns and Aditi Sen (2014). What We've Learned from Horizontal and Vertical Integration of Physicians. The Healthcare Blog. Retrieved August 6, 2014: http://thehealthcareblog.com/blog/2014/04/25/the-way-forward-for-integrated-care-what-weve-learned-from-horizontal-and-vertical-integration-of-physicians/
29. FBI Saint Joseph London (2014, January 28). Saint Joseph London Hospital to Pay $16.5 Million to Settle False Claims Act Allegations of Unnecessary Heart Procedures. Retrieved August 5, 2014: http://www.fbi.gov/louisville/press-releases/2014/saint-joseph-london-hospital-to-pay-16.5-million-to-settle-false-claims-act-allegations-of-unnecessary-heart-procedures?utm_campaign=email-Weekly&utm_medium=email&utm_source=louisville-press-releases&utm_h
30. Becker's Hospital Review (2010, October 26). 50 Largest Hospitals in America. Retrieved August 6, 2014: http://www.beckershospitalreview.com/lists/50-largest-hospitals-in-america.html
31. Mark J Perry (2014). American Medical Association: The Strongest Trade Union In The U.S.A. American Medical Association. Retrieved August 8, 2014: http://www.aei-ideas.org/2012/07/american-medical-association-the-strongest-trade-union-in-the-u-s-a/
32. American Medical Association (2014). Requirements for Becoming a Physician. Retrieved August 8, 2014: http://www.ama-assn.org/ama/pub/education-careers/becoming-physician.page?
33. PM Easton, A Sarma, FLR Williams, CA Marwick, G Phillips, and D Nathwani (2007). Infection Control and Management of MRSA: Assessing The Knowledge of Staff in An Acute Hospital Setting. *Journal of Hospital Infection,* 66(1): 29–33.

34. JC Trim and TSJ Elliott (2003). A Review of Sharps Injuries and Preventative Strategies. *Journal of Hospital Infection*, 53(4): 237–242.

35. David Mechanic, Donna D. McAlpine, and Marsha Rosenthal (2001). Are Patients' Office Visits with Physicians Getting Shorter? *New England Journal of Medicine,* 344:198–204.

36. Ha T. Tu and Paul B. Ginsburg (2004). Losing Ground: Physician Income, 1995–2003. Center for Studying Health Systems Change. Retrieved August 8, 2014: http://v1.tafp.org/News/quickInfo/attachments/physcianPayDropping.pdf

37. US Department of Labor (2014). Physicians and Surgeons. Retrieved August 9, 2014: http://www.bls.gov/ooh/healthcare/physicians-and-surgeons.htm

38. Peter Conrad and Valerie Leiter (2013).

39. Ibid.

40. RJ Cook, A Ortega-Ortiz, S Romans, and LE Ross (2006). Legal Abortion for Mental Health Indications. *International Journal of Gynecology & Obstetrics*, 95(2): 185–190.

41. RJ Cook, A Ortega-Ortiz, S Romans, and LE Ross (2006). Also see, BM Dickens and RJ Cook (2006).

Conflict Of Interest: Legal And Ethical Aspects. *International Journal of Gynecology & Obstetrics*, 92(1): 192–197.

42. Fred Dotzler (2001). Raising Venture Capital: Tips for the Medical Start-Up. DeNovo Ventures. Retrieved August 10, 2014: http://www.denovovc.com/articles/medical_startup_tips.pdf

43. Dev K Mishra (2013, February 26). Opportunities for Physicians in Venture Capital. Non-Clinical Careers for Physicians. Retrieved August 9, 2014: http://www.nonclinicalcareers.com/opportunities-for-physicians-in-venture-capital/

44. Joseph Walker (2013, November 4). Funding Dries Up for Medical Startups Companies Are Squeezed by Venture-Capital Drought. *Wall Street Journal*. Retrieved August 10, 2014: http://online.wsj.com/news/articles/SB10001424052702304470504579164122110690860

45. Cadie Thompson (2013, October 20). Obamacare Is The Chance Of A Lifetime For Venture Capitalists. CNBC: Business Insider. Retrieved August 10, 2014: http://www.businessinsider.com/obamacare-is-the-chance-of-a-lifetime-for-venture-capitalists-2013-10 - ixzz3A07uYWKX

46. Ibid.

47. Medical Device and Diagnostic Industry (2014). Venture Capital Firms Active in the Medical Device Field. Retrieved August 10, 2014: http://www.mddionline.com/links/venture - V

48. Peter Conrad and Valerie Leiter (2013). Pages 266–268.

49. The Free Medical Dictionary (2007). Retrieved August 13, 2014: http://medical-dictionary.thefreedictionary.com/managed+care

50. Michael J Petro (2011, July 1). 42 USC 1320a–7b Medicare Fraud: "Primary Motivation" Doctrine Rejected. 7th Circuit Criminal Law Alert. Retrieved August 13, 2014: http://mjpetro.typepad.com/7th_circuit_alert/2011/07/42-usc-1320a-7b-medicare-fraud-primary-motivation-doctrine-rejected.html

51. Versant Ventures (2014). Ross Jaffe MD. Retrieved August 10, 2014: http://www.versantventures.com/team/ross-a-jaffe-m-d/

52. Rachael Rettner (2013, January 29). Overworked Doctors May Jeopardize Patient Safety. Scientific American. Retrieved August 5, 2014: http://www.scientificamerican.com/article/overworked-doctors-may-jeopardize-patient-safety/

53. Ibid.

54. Atul Gawande (2003). Complications: A Surgeon's Notes on an Imperfect Science. New York: Picador.

55. Ibid.

56. D. Pitteta (2004). The Lowbury Lecture: Behaviour in Infection Control. *Journal of Hospital Infection*, 58(1): 1–13.

57. Atul Gawande, Michael J Zinner, David M Studdert, and Troyen A Brennan (2003). Analysis of Errors Reported by Surgeons at Three Teaching Hospitals. *Surgery*, 133(6): 614–621.

58. Atul Gawande, Michael J Zinner, David M Studdert, and Troyen A Brennan (2003). Also see, JB Sexton, EJ Thomas, and RL Helmreich (2000). Error, Stress, and Teamwork in Medicine and Aviation: Cross Sectional Surveys. *British Medical Journal*, 320: 745–799. NJ Taffinder, IC McManus, Y Gul, RC Russell, and A Darzi (1998). Effect of Sleep Deprivation on Surgeons' Dexterity on Laparoscopy Simulator. *Lancet*, 352:1191–1195.

59. Rachael Rettner (2013, January 29). Retrieved August 5, 2014: http://www.scientificamerican.com/article/overworked-doctors-may-jeopardize-patient-safety/

60. Daniel R Levinson (2010). Adverse Events In Hospitals: National Incidence Among Medicare Beneficiaries. Washington DC: US Department of Health and Human Services. Retrieved December 7, 2014: http://oig.hhs.gov/oei/reports/oei-06-09-00090.pdf

61. Joseph Nordqvist (2012, December 2). Surgical Errors Occur More Than 4,000 Times A Year In The U.S. *Medical News Today.* Retrieved August 5, 2014: http://www.medicalnewstoday.com/articles/254426.php

62. John T James (2013). New, Evidence-based Estimate of Patient Harms Associated with Hospital Care. *Journal of Patient Safety*, 9(3): 122–128.

63. Amy S Collins (2008). Preventing Healthcare-Associated Infections. In Patient Safety and Quality: An Evidence-Based Handbook for Nurses; In RG Hughes (Ed); Agency for Healthcare Research and Quality: Rockville, MD, USA, 2008; Chapter 41, pp. 547–575. Retrieved July 11, 2014: http://www.ahrq.gov/professionals/clinicians-providers/resources/nursing/resources/nurseshdbk/CollinsA_PHCAI.pdf

64. Institute of Medicine (1999).

65. Atul Gawande, Michael J Zinner, David M Studdert, and Troyen A Brennan (2003). Analysis of Errors Reported by Surgeons at Three Teaching Hospitals. Surgery, 133(6): 614–621.

66. Ibid.

67. Daniel Romer, Kathleen Hall Jamieson, and Sean Aday (2006). Television News and the Cultivation of Fear of Crime. *Journal of Communication*, 53(1): 88–104.

68. James W. Kanan and Matthew V. Pruitt (2003). Modeling Fear of Crime and Perceived Victimization Risk: The (In)Significance of Neighborhood Integration. *Sociological Inquiry,* 72(4): 527–548.

69. Jonathan Jackson (2004). Experience and Expression Social and Cultural Significance in the Fear of Crime. *British Journal of Criminology*, 44 (6): 946–966.

70. BJ Doran and MM Burgess (2012). Putting Fear of Crime on the Map: Investigating Perceptions of Crime Using Geographic Information Systems. Springer Series on Evidence-Based Crime Policy. (Page 9).

71. Dennis J. Stevens (1998). Urban Communities and Homicide: Why American Blacks Resort to Murder. *Policing and Society*, 8: 253–267.

72. Dennis J. Stevens (2015) *Women in Solitary Confinement: Health and Recidivism. In Modern American Prisons,* Stephen Richards (Ed). Southern Illinois University Press. Forth coming. Also see, Dennis J Stevens (1999) Interviews With Women Convicted Of Murder: Battered Women Syndrome Revisited. *International Review of Victimology,* 6, 117–135.

73. Dennis J. Stevens (2002). Civil Liabilities and Arrest Decisions. In Jeffery Walker (Ed.) *Policing and the Law*. (Pages 53–70). Upper Saddle River, NJ: Prentice Hall.

74. BJ Doran and MB Burgess (2012). *Putting Fear of Crime on the Map. Springer Series on Evidence-Based Crime Policy*. New York: Springer Science. Page 9.

75. American Foundation for Suicide Prevention (2014). Understanding and Preventing Suicide. Facts about Physician Depression and Suicide. Retrieved August 10, 2014: https://www.afsp.org/preventing-suicide/our-education-and-prevention-programs/programs-for-professionals/physician-and-medical-student-depression-and-suicide/facts-about-physician-depression-and-suicide

76. Daniela Drake (2014, March 14). How Being a Doctor Became the Most Miserable Profession. *The Daily Beast.* Retrieved August 10, 2014: http://www.thedailybeast.com/articles/2014/04/14/how-being-a-doctor-became-the-most-miserable-profession.html

77. US Department of Health and Human Services and US Department of Justice (2014). Stop Medicare Fraud. Retrieved August 5, 2014: http://www.hhs.gov/news/press/2014pres/05/20140513b.html

78. Centers for Medicare and Medicaid Services (2014, June). Report to Congress: Fraud Prevention System, Second Implementation Year. Retrieved August 5, 2014: http://www.stopmedicarefraud.gov/fraud-rtc06242014.pdf

79. FBI (2014). Heath Care Fraud. Retrieved August 4, 2014: http://www.fbi.gov/about-us/investigate/white_collar/health-care-fraud

80. Health Care Fraud and Abuse Control Program Annual Report for Fiscal Year 2013 (2014). The Department of Health and Human Services and the Department of Justice. Retrieved December 7, 2014: http://www.hhs.gov/news/press/2014pres/02/20140226a.html

81. Office of Inspector General (2014). Criminal and Civil Enforcement. Retrieved Augut 10, 2104: https://oig.hhs.gov/fraud/enforcement/criminal/

82. M Brianna Stellpflug (2014). Criminal Prosecutions of Hospitals: Unnecessary Treatment. Cornell School of Law. Retrieved August 10, 2014: http://www.americanbar.org/groups/health_law/membership/law_students_welcome/law_student_writing_opportunities/hot_topics/criminal_prosecutions.html

83. Jonathan Field and Howard O'Leary, Jr. (2014). Criminal Prosecution of Hospitals: Unnecessary Treatment. *The Health Lawyer*, 26(3): 3–5, Retrieved August 10, 2014: http://www.dykema.com/assets/htmldocuments/The Health Lawyer - Feld OLeary Article - February 2014.pdf

84. M Brianna Stellpflug (2014).

85. Health Care Fraud and Abuse Control Program Annual Report for Fiscal Year 2013 (2014).

86. Ibid.

87. US Department of Health and Human Services (2014, May). Medicare Fraud Strike Force Charges 90 Individuals For Approximately $260 Million In False Billing. Retrieved August 11, 2014: http://www.hhs.gov/news/press/2014pres/05/20140513b.html

88. In The United States District Court For The Western District Of Tennessee Eastern Division (2012). Frank R. Pennington, MD v US Department of Health and Human Services. No. 011341. Retrieved August 12, 2014: https://www.tnwd.uscourts.gov/JudgeTodd/opinions/118.pdf

89. Jerome Groopman (2008). *How Doctors Think*. New York: Mariner Books.

90. Jerome Groopman (2008). Page 91.

91. Jerome Groopman (2008). Page 181.

92. Centers for Medicare and Medicaid Services (2014, June).

    FBI (2014). Heath Care Fraud. Retrieved August 4, 2014.

93. Gillian D Sanders (2009). Introduction to Medical Decision Making and Decision Analysis. Retrieved August 4, 2014: http://www.hsrd.research.va.gov/for_researchers/cyber_seminars/archives/hcea-060309.pdf

94. Vili Podgorelec, Peter Kokol, Bruno Stiglic, and Ivan Rozman (2002). Decision Trees: An Overview and Their Use in Medicine. *Journal of Medical Systems*, 26(5): 445–459.

95. Ibid.

96. A Indrayan (2008). *Medical Biostatistics,* 2nd Edition. New York: CRC Press.

97. Daniel P Mears and Sarah Bacon (2009). Improving Criminal Justice Through Better Decision Making: Lessons From The Medical System. *Journal of Criminal Justice,* 37(2):142–154.

98. Laurie Garrett (2000). *Betrayal of Trust: The Collapse of Global Public Health*. New York: Hyperion. Page 567.

99. Susan Rosenthal (ND). Solidarity is the Best Medicine: The Doctor's Dilemma Resolved. *Health Worker.* Retrieved August 9, 2014: http://susanrosenthal.com/about

100. Peter Edelman (2012, July 28). Poverty in America: Why Can't We End It? *New York Times: Sunday Review.* Retrieved January 17, 2014: http://www.nytimes.com/2012/07/29/opinion/sunday/why-cant-we-end-poverty-in-america.html?pagewanted=all&_r=0

101. Karl Marx (1846–1978). The German Ideology. *The Marx Engels Reader*. (Pages 146–200). Robert C. Tucker, Translator. New York: Norton. Karl Marx and Friedrich Engels (1883; 1978). Manifesto of the Communist Party. The Marx-Engels Reader. (Page 473–484). Robert C. Tucker, Translator. NY: Norton.

102. Karl Marx (1845; 1978). The Eighteenth Brumaire of Louis Bonaparte. Die Revolution. The Marx Engels Reader. (Pages 594–617). Robert C. Tucker, Translator. New York: Norton.

103. William G Domhoff (2013). *Wealth, Income, and Power. Who Rules America.* Retrieved July 15, 2013: http://www2.ucsc.edu/whorulesamerica/power/wealth.html

104. GH Talbot, J Bradley, JE Edwards, Jr., D Gilbert, M Scheld, and JG Bartlett, (2006). Bad bugs need drugs: an update on the development pipeline from the Antimicrobial Availability Task Force of the Infectious Diseases Society of America. Clinical Infectious Disease, 42(5): 657–668. Retrieved June 29, 2013: http://www.ncbi.nlm.nih.gov/pubmed/16447111

105. Tara Culup-Ressler (2013, May 7). Report: The U.S. has the Highest First-Day Infant Death Rate in the Industrialized World. Think Progress. Retrieved June 3, 2013: http://thinkprogress.org/health/2013/05/07/1973341/us-infant-mortality-rate/?mobile=nc

106. Consumer Reports.org (2014, May). What to Reject When You're Expecting. Retrieved August 25, 2014: http://www.consumerreports.org/cro/2012/05/what-to-reject-when-you-re-expecting/index.htm

107. Ina May Gaskin (2008). Maternal Death in the United States: A Problem Solved or a Problem Ignored. *Journal of Perinatal Education*, 17(2): 9–13.

108. Ibid.

109. Ibid.

encikcasper/Shutterstock, Inc.

CHAPTER 10

After a Bioweapon Attack on America

Learning Objectives

After you read this chapter, you will be better prepared to:

- Explain the reasons for American hatred by numerous countries and include in your answer why religion might be a possible issue.
- Articulate the focus of this chapter, and explain in what way that focus lends itself to this book.
- Identify the warning signs that the US will be attacked with bioweapons in the near future.
- Describe the various chemical warfare agents highlighted in this chapter. Identify the chemical agent most likely to be utilized in an attack. Why?
- Describe the various infectious warfare agents highlighted in this chapter. Identify the infectious agent most likely to be utilized in an attack. Why?
- Describe the two assumptions about federal and local law enforcement officers.
- Explain the public panic results of the media's sensationalized accounts of truth.
- Identify the various responses of hospitals to bioweapon victims and the importance of early knowledge of a bioweapon attack.
- Describe the various responses of physicians to bioweapon victims.
- Articulate the relevance of physician uncertainty and its results to bioweapon victims and treatment.
- Highlight the various responses of nurses to bioweapon victims.
- Articulate the final thoughts of the author about this chapter. Which point is the most important point and in what way do you agree or disagree with his primary position?

Key Terms

Asymmetric Methods
Biological Warfare Agents
Chemical Warfare Agents
Civil Liberties
Ethnic Bioweapons
Final Solution
Infectious Warfare Agents
Physician Uncertainty
Population Wellness
Public Panic Crisis Event
Surge Capacity
Warning Signs of Surge Capacity
Weapons of Mass Destruction (WMD)

Words of Wisdom

I swear to fulfill, to the best of my ability and judgment, this covenant:

I will respect the hard-won scientific gains of those physicians in whose steps I walk, and gladly share such knowledge as is mine with those who are to follow.

I will apply, for the benefit of the sick, all measures which are required, avoiding those twin traps of overtreatment and therapeutic nihilism.

Hippocratic Oath

Introduction

For the past sixty years, earth's civilized populations have lived in a shadow of a "nuclear holocaust" blasting each of us back to the Stone Age. The recent revolution in molecular biology, the evolution of antibiotic resistant pathogens, and the lack of medical (and pharmaceutical) remedies has unleashed new quality of life hazards producing real live ghouls devouring men, women, children, and their pets; genetically modified viruses and microorganisms including deadly flesh-eating bacteria and chemical compounds can be utilized to develop sophisticated biological weapons that would make nuclear holocausts obsolete.[1]

Some feel that unless chemists and biologists take a hard stand against biological weapons which includes genetically engineered superbugs or obligate carnivores—much as their colleagues in the physical sciences took a forceful stand against nuclear weapons, the end looms near.

A naive and idealized perspective will not guarantee safety. Some of the great minds of the new century write elegant paragraphs about ending terrorisms as though it is a product of a misinformed generation of believers in an eccentric religion;[2] others make ridiculous postulations similar to the way some nations thought about America and her gods, until their skies were filled with Predator drones and Navy F-18 fighter jets delivering an American abyss of divine retribution.[3]

Circumstance, hatred, and ambition whether real or imagined engrained in the everyday thoughts of populations report that enemies of those populations will eventually experience a biological or bioweapons attack. In a Google search for the most hated countries in the world, out of six random websites, America is in the top three if not number one country hated. For instance, one site says that America is one of the most advanced nations of the world. Then why would America be hated? One obvious reason is the military and economic destruction of land, people, and moral of Iran, Afghanistan, and recently in Libya. America is largely hated by the people of the Middle East.[4] From my perspective, the above explanation should include America's military engagements in Vietnam, Somalia, Angola, and nineteen other nations in the past twenty years.[5] Keep in mind that the babies during those American military engagements are in their early twenties today. Some of those young people experienced the loss of family members, their homes, and hear stories of American military's wickedness and its use of excessive fire power enhancing an imperialist empire. It should also be noted that many powerful populations and governments are not Christian or Jewish. Fact is, Israel's strongest defender is the USA. Why talk of religion when discussing politics? (See details below.)

The scholarly literature acknowledges the military power of America, and compares American military engagements with the Ancient Roman Empire a country also hated, (I recall from my studies); scholars also report that a strong hatred toward America exists.[6] America as a democratic nation (with its Christian orientation) has much to defend yet in all fairness when other nations require aid, America and particularly its charitable organizations which includes organizations such as Red Cross and those Christian churches mentioned in Chapter 1 stand ready to provide aid without asking for anything in return.[7] American political explanations about equality and fairness are heard everywhere, yet American political policy tends to protect the wealthy and famous and imprison or antagonize (bill collectors, cable and cell phone company complications, and hollow promises from online universities with educational advancement) the rest of us although admittedly, our quality of life has improved from previous generations.[8] That's really okay if you're rich and famous but most of us aren't, and few of us accept many of the Washington DC, decisions or lack of them. One explanation about the rich getting richer and the poor getting prison comes from Karl Marx who believes that everything is political including the exploitation and invasion of those countries which cannot defend themselves.[9,1] Nonetheless, elegant political rhetoric is an art that has less to do with reality and policy than expected. Politics has not changed over the centuries, and from some individuals' perspective: "war is simply a continuation of political intercourse."[10]

Many populations have experienced a bioweapons attack of sorts, and many populations are currently in the process of a bioweapon experimentation orchestrated by their own government or a distant one without their knowledge.[11] This chapter is not about the history of biological warfare or its effects; nor is it about what nation did what to whom. A more timely contribution lies in briefly describing chemical and infectious warfare agents and how those agents will impact the decisions, occupational risk, and ultimately the performance of first-responders.

Focus of This Chapter

The focus of this chapter relates to issues after a bioweapon attack on America. This chapter is about the response to bioweapon victims by the criminal justice community, specifically law enforcement and corrections, and their collaborative partners specifically hospitals, physicians, and nurses after an attack.[2] Will criminal justice professionals and their partners perform as their counterparts had during Hurricane Katrina as described in Chapter 1? Will American victims experience professional social order, public safety, and treatment or will they experience similar social order, public safety, and treatment consistent with professional behavior prior to an attack? Recall the agents of compliance of criminal justice and their partners discussed in previous chapters consisting of:

- Patient Associated Infections
- Organizational System Policy and Politics[3]
- Government (State and Federal) Compliance Regulation

Will the police professionally manage herds of individuals and provide public safety or will they collect evidence and people and limit civil liberties and freedom? Will jailers provide custody with care or lock-down those jailed and let nature including violence prevail as experienced during Hurricane Katrina (see Chapter 1)? Will hospitals admit and protect patients or will the surge of patients force them to close their doors (see Chapter 9)? Will physicians treat and will nurses care for the survivors of a biological attack or will they choose who will die and will live similar to Hurricane Katrina's victims (see Chapter 8)? Remember, no where does it say that government compliance regulations must conform to the Constitutional rights of constituents. Similar to the picture at beginning of the chapter, will our first responders comply with regulations and simply provide safety to mannequins? Why should we assume that America's first-responders will function effectively and adapt successfully in the aftermath of a bioweapon attack when the evidence from Hurricane Katrina (see Chapter 1 for details), Boston Marathon (see below), and other terrorist attacks says otherwise?[12]

[1] Marx might be right; however, before you accept Marx's perspective in total, consider that Americans in poverty experience a higher quality of life standard than previous poor populations. Also consider that opportunities to rise above poverty are more pervasive in the US than other countries at any time in history. Ask Oprah Winfrey and all the others who hold considerable wealth and privilege but came from very humble origins.
Source: Dennis J. Stevens (2014). *Failure of the American Prison Complex: Let's Abolish It*. Page 37.

[2] Under US law, hospitals may generally not refuse emergency treatment to anyone, whether insured or not.
Source: Competition Law and Policy (2013). Retrieved December 8, 2014: http://www.oecd.org/daf/competition/competition-and-poverty-reduction2013.pdf/ Page 258.

[3] There is a distinction between policy and politics. Politics are necessary in order to go through with policy. Policy is a matter of the authoritative allocation of values; operation statements of values; statements of prescriptive intent Maurice Kogan (1975). *Educational Policy-Making*. London: Allen and Unwin. Page 5. Policy are rules that an organization expects to be followed for the betterment of the organization. Source: Dennis J. Stevens. Also, policy is a definite course of action adopted for the sake of expediency, facility, etc.
Source: Dictionary.com. "Politics are the exploitation of resources, both physical and human, for the achievement of more control over others, and thus of safer, or more comfortable, or more satisfying terms of individual existence." Source: Andrew M. Pettigrew (2014). *The Politics of Organizational Decision-Making*. NY: Routledge. Page 18.

There were warning signs about Katrina's potential which many of us listened to and prepared for accordingly; there are warning signs about an eminent bioweapon attack on America. Finally, there are warning signs about compliance regulations versus Constitutional guarantees. which are not one in the same. There is also a misguided consensus that the US Supreme Court's "primary institutional role is to protect civil rights and civil liberties, particularly the right of disfavored minority groups."[13] Compliance regulations stand alone often lacking democratic principles as guidelines. In part, as expressed in the proceeding chapters, the US justice system has become a sprawling massive enterprise that applies and enforces its compliance regulations regardless of law or method.[14]

Warning Signs of a Bioweapon Attack on America

There are warning signs that the US is a target of a bioweapon attack that are as clear as the warnings received about Hurricane Katrina; government apparently was either unable or similarly refused to respond professionally to those warning signs of Katrina's catastrophic potential. Rather the US government justified their ineffective response through politically elegant rhetoric in order to justify its response or maybe the government did not know how to report its incompetence. For instance, a study conducted for the US Congress says in part that "in the aftermath of Hurricane Katrina there were concerns that federal readiness for the disaster had been hampered by an overemphasis on planning for terrorism at the expense of planning for natural disaster."[15] In a sense, the wars on drugs, immigrants, and poverty have many battlefronts, many survivors, and many violators and apprehension policies do not change because it rains or snows. Also, is that to say that America is losing the war on drugs because our resources are buried in a war on poverty? I am under the impression that a terrorist attack might include battlefronts, many survivors, and many violators.

In a statement released by the US secretary of defense on November 25, 1997, William S. Cohen said, "The United States remains concerned at the threat of proliferation, both of biological warfare expertise and related hardware, from Russia. Russian scientists many of whom are unemployed or have not been paid for an extended period, may be vulnerable to recruitment by states trying to establish biological warfare programs. The availability of worldwide information exchange via the internet or electronic mail facilitates this process. Even beyond such sinister causes, microbial leaks could have occurred if Russians facilities and staff morale were not upgraded."[16]

The Johns Hopkins Center for Civilian Biodefense Studies conducted an exercise engaging key personnel in the management of mock chemical, biological, or cyberterrorist attacks at the request of the US Congress.[17] It was called "TOPOFF," named for its engagement of top officials of the US government. The TOPOFF exercise illuminates problematic issues of leadership and decision-making; the year was 2000– several months before 9/11 and five years before Hurricane Katrina. What was learned at the time was that difficulties lingered linked to prioritization and distribution of scarce resources; when a contagious epidemic crisis happens, the healthcare facilities such as hospitals, outpatient centers, emergency departments, and clinics would not be prepared, the study reports; one recommendation by the researchers is that healthcare providers should develop sound principles of disease containment. The issues of a surprise attack were noted by the government officials by this and other studies; but apparently little was done about the recommendations from the study because both 9/11 and Hurricane Katrina caught the US government off guard, a government reports clarifies.[18] An attack on American soil employing the use of chemical or biological weapons of mass destruction (WMD) will happen, it's only a matter of time.[19, 4, 5]

[4] Weapons of mass destruction (WMD) are defined as any weapon with the capacity to inflict death and destruction on such a massive scale that its very presence in the hands of hostile forces is a grievous threat. Modern weapons of mass destruction are nuclear, biological, or chemical weapons. *Source:* TarbutMUN (ND). Non Proliferation Treaty: North Korea. http://www.tarbut.edu.mx/archivos/tarbutmun/WMDC.pdf

[5] **The Use of Pathogens as Weapons**
Biological warfare agents are defined as "living organisms, whatever their nature, or infected material derived from them, which are used for hostile purposes and intended to cause disease or death in man, animals and plants, and which depend for their efforts on the ability to multiply in the person, animal or plant attacked."
Source: RC Spencer and MH Wilcox (1993). Agents of Biological Warfare. Review of Medical Microbiology, 4:138–143.

The Islamic State in Iraq and Syria (ISIS)

The Islamic State in Iraq and Syria (ISIS) a "hugely successful movement with an apocalyptic, nihilistic philosophy . . . convert (to Sunni Islam), join us, or die" is America's greatest threat.[20] ISIS represents a militant jihad based on strict Sharia law.[6]

ISIS is more media sophisticated than al-Qaeda and excels in using social media as a tool of terrorism. The group's twitter and YouTube postings in American-English show that the West is often their target audience. According to the Heritage Foundation, ISIS has access to a global network of terrorists. "ISIS has evolved into a proto-state, with its own army, civil administration, judiciary and a sophisticated propaganda operation. Al-Qaeda core leaders are fugitives who are forced to live a clandestine existence under the constant threat of drone strikes or commando assaults."[21]

Former director of the CIA and the National Security Agency warned that the "Islamic State of Iraq and al-Sham, ISIS, is destined to launch attacks" on the US in its race to wage jihad and attract followers in the Arab world.[22] ISIS has global ambitions.

New technologies, desires, and threats from biological research developments in biotechnology, genetics, and genomics have created a variety of environmental, ethical, political, and social challenges for today's societies.[23] More recently, Texas Governor Rick Perry says that "the ISIS version of mission creep is to follow through on their threats by sending recruits to this country."[24] He adds that "what rational observer thinks such an attack is not part of their plan?"[25]

[6] Sharia Law covers public behavior, private behavior, and private beliefs. Of all legal systems in the world today, Islam's Sharia Law is the most intrusive and strict, especially against women. According to the Sharia Law:

- Theft is punishable by amputation of the right hand (above).
- Criticizing or denying any part of the Quran is punishable by death.
- Criticizing or denying Muhammad as a prophet is punishable by death.
- Criticizing or denying Allah, the moon god of Islam, is punishable by death.
- A Muslim who becomes a non-Muslim is punishable by death.
- A non-Muslim who leads a Muslim away from Islam is punishable by death.
- A non-Muslim man who marries a Muslim woman is punishable by death.
- A man can marry an infant girl and consummate the marriage when she is 9 years old.
- Girls' clitoris should be cut (per Muhammad's words in Book 41, Kitab Al-Adab, Hadith 5251).
- A woman can have 1 husband, but a man can have up to 4 wives; Muhammad can have more.
- A man can unilaterally divorce his wife, but a woman needs her husband's consent to divorce.
- A man can beat his wife for insubordination.
- Testimonies of four male witnesses are required to prove rape against a woman.
- A woman who has been raped cannot testify in court against her rapist(s).
- A woman's testimony in court, allowed only in property cases, carries half the weight of a man's.
- A female heir inherits half of what a male heir inherits.
- A woman cannot drive a car, as it leads to fitnah (upheaval).
- A woman cannot speak alone to a man who is not her husband or relative.
- Meat to be eaten must come from animals that have been sacrificed to Allah—i.e., be Halal.
- Muslims should engage in Taqiyya and lie to non-Muslims to advance Islam.

Source: Sharia Law (2014). BillionBibles.org. Retrieved August 28, 2014: http://www.billion-bibles.org/sharia/sharia-law.html

Use of Biological Agents as Weapons of Mass Destruction (WMD)

Biological or bioweapon warfare agents are defined as "living organisms, whatever their nature, or infected material derived from them, which are used for hostile purposes and intended to cause disease or death in man, animals and plants, and which depend for their efforts on the ability to multiply in the person, animal or plant attacked."[26]

Biological agents are the most advantageous weapons to employ against America; they are well suited for use in an attack by weak and poor nations against a large, powerful, and wealthy (so-called "asymmetric methods" of attack) nation; other than the research to develop bioweapons toward mass destruction, they are inexpensive, easy to obtain, and disperse easily creating mass casualties with small amounts;[27] full-scale use as a weapon could have limitations but intense (professional) training (from developed nations), insistent networking within American government and global organizations, and practical reasoning will uncomplicate bioweapons delivery at a mass distribution level.

Genetically engineered superbugs that are highly lethal and resistant to environmental impact or medical treatment have been provided by biomedical research, experts say.[28] Also, modern neurobiology provides a broad range of neuroreceptors and manifold psychoactive substances that make non-lethal chemical weapons attractive such as calmative agents like benzodiazepines and α2-adrenoreceptor agonists.[29]

There are several hundred pathogenics that can cause disease but only a few are feasible or adaptable for use as biological weapon agents (see below for details).[30] In addition to microbes, there are several organically produced chemical toxins available as biological weapons. These toxins are not easily destroyed by ultraviolent light. Airborne contamination is the most desirable and those which cause a high rate of fatality.[31]

Ethnic Bioweapons

Finally, ethnic bioweapons target specific ethnic or racial groups based upon genetic markers.[32] While occasional published reports of such research generate public outrage the reality of such bioweapons may well be in full production. Many symptoms of infection or intoxication by biological warfare agents (bacterial, viral, and toxic) are nonspecific and flulike in nature, particularly early in the disease process.[33] In an attempt to briefly explain bioweapons, I will classify two varieties of bioweapon agents, although there are other classifications: chemical and infectious.

Chemical Bioweapon Agents

Chemical warfare agents use toxic chemical substances as weapons. Toxic substances can produce a lethal effect on plants, animals, and humans.[34] They are classified according to their physiological effects; chemical weapons against humans include nerve agents, blistering agents (vesicants), blood agents, choking agents, and toxins. Chemical weapons similar to biological infectious disease weapons (see below) or whatever their source are classified as "unconventional" because they do not rely on an explosive force.

Nerve Agents

Sarin (GA, GB, GD, VX) are the most toxic human-made chemical weapons produced. The most deadly nerve agent is Sarin gas or GB.[35] It is 500 times more lethal than cyanide, and has been known to take lives less than one minute after exposure. Other facts about Sarin advanced by the federal agency (under the supervision of the Department of Health and Human Services—see Chapter 2 for more details) known as the Centers of Disease Control and Prevention (CDC) include:

- Not Found Naturally in the Environment
- Clear, Colorless, Odorless, and Tasteless Liquid
- It Evaporates into a Vapor (Gas) and Spreads into the Environment
- Following Release of Sarin, People Can Be Exposed through Skin Contact, Eye Contact, or Breathing
- Mixes Easily with Water
- A Person's Clothing Can Release Sarin after It Has Come in Contact With Sarin Vapor
- Because Sarin Vapor Is Heavier than Air, It Will Sink to Low-Lying Areas and Create a Greater Exposure Hazard There
- Sarin Is the Most Volatile of Nerve Agents.
- It evaporates quickly and presents an immediate but short-lived threat

For a further list and description of chemical warfare compounds see CDC's website at http://emergency.cdc.gov/agent/agentlistchem.asp

The latest use of Sarin was used in August 21, 2013, in the Damascus suburbs: 1,429 civilians were killed (including 426 children) and 2,200 were injured; rockets with chemical agents fired at about twelve areas in suburbs south and east of Damascus.[36]

Recent technological advances suggest that easy access to raw materials, the Internet, increasing attacks and corruption and state-sponsored terrorism, make chemical warfare a strong possibility to be used as one of the primary weapons against America.[37] I say one of possible more methods to be utilized because it is more likely that more than one bioweapon will be utilized in an attack because of the area to be exposed, the delivery distance, and population density. There are seventy different chemicals or compounds stockpiled as agents of war around the world. Exposure to nerve agents can occur due to accidental release from a military storage facility which is where most nerve agents including Sarin are stored. Deadliest of all options is the specter of deliberate release of supergerms including pesticides that would sweep around the world claiming tens of thousands of lives in man-made epidemics.[38] Public health needs to be—must be—global prevention.[39]

Infectious Bioweapon Agents

The following is a description of infectious bioweapon agents. The Centers for Disease Control and Prevention (CDC) imply that this list represents the most likely bioweapon used by invaders.[40]

- *Anthrax* is a serious infectious disease caused by gram-positive, rod-shaped bacteria known as Bacillus anthracis. Anthrax can be found naturally in soil and commonly affects domestic and wild animals around the world. Although it is rare, people can get sick with anthrax if they come in contact with infected animals or contaminated animal products. Contact with anthrax can cause severe illness in both humans and animals. Anthrax is not contagious, which means you cannot catch it similar to a cold or the flu.

  Genetic engineering has been applied in past weapons programs; for example, the former Soviet Union 'invisible anthrax,' resulted from the introduction of an alien gene into Bacillus Anthracis that altered its immunological properties.[41] Existing vaccines proved to be ineffective against this new genetically engineered strain; however, later scientists imply that a possibility exists through experiments with rabbits that a vaccine might be available in the future.[42]
- *Botulism* is a muscle-paralyzing disease caused by a toxin made by a bacterium called Clostridium botulinum. There are three main kinds of botulism:
  - Food-borne botulism occurs when a person ingests pre-formed toxin that leads to illness within a few hours to days. Food-borne botulism is a public health emergency because the contaminated food may still be available to other persons besides the patient.
  - Infant botulism occurs in a small number of susceptible infants each year who harbor C. botulinum in their intestinal tract.
  - Wound botulism occurs when wounds are infected with C. botulinum that secretes the toxin.

  Botulism is not spread from one person to another.
- *Brucellosis* is an infectious disease caused by bacteria. People can get the disease when they are in contact with infected animals or animal products contaminated with the bacteria. Animals that are most commonly infected include sheep, cattle, goats, pigs, and dogs, among others. Bacteria that cause brucellosis can include occupations such as:
  - slaughterhouse workers
  - meat-packing employees
  - veterinarians
  - laboratory workers
  - hunters

  Game animals that can transmit brucellosis include wild hogs (feral swine), elk, bison, caribou, and moose.
- *Plague* is a disease caused by Yersinia pestis (Y. pestis), a bacterium in rodents and their fleas. It can be used in an aerosol attack. One to six days after being infected, people would develop pneumonic plague. The bacteria can spread to others who have close contact with those infected. Because of the delay between exposure

to showing sickness, a highly contagious situation exists. The Y. pestis bacterium occurs in nature and could be isolated and grown in quantity in a laboratory.

Pneumonic plague can be transmitted from person to person; bubonic plague cannot. Pneumonic plague affects the lungs and is transmitted when a person breathes in Y. pestis particles in the air. Bubonic plague is transmitted through the bite of an infected flea or exposure to infected material through a break in the skin. Transmission can take place if someone breathes in Y. pestis particles, which could happen in an aerosol release during a bioweapon attack. Pneumonic plague is also transmitted by breathing in Y. pestis suspended in respiratory droplets from a person (or animal) with pneumonic plague. Respiratory droplets are spread most readily by coughing or sneezing.

- *Smallpox*: is a serious, contagious, and sometimes fatal infectious disease. There is no specific treatment for smallpox disease; its only prevention is vaccination.

  There are two clinical forms of smallpox: Variola major is the severe and most common form of smallpox, with a more extensive rash and higher fever. There are four types of Variola major smallpox:

  - ordinary (the most frequent type, accounting for 90 percent or more of cases)
  - modified (mild and occurring in previously vaccinated persons)
  - flat
  - hemorrhagic (flat and hemorrhagic are rare and very severe)

  Variola (the virus that causes smallpox) is the most notorious of the poxviruses.[43] Variola major has an overall fatality rate of about 30 percent. Smallpox outbreaks have occurred for thousands of years; the disease has been eradicated after worldwide vaccination programs. There is a heightened concern that the Variola virus might be used as an agent of bioweapon.

  The majority of the US population has no immunity, vaccine is in short supply, and no effective treatment exists for the disease. But, 3 percent of those vaccinated may also develop Variola major.

  Variola virus is highly infectious when released into the air. It is environmentally stable and can retain its ability to infect people for long periods. After a person is exposed to aerosolized virus, the virus multiplies in the person's respiratory tract. After a period of seven to seventeen days, Variola is spread through the bloodstream to lymph nodes where it continues to multiply. Generally, direct and fairly prolonged face-to-face contact is required to spread smallpox from one person to another. Humans are the only natural hosts of Variola.

- *Tularemia*: is a serious illness that occurs naturally in the US. It is caused by the bacterium Francisella tularensis in animals (especially rodents, rabbits, and hares). It can be transmitted in different ways:

  - Bitten by an Infected Tick, Deerfly, or Other Insect
  - Handling Infected Animal Carcasses
  - Eating or Drinking Contaminated Food or Water
  - Breathing in the Bacteria F. Tularensis

  Tularemia is not spread from person to person.

- *Viral Hemorrhagic Fevers* (VHFs): refer to a group of illnesses that are caused by several distinct families of viruses. In general, the term "viral hemorrhagic fever" is used to describe a severe multisystem syndrome (multisystem in that multiple organ systems in the body are affected). Characteristically, the overall vascular system is damaged, and the body's ability to regulate itself is impaired. These symptoms are often accompanied by hemorrhage (bleeding). While some types of hemorrhagic fever viruses can cause relatively mild illnesses, many of these viruses cause severe, life-threatening disease.

  The Special Pathogens Branch (SPB) primarily works with hemorrhagic fever viruses that are classified as biosafety level four (BSL-4) pathogens. A list of these viruses appears in the SPB disease information index.

Chaos before a Bioweapon Attack

Distractions and diversions are required to create chaos and confusion before bioweapons are employed against America. How distractions and diversions are accomplished is beyond the scope of this book and the focus of this chapter. However, there are methods worth considering that link to the focus of this work: criminal justice and their partners as first-responders to bioweapons victims. For example, if another nation orchestrates America's destruction from within first as some 'war experts' suggest by intensifying chaos and confusion before a bioweapon attack, first-responder performance would be compromised. Identifying and manipulating weaknesses of America similar to tinkering with the 'center of gravity,' might be one method.[44] America's weakness and powder keg—race (whites, blacks, and browns). For instance, a Columbine strike at the heart of each racial groups' sacred institutions: church, schools, and shopping centers across the country months before the actual bioweapon attack; the blame of the strike needs to be placed on the 'other' American racial group (i.e., white shopping center, the evidence would show that blacks did it; black school attacked the evidence would show that it was in retaliation of the white shopping center). Allow tempers, ignorance, and hatred among the few individuals of all races who are violent prone to manifest itself into what it truly represents—wickedness, my experience tell me.

Once scientists learn how to prolong Sarin's longevity, it will be part of the first bioweapon assault; yet smallpox has a high mortality rate and can be spread by aerosols or in the dust, and immunity in the American population is low because American terrorist readiness is not up to standards, experts say.[45] Although an initial release of smallpox could infect a large number of people, secondary spread would be slow because of the long incubation period and the close contact required for transmission. Criminal justice professionals especially federal and local law enforcement officers and their partners including hospital personnel, physicians, and nurses are at the greatest risk of becoming infected.

Assumptions about Federal and Local Law Enforcement Officers

There are two assumptions that should be noted before discussing professional personnel response after an attack. The first perspective relates to the myth that federal government agencies are the only agencies that engage violators including terrorists. This myth is projected by the media among others; for example, federal law enforcement agencies such as the Federal Bureau of Investigation (FBI) is all that stands between social order and violent crime including terrorism. One reason for this misconception relates to the number of performances on television such as (some of my favorite series) Bones, The Blacklist, Criminal Minds, and Marvel's Agents of S.H.I.E.L.D. In the US, the FBI boasts that they represent: "An intel-driven national security and law enforcement agency, providing leadership and making a difference for more than a century."[46]

Peter Kim/Shutterstock, Inc.

All total, the FBI has approximately 35,000 agents and staff members whose first priority is "to protect the United States from Terrorists." In 2012 the FBI conducted a little over 25,000 arrests of suspects linked to crimes of every description, processed almost 15,000 indicts, and obtained over 15,000 convictions among all defendants of which terrorists were not significant in number. FBI reports are filled with international terrorist data; the US statistics on terrorism, however, is jammed into a Western Hemisphere report.[47] Finally, another FBI report says: "In 2013, governments in Latin America made modest improvements to their counterterrorism capabilities and their border security. Corruption, weak government institutions, insufficient interagency cooperation, weak or non-existent legislation, and a lack of resources remained the primary causes for the lack of significant progress in some of the countries. … Iran's influence in the Western Hemisphere remained a concern. However, due to strong sanctions imposed on the country by both the United States and the EU (European Union), Iran has been unable to expand its economic and political ties in Latin America. … There were no known operational cells of either al-Qaeda or Hizballah in the hemisphere."[48] No mention of ISIS in their 318-page document covering the 'world's' terrorists data including arrests and strategies; through the FBI files (online) there is no mention of how 9/11 slipped past FBI surveillance, and there was little mention of terrorist activity in the US for 2013 or 2014 including FBI's denial statement.[7]

Most criminal activity is policed by local police departments and most violent crime is prosecuted by state agencies. In 2008, local police, sheriff, and campus agencies employed around 800,000 sworn law enforcement officers.[49] In the nation's 75 largest counties, an estimated 56,000 defendants were charged with a felony offense in 2009. The point is that combating terrorism in the US requires continued reliance on "enhancing cooperation among federal, state, and local authorities as well as mutual trust and partnerships with Muslim communities.[50] The city of New York has one of the largest anti-terrorists departments in the nation. Nonetheless, The Department of Homeland Security (DHS) and Congress must plug gaps to halt terrorist travel, and create a lawful detainment framework for the incapacitation and interrogation of suspected terrorists and put their resources to work where they were intended as opposed to engaging in a turf battle with talented and committed local law enforcement agencies.[51, 8] Little question local law enforcement must have the leading role in local enforcement;[52, 9] for instance, the Boston Police Department was the agency that brought the Boston Marathon killers to justice and because federal agents are not accountable to the communities even when they violate the rule of law such as what occurred in Boston linked to detainment and blocked off part of the city.[53] In the name of justice, the feds freeze liberty. Finally in this regard it isn't merely television, the news media reinforces the myth that federal agencies are 'all that,' my students would say. For instance, *Time Magazine's* September 15, 2014, issue page 76 entitled The Answers Issue reports that the average cost per US federal inmate in 2011 was $28,893.40; then the article goes on to report other alleged facts. The appearance is that as of 2014, there are 214,713 inmates and that almost 50 percent of those inmates were convicted of drug possession or drug trading charges and 81 were convicted of national security charges.[54] On the other hand, approximately 1.2 million prisoners call state prisons their home and another 744,000 are jailed in city or county jails at any given time in 2012.[55] Average prisoner costs are $31,286 and ranged from $14,603 in Kentucky to $60,076 in New York (using the same time period as the BOP, 2011), and the forty states used in this study spend close to $40 billion on corrections each year.[56] When we add state and county probation and parole to dollar counts to those locked down, the number under department of corrections supervision is approximately 6.7 million. Note: If the reporters employed by *Time* were in a university classroom and presented old data and misleading information, they probably would have received a very low grade for their efforts from real professors. Nonetheless, the point is that the media manufactures their own idea of reality.

[7] **October 21, 2013, 11:45 a.m. EDT**
There has been recent reporting relating to whether or not the FBI, Boston Police, Massachusetts, State Police, or other members of the Joint Terrorism Task Force knew the identities of the bombers before the shootout with the alleged marathon bombing suspects and were conducting physical surveillance of them on April 18, 2013. These claims have been repeatedly refuted by the FBI, Boston Police, and Massachusetts State Police.

Source: FBI. Retrieved August 31, 2014: http://www.fbi.gov/news/updates-on-investigation-into-multiple-explosions-in-boston

[8] **Policing Terrorism in the United States: The Los Angeles Police Department's Convergence Strategy**
Local law enforcement agencies around the world face an increasingly complex set of problems with the emergence of globally coordinated criminal networks and national security threats. Modern-day criminals have proved themselves to be transnational in reach, linked by sophisticated networks and highly adaptive in their thinking. In response, local police agencies such as the Los Angeles, California, Police Department (LAPD) are developing strategies that are equally adaptive and networked. The linchpin of these strategies is and must remain convergence.
Source: Michael P. Downing, Deputy Chief and Commanding Officer, Counter-Terrorism and Criminal Intelligence Bureau, Los Angeles, California, Police Department. (2014, September). *The Police Chief.* Retrieved September 3, 2014: http://www.policechiefmagazine.org

[9] Counter-terrorism has to be woven into the everyday workings of every (police) department. We think they must: (a) collect intelligence about possible terrorist activity; (b) ensure that vulnerable targets are protected; and (c) be ready to respond in the event of an attack.

Source: George L Kelling and William J Bratton (2006). See Endnote

The second assumption held by many relates to enforcement control of terrorists. Local police can identify potential terrorists living or operating in their jurisdictions, help to protect vulnerable targets, and can coordinate the first response to terror attacks.[57] Local police which includes state police, sheriff departments, and other sworn officers such as campus police play a critical role in defeating terrorism, which is not much different from other crime.[58] Therein lies the problem. Once terrorists are identified, capturing or killing them—as the main defense against terrorism—might not work. Individuals who are willing to die for their religious belief are unlikely to be deterred by the risk of death or punishment.[59] And if killed, they become martyrized and their death is a potent recruiting symbol among the impressionable young men that terrorists seek to attract; once detected, terrorists feel a gunfight is a good strategy. Catching them is difficult because terrorists are more careful than other criminals to conceal their activities. Even when their identities are known, and they live in other countries, then what? This is not to say that terrorists should not be identified, apprehended, arrested, and if guilty—punished. Bottom line here is that most of the criminological research says the same thing: there is little relationship between severe punishment and reduced criminally violent behavior.[60] It appears that the only consistent expression of severe punishment and crime deterrence is in the media such as television performances, Hollywood productions, and newspapers and magazines. See my earlier book, *The Media and Criminal Justice: The CSI Effect* (Jones and Bartlett, Boston 2011) for more details. Fact is, a small number of people commit a large proportion of violent crimes. Approximately 6 percent of the young males of a given age commit 50 percent or more of all the serious crimes committed by all young males of that age with similar characteristics: dysfunctional families, have close relatives (including parents) who are criminals, have low verbal-intelligence quotients, do poorly in school because they are basely illiterate, are alcohol- and drug-abusers, live in poor and chaotic neighborhoods, begin their misbehavior at a very young age, and have been apprehended by the police. Point is, punishment has nothing to do with the 6 percent crowd or those in abusive relationships, those whose children who have been stanched, those who have no hope or future, those who are mentally ill, those who lack a moral compass (even among the wealthy, see my earlier work, *Wicked Women: A Journey of Super Predators*), those who lack personal accountability, or those who think the world owes them a living.[61]

First-Responder's Performance: Law Enforcement

The first question among law enforcement agencies after any disaster including a bioweapon attack or Hurricane Katrina is how should law enforcement respond to a public panic crisis event.**[10]** For example, from New Orleans and many sounding parishes in Louisiana after Hurricane Katrina in 2005, over one million people migrated to Houston, Texas; Mobile, Alabama; Charlotte, North Carolina; and northern cities as far as Chicago. Local police departments were unprepared for the massive surge of travelers. Many officers in various jurisdictions were unaccustomed to city thugs and urban cultures (not a put-down of officer ability or dedication), although most migrators were respectful; some were relentless in their demands while visiting makeshift camps; one result was that it placed many regions in the country in chaos. How would police respond if multiple cities were biologically attacked; the populations from those places would have no place to run. Some law enforcement jurisdictions are in hot debate with applicable strategies. For instance, Pennsylvania emergency managers debate how they would handle the westward flow of people if biological terrorists attack New York City.[62] Some managers suggest a quarantine of the state. How absurd and exactly how would they enforce such a ridicules plan? Would lethal force become necessary to enforce a quarantine? Two possible means of controlling the flow of people into the region would be to set up checkpoints at the Delaware River crossings or to close interstate exit ramps to force people farther west. But, some say that river checkpoints would create a traffic jam that would extend all the way to New York City and would deny many Monroe County residents access to their homes. As mentioned below can local police suspend the Constitutional rights of Americans even during a bioweapon attack?[63]

> **[10]** Public Panic Crisis Event: An ecological crisis generated by rumors or perceptions of an impending crisis that results in outbreaks of panic response (e.g., hoarding, violence, rioting). Best intervention is preparation.

Hopefully American police will not have to confront an action similar to police at Kenema in eastern Sierra Leone; residents threw stones at a hospital and a police station, spurred by a rumor that healthcare workers were using Ebola as a ruse to kill people and collect body parts.[64] The rumor was spread by a mentally ill former nurse who was in custody; she had gone to the city's main market and told people Ebola was a hoax. Police used tear gas to stop the crowd from destroying the Kenema Government Hospital.

Additionally, the application of prevailing policies led to a quick embrace of punitive policing and incarceration, and journalistic routines ended up supporting this process. Although journalists openly expressed their disgust with state neglect, news conventions nonetheless criminalized much of the New Orleans population and suggested militarized policing and imprisonment as fundamental to restore order. Lacking credible sources, reporters relied on rumors and helped create a racialized 'looter class' that aided state efforts to regain control through existing policies of mass incarceration rather than mutual aid or state welfare.

What remains controversial is whether we must give up civil liberties to deal with this "different kind of war." What steps should the government take 'with consent of the people' to prepare for a bioterrorist attack involving the use of smallpox or another contagious agent, and which level of government, state or federal, should take the lead?[11]

[11] **Large-Scale Crises: Affects Communities or Regions**
Megacrises: Affects Entire Countries
Problem: How To Intervene When Very Large Crises Or Megacrises Affect Neighborhoods, Families, And Individuals?
Source: Richard K James and Burl E Gilliland (2008). Crisis Intervention Strategies, 7th ed. Belmont, CA: Cengage Learning.

The Media's Bit in Establishing Punitive Punishment Policy

A serious problem for criminal justice professionals after Hurricane Katrina, may be similar to the problems in the US after a bioweapons attack. Sensationalized lurid reports offered by the media helped toward legitimate punitive policing and punishment as disaster policy.[65] For instance, there was widespread reporting of murders and rapes by the media that never took place.[66] There was no shortage of individuals who spoke to reporters about horrors: "They are raping babies, raping women, killing people," one said in the Superdome. City authorities repeated these accounts to the news media, leaving the impression that they were factual.[67] At one point, New Orleans Mayor Ray Nagin predicted the death toll from Katrina would be as high as 10,000 people, an estimate that was widely reported. Later, in a television interview, his frustration at the slow pace of evacuation of the Superdome and Convention Center spilled out: "They have people standing out there, have been in that frickin' superdome for five days, watching dead bodies, watching hooligans killing people, raping people," he said. The media picked up these comments and reported some of the rumors of criminal violence as fact. Many of the most sensational reports were untrue.

Rumors, too, add to punitive responses of law enforcement, correctional officers, and the National Guard when involved in local catastrophes such as Hurricane Katrina, for that matter. For instance, the Arkansas National Guardsman patrolling the area said that there was a freezer containing thirty or forty bodies including a seven-year-old with her throat cut, inside the food service entrance of New Orleans' Ernest N. Morial Convention Center.[68] But neither the mass of bodies nor the allegedly dead child would ever be found. The guardsman who repeated the freezer story had heard it in the food line at Harrah's Casino, a law enforcement and military staging area a block away. There were many rumors during Katrina; it was hard to tell the difference between fact or fiction, I learned.

What myths will shape criminal justice response and policy after a bioweapon's attack? An example prior to the US invasion of Iraq might help us better prepare for an answer. "It's hardly controversial to suggest that the mainstream media's performance in the lead-up to the Iraq War was a disaste ... many journalists and pundits wish they had been more skeptical of the White House's claims about Iraq, particularly its allegations about weapons of mass destruction ... media apologists suggest that the press could not have done much better, since 'everyone' was in agreement on the intelligence regarding Iraq's weapons threat."[69] (See Chapter 11 for more details).

Other evidence from the Boston Marathon suggests the popular media offered sensationalized and fake stories about the disaster; products of those sensationalized stories was public panic, vigilantism, and a punitive criminal justice response to the point of violating the civil liberties of many people.[70] Here is one perspective about what happened: An unprecedented manhunt for Dzhokhar Tsarnaev ensued on April 19, (the bomb exploded April 15, 2013) with thousands of law enforcement officers searching the Boston suburb of Watertown, MA. During the manhunt, authorities asked residents to stay indoors. The public transportation system and most businesses and public institutions were closed. Dzhokhar hid in a boat in a family's back yard. During an initial interrogation in the hospital, Dzhokhar alleged that his brother Tamerlan (the individual already shot and killed earlier) was the mastermind. He said they were motivated by extremist Islamist beliefs and the wars in Iraq and Afghanistan, and that they were self-radicalized and unconnected to any outside terrorist groups, one source says.[71]

In prisons, correctional officers make decisions about rendering assistance (both first-aid and protection) to prisoners when a correctional officer hears a rumor about the condition of a prisoner. For example, veteran correctional officers at five prisons participated in a study about exposure to infectious pathogens while at work. What was found was that the more experienced a correctional officer was, the less likely he or she would engage with prisoners or the use of force particularly if the officer thought a prisoner had an infectious condition such as HIV.[72] I take that to include rendering medical assistance to injured prisoners from a prison fight or an accident. "Let'em bleed," one officer told me in confidence. This perspective is consistent with my own experiences at penitentiaries when as a group leader (social services) or a teacher, and battle ensued between prisoners, officers would not intervene if they suspected one of the prisoners had an infectious disease of any sorts. When prisoners fight with each other, correctional officer avoidance is more likely if one of the prisoners is rumored to have HIV or another inflection. If victims from a bioweapon attack are incarcerated or hospitalized, it is very likely that jailers and healthcare providers would avoid them.

The literature suggests that when professionals, including criminal justice and healthcare professionals, internalize risks to their health and believe an individual is perceived as a risk carrier, intervention by those professionals is greatly possible.[73] It may be for those reasons that individuals are medicalized into "healthy patients," subjected to routine control check-ups, preventive medication, indications to lead healthy lifestyle, and show correct comportment in American society. In this manner, an individual's personal health prevention becomes an individual responsibility aimed at avoiding risk and preventing disease. When risk is internalized by providers, there is no major pressure to publicly intervene in social and environmental health-threatening conditions.

An experience of mine supports this perspective. In one of my university (at the University of North Carolina Charlotte) classes, a young man left the classroom early. His close friend followed him through the door. Moments later, the young friend ran up to the podium where I was lecturing to 140 students in a marriage and family sociology course. "Dr. Stevens, Dr. Stevens," he said twice. "Leonard is having an episode." I told the class to prepare an answer to gay marriage in North Carolina, "Talk to your neighbor, and we'll discuss your answers in ten minutes," I mouthed over my shoulder as I headed for the door. In the hall a small crowd had gathered. Campus police were on the scene. Everyone watched Leonard shake, roll, and vomit. No one intervened until I tried to reach out to hold his head from hitting the floor. The officer grabbed my hands, "Don't touch'em, doc," he said and added, "he's got AIDS." With that the crowd backed away. Leonard did not have AIDS, although his sexual orientation was different from most members of the crowd. If we generalize about my experience, is that the way it will be after a bioweapon attack? Professionals will disengage themselves from victims based on their health perceptions of individuals and justify their lack of public safety, treatment, and care on contagion? I asked one of the officers later that day why she did not aid Leonard. Her response was, "Come on, doc. Don't be cruel. You know why? I got a family to think of." Campus police are sworn officers with obligatory responsibilities similar to all law enforcement officers in the jurisdiction.

Issues about Healthcare after a Bioweapon Attack

An outbreak of smallpox, for example, could be controlled through surveillance, containment, vaccination, and isolation of cases—the strategy used to eradicate the disease globally in 1978. My concerns are that the vaccine or the method of application could be compromised. Pre-exposure vaccination for hospital personnel including physicians and nurses and the first-responders who brought victims to a healing center because they are more likely to be exposed to smallpox while engaging victims during an outbreak. Risks are the microbial hitchhikers carried inside immigrants, travelers, and cargo from all over the world.[74] Researchers representing the World Health Organization (WHO) at Geneva, The Kaiser Permanente at Sacramento, California, and the MacColl Institute for Healthcare Innovation in Seattle imply that serious issues exist concerning treatment and care among chronic patients.[75] I read that to mean that global healthcare monitors (i.e., WHO, Kaiser, and MacColl) imply that after a bioweapons attack on the US, hospital admissions and safety, and treatment and care would be a challenging issue for professional providers. Those researchers talk about redesigning health systems in accordance with local resources and demands.

Overview of Government and Healthcare Response

After the attack on the World Trade Center, questions about healthcare treatment and care providers surfaced everywhere. Those concerns involved the public health infrastructure which it was decided must be strengthened to successfully detect and respond to a future terrorist attack, an epidemic, or catastrophe, "which will have the side benefit of enabling the public health system to better fulfill its commitment to protecting the health of the population."[76] Healthcare professionals across the country, the thinking goes, must be trained to recognize and treat diseases that result from the release of a biological weapon; hospitals must be equipped to handle large numbers of infectious and chemically assaulted patients. Yet, four years after 9/11, Hurricane Katrina hit the Gulf coast and based on the evidence in Chapter 1 and my own experience, the level of treatment and care by both government and healthcare providers, little was learned or applied aside from a lot of fancy rhetoric from the experiences of 9/11. The CDC gave a 'C' to the agencies linked to national preparedness of the nation in December 2014.**[12]**

Other evidence from the Center for Biosecurity of the University of Pittsburgh Medical Center and the Society of Critical Care Medicine in 2005 suggests that traditional hospital and clinical care standards in general, and critical care standards in particular, likely could not maintain reasonable clinical guidelines when facing a bioweapons attack.[77]

Surge Capacity

Researchers provide recommendations to hospital and clinical leaders regarding the delivery of critical care services in the wake of a bioterrorist attack resulting in hundreds or thousands of critically ill patients, or what is called surge capacity in hospitals.[78] However, it appears that few if any of those recommendations have been followed.**[13]**

Surge capacity has led to a number of proposals designed to mitigate the effects of crowds as well as deficiencies in patient care capacities.[79] The most controversial of these proposals is to close hospital doors in the wake of a mass casualty terror event. Yet, several specific challenges posed by mass casualty events make closing hospitals doors disadvantageous, say researchers. There remains the need for efficient movement of resources, maintenance of social order, and providing the moral reassurance needed by the general public in times of crisis; to many in the general public a hospital is the cornerstone of quality of life experiences.**[14]** Importantly, these challenges are related to features of terrorist events that distinguish such events from circumstances of "normal" surge that might result in, for example, closure of emergency rooms.

It is expected that management of an attack will be handled primarily by the Department of Health and Human Services (see Chapter 2 for more details), say experts. The federal

[12] The Association of State and Territorial Health Officials (ASTHO), in partnership with the Centers for Disease Control and Prevention (CDC) and more than 35 development partners, released its second report of the National Health Security Preparedness Index (NHSPI™). The NHSPI™ graded the nation's preparedness for natural disasters, terrorism, and disease pandemics at 7.4 out of 10.

Source: CDC and National Health Security Preparedness Index. Retrieved December 16, 2014: http://www.cdc.gov/media/releases/ 2014/ a1209-security-preparedness.html

[13] Surge Capacity—Minnesota Emergency Preparedness Education and Training (MERET)
The MERET site has six modules including one on isolation and one on how to develop Temporary Negative Pressure rooms (TNP). *Source:* MERET http://cpheo1.sph.umn.edu/meret

[14] End-of-Life Care Fact Sheet
What are older adults' mental health needs near the end of life?
The US Supreme Court agreed that Americans should expect palliative care, which combines active and compassionate therapies to comfort and support individuals and families nearing the end of life. End of life is defined as that time period when healthcare providers would not be surprised if death occurred within about six months. Older Americans with chronic illness think about how they would prefer their lives to end, and want a "good death" without burdensome pain, symptoms, and technology. Most Americans die in hospitals (63 percent), and another 17 percent die in institutional settings such as long-term care facilities.
Source: American Psychological Association (2014). http://www.apa.org/pi/aids/programs/eol/ end-of-life-factsheet.aspx

government might suspend private management of the healthcare industry and place them under federal authority.[80,15]

There are government efforts to support the development of vaccines, specifically against anthrax and smallpox. Currently the military possesses a vaccine for anthrax, "but the vaccine is not available for civilians, as there is not even enough for all members of the armed services."[81] Some might say that the government and healthcare failed in their performance of responding to and treating Hurricane Katrina victims; for example, recall from Chapter 1 a report filed by a government researcher says that the Disaster Medical Assistance Teams (DMATs) "are teams of physicians, nurses and other medical professionals who provide medical care. FEMA reports that it deployed all of the nation's more than 50 DMATs in the initial response to Hurricane Katrina. DMAT members from a dozen teams deployed at the airport reported overwhelming numbers of patients, some of whom could not be saved under the austere conditions they faced . . . also robbed the region of 6,000 hospital beds."[82] Imagine what would happen if 100 Hurricane Katrinas hit the US at the same time or a bioweapon attack hit the US? The longer it takes for the public health system to identify that a bioweapon attack has actually happened, the more people will become sick or die, and the costlier it will be to society.[83] In 2004, CDC researchers argued that most evaluations of detection systems and some evaluations of diagnostic systems for bioterrorism responses are critically deficient.[84] In a close search of the literature, I found little that says anything different.

One study tells us that if an anthrax attack on a population of 100,000 is identified and proper doses of antibiotics are distributed to the exposed population within twenty-four hours, then an estimated 5,000 people will die, and the cost to society both in healthcare expenditures and economic loss will be around $128 million, and these numbers are from 1997.[85] If, on the other hand, the attack is not identified by healthcare providers or physicians for six days, and only then are doses of antibiotic prophylaxes given to the exposed population, approximately 33,000 people will die at a cost of $26.2 billion.

Another study indicates that rapid public healthcare providers' response to a large-scale anthrax attack would reduce overall morbidity and mortality of the US. Uncertainty about optimal cost-effective response strategy based on timing of intervention, public health resources, and critical care facilities will make a difference as to who dies and who doesn't. Sound familiar? (See Chapter 1 for details.)[16]

Some researchers conducted a decision analytic study to compare response strategies to a theoretical large-scale anthrax attack on the city of Chicago beginning either Day 2 or Day 5 after a bioweapons attack.[86] Outcomes were measured in costs, lives saved, quality-adjusted life-years and incremental cost-effectiveness ratios; researchers estimated that post-attack antibiotic prophylaxis of all 1,390,000 anthrax-exposed people beginning on Day 2 after attack would result in 205,835 infected victims, 35,049 fulminant (occurring suddenly) victims, and 28,612 deaths. Only 6,437 of the fulminant victims could be saved with the existing

15 When catastrophes overwhelm state and local response capabilities, the President (acting through the Secretary of Homeland Security) can provide assistance to stricken communities, individuals, governments, and not-for-profit groups to assist in response and recovery. Aid is provided under the authority of the Robert T. Stafford Disaster Relief and Emergency Assistance Act (the Stafford Act) upon a presidential declaration. The Secretary of Health and Human Services (HHS) also has both standing and emergency authorities in the Public Health Service (PHS) Act by which he can provide assistance in response to public health and medical emergencies. He has limited means, however, to finance activities that are ineligible, for whatever reason, for Stafford Act assistance.
Source: see endnote. Sarah A. Lister

16 Children represent nearly a quarter of the US population; their unique needs in chemical, biological, radiological, and nuclear (CBRN) emergencies might not be understood by first-responders and healthcare clinicians. Children are different from adults physically, developmentally, and socially.

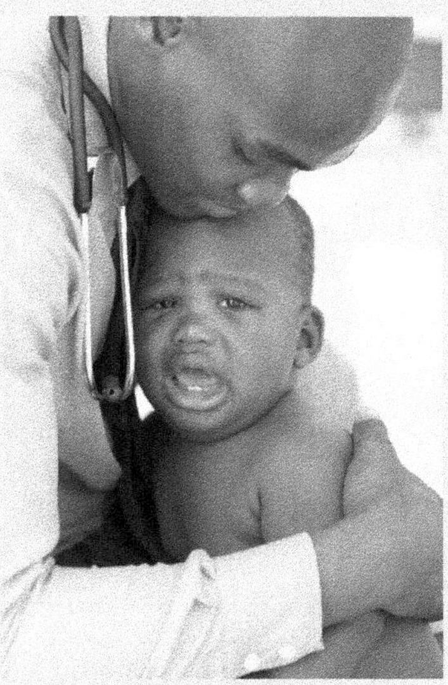

michaeljung/Shutterstock, Inc.

Source: MT Bartenfeld, G Peacock, and SE Griese (2014). Public Health Emergency Planning for Children in Chemical, Biological, Radiological, and Nuclear (CBRN) Disasters. *Biosecurity Bioterrorism*, 12(4):201–207.

critical care facilities in Chicago. Mortality would increase to 69,136 if the response strategy began on Day 5. Including post-attack vaccination with antibiotic prophylaxis of all exposed people reduces mortality and is cost-effective for both Day 2 at an estimated $182 per day and Day 5 at an estimated $1,088 for response strategies for each victim. Increasing hospital bed availability significantly reduces mortality for all response strategies. So how sharp are healthcare providers about bioweapons?

It is predicted that the US government and commercialized healthcare will once again fail the American public unless the US government steps back and promotes private and state sector participation including religious and charitable participation because those are the organizations and the public agencies that pulled the Gulf coast out of Katrina's grip and made life livable (see Chapter 1 for details).

Hospital Response after a Bioweapon Attack

Before a bioweapon invasion, allocation of scarce resources presents an increasing challenge to hospital administrators and health policy makers as of August 28, 2014.[87] For example, intensive care units can present holdups among busy hospitals; their expansion is costly and difficult to gauge. Although many hospital administrators have methods to deal with those issues, imagine what happens when most of the hospital beds become intensive care beds.

Hospital Turn-Away Rates

Rates increased exponentially when utilization of intensive care needs expand. Some administrators justify the turnaway rate through staffing explanations. The random nature of patient flow may falsely lead health planners to underestimate resource needs in busy intensive care units.[88]

Interestingly enough, the evidence shows that inadequate health literacy is an independent risk factor for hospital admission.[89] Individuals with inadequate functional health literacy have a 52 percent higher risk of hospital admission. Hospitals tend to admit individuals who characterize inadequate literacy than those individuals who characterize literacy.[90] The study shows individuals with inadequate literacy as older, were more likely to be non-White, and had lower income and education compared with individuals with adequate literacy. They were less likely to have ever smoked cigarettes and less likely to have used alcohol during the past month, and their health status was worse than those with adequate literacy. In this study, a total of 963 (almost 30 percent) participants were hospitalized one or more times during the study's follow-up. Individuals with inadequate and marginal functional health literacy were more likely to be hospitalized than were those with adequate literacy.

Substantial evidence reports that inadequate functional health literacy adversely affects patients' knowledge, self-care for chronic diseases, health status, and risk of hospitalization. Inadequate literacy is more than just a reading problem. These individuals have global problems with both oral and written communication. Although rewriting healthcare information at a simpler level would greatly increase the number of people who could understand written health information, many patients are unlikely to comprehend even the simplest written materials.

I read the results of a study on illiteracy and a greater possibility toward hospital admission to imply that hospital admission personnel might see literate individuals as individuals who do not need hospital treatment as much as those who are illiterate. These results are congruent in a previous study about illiteracy and hospital, individuals with literacy or in this case a lack of literacy, also have a 52 percent higher chance of admissions (but, interestingly enough a greater chance of imprisonment).[91]

A functional decline in older adults is often linked to acute hospital admissions and can produce devastating consequences such as increased morbidity and mortality.[92] Multiple risk factors such as older age, normal age-related changes, acute illness, and the effects of being hospitalized contribute to this decline. For many older persons, hospitalization can produce a functional decline among those patients despite cure or repair of the condition for which they were admitted.[93] Hospitalization can result in complications unrelated to the problem that caused admission or to its specific treatment for reasons that are explainable and avoidable.

Other evidence comes from the International Journal of Environmental Research and Public Health.[94] Hospitals have been working hard toward "being ready" for a terrorist attack. Yet, at the time (2006) the United States General Accounting Office (GAO) says that US hospitals were not prepared to manage mass causalities resulting from a bioweapons attack or from WMD (defined earlier). Using the State of Mississippi as an example, all acute care hospitals in the state were included in the study. The conclusion of the study states that hospitals in the "State of Mississippi, like a number of hospitals throughout the United States, are still not adequately prepared to manage victims of terrorist attacks involving chemical or biological WMD which consequently may result in the loss of hundreds or even thousands of lives."[95] By 2014, another source reports that "although hospitals have general emergency management plans in place, they may not have planned for a large-scale chemical or biological terrorism incident until federal and state public health groups developed communication plans and networks to address such incidents."[96]

Rather than updating hospital policies, facilities, and the infrastructure to prepare treatment and care to surge capacity linked to the bioweapon attack, the US healthcare system has collectively and individually positioned itself into a profitable machine that operates on its own timetable—not the schedule of its patients;[97] additional evidence supporting this claim can be seen in infant mortality rates (see Chapter 9 for details).

Among hospitals and hospital systems, once their priorities and policies change after a bioweapon attack, in what way will those systems reject admissions to some groups of the population? Must victims have their insurance cards with them or how exactly will that work? The point is that hospitals do reject admission of individuals for a variety of reasons. That is not to suggest that their reasoning is positive or negative, practical or unpractical; yet even when victims are admitted to hospitals or visit a doctor's office will treatment follow?

Age of Bioterrorism: Physicians

While the use of bioweapons initially leads to nonspecific symptoms (among anthrax, smallpox, tularemia, botulism, plague, and hemorrhagic fever), however, a high index of suspicion and clustering of abnormal pathology will often lead only the astute physician in the realm of otolaryngology (ear, nose, and throat) to the correct diagnosis of bioweapons;[98] I take that to mean incompetent, however you wish to define incompetent physicians have difficulty with diagnosis and of course that would include treatment particularly during a bioweapon attack.

Physicians and Misconceptions

Other examples of concern include healthcare professionals who harbor misconceptions or misunderstandings about disease; those misconceptions can lead healthcare professionals to stigmatize patients and deliver "substandard services and propagate such attitudes within the community."[99] Utilizing Ethiopia, for instance, patients with podoconiosis (endemic non-filarial elephantiasis) are challenging; 275 health professionals in public and private health institutions in southern Ethiopia were polled about their attitudes toward podoconiosis. Nearly all of the health participants held at least one significant misconception about the cause of podoconiosis, and nearly all of the participants responded incorrectly to one or more questions about signs and symptoms of podoconiosis. Around one-half of the participants incorrectly considered podoconiosis to be an infectious disease and were afraid of acquiring podoconiosis while providing care. All (100 percent) held one or more stigmatizing attitudes toward people with podoconiosis. At this point you might be right in thinking, well that is in Ethiopia. Yet much to my surprise, there are more Ethiopian physicians in the US than there are in Ethiopia and a high percentage of physicians in Ethiopia were trained by USA or British medical educators.[100]

Medical Residents and Bioweapon Treatment

Medical residents are often faced with uncertainty about treatment and strategies employed to manage their uncertainty and their concerns about the effects on patient care. Data from participants in a study can be placed into three categories:[101]

- Technical Uncertainty (Procedural Skills, Knowledge of Indications)
- Conceptual Uncertainty (Care Transitions, Diagnostic Decision Making and Management Conflict)
- Personal Uncertainty (Goals of Care)

When uncertain, residents report a "hierarchy of assistance" using colleagues and literature for initial management, followed by senior residents, specialty fellows, and the attending physician. There are barriers to seeking input from others particularly the attending physician and fears of losing autonomy, revealing knowledge gaps, and "being a bother." For twelve of the eighteen cases reported, patient care was compromised which included delay in procedure or escalation of care, procedural complications, and cardiac arrest. It would appear that resident uncertainty results in delays of indicated care and, in some cases, patient harm. Despite the presence of a supervisory figure, residents adhere to a hierarchy when seeking advice in clinical matters. Does this finding relate to the 'never events' described in Chapter 9? In the mist of bioweapons attack and hundreds of patients jammed into the emergency department, who would residents consult with when they feel uncertain treatment?

Nonetheless, a recent study suggests that adverse events among hospitals remain prevalent despite efforts by health professionals and hospital managers to improve the quality and safety of healthcare (see Chapter 9 for more details). Certainly, adverse events or 'never events' would have an influence on both the patient and the physician not to mention the fear of prosecution or litigation by the healthcare professional (see Chapter 9 for details). "Clinical supervision is understandably dominated by transferring discipline knowledge and skills but the environment today requires equal attention to integrating patient safety concepts and principles into clinical supervision."[102] However, trainees which can include residents learn from "supervisors who themselves often have inadequate patient safety knowledge and skills." In this study of the physician participants, a high percentile seemed to lack appropriate patient safety knowledge and skills; when residents might ask physicians for guidance in patient safety, I am wondering about the quality of information provided. However, the researchers say that they are in a conundrum partly because there "has been no visible reduction in adverse events" among many hospitals.[103]

Physician Uncertainty

One study shows that few physicians are "well prepared" for bioterrorism; many physicians say they will continue to care for patients in the event of an outbreak of "an unknown but potentially deadly illness."[104] Yet, other researchers suggest that it is not surprising that actual decisions made by physicians about treatment occasionally differs depending on the patient;[105] I would further read that to mean the circumstance such as a bioweapons attack.

The "paradigm of certainty" about medicine in general which knocks on uncertainty's door is inherited from the mechanistic model of scientific knowledge, and applied to medical science in the 1860s. Observation and research admitted as "true" facts were believed to reflect the true organization of matter and determination of disease.[106]

Physicians, nurses, and the general public have been socialized into accepting that knowledge of the mechanisms of disease is sufficient to establish precise diagnoses; to provide accurate prognoses (the forecast of the probable outcome or course of a disease; the patient's chance of recovery, Source Free Medical Dictionary.com: medical-dictionary.thefreedictionary.com/) through application of medical research, cures (see Chapter 3 about the discussion of reductionism versus holistic approaches to medicine). But the cures seem temporary to say the least; medical errors are on the rise, and antibiotic drugs are apparently useless against most superbugs in hospitals.[107] In what way could the healthcare community provide immediate care to surge capacities? Confidence in medicine has faltered. "Some medical interventions which were assumed to be effective have proved to be ineffective, and some untreated patients have fared better than treated patients."[108] There remains a great deal of uncertainty among physicians about how to manage infectious diseases and the pressure from the healthcare organization to step up to organizational policy.[109]

Physicians Refusing to Treat Patients

Are physicians making decisions about patients and refusing treatment? Residents in Alberta, Canada, have been complaining of symptoms such as severe headaches, dizziness, sinus problems, vomiting, muscle spasms, and fatigue, amongst others.[110] The source of symptoms seems to be linked to the tar sands industry. Consequently, some local physicians are reluctant to treat patients who draw connections between the tar sands industry and their personal health problems.

In one report, it says that "there were reports from various sources that physicians would not diagnose a relationship between bitumen exposures and chronic symptoms... Physicians are quite frankly afraid to diagnose health conditions linked to the oil and gas industry."[111] Added to the report is that "analytical services were refused by an Alberta laboratory when told that the proposed analysis was to investigate exposure to emissions related to bitumen extraction."

The literature, too, is consistent with physician treatment refusal. For example, a study shows that physicians are reluctant to treat AIDS patients.[112] A survey was conducted using a questionnaire and semi-structured interviews, to examine why nurses and physicians might be reluctant to care for patients with HIV/AIDS. The findings provide four main themes:

- Perceptions about Sexual Promiscuity
- Blaming Certain Patients with HIV/AIDS
- Belief in the Right to Refuse to Provide Care
- Discriminatory Care

Those findings are congruent with other studies about refusal among nurses and physicians to treat AIDS victims.[113]

Preparedness of Healthcare Professionals: Physicians and Nurses

Physicians and nurses are integral components of the public health bioterrorism surveillance system. Terrorist weapons range from conventional weapons to high explosives, chemical agent weapons, and bioweapon agent weapons all of which have been used in the recent past. While these weapons platforms can cause significant injury requiring critical care by healthcare professionals, pathophysiology, and treatment of these injuries are "unfamiliar to many critical care providers," medical experts suggest.[114]

Bioterrorism training programs are effective methods of enhancing the individual personal confidence among community-based clinicians' (both physicians and nurses) regarding bioterrorism-related disasters and treatment decisions.[115] Research also shows the need and importance of clinical education on the topic of bioterrorism. The Public Health Security and Bioterrorism Response Act helps to provide funding toward clinical education among healthcare providers.

Research shows that previous bioterrorism preparedness education associated significantly with knowledge-based test performance among physicians and nurses.[116] It should be noted that the most important method against bioterrorism is personal reinforcement through education of health and medical teams to diagnose and to apply a rapid and appropriate response during these events. For one reason, there is a huge amount of misinformation about biological attacks. Secondly, before education, almost 97 percent of the participants (sixty-five nurses) had little knowledge about bioterrorism; after education, the majority of them (100 percent) had good knowledge.[117] And the majority of the participants before education had indifferent attitudes toward bioterrorism, but a positive attitude after education. Obviously, these findings lead to the idea that education has a positive effect on nurses' knowledge and attitudes.

Nurses' Preparedness

The anthrax attack in America 2001 resulted in the development of global response strategies for future bioterrorist events. Researchers asked if nurses are prepared to respond to such events.

Seven original research studies were reviewed.[118] Four themes were identified as affecting decisions by nurses to respond professionally to victims after a bioweapon attack:

- Perceptions of Bioterrorism
- Role of Formal Knowledge

- Role of Institutional Plans and Policies
- Personal Factors

Existing nurse education in areas such as infection control can incorporate bioterrorism training to improve preparedness; yet the study makes clear that nurses must prepare themselves personally for a bioweapon attack. These findings are consistent with an earlier study that reports that nursing bioweapons preparedness has much to do with being able to recognize that an attack has indeed occurred and then to respond in a trained manner.[119] To become competent at treating and caring for bioweapon victims, it is advised that nurses participate annually in an educational session and an exercise to meet the minimum requirements of bioweapon preparedness. The researcher points out that recognition of an event and the implementation of an appropriate response action are the two primary issues nurses face.

Early recognition and management of a biological attack are largely dependent on the clinical expertise of front-line healthcare personnel such as nurses. It was urged in 2004 that schools of nursing should integrate bioterrorism education into their curricula to address this growing frontier of healthcare management.[120]

During a bioterrorist attack, healthcare professionals must be prepared to respond appropriately, but many perioperative (before surgery until discharge) nurses do not receive adequate education about bioterrorism, an expert says.[121] Mainly because they had little to no education or training toward bioterrorism, participants report. The literature is consistent with this finding in that studies show nurses at all levels of specialty are ill prepared to deal with agents used in biological warfare.[122]

The Final Solution: The US Constitution is a Suicide Pact

In the fictional book entitled *Executive Orders* written by Tom Clancy, the US is attacked by a strain of airborne Ebola virus.[123] The President declares a state of emergency to contain the epidemic, and orders all nonessential businesses and places of public assembly to be closed; also he suspends all interstate travel by jet, train, bus, and automobile. In defending social order, the fictional President makes a statement that is now often used to justify major changes to Constitutional law: "The Constitution is not a suicide pact." A bioweapon attack aside from the attack itself creates a very thorny circumstance for those of us participating in a Constitutional society. For instance, all adults have the Constitutional right to refuse examination and treatment; such a refusal should not result in involuntary confinement on the whim of public health officials. The thinking goes that persons suspected of having a contagious disease, in a Constitutional society, should have the choice of an examination by physicians at hospitals of their own choice and, if isolation is necessary, of being isolated in their own homes as opposed to a camp or an institution. The requirement that physicians treat patients against their will and against the physicians' medical judgment under penalty of criminal law has no precedent and makes little sense in a democratic environment.

Originally it was Justice Robert H. Jackson who in 1949 talked about the relationship between the Constitution and free speech. Jackson, after serving as a judge at the Nuremburg war crimes trial, saw the dangers of the mob. In one ruling he says, "The choice is not between order and liberty. It is between liberty with order and anarchy without either. There is danger that, if the court does not temper its doctrinaire logic with a little practical wisdom, it will convert the constitutional Bill of Rights into a suicide pact."[124] The problem is the use of biological agents against Americans from the perspectives of the criminal justice community and their collaborative partners (as defined in Chapter 2) presents serious infringements on the American people linked to their public safety and their Constitution rights. Right now, Ebola considerations of a patient by a physician mandate 21 days in isolation. If you were writing a Hollywood movie, what are some of the sensationalized scripts and events you could write to make that movie a financial success? Or you can ask me, my next work for HBO is entitled, *Ebola: Cops and Docs. Will They Protect and Treat Us?*

Final Thoughts

Centered in above evidence reporting enormous civil liberty violations of Americans by local and federal law enforcement officers, hospitals, physicians, and nurses paints a disturbing picture about those enterprises. Intrinsic in the evidence lays the moral violations of hospital systems and personnel to provide effective remedies and reasonable solutions other than to protect their organizational goals and themselves. Finally, considering human error centered in the uncertainty of responsibilities and judgments, healthcare providers and policymakers seem lost when trying to muddle through attempts to comply with government mandates because of a lack of pharmaceutical (i.e., up-to-date bioweapon antibiotic drugs) to products to aid victims. When we consider first-responder performance in the past, we find that local and federal law enforcement develop harsh punitive strategies in part as a product of a sensationalized press and in part through confusion to do the right thing; hospitals reject patients for a variety of reasons including robust profit and loss statements. Physicians and nurses make decisions based on uncertainty and personal agendas, too.

Therefore, in light of these findings, an observation made by this writer is that it is strongly advisable not to allow a bioweapon attack upon America through prevention legal and moral strategies. The best recommendation is prevention rather than to allow an attack and local law enforcement seems to be the safest resource primarily because they are accountable to their jurisdictions and their communities as opposed to federal officers who are accountable to a garrison of federal bureaucracy rules (see Chapter 6 for details). Recommendations enhancing local law enforcement to better suit a democratic America before a bioweapons attack and to combat violent crime in general is provided in Chapter 11.

Summary

Civilized populations live in a shadow of a nuclear holocaust; yet recent revolution in molecular biology, the evolution of antibiotic resistant pathogens, and the lack of medical (and pharmaceutical) remedies has unleashed new quality of life hazards producing real live ghouls devouring men, women, children, and their pets. Genetically modified viruses and microorganisms including deadly flesh-eating bacteria and chemical compounds can be utilized to develop sophisticated biological weapons that would make nuclear holocausts obsolete.

The focus of this chapter relates to issues after a bioweapon attack on America; it is about the response to bioweapon victims by the criminal justice community, specifically law enforcement and corrections, and their partners specifically hospitals, physicians, and nurses. Will American victims experience professional social order, public safety, and treatment or will they experience similar social order, public safety, and treatment consistent with professional behavior prior to an attack?

Biological or bioweapon warfare agents are defined and it is advanced that they are the most advantageous weapon to employ against America by a weak and poor nation. The possible chemical and infectious weapons were described including assumptions about enforcement officers. Before an assault on America, it is predicted that distractions and diversions will be experienced by Americans centered on their race to create confusion and chaos particularly among first-responders. Details about local law enforcement officer response were offered to bioweapon victims leading to government and healthcare reactions. Hospital turn away rates, physician, and nurse responses or refusal to treat were offered along with their ideas about uncertainty and their self-reported lack of bioweapon training. Finally, the notion of denial of individual civil liberties was described leading into the final thoughts of the author about this relationship between bioweapon victims and justice and healthcare professionals.

Name: ______________________________ Date: ____________ School Identification Number: ______

STUDENT WORKSHEETS

Chapter 10 After a Bioweapon Attack on America

Define the following key terms from Chapter 10, and in your answer, show the page number where you found the definition. Provide an example for each key term.

1. Asymmetric Methods

2. Biological Warfare Agents

3. Chemical Warfare Agents

4. Civil Liberties

5. Final Solution

6. Ethnic Bioweapons

7. Infectious Warfare Agents

8. Physician Uncertainty

9. Population Wellness

10. Public Panic Crisis Event

11. Surge Capacity

12. Warning Signs of Bioweapon Attack

13. Weapons of Mass Destruction (WMD)

Name: ______________________ Date: ____________ School Identification Number: ________

STUDENT WORKSHEETS

Chapter 10 After A Bioweapon Attack on America

Discuss and demonstrate in your own words that you comprehend the following learning objectives in this chapter.

1. Explain the reasons for American hatred by numerous countries and include in your answer why religion might be a possible issue.
2. Articulate the focus of this chapter, and explain in what way that focus lends itself to this book.
3. Identify the warning signs that the US will be attacked with bioweapons in the near future.
4. Describe the various chemical warfare agents highlighted in this chapter. Identify the chemical agent most likely to be utilized in an attack. Why?
5. Describe the various infectious warfare agents highlighted in this chapter. Identify the infectious agent most likely to be utilized in an attack. Why?
6. Describe the two assumptions about federal and local law enforcement officers.
7. Explain the public panic results of the media's sensationalized accounts of truth.
8. Identify the various responses of hospitals to bioweapon victims and the importance of early knowledge of a bioweapon attack.
9. Describe the various responses of physicians to bioweapon victims.
10. Articulate the relevance of physician uncertainty and its results to bioweapon victims and treatment.
11. Highlight the various responses of nurses to bioweapon victims.
12. Articulate the final thoughts of the author about this chapter. Which point is the most important point and in what way do you agree or disagree with his primary position?

CHAPTER 10 ENDNOTES

1. Steven Block (2001). The Growing Threat of Biological Weapons. *American Scientist*, 89(1): 28.
2. Seth G Jones and Martin C Libick (2010). *How Terrorist Groups End: Lessons for Countering al Qa'ida.* Santa Monica, CA: Rand. Page 10.
3. Alissa J Rubin, Tim Arango, and Helene Cooper (2014, August 8). US Jets and Drones Attack Militants in Iraq Hoping to Stop Advance. *New York Times*. Retrieved August 30, 2014: http://www.nytimes.com/2014/08/09/world/middleeast/iraq.html?_r=0
4. Top Ten Lists (2013). Top 10 List of Most Hated Nations in the World. Retrieved August 14, 2014: http://listtoptens.com/top-10-most-hated-countries-in-the-world/
5. Politifact.com (2014, March 28). 22 Countries Invaded by the US in 20 Years. *Tampa Bay Times*. Retrieved August 18, 2014: http://www.politifact.com/truth-o-meter/statements/2014/mar/31/facebook-posts/viral-meme-says-united-states-has-invaded-22-count/ Also see, Peter Bergen and Jennifer Rowland (2013). Drone Wars. *The Washington Quarterly*, 36(3): 7–26.
6. Michael Ignatieff (2003). The Burden. *Australian Universities' Review*, 46(1).
7. How To Help Japan: Earthquake Relief Options (2011, March 21). *Huffington Post*. Retrieved August 28, 2014: http://www.huffingtonpost.com/2011/03/21/how-to-help-japan-earthquake-relief_n_834484.html
8. Jeffrey H Reiman and Paul Leighton (2012). *Rich Get Richer and the Poor Get Prison,* The Plus MySearchLab with eText—Access Card Package (10th Edition). Upper Saddle River, NJ: Pearson. Also see, William G Domhoff (2013). Wealth, Income, and Power. Who Rules America. Retrieved August 21, 2014: http://www2.ucsc.edu/whorulesamerica/power/wealth.html
9. Karl Marx (1846–1978). The German Ideology. The Marx Engels Reader. (Pages 146–200). Robert C. Tucker, Translator. New York: Norton. Karl Marx and Friedrich Engels (1883; 1978). Manifesto of the Communist Party. The Marx-Engels Reader. (Pages 473–484). Robert C. Tucker, Translator. NY: Norton.
10. Carl von Clausewitz (2014). The Clausewitz Homepage. Retrieved August 21, 2014: http://www.clausewitz.com/FAQs.htm#Why2
11. Unclassified CIA Data (2014). Use of Toxins and Other Lethal Chemicals in Southeast Asia and Afghanistan. Central Intelligence Agency, Washington, DC. Retrieved August 14, 2014: http://www.foia.cia.gov/sites/default/files/document_conversions/89801/DOC_0000284013.pdf
12. Fran H Norris, Susan P Stevens, Betty Pfefferbaum, Karen F Wyche, and Rose L Pfefferbaum (2008). Community Resilience as a Metaphor, Theory, Set of Capacities, and Strategy for Disaster Readiness. *American Journal of Community Psychology,* 41: 12–150. Also see, Sarah A Lister (2005, September 5). Hurricane Katrina: The Public Health and Medical Response. CRS Report for Congress. Retrieved August 25, 2014: http://fpc.state.gov/documents/organization/54255.pdf/ Page 16.
13. University of Washington (ND). Controversies about the Constitution: Federalism. Retrieved December 16, 2014: https://depts.washington.edu/constday/controversies/
14. Dennis J Stevens (2014). *The Failure of the American Prison Complex: Let's Abolish It.* Dubuque, Iowa: Kendal Hunt. Page 37.
15. Sarah A Lister (2005, September 5). Page 16.
16. Laurie Garrett (2000). *Betrayal of Trust*. New York: Hyperion. Page 518.

17. Donald A. Henderson, Thomas V. Inglesby Jr., Tara O'Toole, Thomas V. Inglesby, Rita Grossman, and Tara O'Toole (2001). A Plague on Your City: Observations from TOPOFF. *Clinical Infectious Disease*, 32(3): 436–445.

18. Special Report (2006). Hurricane Katrina: A Nation Still Unprepared. Retrieved August 25, 2014: http://www.gpo.gov/fdsys/pkg/CRPT-109srpt322/pdf/CRPT-109srpt322.pdf/ Hurricane

19. Russell L. Bennett L. (2006). Chemical or Biological Terrorist Attacks: An Analysis of the Preparedness of Hospitals for Managing Victims Affected by Chemical or Biological Weapons of Mass Destruction. *International Journal of Environmental Research and Public Health.* 3(1):67–75.

20. James Phillips, Charlotte Florance, and Steven Bucci (2014, August 28). 11 Reasons Why ISIS Might be More Dangerous Than al-Qaeda. *The Daily Signal.* Retrieved August 28, 2014: http://dailysignal.com/2014/08/28/11-reasons-isis-might-dangerous-al-qaeda/?utm_source=heritagefoundation&utm_medium=email&utm_campaign=morningbell&mkt_tok=3RkMMJWWfF9wsRonvazBZKXonjHpfsX56OgtUKW%2FlMI%2F0ER3fOvrPUfGjI4DTMBnI%2BSLDwEYGJlv6SgFQrLBMa1ozrgOWxU%3D

21. Ibid.

22. David Martosko (2014, August 28). Former CIA Chief: ISIS Attack Against The West Coming 'Probably Sooner Rather Than Later.' *Daily Mail.com.* Retrieved August 28, 2014: http://www.dailymail.co.uk/news/article-2733962/Former-CIA-chief-ISIS-attack-against-West-coming-probably-sooner-later.html#ixzz3Bh9oKzi7

23. Jan van Aken and Edward Hammond (2003). Genetic Engineering and Biological Weapons. EMBO Reports, 4(1): 57–60.

24. Josh Siegel (2014, August 21). Rick Perry Urges Obama to 'Eliminate' Islamist Terrorists in Iraq. *The Daily Signal.* Retrieved August 22, 2014: http://dailysignal.com/2014/08/21/rick-perry-urges-obama-eliminate-islamist-terrorists-iraq/

25. This is not to say that this writer agrees or disagrees with Governor Perry's viewpoint or solution. It is only to say that America from a high profile politician's perspective has lethal enemies.

26. RC Spencer and MH Wilcox (1993). Agents of Biological Warfare. Review of Medical Microbiology, 4:138–143.

27. K Ganesan, S Raza, and R Vijayaraghavan (2010). Chemical Warfare Agents. *Journal of Pharmacy & BioAllied Sciences,* 2(3): 166–178. Retrieved August 19, 2014: http://www.ncbi.nlm.nih.gov/pmc/articles/PMC3148621/

28. Jan van Aken and Edward Hammond (2003).

29. Ibid.

30. Wladyslaw Kowalski (2009). Bioterrorism Defense. Ultraviolet Germicidal Irradiation Handbook. NY: Springer-Verlag. Page 457.

31. Ibid., Page 458.

32. JM Appel (2009). Is All Fair In Biological Warfare? The Controversy Over Genetically Engineered Biological Weapons. *Journal of Medical Ethics*, 35(7):429–432.

33. Kevin P O'Connell, Bernadette C Menuey, and Dawn Foster (2002). Issues in Preparedness for Biologic Terrorism: A Perspective for Critical Care Nursing. AACN Clinical Issues: Advanced Practice in Acute & Critical Care, 13(3): 452–469.

34. James Geoghegan and Jeffrey L Tong (2006). Chemical Warfare Agents. *Continuing Education in Anesthesia, Critical Care & Pain,* 6(6): 230–234.

35. Centers for Disease Control and Prevention (2014). Facts About Sarin. Retrieved August 19, 2014: http://www.bt.cdc.gov/agent/sarin/basics/facts.asp

36. William R Johnson (2014). Summary of Historical Attacks Using Chemical or Biological Weaspons. Retrieved August 29, 2014: http://www.johnstonsarchive.net/terrorism/chembioattacks.html

37. K Ganesan, S Raza, and R Vijayaraghavan (2010).

38. Laurie Garrett (2000). Page 12.

39. Ibid., Page 14.

40. Centers for Disease Control and Prevention (2014). General Fact Sheets on Specific Bioterrorism Agents. Retrieved August 17, 2014: http://www.bt.cdc.gov/bioterrorism/factsheets.asp

41. AP Pomerantsev, NA Staritsin, YV Mockov, and LI Marinin (1997). Expression of Cereolysine Ab Genes In Bacillus Anthracis Vaccine Strain Ensures Protection Against Experimental Hemolytic Anthrax Infection. Vaccine, 15, 1846–1850.

42. J Enkhtuya, K Kawamoto, Y Kobayashi, I Uchida, N Rana, and S Makino (2006). Significant Passive Protective Effect Against Anthrax By Antibody To Bacillus Anthracis Inactivated Spores That Lack Two Virulence Plasmids. *Microbiology*, 152(Pt 10): 3103–3110.

43. Emedicinehealth (2014). Biological Warfare. Retrieved August 14, 2014: http://www.emedicinehealth.com/biological_warfare/page11_em.htm#smallpox

44. Colonel Dan (ND). Life/Regulator How to Bring Down a Nation. SASS #24025. Retrieved August 21, 2014: http://mddall.com/sbss/1103.htm

45. Fran H Norris, Susan P Stevens, Betty Pfefferbaum, Karen F Wyche, and Rose L Pfefferbaum (2008). Pages 127–150.

46. FBI (2014). Homepage. Retrieved August 29, 2014: http://www.fbi.gov/stats-services/publications/todays-fbi-facts-figures/facts-and-figures-031413.pdf/view

47. National Counterintelligence Center (2009). Report on Terrorism. Retrieved August 29, 2014: http://www.fbi.gov/stats-services/publications/terror_08.pdf

48. US Department of State (2014). Chapter 2. Country Reports: Western Hemisphere Overview. Retrieved August 29, 2014: http://www.state.gov/j/ct/rls/crt/2013/224825.htm

49. Bureau of Justice Statistics (2014). Local Police. Retrieved August 29, 2014: http://www.bjs.gov/index.cfm?ty=tp&tid=71

50. James Jay Carafano, Steven P Bucci, and Jessica Zuckerman (2012). Fifty Terror Plots Foiled Since 9/11: The Homegrown Threat and the Long War on Terrorism. *The Heritage Foundation*. Retrieved August 29, 2014: http://www.heritage.org/research/reports/2012/04/fifty-terror-plots-foiled-since-9-11-the-homegrown-threat-and-the-long-war-on-terrorism

51. Associated Press (2012, March 21). NYPD And FBI Tussle Over Turf, With Consequences For Terror Cases As Police Expand Role: Report. *New York Times*. Retrieved September 3, 2014: http://www.nydailynews.com/new-york/nypd-fbi-tussle-turf-consequences-terror-cases-police-expand-role-report-article-1.1048105#ixzz3CHPGLbi9

52. George L Kelling and William J Bratton (2006). Police Terrorism. Civic Bulletin. Manhattan Institute for Policy Research. Retrieved August 29, 2014: http://www.manhattan-institute.org/html/cb_43.htm

53. Dennis J Stevens (2002). *Civil Liabilities and Arrest Decisions.* In Jeffrey T Walker (Ed.) *Policing and the Law* (Pages 53–70). Boston: Pearson.

54. Federal Bureau of Prisons (2014). Statistics. Retrieved September 13, 2014: http://www.bop.gov/about/agency/

55. Bureau of Justice Statistics (2013). Corrections Populations. 243936. Retrieved September 14, 2014: http://www.bjs.gov/content/pub/pdf/cpus12.pdf

56. Christian Henrichson and Ruth Delaney (2012). The Price of Prisons: What Incarceration Costs Taxpayers. Vera Institute of Justice. Retrieved September 14, 2014: http://www.vera.org/sites/default/files/resources/downloads/Price_of_Prisons_updated_version_072512.pdf

57. Ronald V Clarke and Graeme R Newman (2007). Police and the Prevention of Terrorism. *Policing*, 1(1): 9–20.

58. Ibid.

59. Ibid.

60. Hans Toch (2007). Sequestering Gang Members, Burning Witches, and Subverting Due Process. *Criminal Justice and Behavior* 34(2), 274–281. Also see A von Hirsch (1976). *Doing Justice: The Choice of Punishment*. New York: Hill and Wang. Page 6.

61. Dennis J. Stevens (2014). *Failure of the American Prison Complex: Let's Abolish it*. Iowa: Kendall Hunt. Pages 94–104. Also see, Stanton Samenow (2004). *Inside the Criminal Mind*. New York: Crown. Pages 22–45. Stanton Samenow (2001). *Before It's Too Late*. New York: Three River Press. Pages 4–18; 24–28.

62. Daryl Nerl (2007, September 11). In Event of Biological Weapons Attack, Could Region Take Influx? The Morning Call. Retrieved August 29, 2014: http://articles.mcall.com/2007-09-11/news/3769635_1_mobile-command-centers-biological-weapons-northeast-pennsylvania

63. George J. Annas (2002). Bioterrorism, Public Health, and Civil Liberties. *New England Journal of Medicine*, 346: 1337–1342.

64. Silas Gbandia (2014, July 25). Sierra Leone Police Use Tear Gas to Curb Ebola-Related Riot. Bloomberg. Retrieved August 29, 2014: http://www.bloomberg.com/news/2014-07-25/sierra-leone-police-use-tear-gas-to-curb-ebola-related-riot.html

65. Dan Berger (2009). Constructing Crime, Framing Disaster Routines Of Criminalization And Crisis In Hurricane Katrina. *Punishment & Society*, 11(4): 491–510.

66. Brian Thevenot (2006, December). Myth-Making in New Orleans. *New Orleans' Times-Picayune*. Retrieved August 30, 2014: http://ajrarchive.org/article.asp?id=3998

67. Voice of America (2009, October 27). Rumors of Post-Katrina Anarchy Prove False. Retrieved August 30, 2014: http://www.voanews.com/content/a-13-2005-09-30-voa1-66396247/548807.html

68. Brian Thevenot (2006, December).

69. Media Advisory (2007, March 27). Iraq and the Media. Fairness & Accuracy in Reporting. Retrieved August 30, 2014: http://fair.org/take-action/media-advisories/iraq-and-the-media/

70. Jeremy Stahl (2013, April 15). Thou Shalt Not Stoop to Political Point-Scoring. Slate. Retrieved August 31, 2014: http://www.slate.com/articles/technology/technology/2013/04/boston_marathon_bombing_all_the_mistakes_journalists_make_during_a_crisis.html Also see, Laurie Rodrigues (2013, May 8). Homegrown Terror: The Boston Marathon's Media Coverage. Critical Legal Thinking: Law & Political. Retrieved August 31, 2014: http://criticallegalthinking.com/2013/05/08/homegrown-terror-the-boston-marathons-media-coverage/

71. Katherine Q Seelye, Michael S Schmidt, and William K Rashbaum (2013, April 22). Boston Suspect Is Charged and Could Face the Death Penalty. *The New York Times*. Retrieved August 31, 2014: http://www.nytimes.com/2013/04/23/us/boston-marathon-bombings-developments.html?pagewanted=all

72. Leanne Fiftal Alarid (2009). Risk Factors For Potential Occupational Exposure To HIV: A Study Of Correctional Officers. *Journal of Criminal Justice,* 37(2): 114–122.

73. Miguel Kottow (2012). Public Health Transitions and the "New Public Health." From Justice to Protection. SpringerBriefs in Public Health, 1: 23–31.

74. Laurie Garrett (2000). Page 12.

75. J E Epping-Jordan, SD Pruitt, R Bengoa1, and EH Wagner (2004). Improving The Quality Of Health Care For Chronic Conditions. *Quality and Safety Health Care*, 13:299–305.

76. Rebecca Katz (2001–2004). Biological Weapons: A National Security Problem that Requires a Public Health Response. Office of Population Research Princeton University. Retrieved August 25, 2014: https://opr.princeton.edu/papers/opr0104.pdf

77. Lewis Rubinson, Jennifer Nuzzo, Daniel S Talmor, Tara O'Toole, Bradley R Kramer, and Thomas V Inglesby (2005). Augmentation Of Hospital Critical Care Capacity After Bioterrorist Attacks Or Epidemics: Recommendations Of The Working Group On Emergency Mass Critical Care. *Critical Care Medicine*, 33(10): E2393.

78. Ibid.

79. Thomas May and Mark P. Aulisio (2006). Access to Hospitals in the Wake of Terrorism: Challenges and Needs for Maintaining Public Confidence. *Disaster Management & Response*, 4(3): 67–71.

80. Sarah A Lister (2005, September 5). Page 15.

81. Rebecca Katz (2001–2004). Page 27.

82. Sarah A Lister (2005, September 5). Page 13.

83. Rebecca Katz (2001–2004). Page 30.

84. Dena M Bravata, Vandana Sundaram, Kathryn M McDonald, Wendy M Smith, Herbert Szeto, Mark D Schleinitz, and Douglas K Owens (2001). Evaluating Detection and Diagnostic Decision Support Systems for Bioterrorism Response. *Emerging Infectious Disease*, 10(1): 100–108. Retrieved August 29, 2014: http://wwwnc.cdc.gov/eid/article/10/1/pdfs/03-0243.pdf

85. Arnold F Kaufmann, Martin I Meltzer, and George P Schmid (1997). The Economic Impact Of A Bioterrorist Event: Are Prevention And Postattack Intervention Programs Justifiable? *Emerging Infectious Diseases*, 3(2): 83–94.

86. DN Kyriacou, D Dobrez, JP Parada, JM Steinberg, A Kahn, CL Bennett, and BP Schimtt (2012). Cost-Effectiveness Comparison Of Response Strategies To A Large-Scale Anthrax Attack On The Chicago Metropolitan Area: Impact Of Timing And Surge Capacity. *Biosecurity Bioterrorism*, 10(3):264–79.

87. Michael L McManus, Michael C Long, Abbot Cooper, and Eugene Litvak (2004). Queuing Theory Accurately Models the Need for Critical Care Resources. *Anesthesiology*, 100(5): 1271–1276.

88. Ibid.

89. David W Baker, Julie A Gazmararian, Mark V Williams, Tracy Scott, Ruth M Parker, Diane Green, Junling Ren, and Jennifer Peel (2002). Functional Health Literacy And The Risk Of Hospital Admission Among Medicare Managed Care Enrollees. *American Journal of Public Health*, 92(8): 1278–1283. Retrieved August 21, 2014: http://ajph.aphapublications.org/doi/pdf/10.2105/AJPH.92.8.1278

90. Ibid.

91. Mark V Williams, David W Baker, Eric G Honig, Theodore M Lee, and Adam Nowlan (1998). Inadequate Literacy Is A Barrier To Asthma Knowledge And Self-Care. *Chest Journal*, 114:1008–1015.

92. Carla Graf (2008). The Hospital Admission Risk Profile (HARP). The Hartford Institute for Geriatric Nursing, New York University, College of Nursing. Retrieved August 25, 2014: http://consultgerirn.org/uploads/File/trythis/try_this_24.pdf

93. MC Creditor (1993). Hazards of Hospitalization of the Elderly. *Annals of Intern Medicine*, 118(3): 219–223.

94. Russell L. Bennett L. (2006). Chemical or Biological Terrorist Attacks: An Analysis of the Preparedness of Hospitals for Managing Victims Affected by Chemical or Biological Weapons of Mass Destruction. *International Journal of Environmental Research and Public Health.* 3(1):67–75.

95. Ibid.

96. Emergency Preparedness for Healthcare Facilities (2014). Premier. Retrieved December 7, 2014: https://legacy.premierinc.com/quality-safety/tools-services/safety/topics/disaster_readiness/downloads.jsp

97. Consumer Reports.org (2014, May). What to Reject When You're Expecting. Retrieved August 25, 2014: http://www.consumerreports.org/cro/2012/05/what-to-reject-when-you-re-expecting/index.htm

98. Philip E. Zapanta, and Saba Ghorab (2014). Are You Prepared? Review of Bioweapons and Their Clinical Presentation for Otolaryngologists. *Otolaryngology Head Neck Surgery*, 151(2): 208–214.

99. Bereket Yakob, Kebede Deribe, and Gail Davey (2010). Health Professionals' Attitudes And Misconceptions Regarding Podoconiosis: Potential Impact On Integration Of Care In Southern Ethiopia. *Transactions of the Royal Society of Tropical Medicine and Hygiene*, 104 (1): 42–47.

100. Elias Kifle (2008).There Are More Ethiopian Doctors in the US than In Ethiopia. Ethiopian Review. Retrieved September 1, 2014: http://www.ethiopianreview.com/index/2053/ Also see, William Foreman (2013, September 23). Battling Brain Drain: Training in Ethiopia. University of Michigan. Retrieved September 1, 2014: http://www.ns.umich.edu/new/releases/21706-battling-brain-drain-training-doctors-in-ethiopia

101. JM Farnan, JK Johnson, DO Meltzer, HJ Humphrey, and VM Arora (2008). Education and Training Resident Uncertainty In Clinical Decision Making And Impact On Patient Care: A Qualitative Study. *BMJ Quality and Safety in Health Care,* 17:2 122–126.

102. Merrilyn Walton and Bruce Barraclough (2013). Clinical Supervisors: Are They The Key To Making Care Safer? *BMJ Quality and Safety in Health Care*, 22: 609–612. Retrieved August 21, 2014: http://qualitysafety.bmj.com/content/22/8/609.full.pdf+html?sid=bbe97db2-6a43-472e-a4a2-68606313f506

103. Ibid.

104. G Caleb Alexander and Matthew K Wynia (2003). Ready And Willing? Physicians' Sense Of Preparedness For Bioterrorism. *Health Affairs*, 22(5), 189–197.

105. A Robinson, and RG Thomson (2000). The Potential Use Of Decision Analysis To Support Shared Decision Making In The Face Of Uncertainty: The Example Of Atrial Fibrillation And Warfarin Anticoagulation. *BMJ Quality And Safety In Health Care*, 9:238–244.

106. Alexandra Giraud (1992). Uncertainty In Medicine: Can It Be Reduced? BMJ Quality and Safety in Health Care, 1(3): 150–155. Retrieved August 21, 2014: http://qualitysafety.bmj.com/content/1/3/150.full.pdf+html?sid=bc2592b3-b659-4c2b-b20f-6eaf30737e15. Also see, E Duclay, JB Hardouin, V Sébille, E Anthoine and L Moret (2014). Exploring The Impact Of Staff Absenteeism On Patient Satisfaction Using Routine Databases In A University Hospital. *Journal of Nursing Management*, doi: 10.1111/jonm.12219.

107. Frances H Miller (2013). Medical Errors, New Drug Application, and Patient Safety. In James Hammit, Michael Rogers, Peter Sand, and Jonathan B. Wiener (Eds). *Reality of Precaution: Comparing Risk Regulation in the United States*. New York: Routledge Press (Pages 257–278).

108. Alexandra Girand (1992).

109. I Björkman, J Berg, M Röing, M Erntell, and C S Lundborg (2010). Perceptions Among Swedish Hospital Physicians On Prescribing Of Antibiotics And Antibiotic Resistance. Quality and Safety in Health Care, 19(8). Retrieved August 21, 2014: http://qualitysafety.bmj.com/content/19/6/e8.full.pdf+html

110. Andy Rowell (2014, January 21). Alberta Doctors Reluctant to Treat Patients Who Draw Connection Between Tar Sands and Health. *EcoWatch: Transforming Green*. Retrieved August 21, 2014: http://ecowatch.com/2014/01/21/alberta-reluctant-to-treat-patients-tar-sands-and-health/

111. Ibid.

112. TV McCann (1999). Reluctance Amongst Nurses And Doctors To Care For And Treat Patients With HIV/AIDS. *AIDS Care*, 11(3):355–359.

A survey was carried out, using a questionnaire and semi-structured interviews, to examine why nurses and doctors might be reluctant to care for patients with HIV/AIDS. The findings provided four main themes: perceptions about sexual promiscuity; blaming certain patients with HIV/AIDS; belief in the right to refuse to provide care; and discriminatory care.

113. D Pickles, L King, and I Belan (2009). Attitudes Of Nursing Students Towards Caring For People With HIV/AIDS: Thematic Literature Review. *Journal of Advanced Nursing*, 65(11): 2262–2273.

114. M Hamele, WB Poss, and J Sweney (2014). Disaster Preparedness, Pediatric Considerations In Primary Blast Injury, Chemical, And Biological Terrorism. *World Journal of Critical Care Medicine*, 3(1): 15–23.

115. Robyn RM Gershon, Kristine A Qureshi, Kent A Sepkowitz, Alejandra C Gurtman, Sandro Galea, and Martin F Sherman (2004). Clinicians' Knowledge, Attitudes, and Concerns Regarding Bioterrorism After a Brief Educational Program. *Journal of Occupational and Environmental Medicine,* 46(1): 77–83.

116. AR Katz, DM Nekorchuk, PS Holck, LA Hendrickson, AA Imrie, and PV Effler (2012). Hawaii Physician And Nurse Bioterrorism Preparedness Survey. *Journal of Advanced Nursing,* 68(12):2597–2609.

117. N Aghaei and MB Nesami (2013). Bioterrorism Education Effect On Knowledge And Attitudes Of Nurses. *Journal of Emergency Trauma Shock,* 6(2):78–82.

118. C Smith and A Hewison (2012). Are Nurses Prepared To Respond To A Bioterrorist Attack: A Narrative Synthesis. *Journal of Advanced Nursing*, 68(12): 2597–2609.

119. T Rebmann (2006). Defining Bioterrorism Preparedness For Nurses: Concept Analysis. *Journal of Advanced Nursing,* 54(5): 623–632.

120. CJ Steed, LA Howe, RH Pruitt, and WW Sherrill (2004). Integrating Bioterrorism Education Into Nursing School Curricula. *Journal of Nursing Education*, 43(8):362–7.

121. JR Thomas (2008). Self-Study: An Effective Method For Bioterrorism Training In The OR. *AORN Journal*, 87(5):915–924.

122. AM Nyamathi, A Casillas, ML King, L Gresham, E Pierce, D Farb, and C Wiechmann (2010). Computerized Bioterrorism Education And Training For Nurses On Bioterrorism Attack Agents. Journal of Continuing Education in Nursing, 41(12):531.

123. Tom Clancy (1996). *Executive Order*. NY: GP Putnam. Also see, George J. Annas (2002). Bioterrorism, Public Health, and Civil Liberties. *New England Journal of Medicine*, 346: 1337–1342.

124. Linda Greenhouse (2002, September 22). The Nation; 'Suicide Pact.' *New York Times*. Retrieved August 29, 2014: http://www.nytimes.com/2002/09/22/weekinreview/the-nation-suicide-pact.html

Digital Storm/Shutterstock, Inc.

CHAPTER 11

A Key to a Safer America

Learning Objectives

After you read this chapter, you will be better prepared to:

- Explain in your own words how the fishermen story fits into the discussion of infectious disease control.
- Explain the objectives of the author who wrote this book. In what way have any of those objectives been met?
- Identify the guiding mandates of occupations. Describe in what way those mandates can dictate the performance of a justice and healthcare provider.
- Describe the generalized model relating to the agents of compliance in this chapter. Explain in what way those mandates can influence the performance of a justice and healthcare provider.
- The case study about euthanasia and physician assisted suicide was about a seventy-two-year-old man. Describe the debate about euthanasia and use an eighteen-year-old patient.
- Identify the principles behind the fear of prosecution producing sometimes inappropriate professional conduct from law enforcement and correctional officers, physicians, and nurses among others.
- Discuss the Thomas Theorem and explain in what way the decisions of personnel and students are influenced through this perspective. Use some specific examples.
- Explain the reasoning behind changing the organizational environments of personnel.
- Discuss the reasons to abolish the prison industrial complex and the benefits to society.
- Articulate the reasoning supporting the idea of professionalizing justice and healthcare personnel. What is hoped to be gained through a professionalization process of these professions?
- Explain the idea associated with human beings and errors. In what way do you agree or disagree with this idea?
- In what way does the Power Elite relate to the idea of advancing terrorism and justice?

Key Terms

Amenability to Treatment
Anomie
Blaming the Victim
Decentralizing
Euthanasia
Fear of Prosecution
Guiding Mandates of Occupation
Hieratical Leveling
Organizing for Empowerment
Posse Comitatus Act of 1878
Professionalization
Redefine Circumstances
Thomas Theorem

Words of Wisdom

To learn who rules over you, simply find out who you are not allowed to criticize.

—Voltaire

Introduction

william casey/Shutterstock, Inc.

There were two physicians standing in the middle of a Colorado fishing river. The river has its shallow and deep spots, and the physicians have often fished winding river. They casually move from spot to spot, accepting the morning sunshine and the naturalness of the wilderness mounting high above them. Slowly in nightmarish wakefulness, dead bodies float toward them. At first, there were only a few, and the physicians successfully pulled them onto the riverbank. More bodies floated downstream, and it was impossible to move them all from the river no matter how hard the physicians worked. In desperation, one physician pulled out from the river and struggled at first moving up the bank. "Hey, where ya going?" the physician wading in the river asks and adds, "I can't get all of these bodies from the river myself." With that, the physician on the bank replies, "I am going upstream to find out who's throwing all of the bodies in the river." The physician now chest-deep in the river adds, "It's too muddy. You won't make it." The physician in the river didn't feel the swift and unpredictable currents of floodwater approaching him and the physician moving up the bank didn't see the mounts of earth guiding downward from the slope of the mountain.

Criminal Justice and Public Health

MRSA and Other Deadly Pathogens connects criminal justice personnel, firefighters, and their collaborative partners in healthcare to their occupational exposure to infectious pathogens including MRSA; equally important, their exposure to the 'agents of compliance' described below; in a sense, this work goes upstream to see why so many are dying, and why are they being thrown into the river, before the flood (compliance to regulation behavior) and landslide (prosecution and malpractice lawsuits) overtake them. What caused those individuals in the river to die in the first place, some deadly pathogen; and why were the physicians pulling them from the river?

My Objectives in Writing This Book

My objective in writing this book is to aid readers gain a better understanding of how infectious disease transmission works. However, as a criminologist and sociologist my interests include influences from the social environment which is outside of us, and influences linked to personal goals and objectives nagging away inside of us as a combined 'push and pull' process toward individual and community quality of life opportunities and experiences. as social animals, human beings are goal driven as you know. Now what you have to decide is do your goals contribute to your success or fail in your social world. Another objective is discussing how organizational policy and politics along with government compliance regulation influence the decisions we make about our behavior on the job, at school, and our personnel lives. We often believe that we are in total control of our decisions and, ultimately our behavior. Yes, we think about the rules and laws—we think about our behavior in the classroom and on the highways. Sometimes we don't care, but often we respond to what others might think about our behavior. In the classroom for instance, to demonstrate our intellect, we try not to be too smart or to ask too many questions because we are concerned with what others might think about us. If you were a physician, nurse, healthcare provider, police, or correctional officer, would you think about what your supervisors, peers, and others thought of you when you engage others? Think of it this way, if you think the university would expel an under-aged student for drinking alcohol on campus, would you ignore this thought and take a shot of JD in front of everybody? We all think about the possible outcomes of our behavior before we take action, and often we change our behavior to keep pace with our understanding of the world. Remember Chapter 2's discussion about the Thomas Theorem. We construct our own social reality. Later in this chapter when we discuss the

Fear of Prosecution we will go into more detail about the Thomas Theorem. For right now what you need to know is that justice and healthcare personnel arrive at behavioral decisions in a similar process as you and me. For instance, if you think a student sitting next to you in the library has the plague do you: (a) grab your stuff and walk away; (b) comfort them; (c) call the cops; (d) ignore the person and do your work? Would your answer change if you are obliged by regulation and law to engage that person? What about the quality of your performance with that person?

This book offers a reasonable explanation about justice and healthcare performance. It has been implied that part of that performance can be found in 'guiding mandates' of their occupation which include:

- Laws (local, county, state, and federal) and Rulings
- Obligations, Regulations, and Ethics of the Profession
- Certifications Including State Licensing of the Profession

The above ideas are supported with legal and sometimes criminal consequences if not followed. These guiding mandates are known factors and generally agreed to by potential personnel before accepting a position. Sometimes, potential personnel attend formal training classes prior to performing the job in order for the employer and the potential employee to understand the scope of each other's expectations of job. Once those classes are successfully completed, employees remain on job probation for a period of time in which to adjust to the guiding mandates. It is a very conscious decision in relation to the guiding mandates that an employee must make to move from probation to full-time employment. However, unexpected or latent expectations of the job or what I call 'agents of compliance' are informal in nature and tend to swoop down on personnel as he or she adjusts into his or her position.[1]

[1] It's one thing to let your environment dictate what's going to pierce your umbra in a rainstorm; it's quite another thing when you decide which rainstorm you're going to walk through. It's never the weight of a situation that is difficult, it's how you carry your load that counts.

[2] It is performance and thinking right out of *Robert B. Parker's Damned if You Do*, novel by Michael Brandman (2013). No matter what decision a professional makes, he or she can be damned for the act or damned for failure to perform. For cops that means civil liabilities, for physicians it means malpractice suits. What would a reasonable person do under similar circumstance? But then, isn't it true that any professional can have a different point of view than another professional in the same profession? Who wins? The professional with the most resources (i.e., the Power Elite and conflict theory in Chapter 1 and Chapter 3).

Agents of Compliance

Intrinsic to the guiding mandates toward expectable behavior on the job are agents and contradictions that promote occupational distress and uncertainty which can affect performance or what I call 'agents of compliance.' A very simple example can help clarify how agents of compliance influence performance of justice and healthcare personnel. For many in the justice community and healthcare services, there is a typical perspective held similar to "damn if you do (this or that), or damn if you don't (do this or that)."[2] For example, a domestic violence scenario among police officers: arrest mandates or dictates are in place in many states for domestic violence 9-1-1 calls; most often, law enforcement officers conduct a probable cause arrest when called into a domestic violence incident; often, however, the written laws are ambiguous and arbitrary so much so that officers are not sure what to do next. For instance, a Connecticut General Statute reports the following:

> Arrest: "Whenever a peace officer determines upon speedy information that a family violence crime has been committed within such officer's jurisdiction, such officer shall arrest the person or persons suspected of its commission and charge such person or persons with the appropriate crime. The decision to arrest and charge shall not (1) be dependent on the specific consent of the victim, (2) consider the relationship of the parties, or (3) be based solely on a request by the victim." Connecticut General Statute § 46b-38b(a) (2013). Other times you really wonder if the lawmakers know anything about the place we're in . . . for instance:
>
> - The Nevada statute twice refers to the suspect with the male pronouns "he" and "his." Females therefore aren't perpetrators of domestic violence.
> - The Oregon statute requires arrest in the event of "fear of imminent serious physical injury," a concept that is so ambiguous that it eludes definition.

The examples used above are about law enforcement officers, yet most assuredly, similar ambiguous and arbitrary rules and regulations apply to correctional officers, hospital systems, physicians, and nurses. For instance, abortion guidelines, and physician and nurse assisted deaths.[1] Do each of us have a right to die and can we ask for help if we so elect? Euthanasia has become a subject of public debate and concern. The views of euthanasia among students at an east Texas university and an estimated three-fourths of the general public are in favor of euthanasia.[2] However, assisted suicide is illegal in forty-six states and Washington, DC.[3] Let's consider a case vignette about physician assisted death opinions.

Physician-Assisted Suicide Should Not Be Permitted

When John Wallace was diagnosed with cancer he was seventy-two years old. He was treated with palliative chemotherapy, without success. [4] Later, he became jaundiced, and lost his appetite. He sees a palliative care physician, a social worker, and psychologist. Because of extensive abdominal pain, Mr. Wallace takes high doses of narcotics. He is constipated due to the narcotics. He wants to die. The position from three physicians is that physician-assisted suicide should not be permitted. "We recognize that a patient in Mr. Wallace's situation is in a state of grief. We appreciate his desire to be of sound mind at the end of his life and not to have to suffer as death approaches. We also recognize the obligations of physicians to respect a patient's refusal of treatment, to relieve pain and suffering, and to provide palliative care . . . the art of healing should always remain at the core of medical practice, and the role of healer involves providing patients with hope and renewed aspirations, however tenuous and temporary. . . there exists a well-recognized paradox that one can die healed. Physicians have a duty to uphold the sacred healing space—not destroy it." Other physicians suggest, "beware the beginnings . . . I never knew a patient who really wanted to stop living. We took an oath . . . The act of dying is a process, and we have the tools at our disposal to make it as comfortable and painless as possible, and applying theses judiciously, pain and suffering can be alleviated for both patients and their families."

Other physicians mention the "slippery slope" of a perceived burden on family, loved ones, and finances that the frail and terminally ill might think—"What right do I have to stay alive and cause all this suffering, and burden on my loved ones?"[5] Physician-assisted suicide goes against the very thing—the healing that medical professions are all about. Finally in this regard, another physician uses the phrase 'The Great Euthanasia Con.' "The claim that euthanasia will be restricted to the terminally ill is false." So lobbyists are demanding euthanasia for fifty-year-olds, who are in good health, but "tired of living."

Physician-Assisted Suicide Should Be Permitted

Physicians should explore older adult patients' concerns about dying. "Motivations behind a patient's request for physician-assisted dying should be explored regardless of a physician's personal attitudes."[6] Another physician says that "death appears as a menace, as something we fear and want to avoid at all cost. At the same time, most of us know someone for whom death has come as a relief . . . the opportunity to ask a competent professional for assistance in ending their lives in a legally and socially accepted way would be a clear improvement . . . The role of physicians is not simply to preserve life but also to apply expertise and skills to help improve their patients' health or alleviate their suffering. The latter includes providing comfort and support to dying patients."[7] It is odd however, that physicians as a professional group and police officers have the highest suicide rates of other professionals.[8]

Essentials incorporated into mandates are at-risk consequences; throughout many chapters depending on the profession described, these agents of compliance were specifically linked to the profession discussed; in this chapter I will generalize in an attempt to utilize one model to fit all professionals highlighted in this book—the model below can be used as a pathway to my recommendations.

prudkov/Shutterstock, Inc.

Many individuals are more vulnerable depending on circumstances which could include occupational environments.

I refer to the at-risk consequences as agents of compliance to criminal justice professionals and their partners which include the following categories that can occur at different times, under different circumstances, and can produce different intensities:

- Perpetrator (of a crime), Violator, Victim of Violent Crime, Prisoner, Constituent or Patient-Associated Infections—before person requires professional services has been exposed to deadly pathogens or MRSA and/or is a carrier or host of infectious pathogen. This host may or may not demonstrate the characteristics of the disease for a variety of reasons including an incubation period or colonization—see Chapter 4 for details.
- Organizational System Policy toward Commercialism and Government Politics—(i.e., many hospital systems provide only profitable medical services, not cures; government politics' example—punitive police strategies and get tough on crime criminal sanctions; one reason for political ineptitude is that there is little to no political accountability particularly within government bureaucracies to outsiders.[9]
- Government (local, state, and federal) Compliance Regulation—based in state and federal court decisions with legal consequences by a federal or state agency which is often complex and written in ambiguous legal language.[10] The fear of prosecution is often a determinant of behavior during certain situations (details below).

Despite progress in protecting public and healthcare personnel, substantial gaps remain particularly in comparison to the presumption law benefits of firefighters (each profession in this book should move toward a firefighter union model for their own protection).

Additionally state preparedness to deal with an infectious disease outbreak is below standards; and it goes without saying that the pharmaceutical enterprises plays one of the primary roles in advancing the profitability of healthcare providers at the expense of the suffering and the dead patients from infectious pathogens. As mentioned earlier in this work, neutralizing the plague and preventing crime is an unprofitable venture. (See Chapter 3 and Chapter 4).

Fear of Prosecution

Justice and healthcare personnel should possess the authority to provide public safety, treatment, and care at a professional level in keeping with his or her profession. When Hurricane Katrina hit New Orleans, because officers and healthcare personnel had been mandated prior to Hurricane Katrina to follow hierarchical directives without question, any decision they individually made could be and for many had been scrutinized by local and federal prosecutors (see Chapter 1, 4, and 5). "Since the mid-1980s, the US Department of Justice has increasingly used criminal charges as a means to affect regulatory policy," said experts.[11] Regulatory policy often is a prominent part of justice and healthcare training manuals. Fear of prosecution, similar to the fear of crime, pushes people to make different decisions about their behavior. Among physicians and healthcare providers, for instance, the US Department of Justice has been sending physicians to prison in record numbers for their failure to comply with often ambiguous and inappropriate regulations.[12] Think about earlier discussions in this chapter about topics such as physician-assisted suicide, and other alleged infractions manufactured by the US Department of Justice.

Government utilizes criminalization as a regulatory device. How does the average police officer or physician battle the federal machine that wants a conviction, some might ask? CYA (cover your ass by redefining outcomes) is one answer that many professors including this one, lecture and write about in various courses.[13]

It takes time for officers to learn how to 'redefine' regulations and mandates similar to what the veteran correctional officer below linked to the 'doctor' requirement and handcuffed pregnant female prisoner. Learning to 'redefine' scenarios or conditions is one result of a fear of prosecution and one recommendation around redefining events is professionalization (details below). Redefining scenarios is a craft linked to CYA perspectives. This thought should not be misconstrued as lying about, for instance, a shooting or a harsh arrest strategy.

For example, despite the fact that shackling pregnant women prisoners is degrading, unnecessary, and a violation of human rights, only ten states prohibit the practice by law.[14] For example, up until summer 2014 in Massachusetts, when a female prisoner is giving birth and during labor she is handcuffed, restrained, and often shackled. [15] Generally visitors are not allowed including the father of the child. Professional correctional officers could easily change this regulation but until that happens, 'redefining' events and scenarios is one way to shortcut potential prosecution.[3] Here's one experience from the Massachusetts prison system, a system where I was once a teacher and group leader. I have lectured to my students about this experience at MCI Framingham; I was walking outside toward the academic building during an icy cold winter like only Boston could have when I froze in stride because I couldn't comprehend my observations: a short-haired girl, around sixteen years of age, was handcuffed (behind her back), ankles shackled, lying in a gurney sitting on the ground ready for transportation to a local hospital; the wet snow gathered on her reddened small cheeks and mingled with her tears; her tummy was huge—she was very pregnant. I told the correctional officers standing next to her, "Hey . . ." a little long-winded, "remove those shackles and put the cuffs in front." The younger officer snapped, "Can't do it. It's regulation. Only my supervisor . . . " another officer who I knew had been at the prison forever, cut the young man off and spoke over him . . . "or a doctor," he chimed, smiling at me. "You arrre," he slurred his r's, "a doctor, right, doc?" I replied, "Good call. Right!" My suggestions were followed because the senior officer 'redefined' the situation as discussed above. By the bye, I wanted to reach out and smooth her forehead but that is against regulation, and I already got my way with one action.

[3] Once labor started for Benidalys Rivera's (serving 2½ years for trafficking cocaine) painful contractions were three minutes apart. Her contractions did not dilate her cervix. Traveling to the hospital, the correctional officers clamped on handcuffs. In the hospital room, Rivera was shackled by one ankle; restraints would be removed when she reached "active labor." Rivera was given morphine to rest; Vicki Elson, a volunteer woman's delivery coach, massaged her feet and back.
Later Rivera would say that the restraints hurt her ability to progress with her labor because she could not relax. Rivera asked to have her handcuffs removed but the correctional officer refused. "I remember it bothered me, and I probably should have said something," says Elson. "[The officer] was just kind of going by the book."
Source: see endnote. Meredith Derby Berg (2014).

Theoretically, the degree to which personnel redefine a situation is affected by how he or she views the event at the time. Remember what you learned from WI Thomas and the Thomas Theorem—each of us create our own social reality: "if a person perceives a situation as real, it is real in its consequences."[16] Should we be afraid of traveling aboard an aircraft, we become anxious and nervous prior to the fight. Fear is greater than actual accident records. In other words, conduct most often depends on our subjective (individual) interpretation of an event not on the objective reality of it. Officers would perform to the best of their ability even to the point of following police subculture expectations and then redefine their behavior to fit policy.[17] Factually, it might be easy to imply that physicians and surgeons face similar circumstances while engaged in their occupation. If more of them learned the art of CYA, fewer of them would be going to prison.

"In this turbulent period it is more important than ever that we have a police (and correctional, firefighters, and healthcare providers) capacity that is sensitive, effective, and responsive to the country's unique needs, and that, above all else, is committed to protecting and extending democratic values. That is a high calling indeed."[18] Specifically, the most immediate objective of justice and healthcare personnel is to use a greater range of alternatives to improve their effectiveness. For instance, among police officers, "Quite, simply, mediating a dispute, abating a nuisance, or arranging to have some physical barrier removed—without resorting to arrest—may be the best way to solve a problem."[19]

An observation made by an expert clarifies for us in this regard of meeting the needs of American residents to enhance the democratic enterprise: "the law often, but not always, supports police (correctional officers, physicians, and nurses) deception."[20] This deception can include redefining circumstance as described above. The ends can justify the means.

Finally, recall from previous chapters the civil rights violations of the police during, for instance, the Boston Marathon. Frankly, from what Boston PD officers told me in confidence, professional police officers would not require blocking off one-half of Watertown, MA, to find a terrorist; a blocked strategy is a potential legal liability for local officers; the special agent in charge of the FBIs Boston office provided the blocked off order where he thought the alleged terrorist was hiding.[21] Three questions remain: were the two brothers who lived in Cambridge, MA, really terrorists; do emergencies trump Constitutional Rights; and do federal agencies dictate strategy to local agencies? We see public agencies attempting to comply with compliance regulation which appear to take precedence over liberty and reason particularly when it comes to public health issues.

Linking Infectious Disease Transmission to Prison Populations

Chapter 1 suggests that there is a strong connection between infectious disease transmission, prison and jail populations and releases, and criminal justice personnel, firefighters, and healthcare personnel. The evidence in Chapter 5 implies that disease transmission is extraordinary high among both correctional personnel and recipients of their custodial services. For that reason, I argue that the prison industrial complex is the catalyst of disease transmission and the deciding factor linked to the invasion of super bugs or highly infectious pathogens in America.

In *Failure of the American Prison Complex: Let's Abolish It,* I provide a systematic method to reduce prison populations by abolishing prison sanctions for numerous alleged violations such as drug possession—rather implement a medical model of intervention; reduce length of prison sentences, release the mentally ill; reduce jurisdiction of state authority in local (county and city) jails and prisons. Eliminate private prisons and private healthcare providers because they represent the twenty-first century's slave plantation owners (stock holders and top management of those organizations). Please do not read this to mean that violators should not be punished. The prison industrial complex is morally bankrupt and serves little value toward reducing criminal activities or providing rehabilitation and healthcare or providing community safety. If America is going to retain superpower status, its population must be healthy and happy.

Confinement must be limited: in jails locally for individuals who do not know how to control their behavior, and those awaiting adjudication or transportation to prisons and mental institutions. Prisons should be reserved for the worst of the worst such as pedophiles, sexual homicide offenders, and violent prone individuals who cannot keep their hands to themselves particularly violations against children, women, and elderly beaters (sorry guys, the truth of the matter is that most often it's males violating females). Criminal offensives require redefinition such as drug possession and addiction are punishable through prison sentences. The above explanations are simplified versions of an entire chapter but hopefully the point is made that prisons serve little purpose in controlling crime. High profile violent offenders are not influenced by the threat of capital punishment, and serial rapists—well . . . prisons provide them with new victims. We have to go the root of the problem which is hardly an individual decision since most individuals servicing prison sentences represent members of the social lower class who are illiterate and poor, the literature and government statistics report.[22]

We must also go to the root of the problem similar to what Americans did with the question of slavery. Slavery couldn't be fixed, so we abolished it.

Curing Prisoners and Personnel

There are some assumptions about 'cures' of all varieties; it might help to discuss this assumption before moving on. Similar to others with my experiences in high custody (male and female) penitentiaries, we collectively tend to commonly accept (although we don't like it) that when pontificating about curing prisoners who are violent prone toward conduct such as chronic sexual homicide, we end those intellectual assessments (per say) with a consensus that typically sounds something like this: there is something unsettling about advice from popular writers, god peddling entrepreneurs, and bleeding heart liberals who proclaim rehabilitation is a breath away from every serial murderer, chronic pedophile, and spouse basher.[23] So no matter the future of the prison industrial complex, those genetically abnormal (yes, it's genetic)[24] sexual homicide addicts will always be among us, and have been among civilizations since our early beginnings (see *Inside the Mind of a Serial Rapist* for more details; I wrote a book while at Stateville Penitentiary and at a closed custody prison in North Carolina). Whether we're discussing curing patients including criminal justice personnel, firefighters, and healthcare professionals from a different variety of disease infections, there is another perspective worth your consideration.

Amenability to Treatment

Cures, recovery, or rehabilitation in general is not for everybody. One perspective that can aid in an understanding of this thought is a perspective called an Amenability to Treatment. For the purposes of this discussion, Amenability to Treatment can be defined as a documented willingness and capability toward treatment and recovery. Documentation refers to evidence obtained through interviews, records, and observations. The thinking goes that not every individual (including personnel in this book and discussed below) is amenable toward treatment, and that not every individual wants help. Yet, amenability to treatment determinations are usually associated with past history of an individual particularly law enforcement and correctional officers.[25] Many officers are able to stay under the 'radar' and deal with his or her ills without calling attention to themselves or involving others.[26] They are aware that a physical problem exists. You read in Chapter 8 about nurses who do not report their symptoms of patient associated infection. For that reason alone, it is hard to tell how many justice, firefighters, and healthcare providers have been exposed to infectious pathogens and how many have died or suffer continually from disease transmission.

Which ones are hosts of deadly pathogens?

Kurhan/Shutterstock, Inc.

Unreported Cases of Infection

One reason for their unreported condition, similar to other personnel, is that they would lose their jobs, their income, and there are little or few benefits to aid them once out of work; unlike most full-time firefighters who are protected through presumption laws; few if any physicians and nurses, police and correctional officers, and most healthcare providers generally are not protected. Also, most often, the most important item linked to any treatment or recovery is the participant aside from the ability of those performing the cure or treatment.[27] That means infectious treatment doesn't always work or even work right away. Also consider that once recovery is well underway, there are no guarantees that a professional will not be infected again. After all, treatment is a band-aid and allegedly once cured, the professional returns to the same environment where he or she was first infected.

Blaming the Victim

After everything you have read, you might decide that it's the prisoners or the infected person including the personnel, is the problem; yet virtually anyone in at-risk environments might experience similar situations. For example, once incarcerated regardless of the conviction that brought a person to prison, regardless of innocence or guilt, a person changes. It is difficult to remember this perspective when employed at the department of corrections because most of us want to help those locked down individuals, particularly those wrongfully convicted; but as I lectured in many university classrooms among future counselors, law enforcement, and correctional officers, "Once a sweet and kind person is locked down, there isn't any coming back. Put a dog in a cage for a year and see how fast you run once you release the dog."[28] That can mean, once you're a healthcare provider or a cop, or serving your country in Afghanistan, you're never the same.

William Ryan's classic work refutes the lies we tell ourselves about race, poverty, and those in poverty. We blame victims for their outcomes, for example:[29]

- minority children perform poorly in school because they are culturally deprived (statistics remind us that illiteracy and poverty are pathways to prisons regardless of innocence; as a professor for over twenty-five years, my experience tells me that students from the middle and upper class can do poorly in school; the motivation on the part of lower social class students to succeed is totally awesome)[30]
- African-Americans are handicapped by a family structure that is typically unstable and matriarchal (single women of color and those without color whatever that is—can successfully raise their children)
- Poor people suffer from bad health because of ignorance and lack of interest in proper health care (as though those in poverty possess a monopoly on ignorance)

Nonetheless, it is easy to blame the victim similar to blaming the helpless and abused wives or daughters who see no other way out of their relationship even after numerous 911 calls, reluctant police officer avoiding an arrest of the abuser, and emergency room visits—other than to take the life of their continual abuser; once tried, she is in prison.[31] We have to be careful about blame! [4] There is a vast amount of evidence that shows our criminal justice system is the new home for individuals with psychological problems.[32] Although this may seem like a solution to some, it is creating a dilemma for American society. Once labeled a convict or a professional HIV cured or another serious infection, regardless of the seriousness of the crime or the disease, a stigma is there forever.

Similar to the female prisoners locked down in segregation units who are often raped by correctional officers, visitors, and other prisoners, once they have a label, they are blamed for the attack.[33] Raped females regardless of age, regardless if free or locked down some of the most common emotional responses after rape or attempted rape are guilt, fear, powerlessness, shame, betrayal, anger, denial, and above all blame. Females have no sense of a right to be free from the crimes of violence visited upon them, so she must be the problem! She blames herself, too.

For instance, while writing this section (September 12, 2014), CNN reported on an incident that happened to Ray Rice a football player with the Baltimore Ravens. He punched his wife into unconsciousness, and when you witness the knockout punch on 'YouTube', you can no longer turn this 'incident' into a tiff between drunk lovers or blame the victim: Janay Palmer.[34] "Many people had done just that, and speculated on whether she provoked Rice to knock her out while in an evaluator . . . (even) The Baltimore Ravens blamed her when they suggested in a tweet that she had played a role in the incident. The tweet, . . . read: 'Janay Rice says she deeply regrets the role that she played the night of the incident.' She never posted that tweet. Blaming the victim manifests itself into self guilt which in and by itself perpetuates more victimization. For instance, some believe that it takes two to tango in domestic violence cases. The thinking goes, once a battered woman leaves her abuser, she seeks (allegedly) another abuser. Think of it this way, the poor are lazy and like poverty. Once that perspective is internalized by the victim, guilt and self blame clouds any incentive to work hard? Wait! If someone is arrested and sentenced to prison for killing their abuser, where's the fear of prosecution? Prosecution is a double sword—it validates to the victim that husband killer that was wrong; remember, she is blaming herself just like the parents of the perpetrator or husband who often beat her; sometimes, her own children might blame her for his behavior. This characteristic of blaming the victim as opposed to the real abuser regardless of the action of the perpetrator is typical among many children in dysfunctional families.[35] Just to expand your knowledge on blaming the victim, it is also typical of children who are sexual assault victims to blame themselves for the assaults and protect their attacker.[5] Once victims accept their predicament or situation as their own doing through the self blame and self guilt process, the performance of public service providers changes. For example, the people in New Orleans who thought God was punishing them for their sins during Hurricane Katrina were more likely to accept whatever quality of treatment first responders provided. Victimization has to do with organizational environment.

[4] To blame others is really a process about ourselves and a waste of time. "No matter how much fault you find with another, and regardless of how much you blame him/her, it will not change you. The only thing blame does is to keep the focus off you when you are looking for external reasons to explain your unhappiness or frustration. You may succeed in making another feel guilty about something by blaming him/her, but you won't succeed in changing whatever it is about you that is making you unhappy."

Source: Wayne Dyer (2014). *I Can See Clearly Now*. NY: Hay House. Page 364.

[5] Blame for Child Sexual Assault

- blame placed on perpetrators remained high over time; use of force and/or more frequent abuse was linked with more perpetrator blame
- actual penetration was linked with higher levels of self-blame
- self-blame decreased over time, but initial level of victims' self-blame predicted later level of depression
- youth frequently reported confusion as to why the CSA occurred
- there were no significant gender differences in self-blame
- self-blame and perpetrator blame are both unhealthy because of attributions (i.e., beliefs about causality)

Source: Ola W Barnett, Cindy L Miller-Perrin, and Robin D Perrin (2010). *Family Violence, 3rd edition*. Thousand Oaks, CA: Sage. Page 365.

Organizational Environments

It makes little sense to cure justice or healthcare personnel of an infectious disease and neglect the organizational environment where he or she is employed. Think of it this way, requiring a university student to retake a class with a professor who delivered so much anxiety and animosity toward the student that the student felt totally uncomfortable in every class and was afraid to turn in any assignment for fear of intimidation (the student completed all of the assignments and provided them to her adviser). Another analogy might be an alcoholic working in a crowded neighborhood bar or a drug addict returning to the same cultural environment that promoted and enabled his or her addiction from the beginning.

Drug addiction has more to do with social environments, as does disease transmission. Until the priorities of police agencies, correctional agencies, and healing centers are treatment and care, and inexpensive products are readily available to combat infectious pathogens, as they say in New York City—"forget about it," and in one word.

Once "cured," personnel return to (or never left) the organizational environment and comply with the same hierarchal orders, issued from the same paramilitary mouths, drowned by the same flood of disrespect from courts, federal agencies, and deviants. Cured personnel will be less likely promoted, less likely to be assigned more responsibility, and less likely to be honored for deeds well done, than personnel who never had to be cured. Cured personnel have an "X" branded upon their foreheads through the occupational subculture (as discussed in Chapter 5) and are watched for any sign of faulting by peers, supervisors, and clinicians. They are often blamed for their infection—they didn't take precautions, some might say—similar to blaming the victim thoughts.

Also, when a "cured" person is a litigant in a civil action suit, his or her past medical history play a role and will be used against him or her. One reality is that not all personnel want to be treated because they are aware of these issues; equally important metaphorically, organizations which include police, correctional, and healthcare organizations must be treated and cured for 'infections,' too.

Recall from the previous chapters that 'agents of compliance' among personnel include organization policy (such as hierarchies) and politics which bang the drums toward the wars on poverty, drugs, sex offenders, and terrorism; and ambitious but ambiguous compliance mandates pollute the fishing rivers in Colorado and every other jurisdiction, healing center, and prison across the country.

Changing Justice and Healthcare's Organizational Environment

. . . "agencies (including healing centers) need to be healthy before they can treat the community's illnesses and injuries and aid personnel to provide professional services. Signs of good health among personnel include pride, self-esteem, quality leadership, comprehensive training, and board certification."[36] Environmental changes for organizations also have to do with a new philosophy aimed at organizing for empowerment and hierarchical leveling.[37]

Organizing for Empowerment

Strong unions similar to the firefighters that lobby and win strong presumption laws will aid in an empowerment of justice and healthcare personnel including physicians. Perhaps the same unions! Recall from the chapter on firefighters (Chapter 7) that when unions' bargaining power across the country were put on hold for various reasons, the American worker took a beating and the American economy has yet to regain its previous economy position. For example, although there are many reasons for the fact that university graduates cannot find jobs as easily today as in previous generations including the highly competitive nature of employment but somewhere in the mix is the bothersome notion that personnel have less say or bargaining power in organizations than they used to have.[38] Also consider the difference between the benefits (and pay) among firefighters especially through presumption laws (Chapter 7) who are strongly represented by unions compared with the benefits and pay among police and correctional officers (Chapters 5 and 6). Second on the list of empowerment is hierarchical leveling or professionalism. Obviously physicians and nurses would benefit from an empowerment perspective too. Rather than being blamed for hospital treatment, care, and surgical errors, hospital systems and patients will think twice before setting a lawsuit in motion.

Hierarchical Leveling

It is strongly recommended that authority within police, correctional, and healthcare organizations be flattened (and decentralized across the organization) by empowering personnel to make policy decisions concerning their authority and expectations. Professionals can make decisions about their conduct within certain parameters without concern for being questioned about their performance (we are not talking about criminal conduct, of course; see Fear of Prosecution below for more details). In this manner the agency's environment will be changed coupled with strong bargaining power through a professional union; personnel will come forward more often for treatment rather than infecting others.

Professionalism

Policymakers must circumvent the organization's adversary relationship with their rank-and-file personnel and promote professionalism. We've learned in Chapter 2 about bureaucratic organizations which include police, corrections, and healthcare. Organizations must provide the leadership toward professionalized departments and units. Organizations must support and encourage personnel to practice the primary characteristics consistent of professional personnel. A profession is an occupation requiring extensive education or specialized training.[39] Samuel P. Huntington (1981) writes in his work *Soldier and the State* that a profession displays three primary characteristics to some degree or another: responsibility, expertise, and corporateness.[40]

- Responsibility: The profession consists of practicing experts, who work in a social context, and perform a service, such as the promotion of health, education, or justice, which is essential to the functioning of society. The client of every profession is society, individually or collectively. The profession is a moral unit promoting specific values and ideals that guide its members in their interactions with others. This guide may be a set of unwritten norms transmitted through the professional educational system and it may be codified into written canons of professional ethics.[41]
- Expertise: Professions consist of experts who possess specialized knowledge and skill in a significant field of human endeavor. This expertise is acquired only by a prolonged combination of education, training, and experience. It is the basis of objective standards of professional competence. Professionalism through objectivity (as opposed to subjectivity or a personal agenda) is a goal.
- Corporateness: Professional experts who share a common sense of organic unity and consciousness of themselves as an individual and as a group apart from other occupations. The origin of this collective feeling or set of experiences can be found in their discipline and training necessary for professional competence, the common bond of work, and the sharing of a unique social responsibility.

Organizations employing personnel should encourage them to conduct themselves in a socially responsible manner; personnel should be enjoying freedom, autonomy, and making decisions about their conduct in the best interest of their profession rather than worrying about being disciplined or prosecuted.[42]

Another product of professionalization and unionization is quality services to the individuals whom require their services. It also means better trained personnel.[6] Professionalizing correctional officers would allow them to make decisions about conduct cored in circumstance without concern for being cited or prosecuted. Nurses and physicians along with other healthcare personnel face similar situations that call for decisions not in the manuals. A latent (not expected) result from professionalization would also manifest itself after a terrorist attack because providers could take action according to the situation as opposed to "follow your training." The notion of paramilitary hierarchy within a centralized organization (orders come from the top manager and reports about fulfilling those orders come from the bottom) among providers (and probably every other occupation including the military) is something that served my father's day well; it's time to

[6] The sad thing is that while criminally violent offenders cannot be stopped, the best I can do is study them and train justice professionals to better detect, apprehend, and convict them. For those opportunities, I am pleased with my few accomplishments.

decentralize and professionalize individuals who are employed in a democratic nation. A close analysis would prove that a centralized paramilitary organization is alien to a democratic process, particularly a process encumbered with defending the rule of law and due process as one of its primary objectives. More public service organizations should follow the American Bar Association's (ABA) recent mission change which states: "ABA's purpose is to serve equally its members, the legal profession and the public by defending liberty and delivering justice."[43]

Whatever model of professionalism is tinkered out is meaningless unless a police department, correctional and healing centers adapt it as their own, and they must train and enforce the practices toward the model. Another reality is that if personnel including federal personnel are "bogged down in bureaucracy and agency turf protection," the likelihood of personnel responding according to a specific strategy or model is unlikely.[44] Nonetheless, little has been able to slow the growth of secrecy in American government. "Many suspect it serves the interests of politics, malfeasance, misdeeds, and potential embarrassment . . ."[45] Secrecy is a product of bureaucratic organizations, says a philosophical expert;[46] for instance, middle management keep secrets from lower management, and what is expected from all personnel is passive obedience (see Chapters 3 and 9 for details). Professionalization of both local law enforcement and correctional officers and healthcare providers (including physicians and nurses) would enhance their individual confidence and performance making encounters safer, thereby reducing disease transmission among many constituents, prisoners, and patients. They would also be less likely to redefine their performance to fit compliance regulations.

Hospitals

Basically there are three types of hospital entity types—nonprofit, for-profit, and government-owned hospitals. What is not reliable data are whether hospital types that specialize in different medical services nor how service profitability or even the call toward commercialization affects specialization.[47] The American Hospital Association reports that for every US urban, acute care hospital, more than thirty services were categorized as relatively profitable, unprofitable, or variable. Profitable or profit driven hospitals are most likely to offer relatively profitable medical services. Government hospitals are most likely to offer relatively unprofitable services and often inferior services. Nonprofits such as those hospitals owned by church groups or other organizations that are nonprofit entities such as the Red Cross often fall in the middle.[7] Profitable hospitals are also more responsive to changes in service profitability than the other two types.

Hospitals that are profit driven tend to manage their case-mix more carefully than nonprofit and government hospitals.[48] For example, they differentially locate in areas with relatively well-insured patients. Underlying this concept of profit-making is the assumption that all general hospitals, regardless of ownership, are alike in the types of medical services they provide. They differ in their patient mix.[49] Profitable hospitals are more likely than other types to decide which medical services to offer based on service profitability. There are no regulations for which services must be offered by hospitals. General hospitals do not provide a standard array of medical services. Two-thirds of all US urban hospitals are nonprofit, with the remainder split between for-profit and government ownership.[50] On the other side of the coin, the business model of "non-profit" hospitals, are, in fact, among the most profitable enterprises in the nation.[51]

> [7] DEFINITION of 'Nonprofit Organization' A business entity that is granted tax-exempt status by the Internal Revenue Service. Donations to a nonprofit organization are often tax deductible to the individuals and businesses making the contributions. Nonprofit organizations are also called 501(c)(3) organizations after the section of the tax code that allows them.
> *Source:* Investopedia. Retrieved December 8, 2014: http://www.investopedia.com/terms/n/non-profitorganization.asp

Chargemaster

Every hospital has what is called a "chargemaster," a list of what it charges for everything from a day in the ICU to a single aspirin; it is a lengthy list of the hospital's prices for every single procedure performed in the hospital and for every supply item used during those procedures.[52] Hospitals guard access to its chargemaster like the federal government guarded the Manhattan Project (only with more success, as Stalin knew all about the atomic bomb).[53]

Medicare and insurance companies pay a fraction of the nominal prices. MD Anderson, a high-powered cancer hospital in Houston, charges $283 for a simple chest X-ray and Medicare pays the hospital $20.44. The point is that individuals without insurance, or with limited insurance, who require a simple chest X-ray are charged the full price.

Kirill_M/Shutterstock, Inc.

MD Anderson's operating profit in 2010 was $531 million on revenues of $2.05 billion. That's a 26 percent profit margin, unheard of in any service industry other than hospitals. As a "non-profit" organization, it pays no income taxes.[54]

One recommendation is that hospitals, particularly non-profit hospitals, post their chargemaster lists. If gas stations and automobile dealers are required to post their prices, why shouldn't medical service providers? Once prices become assessable by the public, they could, simply through market forces, competitively 'shop hospitals' toward the lower end.[55] Can you see a groupon for a kidney removal?

The American Hospital Association says that "our goals are to increase the collection of race, ethnicity, and language preference data; increase cultural competency training for clinicians and support staff; and increase diversity in governance and management. Addressing disparities is no longer just about morality, ethics, and social justice: it is essential for performance excellence and improved community health."[56]

Finally, there are no perfect 'types' of hospitals because of size, specialties, and resources. However, one conclusion held by an organization that measures hospital accomplishments and provides a list of those accomplishments is worth mentioning. Truven Health Analytics compares thousands of hospitals in the US comprised of equally weighted measures of key organizational functions and outcomes: [57]

- Financial Stability
- Operational Efficiency
- Patient Safety
- Quality Inpatient and Outpatient Care
- Customer Perception of Care

Based on comparisons between that organization's top 100 winners and a peer group of similar high-volume hospitals that were not winners, Traven argues that if all hospitals performed at the level of 2014's winners the results similar to the following might become a reality:

- Nearly 165,000 additional lives could be saved
- More than 90,000 additional patients could be complication-free
- $5.4 billion could be saved
- The typical patient could be released from the hospital half a day sooner

Traven bases their analysis on the Medicare patients in their study, too. Traven states that if the same standards were applied to all patients, the impact would be even greater. Yet, the obvious absence of, specifically, disease transmission among personnel and patient is missing from Traven's criteria.

Permit one last observation about hospital systems: most often their agendas, policies, and priorities are different and obscure from its medical staff, and healthcare payers have established extensive bureaucracies to control physician-driven costs.[58] It's the physicians under the gun most often as opposed to the hospital systems and yet it's been clarified that most physician and surgeon error is part of the medical process treatment that is the culprit of errors. That means that the agents of compliance particularly hospital policy and fear of prosecution dictate healthcare performance. It is clear that the services of physicians and for that matter nurses are not, in the real world, "separated from the services of other health professionals, nor from the services of a variety of supportive personnel."[59] A final thought about hospitals includes emergency departments and other healing centers, it would seem prudent if reliable screening processes of all patients could be utilized to ascertain the susceptibility of patients to infection before admission and before medical processes or surgery. Therefore, human error is a worthy discussion of your time.

Human Beings and Human Errors

The evidence in Chapter 4 through Chapter 8 suggests that human beings including physicians, nurses, police and correctional officers are subject to making mistakes; most often, it is not the individual who causes an error; rather the performance of many individuals who responded to organizational policy and indifferent government regulation, mentioned above or agents of compliance.[60] Here's how it works: recall driving your vehicle down an unfamiliar country road wondering about the speed limit? Suddenly one sign reads 55 miles per hour, but a few yards further, another sign reads 35 miles per hour. Without hesitation, you slow up because you believe that you have found the local speed trap as you scan your environment looking for the cops.

Nothing . . . you're not sure what to do. Traffic behind you is on your tail. Another sign, 25 miles per hour and another, Yield to Merging Traffic, and another reads 45 Minimum Speed On Highway. Because of so many rules, you're not sure what to do? One thing is sure, you hide your cell and sit straight, almost at attention. From a sociological perspective, this might be what Emile Durkheim advanced some time ago—anomie.[61]

Carsten Reisinger/Shutterstock, Inc.

Too many rules all at one time might cause you to pause as you drive through the countryside

Anomie

Durkheim explains that many of us without intention often engage in what can be perceived as a social imbalance, of sorts, which impacts our decisions about behavior or what Durkheim deems 'anomie.' According to Durkheim, anomie reflects a sense of normlessness, the lack of any societal norms that spurs the tendency to act in a deviant (does not necessarily mean criminal). This writer applies Durkheim's perspective to the vehicle driver above and to the physicians and surgeons described in this chapter. The way my professor Dr. Helena Znaniecki Lopata (her father was Florian Znaniecki who wrote with WI Thomas)[62] at Loyola University of Chicago explains, with so many rules (and regulations) most of us are not sure which rule or which regulation or which expectation to follow. I took that to mean that because healthcare providers may be anxious to follow hospital policy and government compliance regulations. They might be anxious to follow their own oath to themselves to aid others, to make a difference in this world, and to continue the respect of their colleagues and collaborators—which set of rules, regulations, or list of social expectations should they follow? Anomie supports the 'damn if they do and damn if they don't' philosophy, a perspective detailed earlier in the chapter. As previously mentioned, they master the art of redefinition and employ CYA perspectives during their performance.

Nurses

National surveys of the public have repeatedly found nursing to be one of the most trusted professions.[63] The public trusts nurses to provide safe care and to:

- not work while having an infectious illness
- be knowledgeable about the methods to protect our patients from transmission of disease, perform aseptic practice, and monitor patient infections

- participate in quality improvement initiatives reduce infections
- provide care even if it means self-risk from infection.

The general public and researchers hold RN to a higher standard, similar to correctional officer and police officers. And similar to those professions, occupational stress and aiding an officer recover from stress, is one thing; placing him or her back into the same organizational structure that created the stress in the first place results in more acute stress for the officer.[64] He or she now believes that it is his or her fault from the get-go. It is the healthcare organizational structure that must be changed before personnel can change. For example, the working and employment conditions described as determinants of gender inequalities in occupational healthcare studies published between 1999 and 2010 shows that the most common topic analyzed was related to the exposure to work-related psychosocial hazards.[65]

Some Realities: Centers for Disease Control and Prevention (CDC)

CDC reports that declines have been noticed particularly from bloodstream infections (BSI) and surgical site infections since 2008.[66] The report shows no change in the rate of catheter-associated urinary infections. CDC adds that through the efforts of many healthcare organizations awareness of healthcare associated infections has been heightened and its economic implications concerning healthcare personnel and their patients, which is a good sign. Maybe the earlier reports were in error and the present day reports are manufactured to meet those earlier reports—result? No change.

The bad news is that that Methicillin-sensitive Staphylococcus Aureus (MSSA), Methicillin-resistant Staphylococcus aureus (MRSA), and other deadly infections including Ebola remains a significant pathway to unnecessary suffering and death particularly for many patients including premature infants and full-term infants undergoing surgery.[67,8] Nonetheless, despite the reductions and awareness conclusions, Daniel Diekema, President of The Society for Healthcare Epidemiology of America (SHEA)[9] shares:

> "...The CDC estimates that 5–10 percent of hospitalized patients develop a healthcare-associated infection, corresponding to approximately 2 million (hospital associated infections) HCAI with nearly 100,000 deaths each year in US hospitals."[68]

Dedicated professionals have little knowledge that they themselves are hosts or carriers of deadly pathogens (as discussed earlier through colonization). With 2 million reported patients exposed to healthcare associated infections and 100,000 deaths each year, healthcare personnel especially nurses similar to correctional and law enforcement personnel engage any and all persons under their surveillance, supervision, and care every day without knowledge or hesitation should those whom they engage have an infectious disease.

What is the concern about ISIS in comparison to America's at-home assault of infectious pathogens with no ammunition to combat the assault? Our US President says, "The only language understood by (ISIS) killers like this is the language of force."[69] The President has been right about so much and he and his advisers might be right about ISIS, but consider the source of his information—the CIA; isn't that the same source that told President Bush

[8] In Syracuse from 1999–2001, about two-thirds of infant deaths occurred during the neonatal period, with the remaining one-third being post-neonatal deaths. A large proportion of these preterm births resulted from sub-clinical infections, such as bacterial vaginosis. Assisted reproduction has increased the number of multiple births and deaths. A percentage of those multiple pregnancies were conceived with the help of in vitro fertilization or fertility medications. Also, a small percentage of them were conceived with the assistance of reproductive and stimulating medications. Although those conceptions represented a small percent, of the infants who died, almost 37 percent of the infants who were conceived with medical intervention required neonatal intensive care.

Source: Sandra D. Lane (2008). *Why Are Our Babies Dying*. Boulder, CO: Paradigm. Pages 71–73.

[9] SHEA is a professional society representing more than 2,000 physicians and other healthcare professionals around the world with expertise in healthcare epidemiology and infection prevention and control. SHEA's mission is to prevent and control healthcare-associated infections and advance the field of healthcare epidemiology. The society leads this field by promoting science and research and providing high-quality education and training in epidemiologic methods and prevention strategies. SHEA upholds the value and critical contributions of healthcare epidemiology to improving patient care and healthcare worker safety in all healthcare settings. Visit SHEA online at www.shea-online.org.

about nuclear weapons in Iraq? Their announcements change, too, suggesting an inconsistency in obtaining information or those who report the news are saying something different. For example, on September 11, 2014, "The CIA announces that the number of people fighting for ISIS may be more than three times the previous estimates." Analysts and US officials initially estimated there were as many as 10,000 fighters, but now ISIS can "muster between 20,000 and 31,500 fighters across Iraq and Syria," a CIA spokesman tells CNN.[70]

Yet, we know the approximate number of patients and infants, justice and healthcare personnel who will die from infectious pathogens on the day you read this paragraph, and most of those deaths are preventable, says the Centers for Disease Control and Prevention along with scores of researchers (see Chapter 2). Producing weapons of war such as Tomahawk Land-Attack cruise missiles launched from expensive ships such USS Philippine at the Persian Gulf, drones, and fighter jets are as profitable as prisons and hospitals. One answer is finding a balance—not between ISIS and Tomahawk missiles, but between medical treatment and democracy.

After a Bioweapon Attack

There are some thoughts about bioweapons and terrorists worth sharing. Chapters 1 through 9 provided discussions about C. Wright Mills' work on The Power Elite.[71] Mills advances the idea that the Power Elite is comprised of:

- the highest political leaders including the president and a handful of key cabinet members and close advisers
- major corporate owners and directors
- high-ranking military officers.

Is it possible that through the Power Elite that these warlords of an enlarged US military complex have gained decisive political and corporate relevance? War of all types including the wars on poverty and drugs place a premium on the military and criminal justice communities in "their control of men, materiel, money, and power; virtually all political and economic actions are now judged in terms of military (and criminal justice) definitions of reality: the higher warlords have ascended to a firm position within the power elite of the fifth epoch."[72] While writing this chapter, war cries are everywhere—television, radio, Internet, and from the mouths of my neighbors. The mental pictures drawn in everyone's mind about ISIS easily fit the profile of the merciless strange-faced Persian warriors in the ancient Battle of Thermopylae in which King Leonidas and 300 Spartans fought to the death against Xerxes (*300 Men*, 2006).

Anastasios/Shutterstock, Inc.

Sometimes I get lost because there are so many events about US Military engagements and terrorist activity that sound different depending on which news company's account I might hear. For instance, as of September 10, 2014, defense officials say that the total number of US troops in Iraq is 1,213.[73] In September 2014, NATO and the Pentagon estimate that the Taliban has about 20,000 men in Iraq on the other hand, the American military and NATO with a combined force of about 100,000, supplemented by an Afghan force of 350,000, according to NATO.[74]

Also, a spate of highly organized attacks against allied forces, such as the raid in which fifteen Taliban got inside Camp Bastion; this is a major air base in southern Afghanistan's Helmand province; two US Marines were killed and six fighter jets were destroyed; troop numbers do not tell the whole story of what is happening in Afghanistan.[75] No disrespect intended to the men and women who have died or were injured from the fifteen-year war; but these statistics sound like a good weekend in Chicago; for instance over the July 4, 2014, holiday weekend there were eighty-two shootings (reported) in Chicago, in which at least sixteen people were killed (I guess Chicagoans are poor shots). The number of bombings totaled 14, says the Chicago Police Department. There are 25,000 law enforcement officers in my hometown. Thus the question . . . Why does loss of life and resources in Afghanistan take precedence over the needs of American cities such as Chicago? Between New York and Chicago there are more cops (55,000) than there are troops in Afghanistan and Iraq and those brave officers maintain a quality of life experience for most city dwellers that seems more than reasonable. Billions of dollars more are spent on foreign soil than American soil to keep the peace. How reasonable is that expenditure acknowledging that freedom is never free. For the record, federal military cannot perform local police duties centered in '*Posse Comitatus Act of 1878*'.[10]

[10] Whoever, except in cases and under circumstances expressly authorized by the Constitution or Act of Congress, willfully uses any part of the Army or the Air Force as a posse comitatus or otherwise to execute the laws shall be fined under this title or imprisoned not more than two years, or both.
Source: Title 18, U.S. Code, Section 1385

Head Fake

America's attention and resources (Cost of War in Iraq and Afghanistan $1,564,066,412,466) focuses on Muslims in Afghanistan and Iraq;[76] in part this focus can be linked to the Power Elite who can easily 'sell' a continuing holy war of sorts while American cities are rampant with out-of-control violent gang warfare.[77] If the information reviewed is even half true, one explanation for our attention on Afghanistan and Iraq sounds like the 'head fake' described in Robert Pausch's book on *The Last Lecture.*[78] There are two kinds of head fakes. The first head fake description is literal. In sports for example, player one moves his or her head one way to get his or her opponent, player 2, to think that that is the direction of the first player's movement; player 2 moves in the head fake direction when indeed, player 1 moves in the opposite direction.

Christian Bertrand/Shutterstock, Inc.

The second kind of head fake is one that teaches people things they may not realize they are learning "until well into the process," says Pausch. Head fake professionals hold an expertise on hiding real objectives or truths to promote the head fake professional's objective, regardless of the worth of those objectives. Think of it this way: pharmaceutical companies "have seized upon an effective tool for getting their message across to doctors: other doctors."[79] Across the country, thousands of physicians have signed-up as part-time lecturers for pharmaceutical companies. At small meetings, often over lunch or dinner, "these physician-pitchmen tell their peers about diseases and the drugs to treat them, often pocketing $750 or more from the sponsor."

Ljupco Smokovski/Shutterstock, Inc.

In 2004, 237,000 meetings and talks sponsored by pharmaceutical companies featured physicians as speakers, compared with 134,000 meetings led by company sales representatives, according to market researchers.[80] Some physicians have earned remarkable incomes from their part-time speaker job: for instance, Subir Roy, a gynecologist who teaches at the University of Southern California, received $61,250 in fees and an additional $11,117 for expenses in 2002.[81] Pharmaceutical products even those products with a 'black box warning' from Food and Drug Administration (FDA) continue to be prescribed by physicians, and I would imagine, represented by them as well.[82] Feel free to add this explanation to the commercialization perspective linked to physicians and other healthcare providers detailed in Chapters 8 and 9.

One Conclusion

Professional personnel would become a greater asset to the democratic spirit rather than an asset to the Power Elite who dictate law enforcement, correctional, and healthcare policy; professionalized personnel would hold autonomy toward performance and their professional opinions about medical diagnosis, treatment, detainment, arrest, and confinement. This thought might push justice and healthcare power opponents over the edge; yet it's not about power among those in at-risk environments; it's about public safety and democracy and right now, the Power Elite decides who gets rich and who gets prison; who gets quality treatment and who doesn't get quality treatment or treatment at all.[83] The Power Elite trump reason, and are 'circling their wagons' with an emergence of secrecy within government, according to some scholars, resulting in the building of their own Iron Curtain.[84] Recall the Words of Wisdom for this chapter. Here they are again—"To learn who rules over you, simply find out who you are not allowed to criticize." Voltaire, pen name for François Marie Arouet (1694–1778). See, you didn't even know his real name until now!

Summary

This chapter begins with an analogy about a couple of fishermen, and their issues and conduct about dead bodies floating in the river. While one goes off to find why so many people are dying, the other remains chest deep in a river that is about to flood from compliance regulation assuming the landslide or prosecution and malpractice lawsuits doesn't overtake the physician first. That discussion features the guiding mandates of occupations leading to agents of compliance and the fear of prosecution along with its consequences linked to performance. One perspective that arises more than once is that police, corrections, and healthcare providers including physicians should have strong bargaining agents similar to the firefighters. The link was made between the prison industrial complex as a catalyst of disease transmission through the release of prisoners. Blaming victims for their situation or infections is cautioned.

It was said that some individual for various reasons hold an amenability to treatment. It was clarified that curing prisoners and professionals without 'curing' the high risk organizational environments of their employment is fruitless. Changing organizational environments strategies were offered which include organizing for empowerment and hierarchal leveling. Professionalism was reviewed along with the attributes of professionalizing criminal justice personnel and healthcare providers. Hospitals and their charges were discussed along with recommendations. Human beings and human errors suggests that most medical errors had little to do with the practitioner at the time but had more to do with the process overall. Anomie was one explanation used to explain human error. It is clarified throughout the chapter and much of the book that the Power Elite have everything to do with policy in their best interests including the threat of terrorists. I'm sure a very controversial section on the performance of justice and healthcare providers after a bioweapon attack is featured.

Name: ________________________________ Date: ______________ School Identification Number: ______

STUDENT WORKSHEETS

Chapter 11 A Key to a Safer America

Define the following key terms from Chapter 11, and in your answer, show the page number where you found the definition. Provide an example for each key term.

1. Amenability to Treatment

2. Anomie

3. Blaming the Victim

4. Decentralizing

5. Euthanasia

6. Fear of Prosecution

7. Guiding Mandates of Occupation

8. Hieratical Leveling

9. Posse Comitatus Act of 1878

Name: ______________________________ Date: ______________ School Identification Number: ________

10. Professionalization

11. Organizing for Empowerment

12. Redefine Circumstances

13. Thomas Theorem

Name: ____ Date: _________________ School Identification Number: ________

STUDENT WORKSHEETS

Chapter 11 A Key to a Safer America

Discuss and demonstrate in your own words that you comprehend the following learning objectives in this chapter.

1. Explain in your own words how the fishermen story fits into the discussion of infectious disease control.
2. Explain the objectives of the author who wrote this book. In what way have any of those objectives been met?
3. Identify the guiding mandates of occupations. Describe in what way those mandates can dictate the performance of a justice and healthcare provider.
4. Describe the generalized model relating to the agents of compliance in this chapter. Explain in what way those mandates can influence the performance of a justice and healthcare provider.
5. The case study about euthanasia and physician assisted suicide was about a seventy-two-year-old man. Describe the debate about euthanasia and use an eighteen-year-old patient.
6. Identify the principles behind the fear of prosecution producing sometimes inappropriate professional conduct from law enforcement and correctional officers, physicians, and nurses among others.
7. Discuss the Thomas Theorem and explain in what way the decisions of personnel and students are influenced through this perspective. Use some specific examples.
8. Explain the reasoning behind changing the organizational environments of personnel.
9. Discuss the reasons to abolish the prison industrial complex and the benefits to society.
10. Articulate the reasoning supporting the idea of professionalizing justice and healthcare personnel. What is hoped to be gained through a professionalization process of these professions?
11. Explain the idea associated with human beings and errors. In what way do you agree or disagree with this idea?
12. In what way does the Power Elite relate to the idea of advancing terrorism and justice?

CHAPTER 11 ENDNOTES

1. Kathryn A Smith, Theresa A Harvath, Elizabeth R Goy, and Linda Ganzini (2014). Predictors of Pursuit of Physician-Assisted Death. *Journal of Pain and Symptom Management*, In Press. Also see, Courtney S Campbell and Margaret A Black (2014). Dignity, Death, and Dilemmas: A Study of Washington Hospices and Physician-Assisted Death. *Journal of Pain and Symptom Management*, 47(1): 137–153.
2. Sara Horsfall, Cristian Alcocer, C Temple Duncan, and Jonathan Polk (2001). Views Of Euthanasia From An East Texas University. *The Social Science Journal*, 38(4): 617–627.
3. Euthanasia (2014). Pros and Cons. Retrieved September 29, 2014: http://euthanasia.procon.org/view.resource.php?resourceID=000132
4. Clinical Decisions—Comments and Poll (2013). Physician-Assisted Suicide. *New England Journal of Medicine,* 368: 1450–1452. Retrieved September 29, 2014: http://www.nejm.org/doi/full/10.1056/NEJMclde1302615
5. Ibid.
6. Whitney L Carlson and Thuan D Ong (2014). Suicide in Later Life Failed Treatment or Rational Choice? *Clinics in Geriatric Medicine*, 30(3): 553–576.
7. Clinical Decisions–Comments and Poll (2013).
8. Martin R Petersen and Carol A Burnett (2008). The Suicide Mortality Of Working Physicians And Dentists. *Occupational Medicine*, 58(1):25–29. Also see, John M Violanti (2004), Predictors of Police Suicide Ideation. *Suicide and Life-Threat Behavior*, 34: 277–283.
9. Harlan Yu and David G Robinson (2012). The New Ambiguity of 'Open Government.' *UCLA Law Review Discourse*, 178. Retrieved September 8, 2014: http://www.uclalawreview.org/pdf/discourse/59-11.pdf Page 208.
10. Davis D Breaux and Annie I Anton (2008). Analyzing Regulatory Rules for Privacy and Security Requirements. *IEEE Transactions on Software Engineering*, 34(1). Retrieved September 8, 2014: https://www.cs.cmu.edu/~breaux/publications/tdbreaux-tse08.pdf
11. William L Anderson and Candice E Jackson (2006). Criminalization as Policy: Using Federal Criminal Law as a Regulatory Device. *The Journal of Social, Political, and Economic Studies,* 31(1).
12. William L Anderson and Candice E Jackson. (2006).
13. Dennis J Stevens (2016). *An Introduction to American Policing*, 2nd ed. Boston: Jones and Bartlett. (Forthcoming) Page 362.
14. ACLU Briefing Paper (ND). The Shackling of Pregnant Women and Girls in U.S. Prisons. Retrieved September 10, 2014: https://www.aclu.org/files/assets/anti-shackling_briefing_paper_stand_alone.pdf
15. Meredith Derby Berg (2014, April 18). A Pregnant Female Inmate At Western Massachusetts Regional Women's Correctional Center. *Boston Globe*. Retrieved September 9, 2014: http://www.bostonglobe.com/magazine/2014/04/18/taking-shackles-off-pregnant-prisoners/7t7r8yNBcegB8eEy1GqJwN/story.html
16. W I Thomas and Dorothy S Thomas (1928). The Child in America: Behavior Problems and Programs. NY: Oxford University Press.

17. Dennis J. Stevens (2011). *Police Officer Stress: Sources and Solutions*. Upper Saddle River, NJ: Pearson Prentice Hall. Page 170.

18. Herman Goldstein (2002). The new policing: Confronting complexity. In Wilson R. Palacios, Paul F. Cromwell, and Roger G. Dunham (Eds.), *Crime & Justice in America: Present realities and future prospects.* (Pages 102–110). Upper Saddle River, NJ: Prentice Hall. Page 110.

19. Ibid.

20. Jerome Skolnick (1997). Retrieved July 5, 2004: http://www.fact-index.com/j/je/jerome_skolnick.html

21. CNN Library (2014, August 28). Boston Marathon Terror Attack Fast Facts. CNNews. Retrieved September 24, 2014: http://www.cnn.com/2013/06/03/us/boston-marathon-terror-attack-fast-facts/

22. Dennis J Stevens (2013). *Failure of the American Prison Complex: Let's Abolish It*. Iowa: Kendall Hunt.

23. Dennis J. Sevens (2003). *Applied community policing in the 21st century*. Boston: Allyn Bacon. Page 36.

24. Dennis J Stevens (2002). Case Study Of Three Generations Of Incarcerated Sexual Offenders. *Journal of Police and Criminal Psychology*, 17(1), 65–83.

25. CC Cottle, RJ Lee, and K Heilbrun (2001). The prediction of criminal recidivism in juveniles: A meta-analysis. *Criminal Justice and Behavior, 28*, 367–394. Also see J Monahan, HJ Steadman, E Silver, PS Appelbaum, PC Robbins, E Mulvey, LH Roth, T Grisso, and S Banks (2001). Rethinking Risk Assessment: The *MacArthur Study of Mental Disorder and Violence*. NY: Oxford University Press.

26. John M Violanti (2005). Dying For The Job: Psychological Stress, Disease, And Mortality In Police Work. In Heith Copes (Ed.), *Policing and Stress* (Pages 87–102). Upper Saddle River, NJ: Prentice Hall. James Bonta (2002). Offender Risk Assessment: Guidelines For Selection And Use. *Criminal Justice and Behavior, 29*, 355–379.

27. National Association of State Directors of Special Education (NASDSE) (2007). Tools For Promoting Educational Success And Reducing Delinquency. Pages 2–7. Retrieved December 8, 2014: http://www.nasponline.org/advocacy/toolsforsuccess.pdf

    Also see, Jennifer L Ferguson (2002). Putting the "What Works" Research Into Practice: An Organizational Perspective. *Criminal Justice and Behavior*, 29, 472–492.

28. This does not mean that prisoners are dogs. They are persons. Thinking something different is blaming the victim.

29. William Ryan (1976). *Blaming the Victim*. New York: Vintage Press.

30. Lauren E Glaze and Erinn J Herberman (2013). Corrections Populations in the United States. Washington, DC: Bureau of Justice Statistics. Retrieved September 24, 2014: http://www.bjs.gov/index.cfm?ty=pbdetail&iid=4843

31. Dennis J Stevens (1999). Interviews With Women Convicted Of Murder: Battered Women Syndrome Revisited. *International Review of Victimology*, 6, 117–135.

32. Caitlin M Jones (2005, February). Genetics and Environmental Influences on Criminal Behavior. Rochester Institute of Technology. Retrieved September 24, 2014: http://www.personalityresearch.org/papers/jones.html

33. Dennis J Stevens (2015). Women in Solitary Confinement: Health and Recidivism. In Stephen Richards (Ed.), *The Marion Experiment*. Southern Illinois University Press. Forth coming.

34. Mel Robbins (2014, September 9). Lesson of Ray Rice Case: Stop Blaming Victim. CNN News. Retrieved September 10, 2014: http://www.cnn.com/2014/09/08/opinion/robbins-ray-rice-abuse/

35. Dennis J Stevens (2006). Police Apprehension of Sexual Offenders and Sexual Assault Conviction Levels: Why Conviction Levels are Low in Boston. *Police Journal*, 79(2), 125–154.

36. Joseph A Harpold (2000, June). A medical model for community police. *FBI Law Enforcement Bulletin*, Page 26.

37. George L Kelling and Mark H. Moore (2004). The evolving strategy of policing. In Steven G Brandl and David E Barlow (Eds.), *The Police In America: Classical And Contemporary Readings*. (Pages 5–26). Belmont, CA: Wadsworth.

38. James Marshall Crotty (2012, March 1) 60% of College Grads Can't Find Work in Their Field. Forbes. Retrieved September 10, 2014: http://www.forbes.com/sites/jamesmarshallcrotty/2012/03/01/most-college-grads-cant-find-work-in-their-field-is-a-management-degree-the-answer/

39. The Free Dictionary. Retrieved December 8, 2014: http://www.thefreedictionary.com/profession

40. Samuel P Huntington (1981, September). *Soldier And The State: The Theory And Politics Of Civil-Military Relations*. NY: Belknap Press.

41. Samuel P Huntington (1981) was used as a guide. The interpretation of his work is that of this author.

42. Allan R Millett is a Professor of Military History at the Ohio State University and an author of many military books.

43. American Bar Association (2008). ABA Revises Mission. Retrieved September 10, 2014: http://www.bellow-slaw.com/aba-revises-mission-restates-goals-regarding-justice-members-public/

44. Jerry H Ratcliffe (2008). Intelligence-led Policing. Page 230.

45. Timothy L. Ericson (2005). Building Our Own "Iron Curtain:" The Emergence of Secrecy in American Government. *American Archivist,* 68(1): 46–54. Retrieved September 10, 2014: http://archivists.metapress.com/content/9m260j244177p553/fulltext.pdf

46. Karl Marx (2000). Karl Marx: Selected Writings. NY: Oxford Press. Page 37.

47. Jill R. Horwitz (2005). Making Profits And Providing Care: Comparing Nonprofit, For-Profit, And Government Hospitals. *Health Affairs,* 24(3): 790–801. Retrieved May 16, 2014: http://content.healthaffairs.org/content/24/3/790.full

48. Ibid.

49. Ibid.

50. Ibid.

51. Ibid.

52. Uwe E Reinhardt (2006). The Pricing of U.S. Hospital Services: Chaos Behind A Veil of Secrecy. *Health Affairs,* 25(1): 57–69. Retrieved September 9, 2014: http://www.medscape.com/viewarticle/521175_2

53. John Steele Gordon (2013, August 1). Why Non-Profit Hospitals Are So Profitable Commentary Magazine. Retrieved September 6, 2014: http://www.commentarymagazine.com/2013/08/01/why-non-profit-hospitals-are-so-profitable/

54. Steven Brill (2013, February 20). Bitter Pill: Why Medical Bills Are Killing Us. *Time*. Retrieved September 9, 2014: http://www.uta.edu/faculty/story/2311/Misc/2013,2,26,MedicalCostsDemandAndGreed.pdf

55. John Steele Gordon. (2013, August 1).

56. American Hospital Association (2014). Eliminating Racial and Ethnic Disparities. Retrieved August 26, 2014: http://www.aha.org/advocacy-issues/disparities/index.shtml

57. Truven Health Analytics (2014, March 3). 100 Top Hospital: Study Overview, 21st ed. Retrieved August 6, 2014: http://100tophospitals.com/portals/2/assets/100-Top-Study-March-2014.pdf

58. Sandra H Johnson (2008–2009). Regulating Physician Behavior: Taking Doctors' Bad Law Claims Seriously. *St. Louis University of Law Journal,* 53: 973–980.

59. A Donabedian (2005). Evaluating the Quality of Medical Care. *Milbank Quarterly*, 83: 691–729.

60. Atul Gawande, Michael J Zinner, David M Studdert, and Troyen A Brennan (2003). Analysis of Errors Reported by Surgeons at Three Teaching Hospitals. *Surgery*, 133(6): 614–621.

61. Emile Durkheim, (1893/1960). *The Division of Labor in Society*. G. Simpson, Translation. New York: The Free Press.

62. William Thomas and Florian Znaniecki (1926/1996). *The Polish Peasant in Europe and America*. Urbana, IL: University of Illinois Press.

63. Amy S Collins (2008). Preventing Healthcare-Associated Infections. In Patient Safety and Quality: An Evidence-Based Handbook for Nurses; In RG Hughes (Ed); Agency for Healthcare Research and Quality: Rockville, MD, USA, 2008; Chapter 41, Pages 547–575. Retrieved July 11, 2014: http://www.ahrq.gov/professionals/clinicians-providers/resources/nursing/resources/nurseshdbk/CollinsA_PHCAI.pdf

64. Dennis J. Stevens (2011). Pages 360–361.

65. J Campos-Serna, E Ronda-Pérez, L Artazcoz, BE Moen, and FG Benavides (2013). Gender Inequalities In Occupational Health Related To The Unequal Distribution Of Working And Employment Conditions: A Systematic Review. *International Journal of Equity Health*, 12(1):12–57.

66. Statement by The Society for Healthcare Epidemiology of America in Response to Centers for Disease Control and Prevention's State-Specific Healthcare-Associated Infections Summary Data Report (2013). Retrieved July 8, 2014: http://www.shea-online.org/View/ArticleId/193/Statement-by-The-Society-for-Healthcare-Epidemiology-of-America-in-Response-to-Centers-for-Disease-C.aspx

67. CA Jarey, J Duchon, P Della-Latta, and L Saiman (2010). The Epidemiology Of Methicillin-Susceptible And Methicillin-Resistant Staphylococcus Aureus In A Neonatal Intensive Care Unit, 2000–2007. *Journal of Perinatology*. 30(2):135–139.

68. Statement by The Society for Healthcare Epidemiology of America (2013).

69. Josh Siegel (2014, September 24). Obama's 4 Ways For UN To Beat ISIS "Network of Death." *The Daily Signal*. Retrieved September 25, 2014: http://dailysignal.com/2014/09/24/obamas-4-ways-un-beat-terrorists-network-death/

70. CNN Library (2014: September 23). ISIS Fast Facts. Retrieved September 25, 2014: http://www.cnn.com/2014/08/08/world/isis-fast-facts/

71. C. Wright Mills (1956). *The Power Elite*. New York: Oxford University Press.

72. Ibid.

73. Fox News (2014, September 4). 'Frustration And Confusion' Among US Troops Over Mixed Message On ISIS. Retrieved September 10, 2014: http://www.foxnews.com/politics/2014/09/04/frustration-and-confusion-among-us-troops-over-mixed-message-on-isis/

74. Matthew Schofield (2012, October 9). The Afghan war: Do the numbers add up to success? McClathcy Newspaper. Retrieved September 10, 2014: http://www.mcclatchydc.com/2012/10/09/170994/the-afghan-war-do-the-numbers.html

75. Ibid.

76. Information Clearing House (2014, September 9). *World News Daily*. Retrieved September 11, 2014: http://www.informationclearinghouse.info/ Note: I cannot totally depend on this site's information to be 100 percent accurate; use expenditures as a guide. Of course this is a similar statement made by the FBI about their Uniform Crime Report (http://www.ucrdatatool.gov/ranking.cfm). For example: Make valid assessments of crime.

It is incumbent upon all data users to become as well educated as possible about how to understand and quantify the nature and extent of crime in the United States and in any of the more than 17,000 jurisdictions represented by law enforcement contributors to the UCR Program. Valid assessments are possible only with careful study and analysis of the various unique conditions affecting each local law enforcement jurisdiction.

77. Allan Erickson (2014, April 10). The Coming Civil War: Total Government Control at the Point of a Gun. *Clash Daily.* Retrieved September 10, 2014: http://clashdaily.com/2014/04/coming-civil-war-total-government-control-point-gun/ Note: this resource is one perceptive).

78. Randy Pausch (2008). *The Last Lecture*. New York, NY: Hyperion. Page 39.

79. Scott Hensley and Barbara Martinez (2005, July 15). To Sell Their Drugs, Companies Increasingly Rely on Doctors. *Wall Street Journal*. Retrieved September 10, 2014: http://online.wsj.com/articles/SB112138815452186385

80. Ibid.

81. Ibid.

82. Jeff Ventimiglia, Amir H Kalali, Ipsit V Vahia, and Dilip V Jeste (2010). An Analysis of the Intended Use of Atypical Antipsychotics in Dementia. *Psychiatry*, 7(11): 14–17. Retrieved September 10, 2014: http://www.ncbi.nlm.nih.gov/pmc/articles/PMC3010964/pdf/PE_7_11_14.pdf

83. Jeffrey Reiman and Paul Leighton (2012). Rich Get Richer and the Poor Get Prison, The Plus MySearchLab with eText—Access Card Package (10th Edition). Upper Saddle River, NJ: Pearson.

84. Timothy L. Ericson (2005).

Index

A

B

D

E

F

G

H

www.ingramcontent.com/pod-product-compliance
Ingram Content Group UK Ltd.
Pitfield, Milton Keynes, MK11 3LW, UK
UKHW051510290926
15471UKWH00008B/1542

9 781465 267566